REGISTRUM

PRIORATUS DE WETHERHAL.

𝕮𝖆𝖒𝖇𝖗𝖎𝖉𝖌𝖊 :

PRINTED BY J. & C. F. CLAY,

AT THE UNIVERSITY PRESS.

The Priory Gateway Wetheral.

THE

REGISTER

OF THE

PRIORY OF WETHERHAL

EDITED

WITH INTRODUCTION AND NOTES

BY

J. E. PRESCOTT, D.D.

CANON OF CARLISLE CATHEDRAL,
ARCHDEACON OF CARLISLE,
FORMERLY FELLOW OF CORPUS CHRISTI COLLEGE, CAMBRIDGE.

LONDON
ELLIOT STOCK, 62, PATERNOSTER ROW, E.C.
KENDAL, T. WILSON.

1897

PREFACE.

IT is perhaps natural that a member of the Cathedral Church of Carlisle should take a special interest in the *Register of the Priory of Wetherhal*, whose property was transferred to that Church 350 years ago. A careful examination shewed that this *Register* had a more than ordinary value. It did not merely present the ancient deeds of certain lands and privileges. Its early charters, of older date than any local documents now extant, had historic importance. A very incorrect opinion of these charters has been formed even in later days, and from them very erroneous deductions have been drawn. Again, the number of local references was found to be large; and the names of persons recorded in the charters unusually numerous. Some of these are persons who are here mentioned for the first time; others are characters well known in early English History. Much of this importance is, no doubt, due to the connection of the Priory with the famous Abbey of S. Mary at York.

The error in the local histories, which ascribed the conquest of the district to William I. instead of William Rufus, has been refuted by Lappenberg and Dr Luard. It received some support from the ridiculous addition to the *Register* termed "Distributio Cumberlandiæ" (No. **245**), which was quite at variance with the early charters. But the local histories contain other errors which made it impossible to reconcile many of the statements in this *Register*. Two may be mentioned, as each is dealt with later in an Appendix. The foundation of the Priory of Carlisle as early as 1102 seemed very improbable; and the episcopate of the second Bishop of Carlisle, Bishop Bernard, placed in the 12th century, whether beginning in 1156 or 1186, was equally improbable. Further investigation has shewn that these assumptions were clearly mistakes. By their correction, many local characters and incidents fall into their true position, and not a few problems are solved.

Some confusion is caused by the great variations of spelling, both in place names and personal names. When references or quotations are given, the spelling there used is retained and not necessarily that of the charter.

There are mistakes in the language and in the letters of the words of the charters, due to the transcriber or the original writer. These in some very glaring instances have been corrected.

The local histories, ancient and modern, give hardly any authorities for their statements; it is therefore difficult, often impossible, to verify them. I have endeavoured to give early authorities in many cases, such as have come under my own notice, enough to shew how much has yet to be done. Few references are given to the well-known writers of the 17th and 18th centuries; where possible, earlier sources of information have been used.

Great assistance has been obtained from some of the unpublished local manuscripts, which I have reason to think will not long remain in manuscript only.

(1) The *Register of Lanercost* (to be carefully distinguished from the *Chronicon de Lanercost*) is a valuable Transcript now with the Dean and Chapter of Carlisle. Its charters date from about 1169, but their chief interest consists in the local references and in the very large number of witnesses who attest the deeds.

(2) The *Register of Holm Cultram* contains charters dating from 1150, but unfortunately the names of very few witnesses are entered. Some of the charters are of considerable interest. One manuscript, probably of the 14th century, is with the Dean and Chapter of Carlisle; and to this the references in the notes have been chiefly made. Two other old Manuscripts and a Transcript are among the Harleian Manuscripts in the British Museum (Nos. 3891, 3911, 1881). These three differ in many points from one another.

(3) The *Register of the Priory of S. Bega* (Harleian MSS. 434) contains a number of deeds, nearly all of only local importance. Beyond the early charters, little use has been made of this.

(4) The oldest *Registers* of the Bishops of Carlisle, viz. of Bishop John Halton, Bishop John Rosse, Bishop John Kirkby, Bishop Gilbert Welton and Bishop Thomas Appleby. These *Registers* are in two volumes and cover a period from 1293 to 1386; but there are no entries from 1345 to 1353. They contain much valuable information often difficult to decipher. The extracts made from them by Bishop Nicolson were simply copied by Nicolson and Burn in their *History*; and it will be noticed that most of their definite information as to parishes refers only to this period.

Advantage can now be taken of the excellent publications of the Record Commission and of the Rolls Series, as well as of the great facilities offered to persons who are anxious to search at the Public Record Office. All these have been largely used.

The principal note on any place or person will, as a rule, be found under the first mention of the same in the text of the *Register*. These notes, though some of them are long, do not pretend to be exhaustive, but rather to point out the directions in which further information may be found. The General Index and the Index of Personal Names will, it is hoped, be sufficiently copious for all purposes of reference.

I am indebted to the late Rev. James Raine, Canon of York, for some valuable criticisms, especially on the Foundation of the Priory of Carlisle (Appendix B); also to my friend, Dr Henderson, Dean of Carlisle, for not a few important suggestions.

This book cannot be expected to have many readers, but I trust that some may find here matters of value to them, and information which cannot be found elsewhere or which is not readily accessible. There are few parts of England whose history, from Roman days onward, exceeds in interest that of this district. We may look for a more complete and accurate account than any that has yet appeared. To this desired end, the present work is a small contribution.

CARLISLE,
April, 1897.

CONTENTS.

INTRODUCTION.

THE *Register of Wetherhal* throws light upon an important Early point in the early history of the district in which the Priory of History. Wetherhal was placed. A very few years before the Monastery was founded, the boundary of the kingdom had been extended. In the year 1092, William Rufus had swept over this north-western corner of the country, and made it part of England. Its previous history is involved in no little obscurity. The old Stræcled, or Strathclyde, of the Britons had passed through Strath- many changes and troubles. This Strathclyde, when we find clyde. its limits more defined, in 1069, stretched from the Clyde to the Duddon, and afterwards only to the Derwent. It was known also by the name of Cumbria, though this was a later designation, not appearing before the 9th century. After the Romans left at the beginning of the 5th century, it had been harried by Pict and Scot, by Angle and Dane. At length, in the 10th century, in 945, Eadmund, King of Saxon England, who had ravaged the land of Cumbria, ceded it to Malcolm I., to be held as a fief of the English crown. This somewhat uncertain vassalage prevailed until the great expedition of William the Conqueror into Scotland along the east coast in 1072. The out-come of that incursion was that Malcolm III., Malcolm Ceanmor, King of Scots, did homage to the Norman and promised to "become his man." This pledge of homage bound Malcolm but little. When-ever opportunity offered, he laid waste Northumbria, whether the

Conqueror or his successor was King. We can therefore well
understand the desire of William Rufus to secure a "scientific
frontier." He attained this object when he seized the southern
part of Cumbria, began to rebuild Carlisle, and made the
Solway Firth the northern boundary on the western side of his
kingdom. He gave the lordship of the district to one of his
followers, Ranulf Meschin, Viscount of the Bessin in Normandy.
This limit we find mentioned in a royal charter 30 years later as
the "boundary of Ranulf Meschin" (Appendix A, p. 476).
There can be little doubt it was William Rufus who put the
warlike Norman Baron in charge of the new territory, though
none of the Chroniclers register the appointment.

Ranulf was the nephew of Hugh, Earl of Chester. Earl
Hugh was the staunch friend and supporter of William, and, only
the year before, had ceded to the King the fortress of Avranches
in Normandy, a portion of his brother Henry's dominion. We
know that, the year after, in 1093, Ranulf was present at Chester
when Earl Hugh refounded there the Abbey of S. Werburgh.
And now a few years later, our *Register* brings him before us.
He was not an Earl, but he was in full possession as Lord of
the district, the "power" or "honor of Carlisle" (Appendix A,
p. 471). At his castle of Appleby up the valley of the Eden, he
commanded the roads into Yorkshire and the valley of the Tees,
which had been so often trodden by the invading Scots. Some
30 miles lower down, just where the river valley opens out and
debouches on to the plain in which rises the City of Carlisle, he
founded the Monastery of Wetherhal, for a Prior and twelve
monks of the Benedictine Order (Illustrative Docum. LII.).

The situation is well chosen. It is beautiful, like so many of
the sites of the early convents. It is only some 4 or 5 miles from
the ancient city which his Royal Master lately ordered to be
rebuilt out of the ruins in which it had lain for 200 years. It is
close to the direct road, shortly after known as the *Via Regia*
(No. 5) from Carlisle to Appleby, and it is near the eastern road
which runs through the dip in the fells to Hexham and Northumbria.

Marginal notes:

William II.

Ranulf Meschin.

Wether-hal.

Just underneath runs the lovely stream of the Eden, and he takes care that the mill-bay and salmon sluice are secured to the monks by a separate charter. He endows them with the manor and Endow-Church of Wederhal and certain lands near, with the Chapel of ment. Warthwic and the Churches of S. Michael and S. Laurence at Appleby, which his chaplain Radulph has held, also with two-thirds of the tithe of his demesne at Appleby on both sides of the river and of the tithes of Maiburne and Salchild. All these he grants to the Monastery as a Cell, or dependent, of the Benedictine Abbey of S. Mary at York, to which his King, William Rufus, and members of his own family have been liberal benefactors. He names in these charters two of his brothers, Richard and William Meschin, and his wife Lucia, probably present at the time.

Lucia was, no doubt, the link which connected Ranulf more directly with the Abbey of S. Mary. She was the widow of Roger de Romara, and we believe the only daughter of Ivo Ivo Taillebois (Appendix A), who about this time endowed the Abbey Taillebois. at York with Churches and tithes in what was afterwards the Barony of Kendal, which he held immediately to the south of the territory of Ranulf (Illust. Docum. xvi.). Ivo Taillgebosc, as he is called in *Domesday Book*, had no lands near this district at the time of the Domesday Survey in 1085–86, though he possessed some in Lincolnshire and in Norfolk. These possessions on the border of this newly acquired land were at that date in the hands of the Crown, and were, there is little doubt, given to Ivo somewhat later by William Rufus in return for service done. And we can well believe that about the time William made this grant to Ivo on the former border of England, he placed Ivo's son-in-law, Ranulf Meschin, in command of the newly conquered district which he had now included within its bounds.

There is no record of any other monastery existing in the Other district at the beginning of the 12th century. The Convent of Monas-Augustinian Canons at Carlisle was not founded before 1122–23 teries. (Appendix B). The religious House at Hexham on the east had never recovered from the destruction of the Danish inroads, but was to be refounded a few years later, and then to be turned into an Augustinian Convent by Archbishop Thurstin. Of the several monasteries which were to rise around them during the next hundred years, not one was now existing. Much good could be wrought by the monks in those rough and troublous times. There was a call for religion and hospitality, for healing and agriculture, in that comparatively rude state; and these the brotherhood supplied. It was a wise thought which led the Lord of the new district to place here this outpost, and to connect it with the centre of culture and society in the important city of York. The country round was not the barbarous and desolate land which some historians have supposed. War-trodden and harried it had been; some of its towns, like Carlisle, had been left in ruins on the ground. But many Churches were certainly existing, as at Appleby, Kirkby-Stephan, Morland and Wetherhal. Even in the neighbouring wild district of Gillesland, there was a Chapel of wattlework, at Treverman, in the days of the Saxon Bishop Eagelwine (1056–1071). The local incidents which Bede gives us connected with S. Cuthbert, and the famous Saxon cross at Bewcastle tell us the same story[1]. In the earliest records, we have mention of mills and highways, pastures and cultivated lands. And as we go on a few years, there are marks of civilization and social life which must have long existed.

The country round.

Ancient Churches.

Ranulf Meschin.

We learn from other sources that Ranulf Meschin founded certain Baronies in the District, three upon the northern border. These Barons were to guard the way against the Scots, especially when Ranulf was absent in Normandy with his Royal Masters, William Rufus and Henry I. At the great battle of Tinchebrai in September, 1106, he was far away from his northern charge. The wreck of the White Ship in 1120 made a great change in his fortunes. He then became an Earl, succeeding to the Earldom

---

[1] There exist some few remains of probable Saxon work in connection with some of these Churches, as the Saxon hog-backed stone now built into S. Michael's Church, Appleby, also probably the windows in the tower of Morland Church.

and to the estates of his cousin Richard, Earl of Chester. But
he had to yield the lordship of Carlisle to the King (Appendix A,
p. 470). This is borne out by our *Register*, where the charters
of Henry I. granted some 10 years later shew the land to be in
the hands of the Crown (Nos. 5 and 8), and speak of the time
when Ranulph, Earl of Chester, held the "Honor of Carlisle." In
the year 1122 an important event took place. Henry I. came down Henry I.
into the north in October, and, turning aside from York toward the
western sea, inspected the city of Carlisle, and ordered it to be
further fortified. Soon after, it seems clear, the Priory of Carlisle
was founded by the King under the advice of Archbishop Thurstin,
and not as wrongly stated in 1102 (Appendix B). This was a
House of Regular Canons of S. Augustine, and Athelwold, Prior
of Nostell and later the first Bishop of Carlisle, was the first Prior.
Carlisle being made the See of the Bishop, the Prior and Convent
of Carlisle were brought into business relations with the Priory of
Wetherhal, and often appear in this *Register*.

Henry I. endowed Wetherhal with valuable privileges and
certain rights of pasture (No. 5). Other early grants were made
by men of note in their day (No. 14). These grants and privileges
were confirmed by Henry II., and the three succeeding Kings;
but there is no confirmation charter of King Stephen. This Stephen.
omission we might expect. On the death of Henry I., David,
King of Scots, took up arms against Stephen in support of his
niece, the Empress Matilda. He invaded England in 1136, and
seized the newly fortified city of Carlisle. He passed on into
Northumbria, and was then met by Stephen at Durham, where,
however, terms of peace were arranged. The city and a great
part of the District of Carlisle were ceded to David, and became
for a time Scottish possessions. The effect of this cession only
lasted about 20 years; for in 1157 the grant was recalled by
Henry II. and he ruled up to the former boundary of
England. Hence Stephen would have no power to grant a
charter to Wetherhal. But there is during that period the confirmation of a grant of Adam son of Suan by King David of

Scotland (No. **198**). Besides his general confirmation charter,

Richard I. specially confirms the grant given by Henry I. of
pasture between the River Eden and the *Via Regia* within the

bounds of the Manor. The charter of Henry III. is a confirmation and *Inspeximus* of a charter of Henry II. to S. Mary's at
York. There is no charter of Edward I. in the *Register* or of any
succeeding King; though we know that charters were granted in
later times (p. 431).

There were naturally frequent relations between this monastery and the Bishops of Carlisle, and not always of the most
pleasant kind. It is not easy to determine the ecclesiastical
jurisdiction under which the land of Carlisle was placed in early
times. At all events, from the days of S. Cuthbert until 1092, it
would seem to have been under the Bishops of Lindisfarne and
their successors the Bishops of Durham. Many a memorial
connects the name of the seventh century Saint with the district.
The *Fons Sti Cuthberti* near the monastery, so accurately defined
in the *Register* (No. **43**) and now called the Holy Well, is an
instance. The Diocese of Hexham, which ceased to be a See
in 821, never came west of the Eden (p. 399). The claims of
the Diocese of Glasgow, which were pressed during the 11th and
12th centuries, and even up to 1258, seem never to have been
allowed; and we know that the Solway Firth was the acknowledged boundary of that Diocese under Earl David in 1120
(Appendix A, p. 475). From amid the confusion of the time
when this district was added to England, York emerges having
established her jurisdiction, and that, probably at the very beginning of the century under the influence of King Henry I. We
find Michael, Bishop of Glasgow, who was consecrated by Archbishop Thomas II. between 1109 and 1114, acting as the suffragan
of York in the district, and even holding ordinations in the old
Church of Morland, where he later found his grave (p. 43 *n.*). One
of these charters of Henry I. (No. **9**) is addressed to the famous

Archbishop Thurstin, or Thurstan, a year or two before the
foundation at his instigation of the Bishopric of Carlisle by the

King in 1133. We have then two charters by Athelwold, the Bishop
first Bishop (Nos. **15, 16**). He occupied a strange position. He Athelwold.
took an important part in English affairs, and, an English Bishop,
he discharged his episcopal functions for many years in a Diocese
which was under the rule of a Scottish King (Appendix B, p. 488).
His charters afford an early instance of the impropriation of
parish Churches and of the mention of "ancient synodals and
archidiaconal dues."

This *Register* affords strong evidence of the existence of Bishop Bishop
Bernard, the second Bishop of Carlisle, and of episcopal work Bernard.
done by him in the Diocese. Serious doubts have been enter-
tained of both one and the other. Most of those who have
admitted his existence have placed his episcopate at two impos-
sible dates, 1156, when Bishop Athelwold died, and 1186, when
Henry II. was in Carlisle and endeavoured in vain to fill the See
on the supposed death of Bernard. It seems clear now that for
the long period until 1204 the Bishopric was vacant (Appendix D).
Some of its custodians, during the vacancy, such as Archdeacons
Robert, and Peter de Ros, are here brought before us. Then
Bernard, Archbishop of Ragusa, was collated to the See by
Geoffrey, Archbishop of York, at the command of King John.
This post was begged of the King by Pope Innocent III., and
here Bernard remained for about 10 years receiving, besides other
emoluments, a royal annuity of 20 marcs. Thus the second
Bishop of Carlisle was a poverty-stricken foreigner, foisted upon
the district by the Pope of Rome.

Bishop Bernard confirmed (Nos. **117, 122**) a remarkable
composition (No. **119**), which had been entered into not long
before between the monks of Wetherhal and the Canons of
Lanercost, concerning the patronage of the Church of Nether Lanercost.
Denton. This had been a matter of dispute between the two
Priories, and the series of documents in the *Register* shews the
interest which it had excited.

The Priory of Augustinian Canons at Lanercost had been
founded on the banks of the river Irthing, some 8 miles distant

from Wetherhal to the north-east, by Robert de Vallibus, Baron of Gillesland, about the year 1169. The Barony had been granted to his father Hubert by Henry II. in 1157 (Illustrative Docum. XXII., XXIII.); and it extended along the banks of the Eden opposite to Wetherhal. Naturally, there were matters and persons of common interest to the two Houses; and our *Register* receives frequent and valuable illustration from the extant *Register of Lanercost.* Another monastery had been founded in the district, the Abbey of Cistercian monks at Holm Cultram on the Solway Firth, by Earl Henry of Scotland, in January 1150. With this Abbey, Wetherhal seems to have had little to do.

Bishop Hugh. — The third Bishop of Carlisle, Bishop Hugh, appears in several charters, chiefly confirmations. He was the Abbot of the Cistercian Convent of Beaulieu in Hampshire, not, as often stated, of Beaulieu in Burgundy. He was consecrated in February, 1218–19, after a nearly 4 years' vacancy of the See; and, when his episcopate ended, the succession seems to have been clear and continuous.

Bishop Walter. — The fourth Bishop, Walter Malclerk, has but one charter (No. 211) in the *Register*, and that a grant of land in Morland to a private individual, Nicholas Legat. He filled the See for above 20 years, from 1223 to 1246, and was more engaged in the public affairs of the country than in the work of his own Diocese.

Bishop Silvester. — The fifth Bishop, Silvester de Everdon, confirmed (No. 26) in 1247 the impropriation of certain Churches in the Diocese belonging to the Abbey of S. Mary at York. To this Bishop, in the following year, the Abbot and Convent of S. Mary made over the advowson of the Churches of Ormesheved (Ormside), Musgrave, Clibburn and Burgh (under Stanemore), also of the Vicarage of S. Michael, Appleby, reserving the pension of 20 marcs annually received by the Prior of Wederhal (No. 240).

Bishop Thomas Vipont. — The next Bishop, Thomas de Vipont, or de Veteriponte, left only one mark on the *Register* during his short episcopate of a few months. This was an award (No. 27) in March 1256 between the Abbot and Convent of S. Mary and the Vicar of S. Michael's,

Appleby, by which certain curious items of income were assigned to the Vicar and his successors.

Ten years later, the seventh Bishop, Robert de Chauncy, Bishop executed a remarkable document (No. 34). A controversy had Robert de Chauncy. arisen concerning the institution of the Prior of Wetherhal and the custody of the Priory during a vacancy. The Bishop agreed to yield all claim to such custody, and to admit such monk as the Abbot of S. Mary's at York should present, the Priory giving up the annual pension of $2\frac{1}{2}$ marcs which they had received out of the Church of Nether Denton since it had passed into the patronage of the Bishops of Carlisle. There is also a strong letter of excommunication (No. 200), directed by the same Bishop in 1274 against certain "sons of iniquity" who had destroyed the pool and water supply of the mill of Culgaith, in the parish of Kirkland, which belonged to the Priory. No later Bishop appears in the *Register*.

There are but few Papal documents. The earliest is an Papal *Indult* (No. 33) of Pope Alexander III., dated 1165, allowing the Documents. Abbot and Convent of S. Mary at York to appoint Chaplains to serve their Churches which have no Vicars with special pensions from the said Churches. There is a confirmation (No. 18) in 1226 by Pope Honorius III. of the charters of Bishop Athelwold and Bishop Bernard. Pope Gregory IX. in 1240 confirmed (No. 25) to the Abbot and Convent of S. Mary the right to enter upon the Church of S. Michael, Appleby, on a vacancy, notwithstanding the opposition of the Bishop, and allowed the right of patronage which they had for the use of the Priory of Wederhal. Some dispute on the subject appears to have arisen with Bishop Walter Malclerk. This is one of the frequent instances where King, or Bishop, or monk, no doubt for a consideration, secured the Papal sanction in order to further their own ends. The Pope was never unwilling to interfere, as it increased the Papal influence and brought money into the Papal treasury.

Among other ecclesiastical matters, there is a curious contract Corkeby (No. 44) entered into with great solemnity in 1161–65 between Chapel.

Abbot Clement and William son of Odard. He was the Lord
both of Warthwic and of Corkeby, the latter a small demesne
just opposite the monastery on the bank of the River Eden; and
he had built a Chapel at Corkeby within his own curtilage. It
was agreed that Mass should be celebrated there on Fridays and
Sundays, the proper Chaplain or one of the monks to officiate.
The Prior was to have the key, and no one was to enter without
his leave. The service was to be for William and his wife, and
the servants of his household, and any guests who might happen
to be present. But all parishioners of Corkeby, male and female,
great and small, were forbidden; they were to go with their
offerings to the mother Church of Wederhal. On the principal
Festivals, William, his wife and all his household were to go with
their oblation to the Church of Wederhal to hear the Divine
Office. If they were absolutely prevented by the inclemency of
the weather, then, the same day, they were to send their offering
to the Prior, on every occasion 13 pence at the least. When they
were away from home, the Chapel was to be closed. William,
moreover, undertook to pay for ever the tithe of his mill whether
in the territory of Warthwic or of Corkeby; this he appears of
late to have detained. This is an early instance of a private
Chapel, and shews the tight hand which the monastery kept upon
its dues.

Strickland
Chapel.
Somewhat later, about 1235, we find the record of another
private Chapel at Strickland (No. **201**) in Westmoreland, and
Walter de Styrkeland obtained the concession of a Chantry in his
Chapel, the rights of the Vicar and the mother Church of Morland
being carefully guarded.

Altars.
There was in the Church of the Priory of Wetherhal an altar
of the Blessed Virgin Mary and an altar of the Holy Trinity.
This perhaps accounts for the fact that in the charters the dedication of the Church is sometimes given "S. Mary and S. Constantine," sometimes as "Holy Trinity and S. Constantine." For
lights before these altars, or in the Church generally, numerous
gifts were made: 12*d.* annually, lands in Denton, in Melmorby,

in Ulvesby (Nos. 63, 126, 181, 182, 183). John de Wederhal
gave land in Kabergh that one wax light of 8 lbs. weight should
burn every day before the altar of the Blessed Virgin Mary while
Mass was being celebrated there (No. 178). Roger de Bello
Campo gave his body to be buried in the Church, and with it Burials.
land in Cringeldic to find a vestment and light for ever at the
altar of the Blessed Virgin Mary (No. 172). Alan de Langewayt
also gave his body to be buried there, and with it gave all his
land in Warthwic (No. 57). Similar grants of land were made by
Walter the porter at Wetherhal, who is such a frequent witness
(No. 86), and by Anselm de Neuby (No. 141) to secure the right
of sepulture there.

We have, in the first grant of Ranulph Meschin, an early Manors.
example of the territorial jurisdiction of the Norman " Manor " or
Manerium. Though the name is Norman, no doubt the Manor
itself really represented the ancient township, which had existed
long before the coming of the Norman. The change from the
old English village community had begun before the Conquest;
and in the Domesday Survey this territorial lordship, this *Manerium*, is constantly recognized. The free tenants (*liberi homines*,
No. 92) of the lord of the manor answered to the freemen of the
village community: and in both cases there was the servile class,
the slave (*nativus*) whose slavery was hereditary and who, with
his wife and family (*cum sequela sua*) and goods, was absolutely at
the disposal of his master or lord. We have instances in the
Register of the sale or barter of such slaves to the monks of
Wetherhal (Nos. 132, 156). The lord of the manor, whether a
private person or an ecclesiastical corporation, had a separate jurisdiction, independent of other judicial authorities. His men were
free from other courts, so far as the grant of the fief to the lord
permitted, and were judged by the custom of their own manor.
These private courts had also grown up in Anglo-Saxon times,
but were greatly multiplied under the Norman Kings. The
" freemen " held their tenemental lands under the customs of the
manor, and rendered rent and other services to the lord. The

Customs of
Wether-
hal. customs of the Manor of Wetherhal are clearly brought out as
early as the year 1235, when a case came before the King's
Court, between John son of Elmine, a "freeman" of Wetherhal,
who held two bovates of land, and Robert, Abbot of S. Mary's at
York (No. 92). In addition to the payment of 8s. annually, it
was agreed that John and his heirs had to render the following
services :— to carry the corn of the Abbot and his successors at
Wetherhal one day in autumn, to find one man to reap one day in
autumn, to plough one day in the year, to carry wood for the mill
and the fish pool and with the other men of Wetherhal to repair
them, to grind his corn at the mill of Wetherhal giving up to the
thirteenth measure, and to pay pannage. He was to have no
claim by reason of the said tenement on the forest clearings of
the monastery, save the privilege of common of pasture on the
fallows and stubbles. This was the only special privilege that
could be claimed by the "freemen."

Forest
pasture.   These matters of pannage and of pasture are interesting in
connection with the early charter given by Henry I. (No. 5). The
King had granted to the monastery the right of feeding their pigs
in the King's Forest, without payment of pannage. This Forest,
known later as the Forest of Cumberland and the Forest of
Inglewood, came up to the river Eden on the west, and this
manor of Wetherhal was really within its nominal boundaries.
Hence, the anxiety of the monks to secure the confirmation of
their rights by the King as soon as the district passed into the
hands of the Crown ; and especially the confirmation of the right
of pasture in the large tract between the river and the King's
highway or Via Regia, from Wetherhal to the southern boundary
of the manor at Dribec (No. 5). The Via Regia passed through
the manor. This right of pasture was evidently distinct from any
ordinary right of the lord of the manor over commons or wastes,
as we learn more fully from the confirmation charter of Edward
III. (Illustrative Documents, XXXIII., LII.). By that charter the
monks, who seem to have been harassed by the Officers of the
Forest, were empowered to depasture not only their own cattle

and animals of all kinds on the said ground, but also to take on the cattle of other persons, as they pleased, and to apply the profits thereof to their own use without hindrance.

Certain of the tenemental lands were from time to time granted to the Priory absolutely by the tenants; and the charters shew what care was taken to secure a legal conveyance of the property (Nos. 62, 65–70, 84–86 *et al.*) The boundaries of the Bounda-ries of Manor. manor were carefully set out (No. 236) and can still be traced with great accuracy. The bounds of the Wetherhal sanctuary were much narrower than those of the manor, and they are defined, but not so clearly (Appendix C and Illustrative Documents, Sanctuary. xxx.). They were marked by six crosses; the site of one, which stood also on the boundary of the manor, and was called Wetherhal Gryth-Crosse (No. 236), can be clearly determined. This privilege of sanctuary was secured, we find, by the Royal Charter of Henry I., which granted to Wetherhal the same liberties as were enjoyed by the Churches of S. Peter in York and S. John in Beverley (Appendix C). No refuge was allowed to those who had committed felony within the liberty. Felons from without, who sought sanctuary there, had to toll a certain bell in the Church, and swear before the Bailiffs of the liberty that henceforth they would demean themselves well and faithfully. They might then remain as long as they pleased, if they did not leave the bounds. This privilege was of great value in an age when justice moved slowly, and when every man was ready at once to avenge his wrong and to summon his friends to assist him. The sanctuary afforded a refuge at all events until such time as passion might cool down, or friends mediate, or a fair trial could be had. It is clear that numbers resorted to the sanctuary. In the 14th century, we hear of Edward III. pro-mising the Royal pardon to the "grithmen," men who had found the *grith* or peace of Wederhale and of some other sanctuaries, if they went out and fought in Scotland (Illustrative Documents XXVIII.).

Manor of Corkeby.
The proximity of the lords of the manor of Corkeby brought

the monks of Wetherhal into other than ecclesiastical relations with them. The history of this manor is carried back by our *Register* to the beginning of the 12th century. Westcubrict son of William Steffan is mentioned in the charters of Ranulf Meschin and Henry I. and evidently as the lord. The grant of Gillesland by Henry II. to Hubert de Vallibus in 1157 proves that Westcubrict was formerly in possession (p. 8 *n.*). Then Osbert son of Odard, probably Odard Baron of Wigton, appears as lord in the middle of the 12th century (No. 35). His brother William succeeded and, after William, his descendants, until the manor went through a female heir into the family of de Richmund (p. 108 *n*). By sale and grant the manor and house of Corby has since passed through many hands. Naturally the interests of the lords on the opposite sides of the river occasionally clashed; sometimes their relations were very friendly, at others they were a little strained. In the days of old, when the monks were on the spot, they seem as a rule to have got the better of the lords of Corby; but in the time of the Dean and Chapter, the lords of Corby have had the advantage. The Dean and Chapter often took little heed of their business, and their successors have suffered. An instance might be cited in the assumption of the ancient fishery coops in the waters of the Eden.

Fish pool.   Ranulf Meschin, in addition to the manorial fishing rights, had granted by special charter (No. 2) the fish pool and sluice, in the river Eden just below the monastery, which were to be fixed in the opposite bank of Corkeby. No one was to disturb this, or to fish the water on either side below the pool as far down as Munchwath. This was a matter of grave importance to the monks. With the sluice and the "coffins," or coops, placed there, they obtained the salmon which formed such a valuable part of the food of the Priory. It was necessary not only that the holding ground on the opposite bank should be retained but that the fish should not be taken before they reached the coops. As early, therefore, as 1157–67, they got Osbert the son of Odard de Corkeby to grant them (No. 35) the whole of the fishing in the

Eden which belonged to the vill of Corkeby ; and in order that there might be no difficulty about their own fishery, he gave them the whole of the bank on his side as far as Munchwath.   Shortly after William, his brother and successor, and then Robert the son of William, confirmed these grants, enlarging on the point that no one should fish between the pool and Munchwath with hook, or net, or in any other way.   An agreement had, it appears, been entered into by which every eighth fish taken in the coops was to be given to the lord of Corkeby, but this was resigned by Robert son of William (No. 42) in a further charter of confirmation, probably in the year 1208, witnessed by the King's justices itinerant.   Other points, such as the number of boats to be kept on the water (No. 42), the fine to be paid by the person fishing in the water of the monks (No. 46) and the permission to take stone and wood from Corkeby to repair the weir and the bank on that side (No. 42) are carefully set out.   The number and importance of these charters shews the value which was attached to this fishery at that point.

In 1293 the Abbot of S. Mary's was summoned before the justices itinerant for having raised the height of the pool by a foot, and contracted the pass in the river, which by old custom was to be wide enough for a sow with her five little pigs.   The twelve jurors however found that the "pool and engine" were in the state in which they had been from time immemorial.   This and other trials prove how jealously these fishing privileges were watched in the 13th century (Illustrative Documents VI.).

Salt also was an article of great importance to the Monastery. Salt pans. They secured very soon, in the first half of the 12th century (No. 101), two *salinæ*, or salt-pans, at Burgh on the Sands, where salt could be made by evaporation from the waters of the Solway Firth.   These *salinæ* were the gift of Radulph Engahin, who had married Ybri, the daughter of Robert d'Estrivers to whom Ranulf Meschin had given the Barony of Burgh.   They were the subject of several charters.   Another *salina* was obtained later, on the west coast of Cumberland (No. 135).

Nominal rents.

There are several instances of curious nominal rents or tenures to be paid. Thus a pair of white gloves (No. 91); a rose on June 24th (No. 78); and one pound, or half a pound, of cumin, always at Carlisle Fair. The pound of cumin seems to have been valued at 3*d*. (No. 52) about the end of the 12th century.

Land measures.

Certain measures of land, which have been much discussed, are here made clear so far as this district is concerned. The *bovate*, or oxgang, is shewn to be equivalent to eight acres, and more accurately to one half of 15½ acres (No. 138); and the *carucate*, or plough's worth, as equivalent to 8 bovates. The usual *acra*, *roda*, and *pertica*, or *perca*, are mentioned; but we do not hear of the *hide*, though we have *hidagium*.

Places in Wether-hal.

The older charters mark other names and places, besides the well-known mill and fish pool, in the more immediate neighbour-hood of the Monastery, many of which must date from Anglo-Saxon times. The Parish Church of Wetherhal and the Chapel of Warthwic (Warwick) must have long existed. The sites of Munch-wath, the Monks' Ford, and of S. Cuthbert's Spring, and of the piece of land having the strange name of the *Camera Constantini*, can be clearly identified, though the names are no longer known. They seem to point back to some old monastic House near, long before the Norman came into the district. The Via Regia, or Hee Strette, from Carlisle to Appleby (No. 5) can be traced along a present road to the bounds of the manor at Drybec; it is then mentioned again near Renwick on the other side of the river Eden (No. 175), having probably crossed at Armathwaite and then sought the higher ground. Warthwic bridge must have occupied the same position as the bridge at the present day. Just below the bridge still runs into the Eden the little stream which divided the manors and drained the *marsh* between Wetherhal and Warthwic, and was then called Sorbeke or Sawbeke (No. 236). Other places, whose names are still extant, will be found entered in the notes.

Wether-hal Cells.

Not far from the Priory, about 700 yards higher up the river, are three rock-hewn cells which must have existed in the days of the monks, and probably long before. Their large size, each roughly 20 feet by 10 and nearly 9 feet high, and their position overhanging the river at a height of about 40 feet, points to their occupation as a place of concealment and of safety. They may well have been used in times of danger for the goods or grain of the monastery and perhaps to conceal some of their out-lying dependents. Such times were not unfrequent on that border land. They are not mentioned in the *Register*, though from the patron saint they got the modern name of St Constantine's Cells, otherwise Wetherhal Safeguard. It is quite possible that in their beginning they may date from Roman times. The quarry of excellent stone just beyond, so conveniently situated for river carriage, and the Roman inscription on the face of the cliff a few yards above the cells, seem to give colour to the suggestion[1].

We find some interesting references in the 13th century to the neighbouring City of Carlisle. We read as early as 1200 of the *Porta Bochardi* (No. 94), the gate in the southern walls of the City, named, according to tradition, after one Bochard, a Fleming. Then we have the *Vicus Bochardi* (No. 95), the street within the City, the continuation of which is now called Botcher-gate; and the neighbouring hamlet of Bochardby (No. 97). There is also mention of the precincts of the Old Castle (No. 93), and of the Hospital of S. Nicholas, which was outside the City to the south (Nos. 95, 96). The *Register* affords us the name of the earliest Mayor of Carlisle of whom I have found any record, Richard son of Walkelin, *Major*, shortly after 1240; also of another Mayor, in 1270 and in 1280, Alexander de Bolotun. We learn too that Syward, the *Præpositus*, or Provost, of Carlisle was the

(side note: Carlisle.)

(side note: Mayors of Carlisle.)

---

[1] The cells are described with measurements in Hutchinson, *Cumberland*, i. 161. The Roman inscription is given by Dr Bruce (*Lapidarium Septentrionale*, p. 333, No 468), but is now all but obliterated.

　　MAXIMUS SCRI[P]SIT....
　　LE[G]. XX. VV. CONDISIUS...SIUS

with the figure of a stag to the right. "It shews, as elsewhere," he says, "the presence of the xxth legion in the district."

Appleby.

chief officer towards the end of the 12th century, and before 1195 (No. 74). There would not be any Mayor yet appointed. Other towns also come in, such as Appleby with its Castle and Churches at the very beginning of the 12th century; and, in the early part of the 13th, its Burgamote, or Burghers' Court of the Community, and its Hospital of S. Nicholas. Many villages occur also, in connection with which points of interest appear, which are noted under their several names. Some, like Morland and Great Salkeld, are illustrated by the history of the time; others, like Camboc and Carlaton and Eston, have left scarce a record, their Churches vanished, their parishes merged in those adjoining.

Place names.

It is more difficult than in most parts of England to determine the derivation of the place names in this district. The successive immigrations of peoples who supplanted the ancient Celtic inhabitants, or Britons, have all left marks behind them. The Angle or Saxon, the Dane, and the Norseman may be traced by the characteristic name which he occasionally gave to the place of his sojourn. Passing from the south, we enter at Wetherhal upon the more level lands which stretch to the north and west. There, up to the Border and westward to the sea, we find the Saxon terminations *ton* and *stock* and *ham*, and mixed with them most frequently, the Danish suffix *by*. South of Wetherhal, and elsewhere on the higher, rougher grounds, we meet the *thwaite* and *garth*, the *fell* and *bec*, which prove where the Northman has dwelt. Most of the river names would appear to be Celtic. History affords us no record of a Norse immigration, as it does of the inroad of Saxon and Dane. But the Northmen who sailed down the western seas and occupied the western islands did not neglect to throw out settlers on to the mainland. The long estuary of the Solway Firth, not unlike some of their native fiords, would attract many of them; and to it, not improbably, a Norse name was given[1]. Hence in trying to ascribe those place names

---

[1] See Robert Ferguson, *Dialect of Cumberland*, p. 213, and *Northmen in Cumberland*, p. 7 *sq.* who has however too great a leaning to Norse derivations. The Celtic name of the Solway was *Tracht-Romra*.

to their authors, conjectures have to be hazarded, and often
languages are mixed, and some strange mistakes have been made[1].

Numerous officers, both lay and ecclesiastical, are mentioned
in the *Register*. The earliest record of a Sheriff of this district
occurs in the first charter of Ranulf Meschin. Richer was then Sheriffs.
Sheriff of Carlisle, though the existence of a Sheriff in that district
until long afterwards has been much doubted[2]. William is the Arch-
earliest Archdeacon mentioned (No. 2) but he was, it seems most deacons.
probable, Archdeacon of York. Robert, who often occurs in the
Register, was, I at one time thought, the first Archdeacon of
Carlisle, but a charter of Bishop Athelwold in the *Chartulary of
Whitby* speaks of "Elyas, Archdeacon" (p. 64 *n.*). As Robert
was Archdeacon after Bishop Athelwold's death in 1156, Elyas must
have preceded him, and would seem to be the first on record. That
he was an Archdeacon of Carlisle seems clear from the fact that
his name is coupled in the charter with "the Chapter of S. Mary"
(of Carlisle). No Prior is mentioned in that charter; and this Priors of
connection seems to support the view that Bishop Athelwold Carlisle.
was for a time Prior of Carlisle as well as Bishop. Before that
Bishop's death, Walter was Prior of Carlisle, and is often met with
in this *Register*. The *Register* names many of the Archdeacons
and Priors of the 12th and 13th centuries[3]. The Bishop's Official, Bishop's
or Official Principal, appears as early as 1180–92 in the person of Officials.
"Thomas de Thorp, Official of Carlisle," the See then being vacant
(p. 92 *n.*). He was succeeded by Adam de Kirkeby, Gervase de
Louther, and Walter de Ulvesby. The two latter Officials, as
seems to have been often the case, were promoted to be Arch-

---

[1] Thus Torpenhow, sometimes written Thorpenhow, is said by Nicolson and
Burn to be made up of three words, in several languages, all meaning "a hill,"
whereas it simply includes the well-known proper name Thorfin with the suffix
how—Thorfinhow.

[2] Odard and perhaps Hildred are the next Sheriffs of Carlisle on record;
they appear in the Pipe Roll for the 31st year of Henry I. 1130, Odard being
apparently Sheriff the preceding year.

[3] On the jurisdiction of the Archdeacon, and the composition entered into
between the Archdeacon and the Bishop of Carlisle, see my *Visitations in the
Ancient Diocese of Carlisle*, p. 22 seq.

deacons. The Archdeacon, as well as the Bishop, had, it appears, an Official of his own (No. 32), and the seals are mentioned of the Archdeacon, the Chapter and the Official of Carlisle (Nos. 44, 86).

Rural Deans. Rural Deans are frequently witnesses to these charters. At the end of the 12th century, four rural deaneries are named, which are practically the same as those existing in the 18th century, viz. Carlisle, Cumberland, Westmoreland and Allerdale or Alnedale. Then we have at an early period the Dean of Appelby, apparently a somewhat earlier name for the Dean of Westmorland; of Levinton, a large Barony; and of Gillesland, an early division due perhaps to Gillesland being kept so distinct and having been, to some extent, under the episcopal jurisdiction of Durham. The duties of the Rural Deans seem to have been sufficiently onerous. They had to levy the fines imposed in the Bishop's and Arch-deacon's Courts, and to see executed the orders given there; to summon those who had to appear at the Bishop's or the Arch-deacon's Visitation; to collect procurations that were in arrear and, on behalf of the Bishop, such taxes as had been laid upon the Clergy by the Crown. There are instances in the early part of the 14th century of instructions to the four Rural Deans, spoken of above, to carry out all such duties (p. 71 *n*.).

Families. The names of very early members of many well-known ancient families in the district are met with in the *Register*. For example, in the family of de Vallibus, Robert, called the second Lord of Gillesland, Ranulph his brother and Robert his nephew and heir, also Ronald, the Lord of Triermain and bastard brother of this second Robert, and many others. We note too early members of the families of Aglionby, Curwen, Levington, Lucy, Dacre, Tilliol of Scaleby, Strickland and Warwick. Many relationships are established, and not a few of the errors rife in the local histories are corrected. Thus Hugo de Morvilla, Lord of Burgo, is proved to be the son, not the grandson, of Simon de Morvilla (No. 101); and Christiana is shewn to be the wife of the much discussed Ketell son of Eldred. A good deal of light is thrown on the "two Odards" in the 12th century, about whom there has been not a little controversy, Odard son of Hildred and Odard the Sheriff (of Carlisle); several of their descendants also occur. The error which confused Hugh de Morville, Lord of Burgo, with Hugh, one of the assassins of Thomas Becket and Lord of the Honor of Knaresborough, might have been avoided by noting that the latter was the contemporary of Simon the father of the former Sir Hugh (No. 101).

The charters in this *Register* belong almost entirely to the 12th and 13th centuries. After Anglo-Saxon times, it was during these two centuries that the vast majority of the monasteries were founded, and that the chief benefactions were made to them. The number of Anglo-Saxon monasteries in England was, no doubt, large, and some were wealthy; but of these, very many were destroyed by the inroads of the Danes, and in this district some, we know, were swept away. With the Norman Conquest, there came a great increase in the number of Religious Houses and in the amount of property that was granted to them. The honest desire to establish institutions which had much power for good, the belief that such charitable acts would be of spiritual benefit to themselves and their relations and their friends, the strong feelings aroused by the early crusades, these and other causes impelled men to found many of these abbeys and priories, and to make to them gifts and bequests. Hence, above 400 monasteries were founded during the 12th century, and, it is said, 476 besides alien priories, between the Conquest and the first year of Henry III. (1216). After this period, the number of new foundations dwindled rapidly away. The amount of property which had accumulated in the hands of the monastic bodies was enormous. We may judge of the multitude of donors even from this small Priory of Wetherhal. They ranged from the King or the great Lord of the district to the humble tenant or the porter of the monastery. This very accumulation of possessions helped to produce a change of feeling. The lands given to the Religious Houses were held by them free from the services usually due from such lands, and free from other incidents.

Foundation of Monasteries.

The Laws of Mortmain resulted from this condition of things, in order to prevent the loss to the State or the King; and these laws materially restricted the bestowal of land. Then, the sub-servience of the monastic bodies to the Pope, their rapacious dealing with the Vicars, the working clergy, of the parishes, these and other causes produced an ever growing unpopularity. En-

Decline of Grants.

dowments found their way in other directions. Chantries were largely established in the Churches. The Friars who first arrived in 1221, and who did not hold land, before long amassed great wealth. And by the 14th century comparatively little was given to the monks. We are not therefore surprised to find that in this *Register* the charters all but cease at that date; and that the few additional documents are of a different character, and were even added to the manuscript by later hands.

After the 13th century.

The further history of the Priory up to the dissolution of the monasteries can only be gathered from a few scattered records and notices; and these last mainly in connection with the Priors.

Later Priors.

Of the Priors, there is one mentioned in the *Register*, William Rundel, who was promoted to be Abbot of S. Mary's at York, in 1239; but in the next and following centuries, no less than five Priors became Abbots of that great mother foundation (Appendix E). One former Prior, William de Tanefeld, the first of the name, was in 1309 installed as Prior of the Benedictine monastery at Durham. It is evident therefore that the Priory of Wetherhal had an importance which we should scarcely expect from its size and position. It may be that the Benedictine monks took care to have here some one of authority to keep watch on the three rival Houses of Augustinian Canons at Carlisle, Lanercost and Hexham.

The Abbot and Convent of S. Mary at York had, of course, to answer the summons of Edward I. *Quo Waranto?* they held their privileges and property. The pleadings on behalf of the Priory of Wetherhal were put forward before justices itinerant at Carlisle and Appleby in 1292. These pleas as regards certain vills and the Churches of S. Michael and S. Lawrence at Appleby are preserved in the Rolls. Their rights were fully established (Illustrative Documents, VII., XI.).

Two interesting visits were paid to the Priory of Wetherhal by Edward, Prince of Wales, afterwards Edward II. In October, 1301, the Prince had returned from an expedition into the south of Scotland, and was about to proceed through Berwick to join the King. On the 20th, he wrote two letters from Wederhale to the Chancellor, Sir John de Langetone, asking for a protection for his chamberlain and for his "fesicien." On February 19th, 1306-7, the Prince was there again, only a few months before he came to the throne. He there received Dungal MacDowil, who brought with him some prisoners whom he had taken in battle, among them Thomas and Alexander de Brus, two brothers of Robert de Brus, King of Scots. MacDowil also brought the heads of certain Irish and Cantire men who had been slain. He was duly rewarded by the Prince, whose treasurer kept a careful account of the "courser" and fifty marcs which were given (Illustrative Docum. VIII.). The two brothers, with Sir Ranald Crawford, were hanged shortly after at Carlisle, and Robert de Brus led a foray against the MacDowils to avenge them, upon which Dungal and his family had to flee into England. These little historical touches bring vividly before us the rough barbarous character of the times.

The visits of the Prince of Wales to Wetherhal had, not improbably, something to do with the promotion of Prior William de Tanefeld mentioned above. For we learn that when Edward I. was staying in the neighbourhood, the Prior so conducted himself towards the King and his son, Edward de Karnarvan, that they were always afterwards very gracious to him [1].

There was at Wetherhal in the year 1309 one of the numerous cases of "provision," where the Pope wished to provide an incumbent in place of the rightful nominee of the patron. But here a strong opposition was aroused. Pope Clement V. appointed Robert de Gyseburgh to be Prior, John de Thorp being already

Visits of Prince of Wales.

Provision by the Pope.

[1] Robert de Graystanes, *Hist. Dunelm. Scriptores Tres*, p. 85.

in possession on the nomination of the Abbot of S. Mary's. An
appeal was made to the King, who at once sent down two writs
to Bishop Halton charging him not to cite Prior John to any
foreign court, and forbidding the latter to pay any attention to
Robert de Gyseburgh's Papal mandates until the matter in controversy was fully debated and determined in the King's Court in
England. A few years afterwards we find Robert in the office
of Prior, but for some offence he had been excommunicated, and
was compelled to resign.

Another instance occurs about this time of an appeal to Rome
to settle a difference, instead of to the King's Court. A great
contest arose in 1338 between Bishop John de Kirkby and the
Churches claimed 1388. Abbey of S. Mary at York concerning the right to the Churches
of Warwick, Wetherhal and others which had been appropriated to
the Priory of Wetherhal. It would seem as if the point were
clear, but the controversy was only settled when the Abbot and
Convent of S. Mary carried the matter to the court of Rome, and
there gained their cause (p. 15 *n.*). Notwithstanding their inde-
pendence of the Bishops, which these monasteries claimed, they
Visitation of Priory. were from time to time subjected to episcopal visitation. We
have an example in 1358, when the Priory was visited by Bishop
Gilbert de Welton in his ordinary visitation of the Diocese (Illustrative Docum. XXXVII.).

Fishery in 1342. The fishery at the Pool and the rights of the Priory in the
bank at Corkeby, to which they attached so much importance,
came up again in 1342. This was but natural, as a new family,
that of de Salkeld, had lately got possession of Corkeby. A
very complete agreement was then made between Sir Richard de
Salkeld and William de Tanfeld, the second Prior of that name,
Corkeby Manor. and the monks of Wetherhal (No. 244). The manor of Corkeby
had passed into the family of de Richmund by the marriage of
Roald son of Alan de Richmund with Isabella, daughter and heir
of that Robert son of William de Corkeby who appears so often
in this *Register* (p. 304 *n.*). In 1321–22 their descendants Roald,
son and heir of Thomas de Richmund, and Richard de Richmund

concurred in making over the manor of Corkeby to Andrew de Harcla, Earl of Carlisle. The Earl did not hold it long; for on his attainder in March 1323, it was escheated to the King, Edward II. Among those who had been instrumental in the arrest of the Earl was Sir Richard de Salkeld; and the King rewarded him with the manor of Corkeby. This gift of his father, Edward III. confirmed to Sir Richard in October, 1335 (p. 382 *n.*). Salkelds.

Another member of that family comes before us in connection with Wetherhal, another Sir Richard Salkeld, who with his wife Jane was buried in Wetherhal Church, where his effigy still remains. He died in 1503 (p. 382 *n.*). Catherine and Mary, the two eldest of five daughters, had each a moiety of the property. Their descendants remained in possession throughout the dissolution, and sold their two moieties of the manor to Lord William Howard, Sir Walter Scott's "Belted Will," of Naworth, in 1606 and 1624 respectively.

Beyond certain disputes concerning their property, there is little to be learned of the history of the Priory in the 15th century. An interesting Rental of the property in 1490 has been preserved (Illustrative Docum. XLIV.). Like other monasteries, it was gradually going down hill and hastening to the end. The old stones of Wetherhal Parish Church testify to some of the actors in the later scenes. Over the south window of the chancel are the words, "*Orate pro anima Willielmi Thornton Abbatis.*" William Thornton had been Prior of Wetherhal and was Abbot of S. Mary's at York, apparently the last Abbot of that great foundation. Over the chancel door is the inscription, "*Orate pro anima Richardi Wedderhall.*" He was the Prior in 1534–35 when the great valuation was made by Henry VIII. with the view of the transfer of the first fruits and tenths from the Pope to the Crown. This valuation of the property of the monastery is of course preserved to us in the *Valor Ecclesiasticus* (Illustrative Docum. XLV.). Some time during the next three years, the Priory was subjected to the general visitation by Thomas Crumwell's visitors. It was probably made in 1537 by those unscrupulous agents, Church Inscriptions. Visitation and Surrender of Priory.

Dr Layton and Dr Legh, for, together with the neighbouring Religious Houses, the Priory appears in the *Comperta*, or supposed fragments of the Black Book[1]. Of their report of the Monastery as published, like those of many other Religious Houses, it must be said that it is evidently and needlessly foul and false (Illustrative Docum. xxxix.). The deed of surrender of the Priory, examined by Thomas Legh, was signed on October 20th, 1538, by Radulph Hartley, the Prior, and John Clyston, a monk. The property was apparently only given up on December 31st (Illustrative Docum. xxxix.). We have the surveys of the property at the surrender (Illustrative Docum. xLVI.) when the values are put slightly higher than at the survey a few years before. When the property of the Monastery passed into the hands of the Crown, the site of the House and the demesne lands and fishery were leased on March 4th, 1539, to Sir Thomas Wentworth, knight, for a term of 21 years. A statement of the whole property in great detail is given in the King's Ministers' Accounts (Illustrative Documents, xLII.). The tenants of the customary tenements are there set out, very much as in the Rental of 1490 (Illustrative Docum. xLIV.) and often with the same curious additional rent of a cock, two hens and three days' work in autumn. The Rectory of the Parish Church of Wetherhall valued at £26. 13s. 4d. had been assigned to the late Prior Radulph Hartley by Letters Patent dated January 31st, 1539, as part of his pension (Illustrative Docum. xL.). Sir Thomas Wharton and James Rokebie, Commissioners of the King on the surrender, account for the value of divers domestic articles and utensils which had been sold, also of live and dead farm stock. The list is interesting; but the valuables were evidently not forthcoming, or had passed into the hands of the King's Receiver, William Grene. Besides the Prior, Radulph Hartley, the names of three of the monks are given—John Clyston, Thomas Hartleye and John Gaille, as well as of diverse officials, servants and creditors.

---

[1] See *Suppression of the Monasteries*, T. Wright (Camden Society), Letter xlvii, and Dixon, R. W., *Hist. of Ch. of England*, i. 348.

Probably the number of twelve monks on the original foundation had been diminished, especially as the time of dissolution drew near (Illustrative Documents, LII.).

An interesting document dated 1556–7, the report of Commissioners appointed in 3 and 4 Philip and Mary, affords some information as to the bells of the old Monastery. Instructions were given to the Commissioners to enquire what had become of the three " bells of the late Cell of Wetherhal weying vi C pound weight." They learned from Lancelot Saulkelde, the Dean, that one bell came to Carlisle, and was hanged upon the wall called Springall Tower to call the workmen who were making the new Citadel and mending the Castle. The weight of the bell he did not know. The other two bells remained at a house in Wetherhal awaiting the Queen's commands. The two bells he esteemed to be 500 pounds weight. It does not appear what was their ultimate fate[1].

The House and whole demesne, the lands and all the Churches, except those of Wetherhal and Warwick, were granted to the Dean and Chapter of Carlisle by their Endowment Charter dated May 6th, 1541 (Illustrative Docum. XLVII.). The excepted Churches did not long remain in the hands of the King. The Dean and Chapter on March 5th, 1546, petitioned to have the Rectory of Wetherhal in recompense for the decay of the Cathedral Church (Illustrative Doc. XL.). The request was granted, and the Churches of Wetherhal and Warwick, with the Chapels of S. Anthony and S. Severin annexed thereto, were transferred to them by Letters Patent dated January 15th, 1547, a few days before the King's death on the 28th of the month (Illustrative Doc. XL., XLI.). Some arrangement was to be made with the late Prior during his life, and the Chaplains of Wetherhal and Warwick were each to receive a salary of £6. A lease for 37 years of the House and demesne lands, the mill and the fishery, was granted by the Dean and Chapter, Lancelot Salkeld the late Prior being now Dean, on December 14th, 1541,

[1] See Art. by Rev. H. Whitehead in *Cumb. Archæol. Soc. Trans.* IX. 264.

to one John Blaklocke of Henryby (Harraby) at a rent of £20. 0s. 8d., the amount being evidently calculated on the survey made at the surrender (Illustrative Doc. XLVIII.).

More than 350 years have gone by and most of the property of the old Priory remains in the same hands. One instructive interlude there was in the 17th century. At the Revolution, the Commissioners appointed by the Trustees under an Act of the Commons of England made a survey in April, 1650, of the manor of Wetherhal and other possessions "late belonging to the late Dean and Chapter of the Cathedrall Church of S. Maries (*sic*) of Carlisle" (Illustrative Docum. XLIX.). The survey of the Rectory has alone been found. The manor with the House and demesne lands were sold to Robert Banks of Cockermouth for £1044. 5s. 1½d. It is to be feared that it did not prove a good speculation for the purchaser. On the Restoration in 1660, the Dean and Chapter, with other owners of Church property, reentered into possession. A Bill was that year brought into Parliament to confirm sales and to give indemnity to purchasers; but it fell through. The purchasers could only fall back on common law, and with a title so defective they had no remedy[1].

There are few remains of the monastic buildings. The old gateway tower is in good preservation, and there are portions of two or three walls. The monastery must have occupied a considerable space on the large platform artificially formed on the hill side overhanging the river. Hutchinson, the local historian, asserts (vol. i. p. 156) that what was left of the "edifice" was demolished by the Dean and Chapter of Carlisle "who built a prebendal house &c. in Carlisle with the materials." He further states that Mr Howard, "the late beautifier of Corby, offered a sufficient compensation if they would suffer the building to stand." This was written in 1794, and has been diligently copied. It would be interesting to hear the other side. There is no record of such a proceeding in the Chapter Minutes, as there

(margin: Survey and sale 1650.)

---

[1] Hallam, *Constit. Hist.* Chap. XI. A copy of the conveyance is in the Dean and Chapter Office.

naturally would have been. Whatever truth there may be in the story, it is certain that the stone was not used for any prebendal house. The only house to which this could have referred was the house of the second prebendary at the west end of the Cathedral; and there is evidence that this was built in the preceding century, being commenced in 1669. Thus are errors perpetuated.

The long story of this old and retired place, drawn from these documents, is not without its interest and value. Facts are brought before us about which there can be no doubt, and persons about whom little that is certain is now known. These go back to a time when genuine records are very scanty; and they serve to illustrate, sometimes to correct, the local annals of their day. Just 800 years have passed since the Priory was founded. For more than half that period it had fulfilled, more or less well, the part which the Religious Houses were destined to perform in England. It had witnessed the fusion of Norman and Englishman, the growth of English law and of the English language, the long contest for the rights and liberties of the English people. It had seen the increasing hold of Rome upon the English Church, the attempt to make her subservient to the Papal power, and the Nemesis which followed. It had felt the grasping hand of the most arbitrary of English Kings, though its property had not gone, as in some other cases, to enrich his satellites and counsellors. Then it sank into the solitude of the rural village, its site marked by little beyond the farm and the homestead. Amid all, how little the natural scene has changed. The railway and the telegraph within view may tell of 19th century inventions. Fields and woods, the ford and the spring, occupy often, as we can see, their old position, and bear sometimes their old names. The grassy platform on which the Monastery stood can be but little altered. While below the old river runs and murmurs between the same high wooded banks, a type at once of the changes and the continuity of human things above.

———

THE MANUSCRIPT REGISTER OF WETHERHAL AND THE TRANSCRIPTS.

It is fortunate that excellent Transcripts had been made before the original manuscript of this *Register* or *Cartulary* was lost. It was long in the possession of the Dean and Chapter of Carlisle. It was copied in 1693. A controversy about some of the manors in the Forest of Inglewood, chiefly Wetherhal and John de Chapple, arose in 1717 between the Duke of Portland and the Dean and Chapter. The latter, to avoid litigation, laid certain documents before the Duke through the mediation of Bishop Nicolson. The result was satisfactory, and no further steps were taken in Chancery. In their letter to the Bishop, the Dean and Chapter refer to their "Cartulary of Wedderal," "which seems by the writing to be about 400 years old." But in the list of documents, copies of which were enclosed, the references to the pages are not the pages of the old Cartulary, but of the Transcript A which the Dean and Chapter now have. On June 23rd, 1772, the Dean and Chapter ordered "the Register of Wetheral deposited in our inner Treasury" to be exhibited at Kirkby Stephen at a Commission then sitting. In the Appendix (R) to *The First General Report of the Commissioners on Public Records*, dated June 2nd, 1812 (p. 180), it is stated under the head of Carlisle— "The ancient Manuscript Chartulary of the Abbey of Wetherall at Carlisle does not contain any entries of Public Charters or Statutes." A reference is given to page 343 of *The Report of the Select Committee of the House of Commons on Public Records*, where there is an inaccurate return of the manuscripts of the Dean and Chapter of Carlisle made by John Brown, Registrar, and among them "An ancient Manuscript Chartulary of the Abbey of Wetherall." We may conclude therefore that the old manuscript was in the possession of the Dean and Chapter in 1812; and it is to be hoped that it may some day be recovered.

There are fortunately three good Transcripts in existence, and in addition several series of extracts from the *Register*. These have been carefully collated. The Transcripts are :—

A. In the possession of the Dean and Chapter of Carlisle, dated 1693.

B. In the possession of the Dean and Chapter of Carlisle. There is in it the statement that it is copied in 1787 from Bishop Nicolson's Manuscript.

C. In the British Museum, Harleian Manuscripts, No. 1881. It is endorsed "given by Dr Todd, who promised to give three vols. more."

Up to a certain point C is practically the same as A and B. But C contains copies of additional documents, no doubt in the old manuscript, but some of them evidently spurious and all of them full of inaccuracies. Where the latter have been clearly errors of the transcriber, the corrections have been made. There were other matters in the manuscript *Register* which are not in any of these Transcripts. One of them, as copied by Bishop Nicolson, is given among the Illustrative Documents (v.). No doubt, as in many of these monastic Registers, additions were made from time to time by different hands and some on very questionable authority. It is clear that what have been retained in the Transcripts are those charters and records which affected the property and were thought to have a legal value. As to these additions in Transcript C, more information will be found in the notes to them.

The most elaborate of the series of extracts from the *Register* are those of John Stevens published in his *History of Antient Abbeys*, 1772, being two additional volumes to Dugdale's *Monasticon*. They are taken from a "Transcript of the whole Register Book of Wetheral" which he had received from the Rev. Dr Hugh Todd, of Penrith, Cumberland. There are some of the principal charters at length, and brief extracts from many others. There are also some of the additions found in Transcript C. The names are often copied inaccurately. A number of Stevens' extracts are given in the new edition of Dugdale's *Monasticon*, vol. iii. p. 585.

In the Harleian Manuscript, No. 294 (page 209 *seq.*), are extracts made by Roger Dodsworth, *generosus*, in 1638 from the "Chartulary of Wetherall *penes* Lord Wm. Howard, Baron de Naworth." These are often very brief; they are clearly the same as those used by Dugdale in the first edition of the *Monasticon*. The names are often copied incorrectly. This "Chartulary" was probably the same as that which was afterwards with the Dean and Chapter of Carlisle, but there is no record of the transfer having been made. There are extracts in the Harleian Manuscript, No. 2044 (page 105 *sq.*), of much the same character as the preceding, and these are stated to be from Mr Dodsworth's Book, marked B. Similar extracts will be found among the Dodsworth Collections in the Bodleian Library at Oxford in vol. x. fol. 171 and vol. clix. fol. 138. On none of these extracts by Dodsworth can much reliance be placed for accuracy.

Bishop Nicolson, a most accurate transcriber, made several extracts from the old *Register*; they are to be found in his four volumes of manuscripts which are in the possession of the Dean and Chapter of Carlisle. He remarks on the incongruity of some of the late additions (MSS. vol. iii. p. 133). He was consecrated Bishop of Carlisle in 1702. He left another manuscript volume, *Miscellany Accounts of the Diocese of Carlisle*, 1703–4, which has been edited by Chancellor Ferguson. Numerous extracts were also made by Rev. Thomas Machel, Rector of Kirkbythore, in Westmoreland, who died in 1699. They are, nearly all, only abstracts of the charters, and often, like much of his work, inaccurate. They are found mainly in the fourth of the six volumes of his loose papers which were bound up by Bishop Nicolson. They are now in the possession of the Dean and Chapter of Carlisle.

Nicolson and Burn in their *History and Antiquities of Westmorland and Cumberland*, 1777, have given many extracts and references. These seem to be generally taken from Machel's MS. volumes, which they have used largely and which were lent to

Richard Burn, Vicar of Orton, by the Dean and Chapter on Feb. 26th, 1765, the year he was made Chancellor. He gave a formal receipt for the six volumes, which were returned and the receipt given up in 1775. There are numerous references to the *Register* in a parchment manuscript by Hugh Todd entitled *Notitia* &c... now with the Dean and Chapter of Carlisle. They are practically worthless; and a list of 'Priors of Wedderal' which he has drawn out is of no value. Dr Todd appears to have deserved the low estimate which Bishop Nicolson had of his literary talents.

A collation of some of the above extracts with the Transcripts has enabled a correct reading of the text to be made in certain doubtful places; but they have not been sufficient to determine absolutely the crucial case of the King in the first charter. With these extracts references to the pages of the *Register* are often given; but they are generally so confused and contradictory that it seemed no good object would be gained by quoting them.

CORRECTIONS.

Page 8, line 2 *for* de *read* et.

Page 11, line 27 *for* 5th, 1291 *read* 6th, 1292.

Page 144, line 18 *for* Treby *read* Ireby.

Page 250, line 3 from bottom *for* No. **148** *read* No. **87**.

Page 418, note *for* CARLIOLENSIS *read* CARLEOLENSIS.

Page 425, line 8 from bottom
       after Tynemuth *insert* Hextildesham.

CHARTÆ PRIORATUS DE WETHERHAL.

1. Charta Ranulfi Meschyn super Fundatione de Wetheral.

Ranulfus Meschinus[1] Richerio Vicecomiti[2] Karlioli[3] et omnibus hominibus suis Francis et Anglis qui in

1. [1] On Ranulf Meschin and the Honor of Carlisle, see Appendix A.

[2] The *vicecomes* was the Norman equivalent to the Saxon sheriff, or shire-reeve (*scîr-geréfa*). This is the earliest sheriff of Carlisle recorded. It must be remembered that the district was a border land, and had only been a few years brought under Norman rule. It must not be assumed that the sheriff here was a king's officer; nor that the land had been divided into shires or counties. This, we know, took place later (see Appendix A), when the sheriff's duties were clear (compare E. Freeman, *Norman Conquest*, v. 439).

[3] The British name *Caerluel* (from the Celtic "*caer*" "a mound," then "a fort," and "Luel") points to an occupation long before Roman days of the important position on which the city of Carlisle now stands. Whatever the Luel (perhaps a proper name) may mean in Caerluel, this "camp" or "town of Luel," it appears in the Roman name of the place, *Lugubalia*. Later it was called simply Luel, and then Carleol or Carliol (written often with K for C) as Simeon of Durham tells us, writing before 1130—"Lugubaliam quæ Luel vocatur"; "Quorum Luel, quod nunc Carleol appellatur" (*Hist. Dunelm. Eccles*. i. c. 9, ii. c. 5, ed. T. Arnold i. 32, 53). Then it became Carlile and Carlisle, the *s* coming in through the Norman French. Freeman has remarked that "alone among the names of English cities, it remains purely British" (*William Rufus*, ii. 550). In the British idiom *caer* is put before the qualifying name, in the

potestate Karlioli habitant salutem. Sciatis me dedisse in puram elemosinam et sine omni terreno servicio quietum et liberum Manerium quod vocatur Wetherhala[4] et cum alijs terris ad Manerium illud pertinentibus Stephano Abbati[5]

Teutonic after it ; thus, as he shews, *Caer Gwent* became *Winchester*, *Caer Glovi* became *Gloucester*; but *Caer Luel* remained practically unchanged. On the conquest by the Norman, the name was soon applied to all the newly-won district (see Introduction and Appendix A, on Ranulf Meschin).

[4] Wetherhala is spelt here as in Prior Richard's *History of the Church of Hexham* (cap. v. *circ.* 1160 ; see Illustrative Documents, III.) ; sometimes it appears as Wetheral, but generally Wetherhal or Wederhale ; the spelling with the *h* before the *a* is the older form. From the Anglo-Saxon *weðer* "a wether sheep," with the hard *th*, not þ, and perhaps *healh*, "a steep slope" or "bank," which agrees with the locality ; or from *heall* (older form *hal*) "a hall," in Middle English *halle* ; the word *hala*, or *haula*, or *aula* occurs often in *Domesday Book* for the mansion or principal house on the estate. The parish included four townships, Wetherhal, Scotby, and Cum-whinton with Cotehill, on the west of the Eden, and Great Corby with Warwick Bridge on the east.

The bounds of the Manor are given in No. 236, where see the Notes. On the "manor" generally, and its growth from Anglo-Saxon times, see Stubbs, *Constitutional History*, i. 89, 273, 399 ; Sir Henry S. Maine, *Village Communities*, p. 131 sq.; E. Freeman, *Norman Conquest*, v. 460 sq., and Sir Henry Ellis, *Domesday Book*, Introduction, p. lxxii (Record Com.). On the legal aspect and some peculiarities of the border district, see J. Scriven, *Law of Copyhold*, ed. A. Brown, pp. 2, 16 sq. and, on the jurisdiction, F. W. Maitland, *Select Pleas in Manorial Courts*, Introduction, p. xxxvii. The books and rolls of the manor, in the possession of the Dean and Chapter of Carlisle, do not go back earlier than 1680.

[5] This was Stephen de Whitby, the first Abbot, and, with the as-sistance of Alan, Earl of Richmond, the virtual founder of S. Mary's Abbey at York. He became a monk of the Monastery of Whitby under Prior Reinfrid in the year 1078. Some difficulty having arisen on the death of the Prior (see *Chartulary of Whitby*, ed. J. C. Atkin-son, p. lxxi seq.) Stephen and other monks left Whitby, and settled at the Church of S. Olaf, or S. Olave, near York, given them by Earl Alan, and founded there a Benedictine monastery. When the monas-tery was reconstructed, in 1089, Stephen became the first Abbot, and

et Abbachiæ Sanctæ Mariæ Eboraci[6] in perpetuam possessionem pro anima Domini mei Regis Willelmi[7] et pro

thus remained for 24 years till his death in 1112 (see the reff. in
Dugdale, *Monasticon*, iii. 529, 538).

[6] The Church of S. Olaf, or S. Olave, was built by Siward, the
great Earl of Northumbria, in a suburb of York called Galmanho ;
and there he was buried in 1055. Some little time after 1078, the
Church, with four acres of land, was given by Alan, Earl of Richmond,
to Stephen and his brother monks from Whitby (see the note above).
There they commenced to form the Benedictine monastery. In 1088
William Rufus visited the monastery and gave more land to it ; and
in 1089 himself "opened the ground" to lay the foundation of larger
buildings. The dedication was changed from S. Olave to S. Mary ; and
from this point dates the virtual foundation of the great mitred Abbey
of S. Mary at York (Dugdale, *Monasticon*, iii. 529, 545, 548). William I.
had given certain lands to the monastery which were confirmed, with
other lands and privileges, by William II. ; and grants were made by
persons connected with Ranulf Meschin, such as Ivo Taillebois and
Ranulf's brother William.

[7] There is little doubt that this is the correct reading, and not
Regis Henrici. The conclusions, in some histories, that Henry I. was
the King referred to, and that it is he to whom Ranulf Meschin was
indebted for his possessions, are due to the transcript of this Charter
given in the first edition of Dugdale's *Monasticon* (vol. i. p. 398).
There the reading is *Henrici*, and is said to be : *Ex registro de Wetherhall penes D. Williel. Howard de Naworth, an.* 1638. This and some
other charters, though full of evident errors, are, from the numbers of
the folios given, certainly transcribed from this MS. *Register of
Wetherhal*, which at the end of the 17th century had passed into
the hands of the Dean and Chapter of Carlisle (on this *Register*
and the Transcripts, see the Introduction). Numerous copies
of this charter were made from the *Register* about the same time.
Bishop Nicolson, a most careful and accurate transcriber, has the
words "*Regis Willelmi*," with a reference to fol. 7 *a* of the *Register*
(Nicolson MSS. vol. iii. opposite p. 151). Thomas Machel, not by
any means so accurate, speaks of the manuscript as having been
tampered with, and of "Regis Henrici" being written "*in altem.*"
He also says the first charter is "very obscure now in the Booke,"
and speaks of there being a "new copy of this old Deed" written
there (Machel MSS. iv. p. 453). If, as seems evident, Ranulf Meschin
was put in by William II. to rule the district he had conquered, it was

animabus Patris et Matris meæ et Richardi Fratris[8] mei
et pro anima mea et Uxoris meæ Luciæ[9] et pro animabus
omnium fidelium defunctorum. Testibus Osberto Vicecomite[10] et Waldievo filio Gospatricij Comitis[11], et Forna

not unnatural that Ranulf should be an early benefactor of the
Abbey in which that King had shewn such an interest (see above
on note 6). Moreover the father of his wife Lucia, who is mentioned
here, Ivo Taillebois, was also a benefactor to the Abbey about this
time (Illustrative Documents, XVI.) and had strongly upheld the
cause of William II. For the date of the charter to be deduced,
see note 15 below.

[8] Mentioned in the *Liber Vitæ* of Durham (ed. Surtees Society,
p. 78), where his brother William does not appear.

[9] See Appendix A, on Ranulf Meschin and his wife Lucia.

[10] Osbert de Archis, sheriff of Yorkshire (see *Historians of York*,
ed. J. Raine, iii. 22, 29). He appears several times between 1100
and 1109 and as sheriff in 1106 (see Illustrative Documents, II.), also
in *Domesday Book* (Record Com. i. 329 *b*).

[11] Gospatric, Earl of Northumbria, afterwards Earl of Dunbar,
was according to Simeon of Durham (*Hist. Regum*, ed. Arnold, ii.
p. 199) the son of Maldred son of Crinan, of the royal house of
Scotland ; his mother was Algitha, or Ealdgyth, daughter of Uchtred,
Earl of Northumbria, and Elgifa daughter of King Ethelred II.
(Skene, *Celtic Scotland*, i. 394 *n*, 419 ; see also Freeman, *Norman
Conquest*, iv. 134). He obtained the Earldom of Northumbria from
William the Conqueror in 1067, paying a large sum of money, and
probably urging the claims of his descent. The next year he revolted
against William, and fled with Eadgar the Atheling to Scotland. He
submitted and was restored to his Earldom in 1070. In 1072 he
ravaged the district of Cumbria ; and the same year he was finally
deprived of his Earldom by William, and took refuge with Malcolm,
King of the Scots, who granted him Dunbar and the adjacent lands,
with the title of Earl of Dunbar. He retained considerable possessions in England ; and his name, as well as those of his three
sons Dolfin, Waldief and Gospatric, appears in *Domesday Book*.
These three brothers also appear in the Inquisition of King David in
1120, referred to in Appendix A. Skene points out that the name
Gospatric is purely British, and is equivalent to Gwas Patricius,
"the servant of Patrick." The form "Quaspatricius" occurs in an
Inquisition held in 1247 (*Inquis. p. m.* 31 Hen. III. No. 38 ; *Calendar
Documents Scot.* ed. Bain, i. p. 316), where his daughter Juliana is also

Sigulfi filio[12] et Ketello Eldredi filio[13], et Herveio Morini filio[14] et Eliphe de Penrith[15].

mentioned as married to Randulf de Merlaco (Merlay). This form may also serve to explain the name of the place Aspatrick, or Aspatria, in Cumberland (see on No. 30, note 1). He is said to have had another daughter Gunilda, married to Orm the son of Ketell; Etheldreda, and yet another, Octreda, are mentioned.

Waldiev received from Henry I. the Barony of Allerdale or Alredal (*Testa de Nevill*, Record Com. p. 379 *b*), generally called Allerdale below Derwent. From William Meschin, Baron of Copeland, he obtained the land between the Cocker and the Derwent and 5 vills near the valley of the Derwent. There is much about Waldiev in the *Distributio Cumberlandiæ* (Additional Charter, No. 245), but to be received with great caution : see also the very similar document given by J. Bain from the *Tower Miscellaneous Rolls*, and which he suggests is a statement by the monks of Holm Cultram (*Calendar Doc. Scot.* ii. 15). Waldiev was a benefactor to S. Mary's Abbey at York, granting, among other gifts, the Church and manor of Brumfeld (see charter No. 14) ; also to the Priory of Carlisle, to which he gave the Churches of Aspatrick and Crosseby (Cross-canonby) and land near S. Cuthbert's, Carlisle (see extract from the charter of Henry II., Dugdale, *Monast.* vi. 144) ; he also granted to the Church of Bride-kirk in Cumberland, afterwards given by Alice de Rumeley to the Priory of Gyseburne, the vill and church of Apeltun (*Chart. Gyseburne*, ed. W. Brown, ii. 318 ; Dugdale, *Monast.* vi. 270), in which grant his wife Sigrida, or Sigarith, and his sons, Alan and Waldiev, are mentioned. He had a daughter, as well as a sister, called Etheldreda and married to Ranulf Lindsay. This son Alan was also a benefactor to S. Mary's at York, of land in Gosforth and 14 salmon annually from his fishery at Cockermuth. Waldiev and his son Alan also gave land and a herring fishery in Eltadala (Allerdale) to the Priory at Hexham (*Memorials of Hexham*, ed. J. Raine, i. 59).

Of the two other sons of Earl Gospatric, Dolfin was probably the ruler of Cumbria driven out by William II. in 1092 ; Gospatric seems to have been the second Earl of Dunbar, and to have succeeded to his father's estates in Northumberland. The third Earl Gospatric died in 1166 (*Roger de Hoveden*, ed. Stubbs, i. 253).

[12] Forne son of Sigulf, or Liulf, received the Barony of Greystoke from Henry I. (*Testa de Nevill*, p. 379 *b*). Forne was a benefactor to the Priory of Hexham, as was also Ivo his son (*Memorials of Hexham*, ed. J. Raine, i. 59). He died about 1130, for Ivo son of

2. CHARTA RANULPHI MESCHIENS DE EXCLUSAGIO STAGNO EX PISCARIA ET MOLENDINO DE WETHERAL.

NOTUM sit omnibus legentibus vel audientibus litteras has quod Ego Ranulphus Meschinus concessi et dedi in

Forne appears in the Pipe Roll of 31 Henry I. for Yorkshire, paying five pounds for livery of his father's lands. Forne son of Sigulf is mentioned by Simeon of Durham (*Hist. Regum*, ed. Arnold, ii. 261) among a number of principal men in April 1121. The names of the four sons of Ivo often occur in the later Pipe Rolls.

[13] Of Eldred, or Eltred, nothing seems to be known. The local histories which make him the son of Ivo Taillebois are here quite untrustworthy. We know that Ivo had only one child, Lucia (see Appendix A, on Ranulf Meschin). Ketell or Chetell held lands in the Barony of Kendal, which his father may have had before him ; for it appears from an *Inspeximus* of Edward I. that William, son of William de Lancastre, exchanged some land with the Hospital of S. Peter (afterwards S. Leonard) at York for land in Kirkeby (Kendal) which Ketell son of Eltred had given them (Dugdale, *Monasticon*, vi. 613). Ketell was also a benefactor to the Abbey of S. Mary at York, giving them the important church of Morland and the church of Wirchington (see No. 14 and No. 235). From the latter charter we learn that his wife's name was Christiana, and that he had a son William. He had another son Orm, who was married to Gunilda, daughter of Earl Gospatric, well endowed on her marriage by her brother Waldiev. A third son, Gilbert, was said to be the Gilbert who was father to the first William de Lancastre, Baron of Kendal. But for this there is no authority ; in this connection see more on Nigel de Albini in No. 7 and Gilbert son of Reinfrid in No. 209.

[14] There was at a later period Hervicus son of Maurinus who held the Barony of Dalston and the advowson of the Church, which were escheated to the Crown when he was convicted of felony ; these were given to Bishop Walter Malclerk by Henry III. in 1235 (*Assize Rolls*, Cumberland, 1278, *m.* 27 *d.*).

[15] The date of this charter must lie between 1092 when William Rufus conquered this District of Carlisle and 1112 when Abbot Stephen died ; therefore during the last eight years of William's reign or the first twelve years of Henry I., according as we read William or Henry in the charter ; but the former is the probable reading (see note 7 above on *Willelmi*). On the other hand, the witnesses to the charter, especially Osbert the sheriff, would seem to agree better with the later date.

puram et perpetuam Elemosinam Deo et Sanctæ Mariæ et
Sancto Constantino[1] de Wetheral et Monachis ibidem Deo
servientibus exclusagium et stagnum de piscaria[2] et molendino de Wederhale quod scitum est et firmatum in terra
de Chorkeby. Quapropter prohibebo ut nec Dominus de
Chorkeby[3] nec aliquis alius violet ipsum stagnum nec

2. [1] S. Constantine was a King of the Britons who became a
missionary to Scotland and who lived about the end of the 6th century.
He was sent by S. Kentigern to preach in Galwedia and was martyred
in Cantire. Many churches in Scotland were dedicated to him (Bp
Forbes, *Kalendars of Scottish Saints*, p. 314 ; *Dict. of Christian
Biog.* i. 660). These conjoined dedications are not uncommon. The
dedication seems to have been afterwards changed to Holy Trinity
and S. Constantine (No. **35** *et al.*), often written Holy Trinity alone
(No. **43** *et al.*). The monastery was a Cell and subordinate to the
Benedictine Abbey of S. Mary at York. The Church seems to have
been dedicated to the Holy Trinity and to have contained altars of
S. Mary and of the Holy Trinity (see Nos. **126, 183**).

[2] The sluice and pool for the salmon fishery. The weir (Anglo-
Saxon *wer*) or dam forming the pool was fixed in the opposite bank
of Chorkeby. These were afterwards known as "the baye," and
supplied the water for the mill mentioned below (see Illustrative
Documents, VI.). This pool and weir were only done away with in
February 1879, when the mill no longer paid for working. In the
sluice, or opening in the weir, were the salmon traps, called coffins
(from *cophinus* or κόφινος, "a basket") as in No. **38**, or coops (from
Anglo-Saxon *cyfa*, "a basket," and Latin *cupa*, "a tub"). The coop
or *cupa* is mentioned in the Assize Rolls for 1278 (Cumberland, *m.*
32 *d.*), where there is an interesting account of the fixed engines used
in the district for taking salmon, and their abuse ; also of the forma-
tion of a board of conservators (*Calendar of Documents relating to
Scotland*, ed. J. Bain, ii. 38). The use of the word "coffin" in the
sense of a box or chest is shewn in the *Household Books of Lord Wm.
Howard of Naworth* (Surtees Society, vol. lxviii. p. 228): "April 12, 1625.
To Hetherton for fitting iij coffins for iij sammon pyes going to London,
vj*d.*" From the Survey made at the surrender of the monastery (1538)
it appears "the fishyng at the Bay" was reckoned at £10 a year and
the "water corne mill" at 66*s.* 8*d.*; while these together with "the
scite of the howse" and the demesne lands adjoining were only valued
at £20. 0. 8 (Illustrative Documents, XLVI.).

[3] At this time probably Wescubrict, son of William Steffan, one

disturbet illud firmari in terra de Chorkeby. Prohibeo
etiam ne aliquis piscet infra stagnum de Munchewat[4]
præter Monachos.   Testibus hijs, Willelmo Meschino[5],

of the witnesses to this charter (see below on Wescubrict), was the
lord, and held under Ranulf Meschin.   Chorkeby, Korkeby, or Corby,
was a manor on the east side of the Eden in the parish of Wetherhal.
It was afterwards granted by Henry II. to Hubert de Vallibus, *de
incremento*, together with the barony of Gilsland (see also *Testa de
Nevill*, Rec. Com. p. 379 *a*) in these terms : "Sciatis me concessisse
dedisse et confirmasse Huberto de Vallibus in foedo et hereditate sibi
et heredibus suis totam terram quam Gilbertus filius Boet tenuit die
qua fuit vivus et mortuus de quocunque illam tenuisset Et de incremento Korkeby cum piscaria et aliis pertinentiis quam Wescubrich
filius W^mi Steffan tenuit." This charter is given in full in Illustrative
Doc. XXII., and from the witnesses its date must be between 1155—
64, probably in 1157.   There is a list of the lords of Corkeby given
in Hutchinson, *Hist. of Cumb.* i. 170, and elsewhere, said to be preserved at Corby, in the handwriting of Lord William Howard of
Naworth ; but it is incorrect, e.g. it does not mention Osbert, a Lord
of Corkeby who is mentioned in Nos. **35, 191**, the elder brother of
William son of Odard.   In 1323 the vill of Corkeby Magna was given
to Richard de Salkelde by Edward II. after the attainder of Andrew
de Harcla (*Chron. de Lanercost*, ed. Stevenson, p. 251 ; see also on
Additional Charter, No. **244**).   There is a Corby in Lincolnshire,
mentioned in *Domesday Book* (vol. i. p. 371 *b*), which belonged to the
family of Taillebois and came to Lucia, wife of Ranulf Meschin
(*Orderic. Vit.* B. xii. c. 34) ; it is not improbable, therefore, that they
brought the name with them.

[4] Munchwat, or Munchwath as in No. **36**, the Monks' Ford, is
described as below the pool, between Wederhal and Warwick, at the
end of the land known as the *Camera Constantini* (see note 3 on
No. **38**) under S. Cuthbert's Spring (see note 1 on No. **43**).   It is no
doubt identical with the ford still existing, 350 yards below the Railway Bridge, and about 525 yards from the head of the weir where the
sluices would be.

[5] William Meschin was the brother of Ranulf (see No. **3**) who,
according to Camden, gave him the lordship of Gillesland (see
Appendix A on Ranulf Meschin).   From the grant of Henry II.
to Hubert de Vallibus (see note 3 above) it would appear that
William Meschin did not get Gillesland out of the hand of the
original possessor, Gill son of Bueth.   He received the Barony of

Willelmo Archidiacono[6], Odardo[7], Hildredo Milite[8], Wescubrict[9] Godardo[10] et alijs[11].

"Caupaland" or "Coupland" from Henry I. (*Testa de Nevill*, Record Com. p. 379 *a*). It stretched from the Derwent to the Duddon ; and here William Meschin built his castle of Egremunt. He founded near to it the Priory of S. Bega, or S. Bee, as a Cell to the Abbey of S. Mary at York. In the foundation charter he is spoken of as William son of Ranulf, and his wife Cecilia and son Ranulf are also mentioned (see *Regist. S. Begæ*, Harleian MSS. No. 434 ; Dugdale, *Monasticon*, iii. 577, No. III.). Cecilia was the daughter of Robert de Romeli, Lord of Skipton in Craven. His son Ranulf must have died after a short tenure of the Barony ; for his daughter Alice took the property with her in her marriage with William FitzDuncan. The relationships of William Meschin, his wife Cecilia de Romeli, his daughter and granddaughter, both called Alice de Romeli, are shewn in the charters granted to Embsay, later (1151) Bolton Priory in Yorkshire (see Dugdale, *Monast.* vi. 203). Ranulf the son was a benefactor to the Cell of S. Bee and founded Calder Abbey (see the charter of Henry III., Dugdale, v. 340). If Calder Abbey was founded in 1134, as stated in the account of the foundation of Bellalanda or Byland Abbey (Dugdale, v. 349), then William Meschin was probably dead at that date. His foundation of S. Bees was in the time of Archbishop Thurstin, 1119 to 1139. He had also lands in Leicestershire and Northamptonshire (see J. H. Round, *Feudal England*, pp. 210, 221).

[6] Probably Archdeacon of York ; William, Archdeacon, signing directly after Archbishop Thurstin, was also a witness of the foundation charter of S. Bees (*Monasticon*, iii. 577), together with two of the other witnesses here mentioned. Hardy (*Fasti Eccles.* iii. 131) names him as Archdeacon of York, but only on the authority of these charters as given in Dugdale.

[7] The name Odard is very common among persons of distinction in the district during the 12th century, and it is difficult to distinguish them. This Odard may be the same as the Odard who is witness, with Godard, Chetell and others, in two of the three charters of William Meschin to S. Bees ; and he may be identical with Odard, Sheriff of Northumberland in 1121, and was then at York with Forne, son of Sigulf (see above on No. 1). It is not probable that he was identical either with Odard the Sheriff who appears in the Pipe Roll for Carlisle in 31 Henry I. or with Odard, son of Hildred (de Carlel), on whom see No. 72.

3. CHARTA RANULPHI MESCHINI DE DONATIONE ECCLESIARUM SANCTI MICHAELIS ET SANCTI LAURENTII DE APPELBY.

RANULPHUS MESCHINUS omnibus Catholicæ Fidei cultoribus Salutem. Notum sit omnibus quod Ego Ranulphus dedi Abachiæ Sanctæ Mariæ Eboraci Ecclesiam Sancti Michaelis et Ecclesiam Sancti Laurentii[1] Castelli

[8] This may be Hildred mentioned in the Pipe Roll for Carlisle 31 Henry I., and often assumed to be Sheriff of Carlisle, or, as they may be identical, Hildred de Carlel to whom Henry I. gave lands in Gamelsby (see on No. 72); but it is scarcely probable. Neither of them is spoken of as a knight. J. Denton (*Cumberland*, p. 107) speaks of Hildred a knight at the time of the Conquest, afterwards called "de Carliell"; but this is clearly wrong.

[9] Wescubrict or Westubricd was the son of William Steffan, and at one time, probably at the date of this charter, the Lord of Corkeby (see note 3 above). From the charter of Henry I. (No. 8) we learn that he was at Corkeby at the time Ranulf Meschin held the "Honor of Carlisle."

[10] This Godard who attests the two next charters is, no doubt, the Godard who witnesses the three charters of William Meschin granted to S. Bees. J. Denton (*Cumberland*, p. 9) says that William Meschin gave the manor of Millom between the Esk and the Duddon to — de Boyvill, father of Godard Dapifer, whose family held it to the time of Henry III. One of these may well have been the Godard here mentioned. Godard, as appears from the charter of William Meschin (Dugdale, *Monast.* vol. iii. p. 577, No. III.) granted to the Priory of S. Bee the Churches of Witingham (Whicham) and Bothla (Bootle), both in the lordship of Millom.

[11] The date of this and the two following charters cannot be long after the preceding, in any case before 1120, when Ranulf Meschin gave up the district to the King.

3. [1] There seems to be no doubt that these formed a parish or parishes in Saxon times; and some of the remains in the building of the Church of S. Michael confirm this view. The Churches, naturally, appear often in this *Register*. This grant to the Abbey of S. Mary at York, by Ranulf Meschin, was renewed, with the addition of two parts of the tithe of his demesne lands on both sides of the river Eden, by another charter (see No. 4), and was confirmed by Henry I. (see No. 9) and Henry II. (see No. 14), also by Bishop Athelwold (No. 16), Bishop

Bernard (No. 17) and by Bishop Hugh (Nos. 20 and 24). The last mentioned confirmed the grant (1219—1223) on the condition that the house of Wederhale possess the same, saving to the Abbey the accustomed pension, and presenting fit Vicars who should receive, the Vicar of S. Michael 5 marcs and the Vicar of S. Laurence 6 marcs, the Vicars to serve the Churches and pay all Episcopal and Archidiaconal charges. The patronage of the Church of S. Michael was confirmed to the Priory of Wederhale by Pope Gregory IX. on March 14th, 1240 (No. 25), and the right of entry on a vacancy, apparently in consequence of some claim put forward by the Bishop of Carlisle. Bishop Silvester on Feb. 18th, 1247 (No. 26) confirmed the grant of these two Churches made by Bishop Hugh.

On May 8th, 1248, the patronage of the Vicarage of S. Michael was made over to the Bishop of Carlisle and his successors (together with that of the churches of Ormesheved, Musgrave, Clibburn and Burgh) by the Abbey of S. Mary at York, saving the usual pension paid them from the said church by the Prior of Wederhal (see Additional Charter, No. 240). On March 26th, 1256, Walter Scaldewelle being Vicar, Bishop Thomas Vipont ordered what portions the Vicars of S. Michael should have, giving very exact details (see No. 27).

On Jan. 25th, 1251, Bishop Silvester assigned portions to the Vicarage of S. Laurence ; also for the serving of the chapel in the Castle of Appleby every day, and for the service of the chapel of Hoff three days a week ; the payment of 20 shillings pension to the Vicar of S. Michael's was also remitted (see Illustrative Documents, X.).

On November 5th, 1291, an assize was held concerning the right of patronage of the Churches of S. Michael and S. Laurence, which the King, Edward I., claimed ; but judgment was given in favour of the Abbot and Convent of S. Mary at York (see Illustrative Documents, XI.). Other matters of interest connected with the Church of S. Laurence are given among the Illustrative Documents, more especially as to the serving of the Chapel in the Castle of Appleby (see XIII.). There were two Chantrys in the Church of S. Laurence. One the chantry of S. Mary, said to have been founded by William de Goldington (see on No. 157) in the 13th century : the other the chantry of S. Nicholas, founded by Robert de Threlkeld. There is a confirmation by Bishop John de Kirkby, dated March 29th, 1335, among the Levens Hall MSS. (see 10th Report Historical MSS. Commission (iv.) p. 322). It confirms the Letters Patent of Edward III. granting licence to Robert de Threlkeld to alienate in mortmain a yearly rent of 74s. 7d. in Appleby... to a chaplain, who shall celebrate

mei de Appelby[2] cum omnibus quæ ad eas pertinent sicut Radulphus Capellanus meus tenuit quietas et liberas ab omni terreno servicio. Testibus Uxore mea Lucia, et Willelmo fratre meo, et Gilberto Tysun[3], et Godardo.

for his soul in the Church of S. Laurence. It recites the charter of foundation of the chantry, dated the Saturday before March 12, 1335. The reference to this confirmation in Nicolson and Burn, *Hist.* i. 328 is quite incorrect. There are other documents of interest about these chantrys among the Levens Hall MSS.

[2] Judging from the importance of the position, there were probably fortifications here before the Norman conquest of the district. Ranulf Meschin could not neglect a point which commanded the pass into Yorkshire, and the junction of the two roads from Carlisle, one by Penrith, the other up the valley of the Eden. It is also probable that he may have held the castles of Brougham, commanding the road from Penrith along the valley of the Eamont, of Brough, the road over Stanemore, and of Pendragon, the road through the pass of Mallerstang into Yorkshire. There are numerous references to the Castle in old documents. In the earliest Pipe Roll (31 Henry I.), when the district had passed into the hands of the King, a person (name illegible) renders account to the Treasury of 40s. that he may be the porter of the Castle of Aplebi. In 1176 (*Pipe Roll for Yorkshire*, 22 Henry II.) Gospatric, son of Orm, accounts for 500 marcs of amercement because he surrendered the King's Castle of Appelbi to the King of Scots. This was surrendered in 1174 to William the Lion. Others were fined for advising the surrender (see further on Gospatric, Additional Charter, No. 249). In 1194 (*Cumberland*, 5 Rich. I.) 40s. was spent by Royal writ on works on the Castle of Appelbi ; and in 10 Richard I. the same amount was spent in repairs, as well as on the Castle of Burgo (Brough) ; again, in 1 John, 100s. on repairs of the Castle of Appelbi, and £4 on the Castle of Burgo ; and other amounts several times in the same reign. In February, 1227—28, Henry III. issued a writ to the Constable of the Castle to give up the Castle to the bearer, the King having granted to Hubert de Burgo the ward of the land and heir of Robert de Veteripont with the Castles. Similar writs were issued as to the Castles of Malverstang, Bruham and Burgh (*Patent Rolls*, 12 Hen. III. *m.* 6). See further on No. 204. After this date the history of the Castle is clear. On the building itself, see a paper by Chancellor Ferguson, *Transac. Cumberland Archæol. Society*, viii. 382.

[3] Gilbert Tison or Tisun, in a grant of lands made by him to the Church of Selby, is called *summus vexillator* of the King of England

4. CHARTA RANULPHI MESCHINI[1].

RANULPHUS MESCHINUS omnibus Catholicæ Fidei cultoribus Salutem. Notum sit omnibus quia Ego Ranulphus dedi Abbatiæ Sanctæ Mariæ Eboraci Ecclesiam Sancti Michaelis et Sancti Laurentii de Appelby cum omnibus quæ ad eas pertinent sicut Radulphus Capellanus meus tenuit quietas et liberas ab omni terreno servicio et duas partes decimæ Dominij mei ex utraque parte aquæ[2] et duas partes decimæ Dominij mei de Maiburne[3] et

(William I.). This was in the time of Alred, Archbishop of York, 1060—1069. Another grant was made by him to the same Church in the time of Archbishop Thomas, 1070—1100 (Dugdale, *Monasticon*, iii. 500). His name appears as a proprietor in *Domesday Book*, 1085— 86 (vol. i. p. 327 *a*). He was also a benefactor to the Abbey of S. Mary at York (*Monasticon*, iii. 534).

4. [1] This grant is similar to the preceding; there is no mention of the Castle of Appelby, but we have in addition a grant of two parts of the tithe of the demesne lands and of Maiburne and Salchild, with the same witnesses. Such reservation of one third, or two thirds, of the tithe was not uncommon; see examples in *Chron. of Abingdon*, ed. J. Stevenson, ii. p. LXX.

[2] That is of the demesne lands at Appelby on both sides of the water of the river Eden.

[3] Maiburne or Mayburn was in the parish of Crosby Ravensworth in Westmoreland, the Church of which belonged to the Abbey of Whitby. It was called later Mauld's Meaburn from Maud or Matilda, sister of Sir Hugh de Morville, Lord of Burgh, and wife of William de Veteriponte, in the reign of Henry II. (see on No. 204). It was distinguished from Meaburn Regis, or King's Meaburn, in the adjoining parish of Morland, which is mentioned in No. 219. It is also called Gerard's Meaburn, and appears under this name in No. 228, where the Abbey of S. Mary at York allows these two parts of the tithe to the Vicar on the payment of 2*s.* annually, the date being between 1132 and 1161. A convention was entered into concerning these tithes between R. Abbot and the Convent of S. Mary at York, and Peter, Abbot and the Convent of Whitby, the former giving a perpetual lease of the tithe for an annual payment of 10 quarters of wheat; see the Additional Charter, No. 241, and the corresponding charter in the *Chartulary of Whitby* (ed. Atkinson, i. 216), the date being between 1190 and 1211. This payment appears to have been afterwards

Salchild[4]. Testibus Uxore mea Lucia et Willelmo fratre meo, Gilberto Tysun et Godardo.

5. CONFIRMATIO REGIS HENRICI PRIMI DE CELLA SANCTI CONSTANTINI CUM MANERIO DE WEDERHALA.

HENRICUS Rex[1] Angliæ Archiepiscopo Eboraci et Justiciarijs et Vicecomitibus et omnibus Baronibus et Fidelibus suis Francis et Anglis Eboraci scire et de Karleolo[2] salutem. Sciatis me concessisse et confirmasse Deo

commuted for a money pension ; at the dissolution, we find, a pension of £4 was paid by the Rector of Crosby Ravensworth to the Priory of Wetherhal (see Illustrative Documents, XLV.). This grant is confirmed by Henry I. in his charter, No. **9.**

[4] Salchild or Salkeld, called Salkeld Regis in No. **237**; also in later times called Great Salkeld, probably to distinguish it from the manor of Little or Old Salkeld in the parish of Addingham, which belonged to the Priory of Carlisle. Salkeld remained in the King's hands when Ranulf Meschin left the district, and was one of the manors given to Alexander, King of Scots, under treaty by Henry III. in 1242 (see on Scotby, No. **14**). The Church was very early appropriated to the Archdeacon of Carlisle, but in the time of Henry III., it appears from the above grant, the advowson was in the hands of the King. In 1292 it was decided that the advowson was with the Bishop, the Archdeacon (Richard de Wytebi) being *parsona impersonata*, Henry III. having granted it by charter to Bishop Walter Malclerk in 1236—37 (see *Placita de quo war.* Record Com. p. 116 *a*; it is there called Parva Salkeld, the names evidently having being interchanged in error). For Little or Old Salkeld, see on Adam Salsarius, No. **154**. The lands, of which the Priory had two parts of the tithe and the rector one, are set out in No. **237**. At the dissolution, as well as in 1490, the pension for this tithe was reckoned at 15*s.* (see Illustrative Documents, XLIV. XLV.).

5. [1] Henry the First. On these confirmation charters, see the Introduction to the *Charter Rolls* (Record Com. vol. i.) by Sir T. D. Hardy.

[2] The Shire of Carlisle ; the District or Honor of Carlisle was now divided, with certain additions (see Appendix A) into the shires of Carlisle and Westmoreland, *Charleolium* and *Westmarieland,* and the shires or counties appear under these names in the earliest extant Pipe Roll, that of 31 Henry I.

et Ecclesiæ Sanctæ Mariæ Eboraci et Abbati Gaufrido[3] et
Monachis ibidem Deo servientibus Cellam Sancti Constantini cum Manerio de Wederhale et cum Capella de
Warthwic[4] et cum exclusagio et stagno de piscaria et de
molendino de Wederhale quod est scitum et firmatum in
terra de Chorkeby sicut habuerunt quando Randulphus

[3] Gaufrid, the third Abbot, was only Abbot for less than two years,
1131—32. He died according to Dugdale (*Monasticon*, iii. 538) on
July 17th, but Walbran in his *Memorials of Fountains Abbey* (i. 7)
shews that he was alive till after October 6th.

[4] Warthwic, or Warwick, was a distinct parish, as appears from the
charter of Bishop Athelwold (No. 16). The Chapel was probably in
subjection to the Church of Wetherhal (compare Phillimore, *Eccles.
Law*, ii. 1825). We find from No. 14 that this Chapel, as well as the
Church of Wetherhal, was granted by Ranulf Meschin. Later, a
distinct incumbent was appointed by the monastery (see No. 39). A
great controversy on the right of advowson of Wetherhal and Warwick,
claimed by Bishop Kirkby, arose in October, 1338. The Abbot and
Convent of S. Mary, not having appointed to the vacant Church of
Warthwic in time, the Bishop gave the benefit of the lapse to R. de
Bramlay, Doctor of Civil Law, who, as the Bishop's Commissary,
collated Richard de Besyngden (or Resynden) to the benefice. This
was withstood by the Convent, whereupon the Bishop by a notarial
act summoned the Abbot and Convent to prove their title to all the
Churches they claimed in the Diocese of Carlisle ; but they disdained
to put in an appearance. Legal proceedings went on. A declaration
of contumacy was pronounced against the Bishop for not answering a
citation ; but this was revoked by the Official of the Court of York in
December, 1338, and the revocation was confirmed by the Archbishop,
on the Bishop pleading that he was engaged in state business on the
Marches. The Convent appealed to Rome, and in the end the
controversy was settled in their favour (*Register of Bishop Kirkby*,
MS. pp. 380, 385—8). The Chapel was dedicated to S. Leonard, see
Nos. 39, 55. Warthwic parish adjoined the manor of Wetherhal on
the north, and was bounded on the other sides by the river Eden
and Scotby beck. In it were at an early period the two manors and
families of Warthwic and Aglionby, so often occurring in this
Register. Warthwic manor would seem to have been given to Odard
de Corkeby at the same time as Chorkeby (see No. 2, note 3), for we
find it in possession of his son William (see on No. 35) ; they were
probably granted by Hubert de Vallibus.

comes Cestriæ[5] habuit Karleolum[6]. Et confirmo eis ex dono meo totam pasturam[7] inter Edene[8] et Regiam viam[9] quæ ducit de Karleolo ad Appelby[10] et a Wederhale usque ad Dribec[11]. Et concedo eis Forestam meam[12] ad porcos

[5] Ranulf Meschin had lately died, in 1129 (see Appendix A); he is here spoken of as Earl of Chester, and nothing is said of an Earldom of Carlisle.

[6] This is the District or Honor of Carlisle as in No. **8**, not, as above, the Shire.

[7] This pasture was in the Forest; and the monks could also depasture cattle of other persons and take the profits, see the charter of Edward III. referred to below, note 12.

[8] The river Eden, from the Celtic *ed* and *ad* (Sanskrit *ud*) "water," with the formative termination *en* (comp. Robt. Ferguson, *Dialect of Cumberland*, p. 206), rises in one of the mountains of the Pennine range, at the head of the Mallerstang valley on the borders of Westmoreland and Yorkshire; passing through Appleby, it flows in a direction nearly north by Wetherhal and Warwick, when, turning westward, it flows, after a few miles, by Carlisle and on into the Solway Firth. There are two rivers of the same name in Scotland, one near S. Andrews, Fife, the other in Roxburghshire.

[9] It is termed also "Strata Regia quæ vocatur Hee-Strette," in No. **236**, where see its direction determined, running parallel to the river and less than a mile distant. This would be the highway or King's high road; but it is doubtful whether a Roman road ran here. The road is traced further on the other side of the river Eden, see on Nos. **175, 179.**

[10] On the borough of Appleby, see No. **223.**

[11] The southern boundary of the Manor of Wetherhal, as set out in No. **236.**

[12] The King's Forest, of which this is perhaps the earliest record. It is called "my Forest of Carlisle" in No. **9**; it was known later as the Forest of Cumberland and the Forest of Inglewood. In *Testa de Nevill* (p. 379 *b*) we find that Ranulf, Lord of Cumberland, gave the custody of the Forest of Cumberland to Robert de Trivers at an annual rent of x. marcs, and that at the time of that Inquisition the King had the custody of the said Forest in his own hands. A perambulation of the boundaries of the Forest was made in the reign of Edward I., and confirmed by Letters Patent, dated Feb. 14th, 1301 (given in full in Nicolson and Burn, *History*, ii. 522). The same boundaries are shewn by an Inquisition, made in 1380 (see *Escheat,*

4 Ricard. II. No. 115 ; a copy is among the documents in the Dean
and Chapter Office at Carlisle). The Forest of Inglewood then
included the land, omitting the City of Carlisle, between the Shawk
and the Eden, and the Amote (Eamont) on the south ; but no doubt,
at an earlier period, the King's Forest was much larger, and included
roughly most of the Shire that was outside the Baronies and the City
of Carlisle. The earlier Pipe Rolls contain numerous references to
the Forest, especially to the rent paid for its custody ; thus in 1166,
a rent of 5 marks (see the references in the Introduction, *Pipe Rolls for
Cumberland &c.*, p. xxiii.). In 1186 the Pipe Roll gives us the following
entry—" Idem Vicecomes reddit comptum de dimidio marci de Priori
de Wederhala pro warda facta in foresta." In 1211, Richard de Luci
pays 5 marks for the *Census Forestae* and a fine of £100 *de foresta
male custodita*. King John granted the Hermitage of S. Hilda in
" our forest of Englewode" on March 1st, 1214—15, to the Abbey of
Holm Cultram with land which Robert Gobi formerly held and a
vaccaria for 40 cows in the Forest (*Register Holm Cult.* MS. p. 164 sq.
Close Rolls 16 John *m.* 7, and compare *Placita de quo War.* Rec. Com.
p. 130 *a*). We learn from the charter of Edward III. in 1331 (see
Illustrative Documents, XXXIII.) that the King's Officers of the
Forest had disturbed and harassed the monks of Wederhale, and that
the privileges of wood and of pasture in the Forest, granted here and
in No. 9, were fully confirmed by the King.

The disafforesting of a part of the Forest, the manor of Dalston, is
set out in the grant by Henry III. to Bishop Walter Malclerk on July
15th, 1231 ; and a grant of the tithes of certain assart lands in the
Forest to the Priory of Carlisle was made by Edward I. on Dec. 5th,
1293 (these are given in full in Nicolson and Burn, *History*, ii. 541,
546) ; the same King in February, 1286 had granted to the Priory of
Carlisle the tithe of animals taken in the Forest, and other privileges
as to wood, and that the dogs of their men should be *quieti de expedi-
tacione* ; this was confirmed by an *Inspeximus*, dated April 30th, 1331,
by Edward III. (*Patent Rolls*, 5 Edw. III. *m.* 8 ; there is a copy in
the Dean and Chapter Office). On October 26th, 1363, Edward III.,
in consideration of the heavy losses of growing crops caused by the
Scottish army, granted to the men and tenants of Penred, Salkeld and
Soureby in Englewood Forest the right therein of common pasture for
all their animals for ever (*Patent Rolls*, 37 Edw. III. *m.* 22 ; Record
Com. p. 177). On the forest laws and their cruelty about the time of
this charter, see Stubbs, *Const. History*, i. 402 and *Select Charters*,
pp. 156, 206. A Parliamentary survey of the Honor of Penrith and
part of the Forest of Inglewood was made July 16th, 1650 ; a copy is

suos de Wederhal sine pannagio[13]. Et concedo eis et
confirmo Ecclesias res possessiones terras et omnia quæ
eis data sunt et confirmata per cartas meorum proborum[14]
virorum et prohibeo ne aliquis eis inde contumeliam faciat.
Et præcipio ut ita habeant consuetudines suas et terras
suas et res quietas ab auxiliis et tallagiis[15] et ab omnibus
rebus sicut habet Ecclesia Sancti Petri in Eboraco[16] vel
Ecclesia Sancti Johannis in Berverlaco[17] et omnes easdem
libertates habeant quas habent istæ duæ Ecclesiæ. Testi-

in the Office of the Dean and Chapter of Carlisle. A good and full
account of the later history of part of the Forest is given by Chancellor
R. S. Ferguson in *Popular County Histories, Cumberland*, p. 118 sq. ;
see also Hutchinson, *Cumberland*, ii. 465.

[13] *Pannagium*, from Old French *pasnage*, pasture, the food on which
swine feed, such as acorns and beechnuts ; also the payment made for
the privilege of feeding swine in the Forest. The amount paid as
pannage in the King's Forest of Cumberland appears from the Pipe
Rolls to have been considerable ; in 14th Henry II. it was £7, and in
1 Richard I. as much as £17. 3s.

[14] Some of these grants are detailed in the charter of Henry II.
No. **14**.

[15] *Auxilium*, an aid ; *auxilium Regis*, money levied for the King's
use ; *Tallagium*, tallage, a tax, from the French *tailler*, "to cut off" ;
an extraordinary payment assessed on the property of the Crown.
From the Pipe Rolls it appears there was a Tallage in 33 Henry II.,
and several in the reigns of Richard I. and John ; see Thos. Madox,
History of the Exchequer, i. 685.

[16] The Cathedral Church of S. Peter at York, which had important
liberties, especially of sanctuary. These are fully set out in the charter
of liberties granted or confirmed by Henry I. ; see Dugdale, *Monasticon*, No. XXXI. vi. 1180.

[17] The Church of S. John of Beverley, or Beverley Minster, was
founded as a monastery, at the beginning of the 8th century, by John,
Bishop of Hexham, and afterwards Archbishop of York (705—718),
who died in 721, and was canonized in 1037. The Church was
refounded by King Athelstan as a Collegiate Church in 928, and John
of Beverley was taken as the patron saint. A good account of Joannes
Beverlacensis is given by Canon Raine, s. v. in the *Dict. of Christian
Biography*, vol. iii. This Church also had important privileges of
sanctuary ; see Dugdale, *Monast.* vi. 1307 and Appendix C.

bus Roberto de sigillo[18], et Pagano filio Johannis, et
Eustachio fratre ejus[19] et Pagano Peverel[20] apud Windes-
hores[21].

[18] Roberto de sigillo was a monk of Reading and Chancellor of the
King; he became Bishop of London in 1141, and died of eating
poisoned grapes in 1151. See contin. *Florence of Worcester* and
John of Hexham, in ann. 1141, 1150. He is witness to numerous
charters of Henry I., as No. 8; and to the grant of the Church of
Newcastle to the Priory of Carlisle (Dugdale, *Monasticon*, vi. 144),
also to the Foundation Charter of Furness Abbey by Earl Stephen,
afterwards King.

[19] Eustace son of John was, according to Dugdale (*Baronage*, i. 90),
the son of John de Burgh and nephew and heir of Serlo de Burgh,
founder of Knaresborough Castle. Eustace was a well-known character
in the reigns of Henry I. and Stephen, and a favourite of the former
King. He married, first, Beatrix, daugher of Yvo de Vesci, and from
him the family of de Vesci was lineally descended. Eustace and his
brother were among the early justices itinerant. Eustace, together with
Walter Espec, appears in the Pipe Roll for 31 Henry I. as holding
pleas in Carlisle and Westmarieland (ed. J. Hunter, p. 143); and
Pagan son of John as justice itinerant in the western Midland counties.
The brothers are witnesses to a charter of Henry I. in 1133 to the
Abbey of Rievaulx, founded by Walter Espec, together with, among
others, Robert de sigillo and Jordan Paganel (*Chart. Rievaulx*, ed.
Atkinson, p. 141). Eustace, with his second wife, Agneta, daughter of
William son of Nigel, Constable of Chester, founded the Priory of
Watton in Yorkshire (see on No. 208), also the Abbey of Alnwick in
1147, the second of the Premonstratensian houses in England, of
which Shap, or Heppe, Abbey was one (see the charter in Dugdale,
Monasticon, vi. 867). Pagan, who with Athelwold, Bishop of Carlisle,
witnessed King Stephen's Charter of Liberties in 1136, was in command
on the marches of Wales, and was slain by an arrow in the brain when
chastising the Welsh in 1136, see Henry of Huntingdon, *Gesta
Stephani, in ann.* The same witnesses occur in No. 8.

[20] Pagan or Paian Peverel was, probably, the brother of William
Peverel (see on No. 7), whose progenitors as given by Dugdale
(*Baronage*, i. 438) seem somewhat doubtful. He was the standard-
bearer of Robert, Duke of Normandy, in the Holy Land, and died in
London. He founded, or rather moved to Barnwell near Cambridge,
in 1112, a Priory, where he placed Augustinian Canons, but died
before the buildings were completed. To this Priory, a charter of

6. CHARTA DOMINI REGIS HENRICI SECUNDI.

HENRICUS[1] Dei gratia[2] Rex Angliæ et Dux Normannorum et Aquitanorum et Comes Andegaviæ[3] omnibus
Archiepiscopis Episcopis Abbatibus Prioribus et omnibus
Baronibus et Justiciariis Vicecomitibus et ministris suis et
omnibus fidelibus suis Francis et Anglis in Anglia Salutem
Sciatis quod Ego Henricus Rex Angliæ pro salute animæ
meæ et pro salute animarum Henrici Regis Avi mei et
Willelmi Regis Proavi mei et Willelmi Regis secundi filii
ejus et pro redemptione animarum Patris et Matris meæ
et omnium Parentum meorum nec non pro statu Regni
mei concedo et dono in puram Elemosinam Savarico[4]
Abbati et successoribus ejus et Abbachiæ Sanctæ Mariæ
Eboraci et Monachis ibidem Deo servientibus Terras
Ecclesias decimas silvas plana stagna molendina et alias

Henry I. grants certain lands on the petition of Pagan Peverel ; see
Dugdale, *Monasticon*, vi. 87.

[21] Windsor, where the King often held his court. Henry of
Huntingdon tells us that he lay sick there during Christmas 1132.

The date of this charter is fixed by the name of Abbot Gaufrid to
be in 1131 or 1132.

6.   [1] Henry the Second, who was knighted at Carlisle, at Pentecost
1149, by David I. King of Scots (*Ralph de Diceto*, ed. Stubbs, i. 291).
This is only the first part of the charter granted to the Abbey of
S. Mary at York, which is given in full in the Harleian MS. No. 236,
fol. 6 *b* (see also Dugdale, *Monasticon*, iii. 548) ; the part referring to
the Wetherhal grants is given below in No. 14.

[2] This formula is generally a mark of the later charters of
Henry II.

[3] Henry II. was Count of Anjou in right of his father, Geoffrey
Plantagenet. He first took the title of Duke of Normandy in 1150
with the approval of his mother, the Empress Maud. He became
Duke of Aquitaine in 1152 on his marriage with Eleanor, the divorced
queen of Louis VII. of France, and daughter and heiress of William,
Duke of Aquitaine.

[4] Savaricus, or Severinus, was Abbot for 30 years from 1132 to
April, 1161 ; see *Roger de Hoveden*, ed. Stubbs, i. 129 *n*. and Dugdale,
Monasticon, iii. 538.

possessiones possidendas liberas et quietas ab omni terreno
servicio in perpetuam possessionem cum Soch et Sach[5] et
tol et theam[6] et infangentheof[7], cum eisdem legibus et
dignitatibus et libertatibus quas habet Ecclesia Sancti
Petri Eboraci vel Ecclesia Sancti Johannis Beverlaci, et
nominatim ut quum Eboraci scyra fuerit summonita ire
in exercitum Regis tunc inveniet prædicta Abbachia unum
hominem tantum in exercitu Regis cum vexillo Sanctæ
Mariæ sicut faciunt supradictæ Ecclesiæ. Et ne homines
Sanctæ Mariæ eant ad Schiras vel Tridigns[8] vel Wapentachs vel Hundreds[9], nec etiam pro Vicecomitibus vel

[5] *Soc* is the power or liberty to execute judicial authority, also the
district or area within which such liberty is exercised, from the Anglo-
Saxon *socu*, "an inquiry" or "examination"; *sac* is the power of
hearing and determining matters in dispute, the jurisdiction in writs or
causes, from the Anglo-Saxon *sacu*, "a contention" or "dispute." Hence
the law terms "soke," as above, and "socage," the tenure of land within
the lord's soke or franchise. On this, and many of the following
terms, there is much in the General Introduction to *Domesday Book*
by Sir Henry Ellis, published by the Record Commission, 1816.

[6] *Tol*, toll or duty, also the liberty to take, or be free from, toll; from
the Anglo-Saxon *toll*. *Theam* or *team*, the privilege of judging bond-
men, their children and goods, from the Anglo-Saxon *teám*, "a family"
or "offspring."

[7] *Infangentheof*, the privilege of judging a thief taken within the
district or manor to which the right belonged. So *utfangentheof* is
the similar jurisdiction over a thief taken outside the district; from the
Anglo-Saxon *fangen*, "taken," from *fón*, "to take," and *þeóf*, "a thief."

[8] *Tridign*, for Triding or Thriding, the third part of a shire, or the
court held within a Triding, inferior to the *Scira* or county court.
Hence, the three Ridings, or divisions, of the Shire of York, the *th*
being lost in composition with the words North, East and West.
Lincolnshire was similarly divided.

[9] *Wapentachs* and *hundreds*. These were the inferior divisions
into one or other of which the shire was usually divided, also the
courts held in these divisions. The wapentake answered to the
hundred in regard to administration, and occurred chiefly in the
Danish part of England. The word is from the Anglo-Saxon
wæpengetæc or *wæpentác*, borrowed from the Norse. At the election
of the new chief of a wapentake, he raised his *weapon* or spear, which

Ministris eorum, sed si Vicecomites vel Ministri eorum
habent querelam contra homines Sanctæ Mariæ dicant
Abbati et statuto die veniant in Curia Sanctæ Mariæ et
ibi habeant rectum de capitali placito suo et Sancta Maria
habeat quicquid pertinet ad Curiam suam.   Et ne alicujus
Hæres aut successor querat relevamen vel aliquod Dominium præter Orationes et preces et elemosinas animæ suæ
de beneficijs et elemosinis quas aliquis dedit prædictæ
Abbachiæ quæ subscribuntur hic[10].

7.   Confirmatio Henrici Regis de terris, etc.

HENRICUS[1] Rex Anglorum Archiepiscopis Episcopis
Abbatibus et omnibus Comitibus et Baronibus et Justiciariis et omnibus Vicecomitibus et ministris suis per Angliam
Salutem.   Sciatis quod Ego Henricus Anglorum Rex pro
salute animæ meæ, et pro salute quoque animarum Willelmi Regis Patris mei, Matrisque meæ Matildis Reginæ[2]
vel fratris mei Regis Willelmi necnon pro Statu Regni
nostri concedo in puram Elemosinam et do Richardo[3]
Abbati et Successoribus ejus et Abbachiæ Sanctæ Mariæ
Eboraci terras Ecclesias decimas silvas plana stagna mo-

his men *touched* in token of fealty, see Skeat, *Etym. Dict.* s. v. quoting
B. Thorpe, *Ancient Laws*, Glossary.   The *hundreds* were probably
the districts in which the *hundred* warriors originally settled, but it is
not known with certainty ; they were unequal geographical divisions,
see Stubbs, *Const. Hist.* i. 97 and Thorpe, l. c.

[10] As Henry II. began to reign Dec. 19th, 1154, the date of this
charter lies between 1154 and the death of Abbot Savaricus in April
1161.   But the one witness to the charter of Henry II. given in Dugdale (see note above) is Thomas (Becket) Archbishop of Canterbury,
who was consecrated May, 1162 ; this is an error for Theobald, his
predecessor ; see Illustrative Documents, XXXII.

7. [1] Henry the First.   This is another and earlier charter, confirming the property and liberties generally.

[2] Matilda, wife of William I., was a daughter of Baldwin V., Count
of Flanders, she died November 2d, 1083.

[3] Richard, the second Abbot of S. Mary's at York, from 1112 to
his death December 31st, 1130.

lendina et alias possessiones suas possidendas liberas et quietas ab omni terreno servicio in perpetuam possessionem sicut uncquam melius tenuerunt tempore Antecessorum meorum cum eisdem legibus et libertatibus et dignitatibus et consuetudinibus quas habet Ecclesia Sancti Petri Eboraci vel Ecclesia Sancti Johannis Beverlaci. Et ne homines Sanctæ Mariæ eant ad Schiras vel Tridigns vel Wapentas vel Hundredas. Nec etiam pro Vicecomitibus vel ministris eorum sed si Vicecomites vel ministri eorum habent querelam contra homines Sanctæ Mariæ dicant Abbati Eboraci statuto die veniant in Curiam Sanctæ Mariæ et ibi habeant rectum de capitali placito suo et Sancta Maria habeat quicquid pertinet ad Curiam suam. Et ne alicujus hæres vel Successor querat relevamen vel aliquod Dominium præter orationes et preces et elemosinas animæ suæ de beneficijs et elemosinis quas aliquis dedit prædictæ Abbachiæ. Testibus, Ranulpho Episcopo Dunelmensi[4], Nigello de Albenio[5], Willelmo Peverel[6] et Radulpho Basseth[7] apud Clarendunam[8].

[4] Ranulph or Ralph Flambard was Bishop of Durham from June 5th, 1099 to his death, September 5th, 1128.

[5] Nigel of Albini was, like Ranulf Meschin, one of the leaders loyal to Henry I. and distinguished himself at Tinchebrai (1106) and on later occasions in Normandy; he was rewarded with large estates. He had been in the service of William Rufus, and had married, first, Matilda de L'aigle or de Aquila, the wife of the imprisoned Robert de Mowbray, Earl of Northumberland, and niece of Earl Hugh of Chester. He obtained a divorce from her, and then married Gundreda, sister of Hugh de Gournai (*Orderic Vital. Lib.* viii. c. 23), by whom he had a son Roger (Dugdale, *Monast.* vi. 612). Henry I. gave him the Castle of Mowbray, and much of the property of Earl Robert. Hence, his son took the name of Roger de Mowbray. The Barony of Kendal, which had come into the hands of the King after the death of Ivo Taillebois, was also given by King Henry to Nigel of Albini (or d'Aubigni, as Orderic calls him). This appears from a grant by Richard I. to Gilbert Fitz-Reinfrid (quoted from the Rawlinson MSS. by Sir G. Duchett, *Duchetiana*, p. 150). From Roger de Mowbray, son of Nigel, it passed to William de Lancaster. Nigel of Albini was

thus connected with the district. He died at an advanced age, and was buried in the Abbey of Bec in Normandy. The exact date of his death is not known, but his son Roger was a minor, and made a ward of King Stephen very early in his reign. There is much about Nigel and his family in the records of the Abbey of Byland or Bella Landa, which was founded by Roger de Mowbray in 1143 (see Dugdale, *Monasticon*, v. 346 sq.). Grants made by Gundreda and Roger de Mowbray can also be found in the *Chartulary of Rievaulx* (ed. J. C. Atkinson, p. 30 sq.). In the *Chartulary of Whitby* there is an interesting charter of Nigel between 1108 and 1114, which Bishop Ranulf Flambard of Durham also witnesses (ed. J. C. Atkinson, i. 206) ; also a charter of Henry I. of the same date (p. 155), and containing the names of Nigel de Albini and Bishop Ranulf.

[6] This William Peverel was, probably, the Norman who came over with William I., and who, with little authority, is said by Dugdale (*Baronage*, i. 436) to have been a natural son of the Conqueror, see Freeman, *Norman Conquest*, iv. 200. He held the castle of Notting-ham, and the more famous castle of Peak Forest in Derbyshire. He was one of the witnesses to the noted Durham charter in 1091 (Free-man, *William Rufus*, ii. 536), also to a charter of Earl David between 1108 and 1124 (*Calend. Doc. Scotland*, ed. Bain i. 2). He assisted William Rufus in Normandy in 1094 (*Florence of Worcester, in ann.*). The time of his death is uncertain. There is often some confusion with his son, or descendant, William Peverel, the younger, as he is called by Orderic Vitalis (*Lib.* xiii. c. 37), who mentions him, but incorrectly, as one of the rebel lords against Stephen in 1138. Richard of Hexham and John of Hexham speak of this younger Peverel as being on the side of Stephen at the Battle of the Standard (1138) ; and he is supposed to have poisoned the younger Ranulf, Earl of Chester, in 1153. On Pagan Peverel, see No. 5.

[7] Ralph Basset or Basseth was raised by Henry I. from a low station ; he was Justiciar of England and one of the earliest itinerant judges (Stubbs, *Constit. Hist.*, i. 392). A description of his acting as judge at Huntingdon in 1116 is given by Orderic (*Lib.* vi. c. 10). He was one of the King's commissioners with Ranulf Meschin in 1106 (Illustrative Documents II.). He was alive in 1124 ; for, in Leicestershire, he hanged four and forty thieves, "more than had ever before been executed in so short a time" (*Anglo-Sax. Chron. in ann.*).

[8] Clarendon, in Wiltshire ; here was held, under Henry II. in 1164, the Council which the "Constitutions of Clarendon" have made famous. The date of this charter, from Abbot Richard and

8. CHARTA HENRICI REGIS DE EXCLUSAGIO STAGNO, ETC.

HENRICUS[1] Rex Angliæ Archiepiscopo Eboracensi et Justiciarijs et Vicecomitibus et omnibus Baronibus et fidelibus suis Francis et Anglis de Eboraschira et de Karleolo Salutem. Sciatis me dedisse et concessisse in Elemosinam Deo et Ecclesiæ Sanctæ Mariæ Eboraci et Abbati Gaufrido[2] et Monachis ibidem Deo servientibus exclusagium[3] et stagnum de piscaria et de molendino de Wederhal quod est factum et firmatum in terra de Chorkeby sicut ibidem scitum et stabilitum fuit tempore quo Ranulphus Comes Cestriæ honorem de Karliolo[4] habuit et tempore Westutbricd[5]. Et concedo eidem Ecclesiæ terram in Eboraco quam Wigatus Lincolniensis[6] eis dedit et concessit et Alanus filius suus. Et concedo eidem Ecclesiæ Ecclesiam

---

Bishop Ranulf, lies between 1112 and 1128 ; and probably, like the charter of Henry I. to Whitby mentioned above, near to the former date.

8. [1] Henry the First. A third charter, confirming the grant of the fish-pool and mill.

[2] Gaufrid or Godfrid, the third Abbot of S. Mary's at York, 1131—32 ; see on No. 5.

[3] This confirms Ranulf Meschin's grant No. 2, but long after, when Ranulf was Earl of Chester.

[4] A similar clause to that in No. 5, differing in the addition of the word "honor," which meant, not an earldom (see Appendix A), but one of the great baronial jurisdictions or liberties. "It is the most noble kind of seigniory and can be held only of the King"— Jacob, *Law Dict.* It is here applied to the jurisdiction over the whole land or district or power (No. 1) of Carlisle.

[5] This reference to Wescubrict seems to confirm the idea that he was the Lord of Chorkeby or Corby at the time Ranulf Meschin made the grant ; see on No. 2.

[6] In the confirmation charter of Henry II. to S. Mary's at York the name is Wygot, and the land is all the land he had in York in Usgate (Dugdale, *Monast.* iii. 549). In the same charter Alan, son of Wigot, is mentioned as having given land in Lincolnia.

de Hornebia[7] cum terris et decimis et omnibus rebus
adjacentibus eidem Ecclesiæ sicut Radulphus et Wiganus
filii Landrici dederunt et concesserunt eis in Elemosinam.
Et volo et firmiter precipio ut ipsi eas bene et in pace et
honorifice et quiete teneant in Elemosina sicut melius et
quietius alias suas res tenent.   Testibus Roberto de sigillo
et Pagano filio Johannis et Eustachio fratre suo et Pagano
Peverel apud Windesores[8].

9. CONFIRMATIO HENRICI REGIS DE ECCLESIIS
DE APPELBY, ETC.

HENRICUS[1] Rex Angliæ Thurstano[2] Archiepiscopo
Eboracensi et omnibus fidelibus et ministris suis de Westmerland et de Cumberland Salutem. Sciatis me concessisse
et confirmasse Ricardo Abbati et Conventui Sanctæ Mariæ
de Eboraco Ecclesias de Appelby scilicet Sancti Michaelis
et Sancti Laurentii et terras earum cum decimis et dominijs ejusdem villæ ex utraque parte aquæ et decimas[3] de
dominio de Meabrun et de Salchild sicut carta Ranulphi
Meschin testatur. Concedo autem ex dono meo proprio
dicto Abbati et Conventui et Monachis suis de Wederhale
quod ipsi Monachi de Wederhale et homines sui habeant

[7] Horneby in Yorkshire. The grant of this Church by Wigan, son
of Landric, and witnessed by Hugh, the first Dean of York, is given
in Dugdale, *Monast.* iii. p. 551, No. XIII. It was granted in 1220 by
the Abbot and Convent of S. Mary to Archbishop Walter Gray, and
by him in 1231 to the Dean and Canons of York. The latter deed is
in the Appendix to *Archbp Gray's Register* (p. 139 ed. J. Raine).

[8] The date of this charter is fixed by Abbot Gaufrid as 1131—32.
The witnesses are the same as No. 5, and the time is probably the same.

9. [1] Henry the First. A fourth charter, confirming the grant of
the Churches of Appleby.

[2] Thurstan, or Thurstin, of Bayeux, was consecrated Archbishop
of York by Pope Calixtus II. in October 1119, and retired to the
monastery at Pontefract in January 1140, and died in February ; see
his life in *Fasti Eboracenses*, i. 170, by J. Raine.

[3] The *carta Ranulfi Meschin* here referred to (No. **4**) speaks of
only *duas partes* of the tithe.

semper mortuum boscum in Foresta mea de Karliolo[4] ad
ædificandum et comburendum. Et prohibeo ne aliquis
super hoc eis faciat impedimentum. Testibus E. filio
Johannis[5] et Jordano Paganel[6] apud Radings[7].

10. CONFIRMATIO RICARDI REGIS DE TERRIS EC-
CLESIJS, ETC.

RICARDUS[1] Dei Gratia Rex Angliæ Dux Normaniæ
et Aquitaniæ Archiepiscopis Episcopis Comitibus Abbatibus et omnibus Baronibus et Justiciarijs et Vicecomitibus et ministris suis et omnibus fidelibus suis Francis et
Anglis per Angliam Salutem. Sciatis nos concessisse et
dedisse in puram Elemosinam pro salute animæ nostræ et
pro salute animarum Patris nostri Regis Henrici et Matris
nostræ Alienoræ Reginæ[2] et omnium Antecessorum nostrorum necnon pro statu Regni nostri Roberto Abbati[3] et

---

[4] The King's Forest, here called the Forest of Carlisle; and
whereas in No. 5 the King only allows pigs therein without payment of pannage, here he grants wood for building or burning.

[5] Eustace, son of John, as in No. 5.

[6] Probably the brother, or, according to Dugdale (*Baronage*, i.
432), the son of Ralph Paganel, who joined the Empress Matilda in
the reign of Stephen. Another son, Gervase, was in important
command on the same side in 1138. The name of Jordan Painel
occurs in a confirmation charter of Henry I. to Rievaulx in 1133, as well
as that of his co-witness here (*Chart. Rievaulx*, ed. Atkinson, p. 141).

[7] Reading in Berkshire. According to Roger de Hoveden (ed.
Stubbs, i. 90) Henry I. was buried here.

The date of the charter, from Archbp Thurstan 1119—1140, and
Abbot Richard 1112—1131, falls between 1119 and 1131 (see on No.
7), and from Eustace son of John, probably near to the later date.

10. [1] Richard the First. Richard was the first English king
who adopted the plural number in his charters.

[2] Alienor or Eleanor, in her own right Countess of Poitou and
Duchess of Aquitaine, married Henry II. in 1152, being the recently
divorced wife of Lewis VII. of France; in right of his mother,
Richard held the Duchy of Aquitaine.

[3] Robert de Harpham was Abbot of S. Mary's at York from 1184
to his death on April 19th, 1189. Robert de Longo Campo, Prior of

Successoribus suis et Abbachiæ Sanctæ Mariæ Eboraci et Monachis ibidem Deo servientibus terras Ecclesias Cellas maneria decimas silvas plana stagna molendina et alias possessiones suas possidendas liberas et quietas ab omni servicio in perpetuam possessionem sicut unquam melius temporibus Antecessorum nostrorum tenuerunt cum eisdem legibus et libertatibus et dignitatibus et consuetudinibus quas habet Ecclesia Sancti Petri Eboraci vel Ecclesia Sancti Johannis Beverlaci.   Et ne homines Sanctæ Mariæ eant ad Comitatus vel ad Schiras vel Tridigns vel Wapentachs vel Hundreds, Nec etiam pro Vicecomitibus vel ministris eorum.   Sed si Vicecomites vel ministri habent querelam contra homines Sanctæ Mariæ dicant Abbati Eboraci et statuto die veniant in Curiam Sanctæ Mariæ et ibi habeant rectum de capitali placito suo, et Sancta Maria habeat quicquid pertinet ad Curiam suam.   Et sicut aliqua Ecclesia in tota Anglia magis est libera sit et hæc libera.   Et omnes terræ ad eam pertinentes quas nunc habet vel quas rationabiliter adquirere poterit vel maneria vel cellæ vel quæcunque possessiones sint quiete de placitis et querelis et murdro[4] et latrocinio[5] et scutagio[6] et Geldis[7]

Ely, is said to have succeeded him in 1189 (see Dugdale, *Monast.* iii. 538), and died in January, 1239, a very long tenure of the office ; Robert de Longo Campo must be the Robert here mentioned ; but Ralph de Diceto (ed. Stubbs, ii. 151) says he was elected in 1197, which is the more probable date.

[4] *Murdrum* in the time of Henry I. was simply the private killing of a man (Jacob, *Law Dict.*); also, as here, the penalty paid by the district in which a murdered person is found.

[5] *Latrocinium*, here not military service, or robbery, but the penalty to be paid for robbery committed in the district.

[6] *Scutagium*, scutage or escuage, from *scutum* and French *escu*, " a shield," was a tax or contribution paid by those who held lands by knight's service, in proportion to the number of knights' fees, towards a gift, or aid, or other purpose.   Also it was a commutation paid in place of personal service by those who were bound by knight's service ; see Thos. Madox, *History of the Exchequer*, i. 641.   Thus

et danegeldis[8] et hidagiis[9] et asisis[10] et de operacionibus Castellorum et pontium et parcorum et de Ferdwita[11] et

in the 6th year of Richard I. (1195) the Cumberland Pipe Roll gives a payment of 40 shillings of scutage by Ranulf de Vallibus and ten shillings by William de Brus, this scutage being levied on those tenants-in-chief who had not accompanied the King to Normandy (Stubbs, *Constit. Hist.*, i. 507). The next year they paid the same amounts, one for two knights' fees, the other for half a knight's fee. This was the second scutage in that reign for those who had not joined the army of Normandy. The scutage of 20s. raised in 1193—94 for Richard's ransom was properly an aid ; a "hidage" was raised from other tenants for the same purpose.

[7] *Geldum*, geld, a tax of any sort.

[8] *Danegeldum*, danegeld, at first a tax levied for carrying on war against the Danes, or in payment of tribute to the Danes. It was first levied by King Æthelred II., at the instigation of Archbishop Sigeric in the year 991 (*Anglo-Saxon Chronicle in ann.*). In the Laws of Edward the Confessor (Tit. xi.) it is said to have been a yearly payment of twelve pence for every hide of land (B. Thorpe, *Ancient Laws*, p. 192). The danegeld was increased in amount and continued as an oppressive and hated tax long after the time of the Danes. King Stephen promised to abolish it ; but it appears in the Pipe Rolls of Henry II. up to 1163, at the rate of two shillings for the hide of land. It occurs here only as one in a legal list of imposts.

[9] *Hidagium*, hidage, an extraordinary tax to the King assessed on every hide of land. The hide is probably the oldest of the terms representing the division of the land. It occurs in the 7th century. The amount of land in the hide appears to have varied. In *Domesday Book* it has different values. Later it was 100 or 120 acres ; and in the time of Henry II. it was fixed at 100 acres (*Dialogus de Scaccario, Lib.* I. c. xvii. ; Stubbs, *Select Charters*, p. 209). According to Skeat (*Etym. Dict.*) from the Anglo-Saxon *hid*, full form *higid*, which originally meant an estate sufficient to support one family or house-hold ; *hidan* or *hydan*, "to cover" or "conceal." Hide, "a skin," is properly from A. S. *hýd*. Hidage about this time was levied at 2s. the hide (see *Roger de Hoveden*, ed. Stubbs, vol. IV., p. lxxxiv.).

[10] *Assisa*, assize, an assessment, as probably here, also a session of a court, a trial, from the Old French *asseoir*, and Latin *assidere*, "to sit near."

[11] *Ferdwita*, the fine or penalty for not going on military service, from Anglo-Saxon *ferd*, " a military expedition," and *wite*, " a fine."

hengwita[12] et flemenefrenich[13] et de auerpeni[14] et de blodwita[15] et de fuchwita et de hundredpeni[16] et de thethingepeni et de legerwita[17] et de tholonio[18] et de passagio[19] et pontagio[20] et lestagio[21] et stalagio[22]. Concedimus insuper eidem Abbachiæ pacis facturam et pugnam in domo factam et domus invasionem et omnes assultus hominum suorum et forestel[23] et Gridelbreke[24] et soch et sach et tol et theam et infangen-

[12] *Hengwita*, the fine or penalty for hanging a thief without due process of law.

[13] *Flemenefrenich*, or *flymanfyrmth*, receiving or relieving a fugitive or outlaw, from the Anglo-Saxon *flema*, "a fugitive," and *fyrmð*, "a harbouring."

[14] *Averpeni*, money paid to be free from the King's, or lord's, *averia*. The Low Latin *averium* was from Old French *aver*, *avoir*, " to have," and meant that which a man had, his possessions, his cattle. *Averia* was used originally only of cattle or horses employed in husbandry or for carriage, and then a contribution towards the work of carrying for the King or lord. On the word *average*, see Skeat, *Etym. Dict.* s. v.

[15] *Blodwita*, the fine or penalty imposed for bloodshed. *Fuchwita* or *fictwita*, the fine or penalty imposed for fighting, from the Anglo-Saxon *feohte*.

[16] *Hundredpeni*, the tax imposed to support the officer of the hundred. *Thethingepeni*, the tax imposed to support the tithing man, an officer or the head of the "tithing," *tethinga*, a local subdivision of the hundred. The tithing must not be taken as exactly the tenth part of the larger division ; it answered generally to the township in some parts of England, and many tithings still exist in the south ; see B. Thorpe, *Ancient Laws*, Glossary; Stubbs, *Const. Hist.*, i. 86.

[17] *Legerwita*, *lecherwita* or *lairwita*, the fine or penalty imposed for adultery and fornication.

[18] *Tholonium* or *thelonium*, like *thol*, a toll or duty.

[19] *Passagium*, a tax on passengers, generally over water.

[20] *Pontagium*, a bridge toll, a tax for maintaining the bridge.

[21] *Lestagium*, a custom charged on ship's lading or on goods sold and carried away, from Anglo-Saxon *hlæst*, " a burden " or " cargo."

[22] *Stallagium*, payment made for the liberty of erecting a stall in a fair or market.

[23] *Forestel*, and in No. 13 *forestall*, an obstruction or stoppage in the way, originally an assault, used of merchandise on the way to market ; from the A. S. *fore* and *stellan*, "to leap" or "spring."

[24] *Gridelbreke*, or *grudbreke* (as in No. 13), equivalent to *grithbreke*,

theif et utfangentheif[25]. Post obitum vero Abbatis ejusdem Ecclesiæ ex eadem congregatione eligatur alter Abbas qui dignus sit, aliorsin nullus nisi inibi inveniri nequierit qui dignus sit tali fungi officio quod si evenerit de alio noto et familiari loco potestatem liberam habeant elegendi Abbatem idoneum. Testibus hijs Hugone Dunelmensi Episcopo[26], et multis aliis apud Westmonasterium[27].

11. BREVE RICARDI REGIS SUPER CARTAM SUAM.

RICARDUS Dei gratia Rex Angliæ Dux Normaniæ et Aquitaniæ Comes Andegaviæ[1] Justiciarijs et Vicecomitibus de Karleolo salutem. Precipimus vobis quatinus plenarie teneatis Abbati et Monachis Eboraci jura sua et libertates et dignitates suas. Et eisdem habere faciatis in pace et quiete pasturam[2] suam intra Dribec et Edene et Regiam viam quæ ducit de Karleolo ad Appelby sicut carta mea eis confirmat. Testibus Willielmo Cantuariensi[3] nostro Eliensi Electo ix° die Octobris[4].

a breach of the peace, from Anglo-Saxon *griö*, and *brecan*, "to break."

[25] *Utfangentheif,* see on infangentheof in No. 6.

[26] Hugh Pudsey, or Puisse, or Puiset, was consecrated Bishop of Durham in December, 1153, and died in March, 1195. He appropriated the church of Over or Old Denton in Gilsland to the Priory of Lanercost (*Register of Lanercost,* MS. viii. 16).

[27] The date of this charter lies between Sept. 3, 1189, when Richard I. was crowned, and March, 1195 (Bp Hugh). Not improbably it was after June, 1193, when the heavy ransom of King Richard was fixed at 150,000 marcs, and one of the means to obtain this ransom was to order the charters of his subjects to be renewed, for which large sums were charged.

11. [1] This title, Count of Anjou, does not occur in No. **10.**

[2] Confirmation of the pasture, given by Henry I. (see No. **5**), etween the river Eden and the King's Road as far as the manor of Wederhal extended.

[3] William de Longo Campo, or de Longchamp, the famous Chancellor of Richard I., was elected Bishop of Ely in the middle of September, 1189, but was not consecrated until the 31st of December

12. Confirmatio Johannis Regis.

JOHANNES Dei Gratia Rex Dominus Hiberniae[1] Dux
Normaniæ Aquitaniæ Comes Andegaviæ Archiepiscopis
Episcopis Abbatibus Comitibus Baronibus Justiciarijs
Vicecomitibus Prepositis et omnibus Ballivis suis Salutem.
Sciatis nos concessisse et presenti carta nostra confirmasse
Deo et Beatæ [Mariæ] Eboracensi et Roberto Abbati[2] et
successoribus suis et Monachis ibidem Deo servientibus
pro salute nostra et omnium Antecessorum et Successorum
nostrorum omnes donationes et libertates et liberas consuetudines quæ eis ab Antecessoribus nostris vel ab alijs
collatæ sunt. Quare volumus et firmiter precipimus quod
ipsi habeant et teneant omnia prædicta bene et in pace
libere et quiete integre plenarie et honorifice sicut cartæ
Donatorum rationabiliter testantur. Hijs testibus, Comite
David[3], Willelmo Comite de Arundel[4], Rogerio de Toueny[5],

following (*Ralph de Diceto*, ed. Stubbs, ii. 69, 75) ; he would therefore
be elect to Ely on October 9th. He died Jan. 31st, 1197. The word
Cantuariensi is evidently an error for *Cancellario*. The passage
would then read plainly "Willielmo Cancellario nostro Eliensi electo."
An attempt to get over the difficulty is found in the Transcript made
by Stevens from Todd's Manuscript (given in Dugdale, *Monast.* iii.
552) by reading *Willielmo* again for *nostro*. A charter of Richard I.
to certain Cistercian monasteries, November 16th, 1189, has among
the witnesses the same form, *Willielmo Cancellario nostro, electo
Elyens.* (see *Mem. of Fountains Abbey*, ed. Walbran, ii. 18 note).

[4] The date of the charter will be October 9th, 1189.

12. [1] The title *Dominus Hiberniæ* was first used by John, not by
Henry II., and then by all his successors to Henry VIII., who took
the title *Rex Hiberniæ*. John received the dominion of Ireland from
his father in 1177.

[2] Robert de Longo Campo, see on No. **10.**

[3] This was the brother of William I. (The Lion), King of Scotland,
not the Earl David who became David I. in 1124 (see on No. **106**).
He had considerable possessions in England, among them the Honor
of Huntingdon, given him by his brother and confirmed by Richard I.
in 1190 ; see the charter of confirmation in *Calend. Doc. Scotland*,
i. 31, ed. J. Bain, who also gives many interesting facts connected
with the Earl. Earl David died in 1219.

Gyrando de Fornivall[6], Gaufrido de Broillion, Pagano de Rochefort, Willelmo de Cantilupo[7], Huberto de Burgo Camerario[8]. Datum per manum H. Cantuariensis Archiepiscopi Cancellarii[9] nostri apud liram[10]. VIII° Septembris, Anno primo Regni nostri[11].

[4] William de Albini, Earl of Arundel, was the son of William the first Earl by Queen Adeliza, or Alice, widow of Henry I. He was at first on the side of King John at Runnymede, but afterwards joined the Barons. He died in 1221 as he was returning from the Holy Land. He is witness to a charter of King John in *Chartulary of Whitby* (ed. Atkinson, ii. 421) on August 25th of this same year 1199.

[5] Roger de Toueny, or Toeni, or Tony, was the son of William de Toeni and a daughter of Robert, Earl of Leicester. He married Constance, daughter of Richard, Viscount Bellomont, a kinswoman of King John (Dugdale, *Baronage*, i. 470). His castle of Conches in Normandy was taken this very month (*Roger de Hoveden*, iv. 96).

[6] Gyrard, or Girard, de Fornivall or Furnivall, the younger of the same name, took the side of King John against the Barons, and was one of the King's Commissioners to treat with them. He died at Jerusalem in 1219.

[7] Will. de Cantilupe, the well-known noble in the reigns of John and Henry III., and except for a short time, a strong supporter of the former, for which he was well rewarded. There is much about him in Dugdale (*Baronage*, i. 731). He died in 1239 at Reading.

[8] Hubert de Burgo or de Burgh was, as we see here, Chamberlain to King John in the first year of his reign. Two years later he was Warden of the Marches of Wales. He became Justiciar of England after Runnymede in June, 1215, and in this office played such a distinguished part and achieved such a wide unpopularity in the subsequent reign of Henry III. He married, for his fourth wife, Margaret, sister of William the Lion, King of Scotland, at York in 1221. Soon after this marriage he was created Earl of Kent. He died on May 12th, 1243 (*Ann. Monast.*, ed. Luard, i. 130). A large number of documents and references relating to him and his wife will be found in the *Calendar of Doc. Scotland*, ed. J. Bain, vol. i., see Index.

[9] Hubert Walter, or Fitzwalter, was translated from Salisbury to Canterbury in 1193. He was appointed Chancellor by King John in 1199, and held the office till his death July 13, 1205. He was nephew of the famous Ranulf Glanvill, and had been appointed Justiciar in

13. CONFIRMATIO HENRICI REGIS SUPER DONACI-
ONE AVI SUI.

HENRICUS[1] Dei gratia Rex Angliæ Dominus Hiberniæ
et Dux Aquitaniæ Archiepiscopis Episcopis Abbatibus
Prioribus Comitibus Baronibus Justiciarijs Vicecomitibus
Præpositis ministris et omnibus Ballivis et fidelibus suis
Salutem.   Inspeximus cartam quam inclitæ recordationis
Henricus quondam Rex Angliæ Avus noster fecit Abbati
et Monachis Sanctæ Mariæ Eboraci in hæc verba.

Henricus[2] Dei gratia Rex Angliæ Dux Normaniæ et
Aquitaniæ Comes Andegaviæ Archiepiscopis Episcopis
Abbatibus et omnibus Comitibus Baronibus et Justiciarijs
et Vicecomitibus et ministris suis et omnibus fidelibus suis
Francis et Anglis per Angliam Salutem.   Sciatis nos concessisse et dedisse in puram et perpetuam Elemosinam
pro salute animæ nostræ et pro salute animarum Avi
nostri Regis Henrici et Matris nostræ et omnium Antecessorum nostrorum necnon pro statu Regni nostri Roberto
Abbati[3] et successoribus ejus et Abbachiæ Sanctæ Mariæ

1193.   An admirable account of his administration and of his contest
with Archbishop Geoffrey Plantagenet is given in the Preface to the
fourth volume of Bishop Stubbs' edition of *Roger de Hoveden.*

[10] Lira, in the diocese of Evreux, France, where was a Benedictine
monastery.   King John was in France in September of this year (*Rog.
de Hoveden*, iv. 96).

[11] Dated September 8th, 1199.

13.   [1] Henry the Third, who dropped his father's titles of *Dux Normanniæ* and *Comes Andegaviæ* in 1259, when he ceded those provinces
to Louis IX. of France.   This is an *Inspeximus* of a charter of Henry II.,
but of one of a later date than charter No. **6**, and in character more
like charter No. **10**.   These *Inspeximus* charters originated in the 11th
year of Henry III., when all persons had to shew their titles and have
them confirmed.   The amount to be paid was fixed by the Justiciar,
and the King is said to have realised not less than £100,000 (*Charter
Rolls*, ed. T. D. Hardy, Introd. p. v).

[2] Henry the Second.

[3] This must be Robert de Harpham, who was Abbot of S. Mary's

Eboraci et Monachis ibidem Deo servientibus Terras
Ecclesias Cellas maneria decimas silvas plana stagna
molendina et alias possessiones suas possidendas liberas et
quietas ab omni terreno servicio in perpetuam possessionem, sicut unquam melius in temporibus Antecessorum
nostrorum tenuerunt cum eisdem legibus et libertatibus et
dignitatibus et consuetudinibus quas habet Ecclesia Sancti
Petri Eboraci vel Ecclesia Sancti Johannis Beverlaci. Et
ne homines Sanctæ Mariæ eant ad Comitatus vel Schyras
vel Tridings vel Wapentas vel Hundredas nec etiam pro
Vicecomitibus vel ministris eorum. Sed si Vicecomites
vel ministri eorum habent querelam contra homines Sanctæ
Mariæ dicant Abbati Eboraci et statuto die veniant in
Curiam Sanctæ Mariæ et ibi habeant rectum de capitali
placito suo, et sancta Maria quicquid pertinet ad Curiam
suam. Et sicut aliqua Ecclesia in tota Anglia magis est
libera, sit et hæc libera, et omnes terræ ad eam pertinentes quas nunc habet vel quas rationabiliter adquirere
poterit. Et Maneria et Cellæ et quælibet aliæ possessiones
sint quietæ de placitis et querelis et murdro et latrocinio et
scutagio et geldis et danegeldis et hidagiis et assisis et de
operacionibus Castellorum et pontium et parcorum et de
fredwita et hengwita et flemenefrenith et de wardpeni[4] et de
averpeni et de blodwita et de fictwita et de hundredpeni et
de thethingepeni et de leywita et de thelonio et de passagio et pontagio et lestagio. Concedimus insuper eidem
Abbaciæ pacis facturam et pugnam in domo factam et
domus invasionem et omnes assultus hominum suorum et
forestall et Grudbreke haymsoke[5] et soch et sach et tol et
theam et infangenetheif et utfangenetheif. Post obitum
vero Abbatis ejusdem Ecclesiæ ex eadem congregatione

at York from 1184 to his death in April, 1189, not Robert de Longo
Campo as in No. 10, since Henry II. died July 6th, 1189.

[4] *Wardpeni*, money paid to be free from watch and ward.

[5] *Haymsoke*, the privilege of a man's house and home, also the
violation of it.

elegatur alter Abbas qui dignus sit aliunde vero nullus nisi ibi inveniri nequierit qui dignus sit tali fungi officio quod si evenerit de alio noto et familiari loco potestatem liberam habeant eligendi Abbatem idoneum. Testibus hijs Gaufrido Eliensi Episcopo[6], Hugone Dunelmensi Episcopo[7], Willelmo Comite de Maundevill[8], Ranulpho de Glaunvill[9], Hugone Bardulfe[10] apud Wudestok[11].

[6] Geoffrey Ridel or Rydall was Bishop of Ely from October 6th, 1174, to his death August 21st, 1189.

[7] Hugh Pudsey, see note 26 on No. 10.

[8] William de Magnavil, or de Mandevill, Count of Aumâle, succeeded his brother as Earl of Essex in 1167. He married Helewisa, daughter of William le Gros, Earl of Albemarle, and Cecily his wife, in 1180, and in her right became Earl of Albemarle. He carried the Crown at the coronation of Richard I. in 1189, and was made Justiciar of England, but died in November of the same year (*Roger de Hoveden*, iii. 19). Cecilia above mentioned was the eldest daughter and one of the three coheiresses of Alice de Romeli, lady of Copeland and of Skipton, and William FitzDuncan. Helewisa afterwards married William de Fortibus and thirdly Baldwin de Betun, both created Earl of Albemarle (*Chron. de Melsa*, i. 91; Dugdale, *Baronage*, i. 63).

[9] Ranulph de Glaunvill, as he subscribes himself here, or Ranulf Glanvill, was the celebrated lawyer to whom is due the ancient treatise *Liber de Legibus Angliæ*, "on which our knowledge of the Curia Regis in its earliest form depends" (Stubbs). He renders account for Westmoreland, as Sheriff of Yorkshire, from 1176 to 1179 in the *Pipe Rolls* (22—25 Henry II.). He was one of the itinerant justices in the northern counties, including Cumberland, in 1176 and following years, being made Chief Justiciar of England in 1180 (*Roger de Hoveden*, ii. 215, ed. Stubbs). He was deprived of this office by Richard I. on his accession in 1189. He accompanied that King to the Holy Land, and died at the siege of Acre in 1191. See more in E. Foss, *Judges of England*, i. 376; *Dict. of National Biography*, vol. xxi.

[10] Hugh Bardulfe was one of the five Commissioners left in charge of the kingdom when Richard I. went to the Holy Land in 1191, and played an important part during that reign. As Sheriff of Yorkshire, he rendered the accounts for Westmoreland from 1193 to 1199, and he appears as Escheator for Cumberland in 1195 to 1199. He was a

Nos autem predictas concessionem et donationem ratas habentes et gratas eas quantum in nobis est pro nobis et Hæredibus nostris imperpetuum concedimus et confirmamus sicut predicta carta rationabiliter testatur. Volentes insuper predictis Abbati et Monachis pro salute nostra et animarum Antecessorum et Hæredum nostrorum gratiam facere uberiorem ut quietantiæ et libertates prædictæ sibi et Successoribus suis integre et inconcusse remaneant in futurum. Præcipimus et concedimus pro Nobis et Hæredibus nostris quod prædicti Abbas et Monachi et eorum Successores universis et singulis libertatum et quietantiarum articulis supradictis libere et sine occasione et impedimento Nostri vel Hæredum nostrorum Justiciariorum et omnium Ballivorum[12] nostrorum uti valeant de cætero quandocunque voluerint et ubicunque sibi viderint expedire. Quanquam prædictis libertatibus vel quietantijs in aliquo articulo minus plene usi fuerint prout fecisse poterant et debeant secundum continentiam cartæ prædictæ temporibus retroactis. Et prohibemus super forisfacturam nostram ne quis præfatos Abbatem et Monachos contra prædictam concessionem et quietantiam in aliquo vexare inquietare vel molestare præsumat. Hijs Testibus Venerabili Patre Waltero Bathoniensi et Wellensi Episcopo[13], Henrico filio

justice itinerant during the same period, also in 1202—3. He died in 1203 (*Annals of Waverley in ann.*). See also Foss, *Judges of England*, ii. 32.

[11] Woodstock in Oxfordshire, a favourite residence in the reign of Henry II., notorious in connection with the name of Rosamund, daughter of Walter, Lord Clifford. The King had there a collection of wild beasts (*William of Malmesbury, Lib.* v. 409). The date of this inspected charter lies between 1184 (Abbot Robert) and July 6th, 1189 when Henry II. died. He held a council of Bishops at Woodstock August 16th, 1184, which may be about the date of this charter; see R. W. Eyton, *Court and Itinerary of Henry II.* p. 257.

[12] *Ballivus*, Low Latin, from the Old French *bailler*, "to keep in custody"; "a bailiff," an officer put in charge by his superior, as the bailiff of the sheriff or lord of the manor.

[13] Walter Giffard was consecrated Bishop of Bath and Wells

Regis Alemanniæ nepote nostro[14], Rogerio de Leyburñ[15], Johanne de Verdun[16], Willelmo de Grey, Roberto Aguyllun[17], Willelmo de Aecte[18], Nicholas de Leukenor, Galfrido de Perci[19], Radulpho de Bakepuz[20], Petro de Squidemor, Bartholomeo de Bigod[21], et alijs.   Datum per manum

January 4th, 1265, and translated to York the end of the year following.   He died April 22nd, 1279.

[14] Henry was the second son of Richard Plantagenet, Earl of Cornwall, King of Germany and brother of Henry III., by Isabel, daughter of William Marshall, Earl of Pembroke, and widow of Gilbert de Clare, Earl of Gloucester.   Richard was made King of the Roman Empire, or of Germany (*Alemanniæ*) in 1257, and died in 1272 (see J. Bryce, *Holy Roman Empire*, p. 212).   Henry was murdered at Viterbo by one of the sons of Simon de Montfort in 1271.

[15] This was the Roger de Leyburne of Kent, who married his son Roger to Idonea his ward, the younger of the two daughters and coheiresses of the second Robert de Veteripont, Sheriff of Westmoreland and Lord of Appleby (see note 1 on No. 230).   The King granted them their father's property in this 50th year of his reign.   Roger de Leyburne's name appears with a number of these same co-witnesses in a grant by Henry III. of a market at Market Overton, Rutland, dated Sep. 2, 1267 (*Cal. Doc. Scotland*, i. 483).   He saved the life of the King at the Battle of Evesham, August 4th, 1265 (*Chron. de Lanercost*, p. 79).   Some additional incidents will be found in *Annales Monastici*, ed. Luard, iii. 222 sq.   He died in the year 1271 (*A. M.*, iv. 247).

[16] John de Verdun or Verdon was one of the strong supporters of Henry III. against the rebellious Barons, and died in 1274.

[17] Robert Aguyllun occurs frequently in the documents of this period as co-witness with some here mentioned (see the reference given in note 15 above) and even as early as 1232.   He was probably of the family of Aguyllunby, which is so often met with in this *Register*.   Some of the family (see on No. 37, note 3) settled in the parish of Warwick, whence the township of Agillonby, later Aglionby, near Wetherhal.

[18] William de Aecte should be de Aete, or d'Aeth, as in the grant of Henry III. referred to in note 15.

[19] Galfrid de Perci, son of Alan de Percy, and grandson of William, founder of the Abbey of Whitby, and himself a benefactor to it (*Chart. Whitby*, ed. Atkinson, i. 58).

[20] Radulph de Bakepuz, or Bakepuis, occurs with Robert Aguyllun in several charters of Henry III.; see note 15.

nostram apud Kenyllewurth[22] octavo die Septembris Anno Regni nostri L[mo].[23]

14. QUALITER EA QUÆ DONANTUR A PLURIBUS HOMINIBUS RECITANTUR ET SCRIBUNTUR IN CARTA HENRICI REGIS.

IN carta Domini Henrici Regis[1] hæc scribuntur. Randulphus Meschinus Manerium de Wederhal et Ecclesiam ejusdem Villæ[2] cum molendino et piscaria et bosco et certis pertinentijs Capellam de Warthewic terram quæ Camera Sancti Constantini[3] dicitur in Corkeby duas bovatas terræ, aquam de Edene versus Corkeby necnon et ripam versus Corkeby in qua stagnum firmatum est omnino videlicet liberas et quietas sine diminucione. Randulphus Meschinus Ecclesias de Appelby Sancti Michaelis et Sancti Laurentij et terras earum cum decimis de Dominijs ejusdem Villæ ex utraque parte aquæ Adam filius Suani[4] Heremitorium Sancti Andreæ[b] Uctred filius

---

[21] Bartholomew le (not de) Bigod, or le Bigot, was Marshal of the King's Household in 1255, and of the family of the Earl of Norfolk; he was sent to take over the Castle of Werk from Robert de Ros (*Patent Rolls*, 39 Hen. III. m. 3, Record Com., p. 26).

[22] The Royal forces were at this time besieging Kenilworth, which held out until December.

[23] Dated September 8th, 50 Hen. III., 1266.

14. [1] The charter of Henry II., the former part of which is given in No. 6. The grants and grantors to S. Mary's Abbey are not given there, but are in full in Dugdale, *Monasticon*, No. V., vol. iii. p. 548. The grants here seem to be a selection of those belonging more especially to the monastery of Wetherhal. This charter must be a Confirmation charter of Richard or John, see below the words *Henrici Patris mei.*

[2] Hence the Church of the vill of Wederhal was given by Ranulf Meschin, as well as the Chapel of Warthwic mentioned below (see note 4 on No. 5).

[3] On *Camera Sti Constantini*, see No. 38, note 3.

[4] Adam son of Suan, or Suein, appears in the Pipe Rolls for 1159 as receiving 100s. under the King's writ. His brother Henry, who witnesses his charter to Wederhal (No. 196), appears as holding lands in Langwathby and Edenhal in the same year, and as late as

Lyolf[6] tertiam partem Crogline[7] cum Ecclesia et cæteris
1172. Adam held a large tract of country on the east of the river
Eden, including the parishes of Kirkland, Melmorby and Ainstable,
granted by Henry I. on payment of 112s. 8d. cornage. In the reign
of King John it was held by Roger de Montbegon, Simon son of
Walter, and Alexander de Nevill, having previously been held by
William de Nevill (*Testa de Nevill*, pp. 379 b, 380 a). Adam had two
daughters, his heirs, Amabil or Mabilia, and Matilda. Amabil
married first Alexander de Crevequer (see on No. 195) and afterwards
Galfrid de Nevill, who was succeeded by Walter de Nevill, who
married another Amabil (see the charters to Monk Bretton Priory in
Dugdale, *Monast.*, v. pp. 137, 138). Matilda married first Adam de
Montbegon or Munbegun (see note 4 on No. 195) and afterwards John
Malherbe (see *Monast.*, v. p. 138 and on No. 197). She had a son,
Roger de Montbegon, not Robert as Dugdale mistakes (*Baronage*,
i. 618). Adam son of Suan was a large landowner in Southern
Yorkshire, and founded the Priory of Monk Bretton in Yorkshire (see
Dugdale, *Monast.*, v. 136 et seq.) and made grants to it which were
confirmed by different members of his family. To this Priory, Roger
de Montbegon also gave a charter. Adam also confirmed the grant
of his father, Suan the son of Ailrich, to the Priory of Pontefract, of
the church of Silkeston and certain land (*Monast.*, v. 122, see also the
"Progenies Suani" at p. 128 for some of these relationships). Adam
is witness to Bishop Athelwold's charter (No. 15), and made his grant
to Wederhal before 1147 (see No. 196).

⁵ See, on the grant of the Hermitage, No. 196.

⁶ Roger de Hoveden tells us (i. 134 ed. Stubbs) that Liulf lived at
Durham in great friendship with Bishop Walcher (*ob.* 1080), and that
the latter was murdered in revenge for the murder of Liulf by one of
his relatives, Sheriff Gilbert; that Liulf married Aldgitha, daughter of
Earl Aldred, by whom he had two sons, Uchtred and Morekar; also
that through Aldgitha he was uncle to Earl Waldeof.

⁷ Crogline was a parish and manor on the east side of the Eden,
in the Barony of Gilsland, abutting on Northumberland on the east
and on the parishes of Renwick and Kirkoswald on the south. The
first Robert de Vallibus claimed lordship over it (see No. 191). It is
called Croglin Magna, or Kirkcroglin, to distinguish it from Croglin
Parva, in the parish of Kirkoswald, mentioned in No. 157, and referred
to in No. 101 *et al.* Nicolson and Burn (*Hist.* ii. 433) throw doubt on
the Church ever having belonged to the Abbey of S. Mary at York or
to Wetherhal; but the grant is confirmed by the charters of the first
two Bishops of Carlisle (see Nos. 16, 17).

pertinentijs et duas bovatas terræ in Estuna[8] et molendinum de Scoteby[9] in Cumquintina[10] dimidiam carucatam[11] terræ

[8] Eston was an ancient parish, now merged in the parish of Arthuret and the modern parish of Kirkandrews on Esk. In the oldest of the Bishops' *Registers* there are several presentations to the Church ; in 1308 Simon de Beverley was presented by Edward II., as guardian of the son of Sir John Wake, Lord of Lidel (*Regis. of Bp Halton*, MS. p. 113). In 1181—82 the Church was worth 10 marcs yearly and belonged to the manor of Lidel (*Inquis. p. m.* 10 Edw. I. No. 26).

[9] Scoteby was a manor in the parish of Wetherhal, now, with additions, made into an ecclesiastical district. It was one of certain manors in Cumberland, in the Forest of Inglewood, which for a time belonged to the King of Scotland. The others were Penrith (part of the manor), Langwathby, Salkeld (Great), Carlaton and Soureby. David I. took up arms against Stephen on behalf of the Empress Matilda, and marched to Carlisle. Stephen advanced against him in 1136, and they came to terms at Durham, David retaining Carlisle and a large part of the district of that name (*Henry of Huntingdon, Lib.* viii.; *John of Hexham, in ann.* 1136). His son Henry did homage, and was recognised as Earl. In 1157 when Malcolm IV., son of Earl Henry, was King, the grant of this land of Carlisle was annulled, and Henry II. ruled up to the former boundary (*Roger de Hoveden*, i. 216; *Robert de Monte*, ed. J. Stevenson, p. 743). The claims put forward by Scotland were at last set at rest through the mediation of Cardinal Otto, the Papal Legate, and these manors were granted to Alexander II., King of Scotland, on April 22, 1242 (*Charter Rolls*, 26 Henry III. m. 5). They were to be held of the King of England by Alexander and his heirs on yearly rendering at Carlisle one sorhawk. The advowsons of the churches of the manors, and a certain "*rogus*" in the manor of Soureby, were to be retained by the King. The preliminary agreement was made at York, in the presence of the Legate, on September 25th, 1237. The King of Scotland then quitclaimed his hereditary rights to the counties of Northumberland, Cumberland and Westmoreland for ever, and yielded other points. King Henry granted to Alexander and his heirs 200 librates of land within Northumberland and Cumberland (*Patent Rolls*, 21 Hen. III. m. 2, Record Com. p. 18; Rymer, *Fœdera*, new ed., i. 233). Numerous objections were raised before these manors were finally fixed upon in 1242. In 1248 there were five hawks in arrear, and the Sheriff of Cumberland was ordered to see to the matter. In 1251 the farm of the manor of Scoteby was returned as £29. 16. 4½ and the

in Saureby[12] decimam de dominio Constantinus[13] filius
Walteri unam carucatam terræ quæ fuit Durandi in Coleby[14] Ketellus filius Eltreth[15] Ecclesiam de Morland[16] et

farm of the mill as £11. 6. 8. The figures for the other manors are
given in the Pipe Roll for 34 Henry III. The rents and profits in
1286 and later periods (taken from the Pipe Rolls) will be found in
Historical Documents, Scotland, i. pp. 2, 28 seq., ed. J. Stevenson ;
see also F. Palgrave, *Documents illustrating Hist. of Scotland,* i. p. 3.
It appears from an *Inspeximus,* made in 1294, that John Balliol, King
of Scotland, had the year before given these manors to Anthony Bec,
Bishop of Durham (*Patent Rolls,* 22 Edward I. *m.* 3) ; afterwards the
right was disputed, and in 1306—7 the manors were ordered by the
Parliament held in Carlisle to revert to the English crown. In the
Rolls of Parliament (Record Com., i. p. 188) we read " In reply to the
petition of John de Hastinges with regard to the manors of Penrith
and Sowerby, the King replies that he has retaken (*recuperavit*) these
manors formerly given by King Henry, his father, to Alexander, King
of Scotland, to whom no heir *modo Rex* now exists " ; see also the
Assize Rolls quoted in *Historical Doc. Scotland,* i. 359. Scotby does
not, as often supposed, take its name from this special connection with
the Scottish King, for as early as the Pipe Roll of 3 John we find the
men of Scotebi owing one *chaseur* to the Crown. The " mill of
Scotby " was no doubt on the stream separating the manor from that
of Wetherhal, and running into the river Eden, and now called Pow
Maughan beck. The Priory had also the tithes of Scotby (see
Nos. 16, 17) and compounded with the Priory of Carlisle (see No. 31)
for half a silver marc for an alleged right in the same.

    [10] On Cumquintin, see No. 71, note.
    [11] On the carucate and bovate, see No. 55, note.
    [12] This is Temple Sowerby in Westmoreland ; on the place and
these tithes, see Nos. 200, 229. Saureby, or Sowerby, or Soreby, is
derived from *saure* (Old Norse *söggr*) " wet," " swampy," and the
Danish termination *by,* " a dwelling," and is naturally a not uncommon
name in the district.
    [13] *Constantinus* should be Enisant, as copied by Bishop Nicolson,
or Enisand, as in the grant of this carucate of land given in the
Additional Charters, No. 247.
    [14] For Coleby, see on No. 227.
    [15] The grant of the Church of Morland is given in No. 235 ; on
Ketell son of Eltreth, see No. 1, note 13.
    [16] Morland, in Westmoreland, which occurs so often in this *Register,*

tres carucatas terræ Waltef filius Gospatricij Ecclesiam de Brumfeld[17] et corpus ejusdem Manerij in Salchild decimam

appears to have belonged partly to the Priory of Wetherhal, and partly to the first William de Lancastre, in both cases probably derived from Ketell son of Eldred. William de Lancastre, in the latter half of the 12th century, granted, in frank marriage with his daughter Agnes, to Alexander de Windesores what he possessed ("quicquid habeo") in Havershame, Grayrigg and Morlande. This deed is given in full from the Rawlinson MSS. by Sir G. F. Duckett (*Duchetiana*, pp. 16, 267), who has much upon the family of Windesore; see on No. 210, where a dispute with the Priory about the wood at Morland is arranged. The grant of the Church of Morland was confirmed by Bishop Athelwold and Bishop Bernard (Nos. 16, 17), also by Bishop Hugh (No. 19) who expressly says it was for the use and sustentation of the monks of the House of Wederhale, which is a Cell of the said Church of S. Mary at York. Bishop Nicolson (MSS. iii. 127), on the authority of several original grants in his possession, states that Bishop Bernard confirmed the grants of Thomas son of Gospatric to the Abbey of Shap, and that three of the witnesses were Gilbert, Walter, and Thomas, Rectors of the Church of Morland; this would be shortly after 1200. In 1405, John de Stutton, Prior of Wederhala, appointed Roger Peroy, by deed, to the Chapel of the Blessed Mary in le Wyth "in our parish of Morland," reserving the oblations in the same to the Priory (Illustrative Doc. XVIII.). In 1424, a difference arose between the Prior and Sir John Richemont, Vicar of Morland, concerning the oblations in this Chapel, and the right to half an acre of land lying upon Litel Aynesbergh and abutting upon Commune Banc. An agreement was come to in the Parish Church of Morland, by the mediation of William Wellys, Abbot of S. Mary's at York (Illustrative Docum. XIX.). According to Nicolson and Burn (*History*, i. 445) this Chapel was said to have been near the river Lyvennet, midway between Morland and King's Meaburn, "in a place now (1777) called Chapel Garth, belonging to the Vicarage"; the place still bears the name. Michael, Bishop of Glasgow, consecrated by Thomas, Archbp of York 1109— 14, was buried in this church; the year is unknown, but it must have been before 1117, when Bishop John of Glasgow was consecrated. Bishop Michael held ordinations in Morland church for the Archbishop of York (Thos. Stubbs, ed. Twysden, col. 1713).

[17] The Church of Brumfeld, or Bromfeld, in Cumberland, was granted to S. Mary's Abbey at York, but never assigned to Wetherhal.

de dominio[18].   Et confirmo totam pasturam inter Edene et
Regiam viam quæ ducit de Karleolo ad Appelby et ab
Wederhal usque ad Dribec.   Et concedo eis et confirmo
forestam meam ad porcos suos de Wederhal sine pannagio.
Et præcipio quod Abbas Eboraci et Monachi prædicti
teneant omnes terras et res suas quæ per cartam Regis
Henrici Patris mei et meam firmatæ sunt et in pace possideant.   Et non dissaesiantur inde nec ponantur in placitum
nisi coram me.   Et si de aliqua harum rerum dissaesiati
fuerint Justiciarij mei et Vicecomites eos faciant resaesiri
et in pace tenere.   Nec dampnum eorum capiatur nisi
Abbas prius de recto defecerit injuste facere debuerit.

15. CONFIRMATIO EPISCOPI KARLIOLENSIS DE EC-
CLESIA DE WEDERHALE ET CAPELLA DE WARTHEWIC.

NOTUM sit omnibus Sanctæ Ecclesiæ filijs quod ego
Athelwoldus[1] Dei Gratia Karleolensis Episcopus concessi et
præsenti carta confirmavi Abbati de Eboraco et Monachis de
Wederhale Ecclesiam de Wederhale cum Capella de Warthewic Habendum et tenendum in proprijs et perpetuis usibus
eorum cum decimis et obventionibus et omnibus alijs ad
illam pertinentibus sicut eam ab antiquo melius habuerunt
faciendo Sinodalia et Archidiaconalia[2].   Et licebit imperpet-

In 1302, the rectory was appropriated to that Abbey by Bishop
Halton, on condition that 40 marcs of yearly revenue were secured to
the Vicar, and that the right of collation should rest with the Bishops
of Carlisle (*Register of Bp Halton*, MS. p. 72).   Only a portion of the
manor was granted, other portions came into the possession of the
Abbey of Holm Cultram.   There is a concession of the manor, to
farm, July 1st, 1434, by the Abbey of S. Mary to William Osmundyr-
lake in full in Dugdale (*Monasticon*, iii. 567).

[18] This is only a confirmation of the grant by Ranulf Meschin (see
No. **4**), not a grant by Waldief.

15. [1] See Appendix B.—On Bishop Athelwold and the Foundation
of the Priory of Carlisle.

[2] From the mention of Archidiaconals as well as Sinodals, it is
clear that there was an Archdeacon of Carlisle at this time ; see more
on Robert, Archdeacon, in note 3 on No. **28**.

uum dictis Monachis Presbiterum in dicta Ecclesia servi-
turum proprio arbitrio ponere et amovere. Concessi et confirmavi dictis Monachis de Wederhal antiquam pacem loci
illius. Et insuper Ecclesiam de Crokelyn et tertiam partem
ejusdem villæ et Heremitorium Sancti Andreæ cum omnibus
suis pertinentijs liberam et quietam de omnibus ad nos et
posteros nostros pertinentibus, et ab omni subjectione
Ecclesiæ de Kyrkeland[3] quod videlicet Heremitorium A.
filius Suani me et alijs multis coram positis donavit eisdem.
Hanc donationem et tenuram plena autoritate confirmo et
testem me exhibeo. Si quis autem hæc quæ confirmavi
ausu temerario violare præsumpserit vel prædictis Monachis de hijs injuriam fecerit eum excommunicatum esse
decerno. Testibus Ada filio Suani, Warino de Kyrkeland
Roaldo, Ricardo Milite[4] et alijs[5].

16. CONFIRMATIO SUPER ECCLESIIS IN DIŒCESI
KARLIOLENSI.

ATHELWOLDUS Dei gratia Karliolensis Episcopus omnibus legentibus vel audientibus literas has Salutem Notum
sit vobis me intuitu pietatis et Religionis concessisse et
confirmasse Monachis Sanctæ Mariæ Eboraci et usibus
eorum Ecclesias[1] quæ in Diœcesi nostra noscuntur possi-

[3] The Hermitage of S. Andrew (see on No. 196) was in the manor
of Culgaith (see on Nos. 195, 200) and in the parish of Kirkland,
which is on the east of the river Eden in Cumberland, and borders on
Westmoreland. The Church of Kirkland was formerly in the hands
of the Bishop of Carlisle, but was given by King Henry VI. to the
Prior and Convent of Carlisle.

[4] Ricardus Miles appears in the Pipe Roll for Carlisle of 31
Henry I. as paying noutgeld, also 20s. rent of his land; he is a witness
in No. 72.

[5] The date of this charter must lie between 1133, when Bishop
Athelwold was consecrated, and 1147, before which date Adam son of
Suan made the grant mentioned here (see on No. 196).

16. [1] The impropriation of these Churches at this early period,
before 1156, is noteworthy, the only conditions being decent provision
for a priest and the payment of sinodals.

dere, videlicet Cellam de Wederhale cum Parochia de Warthwic et totam decimam de Scoteby et Ecclesias Sancti Michaelis et Sancti Laurentij de Appelby. Et Ecclesias de Kyrkebystephan[2] et de Ormesheved[3] et de Morlund et de Clibbrun[4] et de Brumfeld et de Crokylyn et Hermi-

[2] It is very doubtful whether this name has any connection with S. Stephen. Kirkby, "church town," is usually connected with a locality (see examples in No. 209) or with a personal name, probably the owner. And here the personal name may be Stephan, or Steffan as it is spelt in the next charter. The name we have in William Steffan, the father of Wescubrict, Lord of Corkeby (see note 9 on No. 2). The dedication to S. Stephen, the only one in the diocese, may well have been adopted in later times. This is one of the Churches granted with others to the Abbey of S. Mary at York by Ivo de Taillebois (see Illustrative Documents, XVI.). The charter of Bishop Hugh (No. 19) in 1220 confirms the same on condition that a proper Vicar is appointed with an annual income of 100 shillings. Bishop Walter Malclerk (1223—46) had a controversy about this Church with the Abbey of S. Mary, and, under the arbitration of the Prior of Carlisle and others, it was confirmed to the Abbey on certain conditions. John de Ferentin was then Vicar. At the same time, the patronage of the Churches of Clibburn, Ormesheved and Musgrave was ceded to the Bishop of Carlisle (see Illustrative Documents, XVII.). The cession of these Churches was confirmed to Bishop Silvester de Everdon in May, 1248, by Abbot Thomas and the convent of S. Mary (see Additional Charters, No. 240). After the dissolution of the monasteries, the Rectory and advowson were given by Edward VI. to Sir Richard Musgrave, and sold by him the next year to Lord Wharton (see an abstract of the Indenture in Bp Nicolson, MSS., ii. 337).

[3] Ormesheved in Westmoreland, from the common proper name Orme and Anglo-Saxon *hafod*, "head," since corrupted into Ormside. It is not known how the Church came to the Abbey of S. Mary at York, but it was ceded by them to the Bishop of Carlisle (see preceding note).

[4] Clibbrun, or Clibburn, is spelt Clifburn in No. 218, which probably marks the derivation. It adjoins the parish of Morland in Westmoreland. The Church was appropriated to the Abbey of S. Mary at York; but it does not appear by whom the grant was made, very probably by one of the Taillebois family, who for long possessed one of the two manors into which the parish is divided. It was one of the Churches ceded to Bishop Walter Malclerk (see

torium Sancti Andreæ cum omnibus pertinentijs suis Prædicti vero fratres de beneficijs Ecclesiarum talem proportionem Presbiteris provideant unde decenter sustentari queant Et sinodalia jura persolvere valeant[5].

17. CONFIRMATIO EPISCOPI KARLIOL. DE OMNIBUS ECCLESIJS ET BENEFICIJS ECCLESIASTICIS POSSESSIS IN DIŒCESI KARLIOLENSI.

B.[1] Dei gratia Karliolensis Episcopus universis Sanctæ Matris Ecclesiæ filijs hoc scriptum visuris vel audituris salutem in Domino. Universitati vestre notum facimus nos Divinæ pietatis intuitu et de assensu Capituli Karliolensis Ecclesiæ concessisse et confirmasse Abbati et conventui Sanctæ Mariæ Eboraci et eorum usibus imperpetuum omnes Ecclesias et Ecclesiastica Beneficia quæ in Diœcesi Karliolensi noscuntur possidere. Nominatim Cellam de Wederhale cum Capella de Warthwic et totam decimam de Scoteby et Ecclesias Sancti Michaelis et Sancti Laurentij de Appelby et Ecclesiam de Kirkeby-Steffan cum Capella de Burgo[2] et Ecclesias de

preceding notes). It appears from the obligation of Nicholas Malveysyn, Rector (see No. 218), that the pension reserved out of the living for the Priory of Wederhal was 10s.

[5] The only point to fix the date is the episcopate of Bishop Athelwold, between 1133 and 1156.

17. [1] Bernard, the second Bishop of Carlisle, who succeeded in 1204 after the long vacancy which followed the death of Bishop Athelwold in 1156, and who occupied the see for about 10 years ; see on this Bishop, Appendix D. The first two Bishops are mentioned in the next charter. This confirmation of the right of patronage is referred to in a Faculty of Pope Gregory IX. in 1240 (*Papal Registers*, ed. W. H. Bliss, i. 188), also that of Bishop Hugh in No. **20.**

[2] Burgo, now Brough in Westmoreland, was formerly part of the parish of Kirkbystephan, and appears in 1295 to have been called Burgo subtus Staynemore, or Burgo sub Mora. When the Church of Kirkbystephan was awarded to belong to the Abbey of S. Mary at York in the time of Bishop Walter (see note 2 on No. **16**), the Chapel of Burgo was to go with it on the death of Thomas Boet,

Ormesheved et de Morlund et de Cliburn et de Bromfeld et de Croglyn et Hermitorium Sancti Andreæ cum omnibus pertinentijs suis. Prædicti vero Abbas et Monachi de beneficijs Ecclesiarum talem portionem Clericis provideant unde decenter sustentari valeant, et Episcopalia jura possint persolvere. Et ut hæc confirmatio perpetuæ firmitatis robur obtineat hoc presens scriptum sigilli[3] nostri impressione communimus. Hijs Testibus P. Priore[4], Augustino et Rogero Canonicis Karliolensibus[5], Alexandro de Dacre[6], Henrico de Knaresburg, Thoma de Brunnefeld[7], Waldef de Brigham, et multis alijs[8].

the Chaplain. Nicolson and Burn (*History*, i. 466) assert that Thos. Boet was presented by Richard I., but this is clearly an error. When the three Churches were confirmed to Bishop Silvester in 1248, the patronage of the Church of Burgh was also conveyed to him, without the reservation of any pension to the Abbey (see Additional Charters, No. 240). A great amount of litigation followed as to whether the right of patronage lay with the King, the Bishop, or the family of de Veteriponte. (An account will be found in Bp Nicolson, MSS., ii. 113.) The well-known Robert de Eglesfield, founder of Queen's College, Oxford, was presented to this living in 1332.

[3] This mention of Bishop Bernard's seal is interesting as there is an impression of his seal in existence, attached to a grant among the Duchy of Lancaster Records in the Record Office, Box A, No. 393 (Illustrative Docum., XXI.). There is an illustration of this in the *Transactions of the Cumb. Antiq. Society* (xii. 214), but the grant has no date, as there stated, certainly not 1157.

[4] Probably P. is an error of the copyist for J. John was Prior of Carlisle about this time. He is witness to a charter of Bishop Bernard in the *Register of Lanercost* (MS. viii. 3), and to one of Archdeacon Americ de Taillebois (MS. viii. 2), made Archdeacon in 1196. He witnesses the confirmation of the first-named charter by the Chapter of Carlisle (MS. viii. 4), and confirms the charter of Bishop Bernard as to Denton Church (given below, No. 122). See more on No. 31, note 1.

[5] The two earliest Canons of Carlisle on record, except William Dean, precentor and Canon, who is mentioned in the charter of Henry II. to the Priory of Carlisle, and in the Pipe Roll for 1188.

[6] Alexander de Daker is also a witness to the charter of Bishop Bernard in the *Register of Lanercost* (MS. viii. 3). This is a very early, if

18. CONFIRMATIO SUPER ECCLESIASTICIS POSSESSIONIBUS ET REDDITIBUS CONCESSIS PER EPISCOPOS KARLIOLENSES ABBATI ET MONACHIS EBORACI.

HONORIUS[1] Episcopus servus servorum Dei dilectis

not the earliest, mention of the family of Dacre ; Nicolson and Burn (*History*, ii. 378) give Ranulf de Dacre in 6 Edward I. as "the first of the name that hath occurred to us." He is also a witness with Bp Bernard to the grant of the Church of Bridekirk to the Priory of Gyseburne by Alice de Rumely when she was a second time widow, in 1210—14 (*Chart. Gyseburne*, ed. W. Brown, ii. 319).

[7] Thos. de Brunnefeld granted to the Abbey of Holm Cultram a certain cultivated land, called Northrig, in Brunfeld (Bromfield) with a marsh adjoining, as appears from the *Register of Holm Cultram*, where his wife Agnes and his son Adam are also mentioned. There is a prior grant to the same Abbey by the son Adam, who is probably the same as the witness in No. **48**. These charters are given by Nicolson and Burn, *History*, ii. 166, and in Dugdale, *Monasticon*, v. 612. Thomas is also a witness to the grant of the Church of Burgo by Hugo de Morevilla (who died in 1202) to the same Abbey, together with Thomas son of Gospatric (*Regist. Holm Cultram*, MS. p. 13).

[8] There is little to fix the date of this charter beyond that it was in the time of Bishop Bernard ; and so far as the witnesses go they agree with the period 1204 to 1214 determined in Appendix D.

18. [1] This was Honorius III., Pope from July 1216 to March 1227. He is the Pope who interfered so strongly on behalf of the young King, Henry III., through his Legate Gualo, Cardinal priest of S. Martin. In this district the Legate was especially active against Alexander II., King of Scotland, who in 1215 had taken the town of Carlisle and laid waste Cumberland. In the first year of his Pontificate, January 16th, the Pope had written strongly to King Alexander ; and on April 26th of the same year Henry III. wrote to the Pope complaining of the Canons of Carlisle, who despised the Legate's authority, became subjects of the excommunicated King of Scotland, and had elected a certain excommunicated clerk as their Bishop and Pastor (Rymer, *Fœdera*, i. 147, from the *Patent Rolls*, 1 Hen. III. m. 16 (Record Com. p. 11) also *Papal Registers*, ed. W. H. Bliss, i. 48, 57). The result was that the Canons were exiled by Gualo (*Chronicon de Lanercost*, ed. J. Stevenson, p. 27) and the Pope's mandate was issued for the election, with the royal assent, of Hugh, Abbot of Beaulieu, to be Bishop of Carlisle (1218).

filijs Abbati et Conventui Monasterij Sanctæ Mariæ Eboraci salutem et amplissimam Benedictionem.   Justis peten-
tium desiderijs dignum est nos facilem præbere assensum
et vota quæ a Rationis tramite non discordant effectu
prosequente complere.   Ea propter dilecti in Domino filij
vestris justis postulationibus grato concurrentes assensu
Cellam de Wederhale cum Parochia de Warthwic, et alias
Ecclesias vestras quas de concessione bonæ memoriæ A. et
B.[2] Karleolensium Pontificum Capituli sui accedente consensu canonice proponitis vos adeptos necnon possessiones
redditus et alia bona vestra sicut ea omnia juste canonice
et pacifice possidetis et in prædictorum Episcoporum et
Capituli literis exinde confectis dicitur contineri Vobis et
per nos Monasterio vestro Auctoritate amplifica confirmamus et præsentis scripti patrocinio communimus.   Nulli
ergo omnino hominum liceat hanc paginam nostræ confirmationis infringere, vel ei ausu temerario contraire.   Si
quis autem hoc attemptare præsumpserit indignationem
Omnipotentis Dei et beatorum Petri et Pauli Apostolorum
ejus se noverit incursurum.   Datum Laterani vi° Idus
Aprilis, Pontificatus nostri Anno Decimo[3].

19. CONFIRMATIO EPISCOPI KARLIOL. SUPER EC-CLESIIS DE KIRKEBISTEPHAN ET DE MORLUND CUM CAPELLIS AD EAS PERTINENTIBUS.

HUGO[1] Dei gratia Karliolensis Episcopus omnibus

---

[2] Athelwold and Bernard, Bishops of Carlisle.

[3] Dated April 8th, 1226.

19. [1] Bishop Hugh had been Abbot of Beaulieu in Hampshire
(*Annal. Waverley in ann.* 1218, 1223; Dugdale, *Monasticon*, v. 680)
not in Burgundy, as some have written.   The Cistercian convent of
Beaulieu, or Bellum Locum Regis, was founded by King John in 1204
(*Annal. Waverley*); and in 1213 Abbot Hugh was one of the King's
envoys to the Pope (Innocent III.) with the Bishop of Norwich and
others (see *Papal Registers*, ed. W. H. Bliss, i. 39, 129, 145).   He was
elected by the rebellious Prior and Convent of Carlisle, under pressure
from the Legate Gualo (see note 1 on No. **18**), and the election

Christi fidelibus has literas inspecturis vel audituris salutem
in Domino. Quoniam ex officio nobis injuncto Subjectorum
nostrorum et maxime Religiosorum tenemur utilitati providere et eorum bona augere et confovere, Noscat universitas vestra quod nos Divina ducti pietate de assensu
Capituli Karleolensis Ecclesiæ concedimus et præsenti
pagina confirmamus Deo et Ecclesiæ Sanctæ Mariæ Eboraci et Monachis ibidem Deo servientibus et in posterum
servituris Ecclesias de Kirkebi-Stephan et de Morlund
cum omnibus Capellis ad eas pertinentibus et cum omnibus
alijs pertinentijs suis in proprios usus ipsorum habendas et
possidendas imperpetuum. Ita scilicet quod Ecclesia de
Kirkebi-Stephan cum suis pertinentijs cedat in usus proprios dictorum Monachorum Eboraci ad sustentationem
pauperum et peregrinorum. Et Ecclesia de Morlund cum
suis pertinentijs in usus proprios Monachorum domus de
Wederhale² quæ est cella dictæ Ecclesiæ Sanctæ Mariæ

received the royal assent on August 1st, 1218; he was consecrated
February 24th, 1218—19. The see had been vacant from before
May, 1215, when the custody was granted to the Prior of Carlisle
(see Appendix D). Bishop Hugh was one of those who on June
15th, 1220, gave their promise, *in verbo veritatis*, on the part of
Henry III. to Alexander II. of Scotland, in regard to the marriage of
the latter with the King's sister Johanna (Rymer, *Fœdera*, i. 160). He
granted two charters to the Priory of Lanercost about this time, which
were confirmed by Bartholomew, Prior, and the Convent of Carlisle,
and he fixed the taxation of the Vicarage of Brampton on the collation
of Magister Thomas (*Register of Lanercost*, MS. viii. 6, 7, 8, 10). He
also confirmed the Church of Crosseby Ravenswart in Westmaria to
the Abbey of Whitby, among the witnesses being Bartholomew, Prior
of Karleol, and Suffred, Prior of Wederhala (*Chart. Whitby*, ed.
Atkinson, i. 44). He died at the Abbey of La Ferté in Burgundy,
June 14th, 1223, on his return from Verona, whither he had gone with
the King's help (*Annal. Waverley in ann.* 1223; *Chronicon de Lanercost*, ed. J. Stevenson, p. 30).

² It should be noted that the Church of Kirkebistephan is granted
for the use of the monks of York, and the Church of Morlund for the
use of the monks of Wederhale and for the support of the poor and of
strangers, the vicars (see below) to receive each 100s.

Eboraci ad eorundem sustentationem. Decedentibus vero
vel cedentibus personis vel Rectoribus prædictarum Ecclesiarum qui nunc in eis sunt constituti liceat præfatis
Monachis libere et sine alicujus contradictione vel impedimento eas sibi in usus proprios retinere. Ita tamen quod
in eis vicarios idoneos constituant nobis et successoribus
nostris præsentandos qui de proventibus ipsarum C. solidos
singuli ipsorum de singulis Ecclesiis percipiant imperpetuum. Curamque animarum a nobis et Successoribus
nostris percipere et de Spiritualibus respondere teneantur.
Ut autem hæc nostra concessio et confirmatio perpetuæ
firmitatis robur optineat hoc præsens scriptum sigilli nostri
impressione duximus communire. Hijs Testibus, Domino
J. Abbate de fontibus[3], R. Decano[4] et Magistro J. Romano
Canonico Eboracensi[5], Magistro A. de Kirkeby[6] tunc

[3] John de Cancia was Abbot of Fountains from 1219 to his death,
November 25th, 1247 (*Memorials of Fountains*, ed. Walbran, i. 134).
He was one of the executors of the will of this Hugh, Bishop of
Carlisle, with the Priors of Wederhal and Lanercost (*Close Rolls*,
7 Hen. III. m. 8, ed. Hardy, p. 552). The Church of Crosthwaite,
Cumberland, was granted to the Abbey of Fountains by Alice de
Rumely in 1193—96 (see the ref. in Appendix D), and in 1227 Henry
de Curtenay, parson of Crostwait, quitclaimed his right in the Church
to this John, Abbot, and the Convent.

[4] R., or Roger (as in No. 21) de Insula was Dean of York from
1220 to 1235 ; he was a party in 1220 with John Romanus to an
agreement between the Dean and Chapter of York and the Abbey of
Rievaulx (*Chart. Rievaulx*, ed. Atkinson, p. 255).

[5] John Romanus, or le Romayn, was subdean and afterwards
treasurer of York, and father of the Archbishop of York of the same
name who was consecrated Feb. 10th, 1285—86. He appears to have
been of illegitimate birth, and got a dispensation *super defectu
natalium* from Pope Honorius III., March 1st, 1226 ; on March 22d,
1241, as Archdeacon of Richmond, he attested a grant of Archbishop
Gray (*Historians of Church of York*, ed. J. Raine, iii. 125, 157). He
was named the first subdean in 1228, and died in 1255 according to
Matthew Paris, who adds "avarus et cavillosus, dives valde et senex"
(*Chron. Majora*, ed. Luard, v. 534). He appears in September of this
year, 1220, as witness to the grant of the Church of Horneby by the

Officiali Karliolensi, Johanne de Kirkeby Clerico, Magistris R. de Bridlington, J. de Hampton[7] et R. Benvallet[8], R. Deskegenesse, R. de Apeltun[9], Willelmo de Pontefracto et J. de Bovingtun, Nicholao de Morlund, Samsone Clerico et alijs. Actum XIII° Calend. Novembris Anno Incarnationis Domini MCCXX°.[10]

20. CONFIRMATIO H. EPISCOPI KARLIOL. SUPER ECCLESIIS SANCTI MICHAELIS ET SANCTI LAURENTIJ DE APPELBY.

HUGO Dei gratia Karleolensis Episcopus Venerabilibus fratribus in Christo Roberto[1] Abbati et Conventui Sanctæ Mariæ Eboraci salutem in Domino. Quum plerumque contingit per incuriam negligenter administrantium in Ecclesiis ut quod pejus est per dilapidacionem perperam agentium officia Prelatorum, in eis alienationes possessionum et rerum Ecclesiasticarum in enormem fiant lesionem Piorum locorum. Atque ea quæ ad sustentationem pauperum et peregrinorum et deservientium in eis devotione fidelium sacris cenobijs conferuntur in usus alios qui potius salutem animarum impediant quam promoveant minus licite transferuntur. Cum autem vacante sede[2] Karleolensis

---

Abbey of S. Mary at York with R. de Bridlington, J. de Hamerton, Wm. de Pontefract, Robert de Appelton and W. de Lanum (*Reg. Magnum Album*, ii. 28 quoted in *Archbp Gray's Register*, ed. J. Raine, p. 139 *n.*, see also p. 137).

[6] Adam de Kirkeby, or Kirkbythore, Official of Carlisle, often occurs in the charters of this date, especially those of Bishop Hugh; comp. *Register of Lanercost*, MS. viii. 7, 8, 10; *Chart. of Whitby*, ed. Atkinson, i. pp. 45, 46. There is A. de Kirkeby Junr. in Nos. **211, 213.**

[7] J. de Hampton should be Hamerton as in No. **22**, and see note 5 above on J. Romanus.

[8] R. or Roger de Benvallet, as in No. **22**.

[9] R. or Robert de Apeltun, see note 5 above.

[10] October 20th, 1220.

20. [1] Robert de Longo Campo, see No. **10**, note 3.

[2] That is from the time when Bernard, Archbishop of Slavonia,

Ecclesiæ multa in eodem Episcopatu sint perpetrata et quæ fieri debuerant impudenter omissa Nos reformationi Matricis Ecclesiæ non solum vacare studentes verum et aliarum universitati et præcipue Religiosorum utilitati providentes optamus aliena revocare collapsa reparare et quæ negligenter a Matricibus Ecclesiis sunt separata annuente Domino ex injuncto nobis officio cupimus resarcire. Ea propter karissimi fratres in Christo attendentes devotionem vestram et religiositatem et caritativam in recipiendis hospitibus liberalitatem quam indesinenter habundancius exhibetis. Concedimus vobis ut Ecclesias de Appelby Sancti Michaelis et Sancti Laurentij quas vobis in proprios usus Predecessor noster bonæ memoriæ Adelwaldus Karliolensis Episcopus cum omnibus libertatibus et pertinentijs earundem vobis concessit sicut in originalibus literis quas ab eodem Episcopo recepistis et habetis plenius continetur. Vobis nihilominus de communi assensu capituli nostri Karliolensis presenti scripto perpetuo confirmamus. Habendas et pacifice possidendas in usus proprios salvo jure Diocesano. Ita tamen ut domus de Wederhale nomine universitatis vestræ easdem in proprios usus possideat Salvis tamen consuetis pensionibus quas de eisdem Ecclesiis percipere consuevistis et ministraturi in eis nobis et successoribus nostris Vicarij idonei a vobis præsententur, qui de bonis ipsarum Ecclesiarum congruam recipiant sustentationem. Ita scilicet quod Vicarius in Ecclesia Sancti Michaelis recipiat quinque marcas[3] et Vicarius in Ecclesia Sancti Laurentij recipiat sex marcas. Et ipsi Vicarij jura Episcopalia et Archidiaconalia persolvent et honeste Ecclesijs deservient. Hijs Testibus, B.

resigned or died, before May, 1214, to February, 1218—19 (see on Bishop Bernard, Appendix D).

[3] The Vicar of S. Michael's was to receive 5 marcs or £3. 6s. 8d., if we take the marc at 13s. 4d., and the Vicar of S. Laurence' 6 marcs or £4; but see note 1 on No. 3. The marc varied in value; but in 1225, we have it 13s. 4d., as is shewn in No. 225.

Priore Karliolensi[4], Magistro Adam[5] Officiali, Domino W. Capellano[6], et alijs[7].

21. CONFIRMATIO EPISCOPI KARLIOL. OMNIBUS POSSESSIONIBUS ET PENSIONIBUS INFRA DICŒCESEN KARLIOLENSEM.

HUGO Dei gratia Karliolensis Episcopus omnibus Christi fidelibus ad quorum noticiam præsens scriptum pervenerit salutem in Domino. Noverit Universitas vestra Nos Divinæ pietatis intuitu et assensu Capituli Karleolensis Ecclesiæ concessisse et hac præsenti carta nostra confirmasse Abbati et Conventui Sanctæ Mariæ Eboraci omnes Possessiones et pensiones omnium Ecclesiarum suarum in Diocesi Karliolensi constitutarum quas habuerunt in eadem Diœcesi ante Consecrationem nostram habendas et pacifice possidendas in perpetuum cum omni integritate et statu sicut eas unquam plenius habere et percipere consueverunt. Ut autem hec nostra concessio et confirmatio perpetuæ firmitatis robur obtineat hoc præsens scriptum sigilli nostri appositione una cum sigillo Capituli Karleolensis Ecclesiæ communimus. Qui vero præsentis paginæ tenorem infirmare præsumpserint noverint se sententiam Excommunicationis incursuros. Hijs Testibus, Rogero Decano, Magistris J. Romano et W. de Lanum[1] Canonicis Eboracensibus, Ma-

---

[4] Bartholomew, so frequently mentioned in this *Register*, and elsewhere, in the time of Bishop Hugh (compare *Register of Lanercost*, MS. viii. 7, 8; *Chart. of Whitby*, ed. Atkinson, i. 45). He died in 1231, and was succeeded by Radulph, nephew of Bishop Walter Malclerk (*Chronicon de Lanercost*, ed. Stevenson, p. 41).

[5] Adam de Kirkeby, see note 6 on No. **19.**

[6] Called in No. **118** "our Chaplain" by Bishop Hugh.

[7] The date lies between 1218 and 1223, probably about the same time as the last charter.

21. [1] William de Lanum appears as Canon of York with John Romanus in the charters mentioned in note 5 on No. **19.** In another deed given in the notes to *Archbp Gray's Register* (ed. Raine, p. 186 *n.*) William son of Richard de Lanum occurs (see also p. 245 *n.*). He was afterwards Archdeacon of Durham.

gistro A. Officiali[2], Magistro G. de Louther[3], Thoma de
Wiltun[4] et alijs[5].

22. CONFIRMATIO EPISCOPI KARLIOL. DE OMNIBUS DECIMIS DE DOMINICIS IN DIOCESI KARLIOLENSI.

OMNIBUS Sanctæ Matris Ecclesiæ filijs ad quorum
noticiam presens scriptum pervenerit Hugo Dei Gratia
Karliolensis Ecclesiæ vocatus sacerdos salutem æternam
in Domino. Noscat universitas vestra nos Divinæ Caritatis
intuitu de assensu Capituli Carleolensis Ecclesiæ concessisse
et confirmasse Abbati et Conventui Sanctæ Mariæ Eboraci
et dilectis filijs nostris Priori et Monachis de Wederhale
omnes Decimas de Dominicis quas ab antiquo in Diocesi
nostra fidelium donatione vel concessione noscuntur possidere. Habendas et tenendas inperpetuum in proprios usus
eorum sine alicujus contradictione vel impedimento sicut in
cartis donatorum de prædictis decimis factis et concessis

---

[2] Adam de Kirkeby, see on No. 19.

[3] Gervase de Louther, whose name occurs, in a more or less
abbreviated form, so often in this *Register*. The name appears
without a title here and in Nos. 118, 151 and in the *Register of
Lanercost*, MS. viii. 10, all in the time of Bishop Hugh ; as Official of
Carlisle, in Nos. 46, 93, 131 about 1225 and No. 172 (1223—1229) ; as
Archdeacon, frequently (see Index); for example, in Nos. 54, 129, with
Bartholomew, Prior of Carlisle, therefore before his death in 1231; in
No. 97 with Radulph, Prior, therefore after 1231 ; in *Memorials of
Hexham* (ed. Raine, ii. 121) with Bishop Walter (1223—46), and
Bartholomew, Prior ; in the *Register of Holm Cultram* (MS. p. 17),
being witness to the confirmation of the Church of Burgh by Bishop
Walter in 1234, also witness to an award by the same Bishop
(MS. p. 21) of the tithes of fish caught at Rochclive to the Convent of
Carlisle ; also in the *Register of Lanercost* (MS. iii. 11 ; iv. 14 ; vi. 12).
Hence we gather that he was not made Official till the death of Bishop
Hugh in 1223, and probably soon after by Bishop Walter; and that he
was made Archdeacon shortly before 1230—31.

[4] Thomas de Wilton is called Seneschal of the Abbot in No. 22,
and in No. 180, *Dapifer*.

[5] The date lies in the time of Bishop Hugh (1218—1223), probably
about 1220.

plenius continetur. Et ut hoc scriptum nostræ concessionis et confirmationis perpetuæ firmitatis robur optineat sigillum nostrum eidem fecimus apponi. Hijs Testibus, Domino Petro Capellano nostro, fratre Willelmo, Stephano Dapifero[1], Ricardo Marescallo[2], Roberto de Farendona, Magistris J. de Hamertona[3] et Rogero de Benvallet, Thoma de Wilton Senescallo Abbatis, Thoma Janitore et multis alijs[4].

23. LITERA DOMINI EPISCOPI KARLIOL. DE PENSIONIBUS ET BENEFICIJS DEBITIS SOLUENDIS ABBATI EBORACI.

H. Dei Gratia Ecclesiæ Karleolensis vocatus sacerdos dilectis filijs universis et singulis Clericis beneficiatis de Monasterio Sanctæ Mariæ Eboraci in Diocesi Karliolensis Ecclesiæ constitutis salutem in Domino. Cum ex [officio] nostro subditorum nostrorum et præsertim Religiosorum utilitati et commodo teneamur providere Mandamus vobis firmiter injungentes quatinus Abbati et Monachis dicti Monasterij pensiones solitas quas eis ante consecracionem nostram reddere consuevistis plene et sine difficultate modo et de cetero persolvatis similiter et Beneficia solita in ministrando eidem uberius exhibeatis. Valete.

24. CONFIRMATIO EPISCOPI KARLIOL. SUPER ECCLESIIS ET CAPELLIS.

OMNIBUS Christi fidelibus ad quos præsens scriptum pervenerit Hugo Dei Gratia Karleolensis Episcopus salutem in Domino. Noverit universitas vestra Nos intuitu Pietatis

---

22. [1] *Dapifer*, steward of the household, sometimes the butler. The Dapifer of the Royal household was an officer of great importance.

[2] Richard Mariscallus is a party to a mining lease granted at Hexham by Archbishop Gray in May, 1230 (*Register*, ed. Raine, p. 236).

[3] For J. de Hamertona, see No. **19** on J. de Hampton.

[4] The date of this charter must be about the same as No. **19**, i.e. 1220.

et de assensu Capituli nostri concessisse et præsenti carta
confirmasse dilectis nostris in Domino Priori et Monachis
de Wederhale¹ Ecclesiam de Wederhale cum Capella de
Warthwic Ecclesiam de Morlund Ecclesiam Sancti Michaelis et Ecclesiam Sancti Laurentij de Appelby cum
omnibus pertinentijs earum Habendas et tenendas in proprios usus imperpetuum satisfaciendo integre de Episco-
palibus et Archidiaconalibus. Et eisdem Ecclesiis facient
honeste deservire. Et in hujus rei Testimonium præsentem
cartam nostram eis concessimus sigillo nostro et sigillo
Capituli nostri munitam. Hijs Testibus....

25. BULLA DOMINI PAPÆ DE CONCESSIONE INGRE-
DIENDI POSSESSIONEM ECCLESIÆ SANCTI MICHAELIS
DE APPELBY RECTORE DECEDENTE, ETC.

GREGORIUS¹ Episcopus servus servorum Domini dilectis filijs Abbati et Conventui Monasterij Sanctæ Mariæ
Eboraci Ordinis Sancti Benedicti² salutem et amplificam

24. ¹ There is no reference here to the Abbey of S. Mary at York.
These Churches were separately appropriated to the Prior and Monks
of Wederhale.

25. ¹ Gregory IX., who was Pope from March 21st, 1227 to
August 21st, 1241. It was this Pope who strove so hard to promote
peace between Henry III. and Alexander II. of Scotland, and with
this object wrote to the Archbishop of York and the Bishop of Carlisle
(Walter Malclerk) on January 4th, 1235—36 (see Rymer, *Fœdera*,
new ed. i. 214). This Bull or Faculty is also among the Papal
Registers; see the *Calendar*, Rolls Series, ed. W. H. Bliss, vol. i.
p. 188.

² The Order of S. Benedict, the most important of the monastic
orders, was founded by Benedict, who was born at Nursia in Umbria
about A.D. 480. He betook himself to Monte Cassino, afterwards the
centre of this great Order, about A.D. 530. Here he began his monastery and is said to have composed the famous Benedictine Rule ; he
died probably about A.D. 543. Before his death the Benedictine Rule
had passed into Gaul and Spain, and before long absorbed all the
monastic systems of the West. To this Order is due much of the

benedictionem Referentibus nobis accepimus quod bonæ memoriæ B. et H.[3] Karliolenses Episcopi Monasterium vestrum favore benivolo prosequentes Ecclesiam Sancti Michaelis de Appelby Karliolensis Diocesis in qua jus Patronatus[4] habetis cujusque institutio ad Episcopos dictos pertinebat Capituli sui accedente consensu Monasterio Ipsi pietatis intuitu contulerunt in usus Monachorum Prioratus vestri de Wederhale ejusdem Diocesis cedente vel decedente persona ipsius Ecclesiæ convertendam quæ interim vobis annuam solveret pensionem. Quare nobis humiliter supplicastis ut ingrediendi possessionem Ecclesiæ prædictæ post cessionem vel decessum personæ ipsius vobis licentiam largiremur. Nos igitur vestris supplicationibus inclinati ingrediendi possessionem eandem persona cedente seu decedente prædicta contradictione Diocesani Episcopi non obstante si præmissis veritas suffragatur Vobis authoritate præsentium liberam concedimus facultatem Nulli ergo omnino hominum liceat hanc paginam nostræ Concessionis infringere vel ei ausu temerario contraire. Si quis autem hoc attemptare præsumpserit indignationem Omnipotentis Dei et Beatorum Petri et Pauli Apostolorum ejus se noverit incursurum. Datum Literarum[5] ij Idus Marcij Pontificatus nostri Anno tertio decimo[6].

---

civilization and learning of the middle ages. It is not clear when the Order was introduced into England ; according to some, by Augustine in the 6th century, and others, by Wilfrid in the 7th century. Very many of the finest Abbeys and nearly all the Cathedrals (Carlisle was a Convent of Augustinian Canons) belonged to this Order. See Mabillon, *Annales Ordinis S. Benedicti*, 1703 ; Dugdale, *Monasticon*, vol. i. John Marsham's *Preface* ; for the Rule, Martene, *Præf. Regulæ S. B.* in Migne, *Patrologia*, lxvi.

[3] Bernard and Hugh ; this is an important reference to Bishop Bernard in conjunction with Bishop Hugh, both being dead, and with no mention of Bishop Athelwold.

[4] Some claim had been made by the Bishop, see note 1 on No. 3.

[5] *Literarum*, an error for *Laterani*, the Lateran palace at Rome.

[6] March 14th, 1240.

26. CONFIRMATIO EPISCOPI KARLIOL. SUPER ECCLESIIS DE KIRBYSTEPHAN ET DE MORLUND.

UNIVERSIS Sanctæ Matris Ecclesiæ filijs ad quos præsens scriptum pervenerit Silvester[1] Dei gratia Karleolensis Episcopus salutem in Domino. Noverit universitas vestra nos communi consilio et assensu Capituli nostri Ecclesiæ Sanctæ Mariæ Karlioli concessisse confirmasse et ratas habere concessiones donationes et confirmationes illas quas Venerabilis Pater Hugo[2] Dei Gratia Karleolensis Episcopus Prædecessor noster fecit Abbati et Conventui Sanctæ Mariæ Eboraci super Ecclesias de Appelby Sancti Michaelis et Sancti Laurentij et de Kirkebystephan et de Morlund tenendis [et] habendis in proprios usus imperpetuum integre et plenarie cum omnibus Capellis et pertinentijs suis. Concedimus et confirmamus et ratas habemus omnes concessiones donationes et confirmationes pensionum libertatum procurationum et aliorum beneficiorum Ecclesiasticorum quas idem Venerabilis Pater Predecessor noster fecit Abbati et Conventui prædictis sicut in ipsius Cartis super hijs confectis plenius continetur et sicut temporibus Predecessorum nostrorum habuerunt. Et in hujus rei testimonium et confirmationem præsenti scripto sigillum nostrum una cum sigillo Capituli nostri apposuimus. Testibus, Dominis Waltero de Rudham[3], Willelmo de Swyneford, Henrico de Kyngtun, Magistris Rogero Pepyn[4], Johanne de Aseby,

---

26. [1] Silvester de Everdon, 5th Bishop of Carlisle, was consecrated on October 13th, 1246, in the church of S. Agatha, Richmond (*Chronicon de Lanercost*, ed. Stevenson, p. 53) and died, by a fall from his horse, May 13th, 1254 (*Chron. de Lanercost*, p. 62 ; Matt. Paris, *Chron. Majora*, ed. Luard, v. 431).

[2] These Churches were confirmed by Bishop Hugh (Nos. **19, 20**) but there is no confirmation by Bishop Walter.

[3] Walter de Rudham was guardian of the vacant see of Carlisle on the death of the next Bishop, Thomas Veteriponte, or Vipont, in October, 1256.

[4] Roger Pepyn, or Pepin, was Rector of Kendal in November, 1246, as appears from a grant made to him by Radulph de Ainecurt of land

Domino Gilberto de Kyrketun, Domino J. de Petricurta, Nicholao Spigurnel et alijs. Datum Lundon. xij° kal. Marcij, A.D. MCCXLVII°.[5]

27. TAXATIO VICARIÆ ECCLESIÆ SANCTI MICHAELIS DE APPELBY.

UNIVERSIS Christi fidelibus ad quos præsens scriptum pervenerit Thomas[1] permissione Divina Karliolensis Ecclesiæ Minister humilis salutem in Domino sempiternam. Ad universitatis vestræ notitiam pervenire volumus quod cum inter viros Religiosos Abbatem et Conventum Sanctæ Mariæ Eboraci per fratrem Thomam de Scyreburn[2] Monachum et Galfridum de Grangiis procuratores suos sub alternatione constitutos Priorem et Monachum de Wederhal personaliter comperentes ex parte una et Walterum de Scaldwelle[3] perpetuum Vicarium Ecclesiæ Sancti Michaelis de Appelby personaliter comperentem ex altera super taxatione Vicariæ ejusdem Ecclesiæ coram nobis esset accitatum. Nos de communi consensu utriusque partis non obstante aliqua taxatione prohibita Vicariam memoratæ Ecclesiæ taxavimus in hunc modum, videlicet quod prædictus Walterus et Successores sui qui ministraturi sunt in

in Natelunt (Natland); the charter was among the Strickland deeds at Sizergh copied by Dodsworth (MS. 149, fol. 1421, and quoted in *Duchetiana*, p. 271 by Sir G. Duckett). He was subdean of York in March, 1254 (*Archbp Gray's Register*, p. 122) and in May, 1255; he died in 1266 (Hardy, *Fasti Eccles*. iii. 128).

[5] February 18th, 1247

27. [1] Thomas Vipont, or de Veteriponte, who was formerly Rector of Graistok (*Chron. de Lanercost*, ed. Stevenson, p. 62), was consecrated Bishop of Carlisle on February 7th, 1255—56, and died the 25th of October following, 1256.

[2] Thomas de Scyreburn (probably Sherburn, in Yorkshire) was a monk of S. Mary's, and not to be confounded with a monk of Selby in the next century.

[3] Bishop Nicolson (MSS. ii. 29) has copied this name as Fealdwell, which is probably correct; the error in copying might easily occur; see on this Walter in note 3, No. 205.

dicta Ecclesia habeant nomine Vicariæ omnes agnos lanam omnimodas oblationes decimas quadragesimarum[4] lini ortorum totius albi pullorum vitulorum denarios venientes cum pane benedicto decimas fœni totius parrochiæ molendinorum cerevisiæ et sponsalia mortuaria decimas porcellorum et omnimodas decimas et obventiones ad altaragium qualitercunque contingentes et medietatem totius terræ arabilis et prati. Ita tamen quod tota terra arabilis et pratum per viros fide dignos ad hoc ex utraque parte communiter electos in duas equales partes dividantur et sorte dirimantur. Item dictus Vicarius et Successores sui habebunt totam decimam provenientem de Hospitali Beati Nicholai[5] in eadem Parochia et omnes Toftos et Croftos a domo Astini usque ad domum Roberti Waldi ex Australi parte dictæ Ecclesiæ continuatos et dictus Prior habebit omnes Toftos et Croftos residuos similiter ad Ecclesiam pertinentes cum Capitali Messuagio. In cujus rei Testimonium una cum signis dictorum Prioris et Vicarij mutuis scriptis utriusque partis sigillum nostrum apponi fecimus. Datum apud Bellum locum[6] in crastino Annuntiationis Dominicæ A.D. MCCLVI°.[7]

[4] *Quadragesimæ*, the Lent offerings.

[5] S. Nicholas was the patron saint of children and of sailors; and was Bishop of Myra in Lysia in the 4th century. He was a very popular saint in England and elsewhere, and the chief patron saint of Russia; but his name is not connected generally with lepers, and very few of the leper hospitals in England were dedicated to him; for the legendary account of him, see Jameson, *Sacred and Legendary Art*, ii. 450. This Hospital was granted to the Abbey of Heppe or Shap, in Westmoreland, by John de Veteriponte before 1241, when he died (see on No. 204); and the grant was confirmed by Bishop Walter Malclerk, October 20th, 1240; the confirmation is given in full in the Machel MSS. vol. v. p. 269, and states that the Hospital was for three lepers.

[6] *Bellum Locum* is clearly Bewley, about 2 miles west of Appleby and one of the residences of the Bishops of Carlisle. It is said to have belonged formerly to John de Builli (*ob.* 1213), whose daughter Idonea (*ob.* 1241) was married to the first Robert de Veteri-

Et sciendum est quod dictus Vicarius et Successores sui omnia onera ordinaria consueta et debita sustinebunt. Ex præcepto autem Episcopi et de consensu partium post consignationem hujus literæ fuit ista clausula apposita.

28. CONFIRMATIO PRIORIS ET CONVENTUS KARLIOL. SUPER ECCLESIIS DE WEDERHAL CUM CAPELLA DE WARTHWIC ET MORLUND ET ALIIS.

OMNIBUS Christi fidelibus ad quos præsens scriptum pervenerit Walterus[1] Prior et Conventus Sanctæ Mariæ

ponte (Nicolson and Burn, *History*, i. 456; Dugdale, *Baronage*, i. 455). I have found no real authority for the statement. The subject of the charter agrees well with the place, and *Bellum Locum* seems to point to Beaulieu (Bewley) rather than to the personal name Builli.

[7] March 26th, 1256.

28. [1] Walter, generally taken to be the second Prior of Carlisle as successor to Athelwold, often appears in this *Register* in connection with the witnesses to this charter (see below). He is supposed to be identical with Walter the Chaplain of Henry I., to whom the King gave Linstoc and Carletun, which Walter transferred to the then new Priory of Carlisle on entering that House (*Testa de Nevill*, Record Com. p. 379 *b* and see Appendix B). If he became Prior in 1133, when Athelwold became Bishop, he must have held the office for a very long period. He more probably became Prior later, but before the death of the Bishop in 1156, for we find him witness with Adeluph, Bishop of Carlisle, to the charter granted by Earl Henry to the Abbey of Holm Cultram on January 1st, 1150, and again, with Adeluph, to the confirmation of that charter by David I., King of Scotland, who died in 1153 (Dugdale, *Monasticon*, v. 594, where the charters are given in full, and Illustrative Documents, XXIV.; for the date 1150 see *Chron. de Mailros, in ann.*; *Roger de Hoveden*, ed. Stubbs, i. 211). He was witness to the Foundation Charter of Lanercost, said to be granted in 1169, and no doubt about that time, in which appear the names of all the witnesses to the present charter. His name also occurs in other charters of this period in the *Register of Lanercost*, generally with Robert, Archdeacon of Carlisle; see MS. I. 9, 14; II. 18 (charter of Alexander de Wyndesor as to the tithe of the mill at Corkeby, Gualter for Walter); v. 3 (charter of William son of Odard of land near Warthwyc bridge) and VIII. 5 (G. for Gualter). He was also witness to the confirmation of the Church of Crossby Ravenswart

Karlioli salutem. Noverit universitas vestra nos gratum
præbuisse assensum concessionibus et confirmationibus
quas venerabilis Pater Adelwaldus Episcopus noster fecit
Abbati et Conventui Sanctæ Mariæ de Eboraco super
Ecclesijs de Wederhal cum Capella de Warthwic et de
Morlund et de Brunefeld et alijs bonis Ecclesiasticis sicut
in ipsius Instrumentis super hijs confectis coram nobis in
Capitulo lectis et inspectis plenius continetur. Ad cujus
rei Testimonium et munitionem præsenti scripto sigillum
Capituli[2] nostri apposuimus. Hijs Testibus, Roberto
Archidiacono Karleoli[3], Roberto de Wallibus[4], Petro de
Tillel[5], Willelmo filio Odardi[6] cum alijs pluribus[7].

to the Abbey of Wyteby by Robert, Archdeacon of Carlisle, after the
death of Bishop Athelwold (*Chart. Whitby*, ed. Atkinson, i. 38). He
was succeeded by John, the third Prior, see note on No. 31.

[2] An impression of the seal of the Priory of Carlisle is affixed to a
document dated March 1st, 1484 among the muniments of the city of
Carlisle. The deed is an agreement between the city and Prior
Thomas Gudybour and the Convent. The seal probably dates from the
12th or 13th century. A copy of the seal and an account of it is given
in the *Transactions of the Cumb. Archæol. Soc.* vii. 330. Another
impression much damaged is affixed to a communication dated
September 17th, 1343, from the Priory to the Priory of Conigesheved
(Coniston) among the Duchy of Lancaster Records, Box A, No. 416.

[3] From note 1, on Prior Walter, it appears that Robert was
Archdeacon of Carlisle about 1169, and some time after. He does
not seem to have been the first Archdeacon recorded; he occurs late
in the century, and in the *Chartulary of Whitby* (ed. Atkinson, i. 38)
there is a charter of Bishop Adhelwald addressed to Elyas, Archdeacon, no doubt Archdeacon of Carlisle; and this charter is
confirmed by Archdeacon Robert (i. 39, 42) after the Bishop's death,
under precept from Roger, Archbishop of York (1154—1181), the See
being then vacant. Besides being witness to the Foundation Charter
of Lanercost, he is co-witness to many of the other charters in the
Register of Lanercost together with the persons connected with him in
this *Register*, see MS. I. 9, 14; II. 15 (charter of Ada Engayne, her
father William being dead), 18; III. 1, 2 (charters of Robert son of
Bueth), 13; V. 3, 5; VII. 5; XII. 26 and VIII. 5, where there is a
renunciation before him of rights in the Churches of Irthington and

Brampton by Walter, Prior, and the Convent of Carlisle.   His name occurs in the *Register of Holm Cultram* (MS. p. 36) as ratifying an agreement between the Convent and Adam son of Gospatric son of Orm, parson of Camerton, about the chapel of Flemingby, during the vacancy of the See; to this reference is made in a confirmation of Pope Clement III. dated 1190 (MS. p. 239).   His name does not occur in the charter of Earl Henry to that Abbey in 1150.   He attested the charter of Huctred son of Fergus, 1159—64 (see on Odard son of Hildred in No. **72**).   He is a party to other deeds in this *Register*, two of which should be specially noted—No. **36**, between 1154 and 1175, probably 1160—70, and No. **44** in 1164—65 (on which see below).   Robert was succeeded by Peter de Ros, who was Archdeacon before 1192 and probably from 1180 (see note 3 on No. **31**).   But, in the Pipe Rolls (Cumberland) a Robert, Archdeacon of Carlisle, appears as one of the debtors of Aaron the Jew of Lincoln in 1192, and in the four following years ; he is not among the debtors in 1197, and therefore probably died in 1196.   This can scarcely have been the Robert we are considering, and was probably a second of the name.   Another Archdeacon Robert occurs in this *Register* (see on No. **137**) about 1235—46, Robert de Otterington.   On the Archdeacons of Carlisle generally and their office, see my *Visitations in the Ancient Diocese of Carlisle*, 1888, in which I should now make several corrections as to early dates.

⁴ Robert de Vallibus, or de Vaux, the second Lord of Gilsland, was the son of Hubert de Vallibus, to whom Henry II. gave that Barony (*Testa de Nevill*, p. 379 *a*) to be held for the service of two knights' fees, *per servitium duorum militum* (see Illustrative Documents, XXII. ; No. **191**, note 3), probably in 1157, when Malcolm restored the northern counties.   The King was in Carlisle in 1158, and that year, the 4th of his reign, is the first in which the accounts for Carlisle appear in the Pipe Rolls.   There Hubert de Vallibus is exempted £18. 13s. 3d. for Notegild, or Neatgeld, from which he was free by the terms of the grant of the Barony, thus proving he was in possession of the lands at the time (*quietas ab omni neutegeldo*); and there his name appears until 1164, when, in 1165, Robert de Vallibus takes his place, having succeeded to the Barony.   The important position held by Hubert de Vallibus in 1157 is shewn by another entry in the Pipe Roll for 1158.   The sheriff, Robert son of Troite, pays over to him "the Corredy £11. 3s., prepared against the arrival of the King, by the King's writ"; this was to meet the expenses of the King's visit, who was at Carlisle on Midsummer Day (*Roger de Hoveden*, i. 216 ; *Robert de Monte in ann.*).   The

P.   5

grant made to his father Hubert was confirmed to Robert by Henry II. between 1166 and 1174 (the See of Bath being then vacant, and Henry elect of Bath being one of the witnesses); it was also confirmed by Richard I. in the first year of his reign; these three charters are given in full (taken from some of Dugdale's MSS.) in the Machel MSS. iv. 135—7; see also for Hubert's charter, Illustrative Documents, XXII., or Nicolson and Burn, *History*, ii. 487, taken from Machel's MSS. In the Foundation Charter of Lanercost, the name of the mother of Robert de Vallibus is given as Grecia, or Grace. The Pipe Rolls again afford us important information, with dates. In 1169 he paid 2 marcs for two knights' fees, and in 1172 paid 40s. scutage for the same; in 1175 he was Sheriff of Carlisle, and held the office to 1185 inclusive. He founded the Priory of Lanercost, it is said in 1169 on the authority of an untrustworthy note in the margin of the *Register of Lanercost* (MS. i. 1), but from the witnesses to the Foundation Charter this must have been about the date (see Illustrative Docum. XXIII.). In 1174 he held the Castle of Carlisle for Henry II. against William the Lion, King of Scotland, and was made a Justice Itinerant January 25th, 1176 (*Roger de Hoveden*, ed. Stubbs, ii. 60, 88; *Benedict Abbas*, i. 108). His wife was Ada Engayne, daughter of William Engayne, Lord of Burgh (see the note on No. **101**). In a charter granted by her to the Priory of Lanercost, she speaks of William Engayne, her father, Robert de Vallibus, her husband, Simon de Morville, her former husband, and Hugo de Morville, her son; in other charters Robert speaks of his wife Ada (*Regist. Laner.* MS. i. 2, 3; ii. 11). This and other grants made by her (MS. ii. 15) were confirmed by Pope Alexander III. in 1181 (MS. viii. 17); and Simon de Morville died in 1167 (see note 1, No. **101**). There is no mention of his wife in his Foundation Charter (although his son William is a witness); hence it would appear that he was married between 1170 and 1180. He died in 1195, without issue, and his brother Ranulph succeeded to his property, paying 50 marcs for livery of his lands (*Pipe Rolls*, 6 Ric. I.). His name occurs several times in this *Register*; in No. **44** (1164—65) connected with many names mentioned in the F. C. of Lanercost. Robert de Vallibus, junior, succeeded his father Ranulph in 1199 (see on No. **38** and *Pipe Rolls*, 1 Joh.) and is often confounded with his uncle Robert. For the Priory of Lanercost, see the note on No. **117**.

⁵ Peter de Tillel, or Tyllolf, or Teillol, held the manor of Scaleby, about 5 miles to the north-east of Carlisle. We learn from the Pipe Rolls that he had livery of the lands of his grandfather in 1158, paying 50s. for the same in 1159; and from *Testa de Nevill* (p. 379 b) that

29. CONFIRMATIO PRIORIS ET CONVENTUS KARLIOL. DE DONATIONIBUS ET CONCESSIONIBUS PRÆDECESSORUM SUORUM SUPER ECCLESIIS DE APPELBY KIRKEBISTE-PHAN ET MORLUND.

UNIVERSIS Sanctæ Matris Ecclesiæ filijs ad quos præsens scriptum pervenerit Bartholomeus Prior et Conventus Ecclesiæ Sanctæ Mariæ Karleolensis salutem in Domino. Noverit universitas vestra Nos communi consilio et assensu Capituli nostri ratas et gratas habere donationes et confirmationes illas quas Venerabilis Pater noster Hugo Dei gratia Karliolensis Episcopus fecit Abbati et Conventui Sanctæ Mariæ Eboraci super Ecclesijs de Appelby Sancti Michaelis et Sancti Laurentij et de Kirkebistephan et de Morlund. Tenendum et habendum in proprios usus imperpetuum integre et plenarie cum omnibus Capellis et pertinentijs suis ratas et gratas habemus omnes donationes et confirmationes pensionum libertatum et procurationum et aliorum Beneficiorum Ecclesiasticorum quas idem Vene-

---

this ancestor was Richard Rider or Richard Tyllioll. He attested the charter of Huctred son of Fergus, 1159—64, referred to in the note on Odard son of Hildred in No. 72. He was a witness to the Foundation Charter of Lanercost about 1169; and to one or two other charters of that Priory. A certain land called Holmheim was given him by Henry II. to be held for 20s. yearly, as appears from the *Coram Rege Rolls* (11 Joh. No. 41, m. 9, see *Abbrev. Placit.* Rec. Com. p. 66 *b*). He died in 1184, when his son Simon (see on No. 38) had livery of his lands on payment of 30 marcs. His name appears in Nos. **28, 44**; but that of his grandson Peter de Tyllol occurs very often (see on No. **56**) in this *Register*

[6] On William son of Odard, see note 1 on No. **36**.

[7] The date of this charter turns mainly on the point whether Bishop Athelwold was dead at the time. The language used would seem to imply that he was not, and there is not the usual addition "bonæ memoriæ"; this would have placed the date shortly before his death in 1156; but, as we have seen above, some of the witnesses only come into prominence, and inherit their lands, about 1157—58; and not long after that date, between 1160 and 1170, would seem to agree better with the circumstances of the case.

rabilis Pater noster fecit Abbati et Conventui prædictis
sicut in ipsius cartis super hijs confectis plenius continetur.
Et in hujus rei Testimonium et confirmationem præsenti
scripto sigillum Capituli nostri apposuimus. Hijs Testibus[1].

30. CONFIRMATIO PRIORIS ET CONVENTUS KARLIOL.
DE OMNIBUS CONCESSIONIBUS COLLATIONIBUS CONFIR-
MATIONIBUS, ETC.

UNIVERSIS Christi fidelibus has literas inspecturis vel
audituris B[artholomeus] Prior et Conventus Ecclesiæ
Sanctæ Mariæ Karliolensis salutem in Domino. Noverit
Universitas vestra quod nos ratas et gratas habemus omnes
Concessiones Collationes et Confirmationes Ecclesiasticarum
pensionum reddituum et possessionum procurationum et
aliorum Beneficiorum in Diocesi Karleolensi existentium
specialiter autem Confirmationes Ecclesiarum de Kirkeby
Stephan et de Morlund Abbati et Conventui Sanctæ
Mariæ Eboraci factas sicut continetur in autenticis Venera-
bilis Patris nostri Hugonis Karleolensis Episcopi ipsis
Abbati et Conventui concessis. In cujus rei Testimonium
præsenti scripto sigillum Capituli nostri apposuimus. Hijs
Testibus Magistro A. de Kirkeby tunc Officiali Karleolensi,
A. de Espatric[1] tunc Decano Cumberlandiæ, Odardo
Clerico, S. suppriore de Wederhal et alijs[2].

29. [1] If this charter were granted in the lifetime of Bishop Hugh,
which seems probable, the date would be between Feb. 24th, 1219
and 1223 ; if not, it is certainly before 1231, when Prior Bartholomew
died. In the next charter, of the same date, we have A. de Kirkeby,
Official, who was Official in the time of Bishop Hugh, see on No. **19**.

30. [1] A. de Espatric, or Aspatric, may be the Adam de Aspatric
mentioned in No. **151**. In the *Register of Lanercost* (MS. viii. 3, 4)
the same name appears, in a charter of Bishop Bernard, as Dean of
Allerdale, and in its confirmation by the Chapter of Carlisle; this
cannot be the same person, nor the same as in No. **43** (see note there).
The name of the place, Aspatric, now Aspatria, evidently comes from
Gwaspatricius, or Quaspatricius, the old form of the name of Gospatric,

31. QUIETA CLAMATIO PRIORIS ET CONVENTUS KARLEOL. SUPER QUIBUSDAM DECIMIS DE SCOTEBY

OMNIBUS Sanctæ Matris Ecclesiæ filijs ad quorum notitiam hoc scriptum pervenerit Johannes Prior[1] et Conventus Ecclesiæ Sanctæ Mariæ Karleoli salutem. Noverit Universitas vestra nos per communem assensum Capituli nostri remisisse et quietum clamasse de Nobis et de domo nostra imperpetuum Abbati et Conventui Sanctæ Mariæ Eboraci et Monachis de Wederhale totum jus et clamium quod unquam habuimus vel habere poterimus imperpetuum in quibusdam decimis in campo de Scoteby quas aliquando tanquam ad nos pertinentes vendicavimus. Ita quidem quod dicti Monachi de Wederhale prædictas decimas habeant et percipiant imperpetuum sicut illas quas recognoscimus esse jus Ecclesiæ suæ de Wederhale. Prædicti autem Monachi concesserunt nobis caritative dimidiam

the first Earl of Dunbar, whose son Waldiev had the grant from Henry I. of the Barony of Allerdale below Derwent, in which Aspatric was situated (see also note 11 on No. 1).

[2] The date is evidently like that of the preceding charter.

31. [1] John, usually called the third Prior of Carlisle, succeeded Prior Walter. He is here with Peter de Ros, Archdeacon of Carlisle, which must be before 1192 (see note 3 below). He was defendant in a suit respecting the advowson of Routheclive, May 6th, 1204 (*Pedes Finium*, 5 Joh. ed. J. Hunter, p. 7). In this *Register* he is a witness to No. **94**, about the beginning of the 13th century (see below), and to No. **117**, a charter of Bishop Bernard's, and in No. **122** he is a party to the confirmation of that charter. In the *Register of Lanercost* he is witness to a charter (MS. ii. 12) of Hugo de Morville, who died 1202, among his co-witnesses being Ranulph de Vallibus, which would nearly fix the date, 1195 to 1199, when Ranulph died; also witness to a confirmation (MS. viii. 2) by Americ (de Taillbois) Archdeacon of Carlisle, between 1196 and 1204 (see below on Peter de Ros); also to a charter of Bishop Bernard and a confirmation of the same by the Prior and Convent of Carlisle (same witnesses, viii. 3, 4); also to a charter (v. 4) with Thomas Official (see below on Thomas de Thorp, No. **40**). He must have died before May 6th, 1215, when, the Priory being vacant, King John gave the Church of Rothecliva to Odo de Ledreda (*Charter Rolls*, 15 Joh. ed. Hardy, p. 206 *b*).

markam argenti ad fabricam Ecclesiæ nostræ imperpetuum percipiendam medietatem ad Festum Sancti Martini[2] et medietatem ad Penticosten. Et ut hoc scriptum nostræ remissionis et recognitionis perpetuæ firmitatis robur optineat eidem sigillum Capituli nostri apposuimus. Hijs Testibus Petro de Ros[3] Archidiacono Karlioli, Willelmo de

[2] November 11th.

[3] Peter de Ros was Archdeacon of Carlisle before 1192, but not after; from the evidence of the Pipe Rolls, one Robert was Archdeacon in that year and until 1196 (see note 3 on No. **28**). In 1196 Richard I. gave the Archdeaconry to Aimeric de Taillbois, or Thebert, nephew of Philip of Poitiers, Bishop-elect of Durham, who also gave him the Archdeaconry of Durham (*Roger de Hoveden*, ed. Stubbs, iv. 14). In 1203 King John gave the Archdeaconry to Alexander de Lucy on November 18th, having given him the temporalities of the See on June 8th (*Patent Rolls*, 5 Joh. *m.* 9, *m.* 5, Record Com. i. 30 *b*, 35 *b*); and on February 14th, 1204, the Archdeaconry was again given to Aimeric with the church of Dalston (*Charter Rolls*, 5 Joh. ed. Hardy, p. 119 *b*). In the *Register* of the Abbey of Holm Cultram, Peter de Ros is witness to a grant of Richard son of Anketill made June 17th, 1190 (Dugdale, *Monasticon*, v. 606). In the *Chartulary of Rievaulx* (ed. Atkinson, p. 92) he is witness at York to a deed whose date must be from 1189 to 1194. He is witness, with Simon of Apulia, Chancellor of York, and Roger Arundel, Canon of Suel (Southwell) to a grant by the Priory of Hexham to William, Chaplain of Geoffrey Plantagenet, Archbishop of York (*Mem. of Hexham*, ed. Raine, ii. 88); the date of this grant must also be from 1189 to 1194. We learn from *Benedict Abbas* (ed. Stubbs, ii. 247) that in the troubles which arose in the northern province between Archbishop Geoffrey and Hugh de Puiset, Bishop of Durham, Peter de Ros had been excommunicated, with some of the Canons of York, of whom he appears to have been one, by the Archbishop; but they were restored on their submission in 1192. Peter de Ros was evidently a person of considerable importance in the Diocese of York. In this *Register* Archdeacon Peter de Ros appears in two deeds (Nos. **120**, **123**) as custos of the Bishopric of Carlisle during a vacancy of the See, probably about 1180, in reference to the Church of Denton. The grant of this Church was afterwards confirmed by Bishop Bernard (see on No. **117**). Peter de Ros held the Archdeaconry after the death of the first Archdeacon Robert, and probably from about 1180 to 1192; he died according to *Roger de Hoveden* in 1196 (ed. Stubbs, iv. 14).

Kirkbride[4] Decano Cumberlandiæ, Adam Decano Westmerlandiæ, Bernardo Decano Gilleslandiæ[5], Adam Decano
de Allerdale[6] et alijs multis.

[4] William de Kirkbride, called here Dean of Cumberland, but in
No. 120, about the same period, Dean of Carlisle, is the same as
William, Dean (of Carlisle) in No. 121, perhaps the same as
William, Dean in Nos. 36, 49, but not in Nos. 109, 137, 138,
170. We have here four Rural Deaneries, Cumberland, Westmoreland, Gillesland and Allerdale, near the end of the 12th
century. Whether the Deanery of Cumberland, which, as we have
seen above, existed at this time, was identical with that of Carlisle is
not certain; but probably it was so. Later, the Deaneries of Carlisle
and Cumberland were distinct, Gillesland being apparently included
in the former. The existence of the Rural Deanery of Gillesland may
perhaps be explained by the fact of that Barony having been in early
times kept so distinct and under the acknowledged jurisdiction of the
Bishop of Durham (see my *Visitations in the Ancient Diocese of
Carlisle*, p. 10 n.). Omitting Gillesland, these four Rural Deaneries
appear in the Taxation of Pope Nicholas in 1292, also in the first
formal Visitation Book in the Bishop's Registry. The Visitation of
Bishop Rainbow in 1682 was held for the Deanery of Carlisle in the
Cathedral, for Cumberland at Penrith, for Westmoreland at S. Laurence, Appleby and for Allerdale at Wigton. In 1777, we find the
names of those four towns given to the four Rural Deaneries (Nicolson
and Burn, *History*, ii. 6). At a period prior to this charter, we have
Robert, dean of Appelbi, and Brichetrich, priest of S. Laurence,
witnesses to an early charter of Bishop Athelwold (*Chart. Whitby*, ed.
Atkinson, i. 38), and about 1175 Murdac, dean of Appelby (apparently
an earlier name for Westmoreland) and Robert, dean of Levinton (see
No. 48). The first division of the Diocese into the modern Rural
Deaneries took place under Bishop Villiers in 1858. On the duties
of Rural Deans, see *Visitations in the Ancient Diocese of Carlisle*,
p. 21; *Report of the Eccles. Courts Commission*, Appendix, pp. 25, 32.

[5] Bernard is very probably the same as Bernard, Parson of Ulmsby
(or Ulvesby) in No. 124, for Bernard, Dean is witness to a charter in
the *Register of Lanercost* (MS. vii. 22) concerning land in Ulvesbi.
For an account of Gillesland, see the note on No. 191.

[6] This is probably Adam de Aspatric (see on No. 43). The date of
this charter can only be fixed as being certainly before 1192 and
probably after 1180.

32. LITERA EXCOMMUNICATIONIS ARCHIEPISCOPI EBORACI.

B.[1] Dei Gratia Eboracensis Archiepiscopus et Angliæ Primas G. Officiali[2] Domini G. de Lascy[3] Archidiaconi Karleolensis salutem. Meminimus nos alias excommunicâsse omnes quicunque pacem de Wederhale infregerunt et stagnum Monachorum ibidem Deo servientium dissipaverunt et homines de Ecclesia suo violenter extraxerunt in contemptum Dei et Sanctorum loci illius et præjudicium Monachorum pacem illorum ex antiquo approbatam temere perturbantes. Sed quia nullus delinquentium ad nos veniam petiturus vel satisfacturus accessit, ideo præcipimus Tibi in virtute obedientiæ quatinus eos singulis Dominicis singulis Parochiarum Ecclesijs Episcopatus Karleolensis pupplice denunciare facias esse excommunicatas. Valete.

33. BULLA PAPÆ ALEXANDRI TERTIJ DE ECCLESIJS TAXATIS.

ALEXANDER[1] Episcopus servus servorum Dei dilectis filijs Abbati et Conventui Monasterij Sanctæ Mariæ Eboracensis Ordinis Sancti Benedicti salutem et ampli-

---

32. [1] There is no Archbishop of York with this initial B. within any probable period. It may be an error for R., Roger of Bishopsbridge, 1154—1181, who witnesses the grant connected with this fishpool by William son of Odard, in No. **36**.

[2] Thomas de Foveys was Archdeacon's Official in 1264 (*Chart. Whitby*, i. 285, ed. Atkinson).

[3] I have met with no other mention of G. de Lascy or Lacy as Archdeacon of Carlisle. The name occurs in 1191, when Gilbert de Lacy had charge of Winchester Castle (*Roger de Hoveden*, ed. Stubbs, iii. 136). The See was vacant at this time, between 1156 and 1204. York was vacant from 1181 to 1191.

33. [1] Alexander III., who was Pope from 1159 to 1181. He granted a Confirmation of their Churches to the Priory of Lanercost on August 12th, 1181, very shortly before his death on September 20th (*Reg. of Lanercost*, MS. viii. 17). He was the Pope who was called upon to take such a prominent part in the controversy between Henry II. and Archbishop Thomas Becket.

ficam benedictionem. Ordinis nostri meretur honestas ut votis vestris quantum cum Deo possimus favorabiliter annuamus sane petitionis vestræ series continebat quod vos in Ecclesijs et Capellis eis annexis quas in usus proprios canonice obtinetis in quibus non fuerunt taxatæ hactenus Vicariæ nec perpetui Vicarij instituti a tempore cujus memoria non existit continue fecistis et facilis per Capellanos proprios deserviri. Nos itaque vestris supplicationibus inclinati ut in eisdem Ecclesijs et Capellis veris existentibus supradictis sicut hactenus sic et in posterum possitis facere per Capellanos hujusmodi deserviri. Quodque vobis invitis in futurum Vicariæ taxari seu institui perpetui Vicarij non valeant in eisdem auctoritate vobis præsentium indulgemus. Non obstantibus si aliquibus a sede Apostolica sit indultum vel imposterum indulgeri contigerit ut in Ecclesijs et Capellis quas Religiosi in suis Civitatibus et Diocesibus in usus proprios optinent taxare perpetuas valeant Vicarias et perpetuos instituere Vicarios in eisdem seu quibuscunque literis vel indulgentijs a sede impetratis eadem aut etiam impetrandis nisi eædem impetrandæ de indulgentia hujusmodi plenam et expressam fecerint mentionem. Nulli ergo omnino hominum liceat hanc paginam nostræ concessionis infringere vel ei ausu temerario contraire. Si quis autem hoc attemptare præsumpserit indignationem Omnipotentis Dei et Beatorum Petri et Pauli Apostulorum ejus se noverit incursurum. Datum Anagnie[2] IV° Non. Julij Pontificatus nostri Anno Sexto[3].

34. QUIETA CLAMATIO EPISCOPI KARLEOL. FACTA PRIORI DE WEDERHALE DE JURE CUSTODIÆ PRIORATUS DE WEDERHALE IPSO PRIORATU CARENTE PRIORE.

IN nomine Domini nostri Jesu Christi Amen. Orta dudum inter Venerabilem Patrem Dominum R.[1] Dei Gratia

---

[2] Anagni in Italy, 32 miles from Rome.
[3] July 4th, 1165.
34. [1] Robert de Chause, or de Chauncy, was consecrated 7th Bishop

Karliolensem Episcopum ex parte una et Religiosos viros
Abbatem et Conventum Sanctæ Mariæ Eboraci ex alterâ
super custodia Prioratus de Wederhale dicto Prioratu
carente Priore et super institutione et destitutione ejusdem
Prioris ac quibusdam alijs Articulis materia questionis
Tandem mediantibus communibus amicis Anno Domini
MCCLXVI° pridie Nonas Februarij[2] conquievit hujus controversia super dicta custodia in hunc modum, videlicet Quod
idem Episcopus sollicite considerans quanta dampna et
pericula per hujus custodiam dictis Religiosis possent
accidere et præcipue Cellæ seu Prioratui de Wederhal
antedicto et quod longi temporis questum per hujus custodiam brevis hora consumeret Attendens insuper hujus
occatione parvum emolumenti posse sibi seu Episcopatui
Karleolensi accrescere memoratus Episcopus nomine suo
et Ecclesiæ Karleolensis de consensu Capituli sui expresso
omne jus si quod sibi compecijt super custodia dicti
Prioratus et bonorum ejusdem dictis Abbati et Conventui
favore Religionis tam in possessorio quam in petitorio
undecunque proveniens pro se et Successoribus suis imperpetuum remisit et quietum clamavit. Dicti et Abbas et
Conventus volentes erga tam pium Patrem filij degeneres
reputari eidem Episcopo et Successoribus suis amicabiliter
dederunt et concesserunt ac etiam remiserunt imperpetuum
duas marcas et dimidiam, sibi prius annuatim debitas de
Ecclesia de Denton[3] quæ de Patronatu Domini Karliolensis

of Carlisle April 14th, 1258, and died October 1278 (*Chron. de Lanercost*, ed. Stevenson, p. 101). His tomb in Carlisle Cathedral was said
to have escaped in the great fire of 1292 (p. 145). He was Sheriff of
Cumberland in 55th and 56th years of Henry III. A letter of this
Bishop is given in No. **200**, dated 1274.

    [2] February 4th.

    [3] This is Nether Denton in Gilsland. The Church of the
adjoining parish of "Old," or Over, or "Upper" Denton was given to
the Priory of Lanercost by David son of Terri and Robert son of
Asketill (*Regis. Lanercost*, MS. iii. 13) and confirmed to them by
Robert de Vallibus (MS. i. 4, 5) and by Hugh Pudsey, Bishop of

Episcopi existit dictis Religiosis et Prioratui de Wederhal Durham (MS. viii. 16), also, with other Churches, in 1181 by Pope Alexander III. (MS. viii. 17). It only fell into the Diocese of Carlisle from the Diocese of Durham at the beginning of last century (see Bishop Nicolson, *Miscellany Accounts*, page 4). This Church of Nether Denton was granted by Robert son of Bueth to S. Mary's Abbey at York and the monks of Wederhal (see No. 121). On the presentation of the said Robert, to whom the right of patronage then belonged, about 1180, William, Clerk of Denton, was instituted by Archdeacon Peter de Ros, the See being vacant, to the Church of Denton (see No. 123). Robert having exhibited the charter by which he conceded the advowson of Denton to the Abbot and Convent of S. Mary at York and the monks of Wederhale, Archdeacon Peter de Ros admitted William, Clerk, presented *de novo* by the said Abbot and Monks to the Church of Denton then vacant (see No. 120). But it appears that previously Buethbarn, the father of this Robert, had granted the Church of Denton to the Canons of Lanercost (*Regis. Lanercost*, MS. iii. 1) the grant being confirmed by his son Robert (iii. 2). Difficulty arose from this double patronage, which was met by a composition entered into between the Canons of Lanercost and the Monks of Wederhale (see No. 119); by this it was agreed that Wederhale should have one moiety of the Church of Denton, and Lanercost the other moiety by the name of the Church of Brancton, each house receiving from the two clerks of Buchecastre annually 2s. by way of pension; in case of a vacancy, each to present a clerk to their own mediety. This was in the time of the aforesaid William, Clerk (see No. 124) and the composition was approved and the Church confirmed to the Monks of Wederhale and the Canons of Lanercost by Bishop Bernard (see No. 117) with the assent of the Chapter of Carlisle (No. 122). A charter of confirmation granted to Lanercost by Pope Honorius III. in 1224 speaks of "Ecclesiam de Denton superiorem et beneficium quod habent in Ecclesia de Denton inferiori" (*Reg. Lanercost*, MS. viii. 19). Not long after, an agreement, said to have been the result of a suit, was come to with Bishop Walter, by which the patronage went to the Bishop, he paying annually 2½ marcs of pension to each house. This payment the monks of Wederhale, in this present charter (1266), quit-claim to the Bishop of Carlisle on condition that the Bishop gives up all claim to the custody of the Priory during a vacancy, and institutes as Prior the monk whom the Abbot of S. Mary may present. The charter of Bishop Walter as to the 5 marcs is given in the *Register of Lanercost* (MS. x. 4) dated October 1238.

prius debitas nomine pensionis in utilitatem dicti Episcopatus conventendas. Convenit etiam inter easdem partes quod dicto Prioratu de Wederhale carente Priore Abbas Beatæ Mariæ Eboraci qui pro tempore fuerit Monachum quem suo periclo dictæ domui credidit esse utilem sive dignum dabit Priore et loci Diocesano vel ejus Officiali eo absente præsentabit[4] eundem. Quem dictus Episcopus sine difficultate admittet et curam animarum Parochialium Ecclesiarum duntaxat eidem committet recepta ab eodem canonica obedientia salva dicto Abbati obedientia Regulari. Quod si dictus Episcopus in Diocesi Karleolensi præsens non fuerit dictus Officialis eundem præsentatum absque difficultate admittet. Ita quod post adventum dicti Episcopi in Diocesin dictus præsentatus se eidem Episcopo infra tres dies utroque existente in Diocesi personaliter præsentabit Canonicam obedientiam eidem facturus curamque animarum Parochialium Ecclesiarum ad dictum Prioratum spectantium ab eodem recepturus. Quod si dictus Episcopus Karliolensis vel ejus Officialis dictum præsentatum sine difficultate non admittat liceat eidem dictum Prioratum libere ingredi et ibidem ut Prior commorari. Ita quod ad mandatum Diocesani veniat dictam curam ut dictum est recepturus et obedientiam facturus sine mora. Si vero processu temporis dictus Abbas Priorem de Wederhal ex causa aliqua quam idem Abbas credidit esse sufficientem providerit amovendum dictus Abbas literas suas patentes super ammocione ejusdem prædicto Episcopo destinabit causam quam crediderit ei sufficientem inserendo quam dictus Episcopus sine difficultate aut contradictione approbabit et quod per dictæ cure receptionem et obedientiam Episcopo factas Abbati Eboraci ullum in ammocione hujus fiat præjudicium. Lectis siquidem præmissis dictæ partes hujus compositioni assensum præbentes uberiorem renuntiarunt omnibus processibus et

---

[4] A form of nomination of a Prior as presented to Bishop Halton in 1303 is given in the list of Priors, Appendix E.

literis impetratis et impetrandis omni exceptioni cavella-
tioni et specialiter in integrum restitutioni ac omni juris
remedio per quod poterit presens Compositio imposterum
infirmari seu aliquatenus impugnari. In cujus rei Testimonium huic compositioni dictæ partes alternatim sigilla
sua apposuerunt. Nos vero Prior et Conventus Karliolensis
supradictam compositionem ratam et gratam habentes
ipsam quatenus in Nobis est confirmamus et sigilli nostri
munimine roboramus. Ad majorem securitatem nos
Abbas et Conventus Eboraci dictas duas marcatas et
dimidiam de Ecclesia de Denton nobis debitas eidem
Episcopo et Successoribus suis imperpetuum damus conferimus et assignamus in forma supradicta. Datum apud
Bellum locum[5] Anno et die supradictis. Ponebatur hoc
interlineare nolentes ante consignationem. Teste eadem
manu[6].

35. CARTA OSBERTI FILIJ UDARDI DE PISCARIA IN
EDENE.

NOTUM sit omnibus audientibus vel legentibus literas
suas quod Ego Osbertus filius Udardi[1] assensu et consilio
amicorum meorum in puram Elemosinam dedi Ecclesiæ
Sanctæ Trinitatis et Sancti Constantini de Wederhale et
Monachis ibidem Deo famulantibus totam partem pisca-

---

[5] Bewley, see note 6 on No. 27.
[6] The date of the charter is February 4th, 1266.
35. [1] Udard, or Odard, was no doubt the lord of Corkeby, which
he probably received from Hubert de Vallibus, to whom it was granted
by Henry II. about 1157 (see note 3 on No. 2 and No. 28, note 4). This
Osbert and his brother William were certainly owners of Corkeby (see
No. 191 *et al.*), and their father is called Odard de Corkebi (No. 40
et al.). As it is now in the possession of Osbert, it cannot have come
to William through Osanna, his wife, daughter of Alexander de
Windesores (as Hutchinson, *History Cumb.* i. 170). Osbert seems
to have died without issue and to have been succeeded by his
brother William before 1167 (see note 1 on No. 36). For more on
Odard, see No. 72.

tionis in Edena quæ ad villam meam Chorkeby pertinebat.
Et ut quiete et sine deceptione piscariam² suam possideant,
dedi etiam eisdem Monachis totam ripam contra piscationem
usque ad illum locum qui dicitur Munchewat. De terra
quousque ad mensam meam Dominicam pertinebat dedi
præfatis Monachis in perpetuam Elemosinam duas bovatas³
in eadem Chorkeby solas et quietas ab omni terreno ser-
vicio⁴.

36. Confirmatio de Piscaria Ripa et de Duabus
Bovatis Terræ in Chorkeby.

NOTUM sit omnibus Sanctæ Matris Ecclesiæ filijs tam
præsentibus quam futuris tam Clericis quam Laicis legentibus vel audientibus literas has quod Ego Willelmus filius
Odardi¹ consilio et assensu uxoris meæ Osannæ et amicorum

---

² This is the fishery granted by Ranulf Meschin (see note 2 on
No. 2). Osbert now gives up his own fishing rights, which Hubert de
Vallibus had from the King; and there is again the mention of the
Corkeby bank opposite to the fishery of the Monks, but now the whole
bank is granted, not merely room to fix the sluice.

³ On the bovate, see No. 55.

⁴ The date is almost certainly after 1157, when Hubert de Vallibus
got the Barony, and then probably granted Corkeby to Odard, father
of Osbert, but before 1167, when William had succeeded.

36. ¹ William son of Odard has an important part in this
Register. Of his father Odard, see on Nos. 2 and 72. His brother
Osbert (see No. 35) was formerly owner of Corkeby, and died
apparently without issue. From this charter we learn that his
mother's name was Anna, and that she had given to the Priory land
which she possessed in Warthwic; through her, Warthwic may have
come into the family. His wife's name, we see here, was Osanna,
stated to be the daughter of Alexander de Windesore, through whom
William had Corkeby. The last statement is evidently wrong.
William speaks of the grants made by his antecessors to Wederhale,
of whom his brother Osbert and his mother have been named, and his
father was Odard de Corkebi. The statement comes from a MS. in
the handwriting of Lord William Howard, giving a list of the lords of
the Manor of Corkeby to 1625 (quoted by Hutchinson, *History Cumb.*
i. 170; *Duchetiana*, p. 261). There Alexander de Windesores is made

meorum consessi Deo et Ecclesiæ Sanctæ Mariæ Sanctique
Constantini de Wederhale et Monachis ibidem Deo servientibus in puram et perpetuam Elemosinam omnia bona
quæ Antecessores mei prædictæ Ecclesiæ contulerunt
scilicet totam partem piscationis in Edena quæ ad Villam
meam de Chorkeby pertinebat totamque ripam in qua piscaria firmata est ab illa piscaria usque ad locum qui dicitur
Munchwath et duas bovatas terræ in eadem Chorkeby
liberas et quietas ab omni consuetudine et servitio et hanc
concessionem hac mea propria carta confirmavi et ex meo
proprio dono dedi prædictæ Ecclesiæ de Wederhal tres

to be the 5th Lord by gift of Robert de Vallibus in the time of
Richard I.; and Osanna, wife of William, is called his daughter and heir.
But William held Corkeby long before the time of Richard I., and his
relatives had possessed it before him. Reference is there made to a grant
of Corkeby with a mill and fishery by Robert de Vallibus to the said
Alexander, which explains the error. In the *Register of Lanercost*
(MS. i. 5; ii. 18) we have the grant by Alexander de Wyndesore of the
tithe of this mill to Lanercost, and it is spoken of as "the mill of
Parva Corkeby"; the village of Little Corby is lower down the river
Eden, and this de Windesores may have possessed (see on No. 38).
William, called lord of Corkeby (No. 191), speaks of Robert de
Vallibus as "Dominus meus" (No. 38). From the Pipe Rolls, it
appears that he held the property as early as 1167, when he paid half a
marc for Corchebi; in 1181 William son of Udard rendered account of
3 marcs for recognizance of 3 carucates of land against Udard son of
Adam, which would seem to point to Odard of Wigton being his father
(see on No. 72) and consequently this Udard son of Adam his nephew.
In 1185 he made a payment, and in 1190 paid £1. 13s. 4d. on account
of the mines of Carlisle, and in 1195 he paid 3s. 4d. Shortly after this
date he probably died. He had a son John, whom he speaks of as his
heir (see Nos. 39, 40) and who seems to have inherited Warthwic
(No. 41 *et al.*); a son Robert, afterwards possessor of Corkeby
(No. 42 *et al.*); also other sons Alan (No. 45) and Ranulph
(No. 55). William son of Odard witnessed the Foundation Charter
of Lanercost, and gave to that Priory some land near Warthwic
bridge (*Reg. Lanercost*, MS. v. 3), Walter, Prior, and Robert,
Archdeacon, being among the witnesses. He was also witness to a
grant of Walter de Wyndesore to Farlam Church and its confirmation
by Ranulph de Vallibus, 1195—99 (*Regis. Lanercost*, MS. i. 20; ii. 9).

bovatas terræ in Warthwic Unam scilicet quam Mater mea
Anna eidem Ecclesiæ dederat et duas alias in compactione
pacis quam contraxi cum Monachis in præsentia Domini
Rogerij Eboracensis Archiepiscopi[2] et alijs multis coram
positis liberas et ab omni exactione terrena quietas.
Præterea humagium Thomæ propter quod inter nos controversia erat. Qui Thomas de terra quam de me tenet in
Chorkeby duodecim denarios eidem Ecclesiæ annuatim
reddet. Si aliqua autem interveniente causa contingat me
amittere villam de Chorkeby totidem denarios in aliqua
terra quæ mihi jure hæreditario competit Fratribus sæpe-
dictæ Ecclesiæ assignabo. Hæc autem omnia concessi et
dedi et præsenti carta mea confirmavi pro salute animæ
meæ[3] et uxoris meæ et omnium amicorum meorum tam
vivorum quam mortuorum. Quare volo ut ita libere et
quiete hæc supradicti Monachi teneant ut mihi et omnibus
amicis meis ad salutem animæ et corporis proficiat. Hijs
Testibus, Rogero Archiepiscopo, Ricardo Abbate[4], Waltero
Priore, Roberto Archidiacono, Willelmo Decano[5], Willielmo Capellano Archiepiscopi, Johanne filio Letoldi[6], Petro

[2] Roger de Ponte Episcopi, or of Bishopsbridge, was Archbishop of
York for the long period from October 10th, 1154 to November 22nd,
1181.

[3] It may be noted that this expression *pro salute animæ* is used here
as referring to both "living and dead."

[4] This Richard cannot have been Abbot of S. Mary's, York, as
there was no Abbot Richard of York after 1131. This was probably
Richard de Burgh, Abbot of Whitby, 1148—1175, often connected
with Archbishop Roger (see *Chart. Whitby*, ed. Atkinson, i. lxxxvii.
56 *n.*) and Archbishop Roger is connected with others who attest this
charter, as John son of Letold and Peter de Carkasin (i. 40). Richard
de Waterville, Abbot of Whitby, 1175—1185, would be of later date
than this charter.

[5] Perhaps W. de Kirkbride, see note 4 on No. 31.

[6] John son of Letold is a frequent witness to deeds of this period,
and very often with Archbishop Roger. At times he simply signs his
name, as here, at others as Canon of S. Peter's, York (*Chart. of
Rievaulx*, ed. Atkinson, pp. 33, 165, 166; *Chart. of Whitby*, i. 185) and

de Carcasine[7], Radulpho de Burgo, Aschetillo de Sescales, Huctredo de Carlatun, Roberto filio Roolf, Roberto filio Trute[8], Richardo fratre ejus[9], Willelmo Clerico de Wiga-

again as Archdeacon of York (see the *Chart. of Rievaulx*, pp. 69, 138, 147, the last named charter being certainly before 1174). He is witness as Archdeacon of York to a composition between Archbishop Roger and Hugh Pudsey, Bishop of Durham (see Dugdale, *Monasticon*, Doc. Cathedral of S. Peter, York, vi. 1198); his co-witnesses are A. (Ailred) Abbot of Rievaulx, who died in 1167 and Ralph (de Warneville) Treasurer of York, who became Treasurer in 1163. Hence John was Archdeacon before 1167, and it was probably some years before that he used this simple signature. The list of early Archdeacons of York in Hardy, *Fasti Eccles.* vol. iii. is very confused.

[7] Peter de Carkasin, or Carcasona, also a Canon of York, was witness to a confirmation of the Church of Crosseby Ravenswart to Whitby by Archbishop Roger, John son of Letold and William the chaplain being co-witnesses (*Chart. of Whitby*, i. 40), also to a grant by the same Archbishop to Hexham about 1160, with the same co-witnesses, and Prior Richard of Hexham (*Archbp Gray's Register*, p. 275 *n.*).

[8] The name of Robert, son of Trute, or Troite, appears as sheriff of Carlisle, or Cumberland, in the Pipe Rolls for the 4th (the earliest extant) year of Henry II. (1158) to the 19th year (1173), when his son Adam acted for him, and was himself sheriff the following year. His brother Richard (see below) is also a witness here. The family of Trute had property in Carlisle (see No. 94 and *Pipe Rolls, Cumberland*, 26 & 27 Hen. II.). Robert is witness to a charter of Adam son of Suan (No. 196) about this period, also to the charter William of Scotland granted to Robert de Brus in 1166, and referred to under Bishop Christian in No. 38.

[9] Richard son of Trute is in the Pipe Rolls (5 Ricard. I. 1193—94) as owing 40s. for a covenant, before the Chancellor, with Richard his son. He was therefore alive at that date, but probably died before 1198 when his son got seisin of Gamelby (*Pipe Rolls*, 10 Ricard. I.). See, on his claim to Gamelby and Glassanby, and on Richard his son, No. 73, note 1, and No. 94. A conjecture is made by J. H. Round (*The Genealogist*, New Series, viii. 202) that Trute, or Truite, was one of three daughters of Hildred de Carlel, and therefore that Richard was a cousin of Robert son of Odard, with whom he had the lawsuit about Gamelby. He cites a genealogy drawn from Bracton's *Note Book* (ii. 71, ed. F. W. Maitland); but an examination of the more accurate

tun, Anselmo Milite, Roberto de Thoresby, Gamello de Castelcairoc, Aldwino de Sescales, Siwardo de Karleolo[10].

37. CONFIRMATIO ROBERTI FILIJ WILLELMI FILIJ UDARDI DE OMNIBUS COLLATIONIBUS PRÆDECESSORUM SUORUM.

OMNIBUS Sanctæ Matris Ecclesiæ filijs ad quos præsens scriptum pervenerit Robertus filius Willelmi filij Udardi[1] salutem. Noveritis me concessisse et hac præsenti carta mea confirmasse Deo et Beatæ Mariæ et Sancto Constantino et Cellæ de Wederhal et Monachis ibidem Deo servientibus in puram et perpetuam Elemosinam pro Salute mea et animabus Patris mei et Matris meæ et Antecessorum meorum omnes possessiones et omnia bene-

extract given by J. Bain (*Calend. Doc. Scot.* i. 160) from the *Coram Rege Rolls* shews that this will not hold good.

[10] The date of this charter must lie between 1154 (Archbp Roger, 1154—81) and 1175 when Abbot Richard died. It must be later than No. 28 where William is a witness. Prior Walter appears in 1150 and for many years; Robert, Archdeacon, after 1156. Robert, son of Trute, sheriff 1158—73 does not here add *vicecomes* to his name. If he were not now sheriff, this would bring the date to 1174—5; but 1160—70 seems more probable.

37. [1] Robert son of William was the younger son of William son of Odard; the elder son, John, apparently inherited Warthwic and the younger Corkeby (see on No. 39). He appears often in this *Register* as Robert, son of William de Corkeby. In No. 46 he is called "knight"; and in No. 126 he is named "sheriff," though he does not appear in the Pipe Rolls as such, but in 1213 as paying 30 marks for a trespass. In No. 127 he is called "Seneschal of Gillesland." He married Alicia de Lascels (see No. 54) and succeeded his father at Corkeby shortly after 1195. He had a daughter and heiress Isabella, see on Alan de Lascels in No. 47; where it is shewn that she was in possession in 1252, when her father therefore was dead. He was one of the inquisitors named in the charter granted by Henry III. to the city of Carlisle 1221 (*Fine Rolls*, 5 Hen. III., *m.* 2, given in full in *Royal Charters of Carlisle*, ed. R. S. Ferguson, p. 2), and appears as "knight" in a deed in the *Chartulary of Gyseburne* dated Sept. 30th, 1231 (ed. W. Brown, ii. 320).

ficia, et Elemosinas quas Pater meus et Antecessor meus eis dederunt sicuti cartæ suæ quas de eis habent testantur. Hijs Testibus, Roberto de Dunstun, Alano filio Willelmi[2], Laurentio filio Agyllun[3], Werri de Agyllunby, Radulpho de Stinetun, Petro filio Willelmi, Simone de taligt'.[4] qui cartam scripsit et multis alijs[5].

38. QUIETA CLAMATIO.

NOTUM sit omnibus Sanctæ Matris Ecclesiæ filijs tam præsentibus quam futuris tam Clericis quam Laicis legentibus vel audientibus literas has quod Ego Willelmus filius Udardi consilio et assensu Domini mei Roberti de Väls[1] et Osannæ uxoris meæ et Johannis[2] filij mei et aliorum amicorum meorum quietam clamavi in puram et liberam et perpetuam Elemosinam Deo et Ecclesiæ Sanctæ Mariæ Eboraci et Ecclesiæ Sancti Constantini de Wederhal et

[2] Alan, son of William, son of Odard, and brother of Robert and John; he seems to have been identical with Alan de Langethwayt (see note 7 on No. 46).

[3] Laurence son of Agyllun is identical with Laurence Agelun who signs after Alan son of William in No. 50, and with Laurence Aglunby (the name is in many forms) who gave 4 acres of land in Aglunby to the Priory of Wederhal (No. 99). He is said to have been the son of Walter, but the genealogy is confused; see J. Denton, *Cumberland*, p. 104 and Nicolson and Burn, *History*, ii. 327, though the father of Laurence cannot, as they say, have come in with the Conqueror. Laurence was probably the brother of Werri or Werric, who signs with him here. See also on Robert Aguyllun note 17, No. 13.

[4] Simon de taligt'., the scribe who wrote the charter; the name is perhaps allied to *tallagium*, "an account," hence to tally (Ital. *tagliare*), to keep accounts.

[5] The date is probably not long after 1195 when Robert came into the property.

38. [1] This is the first Robert de Vallibus who was now Lord of Gillesland, in which Barony Chorkeby was. He succeeded his father Hubert in 1164, see note 4 on No. 28.

[2] John (de Warthwic), the eldest son of the grantor, and called his heir in No. 39. He had Warthwic, while his younger brother Robert succeeded to Chorkeby.

Monachis ibidem Deo servientibus totam terram illam
quæ jacet inter Wederhal et Warthewic quæ vocatur
Camera Constantini[3] à fossato quod est juxta domum quæ
fuit Edwyni versus Wederhal sicut fossatum vadit in aqua
Edene et in Occidentali parte tendit versus marescum
quod est inter terram de Wederhal et de Warthewic.
Terra vero à prædicto fossato usque ad Rivilum[4] qui cadit
in Edena juxta pontem quæ terra de eadem calumpnia
fuit mihi et hæredibus meis in perpetuum mihi remanebit.
Illud vero sciendum est quod quando hæc prædictis
Monachis concessi quietas clamaverunt mihi et heredibus
meis duas bovatas terræ[5] quas habebant in Warthewic et
duodecim denarios quos annuatim habere debebant de
terra mea de Chorkeby. Octavum vero piscem quem Ego
et Antecessores mei de coffino[6] Monachorum habere solebamus in manu mea retinui. Sed nec mihi nec Hæredibus
meis piscare licebit nec hamo neque reti[7] nec aliquo modo
piscandi inter Munchewat et stagnum molendini Monachorum Nec impedire poterimus prædictos Monachos

---

[3] The *Camera Constantini* was a piece of land which is pretty
closely defined. It lay towards Wetherhal, bounded on the north by
a ditch which ran into the Eden, and it tended westward to the marsh
between Wetherhal and Warwick under the hill (see also Nos. **55**, **56**);
it was "near Munchwath" (No. **42**), which was at the south end of this
piece of land (No. **43** *bis*), under St Cuthbert's Spring (see note 4 on
No. **2**). In No. **56** it looks as if, at that time, the stream, which divided
Wetherhal and Warwick and fell into the Eden near Warwick
bridge, bounded the *Camera Constantini;* but here in No. **38** there is
land between the ditch on the north of the *Camera* and the dividing
stream.

[4] This stream, which bounded the Manor of Wetherhal was called
Sawbeke (No. **236**) and fell into the Eden just below Warwick Bridge.
The big stone in the bed of the river now marks the point.

[5] Two bovates in Chorkeby are mentioned in No. **36**.

[6] On these coffins or coops, see No. **2**, note 2.

[7] An early mention of fishing with hook and line in England. The
use of the net seems to imply some distance between the millpool and
Munchwath.

firmare stagnum suum in ripa de Chorkeby pro libito suo. Duas vero bovatas terræ[8] quas antea habebant in Chorkeby similiter eis imperpetuum concessi. Testibus hijs Christiano Episcopo de Candidecase[9], Roberto de Vals qui et

[8] These two bovates were granted by his brother Osbert, see No. 35.

[9] Christian was consecrated Bishop of Candida Casa, or Whitherne, on December 19th, 1154, at Bermondsey, by the Archbishop of Rouen acting for the Archbishop of York (Haddan and Stubbs, *Eccles. Doc.* ii. 33). Witerna, now Whitherne in Wigtonshire, on the north side of the Solway Firth, was the place where St Ninian built his church, at the end of the 4th century; and near here founded his famous monastic school, Candida Casa. The See, although in Galloway, existed as an Anglican See under York in the 7th and 8th centuries (Haddan and Stubbs, ii. 7). The See was now revived in Bishop Christian as a suffragan of York; and it continued in subjection to York under his successors until 1359, when it became practically a Scottish See (Haddan and Stubbs, p. 63). In 1177, Cardinal Vivian, the Papal Legate, suspended Bishop Christian, because he refused to attend the Council summoned at Edinburgh; but he pleaded that his bishopric belonged to Roger, Archbishop of York, and denied the supremacy of the Legate over that See (*Benedict Abbas*, ed. Stubbs, i. 166; *Roger de Hoveden*, ii. 135) and disregarded the suspension. He was present at the Council of Northampton in 1176, when many of the Scottish Bishops accompanied William the Lion, and the question of subjection to the English Church was discussed (*R. de Hoveden*, ii. 91). He does not appear to have exercised any episcopal jurisdiction in the Diocese of Carlisle, although that See was vacant during all the years of his Episcopate; and most of the recorded acts seem to have been done by the Archdeacon under the authority of the Archbishop of York. But he was a good deal connected with matters in the Diocese, and was evidently a person of importance elsewhere. In 1159 and the year following he was exempted from the payment of 14s. 8d., Nontgeld, together with Hubert de Vallibus and others (*Pipe Rolls*, 5 and 6 Hen. II.). In 1166, he attested at Lochmaban the grant by William, King of Scots, of the Vale of Anand (Anandale) to Robert de Brus (*National MSS. of Scotland, Facsimile*, i. No. 39). In March, 1177, he attended the great Council held in London on Spanish affairs and was one of the witnesses to the award (*Benedict Abbas*, ed. Stubbs, i. 145, 154). He was witness to the Foundation Charter of Lanercost, and gave to that Priory a Letter testifying that he was present and a witness when

huic cartæ sigillum in testimonium apposuit, Waltero Priore de Karleolo, Alexandro de Wyndesore[10], Willelmo de Cressime[11], Waltero de Windesore[12], Roberto juvene de

certain Churches were granted to them by Robert de Vallibus, Symon being Prior (*Register of Lanercost*, MS. viii. 9). This must have been very shortly after the Foundation, about 1169. He was also witness to a charter of Ada Engayn to Lanercost about the same date (*Regist. Laner.* MS. ii. 15). He attested a charter in the *Register of Holm Cultram* (MS. p. 91); and he granted to that Abbey, where he had chosen to be buried, the Grange of Kirkewinny, using very strong language in regard to any who should fail to carry out his wishes (*Reg. Holm Cult.* MS. p. 112; Dugdale, *Monast.* v. 597). He died October 7th, 1186 (Stubbs, *Regist. Sacrum Anglicanum*, p. 31).

[10] Alexander de Wyndesore, the first of the name who appears in this *Register*, was together with (probably) his brother Walter, who occurs below, a witness to the Foundation Charter of Lanercost. To that Priory he granted the tithe of the multure of his mill at Little Corkby, to which grant Walter was a witness (*Regist. Lanercost*, MS. i. 5, i. 16 and ii. 18) and he attested several of the charters in their *Register*. Osanna, the wife of William son of Odard, was said to have been his daughter; but he was certainly not the Lord of Corkeby (see note 1 on No. 36). A very full account of the family of the Wyndesores is given by Sir G. F. Duckett in *Duchetiana* (pp. 249 sq.); but the connection between these de Wyndesores and Walter Fitz Other, or de Wyndesore, Castellan of Windsor Castle in the time of the Conqueror, is not by any means clearly made out. Little light is thrown by him upon this Alexander beyond what is found in these two *Registers*. Alexander is mentioned in the incorrect list of the Lords of Corkeby, referred to in note 1 on No. 36, as having land at Fentun in Gillesland, which is very possible, Walter having Farlam. The Alexander in Nos. 210, 217 is another person; but he is not improbably the son of William and grandson of this Alexander. This Alexander became Lord of Morland by marrying Agneta daughter of the first William de Lancastre (see on No. 210).

[11] More correctly de la Cressuner., as he is called, with many of his co-witnesses, attesting the grant by Alexander de Wyndesore to Lanercost referred to above; or de la Kersuner. as in the Foundation Charter of that Priory; or de la Kersunara or Kersenere, as in the *Register of Lanercost*, MS. i. 13; iv. 21, 22. There he always appears with these de Wyndesores and other of their co-witnesses to this charter. In the *Pipe Rolls* for 1170, we find William de Kersunera

Vals[13], Ricardo de Heriz[14], Simone de Tyliol[15], Anselmo de

paid ½ marc for some animals of his taken in the Forest; and in 1201, William de la Kersuniere owed 5 marcs for having a writ *de morte antecessoris* concerning a knight's fee in Caterlen against William de Vallibus and Robert his son. These 5 marcs he does not seem to have paid, neither did the manor of Caterlen, in the parish of Newton Reigny, pass out of the family of de Vallibus. John Denton, speaking of Farlam and the two de Wyndesores here mentioned, says "they were both brethren of one William de Kersmier" and speaks of the connection of the latter with Katerleng (*Cumberland*, p. 137).

[12] Walter de Windesore held Farlam in Gillesland and, besides giving land to the Church of S. Thomas the Martyr in Farlam (*Regist. of Lanercost*, MS. i. 20; ii. 9), he made several grants to the Priory of Lanercost about this period (see MS. iv. 8, 13). He attested the Foundation Charter of Lanercost with his brother Alexander (see note 10) and others of his co-witnesses here. He is witness to numerous charters in that *Register;* and in 1166 was witness to the charter of William, King of Scots, together with Bishop Christian; also to the grant to Alexander by William de Lancastre; both referred to above. His father's name was William, and he had a brother of the same name. He is said to have gone with King Richard to Normandy in 1195, and to have died shortly after (see Dugdale, *Baronage*, i. 509; *Duchetiana*, p. 251). His wife's name was Mabilla, or Mabel, who granted to the Priory of Lanercost *one third* of two acres of land near Closegill in Farlam; in the grant she speaks of herself as formerly the wife of Walter de Wyndesore, who had given them the land, and John de Wyndesore is a witness (*Regist. Lan.* MS. iv. 7). Her son Walter confirms the gift of his father Walter of this land in Closegill (MS. ii. 19; iv. 8). He had certainly two sons Walter and John, and a daughter Christiana, who married Duncan de Lasceles. John had lands in Farlam Parva (*Regist. Lan.* ii. 7, 19 *et al.* and below No. 133). See more on Walter and Christiana in No. 134.

[13] This can scarcely be the Robert juvenis de Vallibus who was the nephew of the Robert de Vallibus named above (see note 4 on No. 28), and son of Ranulph who succeeded his brother in 1195 (*Pipe Rolls, Cumb.* 6 Ricard. I.). Ranulph died in 1199, and the second Robert was his heir. Being a minor at the time, he became the ward of Hubert Walter, Archbishop of Canterbury (*Pipe Rolls, Cumber.* 1 Joh.; *Reg. Lanercost*, MS. xiii. 10). In 1206 he was assessed for scutage, having come into his lands; and his name often occurs in the Pipe Rolls of the few following years,

chiefly for fines and debts due. For non-payment, probably, he was thrown into prison by the King in 1212, but released later, and his whole property given into the hands of his mother Alicia, who with Grecia his sister, Hubert his son, Roland his bastard brother and others, were his sureties (*Patent Rolls*, 14 Joh. m. 3, Rec. Com. p. 96 *a*). In 1215, a commutation took place ; and the death of King John in the year following made a difference in his affairs. Other points in his life are given by Dugdale, *Baronage*, i. 525 and Bain *Calend. Doc. Scot.* i. 83, 94, 120 *et al.* As connecting him with others about this time, it may be noted, that he was surety in 1207 for Christiana de Wyndesore and her husband, Duncan de Lascelles, for lands in Buckingham (*Rotul. de Finibus*, ed. Hardy, p. 346). He granted important charters to Wetherhal as Lord of Gillesland (Nos. 192, 193). A Robert de Vall̃. minor, probably this Robert juvenis, was witness to the F. C. of the Priory of Lanercost. The second Robert of Gillesland occurs in other charters in their *Register ;* among his numerous grants, he bequeathed his body to the Canons of Lanercost "ubicunque et quandocunque ex hac vita migraverim" (*Regist. Lan.* MS. ii. 4). His wife's name was Johanna ; and his son Hubert succeeded him soon after 1233—34, when Robert was Sheriff of Devon (Dugdale), which is the last we hear of him.

[14] Richard de Heriz is, perhaps, the son of William de Heriz who was a witness to the Foundation Charter of Holm Cultram (see on No. 71). Richard made a grant to that Abbey of land near the river Waver (*Register Holm Cult.* MS. p. 56). He was witness to the grant of William de Lancastre, Baron of Kendal, on the marriage of his daughter Agneta with Alexander de Wyndesore (on whom see note 10 above) : among his co-witnesses were the daughter of Hubert de Vallibus, Simon de Tilliol, and others mentioned here (see for the grant *Duchetiana*, p. 16 *n.*). He also attests the charter of Huctred son of Fergus, 1159—64, with Peter de Tilliol and other witnesses here (see on Odard son of Hildred No. 72).

[15] Simon de Tyliol, or Tilliol, son of Peter de Tyllol, of Scaleby, who succeeded his father in 1184 (see note 5 on No. 28). We learn from the Pipe Rolls that, though a tenant by cornage, he paid 100s. scutage in 1201 ; and that he died the same year. He had a son Peter who was a minor at the time, and became a ward of Geoffrey, or Galfrid, de Luci (see note 9 on No. 56). On Simon's death his farm of Holwerri (said to be Huthwaite near Cockermouth) was seized by the Crown, and accounted for by the sheriff for some years. In 1205, this Galfrid de Luci paid 20 marcs and one palfrey for permission to marry the widow of Simon. In the *Register of Lanercost* (MS. vi. 4, 11) Simon occurs

Neubi[16], Thoma Clerico de Waltun[17], Roberto et Radulpho Capellanis, Thoma Clerico de Dene[18], Ada de Morland, Henrico Bradfot, Roberto filio Sunnif, Albano nepote Werri, Adam nuper Vicecomite[19], Rogero de Eboraco, et multis alijs[20].

as making a grant of land at Scaleby to the Priory, and as witness with Robert son of Bueth to a grant of Richard junior son of Trute.

The following table will make the succession more clear :

Peter de Tillel or Tyleol
ob. 1184 (No. **28**)
|
Simon de Tyliol
ob. 1201 (No. **38**)
|
Peter de Tillol
ob. 1246 (No. **56**)
|
Galfrid de Tyllol
ob. 1295 (Nos. **56** *n.*, **194**)
|
Robert Tyloll
ob. 1319—20 (No. **47**).

[16] Anselm de Neubi, or Neuby, whose name appears frequently in this *Register* (see his charters Nos. **138, 141**, and No. **86** on the place Neuby), gave to the Priory of Lanercost Henry son of Ledmer, his serf, with all his *sequela* or family ; he was also witness to a charter of Ranulph, son of Hubert de Vallibus, when Lord of Gillesland (*Regist. Laner.* MS. vi. 13 ; i. 18). From No. **138**, we learn that his wife's name was Matilda, and Richard his son and heir.

[17] Walton in Gillesland, 2½ miles west of Lanercost, near the Roman wall, and not far from Castlesteads, where was a Roman station, probably *Petriana.* The vill of Walton, with its Church and Chapel of Treverman (Triermain) was granted by Robert de Vallibus to the Priory of Lanercost (*Register*, MS. i. 1).

[18] Dene, the old form of Dean, near Cockermouth. Thomas was also witness to the Foundation Charter of Lanercost.

[19] Adam was, no doubt, the son of Robert son of Troite (see note 8 on No. **36**). He acted as Deputy Sheriff for his father in 1173, and was himself Sheriff of Carlisle in 1174. Hence this charter cannot be earlier than 1175.

[20] If we can depend on the note above on Adam "lately Sheriff," 1175 must be very nearly the date ; and it agrees with the dates of the witnesses ; Walter Prior could not be much later. Robert juvenis de

39. QUIETA CLAMATIO WILLELMI FILIJ ODARDI DE JURE PRÆSENTATIONIS CAPELLANI DE WARTHWIC.

WILLELMUS filius Odardi omnibus fidelibus tam præsentibus quam futuris salutem. Sciatis me cum consilio et assensu Johannis[1] Hæredis mei et Osannæ uxoris meæ

Vallibus would of course be a difficulty, if he were the 2nd Robert, Lord of Gillesland, who was not of age till 1205 ; but see note 13.

39. [1] John was the eldest son and heir of William ; on the younger son, Robert, see No. 37. John is also called de Warthwic (No. 60), he, apparently, inheriting Warthwic, in connection with which he appears here. His wife's name was Aliva (Nos. 41, 60), and he had a son William who was Lord of Warthewic and often appears in this *Register* (No. 51 *et al.*) A list of his descendants is given in the county histories ; the two following pedigrees will make the earlier members of the two families of Corkeby and Warthwic more clear :

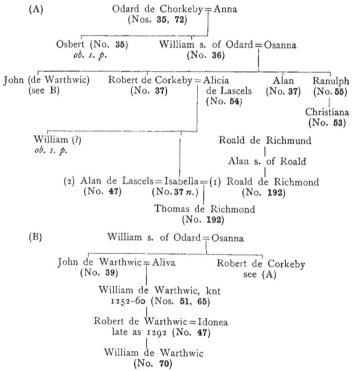

(A)

Odard de Chorkeby = Anna
(Nos. 35, 72)

Osbert (No. 35)   William s. of Odard = Osanna
ob. s. p.   (No. 36)

John (de Warthwic)   Robert de Corkeby = Alicia   Alan   Ranulph
(see B)   (No. 37)   de Lascels   (No. 37)   (No. 55)
                                        (No. 54)
                                                    Christiana
                                                    (No. 53)

William (?)   Roald de Richmund
ob. s. p.
                                   Alan s. of Roald

(2) Alan de Lascels = Isabella = (1) Roald de Richmond
(No. 47)   (No. 37 n.)   (No. 192)

Thomas de Richmond
(No. 192)

(B)

William s. of Odard = Osanna

John de Warthwic = Aliva   Robert de Corkeby
(No. 39)   see (A)

William de Warthwic, knt
1252–60 (Nos. 51, 65)

Robert de Warthwic = Idonea
late as 1292 (No. 47)

William de Warthwic
(No. 70)

et aliorum liberorum et amicorum meorum pro salute
animæ meæ et Odardi Patris mei et pro salute animæ meæ
et filiorum et Parentum meorum quietum clamasse Deo et
Sanctis de Wederhale et Monachis ibidem Deo servientibus
imperpetuum à me et omnibus hæredibus meis quicquid
juris clamavi in præsentatione Capellani de Warthewic[2].
Ita ut a modo liceat Priori et Monachis defuncto Capellano
suo vel forsitan pro culpa sua amoto ibidem sine me et
hæredibus meis Capellanum ponere qui idoneus sit et boni
Testimonij.   Idem vero Capellanus in eadem villa assidue
manere debet ad Divina Officia Deo et Sancto Leonardo[3]
celebranda.   Præterea sciendum est quod Prior et Monachi
concesserunt imperpetuum Patri meo et mihi et Johanni
hæredi meo et Osannæ Uxori meæ in Ecclesijs suis
Anniversarium[4] sicut faciunt pro Monachis suis.   Testibus
hijs...

40.   CARTA DE DECIMIS PANNAGIJ PORCORUM.

NOTUM sit omnibus videntibus vel audientibus literas
has quod Ego Willelmus filius Odardi de Corkebi cum
consilio et assensu Johannis Hæredis mei et Osannæ
uxoris meæ et ceterorum amicorum concessi et dedi et hac
carta mea confirmavi in puram et perpetuam Elemosinam
pro salute animæ meæ et Uxoris meæ et pro animabus
Patrum et Matrum nostrorum et omnium liberorum nostrorum et Antecessorum Deo et Sancto Constantino de
Wederhale et Monachis fratribus meis ibidem Deo servien-

---

[2] On Warthwic Chapel and the right of advowson at a later date
see note 4 on No. **5.**

[3] St. Leonard, the patron saint of prisoners and slaves, was of the
province of Le Mans in France, in the 6th century. For some of the
stories about him, see Jameson, *Sacred and Legend. Art*, ii. 765. The
Bollandists mark his day as October 15th, the day of his death,
others on November 26th. Except the very doubtful one of Crosby
Ravensworth, Warwick is the only dedication to St Leonard in the
ancient Diocese of Carlisle (see No. **55**).

[4] *Anniversarium*, the annual commemoration of the dead.

tibus totam decimam Pannagij mei de porcis hominum meorum et extraneorum omnium quicunque porcos suos in silva mea de Chorkeby posuerunt pascendos de quibus Pannagium accipere debeo. Hanc vero Elemosinam Ego et Hæredes mei Domini de Wederhale in perpetuum concessimus pro animarum nostrarum salutifera redemptione et pro delictorum nostrorum integra absolutione si in aliquo apud præfatam Domum deliquimus ut omnium Orationum et Beneficiorum quæ in Abbatia Beatæ Mariæ Eboraci in omnibus locis ad eandem Abbatiam pertinentibus fient in eternum participes simus. Hijs Testibus Thoma Officiali[1] et multis alijs.

41. DE MESSUAGIO TOFTO ET CROFTO IN WARTHEWIC.

NOTUM sit omnibus videntibus vel audientibus literas has quod Ego Johannes filius Willelmi filij Odardi cum consilio et assensu hæredum meorum et Alivæ sponsæ meæ concessi et dedi et hac præsenti carta confirmavi Deo et Sancto Constantino de Wederhale et Monachis ibidem Deo servientibus in puram et perpetuam Elemosinam pro salute animæ meæ et Antecessorum meorum masagium unum in Warthwic cum tofto et crofto[1] et cum omnibus

40. [1] Thomas de Thorp was Official of Carlisle when Peter de Ros was Archdeacon (see Nos. 120, 123). This would be between 1180 and 1192 (see on Peter de Ros No. 31); and this would agree with his connection here with William son of Odard. He was witness to a grant of the Church of S. Kentigern of Grinesdale by Richard de Neuton to Lanercost (*Reg. Lanercost*, MS. v. 4).

41. [1] There is another grant of this messuage with toft and croft by John de Warthwic (No. 60), probably after the death of his father William, who attests this deed. John is here called son of Odard, not yet de Warthwic. *Toft*, a word of Scandinavian origin, allied to *tuft*, meaning "a knoll"; and so in Middle English; then "a clearing," "a place for a house"; the Anglo-Saxon *croft* is "a small enclosed field." "Toft and croft" is a familiar expression in connection with a messuage, which is from the Low Latin *masagium*, used here, meaning "a dwelling house."

pertinentijs suis et cum omnibus Aisiamentis cum hominibus meis in eadem Villa manentibus liberum et quietum
ab omni terreno servicio et consuetudine et exactione.
Illud videlicet Mesuagium quod Ricardus Carucator in
eadem Villa de me tenuit. Testibus hijs Willelmo filio
Odardi, et multis alijs.

42. CARTA DE OCTAVO PISCE ET ALIJS.

NOTUM sit omnibus legentibus vel audientibus literas
has quod Ego Robertus filius Willelmi de Chorkeby[1] cum
consilio et assensu hæredum meorum concessi et dedi et
hac præsenti carta mea confirmavi et a me et heredibus
meis imperpetuum quietum clamavi Ecclesiæ Sanctæ
Trinitatis Sanctique Constantini de Wederhal et Monachis
ibidem Deo servientibus in puram et perpetuam Elemosinam Octavum piscem[2] quem Ego et Antecessores mei
habere solebamus de Coffino Monachorum de Wederhale
et totam partem piscationis in Edene quæ ad Villam meam
de Chorkeby pertinebat totamque ripam in qua piscaria
firmata est ab ipsa piscaria usque ad locum qui dicitur
Munchewat et quandam terram quæ vocatur Camera
Constantini cum omnibus pertinentijs suis. Et sciendum
quod nec mihi nec heredibus meis piscari licebit neque
hamo neque reti neque aliquo modo piscandi inter Munchewat et stagnum molendini prædictorum Monachorum
nec impedire poterimus prædictos Monachos firmare
stagnum suum in ripa de Chorkeby pro libitu et voluntate
sicut et ubi sibi melius viderint expedire, Et licebit dictis
Monachis imperpetuum capere petram et ramam sufficienter ad prædictum stagnum reparandum in terra de
Chorkeby ubi voluerint sine aliquo impedimento mei vel
hæredum meorum. Insuper vero confirmavi præfatis
Monachis in puram et perpetuam Elemosinam pro salute

---

42. [1] See on Robert son of William son of Odard, No 37.

[2] The eighth fish out of the coops, which William son of Odard
retained (see No. 38), his son now gives up.

animæ meæ et Antecessorum meorum omnes res terras possessiones omnia beneficia et cunctas Elemosinas quas Pater meus et Antecessores mei eis dederunt in Elemosinam sicut cartæ suæ quas de eis habent testantur.   Hanc autem Elemosinam Ego et hæredes mei prænominatis Monachis contra omnes gentes imperpetuum warantiza-bimus.   Hijs Testibus Adam de Port[3], Simon de Patesh.[4], Godefrido de Insulis[5], Henrico de North.[6], Henrico filio Hervei[7], Radulpho Hareng[8], Roberto de Perci[9], Alexandro

[3] Adam de Port', or de Porta, was a justiciary of the King in 1208, Dec. 1st., together with the seven persons following, who are here so termed (see *Fines, sive Pedes Finium*, 10 Joh., ed. Hunter, ii. 9, 10). This would seem to fix the date pretty nearly.   On these itinerating justices, generally, see Stubbs, *Constitutional History*, i. 388 sq.   Adam had been banished from the country by Henry II. in 1172 for treason (*Roger de Hoveden*, ed. Stubbs, ii. 41).

[4] Simon de Pateshill, or Pateshull, was justiciary in 1195 as well as later.   He was Sheriff of Northampton in 1196 and until 1203.   He was witness to the Confirmation Charter of Richard I. to the Priory of Lanercost for the grant of certain Churches by Robert de Vallibus (*Regist. Laner.* MS. viii. 1); also to the Charter of Privileges granted by King John, March 26th, 1200, to the borough of Appleby (see on No. **223**); also to the Charter of King John, dated March 1st, 1204, restoring forest rights to the Abbey of Whitby (*Chart. Whitby*, ed. Atkinson, i. 158).   In 1212, he was one of those appointed to receive the Castle of Fotheringeia, famous in later days, from Earl David on the part of the King (Bain, *Calend. Doc. Scot.* i. 93).   We find him acting as justice so late as 1214 (*Pipe Rolls, Cumberland*).

[5] Godefrid de Insulis, generally written de Insula, was justiciary in 1208.

[6] Henry de Northampton, Canon of S. Paul's, London, was justiciary in 1202, and following years.

[7] Henry son of Herveius, as above, justiciary in 1208.   He fixed the tallage in Cumberland in 1197 (E. Foss, *Judges of England*, ii. 58).

[8] Radulf, or Ralf, Hareng, justiciary as above ; he was also a witness to a charter of Robert de Ros, between 1221 and 1226, granted to his son Robert de Ros (see on No. **44**).

[9] Robert de Perci, as above, justiciary in 1208 ; probably a son, not of Alan de Perci, who would be too early, but of Agnes de Perci,

de Pointū[10] Justiciarijs Domini Regis, Martino Clerico, Ricardo Vicecomite[11], Magistro Adam, Waltero Clerico, et multis alijs[12].

43. CARTA ROBERTI FILIJ W. DE CHORKEBY DE PISCATIONE.

NOTUM sit omnibus legentibus vel audientibus literas has quod Ego Robertus filius W. de Chorkeby cum consilio et assensu hæredum et amicorum concessi et dedi et hac presenti carta mea confirmavi in puram et perpetuam Elemosinam Deo et Beatæ Mariæ et Ecclesiæ Sanctæ Trinitatis de Wederhal et Monachis ibidem Deo servientibus totam partem piscationis in Edene quæ ad terram illam pertinebat quæ vocatur Camera Constantini scilicet à loco illo qui dicitur Munchwat sub fonte Sancti Cuthberti[1]

daughter and heir of Lord William de Perci and Josceline of Louvaine; see Dugdale, *Baronage*, i. 270 and note to *Chart. of Whitby*, ed. Atkinson, ii. 684. He was Sheriff of Yorkshire in 1212.

[10] Alexander de Pointū, or de Pointou, in *Fines*, as above, justiciary in 1203 and 1208. But he is de Pointona, in the *Pipe Rolls*, a Sheriff of Lincolnshire, in 2 John. In March 1204—5 he was one of the custodes of the Honor of Richmond (Bain, *Calend. Doc. Scot.* i. 60).

[11] There is no Richard sheriff of Cumberland anywhere near this time.

[12] The date of this charter must be the beginning of the 13th century, and probably 1208.

43. [1] S. Cuthbert's spring, now called the Holy Well, is in the wood (No. 152, Ordnance Survey Map xxiv. 6) below the mill and weir. The connection with S. Cuthbert is natural in the district; and several Churches are dedicated to him. Ecgfrid, King of Northumbria, and Archbishop Theodore, in 685, granted him "civitatem quæ vocatur Luel, quæ habet in circuitu quindecim milliaria, et in eadem civitate posuit congregationem sanctimonialium, et abbatissam ordinavit, et scholas constituit" (Simeon of Durham, *Hist. de S. Cuthberto*, § 5, ed. J. Arnold, i. 199, and comp. *Hist. Dunelm. Eccles.* Lib. i. c. 9 ed. Arnold, i. 32). This and some other parts of Cumbria were then added to his See of Lindisfarne. S. Cuthbert was at Carlisle that same year, and the citizens shewed him there a wonderful spring or well, constructed by the Romans, and at the time Ecgfrid was being defeated

usque ad fossatum illud quod fuit juxta domum quæ fuit Eduini et sic tendit in aquam de Edene juxta antiquam sedem molendini. Insuper Ego prædictus Robertus de Chorkeby cum consilio et assensu hæredum et amicorum meorum concessi prædictis Monachis imperpetuum aquam meam et ripam meam de Chorkeby inter præfatas divisas ad piscationem suam utendam sine impedimento mei vel meorum ipsi vero Monachi eadem Aisiamenta in aqua sua et ripa sua mihi et hæredibus meis infra præfatas divisas concesserunt. Cognoscendum autem est quod præfati Monachi nichil juris subtus prædictum fossatum Edwini in piscatione de Edene potuerunt exigere nisi concessu mei vel hæredum meorum. Præterea ita convenit inter nos quod Ego Robertus et mei ex parte nostra in prædicta piscatione inter præfatas divisas non poterimus amplius habere nisi quinque naviculas tantum prædicti vero Monachi et sui ex parte sua in præfata piscatione infra prædictas divisas non poterint amplius habere nisi quinque naviculas tantum. De cætero sciendum est quod nec mihi nec hæredibus meis piscari licebit neque hamo neque rethi neque aliquo modo piscandi inter locum illum qui dicitur Munchwat sub fonte Sancti Cuthberti usque ad stagnum molendini prædictorum Monachorum. Hanc vero Elemosinam ego Robertus et Hæredes mei præfatis Monachis contra omnes gentes warantizabimus. Hijs Testibus Roberto de Nuers tunc Vicecomite[2], Gilberto de terribus[3],

---

and slain by the Picts on Nechtansmere (see Bede, *Vita S. Cuthberti*, c. 45, and Simeon, *Hist. Dunelm.*, l.c.). Bede states that he was again at Carlisle (Lugubalia) in 687 where he was visited by his friend Herebert, the anchorite of Derwentwater (Bede, *Hist. Eccles.* iv. 29, and *Vita S. Cuthberti*, c. 48).

[2] Robert de Nuers is not in the ordinary lists of Sheriffs of Cumberland, either as Sheriff or Deputy. His name occurs again with some of the same witnesses in No. 139; while in Nos. 152—4, we have Robert de Miers, or Mihers, Sheriff of Carlisle, with some of the same co-witnesses, where it would seem that evidently Mihers is an error,

forestario, Adam filio Vicecomitis, Anselmo de Dreng, Radulpho de feritate[4], Gilberto fratre ejus, Adam de Aspatric[5], Alexandro filio Radulphi, Willelmo filio Golci et multis alijs[6].

and an easy one, for Nuers ; and Nuers is a name that occurs at this period. We see below he had a son, Adam.

[3] Gilbert de terribus should be de turribus as in Nos. 139, 152, 153; called here and in No. 139 "the Forester."

[4] Radulph de Feritate, or de Ferte, or de la Ferte, "of the waste"; there seem to have been more than one of this name at this period. One appears in the *Pipe Rolls* for Carlisle as early as 1158. Radulph occurs in Nos. 52 and 126, which are about contemporary with the present charter ; also in Nos. 63, 137, 187, the dates of which must be between 1223 and 1247. The first named is probably the same as the one who witnessed the Foundation Charter of Lanercost about 1169 ; and who made two grants to that Priory, one relating to some salt pits given by Ada Engayne who was wife to Robert de Vallibus, the other to some land at Beamund, and a free net in the Eden and, with the men of Brunescayd (Brunskeugh) in the Eden and Esk (*Regist. Lanercost*, MS. vii. 13, 14) ; the former charter, Radulph *juvenis* attests. This agrees with the statement of John Denton, that this family were lords of the manor of Bowness on Solway, and that the family name was le Brun, the first grantee being Gamel le Brun. Their other name arose from the wild wastes near which they lived. Radulph and his brother Gilbert, who is a witness here, are also co-witnesses to a grant of Odard son of Adam to the Priory of Lanercost, which is attested by Bishop Bernard (*Regist. Lanercost*, MS. xiv. 21). This Odard son of Adam appears in the *Pipe Rolls* for Cumberland in 1201 and died in 1208 (see note 5 on No. 72). Gilbert is also a witness to the confirmation by the Chapter of Carlisle of the charter given about the same time by Bishop Bernard to the Priory of Lanercost (*Regist. Lanercost*, MS. viii. 3, 4). Radulph *juvenis*, mentioned above, appears as the son of this Radulph in No. 52, and in the *Regist. of Lanercost* (MS. v. 20 ; vii. 17) with Alan de Caldebec, sheriff (in 1204 and 1215—16) ; he is probably the Radulph of the later charters of this *Register*. We find Gilbert mentioned in 1212 and the later Radulph in 1225 and 1226 in *Calend. Doc. Scot.* (ed. Bain, i. 89, 165) also the latter in the Charter of Henry III. granted to the City of Carlisle Sept. 29th, 1221 (*Royal Charters of Carlisle*, p. 2) and in *Chart. of Gyseburne* (ed. Brown, ii. 320) on Sept. 30th, 1231.

[5] From the co-witnesses, this will be the same as the Adam

44. DE CAPELLA DE CORKEBY.

CLEMENS Abbas Eboracensis[1] dilecto amico suo Roberto Archidiacono Karliolensi et omnibus filijs Sanctæ Ecclesiæ in Domino Salutem. Notificamus discretioni vestræ nos consilio fratrum nostrorum concessisse ut secundum dispositionem Prioris de Wederhale in Capella quam Willelmus filius Odardi const[r]uxit infra curtum suum de Corkeby bis in ebdomada scilicet Dominica die et sexta feria excepta Dominica in ramis palmarum Missa celebretur solumodo sibi et uxori suæ et domesticis familiæ de domo sua et hospitibus suis si forte tunc affuerint, Parochiani autem nostri de Corkeby[2] non ibunt ad illam capellam sed omnes tam viri quam fæminæ tam magni quam parvi venient ad Ecclesiam de Wederhale cum oblationibus et beneficijs matrici Ecclesiæ debitis Matrix enim Ecclesia in nullo minuetur occasione prædictæ Capellæ. Nullus Presbiter nisi proprius Capellanus vel Monachus Prioris de Wederhal ibi Missam celebrabit. Clavem[3] ipsius Capellæ Prior semper habebit nec aliquis

de Aspatric, dean of Allerdale, who attests a charter of Bishop Bernard, and the confirmation of it by the Chapter of Carlisle, granted to Lanercost (*Register of Lanercost*, MS. viii. 3, 4), and is probably the same as Adam, dean of Allerdale in No. **31**, whose date is before 1192; but can hardly be the same as A. de Espatric, dean of Cumberland, in No. **30** or A. de Aspatric, Dean, in No. **151**, which are both about the time of Bishop Hugh 1219—23. He is also witness to a deed of Alice de Rumeli to the Priory of Gysburne in 1210—14 (*Cart. Gysb.* ed. Brown, ii. 319).

[6] All the witnesses seem to mark the date as not long after Robert son of William succeeded to his property in 1195, probably the beginning of the 13th century.

44. [1] Clement was the fifth Abbot of St Mary's at York, from 1161 to August 1184 (Dugdale, *Monast.* vi. 538).

[2] Showing that the inhabitants of Corkeby were parishioners of Wederhale.

[3] It is noteworthy that the Prior of Wederhale is to have the key of the Chapel at Corkeby though built by William son of Odard within his own curtilage.

homo vel fæmina intrabit in eam nisi licentia et voluntate Prioris de Wederhal. Prædicti vero Willelmus et uxor ejus cum omni familia sua in præcipuis Festivitatibus scilicet in Natale Domini in Purificatione Pascha et Pentecoste in Trinitate et in Assumptione Beatæ Mariæ ad Ecclesiam de Wederhale venient cum oblatione sua ad Divinum Officium audiendum. Si vero propter intemperiem aeris nullo modo ad Matricem Ecclesiam venire poterint aliquo horum dierum tunc eodem die sine omni occasione mittant Priori XIII denarios ad minus pro oblatione sua. Si autem Prior aliqua necessitate præventus aliquo horum duorum dierum vel harum Festivitatum Missam ibi celebrari non fecerit prædictus Willelmus nullam inde causam suscitandi litem adversus Priorem habebit. In Festo quoque Sancti Jacobi faciet Prior ibi Missam celebrari. Quando vero alibi manserint interim cessabit omnino prædicta Capella. Illud vero sciendum est quod quando hoc servicium concessimus præfato Willelmo tunc ipse concessit nobis in perpetuam Elemosinam quam antea nobis detinuerat totam decimam de molendino suo ubicunque firmatum fuerit vel in territorio de Warthwic vel in territorio de Chorkeby. Si autem Willelmus vel aliquis suorum contra istud scriptum aliquid facere præsumpserit tunc prædicta Capella omnino cessabit. Willelmus vero et uxor ejus et filij ejus et amici sui coram multis Clericis et Laicis tactis Sacrosanctis juraverunt se inviolabiliter istud observaturos nec aliquid adquisituros contra hoc sine voluntate nostra. Et ut hoc inviolabile permaneat prædictus Willelmus sigillum suum cum sigillo Archidiaconi[4] et Capituli Beatæ Mariæ Karlioli et Roberti

---

[4] The See was vacant at this time (see on Bishop Bernard, Appendix D) hence the Archdeacon is addressed by Abbot Clement, and he may have been custodian of the See. The seal of the Archdeacon of Carlisle used at present is an ancient seal which has been handed down from an unknown past. It is oval and represents

de Ros⁵ huic scripto apposuit.   Testibus hijs, Waltero

the Blessed Virgin and Child with St Peter bearing the keys and has
the legend

    CVSTODIS : SP'ALITATIS : KARLIL : DIOC' : SEDE : VACANTE

It may well have belonged to the long period when the See was
vacant before Bishop Bernard (1204) and when we know that three
Archdeacons at least were custodians of the See—Peter de Ros,
Aumeric de Taillebois and Alexander de Lucy.   There is a poor copy
of the seal given in the *Transactions of the Cumb. Archeol. Society* (vol.
viii. p. 167) and the suggestion is made that it belonged to William de
Ayrmynne, Canon of York, and that he was custodian of the See.
But this is an error.   The said William was entrusted with the
"spiritualities and temporalities" as Bishop not as custodian.   He
was elected in January 1325 (Bishop Halton having died in November
1324), was confirmed and received the temporalities.   Pope John XXII.
nullified the election, and he resigned formally in April.   Soon after he
became Bishop of Norwich.   Another error appears in a note to the
same article, where it is said "the Bishop of Carlisle is his own
Archdeacon."   This by Act of Parliament is the case in the Diocese
of Chester, which formerly embraced the southern part of the Diocese
of Carlisle, but the Archdeacon of Carlisle has always had a separate
jurisdiction ; see my *Visitations in the Ancient Diocese of Carlisle*,
p. 29—32.

    ⁶ There are three persons of the name of Robert de Ros, or Roos,
who come within the range of this *Register*.   The first was the son of
Peter de Ros, a benefactor of St Mary's Abbey, and Adelina, sister
and coheir of Walter Espec, founder of Rievaulx Abbey (Dugdale,
Baronage, i. 545, *Cart. Rievaulx*, ed. Atkinson p. 359).   He had
livery of his father's lands in 1157 ; and he died before 1165 when his
son Everard was in possession.   Everard, who married Rose Trusbut
of Wartre, died before 1185—86, leaving a son, the second Robert,
who was then 13 years of age.   This second Robert got livery of his
father's lands in 1190—91 (Dugdale) and we find him in the *Pipe Rolls*
as Sheriff of Cumberland in 1215 ; in 1216 he was governor of Carlisle
Castle, and he had seisin given him in 1218 by Henry III. of the
manors of Soureby, Hupbrittesby and Karletone till he should recover
his lands in Normandy.   He married Isabel, daughter of William the
Lion of Scotland, and had two sons, William and Robert.   Having
founded the Castles of Hamlake (Helmsley) in Yorkshire and Werke
in Northumberland, he gave by charter the latter to his son the third
Robert, who is generally known as Robert of Werke (see the charter

Priore et toto Capitulo Karliolensi, Roberto Archidiacono Karliolensi, Roberto de Vallibus, Petro de Tyllol, Thoma Clerico Dionisio Bur̃. Capellanis Archidiaconi, Hugone de Neuburg, Roberto de Levington[6], Johanne filio suo, Israël[7], Johanne Camerario, Osberto de Oclande[8], Henrico de Cundale, et multis alijs hujus Conventionis testibus[9].

45. DE CONVENTIONE CONFIRMATA SUPER CAPELLA DE CHORKEBY.

OMNIBUS Christi fidelibus ad quorum noticiam præ-

in *Calend. Doc. Scot.* ed. Bain i. 177). The second Robert is often distinguished as Robert of Hamlake; he died in 1226—27. Robert of Werke was justice itinerant in 1235 (see the note on No. 92); he held the manor of Penrith in 1237, and was concerned in the many changes made about the Cumberland manors in relation to Alexander, King of Scotland (see note 9 on No. 14 and the refs. s. v. in the Index vol i. ed. Bain, *Calend. Doc. Scot.*) He was chief Justiciar of the King's Forests *ultra* Trent. He married Isabella de Albini, and we hear of him as late as 1272, engaged in a plea with his brother William de Ros. In this charter, it must be the first Robert de Ros.

[6] Robert de Levington and John his son are the earliest mentioned members of the family which occurs so often later and in connection with the Barony of Levington (see on Levington No. 48). This is not the same as the justiciary in Nos. 173, 226.

[7] Israel was chamberlain to Robert de Vallibus. In two grants to the Priory of Lanercost (*Register*, MS. iv. 21, 22) of land in Cumquenecath, he calls him "Dominus meus." He attested the Foundation Charter of Lanercost (MS. i. 1) and several others in that *Register*. John was also chamberlain; see *Regist. Lan.* MS. i. 1, 3, where he is co-witness with Israel, *Camerarius*.

[8] This should no doubt be Bocland, as in No. 191, a charter of Robert de Vallibus, with several of the same witnesses. He is witness also to the Foundation Charter of Lanercost, and to another in that *Register* (MS. i. 1, 17).

[9] Clement gives one limit for the date, 1161, and Robert de Ros another limit, 1165, and with this period 1161—65 all the others named in the charter agree, probably better with the later limit. The numerous witnesses here who also occur in the Foundation Charter of Lanercost (Illustrative Documents XXIII) should be noted.

sens scriptum pervenerit Robertus filius Willelmi filij Odardi de Chorkeby æternam in Domino salutem. Noverit universitas vestra quod Ego ratam et gratam habeo pactionem et compositionem quam Pater meus fecit cum Abbate et Conventu Sanctæ Mariæ Eboraci et Monachis de Wederhale super cantaria Capellæ de Chorkeby Ita scilicet quod Ego præsenti scripto obligo me et hæredes meos imperpetuum ad observationem prædictæ pactionis et compositionis sicut scriptum inter prædictas partes confectum et utrinque sigillis munitum plenius in se continet. Ego vero Robertus et hæredes mei de cætero nichil impetrare vel facere poterimus contra voluntatem Monachorum de Wederhal quo minus dicta pactio rata et stabilis permaneat inperpetuum. Quod tamen si aliquo casu processu temporis factum fuerit auctoritate istius scripti irritum et inane sit. Ego autem hæc omnia prædicta fideliter tenenda et observanda imperpetuum pro me et hæredibus meis tactis Sacrosanctis juravi, et eosdem tam præsenti scripto quam dicto juramento pro me et ipsis præstito ad perpetuitatem observationis obligavi et insuper præsenti scripto sigillum meum opposui. Hijs Testibus, Simone Capellano de Wederhal[1], Alano fratre meo[2], Willelmo Clerico, Waltero janitore[3], Odino serviente Prioris, Elya de Aglunby[4], Alano filio suo, Johanne filio coquo et alijs[5].

45. [1] Simon, chaplain of Wederhal, quitclaims certain lands in Ainstapelit, Croglyn and Rucroft to the monastery by No. 158.

[2] Alan, another son of William son of Odard, see note 2 on No. 37.

[3] Porter of the Priory at Wederhal, as in No. 84, where he makes a grant of land ; he is frequently a witness.

[4] Elyas de Aglunby is said by John Denton (*Cumberland*, p. 105) to have been the son of Werri, mentioned with Laurence his brother in No. 37, which agrees with this as being probably a later Charter.

[5] From the witnesses, the date is about that of No. 99, which is 1223—29.

46. Provisio facta inter Monachos de Weder-hale et R. fil. W. de Corkeby super piscatione.

HÆC est provisio facta per Magistrum G.[1] tunc Officia-lem Karliolensem W.[2] Decanum Cumberlandiæ R. de Castle-cairoc[3] A. Buche Milites[4] et Petrum de Brunford Arbitros inter Priorem et Monachos de Wederhale et R. fil. Willelmi Domini de Corkeby communiter electos super statu aquæ eorundem et piscatione in eadem.   Qualiter utraque pars in eadem in posterum indempnis possit conservari.   Scilicet quod si aliquis hominum dicti R. de Chorkeby Militis in Curia prædicti Militis convictus fuerit quod aliquo modo in propria aqua dictorum Monachorum piscatus fuerit vel aliquis hominum dictorum Monachorum in Curia eorum

46.   [1] Gervase de Louther, here Official of Carlisle, see on No. 21.
[2] Walter, dean of Cumberland, as in Nos. 54, 170.
[3] Robert de Castlecairoc, knight, appears often in this *Register*, and there would seem to be more than one of the name. Castlecarrock was a manor in the Barony of Gillesland, about 4 miles from Brampton, under the eastern Fells.   It is said to have belonged to Eustace de Vallibus, and certainly he obtained land in the territory of Castel-cayroc from Robert, son of Hubert de Vallibus (*Register Lanercost*, MS. ii. 8 ; xiii. 6).   We find Robert de Castlecairoc a frequent witness to the Charters of Robert de Vallibus junior, son of Ranulph, and others of his time in the *Register of Lanercost* (MS. ii. 2 ; i. 22 *et al.*) and there making a grant of land (iv. 14) ; and this would be the same as the Robert mentioned here.   We find him in the *Pipe Rolls* paying 30 marks in 1210, and in other years to the end of the reign of John ; also, in 1224—25, he appears as owing 10 marks ; this would be near the time of the present charter.   There is in the *Register of Lanercost* "Robert son of Robert de Castelcayroc" (MS. iv. 15) evidently about the time of a charter dated 1247 (No. 144) in this *Register*; also Richard son of Robert (MS. xiii. 12) and Robert the son and heir of Richard in 1277 (MS. xiii. 8, 9) who calls the first Robert "proavus meus."   This Richard son of Robert we meet in this *Register* (see note 7 on No. 47).   Thus we have in this 13th century the four generations Robert (1), Robert (2), Richard and Robert (3).
[4] Alan Buche, knight, called *Forestarius* in No. 105 (probably 1230—40) ; he was witness to a charter in the *Register of Lanercost* in 1230—33 (MS. xiv. 7).

convictus fuerit quod aliquo modo in propria aqua dicti
Roberti Militis piscatus fuerit ille qui super hoc convictus
fuerit quotiescunque contigerit illum super hoc esse convictum dabit parti conquerenti unam marcam argenti
nomine pænæ si ad hoc ipsius sufficiunt facultates.   Si
autem non suffecerint et conquerenti aliter satisfacere non
possit tunc per unum annum a terra Domini sui fugabitur.
Ita quod in eâ nec hospicium receptaculum nec aliquod
auxilium habebit donec annus integer a tempore quo
convictus erit fuerit terminatus.   Et sciendum est quod ille
in cujus Curia litigabitur parti conquerenti a tempore quo
querela mota fuerit infra quindecim dies Justiciæ plenitu-
dinem exhibebit Quod si non fecerit vel fugatum a terra
sua in eadem infra annum receptari scienter permiserit
licebit Officiali Karliolensi qui pro tempore erit partem
renitentem ad dictæ pænæ solutionem appellatione et
dilacione cessantibus parti compellere conquerenti et illum
qui fugatum ut præscriptum est receptari scienter permiserit
ad solutionem unius marcæ argenti operi Ecclesiæ Sanctæ
Mariæ Karliolensis faciendam similiter compellet.   Hanc
autem provisionem fideliter observandam dictus W. tunc
Prior de Wederhale[5] pro se et Monachis suis et dictus R.
de Chorkeby pro se tactis Sacrosanctis juraverunt renunci-
antes privilegio fori et omni exceptioni tam Ecclesiastici
juris quam Civilis quæ obici potest in factum vel personam.
Et hoc scriptum fieri fecerunt sigillis suis una cum sigillo
Officialis Karliolensis hinc inde munitum.   Testibus R. de
Castlecairoc, A. Buche Militibus, Roberto de Leverisdale[6],
Alano de Langethwaite[7], Simone Capellano, R. de Carla-

---

[5] This is William Rundel, or de Roundell, who was made Abbot
of St Mary's at York, in 1239 ; see the list of Priors, Appendix E.

[6] Robert de Leverisdale, or Laversdale, made a grant of dead wood
in Cumquintin to the Priory, see No. 79.   He is a frequent witness to
the charters of this period granted to Lanercost.   Laversdale was in
Gillesland.

[7] Alan de Langethwaite is probably the same as Alan son of

ton[8], Roberto de Hamton[9], Clerico, Adam Armstrang[10], Johanne et Odardo et alijs[11].

47. QUIETA CLAMATIO WILLELMI SUTORIS ET HAWISIÆ UXORIS EJUS SUPER 4 ACRIS TERRÆ IN CORKEBI.

OMNIBUS Christi fidelibus hoc scriptum visuris vel audituris Willelmus sutor et Hawisia filia Johannis uxor ejus æternam in Domino Salutem. Noverit universitas vestra nos concessisse et quietum clamasse imperpetuum Deo et Ecclesiæ Sanctæ Mariæ Eboraci et Ecclesiæ Trinitatis Sanctæ de Wederhale et Monachis ibidem Deo servientibus de nobis et Hæredibus nostris totum jus et clamium quod habuimus vel aliquo modo habere poterimus in quatuor acris terræ[1] in feudo de Korkebi quæ datæ fuerunt dicto Johanni et hæredibus suis in escambium[2] scilicet toftum et croftum quod Odardus tenuit. et

William de Corkeby, and brother to this Robert son of William, who occurs in No. **45**, and No. **37**. John Denton says that he was Lord of Langthwait (*Cumberland*, p. 133, but as usual without authority); a charter referred to on No. **47** speaks of the grant of a moiety of Langthwaite in Corkby (see note 5 there). He made a grant of his body and of land in Warthwic to the Priory; see No. **57**.

[8] Robert de Carlaton, or Karlaton, is called "knight" in No. **142.** He made grants of land in Little Farlam to the Priory of Lanercost (*Regist. Lanercost*, MS. vi. 6, 7, 8, 22) the deeds being witnessed by Robert de Castelcayroc and others.

[9] Robert de Hamton may be the first sheriff of this name who appears often in this *Register*, see note 4 on No. **54.**

[10] Adam Armstrang, called of Ulvesby (Ousby) in No. **183** (W. de Daker being Sheriff, 1236—47); he attests No. **144**, which is dated 1247.

[11] This deed will be later than the grant by Robert son of William of the Fishery (No. **43**) at the beginning of the century. From W. Prior the date is before 1239; from R. de Castelkairoc not much later than 1225; from G. de Louther, being Official not Archdeacon, before 1230; and we may conclude the date to be 1225—30.

47. [1] These 4 acres in Corkeby were evidently of importance and are the subject of the deeds Nos. **50, 53.**

[2] The exchange is shown in No. **50.**

dimidiam acram proximam terræ Werrici in parte Occidentali et tres acras ultra viam unam quam Reginaldus
molendinarius tenuit et duas acras juxta terram inseph[3]
in parte Orientali Ita quod nec nos nec hæredes nostri nec
aliquis ex parte nostra aliquod jus vel clamium de cætero
in prædicta terra aliquo modo exigere poterimus. In
cujus rei testimonium præsenti scripto sigilla nostra apposuimus. Hijs Testibus Dominis Thoma de Molton[4] et

[3] This word is *Joseph* as in Nos. 50, 53. Transcript MS. C. has
incorrectly *inpepti*.

[4] Thomas de Molton, or Moletona, or Multon, or Maleton, was
one of several of this name in this 13th century. According to
Dugdale (*Baronage*, i. 567) Thomas de Multon came from Lincolnshire, and in 1208 was Sheriff of that county. He married Ada, the
widow of Richard de Luci, in the second year of Henry III. (1217—18)
and that year got seisin of all her lands and of Richard's in Cumberland and Westmoreland (*Patent Rolls*, 2 Hen. III. *p.* 1, *m.* 2). Ada
was the daughter and coheir (with Johanna her sister) of Hugo de
Morville (see the note on No. 101). Richard de Luci died in 1215 or
shortly before (*Pipe Rolls for Cumb.* 16 Joh.) leaving two daughters,
Amabilis, or Amabel and Alicia ; that same year Thomas de Multon had
obtained the wardship of these two daughters and coheirs of de Luci
by the payment of 1000 marks, and then married them respectively to
his two sons by a former marriage, Lambert and Alan de Multon. He
was a witness to the great Charter of Liberties of Henry III. in 1225
(Stubbs, *Select Charters*, p. 354). He paid a fine of 5 marcs in 1227
for a confirmation of King John's charter to Richard and Ada de Lucy
of the Forest of Cumberland and for a charter of a fishery to be made
in the forest of Englewode on the banks of the Eden but not to injure
the neighbouring fishery of the city of Carlisle (*Fine Rolls*, 11 Hen.
III. *m.* 9, ed. C. Roberts, i. 155). In 1233, he was Sheriff of Cumberland,
and had charge of the Castle of Carlisle. He is the Thomas Maleton
mentioned with his wife Ada in No. 174 dated Sept. 9th, 1227, also in
No. 105. He made an agreement with the Abbey of Holm Cultram
concerning pasture and a fishery in the river Eden (*Register Holm
Cult.*, MS. p. 5 ; Dugdale, *Monast.* v. 608). By his second wife, Ada,
he had a son Thomas, who succeeded him, and who had livery of his
lands when he died in 1240 (*Pipe Rolls, Cumberland,* 25 Hen. III.).
This second Thomas de Multon married Matilda de Vallibus, daughter
and heir of the second Hubert de Vallibus, and thus came in for half

Alano de Lascels[5], Roberto de Vaus[6], Ricardo de Castle-

of the Morville property, through his mother Ada, and for Gillesland and other possessions through his wife.   Hence, he is often called " Thomas de Multon of Gillesland," to distinguish him from others of the name.   He and his wife appear in a charter in 1253 (Dugdale). Like his father, he was keeper of Inglewood forest.   He appears with his father and Alan his brother in No. **105**, and is witness to the deed No. **145** (1262—65).   He confirmed a grant of pasture in Laysingby made by his grandfather to the Abbey of Holm Cultram (*Regist. H. C.* MS. p. 22), wrongly ascribed to the father by Nicolson and Burn (*Hist.* ii. 74).   He made important grants to the Priory of Lanercost (see *Regist. Lanercost*, MS. ix. 1 ; x. 6), was a party with his wife to agreements with that Priory in 1255 and 1256 (MS. ix. 4, 12) and with Alan de Maleton was witness to a charter dated 1252 (MS. xii. 22). He died in 1271, leaving a son Thomas (the third) who had livery of the lands which his father had in his own right the same year.   The widow Matilda lived until 1293 (see the note on No. **194**).   This third Thomas became heir to all the de Morville property in 1272 (see Dugdale, *Baronage*, i. 468) in consequence of the failure of the issue of Johanna Gernon, sister of his grandmother Ada (see the note on No. **103**) and came into possession in 1274.   He died in 1293 leaving a son Thomas who died in 1295 (*Inquis. p. m.* 21 & 23 Edw. I. Nos. 36 and 62 ; *Calend. Geneal.* ed. Roberts, ii. 461, 506) and a fifth Thomas came into possession.   In this charter, Thomas de Molton is the second of the name.

The following pedigree will make the relationships more clear :

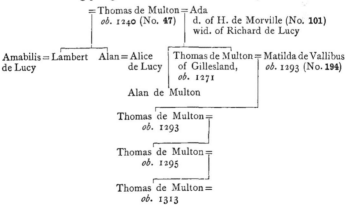

[5] This cannot be the Alan de Laceles who witnessed the Founda-

cairoc[7], Roberto de Warthwic[8], Roberto Tylollf[9], Roberto de Hamton, Johanne de Denton[10] et multis alijs[11].

tion Charter of Earl Henry to Holm Cultram in 1150 (for whom see on Gerald de Lascels, No. 112) but most probably one who married Isabella, daughter and heir of Robert son of William de Corkeby (note 1, No. 37). Her first husband was Roald son of Alan (de Richemund, see the note on No. 192). With him she confirmed in 1252 the agreement with the Priory of Lanercost of wood and pasture between Torcrossoc and Cumquenecach made by Robert son of William, her father (*Regist. Laner.* MS. vii. 8 ; xii. 22). In the *Coram Rege Rolls* for 1266 (50 Hen. III. No. 126, *m.* 8 d.) we find her with her husband Alan de Lascelles and reference made to Roald fitz Alan the first husband of Isabella. In 1265, she had with her husband Alan de Lascels paid a fine of ½ marc for a judicial writ (*Fine Rolls*, 49 Hen. III. *m.* 8, ed. C. Roberts, ii. 420). Alan de Lascels is called "knight" in No. 77 ; and he would seem to have died before 1284 ; for in a deed cited in the incorrect list of Lords of Corkby written out by Lord Wm. Howard (see Hutchinson, *History Cumb.* i. 171) Isabella, relict of Alan de Lascelles and Domina de Corkby makes a grant in 12 Edward I. to her relative John son of Robert (de Warthwic). In Milbourne's copy of John Denton's MS. *Cumberland* (ed. R. S. Ferguson, p. 162) there is a confirmation granted in 1284 by Isabella, relict of Roald son of Alan (her first husband) of the moiety of Langtwaite in Corkby to William de Corkby.

⁶ This cannot be the second Robert de Vallibus who died about 1234 (see note 13 on No. 38), but another of the name.

⁷ This is the son of the second Robert de Castlecairoc (see on No. 46) as in No. 168 ; we find in 1271 he is witness to the dated charter No. 194. He was the King of Scots' bailiff in Cumberland in 1262, see *Calend. Doc. Scot.* ed. Bain, i. 454 and other references there up to 1272 ; in 1266 he appears with Geoffrey and Robert de Tillol (i. 476).

⁸ Robert de Warthwic was the son of William (see No. 56), the son of the John de Warthwic who is noted on No. 39. He occurs frequently in this *Register*, and is witness to No. 194 dated 1271, and No. 203 dated 1292, also Nos. 61, 65 which were in 1259—60. In the *Register of Lanercost* (MS. xii. 19) he is called "seneschal of Gilles-land"; and is witness, with Robert de Tylleoll and John de Denton, to a charter dated 1285 (xiii. 11), to another as late as August 1292 (xi. 6) and to several others. He and his wife Idonea paid ½ marc for a judicial writ in 1269 (*Fine Rolls*, 53 Hen. III. *m.* 5, ed. C. Roberts, ii. 495).

⁹ A Robert Tylolf, or Tyllol, was the son of Geoffrey, or Galfrid,

48. Carta Willelmi filii Udardi facta Monachis de Wederhal de omni piscatione in aqua
de Edene[1].

Notum sit omnibus audientibus vel legentibus literas
has quod Ego Willelmus filius Udardi cum consilio et
assensu uxoris meæ Osannæ et Johannis filij mei et aliorum
hæredum meorum concessi et dedi in puram et perpetuam
Elemosinam Ecclesiæ Sanctæ Mariæ et Sancti Constantini
de Wederhale et Monachis ibidem Deo servientibus
omnem piscationem in aqua Edene ex utraque parte ripæ
sive rethe sive hamo vel aliquo alio modo piscandi quam
Ego solebam habere inter stagnum Monachorum et locum
aquæ qui vocatur Munchwat. Volo itaque et firmiter
præcipio ut hæc Elemosina prædictis Monachis imperpetuum sine omni calumpnia vel impedimento meorum
illibata permaneat pro salute mea et uxoris meæ et
omnium Parentum et amicorum meorum. Illud vero
sciendum est quod octavum piscem quem solebam habere
de Coffino Monachorum retinui in manu mea sicut antea

de Tyllol, whom he succeeded in 1295 at the age of 30 (*Fine Rolls*,
23 Edw. I. *m.* 14 ; *Calend. Genealog.* ed. C. Roberts, ii. 495); and
Geoffrey was the son of the second Peter de Tillol son of Simon (see
note 15 on No. **38**, and note 9, No. **56**), and Robert died in 1319—20.
But the Robert of this charter occurs with Galfrid in No. **194**, dated 1271,
where he is called "seneschal of Gillesland"; he appears with Geoffrey
son of Peter de Tyllyol in the Patent Rolls in 1261, and again in 1266
with Geoffrey de Tillol and Richard de Castlecairoc (see *Calend. Doc.
Scot.* ed. Bain, i. 442, 476). Also in the *Register of Lanercost* (MS. x.
14; xv. 18) he is in 1259 and in 1278 a witness with Geoffrey, and in
1285 a witness with Robert de Warthwic (MS. xiii. 11).

[10] John de Denton is co-witness to No. **194**, with many of those who
attest this deed, in 1271 ; but see on No. **125**.

[11] Most of the witnesses point to the latter half of the 13th century
and Thomas de Multon the second would put the date between 1240 and
1271 ; and near the latter limit of this period we must place the date.

48. [1] This deed is similar to the more formal quitclaim No. **38** so
far as the fishery is concerned.

habui. Testibus hijs Ricardo Capellano, Gamello Diacono, Walterio Priore de Karliolo, Ricardo malæterræ[2], Roberto Decano de Levintona[3], Aschetino Decano, Odardo Decano, Huctredo de Carlatun, Thoma Clerico de Walatona, Radulfo de Laserte[4], Odone de Bocherby[5], Adam de Brunfeld[6], Murdacio Decano de Appelby[7], Roze Engaine[8] et tota Synodo[9].

[2] Richard Mala Terra is witness to the Foundation Charter of Lanercost, and to the charter of Alexander de Wyndesore referred to in note 10 on No. **38**, with many of the same co-witnesses (*Regist. Lanercost*, MS. i. 1 ; ii. 18).

[3] We have here four Deans Rural ; they must have been much more numerous than in later times (see note 4 on No. **31**). The Barony of Levington, some ten miles to the north of Carlisle, was granted (see *Testa de Nevill*, p. 379 *b*) by Henry I. to Richard de Boyvill, whose family took the name of de Levington ; several members occur in this *Register* (see Index). It became divided into Kirk Levington, now Kirklinton, and West Levington or Westlinton.

[4] This is an error for Radulf de la ferte or de la feritate ; see note 4 on No. **43**.

[5] William son of Odo de Bochardeby is given in *Testa de Nevill* (Record Com. p. 380 *a*) as holding by 6*s*. 2*d*. cornage rent the land of Bochardeby, in the time of King John, which land had been given by Henry I. to Wydo the hunter, his ancestor. We also learn (p. 379 *a*) that the name of the wife of Odo de Bochardeby was Alicia. Odo was one of the jurors in 1210 in the trial often referred to before given in the *Coram Rege Rolls* (11 Joh. No. 41, *m*. 9, Rec. Com. *Abbrev. Placit.* p. 66). Bochardby was just outside Carlisle on the east and is said by J. Denton (*Cumberland*, p. 101) to have belonged to one Bochard, a Fleming. He gives an account of the family, but as usual without any authorities, and it contains some evident errors. William was witness to a grant of Radulph de la ferte in the *Register of Lanercost* (MS. vii. 14) ; see No. **43**, note 4.

[6] Adam de Brunfeld was the son of Thomas de Brunfeld before mentioned, see note 7 on No. **17**.

[7] Appelby used here loosely for Westmoreland, of which Murdac appears as Dean in a charter of Torphin son of Robert, granting land in Warcop to the monastery of Bellalanda, or Byland, with Robert dean of York (died 1186), John of Lethold (see on No. **36**) and others about this time ; see Nicolson and Burn, *History*, i. 615 *n*.

49. Carta Willelmi filii Odardi de Corkeby super firmacione stagni de Wederhal in ripa de Korkebi[1]

NOTUM sit omnibus has literas videntibus vel audientibus quod Ego Willelmus filius Odardi de Korkebi cum consilio et assensu Johannis hæredis mei et Osannæ uxoris meæ et aliorum amicorum meorum concessi et dedi et hac carta mea confirmavi Deo et Sancto Constantino de Wederhal et Monachis fratribus meis ibidem Deo servientibus pro salute animæ meæ et uxoris meæ et animabus Patrum et Matrum nostrarum et omnium liberorum et Antecessorum nostrorum quod possint firmare stagnum suum de Wederhale in ripa de Chorkeby pro libito et voluntate sua et capere petram et alia necessaria quantum voluerint ad idem stagnum faciendum sine contradictione et impedimento mei vel hæredum meorum. Concessi insuper dictis Monachis karissimis fratribus meis quod ubicunque Ego vel hæredes mei fecerimus molendinum nostrum de Warthwic super aquam de Edene sive ex una parte aquæ sive ex alia non faciemus nec facere poterimus stagnum molendini de solis vel plankys vel grossis lignis nec de alijs nisi tantum de palis et jugis nec poterimus claudere aquam de Edene nisi ad medium filum prædictæ aquæ vel minus si minus aquæ possit sufficere ad sustentationem prædicti molendini ita quod pro hoc piscis nullum habeat impedimentum veniendi ad piscariam dictorum Monachorum. Nec licebit mihi vel hæredibus meis ad prædictum molendinum vel stagnum piscem capere aliquo modo nisi tantum rethi vel hamo. Et ne Ego vel hæredes

---

[8] This may be an error for Rad. Engaine, who is often witness with others of this period ; see also on No. 101.

[9] The date of this charter must be about the same time as No. 38, probably rather before 1175.

49. [1] This charter is more definite as to the bank and repair of the bay than Nos. 36, 38, and deals with a prospective mill and pool at Warthwic.

mei contra hanc donationem concessionem in posterum venire possimus Ego tactis Sacrosanctis reliquijs juravi. Et insuper ut in perpetuum firmiter observentur præsentem cartam sigillo meo signavi. Hijs testibus Thoma Officiali[2], Willelmo Decano, Willelmo Persona de Soreby[3], Alano Persona de Caldbec[4] et alijs[5].

[2] Thomas de Thorpe, see note 1 on No. 40.

[3] Soreby, or Saureby (Sowerby) in Cumberland was called later Castle Sowerby, and adjoined the parish of Caldbec. The name is derived from *saure* (old Norse *söggr*) "wet," "swampy," with the Danish termination *by* "a dwelling," and is naturally a not uncommon name in the district. It was one of the six manors mentioned in the note on Scotby in No. **14** as allotted to Alexander of Scotland. Despite the retention of the advowsons by Henry III., John Balliol on April 20th, 1294, as appears from *Bishop Halton's Register* (MS. p. 4), presented William de Londors to the Church of Soureby; and in June of the same year Anthony Beck, Bishop of Durham, presented John de Langeton, Chancellor of England, these manors having then passed into his hand. On the petition of the Prior and Convent of Carlisle, the Church was given to them by Edward I. on April 5th, 1307 (*Patent Rolls*, 35 Edw. I. *m.* 17) and the Dean and Chapter still hold the advowson. The same month and year, the tithes were appropriated by Bishop Halton to the Convent for the repair of the Cathedral after the great fire of 1292, on the condition that a Canon Regular of the House held the Vicarage (*Register Bp Halton*, MS. p. 105). The manor of Soureby, together with the manors of Karleton and Hupbrittesby (Upperby), was given by King John in 1214 to Robert de Ros of Werk, till he should recover the lands he had lost in Normandy when in the King's service (*Patent Rolls*, 16 Joh., *m.* 7, *n.* 37). In the transactions with the King of Scotland regarding the Cumberland manors, Robert de Ros junior got part of the manor of Penrith in exchange for the three manors mentioned above; see *Pipe Rolls*, 22 Hen. III. *Rot.* 4, 9, also *Patent Rolls*, 22 Hen. III. *m.* 6. The King undertook to give Robert an exchange of equal value, if Penrith were assigned to the King of Scotland, which took place. In 1257, Soureby was assigned by Alexander II., King of Scotland, to his consort, Queen Margaret, for her chamber (ad cameram suam) (*Patent Rolls*, 41 Hen. III. *m.* 11, Record Com. p. 29).

[4] The parish of Caldbec was about 12 miles south of Carlisle. On the east lay the parish of Sowerby. A hospital was said to have

50. Carta Roberti filii Willelmi de quatuor acris in feodo de Korkeby.

Omnibus literas has visuris vel audituris Robertus filius Willelmi Salutem. Sciatis me concessisse et dedisse et hac mea præsenti carta confirmasse Johanni filio Willelmi et hæredibus suis quatuor acras[1] terræ in feodo de Chorkeby scilicet toftum et croftum quos Odardus tenuit et dimidiam acram proximam terræ Werrici in parte occidentali, et tres acras ultra viam ; unam quam Reginaldus molendinarius tenuit et duas acras juxta terram Joseph in parte orientali quæ quatuor acræ datæ sunt prædicto Johanni et hæredibus suis in esscambium terræ quam Pater ipsius Johannis tenuit in Ernewiolm Tenendum de me et hæredibus meis in feodo et hereditate libere quiete et integre cum omnibus libertatibus pertinentijs et aisiamentis illi terræ pertinentibus quietam de pannagio et multura et merchetto[2] Reddendo inde annuatim mihi et hæredibus meis unam libram cumini ad nundinas Karlioli pro omni servicio consuetudine et exactione forinsecum faciendo servicium quod ad prædictam terram pertinet.

been founded here by the Priory of Carlisle in the time of Radulph Engain, and soon after the Church, and therefore not long before this date, about 1175 ; but the charter of Henry II. shews they were granted, with all appertaining, by Gospatric son of Orm. The advowson was afterwards granted to Bishop Walter Malclerk by the Priory. There is an Alan Persona de Caldebec witness to a grant of William de Fortibus, 2d Earl of Albemarle who died in 1241, to the Priory of S. Bees (Dugdale, *Monast.* iii. 578), but he is of later date than the present.

[5] The date is probably a little later than that of No. **38**, and about 1175.

50. [1] This is the same land as in No. **47**. It is here granted by Robert de Corkeby to John son of William, the father of Hawisia, who was wife of William Sutor, and they granted the land to the Church of Wederhale. It is again referred to in No. **53**.

[2] *Merchettum* or *marchetum* is the sum paid to the lord of the manor for leave to marry a daughter to a freeman.

Testibus Willelmo Capellano de Sancto Nicholao[3], Willelmo Capellano de Warthwic, Roberto filio Adæ, Willelmo de Windeshore[4], Roberto de Lefredal[5], Waltero Baïvi, Alano filio Willelmi[6], Laurentio Agelun, Richardo de Neuby[7], Radulpho de Stiveĩ'[8], Walfrido de Faucuner, Waltero de Bochardbi[9], Willelmo filio Odonis, Elia filio Werrici[10], Ranulpho Clerico, Wulfrid de Wederhale[11].

[3] The Hospital of S. Nicholas at Carlisle, not Appleby ; see on No. 95.

[4] The brother, or more probably the nephew, of the elder Walter de Windeshore, see note 12 on No. 38 and the reff. there. He is co-witness with his brother Walter and this Robert son of William to charters in the *Register of Lanercost* (MS. iii. 7, 12) and is co-witness to other charters with Robert son of William alone (MS. iv. 11 ; v. 18 ; vi. 28). He is not the same with the William de Wyndesoure and his son William who appear in Nos. 203, 220. There seem to have been many of the name.

[5] This may be Robert de Leversdale, see No. 46.

[6] The brother of this Robert and the same as Alan de Langethwaite (see on No. 37 and compare the names in Nos. 51, 52).

[7] From No. 138 we learn that Anselm de Neuby (see note 16 on No. 38) was the father of Richard. For the land in Neuby granted by Richard to the Priory of Wederhal, with consent of his wife Emma, see No. 139. He is witness, with this Robert son of William, in the *Register of Lanercost* (MS. iv. 11) and to several other charters there.

[8] This is Radulf de Stiveton, who appears as Rad. de Stinetun with some of these witnesses in No. 37, and elsewhere in the *Register*. The name Stiveton or Stivetun is well known, see *Calend. Doc. Scot.* ed. Bain, i. p. 495 ; *Cart. of Rievaulx*, ed. Atkinson, pp. 242, 250.

[9] Walter de Bochardbi had a brother Adam (see No. 98) ; but it does not appear what relation he was to William son of Odo (de Bochardby) the next witness, see note 5 on No. 48 and No. 52.

[10] Probably Elias son of Werri de Aguillonebi, who attests the next charter ; Werri was the brother of Laurence Agelun, who is a witness here (note 3, No. 37).

[11] All the witnesses seem to point to the very end of the 12th or beginning of the 13th century, about 1200, as the date ; and we saw that Robert son of William succeeded his father in 1195 (No. 37).

51. CARTA ROBERTI FILII WILLELMI DE CORKEBY
DE TERRA CUM UNO TOFTO IN CONSTANTINECLENE.

OMNIBUS Sanctæ Matris Ecclesiæ filijs præsentes literas
visuris vel audituris Robertus filius Willelmi de Corkebi
Salutem in Domino. Noverit universitas vestra me Divinæ pietatis intuitu pro salute animæ meæ et Antecessorum
meorum et successorum concessisse et dedisse et hac
præsenti carta mea confirmasse Deo et Ecclesiæ Sanctæ
Trinitatis de Wederhal et Monachis ibidem Deo servientibus totam terram illam cum tofto uno in Constantinclene[1]
quam Robertus filius Gerardi[2] de me aliquando tenuit cum
servicio ipsius Roberti et hæredum suorum cum omnibus
pertinentijs suis et aisiamentis et libertatibus ad prædictam
terram pertinentibus in pratis et pascuis in moris et
mariscis in aquis et ripis in bosco et plano in vijs et
semitis et exitibus infra Villam et extra in puram et
perpetuam et liberam Elemosinam Tenendam et possiden-
dam in perpetuum liberam et solutam et quietam ab omni
seculari servicio consuetudine et exactione. Et sciendum
quod Ego Robertus et hæredes mei hanc prædictam terram
cum omnibus pertinentijs suis sicut supradictum est contra
omnes homines prædictis Monachis in perpetuum warantizabimus. Et ut hæc mea donatio et concessio firma et
stabilis in perpetuum perseveret præsenti scripto sigillum
meum apposui in Testimonium. Hijs Testibus Radulpho
de feritate, Simone Capellano, Alano Buche, Alano de
Langethwait, Petro de Corkebi[3], Willelmo filio Johannis de
Warthwic[4], Laurentio et Elia de Aguillonebi[5], Willelmo

---

51. [1] This place was in the vill of Wederhale, see on No. **61**, and
seems to have been a holm near Warthwic Bridge.

[2] Robert son of Gerard de Waverton, see No. **61**.

[3] Peter de Corkebi was in the time of Robert de Vallibus, see
Nos. **192**, **193**.

[4] John de Warthwic was the elder brother of this Robert son of
William de Corkeby. This William de Warthwic often appears in
the *Register*; he appears with his son Robert in No. **56** and Nos. **65**

Clerico de Wederhal, Johanne filio suo, Willelmo de Airunñ[6], Humfredo de Wederhale, Walterio Portario, Johanne Coquo et multis alijs[7].

52. Carta Roberti filii Willelmi de dimidia carucata terræ in Villa de Warthwic.

Sciant omnes tam præsentes quam futuri quod Ego Robertus filius Willelmi dedi et concessi et præsenti carta mea confirmavi Alano fratri meo dimidiam carucatam terræ in Villa de Warthwic scilicet illam dimidiam carucatam terræ quam Hugo de Waltervill[1] tenuit de Patre meo Tenendam et habendam de me et hæredibus meis sibi et hæredibus suis in feodo et hæreditate reddendo mihi et hæredibus meis annuatim unam libram cimini[2] vel tres denarios ad nundinas Karlioli pro omni servicio. Hijs Testibus Adam filio Udardi[3], Roberto de Kyrkebride, Radulpho de Ferte, Radulpho filio suo, Willelmo de Ferte[4], Willelmo de Bochardby, Laurentio de Auguelunby, Elia de Auguelunby et multis alijs[5].

(1259—60), 67 where he is called "knight"; he is witness in two dated deeds in the *Register of Lanercost* 1255 (MS. ix. 12) and 1252 (MS. xii. 22).

[5] The same as Laurence Agelun (No. 50) or son of Aguyllun (No. 37). Elias was his nephew.

[6] Probably the same as William de Airminne, or Eyreminne, in No. 60 *et al.*

[7] The date will be later than the preceding charter, as William the nephew of Robert de Corkeby and son of John de Warthwic is a witness here.

52. [1] Hugo de Wautervilla witnesses one of the deeds of Robert's father, William, No. 55.

[2] For *cumini*, cummin, the seeds of *Cuminum sativum* used as a spice, a certain weight of which is often entered for a nominal payment.

[3] Adam son of Odard (of Wigton), see on Odard the sheriff in No. 72; he got his father's lands in 1208.

[4] William de Ferte is called, by John Denton (*Cumberland*, p. 75), the brother of Radulph (No. 43, note 4).

[5] The date must be after Robert de Corkeby succeeded his father William in 1195, probably early in the 13th century.

53. Quieta Clamatio Christianæ filiæ Ranulphi de Quatuor Acris Terræ in feodo de
Corkeby.

Omnibus Christi fidelibus hoc scriptum visuris vel
audituris Christiana filia Ranulphi[1] Salutem in Domino
sempiternam. Noverit universitas vestra me in libera
potestate mea et in ligia viduitate mea concessisse et
quietum clamasse Deo et Ecclesiæ Sanctæ Mariæ Eboraci
et Ecclesiæ Sanctæ Trinitatis de Wederhale et Monachis
ibidem Deo servientibus de me et hæredibus meis vel meis
assignatis totum jus et clamium quod habui vel aliquo
modo habere potui in quatuor acris terræ[2] cum pertinentijs
in feodo de Korkebi quas Willelmus Tussezemer[3] dedit in
puram et perpetuam Elemosinam domui de Wederhale et
dictis Monachis ibidem Deo servientibus scilicet toftum et
croftum quod Odardus tenuit et dimidiam acram proximam
terræ Werrici in parte occidentali et tres acras ultra viam
unam quam Reginaldus molendinarius tenuit et duas
acras juxta terram Joseph in parte orientali.   Ita quod nec
Ego Christiana nec hæredes mei nec aliquis ex parte mea
aliquod jus vel clamium de cætero in prædicta terra aliquo
modo exigere vel vendicare poterit.   In cujus rei testimonium præsenti scripto sigillum meum apposui. Hijs
Testibus, Roberto de Warthwic, Roberto de Castlecairoc,
Willelmo de Warthwic[4], Hugone de Talkan[5], Johanne

---

53. [1] This is Ranulph, a fourth son of William son of Odard
of Corkeby, see Nos. **55, 149**, where he is mentioned with the eldest
son John ; he may have died before his father and Robert have taken
his place. Christiana would therefore be of the same generation
as William de Warthwic who is a witness here.

[2] These are the same 4 acres that are granted in No. **50** and
No. **47.**

[3] Wm. Tussezemer is the same as William sutor in No. **47.**

[4] William de Warthwic (see on No. **51**) was the son of Robert de
Warthwic the previous witness.

[5] This can hardly be the same Hugh who is witness to No. **110**
and other charters at the end of the century.

Corbet, Alano Armstrang, Johanne Brid de Corkebi⁶ et multis alijs⁷.

54. CARTA ROBERTI FILII WILLEMI DE CORKEBY DE QUADAM PORTIONE TERRÆ AD FACIENDAM GRAN-GIAM.

UNIVERSIS Christi fidelibus ad quorum notitiam præsens scriptum pervenerit Robertus filius Willelmi de Corkeby salutem. Noverit universitas vestra me pro salute animæ meæ et Aliciæ de Lascels uxoris meæ necnon pro salute animarum Predecessorum et successorum meorum dedisse et præsenti carta confirmasse Deo et Ecclesiæ Sanctæ Mariæ Eboraci et Ecclesiæ Sanctæ Trinitatis et Sancti Constantini de Wederhale et Monachis ibidem Deo servientibus quandam portionem terræ in Villa de Korkebi juxta curiam meam ad faciendam ibi grangiam et ad includendum ad curiam faciendam ad commodum suum. Quæ porcio se extendit in latitudinem a semita quæ ducit de Korkebi ad aquam de Edene usque ad sepem curiæ meæ Et in longitudine a dicta sepi usque ad quandam fraxinum quæ stat extra curiam meam juxta angulum sepis et a prædicta fraxino lineariter ex obliquo usque ad finem fossati quod est juxta prædictam semitam quæ ducit de Korkeby ad Edene Habendam et tenendam in perpetuum in liberam et puram et perpetuam Elemosinam cum omni libertate introitus et exitus ad dictam grangiam et curiam. Ego vero R. et hæredes mei hanc Elemosinam prædictis Monachis warantizabimus in perpetuum. Et ut hæc mea donatio perpetuæ firmitatis robur optineat Ego præsens scriptum sigilli mei impressione corroboravi. Hijs Testibus Bartholomeo Priore Karlioli, Magistro G.

---

⁶ John Brid de Corkeby is also witness to No. **145** with Eustace de Baliol, sheriff from 1262 to 1265.

⁷ The date from Robert de Warthwic and John Brid would probably be shortly after the middle of the 13th century.

Archidiacono[1], Magistro T. Werri Officiali[2], Symone[3] et Waltero Decanis de Karliolo et Cumberlandia, R. de Hamtun Vicecomite Karlioli[4], Richardo de Levingtun[5]

54. [1] Gervase de Louther, Archdeacon of Carlisle: he appears first as plain *Magister* in No. 21 (see note 3 there) and as Official of Carlisle in No. **46** *et al.*

[2] T. Werri, Official, succeeded G. de Louther, see next note.

[3] Symon, dean of Carlisle, is witness to a deed in the *Register of Lanercost* (MS. xii. 18) with Robert Sheriff (de Ros 1215—16), Magister G. de Louther and Magister T. Werri.

[4] Robert de Hamtun. One Robert de Hamptone was Sheriff of Cumberland in 1275—77; and Robert son of William de Hamptone was Custos for Bishop Walter Malclerk in 1223—1229. These would seem not to have been the same, and the interval between them is long. It is the earlier Robert who is to be taken here, as Prior Bartholomew died in 1231 (see on No. **20**). Nicolson and Burn (*History*, i. 548) say that Robert de Hampton married Margory, a daughter of Adam de Levington, and therefore sister of Richard de Levington the co-witness here. A Robert appears as juror in an Inquisition *ad quod damnum* in 1268, and is mentioned in another in 1272 as the son and heir of Margory de Hampton (*Calend. Doc. Scot.* ed. Bain, i. 492, 548). This must be the later Robert. He appears as sheriff in an Inquisition in 1276; and in 1277 he was dead, leaving a widow also called Margory (see Bain, ii. 18, 24, 28). The earlier Robert also occurs in this *Register* as Robert son of William, sheriff (No. **75** *et al.*). He is a witness with William de Daker, sheriff (1236—47) in the *Register of Lanercost* (MS. vii. 7). In *Testa de Nevill* (p. 379) Robert de Hampton holds the forest haye of Plumpton.

[5] Richard de Levingtun, or de Boyvill of Levington, appears very often in the affairs of this period. In Nos. **134, 136,** he is called sheriff of Cumberland, but his name does not appear in the lists. It is probable that he was Custos for the sheriff Walter Malclerk in the early years of Henry III., before Walter became Bishop of Carlisle in 1223. He is here called *Constabularius*, but it does not say of what County or Castle or district (on the office, see Stubbs, *Constit. Hist.* i. 354 and Jacob, *Law Dict.* s. v.). From the Pipe Rolls for Cumberland we learn that, in 1212, he rendered account of 300 marcs and three palfreys for having the land of his father Adam, who died the preceding year and that year paid scutage. In 1179—81, we find that this Adam paid 20 marcs to have seisin of Westham or West-

Constabulario, Rolando de Vaus[6], Roberto de Castlecairoc, Symone de Oreṫ[7], Roberto de Leversdale, Elisio de Raveneswic[8], Symone Capellano, W. janitore[9], J. filio Willielmi[10] et alijs[11].

linton ; his brother William is there mentioned, and he is named Adam the son of Adam the son of Richer, or Richard. This agrees with a plea in the *Coram Rege Rolls* (11 Hen. III. No. 27, *m.* 4 ; *Calend. Doc. Scot.* i. 176) in May, 1227, concerning the boundaries between the lands of Richard de Levinton and Peter de Tyllol, where Adam is called Richard's father, and Richer, seized of the property in the time of Henry II., "the father of Adam." This Richard is witness to several charters in the *Register of Lanercost*, perhaps, the most important, one of Roland de Vallibus (MS. ii. 21), other witnesses being Bishop Walter, William (Rundel) Prior of Wederhal and Peter de Tyllol and one (MS. xiv. 8) where William de Daker, sheriff (1236—·47) is witness. In June, 1250, on the death of this Richard, Ranulph, his brother and heir, gave security for £100 for livery of his lands ; Richard left a widow Sara and six sisters who had portions (see reff. *Fine Rolls*, ed. Roberts, ii. 80 ; *Inquis. post mort.* 34 Hen. III. No. 47 ; 28 Edw. I. No. 18). On the Barony of Levington, see No. **48**, note 3 ; this Richard held it in the time of Henry III. as is shewn in *Testa de Nevill* (p. 379). Ranulph's daughter, Helwysa, married Eustace de Ballıol, see on Nos. **145, 103**.

[6] Roland de Vallibus was the natural son of Ranulph de Vallibus, and half-brother of the second Robert, Baron of Gilsland. He was one of the hostages given by Robert to King John in 1212 for the payment of his fine (see, on this Robert, note 13, No. **38**) ; among the hostages named are " Hubert his son and Roland his bastard brother" (*Patent Rolls*, 14 Joh., *m.* 3 ; Record Com. p. 96 *a*). His name appears in the *Register of Lanercost* as Roland de Vallibus of Treverman (Triermain) granting land given to him by his brother Robert (MS. ii. 21); and as son of Ranulph (iii. 4, 5) ; and as uncle of Hubert, son of Robert (iv. 6), with several persons who witness here. He was seneschal and principal forester of the said Robert (xiii. 10) and was succeeded by his son Alexander (ii. 22).

[7] As in No. **63**, Simon de Orreton, or Oreton, or Horeton (No. **75**) ; he is called *Dominus* in No. **126**.

[8] Elisius or Elyas de Raveneswic was one of several members of the family in this *Register*, taking their name from the vill of Ravenswic (Renwick, see on No. **175**) on the east side of the river Eden, though they do not seem to have held the manor at this time.

55. CARTA WILLELMI FILII UDARDI DE UNA BO-
VATA TERRÆ IN VILLA DE WARTHWIC.

WILLIELMUS filius Udardi omnibus hominibus et
amicis suis tam præsentibus quam futuris Salutem. Sciatis
me consilio et assensu Johannis hæredis mei et Osannæ
uxoris meæ dedisse et concessisse et hac carta confirmasse
Deo et Ecclesiæ Sanctæ Trinitatis et Sancti Constantini
de Wederhal et Monachis ejusdem loci et Capellæ Sancti
Leonardi de Warthwic unam bovatam[1] terræ in eadem
Villa de Warthwic scilicet quinque acras in Westcroft et
duas acras in Graistanflat et unam acram juxta holm cum
prato ad prædictam terram pertinente Tenendam et
habendam in puram et perpetuam Elemosinam cum communi pastura et omnibus aisiamentis ejusdem Villæ.
Dedi etiam dictis Monachis totam decimam pannagij mei
et molendini mei ubicunque fuerit situm in terra mea.
Insuper autem remisi et quietum clamavi imperpetuum de
me et hæredibus meis dictæ Domui totum jus et clamium
quod habui in marisco qui jacet inter terram de Wederhal

[9] Walter, porter of Wederhal.

[10] John, son of William who is Clerk of Wederhal in No. **51**.

[11] From the Sheriff, or Custos, R. de Hamtun, the date of the
charter is between 1223—1229; this agrees with the witness Prior
Bartholomew, who died in 1231, and with others such as G. Archdeacon and Richard de Levington.

55. [1] A *bovate* of land is here equal to 8 acres; in No. **138** it is
half of 15½ acres. The bovate, or oxgang, was supposed to be as
much land as an ox could till annually. There has been much dis-
cussion as to the value of the *carucate*, or plough's worth, of land. It
would seem in this district to be equal to 8 bovates, which is the
general rule; although at times elsewhere it is equal to 4 bovates. In
the *Register of Lanercost* (MS. ii. 8; xiii. 6) the carucate is twice
defined "unam carucatam terræ, scilicet sexaginta quatuor acras
terræ." We may therefore take the carucate in this *Register* (No. **14**
et al.) as equal to eight bovates, i.e. in one case 64 acres, in the other
62 acres. On this subject, see *Domesday Book*, de Gray Birch, p. 217;
F. Seebohm, *Village Communities*, p. 62; J. H. Round, *Feudal
England*, p. 35. At a later period we have the bovate in Wetherhal

et terram quæ dicitur Camera Constantini[2] quam prius dictis Monachis coram multis reddidi et quietam clamavi. Ita quod nec Ego nec hæredes mei in dicto marisco aliquod omnino habere vel capere poterimus contra voluntatem dictorum Monachorum ultra rivum qui cadit in dicto marisco inter terram de Wederhal et de Warthwic et dictam Cameram Constantini. Sciendum autem quod quando istam Elemosinam prædictis Monachis donavi concesserunt mihi caritative quod in dicta Capella de Warthwic per Capellanum jugiter in dicta Villa manentem Divina celebrari facerent et me et uxorem meam et filios meos in spirituali fraternitate domus suæ reciperent. Testibus hijs Capitulo Canonicorum Karleoli, Magistro Walkelivo[3], Magistro Reginaldo, Johanne filio meo et hærede[4], Ranulpho filio meo[5], Werrico Senescallo meo, Hugone de Wautervilla, Reginaldo Diacono, Willielmo Clirico et Ranulpho Clirico[6].

56. COMPOSITIO INTER ABBATEM EBORACI ET RO-BERTUM FILIUM WILLELMI ET WILLELMUM FILIUM JOHANNIS DOMINOS DE WARTHWIC DE MARISCO DE WEDERHAL.

HÆC est compositio facta inter Abbatem et Conventum Sanctæ Mariæ Eboraci et Monachos de Wederhale ex una

put at ten acres (see Rental for 1490, Illustrative Documents, XLIV.).

[2] See note 3 on No. **38**, where the grant of this land is made.

[3] This should be Magister Walkelin, who witnesses a charter, with John, Prior of Carlisle, in the *Register of Lanercost* (MS. v. 4), and has a son Richard (MS. vi. 14) probably the Mayor of Carlisle in No. **95**.

[4] Called John de Warthwic ; see on No. **39**.

[5] Ranulph, a 4th son of William, his brothers being John, Robert and Alan (see on No. **36**) ; he was the father of Christiana who made the grant in No. **53** (see note 1 there).

[6] This deed is later than Nos. **48, 49,** which are about 1175, as the two sons of William son of Odard are here witnesses.

parte et Robertum filium Willelmi et Willelmum filium
Johannis[1] Dominos de Warthwic ex altera de marisco[2] qui
jacet subtus condorsum de Wederhal videlicet quod dicti
Abbas et Conventus de consensu dictorum Roberti et
Willelmi et hæredum suorum retinuerunt ad usum proprium
Monachorum suorum de Wederhale totam illam partem
prædicti marisci qui se extendit versus Wederhale á
fossato quod Werricus fecit linealiter ex transverso marisci
usque ad quandam quercum stantem in condorso et sic ex
transverso condorsi usque ad terram de Wederhale cultam
ad includendum pro voluntate sua ad omnimodum commodum suum inde faciendum imperpetuum. Prædicti
vero Abbas et Conventus concesserunt prædictis R. et W.
et hæredibus eorum et hominibus de Warthwic habere
communia pasturæ tantum in altera parte marisci versus
Warthwic sicut dictus mariscus se extendit versus Aquilonem a fossato prædicto usque ad Rivum pluvialem qui
est divisa inter Wederhale et Warthwic qui rivus dividendo
terras prædictarum villarum descendit in dicto marisco
subtus pratum de Westercrouf et inde per transfusum
marisci exit inter terram Monachorum quæ dicitur Camera
Constantini et terram de Warthwic. Ita scilicet quod
nichil omnino capere vel habere poterint in dicto marisco
ultra prædictum rivum nisi communia pasturæ tantum.
Nec aliquis poterit ibi fodere glebas nisi illi qui tenebunt
terram Monachorum quæ dicitur Camera Constantini.
Sciendum est autem quod quando Monachi de Wederhale
totam vesturam marisci quem incluserint plene in usus
suos quolibet anno converterint ex tunc licebit hominibus
de Warthwic habere ingressum in dicto marisco ad pastu-

56. [1] Robert son of William was the son of William son of John
de Warthwic. On the former, see No. 47; and on William de
Warthwic, see No. 51. John was the son and heir of William son of
Odard of the last charter.

[2] On this marsh, adjoining the Camera of St Constantine, see
No. 38; it is here more carefully defined.

ram habendam usque ad tempus illud quo prædicti Monachi voluerint ponere illum in defenso. Sciendum est autem quod hanc compositionem firmiter tenendam et warantizandam utrinque imperpetuum prædicti Abbas et Conventus pro se et suis tenentibus de Wederhal prædicti vero R. et W. pro se et omnibus de Warthwic quolibet modo tenentibus manuceperunt et insuper ijdem R. et W. juramento corporaliter prestito se et hæredes suos sub pæna decem librarum, Abbas vero et Conventus per Priorem suum de Wederhal sub eadem pæna ad præscripta omnia observanda se obligaverunt. Ut autem hæc compositio perpetuæ firmitatis et inconcussum robur optineat prædicti Abbas et Conventus et prædicti R. et W. sigilla sua una cum sigillis B. Prioris[3] et Magistri G. de Louthir[4] Archidiaconi Karliolensis hinc inde apposuerunt. Hijs Testibus, Domino W. Officiali[5], Magistris Ricardo et Helvico Rectoribus Scolarum Theologiæ et decretorum, Domino Thoma de Morlund, Thoma de Graistoc[6], Michaele de Sancto Albano, Symone Decano et Capitulo Karleoli[7],

[3] Bartholomew, Prior of Carlisle, see note 4 on No. 20.

[4] Gervase de Louther, Archdeacon, see note 3 on No. 21.

[5] This is Walter de Ulvesby, or Ulnesby, probably Ulfsby. In No. 183 he is "Parson of Ulvesby, then Official" a witness with William de Daker, Sheriff 1236—47. Ulvesby, *hodie* Ousby, was a vill in Cumberland on the east side of the river Eden, about 9 miles from Penrith. Walter is frequently a witness in this *Register*, both as Official and Archdeacon. A reference to the deeds, such as No. 112 (1231—36) and No. 129 (1230—31) with G. de Louther, Archdeacon, and No. 212, seems to shew that he was Official till about 1239, and after that date Archdeacon. He appears in the *Register of Holm Cultram* (MS. p. 155) about 1250 as Archdeacon, making an award between the Abbey and the Rector of Wygeton.

[6] For Thomas de Graistoc, see on Thomas son of William de Graistoc in No. 137.

[7] That is, the rural Chapter of Carlisle. The meetings of these rural Chapters were held, generally every quarter, under the presidency at first of the rural dean, but soon under that of the Archdeacon. The Chapter was a consultative body, and discussed the more difficult

Thoma filio Johannis Vicecomitis[8], Richardo de Levingtun, Roberto de Castlecairoc, Petro de Tillel[9], Roberto de Hamton, Waltero de Bantun et Comitatu Karleoli.

business brought forward. These Chapters, or meetings of Chapters, fell into disuse before the Reformation. In the early Registers of the Bishops of Carlisle, in the 13th and 14th centuries, there are numerous instances of the Rural Deans executing the orders of the judicial courts, collecting the fines, and getting in the taxes imposed on the clergy by the Crown. See Gibson, *Codex Juris Eccles.* p. 1012, quoting Lyndwood's *Provinciale.*

[8] Thomas son of John was Sheriff of Cumberland, rather Custos, or *pro-Vicecomes* for Bishop Walter, in 1230 and 1231 ; and Custos in 1214. This is no doubt the same as Thomas son of John, who in No. 201 is called "sheriff of Westmoreland" with Richard Brun, "sheriff of Cumberland"; the latter was probably Custos for Bishop Walter 1234—36 (see on No. 97). John de Veteriponte was sheriff of Westmoreland from 1227 to 1241, the office having been granted to Robert de Veteriponte and his heirs for ever by King John in October 1203 (see on No. 204 and Nicolson and Burn, *History*, i. 267 *n.*). It does not appear that John de Veteriponte had a son Thomas ; and in a charter of his to the men of Kirbythore (Nicolson and Burn, i. 24) Thomas son of John, one of the witnesses, is spoken of as *nunc vice-comite meo*, not *filio meo.* In No. 201, therefore, Thomas son of John is Custos for John de Veteriponte. He was one of the justices itinerant in 1235 (see No. 92) when they decided a curious case between Thomas de Lascelles and Gilbert, Abbot of Holm Cultram (*Pedes Finium*, 19 Hen. III. No. 22 ; compare Dugdale, *Monast.* v. 606). He was appointed a justice for special purposes on several occasions (as in 1228) : in 1225, he was one of the collectors of the "Fifteenth" in Cumberland and Westmoreland (see Stubbs, *Select Charters*, p. 355 ; *Close Rolls*, Record Com. i. 245 ; iii. 147 ; *Testa de Nevill*, p. 378 *a*) ; in the *Register of Lanercost*, he attests a deed as sheriff of Carlisle (MS. ii. 19), and another as sheriff of Cumberland (vii. 9).

[9] This is the son of Simon and grandson of the first Peter de Tillel (see note 5 on No. 28). This second Peter was a minor at the time of his father's death in 1201 (see note 15 on No. 38). In 1227, he was engaged in a suit with Richard de Levinton concerning the boundaries o their lands (see note 5 on No. 54). He was one of the special justices with Thomas son of John appointed in 1236. He died in 1246, and we learn that his widow's name was Maria de Tilliol from the order that

57. CARTA ALANI DE LANGEWAYT DE TOTA TERRA SUA IN WEDERHAL (WARTHWIC) CUM ÆDIFICIJS CONSTRUCTIS IN EADEM.

OMNIBUS Sanctæ Matris Ecclesiæ filijs ad quorum notitiam hoc præsens scriptum pervenerit Alanus de Langewayt[1] Salutem æternam in Domino. Noverit universitas vestra me dedisse corpus meum Monachis de Wederhale ibidem sepeliendum Dedi et cum corpore meo Deo et Ecclesiæ Sanctæ Trinitatis et Sancti Constantini de Wederhal et Monachis ibidem servientibus totam terram meam de Warthwic cum omnibus pertinentijs suis libertatibus communis et aisiamentis sine aliquo retenemento et cum ædificijs in eadem terra constructis in liberam et perpetuam Elemosinam Dedi et eidem Ecclesiæ et dictis Monachis cum corpore meo in perpetuam Elemosinam liberam communam in bosco meo de Langewayt[2] ad capiendum ibidem omnimodum boscum tam viridem quam mortuum ad sustentationem Domus suæ. Ita quod dicti Monachi habeant liberum ingressum et egressum prædicti bosci quandocunque et ubicunque voluerint pro voluntate sua cum hominibus carris et carettis suis et bobus et equis ad capiendum prædictum boscum et abducendum pro libitu et voluntate sua ad usus proprios sine alicujus visu contradictione vel impedimento Licebit et dictis Monachis

a dower should be given her out of her husband's lands (*Close Rolls*, 31 Hen. III. *m.* 14). These lands are set out in the *Inquisitio post mort.* dated Dec. 5, 1246, which also states that his heir and son Galfrid was 16 in the first day of Lent in that year (31 Hen. III. *m.* 46, and comp. *Calend. Geneal.* ed. Roberts, i. 18). From the sheriff, the date of this charter is 1230 or 1231 ; evidently from the subject, a little later than No. **54**.

57. [1] See on Alan de Langethwaite in No. **46**, note 7 ; this gift of his body to the Priory is noteworthy.

[2] Langewait, or Langethwaite, was in Corkby, see No. **47**, note 5 ; not improbably this was the adjoining manor of Little Corkby in the parish of Hayton ; a property called at the present day Longthwaite lies partly in Little Corby.

imperpetuum ubicunque et quandocunque voluerint addu-
cere petram in prædicto bosco et fodere fossas in prædicto
bosco et facere sibi clibanos ad calcem faciendam et
comburendam et construere domos in eodem bosco cum
necesse habuerint ad calcem suam reponendam sine alicujus
contradictione vel impedimento Idem autem Monachi
habebunt pasturam bobus suis et equis per totum boscum
meum et per totam aliam pasturam meam sine alicujus
contradictione vel impedimento quicunque boscum vel
calcem vel petram cariabunt. Hæc autem omnia prædicta
dedi prædictis Monachis cum corpore meo in liberam et
perpetuam Elemosinam pro salute animæ meæ et Prædecessorum et successorum meorum. Ita quod hæredes mei
quicunque pro tempore fuerint omnia ista prædicta dictis
Monachis debeant warantizare acquietare et defendere
inperpetuum Nec unquam aliquis hæredum meorum
poterit aliquid facere de prædicto bosco in perpetuum quod
sit ad nocumentum dictorum Monachorum. Et ut hæc
omnia præscripta inconcussæ firmitatis perpetuum robur
optineant hanc cartam sigillo meo signatam dictis Monachis
dedi et concessi. Hijs Testibus, Willelmo de Warthwic[3],
Johanne de Agillunby[4], Johanne filio Willelmi[5], Roberto
Mercatore, Henrico et Radulpho et Ricardo Capellanis,
Gilberto et Nicholao Cliricis, Henrico Thoma Symone
Roberto Johanne servientibus Domini Prioris, Adam fabro
et alijs[6].

58. COMPOSITIO FACTA INTER ROBERTUM FILIUM

[3] This was the son of John de Warthwic and nephew of the
grantor.

[4] John was the son of Adam and the father of Adam de Agellunby,
see on the family No. 37, notes.

[5] Probably John de Warthwic, son of William son of Odard (de
Corkby) and father of William de Warthwic, and brother of the
grantor.

[6] The date is probably not far off that of the preceding and succeeding charters.

WILLELMI ET WILLELMUM FILIUM JOHANNIS DOMINOS
DE WARTHWIC ET ABBATEM EBORACENSEM DE MARISCO
SUBTUS CONDORSUM DE WEDERHALE.

OMNIBUS has literas visuris vel audituris Robertus
filius Willelmi et Willelmus filius Johannis[1] Domini de
Warthwic salutem in Domino. Ad universitatis vestræ
notitiam volumus pervenire nos pro observanda compositione[2] inita inter Abbatem et Conventum Sanctæ Mariæ
Eboraci et Monachos de Wederhale ex una parte et nos ex
altera de marisco subtus condorsum de Wederhale sigillo
ipsorum et nostro signata subjecisse nos et hæredes nostros
imperpetuum jurisdictioni Dominorum Prioris et Archidiaconi Karliolensis qui pro tempore fuerint ut ipsi remota
appellatione et omni exceptione et contradictione cessantibus cessante et cujuslibet privilegio compellant nos per
censuram Ecclesiasticam si necesse fuerit ad ipsius compositionis observationem et ipsa ex parte nostra non observata
ad pœnæ in dicta compositione adjectæ solutionem dictis
Abbati et Conventui faciendam dicta nihilominus compositione si Abbas et Conventus voluerint in suo robore
postmodum duratura. In cujus rei Testimonium præsenti
scripto sigilla nostra apposuimus. Testibus Domino
Bartholomeo Priore Karliolensi, Waltero tunc Officiali
Karliolensi, Adam filio Rogeri[3], Elya de Ravenwic, Waltero
janitore et alijs[4].

59. COMPOSITIO DE MARISCO ET CONDORSO INCLU-
DENDIS INTER WEDERHAL ET WARTHWIC.

OMNIBUS Sanctæ Matris Ecclesiæ filijs ad quorum
notitiam præsens scriptum pervenerit Walterus janitor de
Wederhal Johannes de Agellunebi Johannes filius Willelmi,

58.   [1] These are the same persons as in No. 56.
[2] The composition given in No. 56.
[3] Probably Adam son of Roger de Karliol, see No. 76.
[4] The date must be shortly after that of No. 56.

Johannes de Haṁ[1], Ranulphus filius Unfridi, Robertus de Neubi[2], Robertus Carpentarius Salutem in Domino. Noverit universitas vestra nos ratam et gratam habere compositionem[3] factam inter Abbatem et Conventum Sanctæ Mariæ Eboraci et Monachos de Wederhal ex una parte et Robertum filium Willelmi et Willelmum filium Johannis Dominos de Warthwic ex altera de marisco et condorso includendis qui jacent inter Wederhal et Warthwic sicut in scripto de prædicta compositione inter prædictas partes confecto plenius continetur. Insuper autem totum jus et clamium quod nos in dictis marisco et condorso habuimus vel hæredes nostri habere poterunt dictis Abbati et Monachis remisimus et quietum clamavimus imperpetuum. Et ne nos vel hæredes nostri inposterum contra prædictam compositionem et hanc quietam clamationem venire possimus præsenti scripto sigilla nostra apposuimus. Hijs Testibus B. Priore Karliolensi, Magistro G. Archidiacono Karliolensi, T. filio Johannis tunc Vicecomite, Petro de Tilloil, Roberto de Castro-cairoc, Symone Capellano de Wederhale, Willelmo Capellano de Warthwic, Ricardo Diacono, Radulpho Clirico, J. Coquo, Hamelino, Odardo Clirico de Birescale et alijs[4].

60. Carta Johannis de Warthwic de quodam Mesuagio tofto et crofto in eadem.

Notum sit omnibus legentibus vel audientibus literas has quod Ego Johannes de Warthwic filius Willelmi filij

59. [1] John de Haṁ. may be J. de Hamerton who is a witness to No. **19** in 1220, but it is not probable.

[2] On others of the name of Neuby, but earlier than Robert in No. **148**, see No. **38**, note 16. It does not appear what relation, if any, this Robert was. His widow Beatrix and his sons appear in Nos. **87, 88.**

[3] This is the composition in No. **56**. All these persons seem to have had an interest in this marsh between Wetherhal and Warwick (see below).

[4] The date from the witness Thomas son of John, Sheriff, must be 1230 or 1231, see on No. **56**.

Odardi cum consilio et assensu Alivæ sponsæ meæ et
hæredum meorum dedi et concessi et præsenti carta confirmavi Deo et Sancto Constantino de Wederhale et Monachis
ibidem Deo servientibus pro salute animæ meæ et Parentum
meorum unum mesuagium[1] in terra mea de Warthwic
illud videlicet quod Ricardus carucator de me tenuit
Tenendum et Habendum in liberam puram et perpetuam
Elemosinam cum tofto et crofto et omnibus pertinentijs
suis cum communi pastura et cum omnibus alijs libertatibus et aisiamentis ad Villam de Warthwic spectantibus.
Concessi et confirmavi dictis Monachis inperpetuum
omnes Elemosinas et libertates quas W. pater meus et alij
Antecessores mei eisdem cartis suis dederunt tam in terris
quam in aquis et redditibus et omnibus alijs locis.   Hijs
Testibus Simone de Tillel, Anselmo de Neubi, Laurentio
et Werrico de Agulunebi, Alano fratre meo, Willelmo
Clirico, Willelmo de Eyremine, Henrico filio Weser, Elia
Preposito[2] et multis alijs[3].

61.   Carta Henrici Birkenheued de tribus
acris terræ in holmo juxta pontem de Warthwic.

Omnibus Christi fidelibus ad quos præsens scriptum
pervenerit Henricus Birkenheued et Beatricia uxor sua et
Sibilla filia ejusdem Beatriciæ salutem.   Noverit universitas
vestra nos de consensu et voluntate hæredum nostrorum
dedisse et concessisse et hac præsenti carta nostra confirmasse Deo et Ecclesiæ Sanctæ Trinitatis et Sancti Constantini de Wederhale et Monachis ibidem Deo servientibus

---

60.   [1] This is the same messuage as in No. **41** and the terms of the
charter are very similar; but here, apparently, after the death of the
grantor's father, William, who was then alive and witnessed the dead.

[2] *Præpositus*, whence "provost," the chief officer or headman of
the vill or district, and answering to the Saxon "reeve" (*geréfa*).

[3] The date must be after the death of William son of Odard, which
was probably in 1195 and before the death of Simon de Tillel in 1201
(see note 15 on No. **38**).

tres acras[1] terræ in holmo juxta pontem de Warthwic quas quidem tres acras Robertus filius Gerardi de Waverton Pater dictæ Beatriciæ adquisivit de domo de Wederhal. Tenendum et habendum dictis Monachis quiete integre et pacifice absque omni servitio et calumpnia de nobis et hæredibus nostris in perpetuum in puram et perpetuam Elemosinam Nos vero et hæredes nostri dictas tres acras terræ dictis Monachis contra omnes homines in perpetuum warantizabimus defendemus et acquietabimus inperpetuum. Et ut hæc concessio et præsentis cartæ nostræ confirmatio rata sit et stabilis imperpetuum præsenti scripto sigilla nostra apposuimus. Hijs Testibus Domino Roberto de Mulcastre tunc Vicecomite Karliolensi[2], Dominis Willelmo de Vallibus[3], Roberto de Castlecairoc,

61. [1] From the next charter, we see that this land was in a certain place called Constantineclene (see No. **51**), and here that it was in the holm near Warthwic bridge.

[2] Robert de Mulcastre, or Moelcastre (see on No. **111**) was Sheriff in the latter half of 1259 and in 1260. In 1266, he was bailiff for Hugh le Bigod in Lydel, and in an *Inquisitio p. m.* in 1268, he is named one among several "knights *gladio cinctos*" (52 Henry III. No. 30). He was appointed a justice at Carlisle in July 1273: there is also a convention with Alan de Penintone, in 1278, about the manor of Molecastre (*hodie* Muncaster) given in *Calend. Doc. Scot.* ed. Bain, ii. 29.

[3] This is not William, a son of the first Robert de Vallibus, and a witness to his Foundation Charter of Lanercost, where he is so called, and who was probably Lord of Caterlen and witness to No. **138** (see there). The William who is witness here, and to several other charters, lived half a century later. There was also a William de Vallibus who married Alienora de Ferrers, or de Ferariis, daughter of the Earl of Derby, without the King's license, and was in 1247 fined 200 marcs to have seisin of her lands. His widow having married Roger de Quency, Earl of Winchester, without license, Roger was fined in 1253. At that date, therefore, William was dead, which is prior to the date of this charter. In 1253, John de Vallibus, brother and heir of William, paid part of the fine of 80 marks which his brother had left undischarged; and we have a William de Vaus mentioned in 1254 (see *Fine Rolls* ed. Roberts, ii. 15, 149, 160; *Originalia* 38 Hen. III. m. 9). This will,

Willelmo de Warthwic, Roberto de Warthwic, Roberto de Tyllol, Magistro Johanne de Boulton[4], Johanne Stelfod[5], Laurentio filio Walteri[6], Roberto Minot[7], Thoma de Rochwell, Johanne de Spanton, Roberto de Scupton, Gilberto de Scalremanoc et multis alijs[8].

62. QUIETA CLAMATIO ALANI FILIJ JULIANÆ DE WAVERTON DE IIJˢ. ACRIS TERRÆ IN WEDERHAL.

OMNIBUS Christi fidelibus præsens scriptum visuris vel audituris Alanus filius Julianæ de Waverton Salutem in Domino. Noverit universitas vestra me reddidisse et quietum clamasse pro me et hæredibus meis Abbati Sanctæ Mariæ Eboraci et Monachis Sancti Constantini et Sanctæ Trinitatis de Wederhale ibidem Deo servientibus

probably, be the present witness, and will be the William son of John de Vaux who, about this time, is referred to in a charter in the *Register of Lanercost*, the said John being also the son of a William de Vallibus (MS. vii. 18; ii. 10). In the same *Register*, this William is witness to a charter dated 1255 (ix. 12) and to another dated 1252 (xii. 22). In No. **67** below, he is witness to that charter, the date of which must be 1257—59.

[4] John de Boulton, or Bodilton, is called "citizen of Carlisle" in an *Inquisition* made in 1247 (*Inquis. p. m.* 31 Hen. III. No. 15); and in 1250, there is an Inquisition as to the land which John de Boulton (or Boleton) "holds at farm at the king's will, in the suburb of Carlisle," William de Wardewyk and others being jurors (*Inquis. p. m.* 34 Hen. III. No. 46). In 1251, a plea was entered at Westminster against him and Peter le Legat by Hugh le Bygod (*Calend. Doc. Scot.* i. 337); and he appears, with many of his co-witnesses here, in No. **76**. Alexander de Bolotun, probably one of the family, was Mayor of Carlisle in 1270 (see No. **96**).

[5] John Stelfod, or Stelfot, is very frequently a witness, e.g. in No. **144**, which is dated 1247, and No. **171**, dated 1241; in No. **98**, he is said to be "de Wederhal."

[6] Laurence is called, in No. **146**, "son of Walter le Porter."

[7] Robert Mynot, or Mynoc, is, with this Thomas de Rothewelle, called in No. **87** "servant to the Lord Prior"; and the latter in No. **88**, with Richard Mansel "servant to the Prior of Wederhal."

[8] The date of the charter from the Sheriff will be 1259 or 1260.

tres acras terræ quas habui in villa de Wederhale in quodam loco qui vocatur Constantineclene ut jus Ecclesiæ suæ sine ullo retenemento. Tenendum et habendum prædictis Abbati et Monachis Sancti Constantini et Sanctæ Trinitatis de Wederhal ut Jus Ecclesiæ prædictæ pro nobis et hæredibus nostris imperpetuum. Hijs Testibus Roberto de Warthwic[1], Roberto de Tylloel, Johanne Corbet, Alano Armstrang, Richardo Fenton, Adam de Agillunebi, Roberto de Hederesford, et multis alijs[2].

63. CARTA WERRI DE PONTE DE REDDITU XIJ DENARIORUM AD LUMINARE SANCTÆ MARIÆ.

OMNIBUS Christi fidelibus hanc cartam visuris vel audituris Werri de ponte Salutem in Domino. Noverit universitas vestra me suscepisse fraternitatem in domo Sanctæ Trinitatis et Sancti Constantini de Wederhale et quod nomine Fraternitatis Ego et hæredes mei tenemur solvere annuatim duodecim denarios ad Pentecosten prædictæ Domui specialiter ad luminare coram altari Beatæ Virginis Mariæ Ego vero Werri hunc prædictum redditum me et hæredes meos sine aliqua difficultate ad prædictum terminum soluturos tactis Sacrosanctis juravi Et ad insuper ad majorem securitatem præsenti scripto sigillum meum apposui. Testibus Roberto de Hamton[1] tunc Vicecomite Cumberlandiæ, Ricardo de Levington, Radulpho de Feritate, Symone de Orreton, Adam de Hoton[2], Elya

62. [1] This will be Robert the son of William; both Robert and his son William are mentioned in No. 61.

[2] The date of the charter is later than No. 61; William de Warthwic does not now sign; probably from Robert de Tillol about the date of No. 47.

63. [1] This must be the same as in No. 54 (see note 4 there) when he was Sheriff or Custos, 1223 to 1229, which agrees with the other witnesses here.

[2] Adam de Hoton, or Hutton, is called "knight" in No. 187. Probably of Hutton in the Forest. He was one of the jurors in an

de Agillunebi, Waltero janitore, Johanne filio Willelmi, Johanne de Agillunebi, Elya de Ravenwic, Reginaldo Camerario Prioris Karlioli, Willelmo nepote suo et alijs.

64. CARTA JOHANNIS COQUI DE REDDITU VI DE-NARIORUM PRO QUATUOR ACRIS TERRÆ IN WEDER-HALE.

UNIVERSIS Christi fidelibus ad quorum notitiam præsens scriptum pervenerit Johannes coquus Salutem æternam in Domino. Noverit universitas vestra quod teneo in campo de Wederhal quatuor acras terræ de Abbate et Conventu Sanctæ Mariæ Eboraci et de Monachis de Wederhale in feudo et hæreditate illas videlicet quas emi de Waltero janitore quas idem Walterus janitor ad instantiam meam dictæ domui dedit[1] et quietas clamavit per cartam suam Ego autem Johannes et hæredes mei pro prædictis quatuor acris terrae sex denarios prædictæ domui reddemus annuatim imperpetuum medietatem ad Festum Sancti Martini in yeme et medietatem ad Pentecosten pro omni consuetudine et exactione. Et ad hujus rei securitatem et perpetuam firmitatem præsenti scripto sigillum meum apposui. Hijs Testibus, Willelmo filio Rogeri[2], Symone Sacerdote, Roberto filio Willelmi, Jo-

---

Inquisition in 1246 with Richard de Levington and others (*Inquis. p. m.* 31 Hen. III. No. 4); and in another, in 1268, he is called a "Verdurer of the Forest of Engilwode" (*Inquis. p. m.* 52 Hen. III. No. 30). From *Testa de Nevill* (Record. Com. p. 379 *a, b*) we learn that his wife was Alicia who afterwards married Robert de Neubiggen.

[3] The date of the charter will be from 1223 to 1229.

64. [1] The Quitclaim of Walter the porter is given in No. **84,** with several of the same witnesses.

[2] This must be William son of Roger de Corkeby who is called "knight" in Nos. **159, 187.** In the additional charter No. **243,** he and his wife Osanna speak of their antecessors the Lords of Corkby, and as if they had a like power; but at this time Robert son of William was Lord of Corkby, and Isabella his daughter, who married Alan de Lascels, succeeded him (see note 5 on No. **47**). It is difficult to explain

hanne de Agulluneby, Johanne filio Willelmi, Henrico coquo, Johanne de Hayremynne[3], Suano de Agulluneby, Roberto de Paris, Hamelino nepote Prioris[4] tunc temporis, Radulpho Clirico et alijs[5].

65. CARTA JOHANNIS SPENDLIME ET MARGARETÆ UXORIS SUÆ DE 4ᵣ ACRIS TERRÆ CUM QUADAM DOMO IN WEDERHALE.

OMNIBUS Christi fidelibus ad quos præsens scriptum pervenerit Johannes Spendlime et Margareta uxor sua Salutem in Domino. Noverit universitas vestra nos de consensu et voluntate hæredum nostrorum dedisse concessisse et hac præsenti carta nostra confirmasse de nobis et hæredibus nostris Deo et Ecclesiæ Sanctæ Trinitatis et

his position. I can only conjecture that he may have held the adjoining manor of Little Corkby, lower down the river Eden, in the parish of Hayton; and that it was to his son William de Corkby that Isabella, in 1284, granted the moiety of Langthwaite in (Little) Corkby; see note 5, No. 47, also No. 57, with which the account of the wood in No. 243 should be compared. William son of Roger occurs frequently. He is witness to the charter No. 144 dated 1247; and the same year he is one of the jurors in an *Inquisitio post mort.* with Rouland de Vallibus and with William de Corkebi, probably his son (31 Hen. III. No. 32). In the *Register of Lanercost* he is witness to a charter (MS. ii. 19) with Thomas son of John, Sheriff (1230—31) and Roland de Vallibus, also to one of Roland de Vallibus (ii. 21) with Bishop Walter (1223—46) and William Prior of Wederhale (before 1239). His son William occurs in this *Register* (Nos. 163, 178) and a son Robert (No. 112), and his wife's name was Osanna (No. 116).

[3] John de Hayremine, or Hermine, or Eyremine or Airenmine, was the son of William de Eyremine (see No. 60) and is so called in his two charters Nos. 85, 175. He is witness in 1241 to the dated deed No. 171. They held land "in campo de Wederhal" and in Kaberg on the east of the Eden.

[4] This Prior was probably William Randel, promoted to the Abbey at York in 1239; he appears with William son of Roger in No. 116; and see note 2, also Appendix E.

[5] The date cannot be fixed, but was probably about 1239, see note 4.

Sancti Constantini de Wederhal et Monachis ibidem Deo servientibus pro salute animarum nostrarum quatuor acras terræ in territorio de Wederhal cum domo propinquiore domui suæ et terra ad domum pertinente. Ita scilicet quod Croftum habeat eandem latitudinem in inferiori parte quam habet domus in superiori parte in puram et perpetuam Elemosinam, unam scilicet acram et unam rodam super sabulum inter Wederhal et Warthwic, Et dimidiam acram versus Cumquintin juxta Tranemyre et dimidiam acram ultra Henbuskes et unam rodam super Polimyhuou et unam rodam ex opposito de Brunacre et dimidiam acram ultra le Rig in bank et unum Wandale[1] in Borganes et unum wandale juxta Honbusks et unum wandale super Thabriggelat et unam rodam super Musehou et unam rodam ultra le loning[2] quæ vocatur morode. Tenendum et habendum dictæ domui et dictis Monachis libere quiete pacifice et integre absque omni servicio et calumpnia de nobis et hæredibus nostris imperpetuum. Nos vero Johannes et Margareta et hæredes nostri prædictas quatuor acras cum domo prædicta et cum pertinentijs prædictis Monachis contra omnes homines imperpetuum warantizabimus defendemus et adquietabimus. In cujus rei testimonium præsenti scripto sigilla nostra apposuimus Hijs Testibus Domino Roberto de Mulcastre tunc Vicecomite Karliolensi, Dominis Willelmo de Wallibus, Roberto de Castlecairoc, Willelmo de Warthwic Militibus, Roberto de Warthwic, Roberto de Tyloyl, Johanne Stelefot, Roberto Minnot, Thoma de Rouheb, Johanne de Spanton, Roberto de Scupton et multis alijs[3].

---

65. [1] *Wandale*, from Anglo-Saxon *wang*, "an open field" or "plain," and *dæl*, "a share," was a division, or share of the open arable field of a vill or township.

[2] *Loning*, Cumberland and Yorkshire for a lane or a space between hedges; Scotch *lonnin*; Anglo-Saxon, *lane* or *lone*.

[3] From the witness Robert de Mulcastre, Sheriff, the date is the atter half of 1259 or 1260.

66. Conventio inter Johannem Spendlime et
Henricum de TutesbiR̃. Priorem de Wederhale
de Jª bovata terræ in Wederhale.

Anno Domini MCCLVII°. ad Festum Sancti Martini[1] in
yeme facta fuit haec Conventio inter Johannem Spendlime
et Margaretam uxorem ejus ex una parte et fratrem
Henrici de TutesbiR̃.[2] tunc temporis Priorem de Wederhal
et Monachos ejusdem domus ex altera videlicet quod dicti
Johannes et Margareta de consensu et voluntate hæredum
suorum concesserunt et dimiserunt dictis H. Priori et
Monachis de Wederhale unam bovatam terræ in territorio
de Wederhale de duobus scilicet bovatis quas quondam
tenuerunt in eadem domo de Wederhale quæ jacent ubique
propinquiores terræ Dominæ Dionisiæ de Wederhal. Tenendum et habendum dictæ domui de Wederhale libere
quiete et pacifice integre sine aliquo retenemento usque ad
terminum sexaginta annorum plene completorum Et
sciendum quod dicti Johannes et Margareta et hæredes sui
solvent antiquam firmam et facient antiquum servicium
plene quæ pertinent ad dictas duas bovatas terræ sicut
fecerunt qui eas integras habuerunt in manu sua. Pro
hac autem dimissione et concessione[3] dederunt dicti Prior
et Monachi dictis Johanni et Margaretæ tres marcas
argenti in eorum magna necessitate. Ad hanc vero con-
vencionem fideliter sine dolo et omni cavellatione tenendam
tam dictus Johannes quam Margareta uxor ejus affidav-
erunt et tactis Sacrosanctis juraverunt. In cujus rei

66. [1] S. Martin's day "*in yeme*," November 11th, the supposed
day of the death of S. Martin of Tours, at the end of the 4th century.

[2] Henry de Tutesbiri (as in No. **89**) probably succeeded Richard
de Rothomagus, who was Prior in 1251; see Appendix E.

[3] This is a curious concession for 60 years to the Priory of one
of two bovates held by the grantors as tenants, at the same rent;
and made because of three silver marcs given by the Priory to John
and Margaret " in their great necessity."

Testimonium præsenti scripto cirografphato partes alternatim sigilla sua apposuerunt[4].

67. CARTA JOHANNIS SPENDLIME ET MARGARETÆ UXORIS SUÆ DE UNA BOVATA TERRÆ IN WEDERHALE.

OMNIBUS ad quos præsens scriptum pervenerit Johannes Spendlime et Margareta uxor ejus de Wederhal Salutem in Domino. Noverit universitas vestra nos de consensu et voluntate hæredum nostrorum dedisse et concessisse et hac præsenti carta nostra confirmasse Deo et Ecclesiæ Sanctæ Trinitatis et Sancti Constantini de Wederhale et Monachis ibidem Deo servientibus pro salute animarum nostrarum unam bovatam terræ in campo de Wederhale in puram et perpetuam Elemosinam scilicet unam bovatam de duabus bovatis quas quondam tenuerunt de prædicta Domo de Wederhale Tenendum et habendum dictæ Domui et dictis Monachis libere quiete integre et pacifice absque omni servicio et calumpnia de nobis et hæredibus nostris imperpetuum[1]. Et sciendum quod nos Johannes et Margareta et hæredes nostri solvemus antiquam firmam et faciemus antiquum servicium quod pertinebat ad dictam bovatam terræ sicut melius et plenius fecimus quando ipsam in manu nostra tenuimus. Nos vero et hæredes nostri prædictam bovatam terræ prædictis Monachis contra omnes homines warantizabimus defendemus et acquietabimus imperpetuum. Et ut hæc concessio et præsentis cartæ nostræ confirmatio rata sit et stabilis imperpetuum præsenti scripto sigilla nostra apposuimus. Hijs Testibus Dominis Willelmo de Vallibus, Roberto de Castelcairoc, Willelmo de Warthwic, Militibus, Remigio tunc Vicecomite Karliolensi[2], Johanne Capellano de We-

---

[4] This charter is dated November 11th, 1257.

67. [1] The bovate granted in 1257 (see No. 66) for 60 years is here granted for ever, the grantors still paying the ancient rent and service for the two bovates.

[2] Remigius de Pocklintona was Sheriff of Cumberland, or Custos for William, Earl of Albemarle, from 1255 to the first half of 1259.

derhale³, Roberto de Warthwic, Roberto de Tyllol, Johanne
Stelfot, Laurentio filio Walteri, Roberto Minnoc, Johanne
de Spanton, Gilberto de Scaldermanoc et alijs⁴.

68. Carta Margaretæ Spendlime de unà bovata terræ Messuagio Tofto et Crofto et iiij
acris terræ in Wederhal.

Omnibus Christi fidelibus ad quos præsens scriptum
pervenerit Margareta quondam uxor Johannis Spendlime
de Wederhale Salutem in Domino sempiternam.   Noverit
universitas vestra me remisisse et omnino quietam clamasse
de me et heredibus meis in mea libera viduitate Deo et
Ecclesiæ Sanctæ Trinitatis et Sancti Constantini de Wederhale et Monachis ibidem Deo servientibus pro salute
animæ meæ in liberam puram et perpetuam Elemosinam
unam bovatam terræ in territorio de Wederhale quam
Willielmus le bracur tenet et unum mesuagium cum tofto
et crofto quod messuagium propinquius adjacet domui
meæ versus aquilonem et quatuor acras terræ quas Johannes
Cliricus quondam tenuit in Campo de Wederhale et unam
dimidiam acram illam scilicet per quam aqua ducitur de le
Petemyre usque ad Edene cum omnibus aisiamentis prædictæ terræ intra Villam et extra pertinentibus.   Tenendum
et habendum de me et heredibus meis vel meis assignatis
Ecclesiæ prædictæ et Monachis prædictis libere quiete
pacifice et integre absque omni servicio seculari exactione
et demanda in liberam puram et perpetuam Elemosinam.
Et ut hæc mea remissio et quieta clamatio de me et
heredibus meis in mea libera viduitate facta rata sit et
stabillita remaneat huic scripto sigillum meum apposui.
Hijs Testibus Roberto de Warthwic, Johanne Armstrang,

³ John, Chaplain of Wederhal, is witness in 1241 to No. **171**.
⁴ The date of this charter is later than No. **66**, and therefore from
the Sheriff in 1257—59.

Willelmo de Agulluneby[1], Johanne Robby[2], Willelmo de
Heddresford, Willelmo de Joneby[3], Stephano de porta, et
alijs multis[4].

69.   QUIETA CLAMATIO EVÆ SPENDLIME DE TOTA TERRA QUAM TENUIT IN WEDERHALE.

OMNIBUS hoc scriptum visuris vel audituris Eva Spendlime filia Johannis Spendlime de Wederhale Salutem.
Noverit Universitas vestra me in virginitate mea et libera
potestate mea concessisse remisisse et de me et hæredibus
meis imperpetuum quietam clamasse Dominis meis Abbati
Sanctæ Mariæ Eboraci et Priori et Monachis de Wederhale terram totam illam quam tenui in Villa de Wederhale
de prædicto Domino Abbate et de Priore et Monachis
dictis Dominis meis de hæreditate mea quam habui de
hæreditate Patris mei Johannis Spendlime in Villa de
Wederhale.   Ita videlicet quod nec Ego Eva nec aliquis
hæredum meorum nec aliquis nomine nostro aliquid jus vel
clamium in illis ædificijs et terris vendicare poterimus.   In
cujus rei Testimonium huic scripto meo sigillum meum
apposui.   Hijs Testibus, Willelmo de Agulluneby, Johanne
de Robertby, Nicholao de Thorneheved, Roberto de
Neuby, Willelmo de Hedresford, Roberto de Warthwic,
Roberto Tyllolf, Willelmo de Leversdale[1], Roberto de
Supton et alijs[2].

68. [1] William de Agulluneby was, according to J. Denton (*Cumberland*, p. 105) the son of Alan, who was (see No. **45**) the son of Elyas
de Agulluneby.

[2] John de Robertby, as in No. **69.**

[3] There is a William de Joenebi in the *Pipe Rolls* for 1210 and
following years, and elsewhere about that period, but he can hardly be
the same; this is probably identical with William de Johnsbi who
attests a deed in the *Register of Lanercost* (MS. iii. 8) about this date.

[4] This charter must be later than No. **67** as Margaret Spendlime is
here a widow.

69. [1] William de Leversdale, or Laversdale, is witness to No. **194**,
which is dated 1271, also witness with Robert de Warthwic and Robert

70. Carta Matildæ filiæ Johannis Spendlime de tota terra sua et tofto et curtilagio in Wederhale.

Omnibus Christi fidelibus ad quorum notitiam literæ præsentes pervenerint Matilda de Barrock filia Johannis Spendlime Salutem in Domino sempiternam. Noverit universitas vestra me in pura viduitate et legia potestate mea dedisse concessisse et omnino quietam clamasse de me et hæredibus meis et successoribus meis Abbati et Conventui Beatæ Mariæ Eboraci Cellæque eorundem de Wederhale Priori et Monachis ibidem Deo servientibus totam terram meam cum tofto et curtilagio in Villa de Wederhale, videlicet unam acram terræ et tres rodas cum prato adjacente scilicet unam rodam et dimidiam buttantem super viam Regiam et Tranemire[1] et unam rodam buttantem super fossam Domini Prioris versus portam et unam dimidiam rodam buttantem super busko apud Apiltrehirste et unam rodam jacentem ad Gosgarhis et unam rodam in Suthathe et unam dimidiam rodam jacentem apud Sanctum Serwanum[2] et unam dimidiam rodam jacentem apud

de Tylleol to a charter, among others, dated 1285, in the *Register of Lanercost* (MS. xiii. 11).

[2] The date must be later than the two preceding charters, and not far off the date, 1285, of the witness noted above.

70. [1] Tranemyre was towards Cumquintin (see No. **65**) and thus would be near the Via Regia from Appleby to Carlisle (see No. **5**).

[2] In one transcript (A) altered to *Serwahum*. This name would seem to be a corruption either for S. Servanus or S. Severinus. In the grant by Henry VIII. to the Dean and Chapter of Carlisle, in January, 1547, of the Churches of Wetherhal and Warwick, the Chapels of S. Anthony and S. Severin are mentioned as belonging thereto (Illustrative Docum. XL., XLI.). The Endowment Charter of the Cathedral, granted in May, 1541, speaks of the Chapel of S. Anthony with two closes of land adjoining containing four acres. Tradition identifies this Chapel with a piece of ground marked on the Ordnance Map to the right of the road between Wetherhal and Cumwhinton. The piece of land mentioned in the present charter probably adjoined the other chapel, which has not been identified. This may

Layrpottis et unam rodam jacentem super Solmerithou. Ita quod nec Ego nec aliquis nomine meo hæredes vel assignati mei aliquid jus vel clamium in prædicta terra tofto et prato exigere vel vendicare poterimus imperpetuum. Et ut ista donatio et concessio et omnino quieta clamatio perpetuum optineat robur firmitatis huic præsenti scripto sigillum meum est appensum. Hijs Testibus, Roberto de Warthwic, Willelmo filio ejusdem[3], Ricardo de Fenton, Alano Armstrang, Adam de Agulluneby, Johanne de Roberdby, Roberto de Hedresford et alijs[4].

71. CARTA WILLELMI DE HEŘ. DE DIMIDIA CARUCATA TERRÆ IN CUMQUINTIN.

WILLELMUS de Heř.[1] Omnibus Sanctæ Ecclesiæ filijs salutem. Universitati vestræ clarescat me concessisse Deo et Monachis Sanctæ Mariæ Eboraci in Cella de Wederhale

have been the Chapel of S. Servanus, sometimes written Serwanus, a Scottish saint in the 6th century, about whom there is some confusion, but he is said to have been the instructor of S. Kentigern; and the latter, we are told, sent S. Constantine to preach the word in Galwedia (Galloway). There is thus a connection with the patron saint of Wetherhal, see on S. Constantine in No. 2 and compare Bp Forbes, *Life of S. Kentigern*, pp. 40, 366, and *Dict. of Christian Biog.* s. v. Servanus. Or this may have been the Chapel of S. Severinus, who was a Bishop of Bordeaux in the 4th century and often confused with his contemporary Severinus, Bishop of Cologne (see *Dict. of Christian Biography*, s. v.) but he was little known in England.

[3] William the son of John and father of Robert de Warthwic, with whom he was a frequent witness in the preceding charters, was probably now dead, see on No. 51, note 4. This is William the son of that Robert.

[4] This daughter of John Spendlime was now a widow, hence the date of this charter must be some years later than No. 67 or No. 68.

71.   [1] William de Heriz is a witness to the charter granted by Earl Henry son of King David to the Abbey of Holm Cultram in 1150 (Illustrative Docum. XXIV.). The William de Heriz who is a witness here was probably his son; but see below. The family of Heriz seems to be often connected in different deeds with the family of Brus.

Deo servientibus dimidiam carucatam terræ de Cumquin-
tin² solam et quietam ab omnibus servicijs et commune
pascuum Dominicæ pecuniæ³ eorum simul cum mea.
Testibus Willelmo de Herᵢ⁴ et Gaufrido⁵.

72. CARTA HILDREDI DE CARLEOLO DE TERRA ET SILVA QUIETA CLAMATIO MONACHIS DE WEDERHALE.

NOTUM sit omnibus legentibus vel audientibus literas
has quod ego Hildredus de Carlel¹ terram et silvam illam

---

² Cumquintin, *hodie* Cumwhinton, was a manor in the parish of
Wetherhal lying to the west, and long in the family of de Carleol. This
half carucate of land would seem to be the same as that granted by
Uctred son of Liulf and now confirmed by W. de Heriz with common
of pasture (see No. **14**).

³ "Property," not money here but cattle (*pecus*).

⁴ This is a second William de Heriz, who appears often as a
witness in the beginning of the 13th century, e.g. in a charter of
William de Brus to the monks of Holmcoltram of a fishery in the
Ask (Esk) which would date 1194—1214, also to a grant to Robert de
Brus in Anandale about 1218 (see *Calend. Doc. Scot.* ed. Bain, i. 108,
123), also to a convention in *Chart. of Whitby* (i. 216) with Adam de
Brus and Robert his brother.

⁵ This charter must be in the latter half of the 12th century.

72. ¹ This will be the Hildred de Karleol to whom, and to his son
Odard, Henry I. gave lands in Gamelby and Glassaneby, one Odard
being then sheriff (*Testa de Nevill*, p. 380 *a*; *Coram Rege Rolls*, 11 Joh.
No. 41, m. 9; *Abbrev. Placit.* Rec. Com. p. 66 *b*; *Calend. Doc. Scot.* i.
80). It will be noted that among the first set of witnesses in this charter
are Odard the son of Hildred and Odard the sheriff. This grant
must have been prior to 31st of Henry I., for in the Pipe Rolls for
Carlisle of that year we find Hildred and Odard his son rendering
account of 40*s.* for the grant of the land of Gamel son of Berᵢ.
(Gamelby). Hildred may have been sheriff that year, 1130—31,
though the Pipe Roll is not conclusive. In the earlier part of the
Roll, Hildred seems to be acting as sheriff, but nowhere is he styled
"sheriff"; yet we know from No. 1 that from the beginning of the
century there were sheriffs of this district of Carlisle. Again, in the
same Roll, "Odard the sheriff" is named and appears to have held the
office the previous year or years, and we should be inclined to

unde calumpnia inter me et Monachos de Wederhale fuit Deo et Sanctæ Mariæ et Monachis Eboracensibus in Wederhale degentibus pro salute animæ meæ ab omni calumpnia liberam et quietam clamavi et de jure eorum Ecclesiæ cognovi ac Deo et Sanctæ Mariæ Sanctoque Constantino necnon Monachis prædictis super altare Ecclesiæ de Wederhale præsente Parochia[2] ejusdem Ecclesiæ cum virga[3] dedi secundo vero solario meo Carlel idem concessi coram Monachis et militibus et quibusdam burgensibus de Carlel. Hujus concessionis fuerunt Testes Radulphus Prior de Wederhale[4], Rainaldus Monachus, Odardus Vicecomes[5], Ricardus Miles[6], Ricardus de Meisi

conclude that he rather than Hildred was sheriff in 1130—31. Thus these two Hildreds are probably identical, and one may have been sheriff; these two Odards must be different. This Odard son of Hildred had a son Robert surnamed de Hodelme, in Dumfriesshire, and a grandson Odard de Hodelme who was the grandfather of Christiana de Treby, 2d wife of Robert de Brus the Competitor, and heiress of Gamelby and Glassonby (*Assize Rolls*, Cumb. 20 Edw. I. m. 32; *Regist. Laner.* MS. xiv. 4, also see note 1 on No. 73).

[2] In the presence of the parish of Wederhal. The whole is an interesting instance of the method of proceeding.

[3] Tenure by the virge, or rod, was a species of copyhold, see Jacob, *Law Dictionary*, s. v.

[4] Radulph is the first Prior of Wetherhal, in point of time, that occurs in this *Register*. Richard de Reme is said by Leland (see Appendix E) to have been the first Prior.

[5] This Odard the sheriff is mentioned together with Odard the son of Hildred, not only in this charter, but also, together with Walter Espec and Eustace son of John, in the charter granted to Hildred de Karleol by Henry I. (and referred to in note 1 above), also in the Pipe Rolls for Carlisle of 31 Henry I. They are therefore clearly different persons. Alike in the grant and in the Roll he occupies the place of "sheriff" of Carlisle and not of Northumberland or any other place. Odard the Sheriff received the land and Barony of Wigton from Henry I., under whom he held by cornage of £1. 6s. 4d., as appears from the Inquisition in *Testa de Nevill*, p. 379 b. He had a son Adam, and a grandson Odard son of Adam, and a great-grandson, the second Adam son of Odard. Odard son of Adam appears in the

Constabularius, Willelmus de Herici[7], Anschatillus Odardi filius[8] et Odardus filius Hildredi[9], Willelmus filius Baldwini et Raimbaldus filius ejus, Unspach Hardolf, Rogerus Forestarius. Quod autem hijs duabus vicibus feci tertio nichilominus in præfato loco facere decrevi Ad locum veni et perambulavi cum multis et Radulphum Priorem de prædicta donatione sarsivi usque in Eden. Testibus hijs Vitali Sacerdote et Willelmo Levita, Pagano Milite, Johanne

Pipe Roll of 3 John (1201) as holding his land by cornage ; and the second Adam son of Odard appears as having livery of his father's land in the Pipe Roll of 10 John (1208); he is also a witness to No. 52. This second Adam was witness as Adam de Wygeton to a charter in the *Register of Lanercost* (MS. vii. 17) when Alan de Caldebec was sheriff or custos, i.e. in 1204—5 or 1214—15. He was dead in 1225 when his son, the third Odard de Wigeton, had seizin of his father's lands on payment of 10 marcs to the King (*Fine Rolls*, 10 Hen. III. m. 9, ed. Roberts, i. 134). This Odard the sheriff may have been the father of William son of Odard and Osbert, his brother, Lords of Corkeby (see below on Odard de Corkeby). The local historians call this Odard the sheriff, Odard de Logis, first Baron of Wigton (see Additional Charter, No. 245). In 1238, we find the third Odard (son of the 2nd Adam) who has lately died, and Bishop Walter is given custody of Odard de Wygeton's lands, Christina his widow and Walter his heir ; he occurs also in No. 211. In 1253 Isabella de Muscamps, widow of Adam de Wygeton (apparently a younger brother as Isabella is only 18 and Adam was about 2 years younger than she when they were married), claims $\frac{1}{13}$ of the lands of Wygeton, Melmorby and other places as against the son and heir Walter, to whom however seizin was given. This Walter son of Odard de Wygeton quitclaimed certain lands in Wigeton to the Abbey of Holm Cultram on Feb. 1st, 1265 (see Dugdale, *Monasticon*, v. 611). On the above facts, compare the extracts from the *Coram Rege* and other *Rolls* in *Calend. Doc. Scot.* ed. Bain, i. pp. 264, 362, 415. In *The Genealogist* (New Series, v. 25) J. H. Round discusses the "two Odards"; but while arguing correctly that Odard son of Hildred is different from Odard the sheriff, he seems to identify the latter with the sheriff of Northumberland who, he shows, was Odard of Bamburgh, the son of Sigulf. This identity is very improbable. Where Odard the sheriff appears, as cited above,

Clerico, Waltero Agullun[10], Safrac, Radulpho filio Widonis, Ervisio, Stephano de Corkeby, Acta, Radulfo filio Galfridi,

it is clearly as sheriff of Carlisle. The name was very common at the time.

This seems to be the probable pedigree :

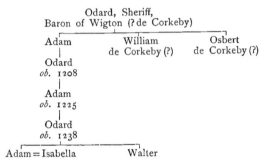

Odard, Sheriff,
Baron of Wigton (? de Corkeby)

Adam   William   Osbert
    | de Corkeby (?)   de Corkeby (?)
Odard
ob. 1208
    |
Adam
ob. 1225
    |
Odard
ob. 1238

Adam = Isabella   Walter

[6] Ricardus Miles is in the Pipe Rolls of 31 Henry I. ; see on No. **15**.

[7] This is probably William de Heriz, the elder of the name, see on No. **71**.

[8] The conjunction between the names helps to show that Odard the father of Anschatill is identical with Odard the son of Hildred.

[9] See the note above on Hildred de Carlel ; from the *Coram Rege Roll* there quoted, it appears Odard held the lands in Gamelby and Glassaneby in the parish of Addingham after his father Hildred ; we learn also that the manors derived their names from Gamel son of Beř. and Glassam son of Brictric, two of the King's *drengs*. His son Robert held them until the King, in 1177, fined him 15 marcs for his rebellion and finally took them from him in 1179. This Robert and his brother Richard occur in No. **73**. In his pleadings before the court in 1199 (see below note 1, No. **73**) Robert asserts that at the siege of Carlisle by William of Scotland in 1174, his father Odard was in Carlisle Castle in the service of King Henry (II.) : and Odard probably died before 1179 when the land being taken from Robert came into the hands of the Crown. Odard is then called Odard de Odelma, or Hodelm, also the title of his son and grandson (*Testa de Nevill*, p. 380 *a*). He is witness, as Hudard de Hodelma, to an important charter granted by Huctred son of Fergus to the Hospital of S. Peter at York (*Calend. Doc. Scot.* ed. Bain, ii. 422) whose date is between 1158 and 1164 ; among his co-witnesses are Hubert de

Roberto fratre Stephani, Odardo de Corkeby[11], Grimchillo preposito de Scoteby, Aschillo, Colfweino, Alnodo, Vivat, Odo, Rogero Forestario, Ranulpho, Unspach de Carlel, Roberto nepote Hildredi[12], Stephano, Helgo, Simulpho Clerico, Roberto Clerico, Werrico Clerico[13].

Vallibus (*ob.* 1164), Robert son of Trute, sheriff (1158—74), Richard his brother, Christian, Bishop of Galloway, Robert, Archdeacon of Carlisle, Everard, Abbot of Holm Cultram, Peter de Tilliol, Richard de Heriz, Robert Dunbredan and others.

The following table may be of use :

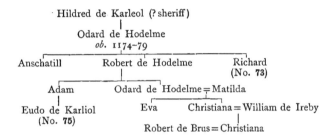

[10] This seems to be the earliest of the family, so many members of which appear in this *Register*; and it is clear that he cannot be put, as by the local historians, at the time of the Conquest ; see also note 3 on No. 37.

[11] Odard de Corkeby is most probably the Lord of Corkeby and father of Osbert and William (see on Nos. 35, 36). The question is whether he is identical with either of the Odards in the first set of witnesses here. Nothing appears to connect him with Odard son of Hildred ; but in the Pipe Rolls for 1181, we found William son of Odard getting recognition of his rights against Udard (Odard) son of Adam (see note 1 on No. 36). This Odard son of Adam was no doubt the grandson of Odard the sheriff, Baron of Wigton (see note 5 above). It is very probable that this younger Odard, if he were the grandson of Odard the Lord of Corkeby, might have put in some claim against his uncle William. If so, Odard de Corkeby was identical with Odard of Wigton.

[12] Robert the *grandson* of Hildred with his brother Richard, sons of Odard, occur in Nos. 73, 74.

[13] All the persons in this charter seem to point to a date about

10—2

73. CARTA RICARDI ET ROBERTI FRATRIS EJUS DE COMMUNA ETC., IN CUMQUINTIN.

NOTUM sit omnibus legentibus vel audientibus literas istas quod Ego Ricardus et frater meus Robertus[1] et Hæredes nostri concedimus Deo et Sanctæ Mariæ et Monachis de Wederhale ibidem Deo servientibus liberam communam in Bosco de Cumquintin ad mortuum boscum capiendum ubi voluerint. Concedimus etiam eisdem Monachis Deo servientibus terram et silvam quam Hildredus Avus noster in vita sua eis prius concesserat in liberam Elemosinam pro salute animæ ejusdem Avi nostri et Matrum et Patrum nostrorum et animarum nostrarum eadem divisa quæ facta fuit coram hijs Testibus Willelmo filio Odardi, Odone de Bossarby[2], Roberto filio Richardi

1130—31 ; and if we hold Odard the sheriff to be the sheriff of Carlisle in 1130 or before, this would give nearly the date of the charter.

73. [1] These were the sons of Odard, and so grandsons of Hildred de Carlel. Nothing is known of Richard except that Robert, a witness, seems to be his son. Robert, as we saw, held the lands in Gamelby (see note 9 on No. 72). He was fined 15 marks in 1177 for having joined the King's enemies (*Pipe Rolls*, 23 Hen. II.). He is called Robert de Hodeuma or Hodelma, and had taken part in the revolt of the younger Henry, the King's son, which had been joined by William the Lion, the King of Scotland, in 1173—4. The lands in Gamelby and Glassaneby were seized by the King, and were accounted for by the sheriff of Cumberland in the Pipe Rolls for 1179 and several subsequent· years. They were claimed against Robert by Richard son of Troite as the next heir. After considerable litigation (see *Coram Rege Rolls*, 1 Joh. m. 9, 11 Joh. m. 9 ; *Abbrev. Placit.* Rec. Com. pp. 22 *a*, 66 *b*) Richard son of Richard son of Truite got seizin of them in 1199 ; but Robert again brought them into court, and in 1210 his son Odard de Hodielma seems to have got possession of them (see *Pipe Rolls*, 12 Joh. ; *Calend. Doc. Scot.* i. 44, 83, 95, 294). Hence Robert died about 1209. This Odard had two daughters, Eva and Christiana, by his wife Matilda who were also his heirs (i. 294). Robert had also a son Adam, see on Nos. 75, 185.

[2] Odo de Boschardeby was one of the jurors in 1210 in the trial

de Karlel, Synardo Præposito de Karlel[3], Osberto Clerico de Bantona[4], Rogero Forestario, Normanno de Penereth, Johanne de Holderness[5].

74. CONFIRMATIO RICARDI ET ROBERTI TERRÆ SILVÆ ETC. FACTA MONACHIS DE WEDERHALE.

NOTUM sit omnibus legentibus vel audientibus literas has quod Ego Ricardus et frater meus Robertus et Hæredes nostri concedimus Deo et Sanctæ Mariæ de Wederhale et Monachis ibidem Deo servientibus terram et silvam[1] quam Hildredus Avus noster in vita sua eis prius concesserat ut liberam et quietam ab omni calumpnia Elemosinam pro salute animæ Avi nostri et animarum Patrum et Matrum nostrarum et animarum nostrarum eadem divisa qua Testes qui præsentes erant porrexerunt eandem de jure eorum esse cognoscentes. Præterea sciendum est quod concedimus eis communem pariter Pasturam in bosco et in plano animalibus de Dominio eorum. Testibus Hijs Willelmo filio Odardi, Odone de Bossarby, Roberto filio Ricardi de Karlel, Sywardo Præposito de Carlel, Osberto Clerico de Bantona, Rogero Forestario, Normanno de Penereth, Johanne de Holderness.

---

as to the lands in Gamelby, see on Hildred de Carlel, No. 72; for Odo, see note 5 on No. 48.

[3] As in No. 74, Syward. On the Mayor of Carlisle, see No. 95. The *Præpositus*, or Provost, would be probably the chief officer of the city before a Mayor was appointed.

[4] Banton, about 5 miles west of Carlisle, in the Barony of Burgh, was divided into Great Banton, now Kirkhampton, and Little Banton. It was said to have been the principal seat of Hildred de Carlel; see also on the Hospital of S. Nicholas, No. 95.

[5] The date of this charter must be mainly drawn from the witness William son of Odard 1167 to 1195, and is, from the other witnesses, near the latter year.

74. [1] This charter conveys, in addition to the grant of the last charter, common pasture.

75. CARTA EUDONIS DE KARLIOLO FACTA MONACHIS DE WEDERHALE AD CAPIENDUM BOSCUM IN CUMQUINTIN.

OMNIBUS Christi fidelibus ad quorum notitiam hoc praesens scriptum pervenerit Eudo de Karliolo[1] Salutem aeternam in Domino. Noverit universitas vestra me Divinae pietatis intuitu concessisse et dedisse et praesenti carta confirmasse Deo et Abbachiae Sanctae Mariae Eboraci et Monachis Sanctae Trinitatis et Sancti Constantini de Wederhal mortuum boscum in bosco de Cumquintin videlicet crescentem et siccum in puram et perpetuam Elemosinam ad capiendum in praedicto bosco ubicunque et quamcunque voluerint ad sustentationem Domus suae sine visu Forestarij. Licebit etiam dictis Monachis accipere quercus stantes quae sunt siccae in croppo ad eorundem sustentationem sine alicujus visu et sine aliquo impedimento meo vel Haeredum meorum. Si autem karri vel carrettae dictorum Monachorum in praedicto bosco fractae fuerint licebit eis capere sufficienter de viridi bosco stante quantum necesse habuerint ad reparationem earum sine alicujus visu vel impedimento. Do autem et concedo quod porci dictorum Monachorum et hominum suorum liberam habeant agistationem in praedicto bosco in perpetuum ubicunque voluerint tam in tempore pessionis quam in alio tempore. Et Ego et haeredes mei hanc Elemosinam sicut

75. [1] Eudo de Karliol is called in No. 186 the son of Adam son of Robert. This is no doubt the Robert mentioned in the two last charters (see on No. 73). We saw that his son Odard had part of his property, and this in Cumquintin had fallen to his son Adam. Eudo seems to have gone over to "the King of Scots, the King's enemy," in 1217 ; and seizin of his lands was given to Robert de Vallibus during the King's pleasure (*Close Rolls*, 2 Hen. III. 2, m. 15, Rec. Com. i. 343 *a*). He was again in possession in 1225, when some litigation as to Cumquintin and Cumbredale had arisen (see the extract from the *Coram Rege Rolls*, 9 Hen. III. No. 22, m. 1 in *Calend. Doc. Scot.* i. 160, ed. Bain). He had a son William (No. 76) and a grandson Eudo (No. 78).

præscriptum est prædictis Monachis contra omnes homines warantizabimus et defendemus imperpetuum. In cujus rei Testimonium præsenti scripto sigillum meum apposui. Hijs Testibus Bartholomeo Priore, Magistro E.[2] tunc Officiali, Roberto filio Willelmi tunc Vicecomite Karlioli[3], Johanne Priore de Lanercost[4], Simone Decano Karliolensi, Waltero Decano de Gillsland, Roberto de Castelcairoc, Roberto de Karlaton, Simone de Horeton, Odardo de Wigeton[5], Simone Capellano, Johanne filio Willielmi, Ricardo Diacono et alijs[6].

76. CARTA AÐÆ FILII ROGERI DE KARLIOL FACTA MONACHIS DE WEDERHAL DE 8s. IN CUMQUINTIN.

OMNIBUS hominibus ad quos præsens scriptum pervenerit Adam filius Rogeri de Karliol[1] Salutem. Noverit universitas vestra me dedisse concessisse et hac præsenti carta mea confirmasse Henrico Priori de Wederhal[2] et Monachis ibidem Deo servientibus octo solidos Argenti annui redditus quos recepi de Thoma de Hubricceby pro

[2] This would seem to be an error for G. Gervase de Louther, who must have been Official about the time of this charter, see on No. 21.

[3] Robert son of William de Hamptone was Sheriff or Custos for Bishop Walter in 1223—29, see note 4 on No. 54.

[4] This is John, Prior of Lanercost (on Lanercost Priory, see No. 117), who is a witness with Robert son of William to a grant in the *Register of Lanercost* (MS. iii. 8) by John, brother of Robert son of Anketin; but he can scarcely be the John, Prior, who occurs in a grant of Matilda de Vallibus (MS. ix. 16) who died in 1295. The latter called John de Galwythia resigned in 1283 and died 1289 (*Chron. de Lanercost*, ed. Stevenson, pp. 113, 133).

[5] This Odard de Wigeton was the son of the second Adam son of Odard; see on Odard the sheriff, No. 72.

[6] The date, from the sheriff, is 1223—1229; and this agrees with No. 54 where there are many of the same witnesses.

76. [1] Probably the same family as Eudo de Karliol in No. 75, but what relation does not appear. William the son of Eudo granted a charter to him, see below.

[2] This is Henry de Tutesbiri who was Prior of Wetherhal in 1257, see Appendix E.

terra illa in Cumquintin quæ vocatur Forlandes et Ofnumes quam terram dictus Thomas hereditarie pro dicto annuo redditu de me tenuit similiter illam partem terræ ubi schalinga³ mea sita fuit una cum communi pastura et communa bosci et alijs omnibus aisiamentis dictæ terræ de Forlandes et Ofnumes pertinentibus quæ excipiuntur et quas mihi reservam quoniam dictum Thomam de dicta terra pro dicto annuo redditu per cartam meam feoffevi. Habendum et tenendum dictis Priori et Monachis et eorum successoribus imperpetuum libere et quiete et integre de me et hæredibus meis reddendo inde annuatim mihi et hæredibus meis sex denarios ad duos anni terminos medietatem ad Festum Sancti Martini in yeme et aliam medietatem ad Pentecosten pro omnibus secularibus servicijs et demandis prout carta Domini Willelmi filij Eudonis de Karliol mihi facta plenius et melius testatur. Et Ego Adam et hæredes mei dictos .8. solidos annui redditus et schalingam cum terra adjacente et communi pastura et communa bosci et omnibus alijs dictam terram cingentibus dictis Priori de Wederhale et Monachis ibidem Deo servientibus contra omnes warantizabimus. In cujus rei Testimonium præsenti scripto sigillum meum apposui. Hijs Testibus Dominis Willelmo de Vaus⁴, Willelmo de Warwick Militibus, Magistro Johanne de Boulton, Roberto de Warthwick, Roberto Tyllol, Ricardo Mansel⁵ et Johanne Stelfot et alijs⁶.

³ *Schalinga*, a temporary building or shelter, a summer hut ; connected with the Norse *skaale*, " a hut." Hence we have, a sheal or shieling, a hut. The word often occurs in place names in the locality; compare Scaleby, Scales, Skelton and Gaitsgill, formerly Gateskale or Gateskill. A *schalinga* beyond Herthingburn is mentioned in a grant of Robert de Vallibus (*Regis. Lanercost*, MS. i. 9).

⁴ This is the second of the name (see note 3 on No. 61) who appears in several charters from 1252 to 1260.

⁵ Richard Mansel, or Maunsel, appears in Nos. **87, 88** as "serving the Lord Prior." He grants the next charter.

⁶ From the witnesses the date will probably be 1250—60.

77. SCRIPTUM RICARDI MANSEL DE ANNUO REDDITU 8s. IN CUMQUINTIN.

OMNIBUS Christi fidelibus hoc præsens scriptum visuris vel audituris Ricardus Mansel Dominus medietatis[1] Villæ de Cumquintin Salutem in Domino sempiternam. Noverit universitas vestra me teneri Deo et Ecclesiæ Sancti Constantini de Wederhale Priorique et Monachis ibidem Deo servientibus in octo solidatis annui redditus soluturi ad dictos anni terminos videlicet medietatem ad Pentecosten et alteram medietatem ad Festum Sancti Martini in yeme pro terra quæ quondam fuit Adæ filij Rogeri in Villa de Cumquintin prout plenius et melius continetur in carta[2] quam idem Prior et Monachi habent de prædicto Ada filio Rogeri. Et si ita contingat (quod absit) quod Ego Ricardus vel hæredes mei in solutione prædictæ Firmæ vel in aliqua parte ejusdem in aliquem terminum prædictorum defecerimus Volo et concedo pro me et hæredibus meis quod præfati Prior et Monachi de Wederhal licite possint me vel hæredes meos per mobilia et immobilia destringere[3] tam intra villam de Cumquintin quam extra scilicet in boscis planis pascuis et pasturis sine contradictione mei vel hæredum meorum. Præterea sciendum quod idem Prior et Monachi de cætero poterint aliquam terram de terra prædicti Adæ filij Rogeri per ullam cartam quam habent de ipso Adam in Villa de Cumquintin exigere vel vendicare. In cujus rei Testimonium huic scripto sigillum meum apposui. Hijs Testibus Domino Alano de Lascels Milite[4],

77. [1] This moiety of the vill seems to have gone out of the Carliol family, and the two moieties to have remained separate, see J. Denton, *Cumberland*, p. 108.

[2] That is charter No. 76.

[3] This power should be noted to distrain on moveables and immoveables, both within and without the vill of Cumquintin, if the rent of 8s. were not paid.

[4] This is the Alan de Lascels who is a witness also with Robert de Warthwic to No. 47.

Roberto de Warthwic, Willelmo de Laversdale[5], Roberto de Tylloel, Willelmo de Joneby, et multis alijs[6].

78. CARTA EUDONIS FILII WILLELMI FILII EUDONIS DE KARLIOL DE OCTO SOLIDIS IN CUMQUINTIN.

OMNIBUS Sanctæ Matris Ecclesiæ filijs ad quos præsens scriptum pervenerit Eudo filius Willelmi filij Eudonis de Karlel Salutem in Domino sempiternam. Noveritis me dedisse concessisse et hac præsenti carta mea confirmasse Domino Abbati et Conventui Beatæ Mariæ Eboraci Priori et Monachis de Wederhale ibidem Deo servientibus octo solidos annui redditus in Villa de Cumquintin percipiendos de terris de Forlandes et Ofnames in eadem Villa Scilicet medietatem ad Festum Sancti Martini in yeme et aliam Medietatem ad Pentecosten. Quem quidem redditum prædicti Abbas et Conventus Prior et Monachi prius habuerunt de dono et Feoffeffamento Adæ filij Rogeri de Karliol de prædictis terris in Villa de Cumquintin. Tenendum et habendum eisdem Abbati et Conventui Priori et Monachis et eorum successoribus de me et hæredibus meis et assignatis libere et quiete et integre. Reddendo inde annuatim mihi et hæredibus meis aut assignatis meis unam Rosam[1] in die Nativitatis Sancti Johannis Baptistæ pro omnibus servicijs consuetudinibus actionibus et demandis. Ita quod liceat prædictis Abbati et Conventui Priori et Monachis districtionem in prædictis terris facere pro illo redditu octo solidorum suis terminis non soluto. Et si

---

[5] William de Laversdale was a witness to No. 194 in 1271, and see on No. 69.

[6] The date must be later than that of the preceding charter to which this grantor is a witness, therefore probably after 1260, but long prior to No. 190, even if that be the charter of this same Richard Mansel. This is also evidently prior to the next charter of the same 8s. rent, which is about the date of No. 190, 1285—98.

78. [1] In No. 76 the sum of 6d. was to be paid annually in lieu of services, customs &c., now a rose on June 24th is substituted.

contingat quod sufficiens districtio in prædictis terris
Forlandes et Oflandes fieri non poterit Volo et concedo
pro me et hæredibus meis et assignatis quibuscunque quod
prædicti Abbas et Conventus Prior et Monachi pro voluntate sua in feodo meo de Cumquintin ad quascunque manus
illud devenerit pro illo annuo redditu ut permittitur suis
terminis non soluto districtiones faciant et prout magis eis
expedit exequantur. Et Ego prædictus Eudo et hæredes
mei vel assignati prædictum redditum octo solidorum
Abbati et Conventui Priori et Monachis supradictis contra
omnes homines et fæminas warantizabimus acquietabimus
imperpetuum defendemus. In cujus rei Testimonium huic
scripto sigillum meum apposui. Hijs Testibus, Michaele
de Hardcla tunc Vicecomite Cumberlandiæ[2], Johanne de
Terriby[3], Thoma de Neuton[4] Coronatoribus[5] ejusdem

[2] Michael de Hardcla, or Hartcla, was Deputy Sheriff of Westmoreland in 1276 and 1277, and Sheriff of Cumberland in part of the
year 1285 and then until 1298. He is witness to two charters in this
Register dated 1291, 1292 (Nos. 199, 203). We learn from No. 234
that his wife's name was Joanna. He was a justice itinerant in
Cumberland in 1300. He was a brother of Andrew de Hardcla, Earl of
Carlisle and Lord Warden of the Marches, who was executed for high
treason in 1323. On hearing of the Earl's arrest, Michael de Hardcla,
who was at "le Peel de Heyhevede" (Highet or Highhead, in the
parish of Dalston), fled into Scotland with others of his friends (*Chron.
de Lanercost*, ed. Stevenson, p. 250). He appears to have had some
claim on the manor of Dalston, and a payment was made to him by
Bishop Irton as late as 1279 (see Nicolson and Burn, *History*, ii.
311). See also on Kirkandrews in No. 195. Harcla (later Hartly)
was a manor in the parish of Kirkby Stephen, long in the possession
of the de Hardcla family.

[3] John de Terriby and Thomas de Neuton were both knights (see
No. 110) and appear together as jurors in Inquisitions in Cumberland
e.g. in 1268 (*Inquis. p. m.* 52 Hen. III. No. 30), in 1280 with Sir Wm.
de Boyville and Alexander de Boulton, Mayor of Carlisle (*Inquis. p.
m.* 8 Edw. I. No. 81); John de Terriby was a juror in 1270 in an
Inquisition on the lands of the late Hellewysa widow of Richard de
Wernune (Vernun) under whom he held land (*Inquis. p. m.* 54 Hen.
III. No. 19); also in 1293 in Tynedale (*Inquis. p. m.* 21 Edw. I. No.

Comitatus, Waltero de Mulcaster[6], Willelmo de Bovilla[7]
Militibus, Roberto de Warthwic, Roberto de Crogelin[8],

13). He appears as a juror in the *Placita de Quo Waranto* in 1292
(Record Com. p. 115,sq.).

[4] Thomas de Neuton (see note above) was also a juror with John
de Stafholle in 1293 (*Inquis. p. m.* 21 Edw. I. No. 13). He appears
with John de Terriby in the *Placita de Quo War.* (see the ref. in the
note above).

[5] The Coroners were officials whose duty it was to watch the
interests of the Crown in several departments of business in the
county. At this time, they were elected by the County Court; see
Stubbs, *Constit. Hist.* ii. 209, 227; Jacob, *Law Dictionary*, s. v.

[6] Walter de Mulcaster, see on No. **111.**

[7] William de Bovilla or Boyvill. Several persons of this name
occur, one as early as the 12th century. This is Sir William, the
knight, who is frequently mentioned. He was one of the jurors in an
Inquisition regarding the lands held of the King by Helewysa, widow
of Eustace de Baylloll, in 1272 (*Inquis. p. m.* 56 Hen. III. No. 35).
In 1274, he was the King's escheator, and was accused of certain
malpractices with regard to the lands above mentioned. In 1291, he
was keeper of the Castles of Dumfries, Wygeton and Kirkcudbrith for
Edward I.; and that year he appears to have died, for he had been
dead some little time in March 1st, 1292 (*Calend. Doc. Scot.* ed. Bain,
ii. 3, 6, 39, 127, 138, also *Doc. illustrative of Hist. of Scot.* ed. J.
Stevenson, i. 241, 282). Frequent mention is made of him, with some
of his co-witnesses here, in 1292, in the *Placita de Quo Waranto*
(Record Com. p. 145 seq.). The family of Boyvill held the Barony of
Levington and a younger member Guido became by marriage Lord of
Thursby near Carlisle (J. Denton, *Cumberland*, p. 151). Sir William
de Boyvill held it at this time. He also held lands in Ainstapelit
(Ainstable) on the east of the Eden (J. Denton, p. 118) which are
referred to in No. **168,** and which his son John is said to have inherited.
In Bishop Halton's *Register* (MS. p. 39) there is the presentation by a
Sir W. de Boyvill, knt., probably the son of the witness here, in 1298,
of Mr R[ichard] de Abindon to the Rectory of Thoresby. In 1305,
the younger Sir William, having died, there was a remarkable Inquisition held *de Jure Patronatus* which is set out in the same Register
(MS. p. 90).

[8] Robert de Crogelin is also witness to No. **194,** which is dated
1271, and where Robert Tyllol is Seneschal of Gillesland; but in
1293, we find Robert holding this office, and witness to a grant under

Johanne de Staffoll[9], Willelmo de Warthwick, Willelmo de Neuby[10], Alano Armstrang et alijs[11].

79. CARTA ROBERTI DE LEVERISDALE FACTA MONACHIS DE WEDERHALE DE MORTUO BOSCO IN SILVA DE CUMQUINTIN.

OMNIBUS Christi fidelibus ad quorum notitiam præsens scriptum pervenerit Robertus de Leverisdale Salutem in Domino. Noverit universitas vestra me Divinæ Caritatis intuitu pro salute animæ meæ et pro salute animarum prædecessorum et successorum nostrorum dedisse concessisse et confirmasse Abbati Sanctæ Mariæ Eboraci et Conventui ejusdem loci et Monachis de Wederhale in puram et perpetuam Elemosinam quod ipsi Monachi habeant mortuum boscum imperpetuum de bosco de Cumquintin ad sustentationem domus de Wederhal et capiant ubi voluerint sine impedimento mei vel hæredum meorum. Et sciendum est quod ego Robertus et hæredes mei hanc Elemosinam prædictis Abbati et Conventui et Monachis de Wederhale imperpetuum defendemus et warantizabimus.

that date by the Priory of Lanercost (*Register of Lanercost*, MS. xii. 25, see also xiii. 17). He was a juror with John de Terriby in the Inquisition in 1270, mentioned in note 3 above. He appears in *Placita de Quo Warant.* with John de Staffoll in 1292 (Record Com. p. 118).

[9] John de Staffoll is mentioned in 1270 as having held a moiety of the vill of Staffol at 40*d.* under Helewysa widow of Richard de Wernune (*Inquis. p. m.* 54 Hen. III. No. 19) and as a juror in 1292 (*Inquis. p. m.* 21 Edward I. No. 13).

[10] William de Neuby was probably the son of Walter and Agnes de Neuby (see Nos. 143—145) who made a grant of land to the Priory by Nos. 146, 147; see notes there on the family. He appears as a juror in the *Placita de Quo War.* in 1292 (Record Com. p. 118) and is witness to a charter of Matilda de Multon dated 1292 in the *Register of Lanercost* (MS. xi. 6).

[11] There is much information concerning the witnesses about the date of the Sheriff, 1285 to 1298, and it does not seem that we can bring the date of the charter within closer limits.

Hijs Testibus Bartholomeo Priore, Magistro E. tunc Offici-
ali[1], Roberto filio W. tunc Vicecomite Carlioli, Johanne
Priore de Lanercost, Simone Decano Karleolensi, Waltero
Decano de Gillesland, Roberto de Castelcairoc, Roberto de
Carlaton, Symone de Ortun, Wardo[2] de Wigeton, Waltero
janitore de Wederhale, Symone Capellano, Johanne filio
Willelmi et alijs[3].

80. CARTA JOHANNIS FILII ROBERTI FACTA GAMELLO WERRERO DE QUINQUE RODIS TERRE ET UNO TOFTO IN CUMQUINTIN.

OMNIBUS ad quos presens scriptum pervenerit Johannes
filius Roberti[1] et Matilda sponsa sua Salutem.   Sciatis nos
concessisse dedisse et hac nostra presenti carta confirmasse
Gamello Werrero et hæredibus suis vel suis assignatis quinque rodas terræ in Cumquintin et Toftum unum in quo
manet, Scilicet unam acram cum tofto in Occidentali parte
terræ quam tenemus de Hospitali Sancti Nicholai de
Karliol[2] et unam rodam ad caput dictæ acræ terræ in parte
Aquilonali.   Tenendum de nobis et hæredibus nostris in
feodo et hæreditate libere quiete et integre cum omnibus
libertatibus pertinentijs et aisiamentis illi terræ pertinentibus Reddendo inde annuatim nobis et hæredibus nostris
duodecim denarios argenti sex ad Pentecosten et sex ad
Festum Sancti Martini pro omnibus servicijs consuetudinibus et exactionibus.   Et nos et hæredes nostri warantizabimus prædictam terram quietam de panagio et mulcta
et de omnibus alijs servicijs per prædictam firmam præfato
Gamello et hæredibus suis vel suis assignatis contra omnes

---

79. [1] E. is an error for G. Gervase de Louther, nearly all these
witnesses also attest the deed of Eudo de Carliol, No. 75.

[2] Wardo is an error for Odardo.

[3] From the Sheriff, the date of this charter is 1223—29; see No.
75.

80. [1] Robert de Cumquintin, see No. 82.

[2] On the Hospital of S. Nicholas, see No. 95.

homines imperpetuum. Testibus Johanne Capellàno de Sancto Nicholao[3], Roberto de Waelpol, Roberto de Aubredam, Radulpho de Kirkebride, Johanne Stilphot[4], Johanne de Agullunby, Simone de Racĩ., Alano de Bubcherby, Willelmo filio Agnetis et alijs[5].

81. Quieta clamatio Johannis filij Gamelli Verrari de 5 rodis terræ et tofto in Cumquintin.

OMNIBUS Christi fidelibus ad quos præsens scriptum pervenerit Johannes filius Gamelli Verrarij[1] de Cumquintin Salutem in Domino. Noverit universitas vestra me Divinæ Caritatis intuitu pro salute animæ meæ et Antecessorum meorum dedisse remisisse et de me et hæredibus meis imperpetuum quietum clamasse Deo et Ecclesiæ Sanctæ Mariæ Eboraci et Domui Sanctæ Trinitatis Sanctique Constantini de Wederhal et Monachis ibidem Deo servientibus totum jus et clamium quod habui vel habere potui vel in posterum habere potero in illis quinque rodis terræ in territorio de Cumquintin cum Tofto quas Gamellus pater meus habuit de dono Johannis filij Roberti et Matildæ uxoris suæ cum pertinentijs in eadem villa. Tenendum et habendum dictæ Ecclesiæ Sanctæ Mariæ Eboraci et Monachis de Wederhal in liberam et perpetuam Elemosinam cum omnibus libertatibus aisiamentis communis et alijs liberis pertinentijs ad prædictam terram pertinentibus intra villam et extra Reddendo inde annuatim Johanni filio Roberti et hæredibus suis duodecim denarios

[3] On John the Chaplain, see No. 95, where he is a party to the deed and is styled *Capellanus Rector.*

[4] John Stilphot is the same as John Stelfot in No. 61, see the note there; a witness in 1241 and 1247.

[5] With John Stilphot and a date about 1240 or a little later, the other witnesses would seem to agree.

81. [1] Gamell Verrar, or Werrer, as he is called in No. 80, referring to the same land.

argenti scilicet medietatem ad Pentecosten et medietatem
ad Festum Sancti Martini in yeme pro omnibus servicijs
consuetudinibus exactionibus et secularibus demandis Et
ut hæc mea donatio et quieta clamatio imperpetuum robur
optineat sigilli mei impressione presens scriptum roboravi.
Hijs Testibus Domino Thoma de'Miltona[2], Domino Roberto
Daniel[3] tunc Vicecomite Cumberlandiæ, Domino W. de
Vallibus, Domino W. de Warthwic Militibus, Magistro
S. de Sancto Nicholao, Adam Armstrang, Willelmo de
Korkeby[4], Roberto de Warthwic, Johanne Stilfot et alijs[5].

82. CARTA JOHANNIS FILIJ ROBERTI DE CUM-QUINTIN FACTA MONACHIS DE WEDERHAL DE ANNUO REDDITU 12*d*.

OMNIBUS Christi fidelibus ad quos presens scriptum
pervenerit Johannes filius Roberti de Cumquintin et
Matilda sponsa sua salutem æternam in Domino. Noveritis
nos dedisse concessisse confirmasse et hac presenti carta
nostra quietum clamasse de nobis et hæredibus nostris
imperpetuum in puram et perpetuam elemosinam Deo et
Ecclesiæ Sancte Marie Eboraci et Domui Sanctæ Trinitatis de Wederhal et Monachis ibidem Deo servientibus
pro salute animarum nostrarum et antecessorum et success-

---

[2] From the period of the charter, this is probably the second
Thomas de Multon (see note 4 on No. **47**) who attests No. **189**, with
several of the same witnesses.

[3] There is no Sheriff, or Pro-sheriff, of the name in the lists; but
there is some confusion about this time, and there is no return for the
years 1257 and 1258 when he may have acted.

[4] Probably the son of William son of Roger de Corkeby; see note 2
on No. **64**, where there is a reference to him with his father in 1247;
they occur together in No. **178**.

[5] The date of this charter must be later than the last, and William
de Vallibus (see No. **61**) and other witnesses agree with a date between
1250 and 1260; and not improbably the date may be the 1257—8
mentioned above in note 3.

orum nostrorum redditum duodecim denariorum[1] annuorum quem Gamellus Verrerus de Cumquintin nobis reddere consuevit pro illis quinque rodis terræ quam idem Gamellus tenuit de nobis in Villa de Cumquintin prout continetur in cartis dicti Gamelli et Johannis filij sui quas dicti Monachi de Wederhal habent penes se. Tenendum et Habendum de nobis et hæredibus nostris imperpetuum libere quiete pacifice integre et honorifice sicut aliquis redditus liberius dari poterit vel elemosinari. Ego vero prædictus Johannes et Matilda uxor mea et hæredes nostri dictum redditum duodecim denariorum dictis Domui et Monachis de Wederhal contra omnes homines imperpetuum warantizabimus acquietabimus et defendemus. In cujus rei Testimonium presens scriptum sigillorum nostrorum munimine roboravimus. Hijs Testibus Domino Willelmo de Karliol[2], Domino Willelmo de Warthwic, Roberto filio suo, Willelmo de Laversdale, Willelmo de Korkeby, Adam filio Rogeri[3], Willielmo de Agullunby, Johanne Stelfot, Thoma de Hobridteby[4] et alijs[5].

83. QUIETA CLAMATIO WILLELMI FILIJ JOHANNIS FILIJ ROBERTI DE CUMQUINTIN FACTA MONACHIS DE WEDERHALE DE REDDITU 12 DENARIORUM IN CUMQUINTIN.

UNIVERSIS Christi fidelibus præsens præscriptum visuris vel audituris Willelmus filius Johannis filij Roberti de Cumquintin Salutem in Domino sempiternam. Noverit universitas vestra me pro me et hæredibus meis relaxasse et

---

82. [1] The 12*d.* referred to in Nos. **80, 81.**

[2] William de Karliol is the son of Eudo de Karliol (No. **76**).

[3] Adam son of Roger is probably the son of Roger de Karliol (No. **76**).

[4] The same as Thomas de Hubricceby in No. **76**. This was one of the various old forms of the place-name Upperby, near Carlisle.

[5] The date must be rather later than Nos. **80, 81,** and probably about 1260.

imperpetuum quietum clamasse Domui Sanctæ Trinitatis de Wederhal et Monachis ibidem Deo servientibus totum jus et clamium quod habui vel aliquo modo habere potui in annuo redditu duodecim denariorum in villa de Cumquintin quem quidem redditum Johannes filius Roberti pater meus et Matilda sponsa sua Mater mea dictæ Domui dederunt et per cartam suam confirmaverunt Ita quod Ego Willelmus filius Johannis nec hæredes mei nec aliquis nomine meo in dictum redditum annuum jus sui vel clamium poterint de cetero vendicare. Et ut hæc mea relaxatio et quieta clamatio robur majoris optineat firmitatis præsens scriptum sigilli mei munimine roboravi. Hijs Testibus Domino Gilberto de Curwen tunc Vicecomite Karlioli[1], Domino Roberto de Laferete[2], Domino Johanne de Terriby, Roberto de Warthwic, Roberto de Tyllol, Roberto de Castlecairoc et alijs[3].

84. QUIETA CLAMATIO WALTERI JANITORIS DE WEDERHAL FACTA MONACHIS DE EADEM DE 4 ACRIS TERRÆ IN CAMPO EJUSDEM VILLÆ.

83. [1] Gilbert de Curwen was Sheriff of Cumberland from 1278 to 1282. Little is known of him. In the *Register of Holm Cultram* (quoted in Dugdale, *Monasticon*, v. 597) his son Gilbert speaks of the charters of Gilbert his father and Patrick, his grandfather, who was the son of Thomas son of Gospatric, son of Orm. A full account of the family is given by W. Jackson in the *Transactions of the Cumberland Archæol. Soc.* v. p. 181 sq. In 1292, Thomas as defendant in a plea affirmed that his name was de Culewen, not de Currewenne (*Assize Rolls for Cumb.* 20 Edw. I. m. 12).

[2] Robert de Laferete, or de la Ferte, or de la Feritate, was a knight (see No. **111**) and a son of the younger Radulph de la Ferte (see note 4 on No. **43**). He appears in 1266 as having a safe conduct to go to the Court, as well as Robert de Tillol and Richard de Castelkaroc (*Patent Rolls*, 50 Hen. III. m. 18); also as one of 4 knights jurors in 1292 in the *Placita de Quo War.* (Record Com. p. 115 *b*). In 1296, as Lord of Beaumont, *apud Bellum Montem*, he presented Elias de Thirlewall to the Church there (*Register of Bp Halton*, MS. p. 27).

[3] From the Sheriff, the date of the charter is between 1278 and 1282.

UNIVERSIS Christi fidelibus ad quorum noticiam præsens scriptum pervenerit Walterus janitor de Wederhale Salutem eternam in Domino. Noverit universitas vestra me de assensu et voluntate Evæ uxoris meæ et hæredum meorum dedisse remisisse et quietas clamasse imperpetuum Deo et Ecclesiæ Sancte Trinitatis et Sancti Constantini de Wederhal et Monachis ibidem Deo servientibus quatuor acras terræ[1] in campo de Wederhal illas videlicet quas Johannes coquus aliquando de me tenuit. Habendas et Tenendas imperpetuum solutas et quietas de me et hæredibus meis absque omni servicio et calumpnia. Ego vero et hæredes mei prædictas quatuor acras terræ prædictis Monachis contra omnes homines warantizabimus imperpetuum. Et ut hoc scriptum meæ donationis et quietæ clamationis firmum sit [et] stabile imperpetuum eidem sigillum meum apposui una cum sigillo uxoris meæ. Hijs Testibus Simone sacerdote, Willelmo filio Rogeri[2], Roberto filio Willelmi, Johanne de Agulunby, Henrico Coquo, Johanne filio Willelmi, Roberto de Paris, Radulpho clerico, Hamelino Nepote Prioris tunc temporis, Suano de Agulunby et multis alijs[3].

85. QUIETA CLAMATIO JOHANNIS FILIJ WILLELMI DE HERM̃INE DE UNO TOFTO ET 4 ACRIS TERRÆ IN WEDERHALE.

UNIVERSIS Christi fidelibus præsentem cartam inspecturis vel audituris Johannes filius Willelmi de Erm̃ine Salutem æternam in Domino. Noverit universitas vestra me pro salute animarum Prædecessorum et Successorum meorum dedisse remisisse et quietas clamasse imperpetuum de me et hæredibus meis Deo et Ecclesiæ Sanctæ Trinitatis Sanctique Constantini de Wederhal et Monachis

---

84. [1] The same four acres in Wetherhal plain mentioned in No. 64.

[2] On William son of Roger, see No. 64, where the witnesses are practically the same.

[3] The date will be the same as No. 64, about 1239.

ibidem Deo servientibus triginta pedes in latitudine de tofto quem Pater meus tenuit in Villa de Wederhal cum tota longitudine illius tofti ad ædificandum ad commodum suum pro libitu suo et quatuor acras terræ[1] in Campo de Wederhal illas videlicet quas Johannes coquus de Patre meo tenuit. Tenendas et habendas imperpetuum quietas ab omni consuetudine et exactione ad me vel hæredes meos pertinente. Et Ego et hæredes mei totam prædictam terram contra omnes homines prædictis Monachis warantizabimus acquietabimus et defendemus imperpetuum. Et ut hoc scriptum meæ donationis remissionis et quietæ clamationis firmum et stabile sit imperpetuum eidem sigillum meum apposui. Hijs Testibus Willelmo filio Rogeri, Simone Capellano de Wederhale, Johanne de Agulunby, Johanne filio Willelmi, Johanne Coquo, Henrico Coquo, Hamelino Nepote Prioris, Suano de Agulunby et multis alijs.

86. QUIETA CLAMATIO WALTERI JANITORIS DE WEDERHAL FACTA MONACHIS EJUSDEM DE UNO TOFTO IN WEDERHAL, ET 1 ACRA TERRÆ, ET DE 2 BOVATIS TERRÆ IN NEUBY.

UNIVERSIS Christi fidelibus ad quorum notitiam præsens scriptum pervenerit Walterus janitor de Wederhal Salutem. Noverit universitas vestra me pro salute animæ meæ et Prædecessorum et Successorum meorum dedisse remisisse et quietas clamasse imperpetuum de me et hæredibus meis Deo et Ecclesiæ Sanctæ Trinitatis et Sancti Constantini de Wederhal et Monachis ibidem Deo servientibus illum toftum[1] in Villa de Wederhal quem emi de Johanne de Ermine et unam acram terræ in territorio ejusdem Villæ. Habendas et tenendas in perpetuum quietas de me et

---

85. [1] The same land as in Nos. 64, 84, where see on John Hermine or Ermine. He had sold this toft to Walter the porter, who quit-claimed it to the Priory, see No. 86.

86. [1] The toft mentioned in No. 85.

hæredibus meis. Et Ego et hæredes mei totam prædictam terram prædictis Monachis contra omnes homines warantizabimus acquietabimus et defendemus. Sciendum est autem quod Ego Walterus janitor dedi predictis Monachis cum corpore meo duas bovatas terræ cum pertinentijs in territorio de Neuby² cum tofto et crofto illas videlicet quas emi de Ricardo de Neuby. Habendas et tenendas imperpetuum quietas et solutas de hæredibus meis ex quo corpus meum tradiderint sepulturæ. Has vero prædictas duas bovatas terræ cum pertinentijs Ego et hæredes mei prædictis Monachis warantizabimus imperpetuum. Hijs Testibus Simone Capellano de Wederhale, Willelmo filio Rogeri, Johanne de Agulunby, Johanne filio Willelmi, Johanne Coquo, Hamelino nepote Prioris, Suano de Aguluneby et multis alijs.

87. Carta Beatricis uxoris Roberti de Neuby facta Alano filio suo de tota terra sua quam habuit in Wederhale.

Omnibus Christi fidelibus ad quos præsens scriptum pervenerit Beatrix quondam uxor Roberti de Neuby[1] Salutem. Noveritis me in libera mea viduitate dedisse concessisse et hac præsenti carta mea confirmasse Alano filio meo pro homagio et servicio suo totam terram meam in Villa de Wederhal cum tofto et crofto et alijs pertinentijs quam habui de dono Agnetis matris meæ in eadem villa. Tenendam et habendam sibi et hæredibus suis vel

---

² This is the Neuby, or Newby, which was in the Barony of Linstock and in the parish of Irthington, about 3 miles north of Wetherhal on the east of the Eden, and on the north bank of the river Irthing. Grants in this Neuby were confirmed by the Bishops of Carlisle as Lords of the Barony, see on No. **94**, note 1. But this property is confirmed to the Priory by Robert de Vallibus in No. **193**. J. Denton (*Cumberland*, pp. 135, 157) is in great confusion about this place.

87. [1] Robert de Neuby occurs in No. **59** in the year 1230 or 1231: from the witnesses, he belonged to Neuby in Morland. Alan his son is called "*Clericus*" in No. **90**.

suis assignatis libere et pacifice cum omnibus pertinentijs
et libertatibus dictæ terræ pertinentibus infra Villam et
extra Reddendo inde annuatim Ecclesiæ de Wederhale et
Monachis ibidem Deo servientibus quatuor solidos scilicet
medietatem ad Pentecosten et medietatem ad Festum
Sancti Martini in yeme Et mihi et hæredibus meis vel
meis assignatis unum denarium die Natali Domini super
eandem terram pro omnibus servicijs et demandis. Ego
Beatrix et hæredes mei vel mei assignati totam prænominatam terram cum pertinentijs per prædictum servicium
dicto Alano et hæredibus suis vel suis assignatis contra
omnes warantizabimus imperpetuum. Et ut haec mea
donatio et concessio stabilis permaneat huic scripto sigillum meum apposui. Hijs Testibus, Domino Ricardo de
Rotomago tunc Priore de Wederhal[2], Dominis Johanne
de Langecost, Thoma de Walmegaꝧ, Roberto de Ripon et
Thoma de Scirburn Monachis, Ricardo Mansel, Thoma de
Rothewelle et Roberto Mynot servientibus Domini Prioris,
Johanne Stelphot, Roberto Pincerna et Willelmo Tutzeɱ[3]
et alijs[4].

88. QUIETA CLAMATIO THOMÆ FILIJ ROBERTI DE NEUBY FACTA ALANO FRATRI SUO DE TOTA TERRA QUAM HABUIT IN VILLA DE WEDERHALE.

OMNIBUS Christi fidelibus ad quos præsens scriptum
pervenerit Thomas filius Roberti de Neuby[1] Salutem.
Noverit universitas vestra me confirmasse et quietum

---

[2] Richard de Rotomago, or de Rouen, was Prior of Wederhal in
1251; see Appendix E.

[3] William Tutzemer or Tussezemer as in No. 53.

[4] The date of the charter would probably be 1250—60.

88.   [1] Thomas son of Robert de Neuby granted a toft in Neuby to
William his son, a witness here; the deed is witnessed by Thomas de
Musgrave, also by Robert son of Adam de Slegill, Gilbert de Slegill
and William his brother, and William son of William de Neuby; it is
among the Levens Hall MSS. see the 10th Report Hist. MSS. Com.
(iv.) p. 324.

clamasse Alano fratri meo totum jus et clamium quod
habeo vel habere potero in tota illa terra cum pertinentijs
quam dictus Alanus tenet in Villa de Wederhale de dono
Beatricis Matris meæ prout carta testatur quam habet de
dono dictæ Beatricis Matris meæ in libera viduitate Matris
meæ dicto Alano data et concessa. Tenendam sibi vel
cui assignare voluerit libere et quiete Ita quod nec Ego
nec hæredes mei nec aliquis per me vel pro me aliquid jus
vel clamium in dicta terra cum pertinentijs de cetero
exigere poterimus. In cujus rei Testimonium huic scripto
sigillum meum apposui. Hijs Testibus Domino Ricardo
de Aquila[2] tunc Vicario de Morland, Adam de Selegile[3],
Willelmo de Neuby, Thoma de Aselakeby, Roberto Pincerna, Johanne Stelfot de Wederhal, Ricardo Mansel et
Thoma de Rothewell servientibus Priori de Wederhal et
alijs[4].

89. QUIETA CLAMATIO ADÆ FILIJ RICARDI DE
NEUTON FACTA ALANO FILIO ROBERTI DE NEUBY.

OMNIBUS Christi fidelibus ad quos præsens scriptum

---

[2] Richard de Aquila is witness with Thomas de Musegrave, Sheriff
(deputy for Robert de Veteriponte in his minority) in No. 205.

[3] Adam de Selegile, or Slegyle, was forester of Stanemore in Westmoreland until the death of John de Veteriponte in 1241 (see on No. 204
and Nicolson and Burn, *History*, i. 578). The family held the manor of
Slegill which was in the parish of Morland and adjoining Neuby in that
parish. A messuage in Selegile was granted to the Priory by Gilbert
de Sleygile and confirmed by his widow (see on No. 220). Another
Adam appears with Margaret daughter of Gilbert, as late as 1292, in
the *Placita de Quo War.* (Record Com. p. 788) defending their rights
in Thybeya (Tebay); but he must be of a later generation, for Adam
de Slegile is witness with Thomas de Aslachby, who attests this deed,
to No. 201 whose date is probably 1231—40 (see there). See also the
Levens Hall MS. referred to above, where the present Adam and his
son Robert (No. 207) are mentioned, with Gilbert and William, also
William de Neuby, probably the son of the grantor.

[4] The date would probably be a little later than No. 87 or about
the same time.

pervenerit Adam filius Ricardi de Neuthona[1] Salutem in Domino. Noverit universitas vestra quod cum motum esset placitum per Breve Domini Regis de recto in Curia Domini Abbatis Eboraci apud Wederhal inter me peten-tem et Alanum filium Roberti de Neuby defendentem Ego Adam totum jus et clamium quo aliquo jure habui vel habere potui in dicta terra cum pertinentijs dicto Alano et hæredibus suis vel cuicunque dictam terram assignare voluerit Concessi et quiete clamavi de me et hæredibus meis imperpetuum Ita scilicet quod nec Ego nec hæredes mei nec aliquis pro me vel per me jus vel clamium in dicta terra de cetero exigere poterimus pro ista vero quieta clamatione dictus Alanus mihi quadraginta solidos argenti pacavit. In cujus rei Testimonium huic scripto sigillum meum apposui. Hijs Testibus Domino Henrico de Tutes-biri[2] tunc Priore de Wederhal, Domino Radulpho de

89. [1] Adam de Neuthona, or de Neuton, is witness to No. 137 which dates 1236—47. His father Richard lived in the time of King John, and was a juror in 1210 in an inquisition often referred to (*Coram Rege Rolls*, 11 Joh. No. 41, m. 9). They held the manor of Newton, or West Newton, in the parish of Bromfield (see Nicolson and Burn, *Hist.* ii. 163). Adam appears in a Final Concord between Lambert and Alan de Muleton in 1230, as holding land in Ormesby (*Feet of Fines, Cumb.* 15 Hen. III. No. 12) and as one of the justices of a special assize at Carlisle in 1237 (*Patent Rolls*, 21 Hen. III. m. 8 d.). He confirmed a grant of his grandfather Adam son of Odard to the Abbey of Holm Cultram (*Regist. Holm Cultram*, Harleian MSS. 1181, p. 386). The manor of Grinsdale near to Carlisle appears to have come by marriage in part to Richard de Neuton, and part to William le Sor (J. Denton, *Cumberland*, p. 81). In the *Register of Lanercost* (MS. v. 4) we have a grant to that Priory by Dominus Richard de Neuton of the Church of S. Kentigern of Grenesdale in the time of John, Prior of Carlisle (the end of the 12th century), and Adam de Neuton is witness to several charters of William le Sor granting lands in Grenesdale (MS. v. 9—15). Richard de Neuton, son of Adam, made a convention with Henry, Abbot of Holm Cultram in 1262 (*Register*, Harleian MSS. 1181, p. 387). He died in 1267, and his son William then did homage for his lands (*Fine Rolls*, 52 Hen. III. m. 12, ed. Roberts, ii. 462).

[2] Prior Henry de Tutesbiri is a party to No. 66 which is dated 1257.

Notingham, Ricardo Buche[3], Adam de Langerig, Laurentio dicto janitore, Gilberto de Schalermanoc, Thoma de Grimeston tunc serviente Domini Prioris et alijs[4].

90. QUIETA CLAMATIO ALANI DE NEUBY FACTA MONACHIS DE WEDERHAL DE TOTA TERRA SUA IN EADEM.

OMNIBUS hoc scriptum visuris vel audituris Alanus de Neuby[1] Clericus Salutem. Noverit vestra universitas me pro salute animæ meæ et animarum Patris mei et Matris meæ et Parentum meorum reddidisse et omnino de me et hæredibus meis quietam clamasse Abbati Sanctæ Mariæ Eboraci et Monachis suis apud Wederhal Deo servientibus totam terram meam cum Tenemento quam tenui de eisdem Abbate et Monachis in Villa de Wederhal cum omnibus aisiamentis prædictis terræ et tenemento pertinentibus infra Villam et extra. In cujus rei Testimonium presenti scripto sigillum meum apposui. Hijs Testibus Willelmo de Agu-lunby, Johanne de Roƀby, Willelmo de Hederesford, Stephano de Porta, Roberto de Warthwic, Johanne Armstrang, Johanne Caperun de Corkeby et alijs[2].

91. QUIETA CLAMATIO WILLELMI DE AGUILLUNBY FACTA MONACHIS DE WEDERHAL DE UNO PARI CIRO-TECARUM.

OMNIBUS Sanctæ Matris Ecclesiæ filijs hoc scriptum

---

[3] Richard Buche was one of the jurors in an Inquisition in 1268 with Adam de Langerig concerning the bounds of Penrith, there called "freeman of the County of Cumberland" (*Inquis. p. m.* 52 Hen. III. No. 30).

[4] The date of this charter may be a little later than the two preceding, but is probably from 1250 to 1260.

90. [1] Alan de Neuby, the son of Robert whose widow Beatrix made the grant in No. 87, here grants the same land to the Priory.

[2] The witnesses to this charter are almost identical with those to No. 68 which was after the date 1257—59. That agrees with the present charter, which must be not long after the three preceding, 1250—60.

visuris vel audituris Willelmus de Aguillunby[1] Salutem in
Domino sempiternam. Noveritis me concessisse dedisse et
hoc presenti scripto confirmasse ac omnino de me et
hæredibus meis imperpetuum quietum clamasse Simoni[2]
Abbati et Conventui Monasterij Sanctæ Mariæ Eboraci ac
Prioratui Sanctæ Trinitatis de Wederhal totum jus et
clamium quod habui vel habere potui in annuo redditu
unius paris cirotecarum albarum quas Walterus de Mitoñ
mihi debuit vel annuatim reddere consuevit. Tenendum
et Habendum dictis Abbati et Conventui Prioratui et
eorum successoribus universis in liberam puram et perpetuam Elemosinam quiete et pacifice Ita quod nec Ego
Willelmus vel hæredes mei nec aliquis ex parte nostra
aliquid jus vel clamium in prædicto annuo redditu aliquo
casu contingente de cetero exigere vel vendicare poterimus
imperpetuum. In cujus rei Testimonium presenti scripto
sigillum meum apposui. Hijs Testibus Roberto de
Warthwic, Willelmo filio suo, Ricardo de Brakenthwait[3],
Ricardo de Fenton, Roberto de Hedresford, Roberto de
Yupton[4], Stephano de Porta et alijs[5].

92. Finis in Curia Domini Regis inter Johan-

91. [1] William de Aguillunby was the son of Alan, see on No. **68**.

[2] Simon de Warwick was Abbot of S. Mary's at York from July
1258 to July 1296. He wrote a continuation of the history of the
Abbey; see Dugdale, *Monast.* iii. 538. He is a party to No. **234**, but
evidently at a later date than the present charter.

[3] Richard de Brakenthwayt is witness to Nos. **111**, **190** with
Michael de Hartcla, Sheriff, from 1285—1298. He is witness to two
charters of the daughters of Michael del Dale granting land in
Ainstapell (Ainstable) to the Priory of Lanercost (*Regist.* MS. iv.
9, 10).

[4] Yupton is probably an error for Robert de Scupton, a witness to
No. **61** *et al.*

[5] The date of the charter lies between 1258 and 1296; the witnesses
seem to point rather to the later period: Robert de Warthwic, we know,
appears in 1259 and 1292.

NEM FILIUM ELMINE ET ROBERTUM ABBATEM EBORACI
DE DUABUS BOVATIS TERRÆ IN WEDERHALE.

HÆC est finalis Concordia facta in Curia Domini Regis
apud Cumberland in crastino clausi Pasche[1] Anno Regni
Regis Henrici filij Regis Johannis decimo nono coram
Rogero Berteram[2] Roberto de Ros[3] Willelmo de Eboraco[4]
Ranulpho filio Henrici et Thoma filio Johannis[5] Justiciarijs
itinerantibus et alijs Domini Regis fidelibus tunc ibi
præsentibus inter Johannem filium Elmine petentem et

92. [1] The morrow of the close of Easter, or the Monday following
the Sunday after Easter; in 1235 this was April 16th. *Clausum Pasche*
is the octave of Easter, sometimes called Low Sunday, or *Quasimodo*,
from the beginning of the Introit *Quasi modo geniti*, see *Sarum
Missal*, ed. Dickinson, col. 385.

[2] Roger Bertram was also justice itinerant in 1227 in Cumberland,
see No. **174**. He was an important person in the reign of Henry III.
We hear of him in the time of King John (1211—12) as being excused
scutage (*Pipe Rolls for Northumberland*, 13 Joh.). In 1220 he was
one of those who with Hubert de Burgo, chief justiciary, gave their
charters of good faith to Alexander II. of Scotland on the part of King
Henry III. (Rymer, *Fœdera*, new ed. i. 160); and in 1229 he was one of
those appointed to conduct Alexander to meet the King at York; and
again in 1235 to conduct Alexander and his Queen to London (Rymer,
Fœdera, new ed. i. 221). He was a witness to the famous agreement
between the two Kings at York in 1239, in the presence of the Cardinal
Legate Otto (*Fœdera*, i. 234). He appears to have lived until about
1263, when his widow Laderana laid claim to certain lands before the
King's Court (*Coram Rege Rolls*, 47 Hen. III. No. 120, m. 8 d.).

[3] See on No. **44**. This is not the second Robert there mentioned,
Robert of Hamlake who died in 1226—27, but his son, Robert de Ros
of Werke.

[4] William de Eboraco, often called Provost of Beverley, appears
in 1231—32 as witness to a grant of Henry III. to Hubert de Burgo,
Earl of Kent, and Margaret his wife, on a yearly rent of a pair of gilt
spurs; Bishop Walter of Carlisle is also a witness (*Calend. Doc. Scot.*
ed. Bain, i. 211). He is again a witness, with the same Bishop, in
1242, to the grant of Henry III. to Alexander of Scotland of the five
manors in Cumberland (see on Scotby in No. **14**).

[5] The same who was Sheriff of Cumberland in 1230—31; see
note 8 on No. **56**.

Robertum Abbatem[6] Sanctæ Mariæ de Eboraco tenentem de duabus bovatis terræ cum pertinentijs in Wederhal unde assisa mortis Antecessorum[7] summonita fuit inter eos in eadem Curia scilicet quod predictus Johannes recognoscat totam predictam terram cum pertinentijs esse jus ipsius Abbatis[8] et Ecclesiæ suæ de Eboraco. Et pro hac recognitione fine et concordia idem Abbas concessit prædicto Johanni totam prædictam terram cum pertinentijs. Et præterea idem Abbas concessit prædicto Johanni de Tenemento quod Margareta filia Elmine tenuit in eadem Villa quatuor solidos per annum. Habendam et Tenendam eidem Johanni et hæredibus suis de prædicto Abbate et Successoribus suis et Ecclesia sua de Eboraco imperpetuum, Reddendo inde annuatim octo solidos sterlingorum ad duos terminos anni scilicet medietatem ad Pentecosten et alteram medietatem ad Festum Sancti Martini. Et sciendum quod idem Johannes et hæredes sui cariabunt bladum prædicti Abbatis et Successorum suorum de Wederhale una die in Autumpno et invenient unum hominem ad metendum una die in Autumpno et arabunt una die per annum et cariabunt meremium[9] stagni et molendini de Wederhale et reparabunt molendinum et stagnum de

[6] This was Robert de Longo Campo, Abbot from 1197 to 1239; see on No. 10.

[7] The "Assize of Mort d'ancestor" was an action by which a person who alleged that he was the heir of an "ancestor," being his father, mother, uncle, aunt, brother or sister, in respect of a freehold of which that "ancestor," as he alleged, died seized after a period variously limited, claimed possession of his inheritance against one by whose alleged entry into it he had been prevented from taking possession (Haydon). If the "ancestor" were more distantly related, a different writ had to be obtained.

[8] That is his right as lord of the manor. This is an important document as showing the manorial customs in the manor of Wetherhal, in which there is no mention of fishery rights. On these *liberi* or freemen, see the reffs. on the word *Manerium* in No. 1, note 4.

[9] *Meremium*, Low Latin, "timber," contracted from *materiamen*.

Wederhale cum alijs hominibus de prædicta villa de
Wederhale Et molent ad molendinum dicti Abbatis et
successorum suorum de Wederhal ad tertium decimum
vas et dabunt pannagium sicut alij liberi homines de prædicta villa de Wederhale.   Nec idem Johannes vel hæredes
sui aliquid clamare vel exigere poterint in assarcis[10] dicti
Abbatis et Successorum suorum de Wederhal factis vel
imposterum faciendis occasione dicti Tenementi Salva
tamen eidem Johanni et hæredibus suis communia Pasturæ
in stipulis et warettis[11].   Et hæc Concordia[12] facta fuit
presente prædicta Margareta et agnoscente se debere prædictum redditum quatuor solidorum per annum.   Et
sciendum est quod si prædictus Johannes vel hæredes sui
implacitentur de prædicta terra vel de prædicto redditu
quatuor solidorum per annum aliquo tempore imposterum,
dictus Abbas nec Successores sui prædictam terram nec
prædictum redditum prædicto Johanni nec hæredibus sui
tenentur warantizare[12].

93. CARTA H. DE THEBAY DE REDDITU 12ᵈ. PRO TRIBUS ACRIS TERRÆ EXTRA MUROS KARLIOLI.

OMNIBUS Sanctæ Matris Ecclesiæ filijs ad quorum
noticiam presens scriptum pervenerit H. de Thebay
æternam in Domino Salutem.   Noverit universitas vestra

---

[10] *Assartum,* or *essartum,* is "a clearing" grubbed up in a forest,
from O. French *assarter, essarter.*

[11] *Warettum,* or *warectum,* "a fallow" or a "stubble" to be ploughed
up next spring; here with stipulis means "fallows and stubbles."
Terra novalis seu requieta, quia alteriis annis requiescit.—Ducange,
Gloss.   These are the only claims allowed to the customary tenant by
reason of the said tenement.

[12] There was a similar assize concluded on the same day, before
the same justices, concerning 60 acres of wood in Inglewood Forest,
between Thomas de Lascelles and Gilbert, Abbot of Holm Cultram
(*Feet of Fines,* 19 Hen. III. No. 22, *Cumberland*).

[13] The date is Monday after 1st Sunday after Easter, or April 16th,
1235.

me tenere de Abbate et Conventu Sanctæ Mariæ Eborum
et de Domo Sanctæ Trinitatis et Sancti Constantini de
Wederhal tres acras terræ extra muros Karlioli versus
Orientem quæ jacent inter vetus Castellarium et terram
Petri Tillel quas Richer de Levingtun[1] prædictæ Ecclesiæ
dedit in Elemosinam. Pro hijs autem tribus acris terræ
Ego H. et hæredes mei reddemus annuatim duodecim
denarios Domui de Wederhal ad Pentecosten.   Et ad
prædictum redditum fideliter solvendum et ad terminum
prædictum Ego H. me et Hæredes meos et assignatos
Sacramento corporaliter prestito obligavi et insuper præ-
sentem cartam sigillo meo signatam Monachis de Wederhal
tradidi. Hijs Testibus B. Priore Karleoli[2], Magistro G. de
Louther[3] Officiali, R. filio Willelmi[4], Willielmo Clerico,
Johanne filio Willelmi, Johanne de Agluneby, Waltero
Janitore, Richardo Præposito et multis alijs[5].

94. Carta Ricardi filij Ricardi filij Trute de Jº tofto extra Portam Bochardi de Karleolo.

· Omnibus Sanctæ Matris Ecclesiæ filijs tam præsentibus quam futuris Ricardus filius Ricardi filij Trute[1]

93. [1] Of the family, see note 5 on No. 54; Richer was the great-
grandfather of Richard and grandfather of Adam de Levington, and
was seized of the property in the time of Henry II.

[2] Bartholomew, see note 4 on No. 20. He died in 1231.

[3] Gervase de Louther, see note 3 on No. 21; here "Official," and
therefore probably between 1223 and 1229—30.

[4] This is probably Robert who with John son of William, also a
witness, was a son of William son of Odard of Corkby.

[5] The date of the charter will be between 1223 and 1230.

94. [1] Richard son of Richard son of Trute was the nephew of
Robert son of Troite, Sheriff of Carlisle, 1158—73, and the son of his
brother Richard (see notes 8, 9 on No. 36). He appears with his father
in the Pipe Roll for 1194 on a payment of 40s. for a covenant between
them. His father Richard had claimed Gamelsby and Glassanby which
had been seized by the Crown from Robert de Hodelme, son of Odard de
Karleol; on this claim Robert was charged 20 marks in 1177, although
it is stated he had not got the property (*Pipe Rolls*, 23 Hen. III.).

Salutem. Notum sit vobis me dedisse concessisse et hac præsenti carta mea confirmasse Deo et Beatæ Mariæ et Sancto Constantino de Wederhal et Monachis ibidem Deo servientibus pro salute mea et animæ uxoris meæ Antigonæ et Antecessorum meorum et successorum unum toftum extra portam Bochardi[2] quem Radulphus Clericus

Richard the son of Richard got seisin of the property in 1199 on payment of 100 marks (*Pipe Rolls*, 10 Ricard. I. and 1 Joh., and see the other reff. on Robert son of Odard in No. 73). This Richard, the son, seems to have been concerned in the rebellion of John de Curcy, the conqueror of Ireland in the time of Henry II. (*Pipe Roll*, 9 Joh.); his lands were seized by King John in 1202; some that he had in Crogelin and Niewebiggige (Newbiggin) were restored in 1208, but Gamelsby went back to the other family (see *Pipe Roll*s, 4 and 9 Joh.). His name often appears in the *Pipe Rolls*, e.g. as paying 100s. for a hearing before the justices at Westminster, in 1195 and following years; as paying scutage in 1205; as paying 2 marcs in 1200 and other years for hunting hares and foxes. From the *Register of Holm Cultram* (MS. p. 22) we learn that this Richard conceded Neuby in the Barony of Linstock to Reginald de Karlel on his paying 10s. rent and 16s. cornage; and Reginald granted (MS. p. 23) Neuby to the Abbey, the same terms being specified; also Margaret, wife of Robert de Wathepol, daughter and heir of Richard son of Trute (i.e. the second Richard), released her rights in Neuby which her father had conceded (MS. p. 23). This charter, from some of the parties named, was about 1236. These grants were confirmed by Bishop Walter (MS. p. 24) and other Bishops of Carlisle, who were lords of the Barony. Richard the son by a charter in the *Register of Lanercost* (MS. vi. 11) confirms a grant which his father (called de Bampton) had made (MS. vi. 10) of two tofts outside the Porta Bochardi at Carlisle to the Priory. The father's grant speaks of Alicia his daughter, who was buried there. The son in this charter speaks of his wife Antigone. This Richard the son of Richard is often spoken of as Richard son of Trute, a not uncommon abbreviation of a name, as in the case of Gilbert son of Roger son of Reinfrid (see No. 209), but some confusion results.

[2] This toft is in the same locality as the two which passed from Richard to the Priory of Lanercost (see the note above). The *Porta Bochardi* was the gate of the city of Carlisle on the south, and was said to have its name from Bochard a Fleming, one of the early settlers brought from the south, and from whom was also named the

et David filius ejus aliquando tenuerunt illum scilicet qui jacet inter toftum Willelmi Palmeri et toftum Walteri de Haitun in puram et perpetuam Elemosinam liberum et quietum ob omni servicio et exactione seculari. Ego autem Ricardus et hæredes mei prædictum toftum prædictis Monachis contra omnes homines warantizabimus. Et ut hæc mea donatio rata et illibata permaneat illam sigilli mei appositione roboravi. Hijs Testibus Johanne Priore Beatæ Mariæ Karleoli, Magistro Adam tunc temporis Officiali[3], Henrico Capellano de Hotun[4], Stephano Mercenario, Adam filio Willelmi, Henrico fratre ejus et multis alijs[5].

95. CARTA RECTORIS ET FRATRUM HOSPITALIS SANCTI NICHOLAI DE KARLIOLO FACTA JOHANNI DE SANCTO NICHOLAO.

OMNIBUS has literas visuris vel audituris Johannes Capellanus Rector Hospitalis Sancti Nicholai[1] de Karleolo

neighbouring vill of Bochardby. In the next charter, we have the *vicus Bochardi*, or Bochard's Street, which led through this port or gate; the Street being called later Bochard's gate or Bochergate.

[3] Adam de Kirkeby, see note 6 on No. **19**.

[4] Hotun is probably Hutton in the Forest, or Haitun as the personal name is given in the charter; but often spelt Hotun in early times. It lay some five miles north-west of Penrith and was granted by Henry I. to one Ediñ (*Testa de Nevill*, p. 379 b). The Chapel, which was afterwards reckoned a Rectory, was granted by Robert de Vallibus with a carucate of land to the Priory of Carlisle (see charter of Henry II. Dugdale, *Monast.* vi. 144).

[5] The date of this charter from Prior John must be the end of the 12th or the beginning of the 13th century.

95. [1] The Hospital of S. Nicholas at Carlisle (referred to in No. **80** with John the Chaplain) was founded by one of the Kings of England, but the name is not recorded. It was founded and endowed for the sustentation of thirteen lepers, both men and women, one Master (or Rector) Chaplain to reside, and to keep the common seal, and to sing mass at his discretion, also a Chaplain to sing mass daily for the benefactors of the Hospital. It appears that after a time other poor persons, not lepers, but *debiles et impotentes*, were by consent admitted and sustained under the same rules; see *Patent Rolls*

et Fratres ejusdem Loci Salutem. Noveritis nos concessisse dedisse et hac nostra presenti carta confirmasse

15 Edw. III. m. 48, where a summary of the rules is also given.
Hugh Todd in his MS. *Notitia Cathedralis Carleol.* (p. lxvii.) says
with his usual inaccuracy "Hospitale hoc fundavit Willielmus II., Rex
Angliæ &c. prout conjicere fas est: nam sub ejus tempus constat
Prioratum de Wedderhal de hac Domo Terras et Redditus tenuisse";
but it need hardly be said that the Priory of Wederhal held no lands
or rents from the Hospital in the time of William II. The earliest
notice appears to be in the *MS. Register of Bishop Kirkeby* (p. 482)
that a moiety of the tithes of Little Bampton (in the parish of Kirk-
bampton) was, with the consent of Bishop Bernard, given to this
Hospital by Adam son of Robert on condition to have always two
almsmen from that parish. This Adam was the son of Robert son of
Odard, and great grandson of Hildred de Carlel (see on No. **73**), and
he lived in the time of Bishop Bernard, 1204—1214. In the pleading,
in answer to the summons of Edward I. in 1292 *Quo Waranto*, the
Bishop of Carlisle, Bishop Halton, claimed the advowson of the
Hospital. It was asserted that King John was seized thereof in fee,
and conferred it upon Robert son of Ralph his clerk (*Placita De Quo
Waranto*, Record Com. p. 122) and the jury found for the King.
Besides the present charter, we have in this *Register* the convention
dated 1270 between the Master of the Hospital and the Prior of
Wederhal (see No. **96**) and a grant made by the Hospital (see
No. **170**). An account of certain endowments and other matters is
given in Bp Nicolson's MSS. (iii. 65); and see a paper on Local Leper
Hospitals by H. Barnes, M.D. in the *Cumb. Archæol. Soc. Transac.*
(x. 95), but some points in the latter require revision; at the end, the
part of the Patent Roll of Edward III. referred to above is given in
full. In 1377, the Scots attacked Carlisle, but finding it strongly
defended burnt the Hospital of S. Nicholas in the suburbs of the town
and then went off "ad Manerium de Rose" (*Chron. de Lanercost*, ed. J.
Stevenson, p. 292). On May 10th, 1477, the Hospital was granted by
Edward IV. to the Prior and Convent of Carlisle in consequence of
their petition (both documents are set out, apparently from the
Liberate Rolls, in Nicolson, MSS. iii. 67 and i. 297). It passed to the
Dean and Chapter of Carlisle under the Endowment Charter of
Henry VIII. on May 6th, 1541; and among the charges on their
estate, that Charter names 46*s.* 8*d.* annually to a Chaplain celebrating
Divine service in the Hospital "coram tribus Bedellis et hominibus
leprosis," and £5. 17*s.* to the said poor Bedells. The Hospital lay to the

Johanni de Sancto Nicholao et assignatis suis terram cum
ædificijs infra Civitatem Karleoli in Vico Bochardi in qua
Gilbertus Collan mansit inter terram David de Blachale et
terram Alexandri Bakun[2] Tenendam de nobis et de domo
nostra in feodo et hæreditate libere quiete et integre cum
omnibus libertatibus pertinentijs et aisiamentis illi terræ
pertinentibus Reddendo inde annuatim nobis et domui
nostræ quinque solidos argenti medietatem ad Pentecosten
et medietatem ad Festum Sancti Martini pro omni servicio
consuetudine et exactione.   Et prædictus Johannes et

south of Carlisle, in the suburbs of the city, and often suffered in the
incursions of the Scots.   At length, as we learn from the Parliamentary Survey of the Manor of John de Chapple, dated June 11th,
1650, "it was alltogether ruynated in the tyme of the leaguer before
Carlyle" (1645).   The Survey states the extent of the property, together with "the Church Yarde abuttinge upon the highe waye on the
easte and southe" to be 2½ acres.

Among the Chaplain Masters or Rectors, besides John mentioned
in this charter, we have:

William (?), about 1200 (No. **50**).
William, about 1240—47 (No. **170**).
Symon, in 1270 (No. **96**).
Thomas de Goldyngton, 1336 (*Register Bp Kirkby*, p. 329).
      ,,   ,,   1341   (*Pat. Roll*, 15 Ed. III. m. 48).
Richard Orielle, *temp*. Ed. I.   ,,   ,,   ,,   ,,
John de Crosseby, *temp*. Ed. I.   ,,   ,,   ,,   ,,
Thomas de Wederhale, *temp*. Ed. II. ,,   ,,   ,,   ,,
Radulph .... *temp*. Ed. II.   ,,   ,,   ,,   ,,
William de Northewell, *temp*. Ed. III. ,,   ,,   ,,   ,,
John Thorpe, 1477 (*Nicolson, MSS*. iii. 67, *Liberate Rolls*).

There are three or four others given in Dugdale, *Monast.* vi. 757.

[2] Alexander Bakun is also a witness in Nos. **134**, **136** where he is
named Seneschal of Gillesland.   He has the same title in two charters
in the *Register of Lanercost* (MS. iv. 14, 16) which, from the witnesses,
are about the same date (1230) as No. **211**, where he is again a
witness.   He was appointed a temporary justice on an assize at
Appelby in Sept. 1236 (*Patent Rolls*, 20 Hen. III. m. 2 d.).   In 1232 he
paid £10 for having custody of the land and heir of William de
Ulvesby, and 10 marcs in 1235, similarly of Radulph de Bochardeby
(*Fine Rolls*, ed. Roberts, i. 222, 280).

Assignati sui dabunt Husgavel[3] de prædicta terra sicut de Burgagio libero.   Et licebit eis dictam terram dare vendere et invadiare cuicunque et quandocunque voluerint sine contradictione nostra salva nobis et domui nostræ Fina prænominata scilicet quinque solidis per annum ad terminos præscriptos de predicta terra.   Et nos warantizabimus prædictam terram cum omnibus pertinentijs suis præfato Johanni et assignatis suis quamdiu eam nobis ipsis warantizare poterimus.   Testibus R. filio Walkelini Majore[4], Johanne de Crofton[5], Alexandro Bakun, Johanne de Mora[6], Adam Magistro, Johanne de Bohalton[7], Roberto de Tibay[8], Willelmo Capñ[9], Jordano Porter, Willelmo Tymparun, Alexandro Clerico et Alano Thorfiñ et alijs[10].

[3] *Husgavel*, sometimes *husgable*, is house tenure, and then a tax laid upon houses.   The word *gavel* is Celtic, not Anglo-Saxon, from *gabhaim*, "to take" or "receive."   Conf. *gavelkind*, and see Skeat, *Etymol. Dict.* s. v.

[4] This is the earliest Mayor of Carlisle of whom I have seen mention made.   His name was Richard, as he is given in the *Register of Lanercost* (MS. vi. 12, 14; xv. 1) though not as Mayor, with several of the present witnesses, the grants being for land in the *Vicus Francorum* and a house next to the Castle fosse ; see also No. **55**, note 3, and No. **96**.

[5] John de Crofton granted the charter to Lanercost named above (vi. 12) and attested the two other charters ; see also on No. **215**.

[6] John de Mora was Sheriff of Cumberland, or Custos, in 1236.   He is called Seneschal of Gillesland in the *Register of Lanercost* (MS. iv. 15, 17) and appears in 1250 in an Inquisition as to the King's lands held by John de Boulton (who is named below) in the suburbs of Carlisle (*Inquis. p. m.* 34 Hen. III. No. 46).

[7] John de Bohalton was "a citizen of Carlisle," see on John de Boulton, No. **61**, note 4.

[8] Robert de Tibay was the son of Herbert, perhaps the H. de Thebay of No. **93**; and in 1200 they appear in the Pipe Roll for Westmoreland as paying 10 marcs for putting the son in possession of his land.   He appears in the Inquisition mentioned above as holding land under John de Boulton in the suburbs of Carlisle.

[9] William Caprun, or Caperun, is a witness with Richard son of Walkelin and John de Mora to the grants to Lanercost mentioned above.

96. CONVENTIO FACTA INTER PRIOREM DE WEDER-
HALE ET MAGISTRUM HOSPITALIS SANCTI NICHOLAI
DE KARLIOLO DE QUINQUE SOLIDIS SOLVENDIS EIDEM
HOSPITALI PER ANNUM.

UNIVERSIS ad quorum notitiam præsens scriptum pervenerit Thomas de Wymundham Prior de Wederhal et
Symon Magister Hospitalis Sancti Nicholai juxta Karliolum
æternam in Domino Salutem.   Ad vestræ volumus universitatis notitiam pervenire quod cum inter nos orta esset
cujusdam contentionis materia in Curia Civitatis Karlioli
super quadam vasta placia inter murum Fratrum prædictorum et domum Ricardi quondam de Mora jacente quam
Abbas et Conventus Beatæ Mariæ Eboraci tenent de
prædicto Hospitali pro quinque solidis ad duos Terminos
videlicet duobus solidis et dimidio ad Festum Sancti
Martini in yeme et totidem ad Festum Pentecosten reddendis de voluntate et consilio dicti Abbatis una cum
consensu nostro expresso conquievit in hunc modum :
videlicet Quod Ego Symon Magister Hospitalis pro me
et fratribus meis remitto et quietum clamo memoratis
Abbati et Conventui et Vobis Domino Thomæ Priori de
Wederhal omnia arrearagia firmæ prædictæ placiæ usque
ad diem confessionis præsentis scripturæ pro decem solidis
quos mihi solvistis.   Et ego Frater Thomas de Wymundham ex nunc in posterum pro Abbate meo et Conventu et
me firmam predictæ placiæ ad Terminos suprascriptos
vobis Magistro Symoni et Fratribus vestris vel vestro certo
Attornato pro tempore meo sic faciet quilibet successor
meus pro tempore suo sive placia jam dicta fuerit hos-
pitata sive non sine contradictione persolvam.   In cujus
rei Testimonium huic scripto in modum Cirograffi confecto alternatim sigilla nostra apposuimus.   Hijs Testibus

---

[10] The date of this charter would seem to be, from the witnesses,
from about 1240 to about 1250 ; from John de Mora, Robt. de Tibay
and Alex. Bakun, probably, near the earlier date.

Dominis Alexandro de Bolotun Majore Karlioli[1], Willelmo filio Yvonis, Gilberto de Grenesdale[2], Willelmo de Tymparun, Willelmo filio Hysmay, Thoma de Tybay, Johanne Waster, Roberto de Kirkeof, Wald. Clerico et alijs. Datum Karlioli die Lunæ proxima ante cineres Anno Domini Millesimo Ducentesimo Septuagesimo.

97. CARTA WALTERI DE BOCHARDBY DE TOTA TERRA SUA QUÆ VOCATUR ELDWRICFLAT CUM PRATO ETC.

OMNIBUS Christi fidelibus ad quorum notitiam præsens scriptum pervenerit Walterus de Bochardby Salutem æternam in Domino. Noverit universitas vestra me caritatis intuitu et pro salute animarum Prædecessorum et success-

96. [1] Alexander de Bolotun, or Bouilton, was also Mayor of Carlisle in 1280, as appears from an Inquisition held before him and others concerning certain customs in Cumberland (*Inquis. p. m.* 8 Edw. I. No. 81). The family seems to have been numerous in Carlisle.

It may be useful to give here a list of such early Mayors of Carlisle as are known ; the list in the Appendix to *Royal Charters of Carlisle*, ed. R. S. Ferguson, is incorrect :

Richard son of Walkelin, circ. 1240.—No. 95.

Alexander de Bolotun, or Bouilton, 1270, 1280.—No. 96 and *Inquis. post mortem*, 8 Edw. I. No. 81.

Alan de Penington, 1287.—*Register of Lanercost*, MS. x. 19. He died in 1291 or 1292, leaving lands in Cumbresdale and Carlisle (*Inquis. p. m.* 20 Edw. I. No. 24); he had a wife Johanna and a son John (*Calend. Geneal.* ed. Roberts, ii. 459).

Thomas de Alaynby, will dated 1362.—*Register of Bp Welton*, p. 96.

William de Arthureth, will dated 1369.—*Register of Bp Appleby*, p. 173.

William de Loudon, 1375,—witness to a deed of trust. *Bishop's Miscellan. Registers*, vol. 2 (Bp Nicolson, MSS. iii. 284).

Alan de Blenerhasset, 1382,—witness to a deed. Reff. *ut sup.*

[2] Gilbert de Grenesdale granted land *in Via Francorum* in Carlisle to the Priory of Lanercost by a charter dated 1287; Alan de Penington was then Mayor of Carlisle (*Regist. Lan.* MS. x. 19).

orum meorum dedisse concessisse et præsenti carta mea
confirmasse Deo et Abbachiæ Sanctæ Mariæ Eborum
necnon et Monachis Sanctæ Trinitatis et Sancti Constantini de Wederhal totam illam terram in territorio de
Bochardby[1] quæ vocatur Elwricflat cum prato eidem terræ
adjacente quæ terra jacet inter divisam de Scoteby et
Rivum fontis Sanctæ Elenæ ita scilicet quod dicti Monachi
habebunt totam prædictam terram et pratum in liberam
puram et perpetuam Elemosinam cum omnibus communis
et aisiamentis Villæ de Bochardeby tantæ terræ pertinentibus.   Licebit autem prædictis Monachis prædictam
terram et pratum includere muro fossato et construere
ædificia in prædicta terra sicut sibi melius viderint expedire.   Insuper habebunt prædicti Monachi quandam
portionem terræ meæ continentem duodecim pedes in
latitudine et in longitudine a communi via de Bochardby
usque ad predictam terram de Eldewricflat ad faciendum
sibi liberum introitum et exitum ad prædictam terram sine
impedimento mei vel hæredum meorum.   Et ego Walterus
et hæredes mei totam hanc prædictam donationem et
concessionem omnino sicut præscriptum est dictis Monachis
imperpetuum warantizabimus, defendemus et acquietabimus.   Et ego Walterus sacramento corporaliter præstito
ad observationem omnium præscriptorum me et hæredes
meos perpetuo obligavi; et insuper ad majorem securitatem præsenti scripto sigillum meum apposui.   Hijs Testibus Radulpho Priore[2], Gervasio Archidiacono[3], Waltero

---

97.   [1] Bochardby lies on the east of Carlisle, between that city and
Scotby; see on Odo de Bochardby, No. **48**, note 5.

[2] Radulph was Prior, no doubt, of Carlisle ; he often occurs in this
Register, and with several of these witnesses ; in Nos. **109, 112** with
the same Archdeacon and Official.   The *Chronicon de Lanercost* (ed.
J. Stevenson, pp. 41, 53) says that his name was Radulf Barri, being a
nephew of Bishop Walter, that he succeeded Prior Bartholomew in
1231 and died February 9th, 1247.   He is witness, with Bishop
Walter and most of these witnesses, to a charter of Rolland de

Officiali[4], Ricardo Brun tunc Vicecomite Karlioli[5], Ricardo de Levington, Petro de Tyllol, Roberto de Castelkairoc, Johanne de Aglunby, Johanne filio Willelmi, Ricardo et Radulpho Clericis, Gilberto Diacono et alijs[6].

98. CARTA ADÆ FRATRIS WALTERI DE BOCHARDBY DE QUADAM PORTIONE TERRÆ JACENTIS JUXTA RIVUM FONTIS SANCTÆ ELENÆ.

OMNIBUS Christi fidelibus ad quorum notitiam præsens scriptum pervenerit Adam frater Walteri de Bochardby Salutem æternam in Domino. Noverit universitas vestra me dedisse Priori et Monachis de Wederhal in puram et perpetuam Elemosinam quandam perviunculam portionem terræ quæ jacet ad caput crofti mei juxta rivum fontis Sanctæ Elenæ ad faciendum fossatum suum in prædicta portione. Ita quod nec Ego nec hæredes mei aliquo tempore imperpetuum prædicto Priori et Monachis aliquam litem movere poterimus. Immò ego et hæredes mei prædictam terram eisdem Monachis warantizabimus imperpetuum acquietabimus et defendemus. In cujus rei Testimonium præsenti scripto sigillum meum apposui. Hijs Testibus, Domino Waltero tunc Officiali Karlioli,

Vallibus in the *Register of Lanercost* (MS. ii. 21); also to a charter of Bishop Walter, dated 1234, in the *Register of Holm Cultram* (MS. p. 17).

[3] Gervase de Louther, see on No. **21**, note 3.

[4] Walter de Ulvesby, see on No. **56**, note 5.

[5] Richard Brun, or Le Brun, appears several times as Sheriff of Carlisle or of Cumberland in this *Register*; but his name does not occur in the official lists of the Sheriffs. He was probably "custos" for Bishop Walter, who was Sheriff until his resignation in 1246, and it may be "custos" in 1233—35, and not Thomas de Multon as usually stated. He was a justice to hold a special assize at Carlisle in May, 1237 (*Patent Rolls*, 21 Hen. III. m. 8 d.). The family seem to have been lords of the manor of Bowness on Solway (see on Radulph de la Ferte, No. **43**), also of Bothill in the parish of Torpenhow.

[6] The date of the charter is after 1231 when Radulph became Prior, and probably not later than 1235.

Henrico Capellano de Wederhal, Willelmo de Warthwic, Johanne de Aglunby, Henrico de Terreby[1], Alano de Langthwait, Johanne Stelfot de Wederhal, Johanne Coco, Henrico Wrene, Roberto Corte et alijs[2].

99. CARTA LAURENTIJ AGULLUNBY DE QUATUOR ACRIS TERRÆ IN TERRITORIO DE AGLUNBY.

UNIVERSIS sanctæ Matris Ecclesiæ filijs ad quorum notitiam præsens scriptum pervenerit Laurentius Aglunby[1] Salutem æternam in Domino. Noverit universitas vestra me Divinæ pietatis intuitu et pro salute animæ meæ et Prædecessorum et Successorum dedisse concessisse et hac præsenti carta mea confirmasse Abbati et Conventui Sanctæ Mariæ Eboraci et Domui Sanctæ Trinitatis et Sancti Constantini de Wederhal et Monachis ibidem Deo servientibus quatuor acras terræ cum pertinentijs in territorio de Aglunby[2] scilicet toftum et croftum quod Rogerus filius Duvæ tenuit pro una acra et unam acram in cultura mea quæ est ad Brimblimere ultra viam et unam acram in cultura mea quæ dicitur Grensicflat et dimidiam acram in Langlandes et dimidiam acram de butto[3] subtus Mirebrige. Habendas et Tenendas in puram liberam et perpetuam Elemosinam cum omnibus libertatibus communis et aisiamentis prædictæ villæ adjacentibus. Ego vero Laurentius et hæredes mei hanc prædictam Elemosinam prædictis Monachis contra omnes homines imperpetuum warantizabimus acquietabimus et defendemus. Et ut hoc scriptum perpetuæ firmitatis robur optineat illud sigilli mei

---

98. [1] Henry de Terribi held lands in Ainstable, on the east of the river Eden, and made grants to the Priory, see Nos. 166, 167.

[2] The charter is of nearly the same date as the preceding.

99. [1] See on Laurence son of Agyllun, No. 37, note 3.

[2] Aglunby was the more western of the two manors into which the parish of Warwick was divided, and where the family were said to have first settled; see also on No. 5, note 4.

[3] *Buttum terræ*, "a butt of land," was a short piece of land, the end of an arable ridge and furrow; see Jacob, *Law Dict.* s. v.

impressione roboravi.   Hijs Testibus, Roberto de Hamton tunc Vicecomite Karlioli⁴, Ricardo de Levington Constabulario, Roberto filio Willelmi de Corkeby, Willelmo de Warthwic, Eliseo de Aglunby, Alano filio ejus, Alano de Langethuet, Waltero Portario, Radulpho filio Umfridi et multis alijs⁵.

100. CARTA ROBERTI ABBATIS EBORUM FACTA SUAINO CARPENTARIO DE AGLUNBY DE 4. ACRIS TERRÆ IN EADEM.

SCIANT omnes qui viderint vel audierint litteras has quod Ego Robertus Abbas¹ Sanctæ Mariæ Eborum cum communi consilio et assensu Capituli nostri dedi et concessi et præsenti carta confirmavi Suano carpentario de Aglunby quatuor acras terræ in Villa de Agullunby illas videlicet quas Laurentius de Agullunby Domui nostræ dedit in Elemosinam sicut in carta dicti Laurentij² plenius continetur.   Habendas et Tenendas sibi et hæredibus suis in feodo et hæreditate imperpetuum cum omnibus libertatibus et aisiamentis infra Villam et extra ad prædictam terram pertinentibus Reddendo inde annuatim Domui nostræ de Wederhale duodecim denarios Sterlingorum medietatem ad Festum Sancti Martini in yeme et medietatem ad Pentecosten pro omni servitio consuetudine et exactione ad Nos pertinente.   Hæc autem ei et hæredibus suis concedimus quamdiu se legaliter erga nos habuerint et prædictam firmam bene reddiderint.   Si vero contigerit ipsum vel hæredes suos prædictam terram vi vel ratione amittere non dabimus eis escambium.   Testibus hijs,

---

⁴ This must be when Robert de Hamton was custos for Bishop Walter from 1223 to 1229, with which the other witnesses agree ; see on No. **54**, note 4.

⁵ The date, from the Sheriff, will be 1223—29.

100. ¹ Robert de Longo Campo who was Abbot from 1197 to 1239; see note 3 on No. **10.**

² Charter No. **99.**

Roberto de Skegnes[3] tunc Senescallo nostro, Magistro J. de Hamͭton, Magistro Eustachio de Kyma, Waltero de Gaugi[4], J. de Selebi[5] Clericis, Waltero de Asch, Theobaldo, Johanne filio Turgis, Galfrido de Torrenton et multis alijs[b].

101. CONFIRMATIO SIMONIS DE MORVILLA FACTA MONACHIS DE WEDERHALE DE DIMIDIA CARUCATA TERRÆ IN CROGLIN.

SCIANT omnes qui viderint vel audierint literas has quod Ego Symon de Morvilla[1] concessi Monachis de

[3] Robert de Skegnes, or Skegnesse, is witness with J. de Hamerton (Hamͭton) in 1220 to No. 19, where see note 7 on the name of this next witness.

[4] Walter de Gaugy, clerk, was instituted to the Church of Kirkeby in Hundovedal, on the presentation of the Convent of S. Mary, at York, in March, 1229 (*Archbp Gray's Register*, ed. J. Raine, p. 29).

[5] John de Selebi, clerk, was instituted to the Church of Foston, on the presentation of the Abbey of S. Mary, at York, in January, 1231 (*Archbp Gray's Register*, ed. J. Raine, p. 42).

[6] This charter is of later date than the preceding and must therefore be after 1223 and prior to the death of Abbot Robert in 1239. With this the witnesses agree, who seem to be all from the York district.

101. [1] Little or nothing seems to be known of the immediate ancestors of Symon de Morvilla. A Hugh de Moravilla is witness with William Engaine to the charter of Earl Henry, son of King David, to the Abbey of Holm Cultram in 1150, and may have been the father or other relative (Illustrative Doc. XXIV.). Simon married Ada, the daughter of William Engaine, through whom he obtained the great barony of Burgo, or Burgh, by Sands. This barony was granted by Ranulph Meschin, "Lord of Cumberland," to Robert de Trivers (said to be his brother-in-law) together with the custody of the Forest of Cumberland (*Testa de Nevill*, p. 379 *b*); his daughter and heir Ebria (the *Domina Ybri* of this charter) married Radulph Engaine, or Engahin. It was their son William whose daughter and heir, Ada, by his wife Eustachia (*Regist. Lanercost*, MS. ii. 15) married, for her first husband, Simon de Morvilla; her second husband was Robert de Vallibus, see note 4 on No. 28. Simon had, by his wife Ada, a son Hugo de Morvilla, often called wrongly his grandson; see No. 102, where Hugo speaks of *Symon pater meus*; moreover, in the *Register*

Wederhal eandem dimidiam carucatam terræ in Croglyn[2] quam Domina Ybri[3] eis dedit in Elemosinam cum omnibus quæ ad eam pertinent Et duas salinas[4] in Parochia de

of Lanercost (MS. ii. 11) in a charter of Ada daughter of William Engayne, mention is made of Robert de Vallibus, her husband, Hugo de Morvill, her son, and Simon de Morvill, her former husband; also in another charter in the same *Register* (MS. ii. 14, also 16) Hugo de Morvill, granting the Church of Laysingby, twice speaks of Ada Engayne as *mater mea.* And yet almost all the local histories call Hugh de Morvill the *grandson* of Simon, and son of one Roger. The error seems to be due to Dugdale (*Baronage,* i. 612) who also says that Simon had two sons Richard and Roger; and the other writers have diligently copied him; for once J. Denton (*Cumberland,* p. 68) is right. In the Pipe Roll for 1158, Simon de Morevilla is noted as owing 50 marcs for the land of Radulf Engaigne, which he paid the next year. He had therefore lately got livery of this property. It appears also that he held Leysingby in 1166, when the Sheriff granted him by Royal writ an abatement of 18*s.* 4*d.* The next year the abatement was 13*s.* 9*d.* paid *dum idem Simon vixit,* shewing that he died in 1167. There were several other persons of the name of Morvill about this time connected with the district, besides the Hugh de Moravilla in 1150 mentioned above. The Hugh de Morvill, who was one of the knights that slew Thomas Becket in 1170, has been confused (as by Dugdale) with Hugh the son of Simon; but he was lord of Knaresburg in Yorkshire, which he got as early as 1158; and he is said to have died in the Holy Land. A Hugh de Morville and a Richard de Morville were witnesses to the charter given by David, King of Scots, to Robert de Brus referred to in note 1 on No. **106.** Richard de Morville, Constable of Scotland, often occurs about this time; and John de Morville was fined £20 for advising the surrender of the castle of Appleby in 1174 (*Pipe Rolls, Westmoreland,* 22 Hen. II.).

[2] Croglyn, i.e. Little Croglyn in the parish of Kirkoswald.

[3] On Ybri, or Ebria, de Trivers, see note 1 above; she seems to have given a tenth part of the vill of Croglyn to the Priory, see No. **152.**

[4] These *salinæ* or salt pans were used for producing the indispensable article of salt by evaporation from the sea-water. The monastery had another on the west coast (see No. **135**). A great number are mentioned in *Domesday Book* (see ed. Ellis, Record Com., Introduction, p. XL). In the more inland counties, such as Cheshire and Worcestershire, the salt was obtained by boiling the water of the brine springs.

Burgo[5], unam scilicet quam Radulphus Engahin[6] dedit eis, alteram vero quam Willelmus filius ejus[7] dedit eis. Hanc terram et has salinas pro animabus Prædecessorum meorum ab omni terreno servitio liberas quod ad me pertinet predictis Monachis in Elemosina concedo et præsenti carta confirmo. Testibus hijs, Hugone de Morvilla[8], Radulpho Clerico de Burgo et alijs multis[9].

The workmen were called *salinarii*. The rock salt does not seem to have been worked until quite a recent period.

[5] Burgo, or Burgh, upon Sands, *supra sabulones* or *juxta arenam*, is a parish on the shores of the Solway Firth, near where the river Eden enters that estuary, and about 8 miles from Carlisle, well situated for these *salinæ* or salt pans.

[6] Radulph Engahin, or Engaine, was Lord of the manor of Isel on the Derwent, and married Ybri or Ebria de Trivers; see note 1 above. Through her, he came into the Barony of Burgh and other large possessions. He was dead in 1158, when, it appears from the Pipe Rolls, Simon de Morvilla had livery of his lands. The name, together with that of Gilbert Engaine, is given in the Foundation Charter of Lanercost about 1169, but this must be another Radulph.

[7] William the son of Radulph Engahin witnessed the charter of Earl Henry to the Abbey of Holm Cultram in 1150 (Illustrative Docum. XXIV.). In the *Register of Lanercost* (MS. ii. 15 and vii. 25) his wife Eustachia is mentioned, also his daughter and heir Ada, who married first Simon de Morvilla and then Robert de Vallibus. He must have died before 1158 (see note 6), perhaps before his father Radulph.

[8] Hugo de Morvilla was the son of Simon and of Ada Engaine; see the note above on Simon. We learn from *Testa de Nevill* (p. 379 *b*) that Hugh held his lands by payment of £10. 2s. 10d. cornage, which lands came to him from his ancestor Robert de Trivers, and therefore through his mother Ada Engaine. These would include, besides the barony of Burgh, the manors of Kirkoswald and Laysingby, which his father Simon held (*Pipe Rolls*, 13 Hen. II.) and in connection with which Hugo often appears. He married Helewisa de Stuteville, of the family of the Barons of Lyddale, whose ancestor Turgis Brundis got that Barony from Ranulf Meschin (*Testa de Nevill*, p. 379 *b*). She was a daughter of Robert de Stuteville, whose wife's name was also Helewisa (see Dugdale, *Baronage*, i. 456), and who is a co-witness with Hugo de Morvil to the charter granted by Henry II.

102. CONFIRMATIO HUGONIS DE MORVILLA FACTA MONACHIS DE WEDERHALE DE DUABUS SALINIS IN PAROCHIA DE BURGO.

SCIANT omnes qui viderint vel audierint literas istas quod Ego Hugo de Morvilla[1] reddidi et hac carta mea confirmavi Monachis de Wederhale duas salinas in Parochia de Burgo quas Symon Pater meus confirmavit eis ex dono Radulphi Engahin et Willelmi filij ejus. Tenendas imperpetuum quietas et liberas ab omni terreno servitio. Sciendum vero quod una istarum salinarum jacet juxta

to Hubert de Vallibus (Illustrative Documents XXII.). Hugo had two daughters, who inherited his property, Alda or Ada, who married Richard de Lucy, and Johanna, who married Richard Gernun (see below on Nos. 103, 104). He held also the forestry of the Forest of Cumberland (*Pipe Rolls*, 6 Ric. I.). He paid two destriers for leave to make a marriage between his daughter, Ada, and Richard (de Lucy) of Egremunt (*Pipe Rolls*, 2 Joh.). He died in 1202—3; when his wife paid 60 marcs that she might not be compelled to marry and might have her dower; and William Briewere paid 500 marcs for having the custody of his younger daughter, Johanna, and other privileges (*Pipe Rolls*, 4 Joh.; and see on Nos. 103, 104). It appears from a convention between William Briewere and Helewisa de Stuteville that William quitclaimed to her of her dower the manors of Chircoswarde (Kirkoswald) and Lesingebi (Lazonby), and she quitclaimed to him the manor of Hisale (Isel) (*Calend. Doc. Scot.* ed. Bain, i. 57). Hugo de Morvilla also made grants, or confirmed the grants of his mother Ada, to the Priory of Lanercost, of the Churches of Laysingby and Grenesdale, pasture and two salt pans in Burgh, a free net in Eden and lands (Hærasion or Hareskeugh) in the manor of Kirkoswald (*Regist. Lanercost*, MS. ii. 12, 13, 14, 16, 17); also to the Abbey of Holm Cultram, the Church of Burgh and lands and pasture in Laysingby, the grant being witnessed by Thomas son of Gospatric (*Regist. Holm Cult.* MS. pp. 13, 14, 22) and Thos. de Brunefeld, and confirmed by Bishop Bernard. After his death, his wife Helewisa married William son of Ranulph of Graystoc; and in 1210 she was again a widow, and was in the custody of Robert de Veteriponte (see *Pipe Rolls*, 11 Joh.).

[9] The date of this charter can only be fixed by the time during which Simon de Morvilla had the property, from 1158 to 1167.

102. [1] On Hugo de Morvilla, see note 8 on the preceding charter.

salinam Ecclesiæ versus Occidentem altera vero ex alia parte versus Orientem. Hanc concessionem feci præfatis Monachis in puram et perpetuam Elemosinam pro salute mea et uxoris meæ et Patris et Matris meæ et Parentum meorum. Concessi et eisdem Monachis sufficienter sumere necessaria ad salem faciendum de meliori turbaria mea. Testibus hijs, Ricardo Capellano de Burgo, Roberto Dunbredan[2], Radulpho de Folevile[3], Willelmo Dereman, Waltero Clerico, Huctredo Cabiaca, Adam de Karliol[4], Hugone de Levington, et multis alijs[5].

103. CARTA RICARDI GERNUN FACTA MONACHIS DE WEDERHAL DE 2 SALINIS IN PAROCHIA DE BURGO.

SCIANT omnes qui viderint et audierint Literas istas quod Ego Richardus Gernun[1] cum consilio et assensu

---

[2] Robert de Dunbredan rendered account of 20s. in 1210, for pannage in the Forest (*Pipe Rolls*, 11 Joh.), but may be son of this witness; Robert is witness to three of the charters of Hugh de Morvill in the *Register of Lanercost* (MS. ii. 12, 14, 16) and to the charter of Huctred son of Fergus, 1158—64 (see note 9 on No. **72**).

[3] Radulph de Folevile is also witness to two of Hugh's charters in the same *Register* (MS. ii. 14, 17).

[4] Adam de Karliol was the son of Robert and father of Eudo: see on No. **75**. He renders account of a sum for a charter in the Pipe Rolls for 1195.

[5] The date of this charter lies between the deaths of Simon and Hugh, i.e. 1167 and 1202—3.

103. [1] On the death of Hugo de Morvilla, his daughters, Ada and Johanna, inherited his great property. The elder Ada was already married to Richard de Lucy of Egremunt (see note 8 on No. **101**, also No. **104**), the younger, Johanna, was afterwards married to Richard Gernun or de Vernun, the nephew of William Briewere. This William Briewere was a person of great importance in the reigns of Richard I. and John; he was made Justiciar by the former (*Roger de Hoveden*, ed. Stubbs, iii. 16); as in this case, he seems often to have secured the wardship of minors with a view to profit; he died in 1226—27 (see Dugdale, *Baronage*, i. 700). In the 4th year of John, William Briewere accounted for 500 marcs to have the daughter (Johanna) of Hugo de Morevill with her inheritance, the right to

Johannæ uxoris meæ et amicorum meorum concessi et hac mea carta confirmavi Deo et Beatæ Mariæ et Monachis de Wederhal duas salinas in Parochia de Burgo quas Simon de Morvilla et Hugo de Morvilla confirmaverunt eis ex dono Radulphi Engayne et Willelmi filij ejus. Tenendum imperpetuum quietas et liberas ab omni terreno servicio. Sciendum vero quod una istarum salinarum jacet juxta salinam Ecclesiæ versus occidentem, altera ex alia parte versus orientem. Hanc concessionem feci præfatis Monachis in puram et perpetuam Elemosinam pro salute mea et uxoris meæ et pro animabus Antecessorum et Parentum meorum Concessi etiam eisdem Monachis sufficienter sumere necessaria ad salem faciendam de meliori turbaria mea. Testibus hijs, Radulpho de Laferte, Willelmo Gernun[2], Warino Presbitero, Willelmo filio

marry her to his son Richard or his nephew Richard Gernun, and the forestry of the Forest which Hugh had (*Pipe Rolls*, 4 Joh.). Two years afterwards, we find that Richard de Lucy had got all these privileges, with the reasonable share of his wife Alda in her father's land, on the payment of 900 marks and five palfreys; and Richard Gernun had the younger daughter Johanna and the reasonable share falling to her, on the payment of 500 marcs (*Pipe Rolls*, 4 & 6 Joh.). Richard Gernun and his wife Johanna had two daughters, Helewisa who became the wife of Richard de Vernun, dying in 1269—70 (*Inquis. p. m.* 54 Hen. III. No. 19), and Ada who married first Ranulph Boyvill of Levington, and then William Furnival, and outlived them both, dying in 1270—71 (*Inquis. p. m.* 55 Henry III. No. 9); the daughter of Ada, named Helewisa de Levington, became the wife of Eustace de Bailliol and died 1270—71 (see *Pipe Rolls*, 31 Hen. III.; *Inquis. post mort.* 56 Hen. III. No. 35, *Calend. Geneal.* ed. Roberts, i. 157; *Patent Rolls*, 45 Hen. III. m. 8 d.). Johanna de Morvilla (or Gernun) died in 1246—7, when the first Richard and Radulph Boyvill did homage for her property (*Pipe Rolls*, 31 Hen. III.; *Inquis. p. m.* 31 Hen. III. No. 32; *Fine Rolls*, 31 Hen III. ed. Roberts, ii. 10 and *Calend. Geneal.* i. 16). In 1227, Richard and Johanna entered into an agreement with the Abbey of S. Mary, at York, in regard to lands at Cringledic (see on No. **174**). The manor of Aikton in the Barony of Burgh, which fell to them, was said to be their chief residence.

[2] William Gernun was witness to the famous agreement at York

Vernun, Alano Senescallo, Uctredo Caleware, Willelmo Clerico de Wederhal, Willelmo de Airminne et multis alijs[3].

104. CARTA RICARDI DE LUSEY FACTA MONACHIS DE WEDERHALE DE DUABUS SALINIS IN PAROCHIA DE BURGO.

SCIANT omnes qui viderint et audierint litteras istas quod Ego Richardus de Lucy[1] cum consilio et assensu Adæ uxoris meæ et amicorum meorum concessi et hac carta mea confirmavi Monachis de Wederhal duas Salinas

between Henry III. and Alexander II., King of Scotland, Sept. 25th, 1237 (Rymer, *Fœdera*, new edn. i. 233).

[3] The date of the charter is probably not very long after the marriage of the grantors about 1204—5, though the witnesses Radulph de la Ferte and William Gernun point to a somewhat later date.

104. [1] Richard de Lucy and Ada his wife have already been spoken of in the notes on Nos. **101** (note 8) and **103** (note 1). In *Testa de Nevill* (p. 379 b) he is mentioned as holding, with Richard Gernun, the land of Hugo de Morvill on a cornage rent. He was not the Richard de Lucy who was Chief Justiciar of England for so long in the 12th century, but the son of Reginald de Lucy and Amabilia "Countess of Copland," the second of the three daughters and coheirs of William FitzDuncan and Alicia de Romely, daughter of William Meschin (see on No. **2**, note 5). In 1200—1, he accounted for 300 marcs for having his land in Coplanda and Cambridge, for leave to marry whom he will, and other privileges. In 1204—5, he had married Ada de Morville and got her property and the forestry of the whole Forest of Cumberland (see on No. **103**, and for the preceding relationships the Pipe Rolls for 2, 3, 4 and 6th of John, and Dugdale, *Baronage*, i. 563). He died in 1215 or shortly before, and his widow then obtained livery of her lands (*Pipe Rolls*, 16 Joh.). He left two daughters, Amabilis and Alicia, of whom Thomas de Multon the elder (see note 4 on No. **47**) obtained the wardship; their mother Ada married this Thomas; and his two sons, Alan and Lambert de Multon, respectively married the daughters Amabilis and Alicia, though under age (see *Testa de Nevill*, p. 378 b; *Coram Rege Rolls*, 7 and 8 Hen. III. No. 17 m. 22 d.; *Feet of Fines, Cumb.* 15 Hen. III. No. 12). Ada became the mother of Thomas de Multon the younger, who married Matilda de Vallibus.

Descent of the parties referred to in the preceding note:—

in Parochia de Burgo quas Simon de Morvilla et Hugo de Morvilla confirmaverunt eis ex dono Radulphi Engayne et Willelmi filii ejus Tenendas imperpetuum quietas et liberas ab omni terreno servicio. Sciendum vero quod una istarum salinarum jacet juxta salinam Ecclesiæ versus Occidentem, altera ex alia parte versus Orientem. Hanc concessionem feci præfatis Monachis in puram et perpetuam Elemosinam pro salute mea et uxoris meæ et pro animabus Antecessorum et Parentum nostrorum. Concessi et eisdem Monachis sufficienter sumere necessaria ad salem faciendum de meliori turbaria mea. Testibus hijs Willelmo de Johanbi, Reginaldo Milite, Warino Capellano, Ricardo Clerico, Adam Diacono, Willelmo Clerico, Umphrido de Wederhal, et multis alijs[2].

105. CARTA THOMÆ DE MULTON FACTA MONACHIS DE WEDERHAL DE UNA SALINA CUM COMMUNA TURBARIE DE DRUMBOC.

OMNIBUS Christi fidelibus ad quos presens scriptum pervenerit Thomas de Multon[1] Salutem. Noverit universitas vestra me recepisse de Priore et Monachis de Wederhale quandam Salinam in territorio de Burgo quæ est

Robert de Trivers = (?) sister of Ranulph Meschin
Rad. Engaine = Ybri or Ebria de Trivers
William Engaine = Eustachia
Simon de Morvill = Ada Engaine = Robert de Vallibus
Hugh de Morvill = Helewisa de Stutevill
Rich. de Lucy = Ada = Thos. de Multon   Johanna = Rich. Gernun
Amabilis   Alicia   Thos. de Multon   Ada = (1) Ranulph Boyvill
m.   m.   m.   = (2) Wm Furnival
Alan de   Lambert   Matilda   Helewisa = Eustace de Bailliol
Multon   de Multon   de Vallibus

[2] The date of this charter is probably at, or about, the date of the preceding.

105. [1] Thomas de Multon the elder, who married Ada de Morvill, widow of Richard de Lucy; see note 4 on No. **47.**

propinquior Salinæ Ecclesiæ versus Orientem quam quidem
Salinam dicti Monachi mihi et hæredibus meis quietam
clamaverunt imperpetuum.   Et Ego pro prædicta Salina
dedi prædicto Priori et Monachis de Wederhal quandam
aliam Salinam versus occidentem in Escambium illam
videlicet quam Michael aliquando tenuit ad firmam.   Habendam et Tenendam imperpetuum in liberam puram et
perpetuam Elemosinam cum communa turbarie de Drum-
boc² ubicunque sibi magis viderint expedire, et cum
omnibus alijs aisiamentis quæ meæ propriæ Salinæ ibi
habent vel habere poterunt.   Et Ego et Hæredes mei
prædictam Salinam prædictis Monachis imperpetuum warantizabimus acquietabimus et defendemus.   Et ut hoc
scriptum perpetuæ firmitatis robur optineat eidem sigillum
meum apposui.   Testibus hijs, Alano de Multon fratre
meo, Thoma et Alano filijs meis, Alano Buche tunc
Forestario, Roberto Kyime, Stephano Clerico, Thoma
Bec, Johanne filio Willelmi, Petro Vicario de Burgo et
alijs³.

106. Carta David Comitis facta Monachis de Wederhal de Villa de Karkarevill et Ecclesia ejusdem.

Omnibus videntibus vel audientibus litteras has David
Comes¹ Salutem.   Sciatis me concessisse Deo et Sanctæ

---

² Drumboc, or Drumbegh, said to be "the bog of the bitterns,"
was in the parish of Bowness on Solway.   Here was a Roman station,
not certainly identified, but near the end of the great Roman wall.

³ The date of this charter must be before 1240 when Thos. de
Multon died, and after his marriage in 1217—18.

106.   ¹ This was apparently the Earl David who was afterwards
David I., King of Scotland from 1124 to 1153, and not the Earl David
who was brother to King William the Lion.   He was the youngest son
of Malcolm Ceanmor and Queen Margaret, and ruled over Scotland
south of the Forth and Clyde to the Solway Firth with the title of
Comes or Earl, from 1107 to 1124 (see Skene, *Celtic Scotland*, i. 445,
455).   His sister Matilda had married Henry I.; his wife was also

Mariæ et Abbachiæ Eboraci in pura Elemosina Villam quæ vocatur Karkarevill[2] et Ecclesiam ejusdem Villæ quam dedit Robertus de Brus[3] prædictæ Abbachiæ pro salute mea et uxoris meæ et pro salute animarum Patris et Matris meæ et pro animabus omnium fidelium defunctorum. Valete[4].

107. CONFIRMATIO ROBERTI FILIJ BUEC FACTA MONACHIS DE WEDERHALE DE TOTA TERRA QUAM PATER SUUS DEDIT EIS IN BUCHASTRE.

UNIVERSIS Sanctæ Matris Ecclesiæ filijs hoc scriptum visuris vel audituris Robertus filius Buec[1] de Buchastre

called Matilda. He founded the monastery of Selkirk in 1113, and among the Norman Barons who are witnesses to the charter is Robert de Brus (quoted by Skene *l.c.*). There are two original charters extant, copied in facsimile in *National MSS. of Scotland*, i. Nos. xix., xx., by which King David gave to Robert de Brus Anandale (Estranent or Strathanan) with the rights of forest therein; see also Illustrative Docum. I. For his charter to Wederhal when King, see No. **198**.

[2] Karkarevill was probably in Anandale, but I have been unable to identify the place. There was a Kirkonevill in Galloway, mentioned in the *Register of Holm Cultram*.

[3] This Robert de Brus was the first of the many of the name connected with this part of the kingdom, but scarcely as Dugdale (*Baronage*, i. 447) makes him, the one who came from Normandy at the Conquest. The family had settled in Yorkshire, but this Robert was welcomed to Scotland by David as his friend and brother in arms. He was a considerable benefactor to S. Mary's Abbey at York (*Monasticon*, iii. 549); he died in May 1141, and was buried in the Priory of Gyseburn which he had founded in 1119.

[4] The date of the charter will be during the time David ruled as Earl, 1107 to 1124.

107. [1] Bueth, or Buec, or Boed, would seem to have held the district which afterwards formed the Barony of Gilsland, or Gillesland, and the country immediately to the north of it. The name appears here in the place name Buchastre, Buchecastre, or Buethcastre. But Gille, or Gilles, the son of Bueth, brings us more into historic times. In an *Inquisition* found in the *Register of Glasgow*, and made in 1120—21 by Earl David concerning the lands of the Church of Glasgow, one of

Salutem. Noveritis me intuitu caritatis pro salute animæ
meæ et prædecessorum meorum et successorum concessisse
et presenti carta confirmasse Deo et Ecclesiæ Sanctæ
Trinitatis et Sancti Constantini de Wederhale et Monachis
ibidem Deo servientibus totam terram cum pertinentiis

several "*Cumbrenses judices*" was *Gill. filius Boed* (Haddan and Stubbs,
Eccles. Doc. ii. 17). From him, no doubt, Gillesland took its name.
In the charter of Henry II. in 1157 granting this district to Hubert de
Vallibus, the district is described as "totam terram quam Gilbertus
filius Boet tenuit" (Illustrative Docum. XXII.). Gilbert would be an
incorrect rendering of Gille or Gilles, but there is no doubt who is
meant. On Gillesland, see No. 191. In the Foundation Charter of
Lanercost (Illustrative Documents XXIII.) and in the Confirmation by
Pope Alexander III. in 1181 (*Register*, MS. viii. 17) certain lands are
described—"per has divisas per quas Gille filius Bueth illam melius et
plenius in vita sua tenuit," and again—"Dedi autem eis omnem
corticem de merremio meo proprio...in boscis meis infra Baroniam
meam de terra quae fuit Gille filii Bueth." There is abundant
evidence, therefore, of Gillè the son of Bueth holding part of the
territory before Hubert de Vallibus obtained the grant from Henry II.
In the *Register of Lanercost* (MS. iii. 1) there is a charter of one
Buethbarn, granting the church of (Nether) Denton to the Priory of
Lanercost. This is confirmed in the next charter (MS. iii. 2, also xii.
26) by Robert son of Bueth who speaks of Buethbarn as his father.
To both these charters, Robert, Archdeacon (of Carlisle) and Robert
de Vallibus are witnesses. In the charter following (iii. 3) also by
Robert son of Bueth, he speaks of his father Bueth and John his
nephew. Buethbarn and Bueth are therefore identical, but must be
different from that Bueth whose son Gille lived in 1120. Bueth seems
to be the family name, and Buethbarn, or Bueth's child, one of the
family. Robert son of Bueth was the brother-in-law of Robert son of
Asketill (or Anketin or Asketin) who was father of the "nephew John"
spoken of above (*Register*, MS. iii. 5, 8). They join in two grants to
the Priory of Lanercost (MS. iii. 6, 10); and in the latter mention is
made of Bueth, also of Eda and Sigrida, one of whom Robert son of
Asketin had married. In the Pipe Rolls, we find that Robert son of
Bueth was fined one marc in 1177, for having been with the enemies
of the King. He is witness to several of the charters of Robert de
Vallibus and others of the period (*Regist. Lanercost*, MS. i. 6, 8; ii.
9, 12). Robert de Buethcastre is said to have given the Church of
Bewcastle to the Priory of Carlisle.

quam Pater meus dedit eis in Villa de Buchastre[2], Insuper et pasturam sicut in ejus carta[3] plenius continetur.
Ego autem de dono meo proprio dedi et concessi et
presenti carta confirmavi dictæ Domui et Monachis de
Wederhal quatuor acras terræ in dicta Villa de Buchcastre
cum pertinentijs quæ jacent versus occidentem propinquiores sicheto[4] juxta terram quam Pater meus dedit eis
et pasturam trecentis ovibus ubique in communi pastura
de Buchecastre. Hæc autem præscripta omnia dedi eis
in puram liberam et perpetuam Elemosinam sicut aliqua
Elemosina potest dari liberius. Et Ego et Hæredes mei
hanc meam Elemosinam imperpetuum warantizabimus.
Hijs Testibus, Adam de Raveneswic[5], Willelmo fratre
ejus[6], Gilberto Sacerdote de Camboc[7], Rogero Capellano,

---

[2] Buchastre, or Buethcastre, is now Bewcastle; the name Bueth
appears in other places in Gilsland, as Buetholme and Buethby
(*Regist. Lanercost*, MS. iii. 8 *et al.*). The manor of Buchecastre is
mentioned in No. **109**. It lies about 7 miles due north of Lanercost
and is the northernmost parish of the county of Cumberland, touching
Scotland on the north-west and Northumberland on the east and
north-east. Here was a Roman station, not far from the Maiden Way;
and in the churchyard is the famous Saxon Runic Cross. The castle,
of later date than the time of Gille son of Bueth, probably occupies the
site of the castle where the family of Bueth resided, and where Gille
son of Bueth held the district until his death. We find the family now
holding the vill and manor, in the days of Robert de Vallibus. It was
called Bewecastell as early as 1488 (*Cal. Doc. Scot.* ed. Bain, iv. 315);
see also on Adam de Swynburne, No. **111**.

[3] There is no charter granted by Bueth himself in this *Register*.

[4] *Sichetum* from the Anglo-Saxon *sich*, "a furrow" or "watercourse," "a syke."

[5] Adam de Raveneswic appears in the *Pipe Rolls* in 1178, and
again in 1185.

[6] William de Raveneswic, and Adam his son (mentioned in No.
108) are witnesses to a charter of Robert son of Bueth in the *Register
of Lanercost* (MS. iii. 10).

[7] This is no doubt the same as the Gilbert de Camboc in Nos. **120**,
123. Camboc, or Kirkcamboc, was a small parish lying to the north-
west of Lanercost on the Cam Bec, a stream running into the river

Clemente Capellano, Eustachio Diacono, Willelmo Clerico de Wederhal, Waltero Flamāc[8], Alano filio Adæ de Raveneswic, Thoma fratre suo, Alano filio Willelmi[9] et aliis multis[10].

108. CARTA ROBERTI FILIJ BUEC DE BUCHECASTRE, FACTA WILLELMO CLERICO DE ECCLESIA DE DENTON.

UNIVERSIS Sanctæ Matris filijs visuris vel audituris has litteras Robertus filius Buec de Buchastre Salutem. Noverit universitas vestra me intuitu caritatis et pro salute prædecessorum meorum et successorum dedisse et concessisse et hac præsenti carta mea confirmasse Willelmo Clerico Ecclesiam de Dentun[1] in puram et perpetuam

Irthing. This parish has practically died out, and has become merged in the neighbouring parishes of Lanercost and Stapleton. The Church was originally a rectory; in March 1259, Radulf de Tyllioll was rector, and entered into an agreement with the Priory of Lanercost in regard to the tithe and the division between Cambok and Lanercost (*Register of Lanercost*, MS. xv. 18). In 1304, there was an inquisition as to the right of patronage, when it was determined that Richard de Tyrer and the Priory of Carlisle had alternate right of presentation; on the presentation of the latter, Alexander de Crokedayke was instituted; and in 1305, on the presentation of the former, Simon de Tyrer was instituted, an annual pension of 2s. customary *ab antiquo* being allowed to the Cathedral of Carlisle (*Register Bishop Halton*, MS. pp. 78, 91). There was no Church, only "very small remains," or any Rector, in the time of Bishop Nicolson, 1703. It does not appear in the *Valor* of Henry VIII.

[8] Walter Flamanc, or Flamang, or Flandres, i.e. Walter the Fleming, is a witness to the charter, mentioned above, of Robert son of Bueth in the *Register of Lanercost* (MS. iii. 2), and is a co-witness with him to other charters (MS. ii. 9, 12) also a witness to the Foundation Charter. In No. **108**, he is called de Camboc.

[9] Alan son of William de Raveneswic, and therefore nephew of Adam.

[10] This and the next charter are evidently of the same date. We find Robert son of Bueth and Adam de Raveneswick both in 1177—78, the former a contemporary of Robert, Archdeacon; and this is probably not far from the date.

108. [1] This is Nether or Lower Denton in Gilsland; see on No.

Elemosinam cum libertatibus et pertinentijs ad eandem Ecclesiam pertinentibus. Et ut ista Concessio rata et illibata consistat eam presentis scripti Patrocinio communivimus. Hijs Testibus Adam de Raveneswic et fratre suo, Waltero Flamāc de Camboc, Clemente Capellano, Rogero Capellano, Eustacio Diacono, Thoma Capellano, Thoma filio Adæ, Alano filio Willelmi et Adam fratre suo, Hugone filio Willelmi et multis alijs[2].

109. CARTA MABILIÆ FILIÆ ADÆ FILIJ RICHERI DE BUCHCASTRE FACTA MONACHIS DE WEDERHALE DE XIV ACRIS TERRÆ IN BUCHCASTRE.

OMNIBUS Christi fidelibus ad quorum noticiam hoc præsens scriptum pervenerit Mabilia filia Adæ filij Richeri de Buchastre[1] Salutem. Noverit universitas vestra me in libera viduitate mea et ligia potestate mea pro salute animarum Prædecessorum et Successorum meorum dedisse concessisse et præsenti carta confirmasse Deo et Abachiæ Sanctæ Mariæ Eboraci et Monachis Sanctæ Trinitatis et Sancti Constantini de Wederhal quatuordecim acras terræ in territorio de Buchecastre quæ jacent inter divisas de Maspaynen[2] Habendas et Tenendas in liberam puram et perpetuam Elemosinam cum duobus toftis et cum omnibus pertinentijs libertatibus communis et aisiamentis ad

---

34, and the account there given of the presentations to this Church. The advowson of the Church was granted about this time to the monks of Wederhal (No. 121) and William, clerk, now presented by Robert son of Bueth, was presented anew by them and instituted by Archdeacon Peter de Ros (No. 120). This presentation by Robert is confirmed by Peter de Ros in No. 123.

[2] The witnesses are practically the same as in the last charter, and the date must be about the same, 1170 to 1180 and nearer the latter year.

109.   [1] Richer was the parson of Buchcastre, see Nos. 110, 111.

[2] Or "Dykes of Maspeyaneu" as Bp Nicolson translates (MSS. iii. 150) and adds that in the margin of the charter a later hand explains—"Rivulus currens de Mora."

Manerium de Buchecastre ubique spectantibus intra Villam et extra absque aliquo retenimento adeo libere et quiete sicut aliqua Elemosina liberius aut quietius dari possit aut possideri. Et Ego Mabilia et hæredes mei prædictam Elemosinam dictis Monachis contra omnes homines imperpetuum warantizabimus adquietabimus et defendemus. In cujus rei testimonium presenti scripto sigillum meum apposui. Hijs Testibus Radulpho Priore[3], Waltero Officiario[4], W. Decano Karlioli, Willelmo de Dacre tunc Vicecomite[5], Roberto de Castlecayroc, Adam de Hotun, Richard de Cleterne tunc forestario Cumberlandiæ, W. filio Rogeri, W. de Warthwic, Alano de Langwayt, Johanne de Agulunby, Johanne filio Willelmi, Rogero clerico et alijs[6].

110. QUIETA CLAMATIO JULIANÆ FILIÆ ADÆ FILII PARSONÆ DE BUCHCASTRE FACTA MONACHIS DE WEDERHALE DE TERRA QUAM ADAM PATER SUUS TENUIT IN EADEM.

OMNIBUS Christi fidelibus ad quorum noticiam litteræ presentes pervenerint Juliana filia Adæ filij Parsonæ de Buchcastre Salutem in Domino sempiternam. Noverit universitas vestra me in pura viduitate et ligia potestate mea concessisse remisisse et omnino quietam clamasse Abbati et conventui Beatæ Mariæ Eboraci Cellæque eorun-

---

[3] Radulph was Prior of Carlisle 1231—47, see on No. **97**.

[4] Walter de Ulvesby, see note 5 on No. **56**.

[5] William de Daker, or Dacre, was Sheriff of Cumberland, or 'Custos,' between 1236 and 1247. He was also Sheriff of Cumberland and governor of Carlisle Castle in 1268 (*Inquis. post mort.* 52 Hen. III. No. 30) and was succeeded in the office of Sheriff by his son Ranulph de Dacre (*Pipe Rolls, Cumberland*, 53 Hen. III.), and he died in that year. It was his great grandson, also Ranulph, who carried off the heiress Margaret de Multon in the time of Edward II. and brought the Barony of Gilsland into the family of the Dacres. Compare on Thomas de Multon in No. **47**, note 4.

[6] The date of this charter must be from 1236 to 1247, and probably, from the Official, before 1240.

dem de Wederhal Priori et Monachis ibidem Deo servientibus totum jus meum quod habuero vel habere potero in tota illa terra quam Adam prædictus Pater meus tenuit in Villa de Buchecastre quondam de prædictis Abbate et Conventu Priore cellæ supradictæ. Ita quod nec Ego nec aliquis nomine meo Hæredes vel assignati mei aliquod jus vel clamium in prædicta terra exigere vel vendicare poterimus imperpetuum. Et ut ista mea concessio remissio et omnino quieta clamatio perpetuum optineat robur firmitatis huic præsenti scripto sigillum meum est appensum. Hijs Testibus, Domino Michaele de Hartcla tunc Vicecomite[1], Domino Johanne de Teribi, Domino Thoma de Neuton Militibus, Roberto de Warthwic, Willelmo filio ejusdem, Adam de Ulnesby[2], Johanne Tylliol[3], Hugone de Talkan et alijs[4].

111. QUIETA CLAMATIO RADULPHI FILIJ ADÆ DE BUCHCASTRE FACTA MONACHIS DE WEDERHALE DE TERRA QUAM DE EIS TENERE SOLEBAT IN EADEM.

UNIVERSIS Christi fidelibus ad quorum notitiam præsens scriptum pervenerit Radulphus filius Adæ de Buchcastre Salutem in Domino sempiternam. Noverit universitas vestra me reddidisse et remisisse resignasse et omnino pro me et Hæredibus meis quietam clamasse imperpetuum Deo et Ecclesiæ Sanctæ Mariæ Eborum et Domui Sanctæ Trinitatis et Sancti Constantini de Wederhal et Monachis ibidem Deo servientibus totam terram illam in Villa de

---

110. [1] Michael de Hartcla was Sheriff of Cumberland 1285 to 1298; see note 2 on No. **78.**

[2] Adam de Ulnesby, or Ulvesby, appears with Michael de Hartcla in No. **199,** which is dated 1291.

[3] John Tylliol was one of the Coroners of Cumberland in 1301 (*Calend. Doc. Scot.* ed Bain, ii. 309); he is witness to a charter dated 1293 in the *Register of Lanercost* (MS. xiii. 17) with Hugh de Talkan, who also witnesses several other dated charters about the same time; an elder Hugh is mentioned in No. **53.**

[4] From the sheriff, the date is 1285—98, probably about 1290.

Buchecastre cum edificijs pratis pasturis et omnibus alijs
pertinentijs suis sine aliquo retenemento quam quidem
terram aliquando de prædictis Monachis in prædicta Villa
usque ad terminum vitæ meæ tenui et quam quidem terram
Adam filius Parsonæ[1] de Abbatia Sanctæ Mariæ Eborum
et Domo Sanctæ Trinitatis et Sancti Constantini de
Wederhale aliquando tenuit, Ita videlicet quod nec Ego
Radulphus nec Hæredes mei nec aliquis alius nomine mei
vel Hæredum meorum in prædictis edificijs terris pratis vel
pasturis seu eorum aliquibus pertinentijs de cætero aliquod
jus vel clamium habere exigere vel vendicare poterimus
imperpetuum.   In cujus rei Testimonium præsenti scripto
sigillum meum apposui.   Hijs Testibus, Dominis Michaele
de Hartcla tunc Vicecomite Cumberlandie, Thoma de
Neuton, Johanne de Teribi tunc Coronatoribus ejusdem
Comitatûs Cumberlandiæ, Roberto de Feritate, Waltero
de Mulcaster[2], Willelmo de Boyvill Militibus, Adam de
Swynburne[3], Roberto de Warthwic, Willelmo filio suo,

111.   [1] This *Parsona* was Richer the Parson of Buchcastre (see
Nos. 109, 110) and the word Buchcastre is probably omitted here.

[2] Walter de Mulcaster, or Molecastre, is mentioned with the above
Robert de la Feritate in an Inquisition held in 1281—82 with regard to
the manor of Lydel on the Scotch border (*Inquis. post mort.* 10 Edw.
I. No. 26).   He there is said to hold North Eston and a tenement in
Arthuret.   He seems to have been known as Sir Walter de Mulcaster
of Arthuret, to the north of Carlisle; but Mulcaster, or Moelcastre
(*hodie* Muncaster), connected with other members of the family, was
on the west coast, south of the Derwent.   The word is derived from
the Celtic *moel*, "a bare hill" or "headland"; compare the Mull of
Cantire.

[3] Adam de Swynburne, or Sir Adam as he is called later, held the
manor of Buchecastre.   It appears to have been in the hands of
Richard de Levington; as he died without issue, it passed to Juliana
de Carrig, one of his six sisters; her daughters Matildis and Emma
sold Bothecastre "before the war" to Sir John de Swyneburne, who
was Sheriff of Cumberland in 1278.   In 1296, it had passed to Adam
de Swynburne, apparently the son of Sir John; but it was seized by
the King (Edward I.) because Adam had joined the Scots and was a

Roberto de Crogelyn, Hugone de Talkan, Richardo de Brakentwayt et alijs⁴.

112. CARTA GERARDI DE LASCELS FACTA MONACHIS DE WEDERHALE DE XX ACRIS TERRÆ IN HEDRESFORD.

OMNIBUS Christi fidelibus ad quorum notitiam præsens scriptum pervenerit Gerardus de Lascels¹ Salutem eternam in Domino. Noverit universitas vestra me Divinæ Pietatis

party to the plundering of the Priory of Hexham. He seems later to have made peace with the King. In 1338, or shortly before, Adam died, as well as his son Henry; and his daughter Barnaba, wife of Sir John de Strivelyn, succeeded to Bothecastre and his other property. This daughter Barnaba was living in 1357—58, and her lands in Cumberland were restored by the King, Edward III., on account of the services of her husband, although in the time of the King's father she had been in allegiance with the Scots, and lived in the family of Robert de Brus. In 1401, the Castle of Bothe belonged to John, son and heir of Sir John de Middelton. See the numerous refs. in *Calend. Doc. Scot.* ed. J. Bain (especially ii. 32, 172; iii. 238; iv. 1, 2, 121). The account in Nicolson and Burn (*History* ii. 476) is strangely incorrect.

⁴ From the Sheriff and other witnesses, the date must be nearly the same date as the preceding charter, probably about 1290.

112. ¹ It does not appear exactly who this Gerard de Lascels was. He held lands in Levington (see below on Hedresford) by agreement with the Lord of Levington (see on No. **114**). As we have seen, the family of Lascels was connected with the Corkeby family, not far from this time, Isabella, daughter of Robert son of William, having married Alan de Lascels for her second husband (see on Nos. **37, 47**). Gerard had a son Elyas who appears in No. **116**. There was a Gerard de Lasceles in the preceding century, who held lands in Asby, Westmoreland. In a grant of lands made by him about 1160—70 to the monks of Byland, his brother Alan de Lasceles is mentioned, his son Alan, his son-in-law Richard de Crosby and a Robert de Lasceles a party to the agreement. It is attested by Robert Archdeacon of Carlisle, also by Maureward de Appleby. The elder Alan of these may well have been the Alan de Lascels who with Archdeacon Robert witnesses the charter of Earl Henry to Holm Cultram in 1150. The original charter of this Gerard de Lasceles is one of the Levens Hall MSS.; see 10th *Report Hist. MSS. Commission* (iv.) p. 321.

intuitu et pro salute animarum Prædecessorum et Successorum meorum dedisse concessisse et præsenti carta mea
confirmasse Deo et Abachiæ Sanctæ Mariæ Eboraci necnon et Monachis Sanctæ Trinitatis et Sancti Constantini
de Wederhal viginti acras terræ arabilis in territorio de
Hedresford[2] in cultura quæ vocatur Scalingrig et unam
acram et unam rodam terræ in eodem territorio in alio loco
in eadem Cultura quæ dicitur Scalingrig. Habendas et
Tenendas in liberam puram et perpetuam Elemosinam, et
dicti Monachi habebunt in perpetuam Elemosinam in
prædicta Villa de Hedresford ex dono meo et concessione
pasturam ad trecentos multones[3] vel ad trecentas oves.
Et habebunt imperpetuum ex dono meo et concessione
pasturam in prædicta villa ad novem boves et ad quatuor
vaccas cum sequela unius anni et ad unum Equum et unam
Equam cum sequela unius anni et ad quatuor porcos vel
quatuor sues cum porcellis suis usque ad tempus separa-
tionis. Et insuper capient sufficienter omnia estuveria[4]
sua ad edificandum claudendum et comburendum in boscis
et moris et in omnibus alijs locis ad Villam de Hedresford
spectantibus sine alicujus visu vel impedimento scilicet
quantum pertinet ad prædictum Tenementum. Et sciendum est quod si quid de prædictis acris in prædicta cultura

[2] Hedresford was a vill in the Barony of Levington, as appears
from the grant (No. 113) to the monks to grind free of multure in the
mill of Levington, also from an inquisition in 1272 concerning the
lands of Helewysa widow of Eustace de Baylloll (*Inquis. post mort.*
56 Hen. III. No. 35). Hedresford is probably another form of
Hethersford; so we have now Hethersgill in Kirklinton (Kirklevington)
and the Hether Burn.

[3] *Multones* were sheep for food, from the Low Latin *multonem*,
accusative of *multo*, "a sheep"; *oves* were sheep for breeding. The
whole passage is interesting as shewing the kinds of animals fed on
the common pasture to which the right is here given.

[4] *Estuveria*, or *estoveria*, "firewood," the allowance of wood to
tenants, originally allowance of provisions or stuff generally, from the
French *estover, estoffer*.

de Scalingrig dictis Priori et Monachis defuerit Ego vel
Hæredes mei in cultura mea de Selesete in loco competenti ad commodum suum prædictas acras eis sine aliqua
occasione plene perficiemus.   Ego autem Gerardus et
Hæredes mei totam prædictam terram cum pertinentijs
sicut prædictum est, et totam prædictam pasturam sicut
supradictum est prædictis Monachis contra omnes homines
imperpetuum warantizabimus acquietabimus et defendemus.
Et ut hoc scriptum meæ donationis et concessionis per-
petuæ firmitatis robur optineat ad omnium prædictorum
observantiam Sacramento corporaliter prestito me et
Hæredes meos perpetue obligavi.   Et insuper ad majorem
securitatem præsenti scripto sigillum meum apposui.   Hijs
Testibus Domino Radulpho Priore Karlioli, Magistro G.
Archidiacono[5], Domino Waltero Officiario[6], Ricardo Brun
Vicecomite Karlioli, Domino Ricardo de Levington, Domino
Roberto de Castelkairoc, Domino Petro de Tyllol, Domino
Willelmo filio Rogeri de Corkeby[7], Roberto filio suo,
Willelmo de Warthwic, Radulpho Clerico, Johanne Stelfot,
Henrico Wrenne et alijs[8].

113. CARTA GERARDI DE LASCELS DE QUIETANCIA
MULTURÆ TERRÆ QUAM DEDIT MONACHIS DE WEDER-
HALE IN HEDRESFORD.

OMNIBUS Christi fidelibus ad quorum noticiam præsens
scriptum pervenerit Gerardus de Lascels Salutem æternam
in Domino.   Noverit universitas vestra me Divinæ pietatis
intuitu et pro salute animarum Prædecessorum et Successorum meorum dedisse concessisse et presenti carta mea

5 Gervase de Louther, Archdeacon of Carlisle, see on No. **21**.

6 Walter de Ulvesby, see on No. **56**.

7 William son of Roger, here first called de Corkeby, see note 2
on No. **64**.

8 The date of the charter must be after 1231 when Radulph was
made Prior; see No. **97**, where are many of the same witnesses with
Richard Brun as Sheriff, probably before 1235—6.

confirmasse Deo et Abaciæ Sanctæ Mariæ Eboraci necnon et Monachis Sanctæ Trinitatis et Sancti Constantini de Wederhal libertatem istam scilicet quod molent totum bladum suum quod crescet in territorio de Hedresford scilicet in illa terra quam dedi eis in liberam puram et perpetuam Elemosinam ad molendinum de Levington quietum de multura. Et Ego et Hæredes mei prædictam libertatem prædictis Monachis contra omnes homines imperpetuum warantizabimus acquietabimus et defendemus. Et ut hoc scriptum meæ Donationis et Concessionis perpetuæ firmitatis robur optineat ad prædictæ libertatis observantiam juramento corporaliter præstito me et Hæredes meos perpetue obligavi. Et insuper ad majorem securitatem presenti scripto sigillum meum apposui. Hijs Testibus Domino Radulpho Priore Karlioli, Magistro Waltero Officiario, G. de Louther Archidiacono, Ricardo Brun Vicecomite Karlioli, Domino Ricardo de Levington, Domino Roberto de Castelkairoc, Domino Petro de Tyllol, Domino Willelmo filio Rogeri de Korkebi, Roberto filio suo, Willelmo de Warthwic, Radulpho Clerico, Johanne Stelfot, Henrico Wrenne et alijs.

114. CARTA GERARDI DE LASCELS FACTA MONACHIS DE WEDERHAL DE UNA ACRA PRATI IN HEDRESFORD.

OMNIBUS Christi fidelibus ad quorum notitiam hoc præsens scriptum pervenerit Gerardus de Lascels Salutem æternam in Domino. Noverit universitas vestra me Divinæ Pietatis intuitu et pro salute animarum prædecessorum et successorum meorum dedisse concessisse et præsenti carta mea confirmasse Deo et Abbachiæ Sanctæ Mariæ Eboraci necnon et Monachis Sanctæ Trinitatis et Sancti Constantini de Wederhal unam acram Prati in territorio de Hedresford in Prato quod vocatur Cumberhait, Habendam et Tenendam in puram et perpetuam Elemosinam. Et quia dictam acram tempore confectionis istius cartæ in manu mea non habui tradidi eis unam acram prati quæ est in prato sub crofto meo de Hedresford juxta Fontem quam dicti Monachi habebunt et pacifice possidebunt donec terminus Cirographi (inter Dominum -⊕-[1] de Levington et A. uxorem suam ex una parte et me ex altera super terra et prato de Cumberhait confecti) plene compleatur et donec prædictam acram de bosco plenarie deliberavero. Et Ego Gerardus et Hæredes mei prædictam acram prati cum pertinentijs prædictis Monachis contra omnes homines imperpetuum warantizabimus acquietabimus et defendemus. Et ut hoc scriptum meæ Donationis et concessionis perpetuæ firmitatis robur optineat ad omnium præscriptorum observantiam Sacramento corporaliter præstito me et hæredes meos perpetue obligavi. Et insuper ad majorem securitatem presenti scripto sigillum meum apposui. Hijs Testibus Domino Radulpho Priore Karlioli, Magistro G. de Louther Archidiacono, Domino Waltero Officiario, Ricardo Brun Vicecomite Karlioli, Domino Ricardo de Levington, Domino Roberto de Castelkairoc, Domino Petro de Tyllol, Willelmo filio Rogeri de Korkeby, Roberto filio suo, Willelmo de Warthwic, Radulpho Clerico, Johanne Stelfot, Henrico Wrenne et multis alijs[2].

115. Quieta Clamatio Gerardi Lascels facta

114. [1] This is, no doubt, R. for Ranulph de Boyvill of Levington, the brother and heir of Richard de Levington (see note 5 on No. 54). He would obtain this property, which he and A. his wife had here leased to Gerard de Lascels, through his wife Ada. She was one of the two daughters of Johanna, daughter of Hugh de Morville, and Richard Gernun; she married William Furnival on the death of Ranulph de Levington (see note 1 on No. 103). Ranulph had livery of the lands of his brother Richard de Levington in 1250; but he did not keep them long, as he was dead in January 1253—54, leaving a daughter and heir Helewisa, who married Eustace de Balliol. Ada, his widow, became heir to her sister Helewisa, widow of Richard de Vernun, in 1270 (*Inquis. post mort.* 54 Hen. III. No. 19) and died shortly after.

[2] This charter has the same witnesses and date as the two preceding charters.

PRIORI DE WEDERHALE DE UNO BISANCIO QUOD
RECIPERE SOLEBAT AB EODEM.

OMNIBUS hanc cartam visuris vel audituris Gerardus
de Lascels Salutem æternam in Domino. Noverit universitas vestra me remisisse et quietum clamasse de me
et Hæredibus meis imperpetuum Deo et Beatæ Mariæ
Eboraci nec non et Priori et Monachis Sanctæ Trinitatis et
Sancti Constantini de Wederhale unum Bisancium[1] quod
solebam annuatim percipere de Camera prædicti Prioris
de Wederhal prout continebatur in quadam carta quam
habui de Abbate et Conventu Eboraci quam prædicto
Priori in confectione hujus cartæ reddidi. Et pro hac
remissione et quieta clamatione dederunt mihi in magna
necessitate mea de bonis Ecclesiæ suæ viginti quinque
solidos et octo denarios. Et ne Ego vel aliquis Hæredum
meorum contra hanc cartam venire poterimus illam sigilli
mei impressione roboravi. Hijs Testibus Domino R. Priore
Karlioli[2], Domino W. Archidiacono Karliolensi[3], Domino
W. Vicecomite Karlioli[4], Domino Ricardo de Levington,
Domino Petro Tyllol, Domino Willelmo filio Rogeri de
Korkebi, Willelmo de Warthwic, Johanne Stelfot, Roberto
de Horneby[5], Willelmo de Langcost et alijs[6].

115. [1] *Bisancium,* "a besant" or "byzant." The silver besant,
which is evidently meant here, was worth about two shillings. The
gold besant was worth about £15, and was so called from the place
where they were first struck, Byzantium (Constantinople). The word
has come to us from the Latin, through the Old French. Gerard
makes here a curious quitclaim of this annual besant for the sum of
25s. 8d. given to him by the Convent in his great necessity.

[2] Radulph Prior, see note 5 on No. **97.**

[3] Walter de Ulvesby, formerly Official, now Archdeacon, see on
No. **56.**

[4] William de Daker is here meant; he was custos from 1236 to
1247, and probably followed Richard Brun; see note 5 on No. **109.**

[5] Robert de Horneby is witness with John Stelfot to charter No.
171, in 1241.

[6] The date of this charter must be between 1236 and 1247, and is
probably not later than 1240.

116. Obligatio Gerardi de Lascels de non movenda lite contra Priorem de Wederhale vel aliquem de suis.

Omnibus Christi fidelibus presentes litteras inspecturis vel audituris Gerardus de Lascels Salutem æternam in Domino. Noverit universitas vestra quod Ego tactis Sacrosanctis juravi pro me et Elya filio meo quod nunquam Ego nec ipse movebimus calumpniam, vel litem contra Willelmum Priorem de Wederhal[1] vel aliquem hominum suorum coram Justiciarijs vel aliquo alio Ballivo in mundo Ratione alicujus Controversiæ motæ inter dictum Priorem et homines suos et me et filium meum. Et si (quod absit) instigante Diabolo quandoque contra tenorem presentis scripti Ego vel filius meus venire presumpserimus tanquam perjuri et excommunicati in omnibus locis repellemur. Et insuper Ego Gerardus sub prædicto juramento, prædicto Priori Centum solidos nomine pœnæ persolvam, Renunciando Civilis Fori privilegio et omni juris auxilio. In cujus rei Testimonium presenti scripto sigillum meum apposui. [Testibus] Domino Willelmo filio Rogeri et Osanna uxore sua, Alano de Langetheit, Alano Malekat[2], Willelmo Clerico de Agulunby, Willelmo et David de Korkeby[3], Galfrido, Hamelino, Henrico, Adam, Ricardo Clerico servientibus de Wederhale, Stephano et Alexandro de Neuby[4] et alijs[5].

---

116.   [1] William Rundel, Prior of Wederhal, who was made Abbot of S. Mary's, York, in 1239, see Appendix E.

[2] This is probably Alan Malekak; as Alan Malecake he granted lands in Brampton to the Priory of Lanercost (*Regist. Lanercost*, MS. ii. 7) and William son of Roger attests the deed. The name occurs in the *Chart. of Whitby* (ed. Atkinson, i. 112) and the *Chart. of Rievaulx* (ed. Atkinson, p. 118 *et al.*).

[3] William was a son of William son of Roger, and probably David also, see on No. **64.**

[4] Alexander de Neuby, see on No. **148.**

[5] The date of the charter is probably not long before 1239.

117. Confirmatio Episcopi Karliolensis super compositionem factam inter Monachos de Wederhale et Canonicos de Lanercost de Ecclesia de Denton[1].

OMNIBUS Christi fidelibus ad quorum notitiam hoc presens scriptum pervenerit W.[2] Dei Gratia Karliolensis Episcopus Salutem æternam in Domino. Noverit universitas vestra Nos compositionem factam coram judicibus a Domino propterea delegatis inter Monachos Sanctæ Mariæ Eboraci et de Wederhal et W. et R. de Buchecastre Clericos[3] ex una parte et Canonicos de Lanercost[4]

---

117. [1] This is a Confirmation by Bishop Bernard of the Composition made in No. 119 between the Monks of Wederhale and the Canons of Lanercost, and confirms the Church of (Nether) Denton to them for ever ; see note 3 on No. 34.

[2] There is no doubt W. is an error for " B. (*Bernardus*) Episcopus." The Transcript C reads $_W^B$ and has *Bernardus* in the margin. There is no Bishop W. except Bishop Walter Malclerk, who succeeded Bishop Hugh, whereas in No. 118 Bishop Hugh refers to this Confirmation as that of his predecessor, who must be either Bishop A. (Athelwold) or Bishop B. (Bernard). The witnesses to this charter belong undoubtedly to the period which we have fixed as being that of Bishop Bernard. The error in the initial W. is repeated in No. 118 ; but in No. 122 this Confirmation is mentioned as that of " B. Episcopus."

[3] The term "clerks" is, apparently, not here the law term, but is used of the incumbents of the two moieties of the living. The legal "clerk" was very generally in the ministry. The term was also used to denote a secular in opposition to a regular priest.

[4] Lanercost was a Priory of Augustinian Canons, beautifully situated on the river Irthing, about 10 miles north east of Carlisle. It was founded by Robert de Vallibus about 1169 (see note 4 on No. 28). The grants of their possessions are given in the *Register of Lanercost* (MS. with the Dean and Chapter of Carlisle) to which reference has been so often made. The points of greatest interest in the history of the Priory were the visits of Edward I. with Queen Eleanor in September 1280 and with Queen Margaret to stay some months, from September 29th, 1306 to March 26th, 1307. The King died at Burgh upon Sands the following July 7th (*Chronicon de Lanercost* ed. J. Stevenson, pp. 105, 205 ; Lysons, *Cumberland*, pp. xv, 131).

et W. Archidiaconum de Notingham[5] ex altera super Ecclesia de Denton[6] ratam habere et firmam. Et quia volumus conditionem dictorum Monachorum et Canonicorum intuitu Dei et Caritatis in dicta Ecclesia meliorare Noveritis quod de assensu Capituli nostri concessimus et confirmavimus dictis Monachis de Wederhal et Canonicis de Lanercost prædictam Ecclesiam de Denton in usus proprios imperpetuum. Ita quidem quod liceat dictis Monachis et Canonicis post decessum W. et R. Clericorum in dictam Ecclesiam ingredi auctoritate propria et eandem pacifice possidere imperpetuum sine aliquorum contradictione vel impedimento salvis Nobis et Successoribus nostris Sinodalibus et Archidiaconalibus. Et ut hoc scriptum nostræ concessionis et confirmationis perpetuæ

[5] This was William Testard, Archdeacon of Notingham (on the one t being correct, see Skeat, *English Etymology*, i. 258), which was then in the province and diocese of York. He took an active part in the violent controversy between the Chapter of York and Archbishop Geoffrey Plantagenet, brother of Richard I. He had been the agent of Archbp Geoffrey at Rome in 1190, when the quarrel began ; but with Hamo the Treasurer (who attests No. **119**) he joined the others against him in 1194, and in September of that year was one of those who, with Simon of Apulia (who attests No. **119**) and Geoffrey de Muschamp, carried the appeal to Rome. In 1199, he was present when the dispute was submitted to the arbitration of the Bishop of Lincoln and others ; but it was not settled until 1200, when at Westminster William Testard and others were received by the Archbishop to the kiss of peace (*Roger de Hoveden*, iii. 272, iv. 98, 126 and see Bishop Stubbs' excellent account of the controversy in his Preface to vol. iv.). He is a witness to the confirmation charter of Archbp Geoffrey to the Priory of Lanercost (*Register*, MS. viii. 15) with Geoffrey (de Muscamp) Archbishop of Cleveland, who was made Bishop of Lichfield in 1198, and J. (John) Bishop of Whiterne or Candida Casa, who was certainly at York with G. de Muscamp in 1195 (*R. de Hoveden*, iii. 286). William Testard was made Dean of York October 29th, 1214 (*Patent Rolls*, 16 Joh. Record Com. p. 123a) and died before 1221.

[6] Nether Denton, or Denton Inferior, see the account of the Church in note 3 on No. **34**.

14—2

firmitatis robur optineat eidem sigillum nostrum fecimus apponi. Hijs Testibus, Johanne Priore Karlioli, Adam Decano[7], Magistro Adam de Kirkebithore[8] Veregario, Adam Clerico, Michaele Serviente, Willelmo Clerico, Willelmo de Eyreminne, Umfrido, Laurentio de Aguluneby et multis alijs[9].

118. CONFIRMATIO EPISCOPI KARLIOLENSIS DE CONCESSIONE PRÆDECESSORIS SUI SUPER ECCLESIA DE DENTONA.

UNIVERSIS Sanctæ Matris Ecclesiæ filijs ad quorum notitiam hoc præsens scriptum pervenerit H. Dei Gratia Karliolensis Episcopus[1] salutem æternam in Domino. Quoniam ex injuncto nobis Curæ Pastoralis Officio tenemur subjectorum nostrorum et præcipue Religiosorum commoditati misericorditer providere, Noverit universitas vestra Nos Divinæ Pietatis intuitu de assensu Capituli Nostri Karliolensis Ecclesiæ Ecclesiam de Dentona quam felicis memoriæ prædecessor noster W.[2] quondam Karlio-

---

[7] Adam de Aspatric, Dean of Allerdale, see note 5 on No. **43**.

[8] Adam de Kirkebithore was lord of the manor of Kirbythore in Westmorland, the son of Waldiev son of Gamel son of Whelp; he and his father granted certain lands there to the Abbey of Holm Cultram (*Register Holm Cultram*, p. 126, seq.; the charters are also set out in Nicolson and Burn, *History* i. 376 from *Machel MSS.* v. 471, 479). In 1206 he appeared as defendant in an action brought against him by Matilda, wife of William Mauchael, concerning lands in Crackenthorp (*Pedes Finium*, 8 Joh. Westmorland). From the above-named charters it appears that he had a brother Alan and a son Gilbert (see also on No. **200**). His father Waldiev in witness to a grant of lands in Coleby by William de Bretton in the time of Abbot Clement 1161—84 (Additional Charters No. **252**).

[9] We have John, Prior in 1204 (see on No. **31**), and the other witnesses occur about the early years of the century. They agree with the date assigned to Bishop Bernard in Appendix D, 1204—14.

118. [1] Hugh de Beaulieu, 3rd Bishop of Carlisle, February, 1218—19 to 1223, see note 1 on No. **19**.

[2] W. is clearly an error for B. (Bernardus) as shown in note 2 on No. **117**.

lensis Episcopus Domibus de Wederhale et de Lanercost communiter concessit sicut in ipsius autentico scripto et carta Capituli super hoc confectis plenius continetur, eisdem domibus et viris Religiosis in eisdem manentibus cum omnibus suis pertinentiis ad eorum proprios et communes usus perpetuo concessisse et præsentis scripti patrocinio confirmasse. Ita scilicet quod cedente vel decedente Rectore dictæ Ecclesiæ liceat eis dictam Ecclesiam Auctoritate propria ingredi et pacifice possidere sine contradictione nostra vel Successorum nostrorum Salvis tamen Sinodalibus et Archidiaconalibus. In cujus rei Testimonium præsenti scripto sigillum nostrum apposuimus. Testibus W. Priore[3], Magistro A. Officiali Karliolensi[4], Magistro Phillipo de Ardenne[5], Magistro G. de Louthir, Domino W. Capellano, nostro fratre Willelmo, Odardo Clerico, Stephano serviente[6].

119. COMPOSITIO INTER MONACHOS DE WEDERHALE ET CANONICOS DE LANERCOST SUPER ECCLESIA DE DENTON[1]

UNIVERSIS Sanctæ Matris Ecclesiæ filijs ad quos præsens scriptum pervenerit R. de Gysburne[2] et W. de Novo Castro[3] Priores et P. Supprior de Dunelmo æternam

[3] William Rundel, now Prior of Wederhal, see Appendix E.

[4] Adam de Kirkeby, see note 6 on No. 19.

[5] Philip de Ardenne, or Arderne, was one of the emissaries of Henry III. in 1228 to the Pope about the affairs of the Bishopric of Durham (*Close Rolls*, 11 Hen. III. m. 20, Record Com. i. p. 207 *b*).

[6] The date of the charter lies between 1218 and 1223.

119. [1] This is the Composition which is confirmed in the two preceding Charters.

[2] Roald was Prior of Gyseburne in 1199, and a contemporary of Archbishop Geoffrey Plantagenet (see *Chart. Gyseburne*, ed. Brown, p. xxvii).

[3] The margin of Transcript A has *Burgo* for *Castro*; Newburgh was a Priory of Austin Canons in Yorkshire; at Newcastle there was only a nunnery. The historian William, a monk of Newburgh, wrote

in Domino Salutem.   Noverit universitas vestra quod
causa quæ vertebatur inter Monachos Sanctæ Mariæ
Eboraci et Monachos de Wederhal et W. et R. de Buchecastre Clericos ex una parte et Canonicos de Lanercost
et Magistrum W. Archidiaconum de Notingham ex alia
super Ecclesia de Denton nobis a Domino propterea commissa amicabiliter sopita est.   Ita scilicet quod præfati
Monachi de Eboraco et de Wederhal habebunt totam
medietatem prædictæ Ecclesiæ de Denton et Canonici de
Lanercost aliam medietatem nomine Ecclesiæ de Brancton,
Et prenominati W. et R. clerici de Buchecastre persolvent
annuatim jam dictis Monachis apud Wederhal duos solidos
nomine pensionis prædictæ Ecclesiæ, et alios duos solidos
Canonicis de Lanercost nomine pensionis ejusdem Ecclesiæ
de Denton.   Et si contigerit eandem Ecclesiam vacare
Monachi prædicti præsentabunt Clericum ad suam medietatem, et Canonici de Lanercost præsentabunt Clericum
ad suam medietatem.   Et si contingat Deo volente quod
alterutra portio....sive Monachorum sive Canonicorum præfatorum quocunque modo eisdem melioretur et Monachi
et Canonici jam dicti communiter percipient emolumentum
inde proveniens et inter se dimidiabunt.   Et ut ratum
permaneat quod coram nobis sollempniter actum præsenti
scripto sigilla nostra dignum duximus apponere.   Hijs
Testibus S. Decano[4], H. Thesaurario[5], Magistro G.

just at this time, 1198, and died in 1208.   No Prior W. is given in
Dugdale, *Monasticon.*

[4] Simon of Apulia, Dean of York.   We have in this charter the
three great opponents in the Chapter of York to Archbishop Geoffrey,
who had all been his confidential agents in 1190, Simon the Dean,
Hamo the Treasurer (see below) and William Testard (see note 5
on No. 117).   Simon, who had been an Italian lawyer and Chancellor
of York, being disappointed in regard to his appointment to the
Deanery in 1193, about which the Archbishop played fast and
loose, took a hostile part, and was elected by the discontented Chapter.
There were appeals to Rome, Simon going in person, and he was
confirmed in the office in February, 1194 (*Roger de Hoveden,* ed.

Canonico Eborum[6], Magistro R. de Karliolo Canonico de Lanercost[7].

Stubbs, iii. 283 sq.). Concerning the subsequent contest, see note 5 on No. 117. Other details concerning Simon are given by Roger de Hoveden. He was made Bishop of Exeter in October, 1214, and died in September, 1223.

[5] Hamo, or Hamund, was Treasurer of York and a party to the troubles mentioned above on William Testard and Simon of Apulia. From 1186 to 1189, when Hubert Walter was Dean and Geoffrey Plantagenet was Treasurer, Hamo was precentor of York. *Benedict Abbas* (ed. Stubbs i. 352) names him as one of the five nominated to Henry II. by the Chapter of York, in September 1186, to fill the long vacant See of York, all of whom the King rejected. When Geoffrey was elected to the See in 1189, Hubert Walter the Dean, who was disappointed of the office, led the Chapter in hostile action against him. Hamo had held the office of Precentor many years, and had been promised the treasuryship by Archbp Roger before his death in 1181 (see *Benedict Abbas* ii. 88). When Geoffrey was appointed in 1181, Hamo too was a disappointed man ; and when the office was given to Bouchard de Puiset in 1189, he refused to instal him. At first he was friendly with Archbp Geoffrey, and took his part against the Chapter in 1190, and was one of his agents in Rome. In 1194 on the renewed quarrel of the Archbishop with the Chapter, Hamo took active part against him. On the peace which was made, see above on W. Testard. When Bouchard de Puiset died in 1196, Eustace, the keeper of the king's seal, was made Treasurer ; and Hamo was again disappointed ; but when Eustace was made Bishop of Ely in March 1198, Hamo at last became the Treasurer of York, and Reginald Arundel succeeded as Precentor (*R. de Hoveden*, iv. 41, 98). He appears to have held the office as late as July 1215 (*Patent Rolls*, 17 Joh., Record Com. p. 151 a). Hamo and Simon the Dean attest three charters of Bishop Bernard in the *Chartulary of Whitby* (ed. Atkinson, i. 41).

[6] This is most probably Godard, a canon of York, also Pœnitentiarius or Penancer, who attests a grant of Archbp Gray to Nostel Priory, with Hamo, Dean of York and William, Archdeacon of Notingham (*Archbp Gray's Register*, ed. Raine, p. 128) ; see also on No. 225.

[7] The date of this Composition, from Simon, Dean, must be after 1194 and before 1214, and from Hamo, Treasurer in or after 1198 ; probably, like the charters to Whitby referred to above, in the time of Bishop Bernard. It is naturally later than No. 120.

120. CONFIRMATIO CUSTODIS EPISCOPATUS KAR-
LIOLI SUPER INSTITUTIONE WILLELMI CLERICI PRÆ-
SENTATI AD ECCLESIAM DE DENTON[1].

PETRUS DE ROS Archidiaconus Karliolensis et custos
Episcopatus[2] ejusdem Universis Clericis et Laicis per Episcopatum Karlioli constitutis litteras has visuris vel audituris
in Domino Salutem.   Quoniam ea quæ coram nobis gesta
sunt ad præsentium et posterorum memoriam volumus pervenire, Noverit universitas vestra Robertum filium Buec
de Buchcastre in præsentia mea et aliorum multorum fide
dignorum advocationem Ecclesiæ de Denton Abbati et
Conventui Sanctæ Mariæ Eborum et Monachis de Wederhale carta sua concessisse et confirmasse et eundem
Abbatem de jure Patronatus ejusdem Ecclesiæ coram nobis
sansisse.   Unde ad hujus rei evidentiorem firmitatem
Willelmum Clericum per prædictum Abbatem et Monachos
de Wederhal de novo præsentatum ad dictam Ecclesiam de
Denton Canonice admisimus, et eundem in dicta Ecclesia
tunc vacante cum omnibus pertinentijs suis instituimus unde
dictam Collationem et Institutionem præsenti carta confirmavimus salvo jure Episcopali et Archidiaconali et Officialium nostrorum.   Hijs Testibus, Thoma de Thorp Officiali
Karliolensi, Willelmo de Kirkebride Decano Karleoli,
Adam de Levington[3], Gilberto de Camboc[4], Ricardo de

120. [1] This is the Confirmation of the institution of William, Clerk,
to the Church of Denton, to which he had been presented *de novo* by
the Abbot of York and the monks of Wederhal, to whom Robert son
of Bueth had granted the advowson (see below and No. 121).   Robert
had previously presented William, Clerk (No. 108), and the institution
had also been confirmed by Peter de Ros (No. 123).

[2] Peter de Ros, Archdeacon, was Custos of the See in the vacancy
before Bishop Bernard.   He ceased to be Archdeacon before 1192
when Robert held the office (see note 3 on No. 31).

[3] Adam, the father of Sir Richard de Levington, who succeeded him
in 1211 ; see note 5 on No. 54, where Adam is shewn to be the son of
Adam the son of Richer or Richard.   The family name was de
Boyvill.   His mother's name was Juliana, and he is mentioned in the

Harton, Alano de Raveneswick, Thoma frate ejus, Rogero Sacerdote de Buchecastre[5] et alijs multis[6].

121. CARTA ROBERTI FILII BUEC FACTA MONA-CHIS DE WEDERHAL SUPER DONATIONE ECCLESIÆ DE DENTON[1].

SCIANT omnes tam præsentes quam futuri quod Ego Robertus filius Buec cum consilio uxoris meæ et amicorum meorum concessi et dedi et hac mea carta confirmavi Deo et Sanctæ Mariæ Eborum et Monachis de Wederhal Ecclesiam de Dentona cum terra eidem Ecclesiæ pertinente et cum omnibus pertinentijs suis et octo insuper acras terræ in omnibus aisiamentis intra Villam et extra quas David[2] tenuit in liberam puram et perpetuam Elemosinam pro animabus Patris et Matris meæ et pro salute mea et Uxoris meæ et omnium Parentum meorum. Hanc vero donationem Ego Robertus et hæredes mei warantizabimus eis contra omnes homines. Testibus, Thoma Officiali Karliolensi[3], Willelmo Decano[4], Johanne Parsona de Arturet[5],

Pipe Rolls for 1177 and 1178 as not having yet got seisin of Westham (Westlinton). As Adam son of Adam de Leventon, he is witness to a charter of Robert son of Bueth in the *Register of Lanercost* (MS. iii. 10).

[4] Gilbert de Camboc is the same as Gilbert, Priest of Camboc, in Nos. **107, 124.**

[5] Roger, priest of Buchecastre is probably one of the two clerks of Buchecastre, W. and R. mentioned in Nos. **117, 119.**

[6] From Archdeacon Peter de Ros, the date of the charter must be before 1192 and probably very shortly after 1180, with which date the witnesses agree.

121. [1] This is the grant of the advowson of the Church of Denton to the monks of Wederhal, which necessitated the presentation *de novo* of William, Clerk, and the Confirmation in the preceding charter.

[2] David de Denton, see No. **126.**

[3] Thomas de Thorp, see on No. **40.**

[4] William de Kirkbride, Dean of Carlisle, as in No. **120**; see note 4 on No. **31.**

[5] Arturet, or Arthuret, or Ardderyd (qu. Arthur's head) was on the river Esk, in the Barony of Liddell, or Lyddale, which was given

Johanne Parsona de Levington, Roberto fratre ejus, Thoma
de Brunef, Johanne de Aschetil filio Roberti[6], Hugone
Nepote Roberti et Adam fratre Hugonis, Ricardo Mazun,
Johanne Scott et alijs multis[7].

122. CONFIRMATIO PRIORIS ET CONVENTUS KARLIOLENSIS SUPER ECCLESIA DE DENTON[1].

OMNIBUS Christi fidelibus ad quorum notitiam hoc
præsens scriptum pervenerit Johannes Prior et Conventus
Sanctæ Mariæ Karlioli Salutem.   Noverit universitas vestra
nos ratum et gratum prebuisse assensum collationem et
concessionem quam Venerabilis Pater B. Episcopus noster[2]

by Ranulf Meschin to Turgis Brundis, a Fleming, and which was in the
time of King John and Henry III. held by Nicholas de Stutevill, his
descendant (*Testa de Nevill*, Record Com. p. 279 *b*).   Arthuret Church
lies about 8 miles north of Carlisle.   It was the border parish from which
the parish of Kirkandrews on Esk was taken ; and it included the
ancient parish of Eston, mentioned in No. 14, but it does not appear
when the latter was absorbed.   The advowson of the Church of Arthuret,
according to the *Register of Bishop John de Rosse*, in 1330 (page 262),
was given by Turgis de Russedale, " Lord of the manor of Lydale," to
the Abbey of Jeddwerth (Jedburgh), which grant was confirmed by
Bishop Bernard (see on No. 247, also *Inquis. ad quod dam.* 2 Edw. III.
No. 3, Record Com. p. 288).   It was here the great battle of Ardderyd
was fought in 573, the last between the Christians and the pagans ;
the victory gave Rydderch, the friend of Kentigern and Columba, the
whole kingdom of Cumbria, and he placed his capital at Alcluyd or
Dumbarton (see Skene, *Celtic Scotland* ii. 190 ; *Chron. Pict.* pp.
xciii, 161).

[6] John de Aschetil was the son of Robert son of Asketill, or
Asketin, and was the nephew of Robert son of Bueth, see on No. 107 ;
see also on No. 125, where he is called John de Denton.

[7] The date of this charter must be shortly before that of No. 120,
and after that of No. 108 ; probably shortly after 1180, certainly
before 1192.

122.   [1] This is the Confirmation by the Prior and Convent of
Carlisle of the act of Bishop Bernard in No. 117.

[2] *Episcopus noster* shews that Bishop Bernard was alive at this
time.   We note that his concession is to the Houses of Wederhal and
Lanercost.

fecit Abbati et Conventui Sanctæ Mariæ Eborum et Domibus de Wederhal et Lanercost super Ecclesia de Denton in proprios usus eorum habenda sicut in ejusdem Episcopi nostri Instrumento super hoc confecto plenius continetur. Ad cujus rei perpetuam confirmationem præsenti scripto sigillum Capituli nostri apposuimus[3].

123. CONFIRMATIO WILLELMI CLERICI INSTITUTI IN ECCLESIAM DE DENTON PER PETRUM DE ROS CUSTODEM EPISCOPATUS KARLIOLI SEDE VACANTE[1].

PETRUS DE ROS Archidiaconus Karliolensis Custos Episcopatus ejusdem Universis Clericis et Laicis per Episcopatum Karliolensem constitutis Litteras has visuris vel audituris in Domino Salutem. Sciatis nos recepisse Willelmum Clericum de Denton in Ecclesia de Denton vacante ad præsentationem Roberti filij Buec de Buchecastre ad quem jus Patronatus de jure spectare dinoscitur, et eum in ipsam Ecclesiam cum omnibus pertinentijs suis Canonice instituisse et institutionem ipsius præsenti carta nostra confirmasse salvo jure Episcopali et nostro et Officialium nostrorum. Hijs Testibus, Thoma de Thorp Officiali Karliolensi, Willelmo Decano Karliolensi, Adam de Levington, Gilberto de Camboc, Ricardo de Harton, Alano de Ravenwic, Thoma fratre ejus, Randulpho de Raneswic, Thoma Diacono de Warthwic et multis alijs[2].

124. QUIETA CLAMATIO FACTA WILLELMO CLERICO SUPER MEDIETATEM ECCLESIÆ DE DENTON PER CANONICOS DE LANERCOST.

[3] The date of this charter must be very shortly after No. 117.

123. [1] This is the Confirmation of the institution of William, Clerk, to Denton on the presentation of Robert son of Bueth, and must have preceded that of No. 120 when William had been presented *de novo* by the Abbey of S. Mary, York, and the monks of Wederhal.

[2] The date of this charter must be shortly before that of No. 120, where there are nearly the same witnesses, about 1180.

S.[1] PRIOR de Lanercost humilisque Conventus ejusdem loci Universis Sanctæ Matris Ecclesiæ filiis Salutem. Noverit universitas vestra nos Divinæ Pietatis intuitu concessisse dedisse et hac præsenti carta confirmasse Willelmo Clerico de Denton totam medietatem[2] Ecclesiæ de Denton cum omnibus pertinentijs suis reddendo nobis inde annuatim duos solidos quos de Vicario suo recipiet ad Nundinas Karleoli. Et ut hæc nostra concessio rata et illibata permaneat eam præsenti scripto et sigilli nostri appositione roboravimus. Hijs Testibus, Ricardo de Heiton[3] Parsona, Stephano fratre ejus, Bernardo Parsona de Ulmsby[4], Reginaldo filio ejus, Fabiano Clerico et Willelmo fratre ejus, Gilberto Parsona de Camboc, Clemente Sacerdote et multis alijs[5].

125. CARTA JOHANNIS DE DENTON DE OCTO ACRIS TERRRÆ IN EADEM.

UNIVERSIS Sanctæ Matris Ecclesiæ filijs tam præsentibus

124. [1] This is Symon, Prior of Lanercost, who appears in the Confirmation to that Priory by Pope Alexander III. in 1181 and Pope Lucius III. in 1184 (*Regist. Lanercost* MS. viii. 17, 18). There was another Prior Simon, Simon de Driffeld, who succeeded John de Galwythia (see on No. 75) August 16th, 1283 (*Chron. de Lanercost* ed. Stevenson p. 113).

[2] The Priory of Lanercost quitclaim their moiety of the Church of Denton, secured to them by the Composition of No. 119, on the payment by William, Clerk, of the 2s. pension there mentioned, see also note 3 on No. 34.

[3] Richard de Heiton was parson, probably, of Haiton, see on No. 168.

[4] Ulmsby, Ulvesby or Ulfsby, now Ousby, was a parish in Cumberland on the east side of the river Eden, between Kirkland and Melmorby.

[5] The date of this charter would be shortly after that of the Composition, No. 119, as William, Clerk, had been some time instituted.

The following would seem to be the order of this series of charters:—(1) No. 108, (2) No. 123, (3) No. 121, (4) No. 120, (5) No. 119, (6) No. 117, (7) No. 122, (8) No. 124, (9) No. 118, and (10) No. 34.

quam futuris ad quorum notitiam hoc præsens scriptum pervenerit Johannes de Denton[1] salutem. Noscat universitas vestra me Caritatis intuitu dedisse concessisse et hac præsenti carta mea confirmasse Deo et Ecclesiæ Sanctæ Mariæ Eborum et Monachis Sanctæ Trinitatis et Sancti Constantini de Wederhal et Luminariis Ecclesiæ suæ octo acras terræ in territorio de Denton in cultura scilicet quæ vocatur Werduthel in escambio illarum octo acrarum quas Robertus filius Bueth Avunculus meus prædictis Monachis in liberam puram et perpetuam dedit Elemosinam. Habendas et Tenendas sibi in liberam puram et perpetuam Elemosinam cum omnibus pertinentijs libertatibus et aisiamentis suis infra Villam et extra adeo libere et quiete in omnibus ut aliqua Elemosina liberius et quietius dari possit aut possideri. Et ego et Hæredes mei warantizabimus prædictis Monachis prædictas octo acras terræ cum pertinentijs contra omnes homines imperpetuum. Et ne quis Hæredum meorum contra hoc factum meum venire imposterum possit præsenti scripto cum sigilli mei appositione illud corroboravi. Hijs Testibus, Bartholomæo tunc Priore Karlioli, Thoma filio Johannis tunc vicecomite Cumberlandiæ et Senescallo Gilleslandiæ, Roberto filio Willelmii, Roberto de Castelkairoc, Willelmo filio Rogeri, Roberto

---

125. [1] John de Denton was the son of Robert son of Asketill, or Asketin, or Anketin ; his father had married a sister (Eda or Sigrida) of Robert son of Bueth ; hence below he calls the latter *avunculus meus* (see note 1 on No. 107) ; in the different form of his name, he attests the charter of Robert son of Bueth, No. 121. His name occurs often in the *Register of Lanercost* under both forms ; thus (MS. v. 26) John son of Robert son of Anketin grants land in Pirihon to Agnes his sister and her husband Eustachius ; Robert and Anketin his brothers being witnesses ; as John de Denton, he grants the whole land of Pirihon to the Priory (MS. iii. 7). He had a son John who (MS. iii. 9) confirmed the grants of his father John to the Priory of Lanercost ; this son John de Denton granted them charters in 1273 (MS. ix. 15) and 1278 (MS. x. 14), and is the John de Denton mentioned in this *Register* in No. 47, and in No. 194 in the year 1271.

filio Roberti de Denth[2], Simone fratre ejus, Radulpho de
Bordeswald, Anketin fratre meo[3], et multis alijs[4].

126. QUIETA CLAMATIO ELYE FILIJ DAVID DE
DENTON FACTA MONACHIS DE WEDERHALE DE TOTA
TERRA QUAM DE EIS TENUIT IN DENTON.

UNIVERSIS Sanctæ Matris Ecclesiæ filijs tam præsentibus quam futuris Elyas filius David de Denton[1] Salutem.
Noverit Universitas vestra me Dei amore et pro salute
animæ meæ resignasse et quietam clamasse Deo et
Ecclesiæ Sanctæ Trinitatis de Wederhale et Monachis
ibidem Deo servientibus totam terram cum pertinentijs
quam aliquando de prædictis Monachis tenui in Denton.
Habendam et Tenendam sibi imperpetuum ad sustentamentum luminis coram altari Sanctæ Trinitatis in eadem
Ecclesia Ipsamque pro me et hæredibus meis et in pleno
Comitatu Karleoli abjurasse. Et ne aliquis hæredum
meorum possit in posterum aut debeat contra hanc resig-
nationem et quietam clamationem venire Ego prædictus
Elyas de Denton prædictis Monachis de Wederhal præsens
scriptum cum appositione sigilli mei confirmavi et corroboravi imperpetuum. Hijs Testibus, Domino Roberto filio

[2] Denth. will be a contraction for Denton. Robert, son of
Robert de Denton, and brother of John, is mentioned in the note
above, and Simon son of Robert de Denton occurs with John, Prior
of Lanercost, in the *Register of Lanercost* (MS. xv. 19).

[3] Anketin, the son of Robert son of Anketin de Denton, and
brother of John, granted two charters to the Priory of Lanercost
(*Regist. Lanercost*, MS. iii. 12, 18) in which his brothers John de
Denton and Robert are mentioned.

[4] The date of this charter from the sheriff or 'custos' Thomas son
of John (see No. 56, note 8) must be 1214 or 1230—31 ; as John de
Denton occurs in 1180—92 (see No. 121) the former date seems
the most probable, and with this the other witnesses agree.

126. [1] David de Denton held this land in the time of Robert son
of Bueth (see No. 121) but it does not appear what relation he was
though several of the family attest this deed.

Willelmi de Korkeby[2] tunc Vicecomite, Domino Radulpho de Feritate[3], Domino Symone de Oreton, Willelmo de Warthwic, Johanne de Denton[4], Willelmo Parsona[5] Ecclesiæ de Denton, Adam de Camboc, Astino fratre Johannis de Denton[6], Eustachio de Denton[7], Gilist, Adam filio Willelmi Parsonæ de Denton et multis alijs[8].

127. CARTA WALTERI BAYNINI DE VIGINTI ACRIS TERRÆ IN CAMPIS DE BORDDOSWALD.

SCIANT præsentes et futuri quod Ego Walterus Bayninus[1] consilio et consensu uxoris meæ et Hæredum meorum dedi et concessi et hac præsenti carta mea confirmavi Deo et Beatæ Mariæ et Ecclesiæ Sanctæ Trinitatis de Wederhal et Monachis ibidem Deo servientibus viginti acras terræ in campis de Borddosewald[2] cum omnibus pertinentijs et libertatibus infra Villam et extra prædictæ Villæ pertinentibus Scilicet in Bosco in Plano et in omnibus Aisiamentis in puram et perpetuam Elemosinam pro

---

[2] Robert son of William de Korkeby does not appear in the lists of sheriffs ; he was probably ' custos' at this time ; see note 4 on No. 37.

[3] This is the elder Radulph of the name ; see on No. 43.

[4] John de Denton, the elder of the name ; see on No. 121.

[5] This is the same as William, Clerk, of Denton, referred to so often in No. 108 and succeeding charters concerning Denton ; he is now older and has a son Adam, who witnesses below.

[6] Astin i.e. Asketin, brother of John de Denton ; see on No. 125.

[7] Eustachius married Agnes, sister of John de Denton.

[8] Probably the date is early in the 13th century, and not far from that of No. 125.

127. [1] Walter Baynin, Beinin, or Benn, occurs frequently in the *Register of Lanercost* ; he makes a grant to the Priory (MS. iv. 20) ; is witness to a charter of Ranulph de Vallibus (MS. i. 19) also of Robert de Vallibus (MS. i. 6 *et al.*) ; is co-witness with Bishop Bernard to a Confirmation of Odard son of Adam (MS. xiv. 21) ; and he appears in the Pipe Rolls as late as 1214.

[2] Borddosewald, now Birdoswald, was about 4 miles from Lanercost on the Roman wall, and was the site of the well known Roman station *Amboglanna*.

salute animarum Dominorum meorum Ranulphi de Vallibus et Roberti[3] filij sui et pro salute animæ meæ et
omnium antecessorum meorum libere et quiete ab omni
terreno servicio et exactione sicut aliqua Elemosina liberius
dari vel confirmari potest. Scilicet terra quæ dicitur
Haithwait usque ad magnam quercum quæ stat supra
antiquum fossatum et ab illa quercu usque ad fracturam
muri[4] in qua semita jacet quæ venit de Trewermain[5] et ab
illa fractura muri usque ad quercum quæ stat super
murum versus orientem, et ab illa quercu usque ad
fossatum quæ ducit ad Cundois[6] de Hyrchin. Et sciendum
est quod Ego Walterus prædictus et Hæredes mei prædictam Elemosinam præfatis Monachis contra omnes
gentes warantizabimus imperpetuum. Et ut hæc mea
donatio et concessio rata et inconcussa perseveret in
posterum præsens scriptum sigilli mei appositione roboravi.
Hijs Testibus, Roberto de Korkeby tunc temporis Senes-

[3] This is the second Robert de Vallibus, son of Ranulph and
nephew of the first Robert ; his father died when he was a minor,
in 1199, and he came into possession of Gillesland in 1206 ; see note
18 on No. 38.

[4] That is of the Roman wall.

[5] Trewermain, or Tryermain, formerly written Treverman. The
Register of Lanercost (MS. xv. 17) gives an interesting *Veredictum
antiquorum* wherein it is stated that Gilemor filius Gilandri, Lord of
Treverman and Torcrossoc, made a chapel of wickerwork (*capella de
virgis*) at Treverman, and procured the celebration of the Divine
Offices there with the consent of Bishop Edelwan (Eagelwine, Bishop
of Durham 1056—71). This Gilemor, or Gille the great, is connected
by name with the Gille son of Bueth and Gillesland (see note 1 on No.
107). The chapel of Treverman was granted to the Priory of Lanercost by Robert de Vallibus in their Foundation Charter. Treverman
passed to Roland de Vallibus, the brother of the second Robert (see
No. 54, note 6). He is called "of Treverman" (*Regist. Lanercost*, MS. ii. 21) and he granted land there for the chaplain and clerk,
which his nephew Hubert confirmed (MS. iv. 6). His son Alexander
also gave rights to the Priory in his turbaries of Treverman (MS. ii. 22).
The castle of Tryermain is rather more than a mile from Birdoswald.

[6] *Cundois* or *cundoys*, "a conduit" or "watercourse."

callo de Gillesland, Johanne de Denton, Alano de Cumreu[7], Alfredo de Camboc, Willelmo de Aireminne, Willelmo Clerico de Wederhal, Waltero Porter[8].

128. Confirmatio Radulphi Baynin de viginti acris terræ in Bordoswald.

Notum sit omnibus tam præsentibus quam futuris quod Ego Radulphus Baynin[1] concessi et hac præsenti carta confirmavi Deo et Beatæ Mariæ et Ecclesiæ Sanctæ Trinitatis de Wederhal et Monachis ibidem Deo servientibus viginti acras terræ in campis de Bordoswald cum omnibus pertinentijs et libertatibus infra Villam et extra prædictæ Villæ pertinentibus Scilicet in bosco in plano et in omnibus aisiamentis in puram et perpetuam Elemosinam pro Salute animarum Dominorum meorum Ranulphi de Vallibus et Roberti filij sui, et pro Salute animæ meæ et omnium antecessorum meorum libere et quiete ab omni terreno servicio et exactione sicut aliqua Elemosina liberius confirmari potest Scilicet terram quæ dicitur Haithwait et ab Haithwait usque ad magnam quercum quæ stat super antiquum fossatum et ab illa quercu usque ad fracturam muri in qua Semita jacet quæ venit de Treverman, et ab illa fractura usque ad quercum quæ stat super murum versus Orientem et ab illa quercu usque ad

---

[7] Alan de Cumreu appears in 1212, with Robert son of William (de Korkeby) and Ranulph de Daker, as sent to Alicia de Rumelli to obtain the appointment of a person to represent her in a suit, when she appointed Hugh de Moricebi (*Coram Rege Rolls* 13 Joh. No. 43, m. 13). He is witness to a charter of Walter de Wyndesore in the *Register of Lanercost* (iv. 11) with this Walter Benin, Robert son of William, and John de Denton.

[8] All the witnesses point to the end of the 12th or the very beginning of the 13th century as being the date of this charter; probably not long after the death of Ranulph de Vallibus in 1199.

128. [1] Walter Baynin, who granted the preceding charter, was, as appears below, the uncle on the mother's side of this Radulph, who was apparently his heir.

fossatum quod ducit ad cundoys de Hyrchin. Et
Sciendum est quod Ego Radulphus Baynin et Hæredes
mei prædictam Elemosinam præfatis Monachis contra
omnes homines imperpetuum warantizabimus sicut carta
Walteri Bainin Avunculi mei inde facta testatur. Et ut
hæc mea concessio et confirmatio rata et inconcussa
perseveret in posterum præsens scriptum sigilli mei appositione corroboravi. Hijs Testibus, Roberto filio Willelmi,
Johanne Museihe², Johanne de Denton, Roberto fratre ejus,
Alano de Cumreu, Willelmo de Airminne, Waltero Janitore de Wederhal, Umfrido de Wederhale et multis
alijs³.

129. QUIETA CLAMATIO SIMONIS CAPELLANI DE WEDERHALE DE TOTA TERRA QUAM TENUIT IN BORD-OSWALD DE MONACHIS DE WEDERHALE.

OMNIBUS Christi Fidelibus ad quos præsens scriptum
pervenerit Symon Capellanus de Wederhal¹ Salutem.
Noverit universitas vestra me remisisse et quietam clamasse
imperpetuum Abbati et Conventui Sanctæ Mariæ Eborum
et Monachis de Wederhal totam terram quam tenui de
eisdem in Bordoswald. Ita quod dicti Monachi habeant
et teneant dictam terram imperpetuum quietam de me et
omnibus heredibus et successoribus meis. Et quia tempore
confectionis hujus instrumenti cartam quam habui de

---

² John Museihe, or perhaps his son of the same name, had
property in Ainstapelit (Ainstable) and, with Matildis his wife,
granted 7 acres there to the Priory of Wederhal (Nos. **164, 165**). He
is witness to a charter of Anketill son of Robert in the *Register of
Lanercost* (MS. v. 23) with Walter Benn and John, Prior of Lanercost.

³ From the witnesses, the date of this charter must be shortly after
the preceding.

129. ¹ Symon, Chaplain of Wederhal, seems to have held the 20
acres in Bordoswald granted to the Priory by the two preceding
charters, and as he has lost the charter he had from the Chapter
of S. Mary's at York, he quit-claims the property he undertook to
resign.

Capitulo Sanctæ Mariæ Eboraci penes me non habui nec habere potui ut eam dictis Monachis resignarem, Si ipsa aliquo tempore ad nocumentum dictorum Monachorum quominus ipsi prædictam terram in pace possideant imperpetuum per me vel aliquem hæredum meorum vel assignatorum vel successorum meorum fuerit ostensa careat viribus imperpetuum et habeatur tanquam inanis et frivola. Et ut hoc scriptum meæ resignationis et quietæ clamationis perpetuæ firmitatis inconcussum robur optineat illud sigilli mei impressione roboravi. Hijs Testibus, Domino Bartholomæo Priore Karleoli, Magistro Gervasio[2] Archidiacono Karleolensi, Waltero tunc Officiali Karliolensi[3], T. Parsona de Morland, T. filio Johannis tunc Vicecomite Karlioli, Adam filio Rogeri, Elya de Raveneswick, Waltero Janitore et alijs[4].

130. Carta Alani filij Willelmi Raveneswick de duabus bovatis terræ in Talcan.

Notum sit omnibus audientibus vel videntibus has literas quod Ego Alanus filius Willelmi de Raveneswick[1] concessi et dedi in puram et perpetuam Elemosinam Sanctæ Trinitati et Sancto Constantino de Wederhal et Monachis ibidem Deo servientibus pro Salute animarum Patris et Matris meæ et mei ipsius et uxoris meæ et Parentum meorum duas bovatas terræ in Talcan[2] quas

---

[2] Gervase de Louther is now Archdeacon, so after the death of Bishop Hugh ; see note 3 on No. 21.

[3] Walter de Ulvesby, see on No. 56.

[4] From the sheriff, Thomas son of John, the date of this charter must be 1214 or 1230—31 (No. 56) ; as Gervase is now Archdeacon it will be the latter date, before the death of Prior Bartholomew in 1231.

130. [1] Alan son of William de Raveneswic appears in Nos. 107, 108, where we saw Adam, the brother of Alan, witnessing a charter of Robert son of Bueth ; also Adam the brother of William living in 1178 and 1185.

[2] Talcan, or Talkin, is in the parish of Hayton, adjoining Brampton.

Willelmus Rufus tenuit cum omnibus aisiamentis ejusdem Villæ. Et notandum quod concessi cum eisdem bovatis pasturam in eadem Villa sexaginta ovibus et octo Vaccis et quatuor Bobus et duabus Equabus cum pullis earum duorum annorum vel duobus equis. Hijs Testibus, Willelmo Capellano de Warthwic, Radulpho de Stineton, Willelmo de Eyreminne, Willelmo Clerico, Ricardo Portario, Gilberto de Talcan[3], Willelmo filio, Alden Fulcheno, Anselmo de Neuby, Laurentio de Agullunby et multis alijs[4].

131. Confirmatio Adæ filij Alani de Cumreu de duabus bovatis terræ in Talcan.

Notum sit omnibus videntibus vel audientibus Literas has quod Ego Adam filius Alani de Cumreu[1] concessi et confirmavi Deo et Ecclesiæ Sanctæ Mariæ Eboraci et Monachis Sanctæ Trinitatis et Sancti Constantini de Wederhal pro Salute animæ Patris mei et Antecessorum meorum et pro salute animæ meæ in puram et perpetuam Elemosinam duas bovatas terræ cum pertinentijs in territorio de Talcan cum tofto et crofto illas videlicet quas Willelmus Rufus tenuit. Sciendum est autem quod ego Adam ex dono meo proprio dedi prædictis Monachis vel cuicunque nomine eorum prædictas bovatas tenuerit omnia aisiamenta et omnes communas et omnes libertates infra Villam et extra Ita quod prædicti Monachi illas duas bovatas adeo libere habeant sicut aliqua Elemosina

---

[3] Gilbert de Talkan attests two charters of Robert son of Ranulph de Vallibus in the *Register of Lanercost* (MS. ii. 2, 5) and his two other sons, Adam and Alan, grant land in Talkan (MS. v. 16, 17).

[4] William, Chaplain, appears with several of these witnesses in No. **50**, about 1200 ; and 1195—1200 is probably the date here.

131. [1] Adam de Cumreu is witness to several charters in the *Register of Lanercost*, one of Hubert, nephew of Rolland de Vallibus, for land in Treverman (MS. iv. 6), and one of Robert de Castelkayroc for a serf, Gamel de Walton, *cum tota sequela ejus* (MS. iv. 17), similar to No. **132**. On his father Alan, see No. **127**, note 7.

liberius potest dari vel teneri. Ego vero Adam et Hæredes
mei prædictas duas bovatas terræ cum pertinentijs prædictis Monachis contra omnes homines imperpetuum
warantizabimus et defendemus. Et ad majorem securitatem Ego tactis Sacrosanctis illud juravi, et insuper
præsenti scripto sigillum meum apposui. Hijs Testibus,
B. Priore Karlioli, S. Priore de Lanercost[2], Magistro G.
Officiali[3], R. filio Willelmi tunc Vicecomite[4], Roberto de
Castelkairoc, Eudone de Karleolo, Roberto de Leversdal,
Roberto de Carlaton, W. Janitore, S.[5] filio Willelmi Clerici,
J. de Agullunby et alijs[6].

132. Quieta Clamatio facta Monachis de We-derhal per Adam de Cumreu de nativo suo.

Omnibus Christi fidelibus ad quorum notitiam hoc
præsens scriptum pervenerit Adam de Cumreu Salutem
æternam in Domino. Noverit universitas vestra me dedisse et quietum clamasse Deo et Monachis Sanctæ
Trinitatis et Sancti Constantini de Wederhal Rogerum
filium Huctredi[1] cum omnibus Catallis suis et cum tota

---

[2] This can hardly be Symon, who was Prior at the end of the 12th
century (see on No. **119**), but it is possible. More probably, it should
be J. for John, as in Nos. **75, 79**; see note 5 below.

[3] Gervase de Louther, not yet Archdeacon as in No. **129**.

[4] Robert son of William de Hampton who appears, with so many
of the same witnesses, in Nos. **75, 79**, was sheriff in 1223—29 (No. **54**).

[5] This should be J. for John son of William, as in Nos. **75, 79**.
This error in the initial seems to point to the same error in S. Prior
above.

[6] From the sheriff, the date is 1223—29 ; and from the witnesses,
probably about 1225.

132. [1] This Roger son of Huctred was a *nativus*, serf, or villein,
who is here handed over with all his chattels and his whole family
(*sequela*). The serfdom of the Anglo-Saxon period was transferred
with the lands to the Normans. The class of serfs to which Roger
belonged was that of the prædial slaves, or slaves of the estate.
They were more independent than the domestic slaves, and could even
hold an amount of land and other property ; but they and all their

sequela sua Ita quod dicti Monachi habeant dictum Rogerum sicut prædictum est in perpetuam Elemosinam quietum et solutum absque omni calumpnia mea mei et hæredum meorum. Et si in posterum per aliquem hære- dum meorum contra dictum Rogerum aliqua calumpnia moveatur autoritate istius scripti irrita sit et inanis Immo ego et hæredes mei dictum Rogerum sicut prædictum est dictis Monachis warantizabimus et defendemus im- perpetuum. In cujus rei Testimonium præsenti scripto sigillum meum apposui. Hijs Testibus, R. Priore[2], G. Archidiacono[3], W. Officiali Karliolensi[4], W. de Daker Vicecomite Cumberlandiæ, Ricardo de Levingtun, Petro de Tylloyl, Elya de Raveneswic, Ricardo de Halneburch, W. de Warthwic, Roberto de Brakenthwayt, Johanne de Aguluneby et alijs[5].

133. Carta Salamonis de Farlam facta Monachis de Wederhal de duabus acris terræ in
Farlam.

Omnibus Christi Fidelibus præsentem cartam inspecturis vel audituris Salamon de Farlam[1] Salutem in Domino.

belongings were entirely at the disposal of the lord, who could sell or transfer them at will. There is another grant of a *nativus* and his wife in No. **156.** Besides the instance in the *Register of Lanercost* mentioned in No. **131**, note 1, there are others (as in MS. vi. 13 and xiv. 8) and one (MS. i. 17) where Robert de Vallibus himself grants to the Priory Galfrid Pich, his wife and children. How these *nativi* often passed into the tenants of the manor, see Sir Henry Ellis, Intro- duction to *Domesday Book*, p. xxiv. (Record Com.).

[2] Radulph, Prior of Carlisle, succeeded Prior Bartholomew in 1231, see note 2 on No. **97.**

[3] Gervase de Louther ; see on No. **21.**

[4] Walter de Ulvesby ; see on No. **56.**

[5] From the other witnesses, the date of the charter must be during the first period that William de Daker was Sheriff or Custos, from 1236 to 1247, and from the Official, not being yet Archdeacon, before 1240.

133. [1] Salamon de Farlam, also a witness to No. **136**, may have been of the family of de Windesore ; but there seems to be little

Noverit Universitas vestra me Divinæ Caritatis intuitu pro salute animæ meæ et prædecessorum meorum et successorum meorum dedisse et concessisse et præsenti carta confirmasse Deo et Ecclesiæ Sanctæ Trinitatis et Sancti Constantini de Wederhal et Monachis ibidem Deo servientibus duas acras terræ in territorio de Farlam[2] Illas videlicet quæ jacent inter duos sickes de Colledaykelehe versus Aquilonem. Habendas et Tenendas in liberam puram et perpetuam Elemosinam cum pertinentijs et communis et aisiamentis infra Villam et extra Villam de Farlam pertinentibus sicut aliqua Elemosina liberius dari possit aut possideri. Et Ego Salamon et hæredes mei prædictas duas acras terræ cum pertinentijs contra omnes homines imperpetuum dictis Monachis warantizabimus acquietabimus et defendemus. Et ut hæc mea donatio firma sit et stabilis sigillum meum præsenti scripto apposui. Hijs Testibus, Symone Capellano, Gilberto Clerico, Radulpho Clerico, W. Janitore, J. Stelfot, J. de Agulunby, Hamelino nepote Prioris, Henrico Coquo, Thoma Clavigero et multis alijs[3].

evidence that he was. J. Denton (*Cumberland*, p. 138) followed by Nicolson and Burn (*History*, ii. 507) makes him a son of John, the brother of Walter de Windesore the younger. In the *Register of Lanercost* Salamon de Farlam is witness with Walter the younger, to a grant of Robert son of Ranulph de Vallibus (MS. ii. 1). He is very probably identical with Salomon son of David, who appears in that *Register* (MS. v. 18, 19) in connection with Farlam; but see more on No. 136.

[2] Farlam in Gillesland, about 3 miles south of Lanercost Priory, was held by Walter de Wyndesore the elder, to whom it was probably granted by the first Robert de Vallibus; the said Robert by his Foundation Charter granted or confirmed the Church of S. Thomas the Martyr of Farlam to the Priory of Lanercost, which Walter had granted (*Regist. Lanercost*, MS. iv. 13). Walter de Wyndesore and his son Walter the younger made grants of land in Farlam (MS. ii. 9, 19, 20) which were confirmed by Ranulph and Robert de Vallibus (i. 20, 21).

[3] The date, from the witness John de Agulunby, is probably nearly that of the succeeding charter.

134. Carta Salomonis de Farlam de quatuordecim acris terræ de Dominico suo in parva
Farlam.

Omnibus Sanctæ Matris Ecclesiæ filijs ad quorum
notitiam hoc præsens scriptum pervenerit Salomon de
Farlam Salutem. Noverit universitas vestra me caritatis
intuitu et pro salute animæ meæ dedisse concessisse et hac
præsenti carta mea confirmasse Abbati et Conventui Sanctæ
Mariæ Eborum et Monachis Sanctæ Trinitatis et Sancti
Constantini de Wederhal quatuordecim acras terræ de
Dominico meo in parva Farlam[1], scilicet octo acras terræ
in parte occidentali cujusdam divisæ quæ tendit a loco ubi
Domus Willelmi Clerici quondam sita fuit versus Aquilonem usque in Gaytesigemire et sex acras terræ in campo
qui vocatur Ruthait. Habendas et Tenendas sibi in
liberam puram et perpetuam Elemosinam cum omnibus
pertinentijs libertatibus communis et aisiamentis suis infra
Villam et extra adeo libere et quiete in omnibus ut aliqua
Elemosina liberius et quietius dari possit aut possideri.
Et Ego et Hæredes mei hanc Elemosinam dictis Monachis
contra omnes homines imperpetuum warantizabimus acquietabimus et defendemus. Et ne quis hæredum meorum
possit imposterum contra hanc donationem meam venire
præsenti scripto cum sigilli mei appositione eam corroboravi.
Hijs Testibus, Ricardo de Levington tunc Vicecomite
Cumberlandiæ, Alexandro Bacon tunc Senescallo de
Gilleslandiæ, Roberto filio Willelmi, Roberto de Castel-
kairoc, Rollando de Wallibus, Willelmo filio Rogeri,
Waltero de Wyndesour[2], Johanne de Denton, et alijs[3].

---

134. [1] On Farlam, see note 2 on No. **133**; this was apparently a
vill in the east part of Farlam. A good many of its localities are
mentioned in two grants of Salomon son of David (*Regist. Lanercost,*
MS. v. 18, 19), and in a confirmation by Walter de Wyndesore (MS.
iv. 11); the former speaks of the *Via Regia* and of the land between
the Lake (*Tindale Tarn*) and the place called Hallebanke.

[2] This Walter de Wyndesour appears here in a charter whose

135. CARTA MAURICII DE MAN DE QUADAM PLACEA AD FACIENDAM SALINAM IN TERRITORIO DE AERMGTHUAIT.

UNIVERSIS Christi fidelibus ad quorum notitiam hoc præsens Scriptum pervenerit Mauricius de Man Salutem

date, from the witnesses, must be well on in the 13th century; and similarly in No. 136. We should naturally suppose that he was the son of the Walter who died about 1195, and who is mentioned in No. 38 (see note 12 there); but a difficulty arises in connection with the early date of Christiana who is believed to be the daughter of that first Walter. In the Pipe Rolls for Cumberland, in 1200, Duncan de Lasceles and his wife Christiana (see on No. 185) account for £10 for having her land in Boulton which was a part of her inheritance. In the year 1202, Christiana de Wyndleshore granted land in Scotland to the Priory of Lanercost for the souls of William the King (of Scotland), of her husband, her children and Walter de Wyndleshore her brother. Walter may have been alive, the King and her husband certainly were (*Regist. Lanercost*, MS. iv. 18). Again, in 1203, Christiana de Wyndesore accounts for 220 marcs that she may have seisin of all the land, and be reckoned the next heir, of Walter de Wyndesore in Essex and Hertford (*Pipe Rolls*, Essex, 5 Joh.); and in 1206, with her husband, Duncan de Lasceles, and Radulph de Hodeng, she pays 240 marcs for land held by Walter of the King in Beds and Bucks, Robert de Vallibus (the younger) and Ivo de Veteriponte being pledged (*Fine Rolls* 7 Joh. m. 5, ed. Hardy p. 346). This signifies that Christiana was the heir either of her father Walter, or of her brother Walter, who must have died soon after his father. Who then is this Walter, and the Walter son of Walter, who occurs at this and at a later period? Thus in the Pipe Rolls for Cumberland, Walter de Windlesore pays 46s. 8d. in 1214, and William pays 2½ marcs; in the *Register of Lanercost* (MS. ii. 19) Walter son of Walter de Wyndesore grants to the Priory the right of patronage in Farlam Church and two acres in Closegill, Thomas son of John being sheriff, i.e. in 1214 or 1230—31; he grants (MS. ii. 20) to the Priory all his demesne in Farlam, William de Daker being sheriff, i.e. in 1236—47, John his brother being witness to both these charters; he confirms a grant of Salomon son of David of land in Little Farlam (MS. iv. 11), William de Wyndesore being witness; and he grants (iv. 12) land in Severig (in Farlam), both of these charters being about the present date; he is witness to charters of Robert son of Ranulph de Vallibus (MS. ii.

æternam in Domino. Noverit Universitas vestra me pro
salute animæ meæ et pro salute animarum Prædecessorum
et Successorum meorum dedisse concessisse et præsenti
carta confirmasse Deo et Abbachiæ Sanctæ Mariæ Eborum
et Priori et Monachis de Wederhal unam placeam in
territorio de Aermgthuait[1] in puram et perpetuam Elemosinam ad construendam Salinam sicut sibi viderit
melius expedire, cum libero introitu et exitu per illud iter
quod dedi Priori et Monachis de Sancta Bega[2]. Prædictus
autem Prior et Monachi et homines sui capient omnia
estoveria sua et aisiamenta tam in terra quam in aqua
sicut sibi viderint melius expedire ad prædictam Salinam
tenendam sine aliqua contradictione mei vel Hæredum
meorum. Solvent autem mihi et Hæredibus meis annuatim
pro prædicta Salina sex denarios ad Natale Domini in
Ecclesia Sanctæ Begæ pro omni servicio consuetudine
et exactione. Et ego et hæredes mei hanc prædictam

1, 2, 3) with Duncan de Lasceles, Salomon de Farlam and others ; he
appears, in a charter of Christiana, daughter of Adam (MS. xiii. 14)
with his father Walter, and with him again in a charter of his son
Adam de Farlam for land in Clovesgill, *ante* Closegill (MS. xiii. 16).
That he is identical with the Walter de Wyndesour of this charter,
there can be little doubt, but his exact connection with the Walter of
Henry II.'s time is not determined. The accounts of Sir G. Duckett
(*Duchetiana* p. 251 sq.) recognise the difficulty, but only show the
contradictory character of the pedigrees.

[3] It is not probable that John de Denton, Robert son of William,
and other of the witnesses who were alive in the 12th century, lived
much beyond 1213—14 when some of them appear ; and we may put
the date of this charter pretty certainly in the first 20 years of
the 13th century.

135. [1] Aermgthuait is not identified ; it was on the west coast of
Cumberland ; not Armathwaite in the valley of the Eden, nor near
Bassenthwaite lake.

[2] The Priory of S. Bega, or S. Bee, was also a Cell of the Abbey
of S. Mary at York, founded by William, the brother of Ranulph
Meschin ; it was on the west coast of Cumberland, and south of
Wirkington and the other places mentioned below ; see Dugdale,
Monast. iii. 576.

Elemosinam prædictis Monachis contra omnes homines
warantizabimus. Sciet et hoc sciendum est quod si Prior
et Monachi processu temporis dictam placeam ad opus
suum habere noluerint amplius cessabunt à solutione sex
denariorum. Et Ego et hæredes mei de prædicta placea
commodum nostrum faciemus. In cujus rei Testimonium
præsenti scripto sigillum meum apposui. Hijs Testibus
Domino Patricio de Wirgington[3], Domino W. Decano,
Hugone de Moriceby[4], Adam de Haverington[5], Ricardo de
Cleterne, Roberto de Bromthoit, Johanne de Boyvill[6],

[3] Patrick de Wirgington was the younger son (Thomas being the
elder) of Thomas son of Gospatric son of Orme, who held Camerton
and other manors on this west coast. Workington came to Orme
from the first William de Lancastre by exchange. Patrick received
from his father the lordship of Culwen in Galloway, and came in for
the other estates on the death of his elder brother. He is often called
Patrick de Culwen, and was ancestor of the Culwen or Curwen family,
of whom a good account is given by W. Jackson, *Trans. Cumberland
Archæol. Soc.* v. p. 181 *seq.* W. Jackson refers, among others, to a
grant to Patrick about 1210; but he does not mention the important
grants in Seton to the Abbey of Holm Cultram by Thomas son of
Gospatric, their confirmation by this, his son Patrick, and by Thomas
son of Gilbert de Culwenne, grandson of Patrick (*MS. Register H. C.*
pp. 35, 47, 127).

[4] Hugh de Moriceby is witness with Adam de Haverington (a
witness below) to a confirmation charter of William de Fortibus, 2nd
Earl of Albemarle (*ob.* 1241) to the Priory of S. Bee (Dugdale,
Monast. iii. 578). He gave land in Distington to the Abbey of Holm
Cultram (*Register*, MS. p. 65). He appears in 1211—12 as the legal
representative of Alice de Rumelli (see note 7 on No. 127), and, with
Richard de Cleterne (a witness below) and others, as making an
inquisition in 1246 of the lands of Lambert de Muleton (*Inquis. post
mort.* 31 *Hen. III. No.* 4).

[5] Adam de Haverington or Harrington (see previous note) must be
different from the Adam de Hairington of No. 203 in 1292, and of
Nos. 207, 220. The family seems to have been connected with that
of Culwen or Wirgington. The manors of Haverington, Distington
and Moriceby (Moresby) lie in order to the south of Wirkington.

[6] John de Boyvill is probably the John who was son of Guido,
Lord of Thursby, referred to in note 7 on No. 78.

Willelmo et David de Kirkeby, Radulpho de Preston et alijs[7]

136. CARTA RICARDI FILIJ BERNARDI DE FARLAM FACTA MONACHIS DE WEDERHALE DE QUINQUE ACRIS TERRÆ IN PARVA FARLAM.

OMNIBUS Sanctæ Matris Ecclesiæ filijs ad quorum notitiam hoc præsens scriptum pervenerit Ricardus filius Bernardi de Farlam[1] salutem in Domino. Noverit universitas vestra me pro salute animæ meæ et Parentum meorum dedisse concessisse et hac præsenti carta mea confirmasse Abbati et Conventui Sanctæ Mariæ Eborum et Monachis Sanctæ Trinitatis et Sancti Constantini de Wederhal quinque acras terræ in territorio de parva Farlam in campo qui vocatur Ruthait. Habendas et Tenendas sibi in liberam puram et perpetuam Elemosinam cum omnibus pertinentijs libertatibus communis et aisiamentis suis infra Villam et extra adeo libere et quiete in omnibus sicut aliqua Elemosina liberius dari possit et possideri. Et ego et hæredes mei warantizabimus prædictam terram cum pertinentijs supranominatis Deo et Abbachiæ Sanctæ Mariæ Eborum et Monachis de Wederhal contra omnes

---

[7] From Richard de Cleterne, a witness to No. **109**, between 1236 and 1247, and the other witnesses here, the date must be in the first half of the 13th century, and probably not long before 1240.

136. [1] Richard son of Bernard de Farlam is stated by Nicolson and Burn (*History*, ii. 507) following J. Denton, to be the great grandson of John de Wyndesore, who had two sons Rayner and Salomon, and Rayner a son of Bernard; but they give no authority. In the *Register of Lanercost* (MS. v. 18) Salomon son of David and Bernard son of Ratmer grant to the Priory land in Little Farlam, called Raven, which grant is confirmed (MS. iv. 11) by Walter de Wyndesore. It is much more probable that this is the Bernard here referred to, and that Salomon son of David is identical with Salomon de Farlam (see Nos. **133, 134**) who is a witness here. The witnesses to these three charters and to those in the *Lanercost Register* are similar, and point to the same conclusion.

homines imperpetuum. Et ne quis Hæredum meorum possit in posterum contra hanc donationem meam venire præsenti scripto cum sigilli mei appositione eam roboravi. Hijs Testibus Ricardo de Levington Vicecomite Cumberlandiæ, Alexandro Bacun tunc Senescallo de Gilleslandiæ, Roberto filio Willelmi, Roberto de Castelkairoc, Willelmo filio Rogeri, Rollando de Vallibus, Johanne de Denton, Waltero de Wyndshor, Salomone de Farlam et alijs[2].

137. CARTA ROBERTI DE CASTELKAIROC FACTA MONACHIS DE WEDERHAL DE PETRA AD FACIENDAM CALCEM.

OMNIBUS Christi Fidelibus ad quorum notitiam hoc præsens scriptum pervenerit Robertus de Castelkairoc[1] Salutem æternam in Domino. Noverit universitas vestra me pro salute animæ meæ et pro salute animarum Prædecessorum et Successorum meorum dedisse concessisse et præsenti carta confirmasse Domui Sanctæ Trinitatis et Sancti Constantini de Wederhal et Monachis ibidem Deo servientibus petram ad faciendam calcem[2] in territorio de Castelkairoc in puram et perpetuam Elemosinam. Habendam et capiendam imperpetuum in prædicto territorio extra terram aratam ad commodum suum faciendum cum libero ingressu et exitu sine aliqua contradictione vel impedimento. Dedi et concessi quod boves et equi dictorum Monachorum et aliorum qui trahent petram ad opus eorum habeant ubique pasturam in communi pastura in prædicto territorio sine aliquo impedimento excepto nocumento

---

[2] The date, from the witnesses, is probably almost the same as No. **134**, in the first 20 years of the 13th century; and it is not improbable that Richard de Levington was then custos for Walter Malclerk I. after 1216 in the early years of Henry III.

137. [1] This is the second Robert de Castelkairoc; see note 3 on No. **46**.

[2] There is limestone now got in the territory of Castlekairoc. We note that they were to keep outside the arable land in getting the limestone, and that oxen as well as horses were used in drawing it.

bladorum et pratorum eo tempore quo cariabunt prædictam petram. Ego autem et hæredes mei hanc Elemosinam
prædictis Monachis warantizabimus et defendemus imperpetuum. In cujus rei Testimonium præsenti scripto
sigillum meum apposui. Hijs Testibus, Roberto Archidiacono Karleoli[3], Radulpho Priore[4], Waltero Officiali[5], W.
Decano, Thoma filio Willelmi de Graistoc[6], Willelmo de
Daker tunc Vicecomite, Ricardo de Levington, Radulpho
de Feritate[7], P. de Tillol, Roberto de Hamton, Adam de
Hotun, Adam de Neuton, Willelmo filio Rogeri et alijs[8].

138. CARTA ANSELMI DE NEUBY FACTA MONACHIS
DE WEDERHAL DE UNO TOFTO ET CROFTO CUM QUIN-
DECIM ACRIS TERRÆ ET DIMIDIA IN NEUBY.

[3] This is Robert de Otterington, not the Robert who is so often
mentioned in the 12th century. A Papal Bull, dated April 12th, 1238,
gave him authority to hold the office ; see Hardy, *Fasti Eccles.*
iii. 249 and *Calendar of Papal Registers*, ed. W. H. Bliss, i. 170.
Robert de Oterington was witness with Gervase de Louther, Archdeacon of Carlisle, to an agreement between Radulph, Prior of
Carlisle, and the Abbey of Holm Cultram about a fishery in the Eden
(Dugdale, *Monasticon*, v. 607).

[4] Radulph, Prior of Carlisle, died Feb. 9th, 1247; see note 2
on No. **97**.

[5] Walter de Ulvesby ; see note on No. **56**.

[6] Thomas son of William de Graistoc was one of the Barons
of Graystock, and got livery of his father's lands in 1217 ; he married
Christiana, daughter of the first Robert de Veteriponte of Appleby
(see on No. **204**). The Barony was formed by Henry I. when Ranulf
Meschin became Earl of Chester in 1120, and was given to Forne son
of Sigulf or Liulf ; see *Testa de Nevill*, p. 379 *b* and note 12 on No. **1**.
This was one of his descendants. Thomas died in 1247, when his son
Robert did homage for his lands (*Fine Rolls*, 31 Henry III. m. 5,
ed. Roberts, ii. 14).

[7] Radulph de Feritate, the later person of this name ; see note 4
on No. **43**.

[8] From the Sheriff, William de Daker, the date must be from
1236 to 1247 ; as Walter was not yet made Archdeacon, which took
place about 1239 (see note 6 on No. **56**), the date will be from 1236
to 1239.

SCIANT omnes tam præsentes quam futuri quod Ego Anselmus de Neuby[1] cum consilio et assensu Matildis Uxoris meæ et Ricardi hæredis mei et cæterorum hæredum meorum et amicorum concessi et dedi et hac mea carta confirmavi Deo et Sanctæ Mariæ Eborum et Sancto Constantino de Wederhal et Monachis ibidem Deo servientibus in liberam puram et perpetuam Elemosinam unum toftum in Neuby[2] cum crofto adjacente quæ Elyas aliquando tenuit cum quindecim et dimidia acris terræ quæ faciunt duas bovatas in eadem Villa cum omnibus aisiamentis et pertinentijs suis sine retenemento aliquo et communem pasturam quatuor scilicet equis et viginti animalibus et quater viginti ovibus et octo porcis cum tota sequela prædictorum averiorum scilicet duorum annorum pro salute animæ meæ et uxoris meæ Matildis et Antecessorum et Successorum meorum. Et hanc Elemosinam ego Anselmus et hæredes mei warantizabimus prædictis Monachis ab omni terreno servicio et exactione. Testibus Hijs, Elia Senescallo de Gillesland, Willelmo de Vaus[3], Waltero Beinin, Roberto de Laversdal, Radulpho de Stineton, Laurentio de Agulunby, Willelmo Clerico de Wederhal, Willelmo filio ejus, Willelmo de Kaberge[4], Humfrido, Willelmo Decano, Michaele Dispensario[5], Waltero Portario et multis alijs[6].

138. [1] Anselm de Neuby lived in the time of William son of Odard (see note 16 on No. 38) who is a witness to his charter No. 141.

[2] Neuby, in the Barony of Linstock ; see on Nos. 86, 139.

[3] This is not the William de Vaus, or de Vallibus, who is a witness to No. 61 (see note 3 there) nor, probably, William, son of the first Robert de Vallibus, so called in the Foundation Charter of Lanercost, as Robert died without issue in 1195. He appears in the Pipe Rolls for 1201.

[4] Others of the family of Kaberge appear in this *Register*, as belonging to Westmoreland, see on No. 177. They probably belonged to Kaberg (*hodie* Kaber), a manor in the parish of Kirkbystephen.

[5] *Dispensarius* or *Dispensator* (see on No. 158), a steward generally.

139. CARTA RICARDI DE NEUBY FACTA MONACHIS DE WEDERHAL DE DUABUS BOVATIS TERRÆ IN TERRITORIO DE NEUBY.

OMNIBUS Sanctæ Matris Ecclesiæ filijs qui hanc cartam viderint vel audierint Ricardus de Neuby[1] Salutem. Noverit Universitas vestra me Divini amoris intuitu de consensu et assensu Emmæ uxoris meæ et Hæredum meorum pro salute animæ meæ et pro salute animarum Antecessorum et Successorum meorum dedisse et concessisse et hac præsenti carta mea confirmasse Deo et Beatæ Mariæ et Ecclesiæ Sanctæ Trinitatis de Wederhal et Monachis ibidem Deo servientibus duas bovatas terræ in Neuby[2] cum omnibus pertinentijs suis in liberam puram et perpetuam Elemosinam, Illas scilicet duas bovatas terræ quas Normannus Capellanus de Crosby[3] aliquando tenuit. Habendas et Tenendas integre et plenarie cum omnibus aisiamentis ad prædictam Villam spectantibus libere et quiete ab seculari servicio et consuetudine et exactione sicuti aliqua elemosina liberius haberi vel teneri potest. Et Ego et hæredes mei hanc Elemosinam prædictæ Ecclesiæ et prædictis Monachis contra omnes homines warantizabimus. Hijs Testibus, Roberto de Nuers tunc Vicecomite[4],

---

[6] The date of this charter will be before 1195, when William son of Odard, who attests No. **141**, died (see note 1 on No. **36**); from Walter Beinin and other witnesses, probably not long before.

139. [1] Richard de Neuby, son of Anselm, who granted the preceding charter.

[2] This is Neuby, in the Barony of Linstock (see on No. **86**), which is further proved by the land being held here by Norman, Chaplain of Crosby adjoining, and by the Seneschal of Erdington (Irthington) being witness to No. **140**.

[3] Crosby on Eden, in the Barony of Linstock, but abutting on the parish of Irthington in Gilsland.

[4] Robert de Nuers does not occur in the lists of sheriffs, see note 2 on No. **43**, where he appears with some of these witnesses in the beginning of the 13th century.

Gilberto de Turibus tunc Forestario, Roberto filio Willelmi de Korkeby, Roberto filio Adam, Alano de Langethech[5], Laurentio de Agulunby, Willielmo Clerico de Wederhal, Willielmo et Johanne filijs ejus, Humfrid de Wederhal et multis alijs[6].

140. Scriptum Radulphi filij Theobaldi annui redditus XII^d pro duabus bovatis terræ in Neuby.

SCIANT tam presentes quam futuri quod Ego Radulphus Theobaldi filius teneo duas bovatas terræ in Neuby de Priore et Monachis Dominis meis de Wederhal illas scilicet quas Anselmus de Neuby eis dedit in Elemosinam et teneor reddere eisdem Monachis pro prædicta terra duodecim denarios annuatim ad duos terminos, medietatem in festo Sancti Martini et medietatem ad Pentecosten. Uxor quoque mea[1]...si me supervixerit tenebit terram illam de prædictis Monachis eadem conventione. Post obitum vero meum et uxoris meæ remanebit terra illa cum omnibus melioracionibus quas fecimus in ea prædictis Monachis imperpetuum sine omni calumpnia alicujus vel impedimento. Et Sciendum quod si quis nostrum alterum supervixerit et vitam suam voluerit mutare dabit Domui de Wederhal in Elemosinam omnia catalla sua quæ eum tunc contigerit habere. Si autem alter nostrûm in seculo in fata concesserit medietas catallorum quæ eum contigerit tunc habere erit Domui de Wederhal et aliam medietatem licebit ei dare ubicunque voluerit. Præterea sciendum est quod

---

[5] Alan de Langethech is probably identical with Alan de Langethwaite, who appears in the charters of Robert son of William de Korkeby (see Nos. 46, 51) with Laurence de Agulunby and other of these witnesses.

[6] The date of this charter must be in the early part of the 13th century; the sheriff Robert de Nuers does not help us.

140. [1] After *Uxor quoque mea* there is a blank in all three Transcripts; but Machel who copied the charter (MSS. iv. 503) has the word "*Aicus*" carefully written.

neuter nostrum poterit obligare se alij Domui quam Domui
de Wederhale nisi de voluntate Prioris et Monachorum. Et
[ut] hoc ratum sit et firmum huic scripto sigillum nostrum
apposuimus in testimonium et juramento devoto præstito
confirmavimus. Testibus hijs, Elya Senescallo de Erdington[2], Willelmo Capellano de Warthwic, Anselmo de Neuby,
Ricardo filio ejus, Radulpho de Stiveton, Laurentio Agulunby, Willelmo Clerico de Wederhal, Willelmo filio ejus,
Willelmo de Eirminne, Ricardo Cemetario et multis alijs[3].

141. CARTA ANSELMI DE NEUBY FACTA MONACHIS DE WEDERHAL DE UNO MESSUAGIO ET TOFTO ET CROFTO IN NEUBY.

SCIANT omnes tam præsentes quam futuri quod Ego
Anselmus de Neuby cum consilio et assensu Matildis
uxoris meæ et hæredum meorum concessi et dedi et hac
mea carta confirmavi Deo et Sancto Constantino de Wederhal et Monachis ibidem Deo servientibus in puram et
perpetuam Elemosinam pro salute animæ meæ et Uxoris
meæ et Patris mei et Antecessorum nostrum mesuagium
illud cum tofto et crofto quod Rogerus filius Elwini de me
tenuit in Neuby et Elwinus Pater ipsius Rogeri post eum
liberum et quietum ab omni servicio cum communi pastura
et omnibus aisiamentis cum hominibus quantum una bovata
terræ in eadem Villa sustinere potest. Hanc vero terram
prædictus Elwinus in vita sua de Priore de Wederhal tenebit,
Reddendo inde sexdecim denarios, octo scilicet ad Festum
Sancti Michaelis et octo ad Pascham. Post obitum vero
prædicti Elwini Prior illam terram cuicunque voluerit

---

[2] Erdington (*hodie* Irthington) is the parish of which Neuby was a
part, but then in the Barony of Linstock (see note 2 on No. 86) and is
bounded on the east by the river Irthing. The Church of Irthinton
was granted by Robert de Vallibus to the Priory of Lanercost (*Regist.
Lanercost*, MS. i. 1).

[3] Anselm de Neuby is a witness, and the land is the same as in
No. 138 ; the date is therefore, probably, a little later.

locabit cum prædictis aisiamentis. Præterea sciendum est quod Ego A. et Uxor mea M. corpora nostra Ecclesiæ de Wederhal damus in sepulturam. Testibus Hijs, Willelmo filio Odardi de Korkeby, Johanne filio ejus, Willelmo Clerico de Wederhal, Willelmo de Airminne et multis alijs[1].

142. CARTA WALTERI DE NEUBY FACTA MONACHIS DE WEDERHAL DE XVI ACRIS TERRÆ IN TERRITORIO DE NEUBY.

OMNIBUS hanc cartam visuris vel audituris Walterus de Neuby[1] Salutem. Noveritis me pro salute animæ meæ et omnium Parentum meorum concessisse dedisse et præsenti carta mea confirmasse Deo et Ecclesiæ Beatæ Mariæ Eboraci et Monachis Sanctæ Trinitatis de Wederhal sexdecim acras terræ in territorio de Neuby quas Ricardus filius Petri aliquando tenuit de me ad firmam cum tofto et crofto quæ Ricardus filius Petri tenuit in villa de Neuby et unam acram terræ in holmo et dimidiam acram terræ in Garbrades quas Ego aliquando tenui in Dominico meo. Tenendas et Habendas dictis Ecclesiæ et Monachis in liberam puram et perpetuam Elemosinam in perpetuum cum omnibus pertinentijs suis libertatibus et aisiamentis ad prædictam terram pertinentibus infra Villam de Neuby et extra absque ullo retenemento sicut aliqua terra liberius potest dari vel teneri. Et sciendum est quod tota dicta terra quieta erit de multura et pannagio et de omnibus secularibus accionibus et demandis imperpetuum. Hanc itaque Elemosinam Ego et hæredes mei prædictis Ecclesiæ

141. [1] From the witness William son of Odard de Corkeby, and his son John de Warthwic, the date, like that of No. **138**, will be not long before 1195.

142. [1] Walter de Neuby was dead in 1247, as appears from the dated charter of his widow Agnes, No. **144**. It is not clear whether he was the son of Richard, the grantor of No. **139**, but probably he was, as his wife Agnes, in No. **145**, quitclaims her third share in the property granted by Anselm.

et Monachis contra omnes gentes warantizabimus defendemus et acquietabimus imperpetuum.   Hijs Testibus, Domino Waltero Archidiacono², Domino Willelmo Vicario de Hyrthington Decano, Adam Monacho, Domino Roberto de Karlaton Milite, Willelmo de Warthwic, Willelmo de Korkeby³, Willelmo Pollard, Silvestro, Johanne filio Willelmi de Wederhal, Ricardo Maysel, Adam Janitore et alijs⁴.

143. CARTA WALTERI DE NEUBY FACTA MONACHIS DE WEDERHAL DE XVI ACRIS TERRÆ CUM TOFTO ET CROFTO IN NEUBY.

OMNIBUS hanc cartam visuris vel audituris Walterus de Neuby Salutem.   Noveritis me pro salute animæ meæ et omnium Parentum meorum concessisse dedisse et præsenti carta confirmasse Deo et Ecclesiæ Beatæ Mariæ Eboraci et Monachis Sanctæ Trinitatis de Wederhal sexdecim acras terræ in territorio de Neuby quas Alexander de Neuby tenuit de me ad firmam cum tofto et crofto quod Rogerus filius Hugonis tenuit in Villa de Neuby.   Tenendas et Habendas dictis Ecclesiæ et Monachis in liberam puram et perpetuam Elemosinam imperpetuum cum omnibus pertinentijs suis libertatibus et aisiamentis ad prædictam terram pertinentibus infra Villam et extra absque ullo retenemento.   Et sciendum est quod ista terra quieta erit de multura et pannagio imperpetuum de me et heredibus meis.   Hanc itaque Elemosinam Ego et hæredes mei prædictis Ecclesiæ et Monachis contra omnes gentes warantizabimus defendemus et acquietabimus imperpetuum. In cujus rei Testimonium præsenti scripto sigillum meum apposui.   Hijs Testibus Roberto de Castelkairoc, Adam de

---

² Walter de Ulvesby was promoted from Official to Archdeacon in or about 1139 ; see note 5 on No. **56.**

³ William de Korkeby was probably the son of William son of Roger de Korkeby, about this date ; see on Nos. **64, 81.**

⁴ From the notes above, the date of the charter will be 1239—47.

Cumreu, Henrico de W[i]deburn[1], Jordano de Blaterne[2], Waltero de Camboc[3], Nichol de Waliford[4], Thoma Forestario, Roberto de Horneby[5], Roberto Clerico de Cucun[6], Johanne Stelfot, Stephano Wagbrakan et alijs[7].

144. QUIETA CLAMATIO AGNETIS UXORIS WALTERI DE NEUBY DE TERTIA PARTE IV BOVATARUM TERRÆ IN EADEM.

OMNIBUS Christi Fidelibus ad quorum notitiam præsens scriptum pervenerit Agnes quæ fuit uxor Walteri de Neuby Salutem æternam in Domino. Noverit universitas vestra me in libera potestate et viduitate mea remisisse et quietum clamasse imperpetuum Deo et Beatæ Mariæ Eboraci et Domui de Wederhal et Monachis ibidem Deo servientibus totum jus et clamium quod habui vel habere potui nomine Dotis in tertiam partem quatuor bovatarum terræ cum pertinentijs in territorio de Neuby quas Walterus Maritus meus dedit Domui de Wederhal in puram et perpetuam

143. [1] Transcript C has Wideburn. In the *Register of Lanercost* we have Henry de Wodeburn (MS. xiv. 10).

[2] Jurdan de Blaterne, or Blacerne, appears in an Inquisition made concerning the King's lands held by John de Boulton of Carlisle in 1247 (*Inquis. p. m.* 31 Hen. III. No. 25) ; he is also witness to a charter of Robert de Castelcairoc in the *Register of Lanercost* (MS. iv. 16).

[3] Walter de Camboc is also a witness in the same *Register* (MS. vi. 19).

[4] Nichol de Waliford is probably identical with the Nicholas de Walingford who attests two charters in the *Register of Lanercost* (MS. ii. 19; iv. 6) about this period, with several of the same co-witnesses.

[5] Robert de Horneby, with several of his co-witnesses here, attests charter No. **171**, dated 1241.

[6] Cucun is evidently identical with Cutun in Nos. **160, 171** and elsewhere. This is Cutun, or Cuton (*hod.* Cowton) in Yorkshire. Robert de Cuton, clerk, was instituted to Gerford, May 1248, see *Archbp Gray's Register*, ed. Raine, p. 103.

[7] The date of this charter, from what is known of many of the witnesses, must be very nearly the same as the last, 1239—47.

Elemosinam. In cujus rei Testimonium præsenti scripto sigillum meum apposui. Hijs Testibus, Domino Willelmo filio Rogeri, Domino Roberto de Castelkairoc, Willelmo de la Blamyre[1], Adam Armstrang, Willelmo de Croklyn[2], Johanne Stelfot et alijs. Datum apud Karleolum die Martis proximo post Festum Sanctæ Trinitatis Anno Gratiæ M°cc°xlvii°.

145. QUIETA CLAMATIO AGNETIS UXORIS WALTERI DE NEUBY DE TERTIA PARTE MULTURÆ ET PANNAGIJ DUARUM BOVATARUM IN NEUBY.

OMNIBUS Christi Fidelibus ad quorum notitiam præsens scriptum pervenerit Agnes quondam Uxor Walteri de Neuby Salutem æternam in Domino. Noverit universitas vestra me in ligia potestate et libera viduitate mea remisisse et quietum clamasse imperpetuum Deo et Sanctæ Mariæ Eboraci et Domui Sanctæ Trinitatis et Sancti Constantini de Wederhal et Monachis ibidem Deo servientibus totum jus et clamium quod habui vel aliquo modo habere potui nomine Dotis in tertiam partem multuræ et pannagij duarum bovatarum terræ in Neuby quas Normannus Capellanus de Crosseby aliquando tenuit Et insuper tertiam partem meam quindecim acrarum terræ et dimidiæ cum tofto et crofto in eadem Villa quas Anselmus de Neuby dedit Domui de Wederhal quas Elyas aliquando tenuit cum messuagio tofto et crofto quæ faciunt dimidiam acram terræ in eadem Villa in liberam puram et perpetuam Elemosinam. Ita quod nec Ego nec aliquis ex parte mea aliquo tempore vitæ meæ in dictis duabus bovatis et dictis quindecim acris

---

144. [1] William de la Blamyre appears as a sub-tenant of the King's lands at Carlisle under John de Boulton in an Inquisition held September, 1250 (*Inquis. p. m.* 34 Hen. III. No. 46). He also attests several charters in the *Register of Lanercost* (MS. ii. 7 ; iv. 5, 7) with some of these co-witnesses. The name has remained to the present day as that of a well-known Cumberland family.

[2] For William de Croklyn, see on No. **150**.

terræ et dimidia et toftis et croftis cum mesuagio ullum jus vel clamium nomine Dotis multuræ et pannagij quod me contingebat numquam vendicabo vel vendicabit. Hijs Testibus, Domino Thoma de Multon[1], Domino Eustachio tunc Vicecomite Karlioli[2], Domino Hugh de Multon[3], Ricardo de Castelkairoc, Roberto de Tyllol, Roberto de Warthwic, Thoma de Beuchamp[4], Johanne de Spaunton,

145.   [1] This Thomas de Multon is the son of the Thomas in No. **47** (see note 4 there) and succeeded to his father's lands in 1240, generally called Thomas de Multon of Gillesland.   He died in 1271.

[2] This is Eustace de Balliol, as in the next charter.   He was Sheriff of Carlisle in 1262—1265, and keeper of Carlisle Castle, on which he spent large sums and incurred debts with which his executors had to deal (*Liberate Rolls*, 2 Edw. I. m. 2).   He appears as Justiciary in September, 1268 (*Pipe Rolls*, 1268—69; *Patent Rolls*, 52 Hen. III. m. 4).   He married Helewisa (or Hawisa) de Levington, daughter of Radulph Boyvill of Levington and Ada Gernun (see note 1 on No. **103**).   He was a crusader, and went in 1270 with Prince Edward to the Holy Land (*Patent Rolls*, 54 Hen. III. m. 10, 11); there he probably died in 1271—72.   In November of 1272 important Inquisitions were held concerning the lands of his widow Helewysa who was then dead.   Her heir was determined to be "Thomas son of Thomas de Multon de Gillesland" who was of full age (see No. **47**, and *Inquis. p. m.* 56 Hen. III. Nos. 35, 36); hence Eustace de Balliol left no son, and clearly did not marry again, as Dugdale asserts (*Baronage*, i. 524).

[3] Hugh de Multon was the son of the second Thomas, or Thomas de Gillesland, mentioned above, and brother of Thomas and Hubert (*Regist. Lanercost* xiii. 16, 17, 18).   He is witness to No. **203**, dated 1292, where he is called "knight." He is also witness, with his brother Hubert, both "knights," and William de Neuby to a charter dated 1292 in the *Register of Lanercost* (MS. xi. 6), where he is called "Lord of Hoffe " (in the parish of S. Laurence, Appleby).   He appears as a juror in 1292 in the *Placita de Quo Waranto* (*Record Com.* pp. 115, 118).

[4] Thomas de Beuchamp, or Beauchamp, is elsewhere in this *Register* Thomas de Bellocampo (as in No. **176**).   He is called "Seneschal of Gillesland" in the *Register of Lanercost* (MS. ii. 22) where he is a frequent witness, and co-witness to one charter (MS. xiv. 3) with Thomas and Hugo de Multon as here.   From Inquisitions held in 1268 and 1270, he appears to have been a

Roberto Minoc, Willelmo de la Blamyre, Johanne Stelfot, Johanne Armstrong, Johanne Briđ. de Korkeby, et alijs[5].

146. CARTA WILLELMI FILIJ WALTERI DE NEUBY FACTA MONACHIS DE WEDERHAL DE DUABUS BOVATIS TERRÆ IN NEUBY.

OMNIBUS Christi Fidelibus hanc cartam visuris vel audituris Willelmus filius Walteri de Neuby[1] Salutem æternam in Domino. Noveritis me pro salute animæ meæ et omnium Parentum meorum dedisse concessisse et hac presenti carta mea confirmasse Deo et Ecclesiæ Sanctæ Mariæ Eboraci et Monachis Sanctæ Trinitatis et Sancti Constantini de Wederhal illas duas bovatas terræ in Neuby quas Normannus Capellanus de Crosseby aliquando tenuit, et alias quindecim acras terræ et dimidiam cum tofto et crofto quæ faciunt duas bovatas terræ in Neuby quas Elyas aliquando tenuit quas Anselmus de Neuby dedit Domui de Wederhal cum uno mesuagio tofto et crofto quæ faciunt dimidiam acram terræ in Neuby quietas et liberas de multura et pannagio imperpetuum de me et hæredibus meis dictis Ecclesiæ et Monachis in puram liberam et perpetuam Elemosinam possidendas sicut aliqua Elemosina melius et liberius poterit dari vel possideri. Ego vero Willelmus supradictam terram cum toftis et croftis dictis Ecclesiæ et Monachis de multura et pannagio contra omnes homines et fæminas warantizabimus acquietabimus et defendemus imperpetuum. Insuper Ego Willelmus

Verdurer of the King's Forest, and to have held land under Helewisa, widow of Richard de Vernun (*Inquis. p. m.* 52 Hen. III. No. 30, and 54 Hen. III. No. 19). He is witness to the charter of Matilda de Vallibus, No. **194**, dated 1271.

[5] From the Sheriff, the date of this charter is 1262—65, which agrees with what we know of the witnesses. Thomas de Multon died in 1271.

146. [1] William de Neuby (see note 10 on No. **78**) confirms the preceding grants of his ancestors, as set out in the charters of his mother Agnes, Nos. **144**, **145**.

omnes terras et possessiones quas Anselmus de Neuby et Ricardus de Neuby dederunt et concesserunt Domui de Wederhal in puram et perpetuam Elemosinam ratifico et confirmo pro me et hæredibus meis imperpetuum. In cujus rei Testimonium presenti cartæ sigillum meum apposui. Hijs Testibus, Eustachio de Baliolo tunc Vicecomite Karleoli, Roberto de Mulcastre, Alano de Horeton[2], Ricardo de Castelkairoc, Roberto de Warthwic, Roberto de Tyllol, Ricardo Maunsell, Roberto Mynoc, Johanne Mynoc, Willelmo de Blamyre, Johanne Stelfot, Laurentio filio Walteri le Porter, Roberto de Scupton, et multis alijs[3].

147. CARTA WILLELMI FILIJ WALTERI DE NEUBY FACTA MONACHIS DE WEDERHAL DE 2[us] ACRIS TERRÆ QUIETIS DE MULTURA ET PANNAGIO IN NEUBY.

OMNIBUS Christi fidelibus præsens scriptum visuris vel audituris Willelmus filius Walteri de Neuby Salutem æternam in Domino. Noverit universitas vestra me dedisse et concessisse et hac præsenti carta mea confirmasse Deo et Beatæ Mariæ Eborum et Domui Sanctæ Trinitatis et Sancti Constantini de Wederhal duas acras terræ in territorio de Neuby quarum una jacet juxta le pot et dimidia acra abuttat super le pot et dimidia acra abuttat super hevedland[1] Alexandri de Neuby ad viridem viam. Tenendas

[2] Alan de Horeton, or Orreton, was, with Thomas de Lascels, Robert de Castelkayroc, and William de Derwentwater, appointed in October 1255 to report on the state of the Castle of Carlisle, when the county and the castle were delivered up by Robert de Brus, and delivered by the king to William de Fortibus, Earl of Albemarle (*Patent Rolls*, 40 Hen. III. m. 22); the interesting report of its bad condition is given in *Calend. Documents Scot.* ed. Bain, i. 391. He was witness to a charter of Matilda de Vallibus in the *Register of Lanercost* (MS. x. 7) with several of the witnesses here. He and Robert de Mulcastre were appointed justices at Carlisle in July, 1273.

[3] From the Sheriff, the date of the charter is 1262—65, like the preceding, though probably somewhat later.

147. [1] *Hevedland* or "headland."

et Habendas dictis Domibus de Eboraco et de Wederhal in liberam puram et perpetuam Elemosinam quietas de multura et pannagio et ab omni terreno servicio imperpetuum. Et Ego Willelmus et hæredes mei dictas duas acras cum omnibus pertinentijs suis et cum communi pastura Villæ de Neuby dictis Domibus de Eboraco et de Wederhal contra homines omnes imperpetuum warantizabimus acquietabimus et defendemus. In cujus rei Testimonium præsenti scripto sigillum meum apposui. Hijs Testibus, Roberto de Warthwic, Roberto de Tyllol, Waltero de Thorheved, Willelmo de Agulunby, Roberto de Mynot[2], Johanne de Spaunton, Johanne Stelfod, Johanne de Aqua, Johanne Spendluve, Ranulpho Præposito et multis alijs[3].

148. CARTA ROBERTI FILIJ ALEXANDRI DE NEUBY FACTA ROGERO FILIO SUO DE TOTA TERRA SUA IN NEUBY.

OMNIBUS Sanctæ Matris Ecclesiæ filijs ad quorum notitiam hoc præsens scriptum pervenerit Robertus filius Alexandri de Neuby[1] salutem in Domino sempiternam. Noveritis me dedisse concessisse et hoc præsenti scripto confirmasse Rogero filio meo totam terram meam cum ædificijs sine ullo retenemento quæ habui in territorio de Neuby una cum libero servicio Willelmi et Rogeri fratrum meorum. Tenendam et Habendam eidem Rogero et Hæredibus suis de Abbate Ecclesiæ Sanctæ Mariæ Eborum et Conventu ejusdem loci libere quiete bene in pace et hæreditarie cum omnibus libertatibus et aisiamentis dictæ

---

[2] Robert *de* Mynot, or Mynoc, the "de" is probably an error, as it does not occur elsewhere with the name of this "servant of the Lord Prior" (No. **87**).

[3] The date must be somewhere near the date of the last charter.

148. [1] Alexander de Neuby appears in Nos. **143** and **147** as holding land under Walter de Neuby. Robert, his son, must be different from the Robert de Neubi in Nos. **59, 148**, at the earlier period 1230—31. The brothers of Robert, William and Roger, are mentioned in this charter.

terræ infra Villam de Neuby et extra prope et procul
pertinentibus Reddendo inde annuatim Cellæ de Wederhal
tres solidos argenti scilicet medietatem ad festum Sancti
Martini in yeme et aliam medietatem ad Pentecosten.   Et
faciendo eisdem Abbati et Conventui et Cellæ prædictæ alia
servicia inde debita et consueta.   Et Ego vero prædictus
Robertus et hæredes totam prædictam terram cum ædificijs
et libero servicio prædicto dicto Rogero et hæredibus suis
contra omnes gentes warantizabimus et defendemus imperpetuum.   Hanc autem donationem concessionem confirmationem concedo eidem Rogero et hæredibus suis dum
erga prædictos Abbatem et conventum fideliter se habuerint
et servicia fecerint, et firmam suam prædictæ Cellæ bene
reddiderint.   In cujus rei Testimonium præsenti scripto
sigillum meum apposui.   Testibus, Roberto de Warthwic,
Willelmo de Neuby, Willelmo de Warthwic[2], Johanne
Tyllolf, Alano Armstrang, Ricardo de Fenton, Thoma
Clerico et alijs[3].

149. Carta Elyæ de Croglyn facta Monachis
de Wederhal de v acris terræ juxta divisas
Domini sui.

Elyas de Croglyn[1] omnibus Sanctæ Matris Ecclesiæ
filijs salutem.   Sciatis me dedisse et hac presenti mea
carta confirmasse Deo et Ecclesiæ de Wederhal et Monachis ibidem Deo servientibus pro anima Patris et Matris
meæ et Antecessorum meorum in puram et perpetuam
Elemosinam quinque acras terræ juxta divisas Domini
mei.   Hijs Testibus, Willielmo filio Odardi, Johanne filio
ejus, Randulpho filio ejus, Ricardo de Haiton, Johanne de

---

[2] William the son of Robert de Warthwic as in No. **70** where are
some of the same witnesses.

[3] From John Tyllol, or Tyllolf, who appears with the two de Warth-
wics in No. **110**, the date of this charter will probably also be about 1290.

149. [1] On the family and demesne of Elyas de Croglyn, see
the next charters.

Graistoc[2], Stephano Capellano, Augustino Capellano, Ricardo de Ulnesby, Gilberto fratre Prioris, Johanne de Rokesburg et multis alijs[3].

150. CARTA WILLELMI DE CROGLYN FACTA MONACHIS DE WEDERHAL DE DUABUS BOVATIS TERRÆ ETC. IN CROGLIN.

OMNIBUS Christi fidelibus ad quos præsens scriptum pervenerit Willelmus de Croglyn[1] salutem in Domino. Noverit universitas vestra me Divinæ caritatis intuitu pro salute animæ meæ et Antecessorum Successorumque meorum dedisse concessisse et hac præsenti carta mea confirmasse Deo et Beatæ Mariæ de Eboraco et Beato Constantino de Wederhal et Monachis ibidem Deo servientibus duas bovatas terræ in Villa mea de Croglyn[2] cum tofto et crofto et cum prato quod jacet inter terram Ybri et terram Walteri portarij descendens usque ad rivulum qui cadit in rivulo molendini ejusdem Villæ versus Orientem Illas scilicet bovatas terræ quas Elvina Vidua quondam tenuit. Habendas et Tenendas in puram

---

[2] John de Graistoc'is not in the lists of the Barons of Graystock (see note 6 on No. 137) at this period, though there is one of the name at the end of the 13th century.

[3] Five of these witnesses, after the first three, do not appear elsewhere in this *Register*. The first three occur in No. 55, and, probably, this charter is about the same date i.e. shortly after 1175, and certainly before 1195, when William son of Odard died.

150. [1] This William de Croglyn is not the son of Elyas as in Nos. 152, 153, but of a later date, probably identical with the William of Nos. 155, 156, his son and heir being also called William (No. 155). He was witness to the charter No. 144, dated 1247, and to the convention No. 171, dated 1241.

[2] This is not the Croglyn, the parish, of No. 14 (note 7), but Little Croglyn, or Parva Croglyn (see No. 157), a manor in the parish of Kirkoswald on the opposite side of the little river Croglin. It was held by Ebria or Ybri, daughter of Robert d'Estrivers (see on Simon de Morvilla, No. 101) referred to below ; but it does not appear how it came to her.

liberam et perpetuam Elemosinam cum omnibus communis libertatibus et aisiamentis infra Villam et extra adeo libere honorifice et integre sicut aliqua Elemosina liberius possit dari vel possideri. Ego vero Willelmus et hæredes mei hanc Elemosinam prædictis Monachis sicut prædictum est contra omnes homines warantizabimus acquietabimus et defendemus imperpetuum. Et ut hoc scriptum perpetuæ firmitatis robur optineat Ego illud sigilli mei impressione corroboravi. Hijs Testibus, Roberto de Hamton tunc Vicecomite Cumberlandiæ, Roberto filio Willelmi de Ulsisby, Adam de Cumreu, Michaele de Wallibus[3], Johanne de Ermin, Thoma de Rafneswic[4], Waltero janitore, Johanne filio Willelmi, Johanne Agulunby, Johanne Clerico et alijs[5].

151. Carta Willelmi de Croglyn facta Monachis de Wederhal de quinque acris terræ in Croglin.

Omnibus Sanctæ Matris Ecclesiæ filijs ad quos præsens scriptum pervenerit Willelmus de Croglyn salutem in Domino. Sciatis me concessisse et dedisse et hac præsenti carta mea confirmasse Deo et Ecclesiæ Sanctæ Trinitatis de Wederhal et Monachis ibidem Deo servientibus in puram et perpetuam Elemosinam quinque acras terræ cum pertinentiis in territorio de Croglyn, scilicet duas acras in uno crofto quas Ricardus filius Lewini tenuit, et tres acras inter terram dictorum Monachorum et terram Henrici de

---

[3] I have not been able to determine what member of the family of de Vallibus this is ; Nicolson and Burn (*Hist.* ii. 429) seem to make him identical with Michael de Valle of Ainstable (Nos. **168, 170**).

[4] Thomas de Rafeneswic, or Raveneswic, is given in No. **107** as the brother of Alan son of Adam de Raveneswic ; see note 5 on No. **107** (about 1178) where Adam is mentioned as late as 1185.

[5] We have the same Sheriff in No. **63**, with John de Agulunby, John son of William, and Walter janitor. As in that charter, therefore, the reference is to the earlier Robert de Hamton (see note 4 on No. **54**) who was Sheriff 1223—29. This agrees also with the time of Bishop Hugh in the next charter.

Ulnesthwait[1] pro quieta clamacione quam Prior et prædicti Monachi fecerunt mihi de quinque acris terræ quas Pater meus dedit eis in liberam Elemosinam. Tenendas et Habendas in puram et perpetuam Elemosinam cum omnibus pertinentijs adeo libere ut aliqua Elemosina liberius ab aliquibus poterit optineri. Ego vero Willelmus et hæredes mei præfatas quinque acras terræ cum pertinentijs prædictis Monachis contra omnes homines warantizabimus. Hijs Testibus, Domino H. tunc Episcopo Karliolensi[2], B. tunc Priore[3], Magistro A. tunc Officiali Karliolensi[4], A. de Aspatric Decano, Magistro G. de Louther, W. et R. Monachis de bello loco[5] Sacerdotibus Domini Episcopi, Thoma de Morland, Odardo Clerico, Stephano le Burgeigium, Johanne Ausing et multis alijs[6].

152. QUIETA CLAMATIO WILLELMI FILIJ ELYÆ DE CROGLYN FACTA MONACHIS DE WEDERHAL DE DIMIDIA PARTE VILLÆ DE CROGLYN.

NOTUM sit omnibus legentibus vel audientibus litteras has quod Ego Willelmus filius Elyæ de Croglyn cum consilio et assensu Ysoudæ Uxoris meæ et hæredum meorum dedi et concessi et hac præsenti carta mea confirmavi et a me et hæredibus meis quietam clamavi Deo et Beatæ

151. [1] For Henry de Ulnesthwait, see on No. 157.

[2] Hugh, Bishop of Carlisle; see note 1 on No. 19.

[3] Bartholomew, Prior of Carlisle, who died in 1231; see note 4 on No. 20.

[4] Adam de Kirkeby, Official; see note 6 on No. 19.

[5] Beaulieu (Bellum Locum Regis) in Hampshire, of which Bishop Hugh had been Abbot. It was founded by King John in 1204; see Dugdale, *Monast.* v. 680, also *Close Rolls*, 3 Hen. III. m. 11 (Rec. Com. i. 405), where there is no mention of Beaulieu in Burgundy, though the King in his letter to Pope Honorius III. mentions Hugh, Abbot of Beaulieu.

[6] The last charter cannot have been earlier than 1223, hence this charter, which was probably about the same time, would be probably in 1223, the last year of Bishop Hugh.

Mariæ et Ecclesiæ Sanctæ Trinitatis de Wederhal et
Monachis ibidem servientibus Deo terram illam in Croglyn
quam Domina Ybri dedit prædictis Monachis in perpetuam
Elemosinam, scilicet totam dimidiam[1] partem Villæ de
Croglyn cum omnibus libertatibus aisiamentis decimæ parti
Villæ pertinentibus infra Villam et extra sine aliquo retene-
mento, Et quinque acras terræ quas Pater meus dedit
prædictis Monachis in perpetuam Elemosinam. Hanc vero
Elemosinam Ego et hæredes mei prædictis Monachis contra
omnes gentes imperpetuum warantizabimus. Hijs Testibus,
Roberto de Mihers tunc Vicecomite[2], Gilberto de Turibus,
Alano de Caldebec[3], Roberto de Castelkairoc[4], W. de
Aireminne, W. Clerico de Wederhal, Radulpho Clerico,
Unfraio et multis alijs[5].

152. [1] This should apparently be "*decimam*" *partem*, as shewn in
the words following and in the next charter. It was granted by Lady
Ybri, or Ebria, d'Estrivers, see No. 101, where it is called a carucate of
land.

[2] Robert de Mihers, probably the same as de Nuers (see on
Nos. 43 and 139) neither of which names is in the lists of Sheriffs.
The number of witnesses common to these three charters, and the two
above-named, seems conclusive.

[3] Alan de Caldebec was pro-Sheriff or Custos in the years 1204—5,
1215 and for Walter Malclerk in 1222. He appears in the Pipe
Rolls, in 1201, making payment for the land of Grenewra, and often in
subsequent years. He was witness to the grant of the Church of
Crosthwaite by Alicia de Rumeli to Fountains Abbey (Cotton MSS.
Tiberius C. xii. p. 97 ; also in full in *Archbp Gray's Register*, p. 58 *n.* ;
the date of which must be 1193—96; he also attests a grant by her of
Borcherdale (Borrowdale) to Furness Abbey in her second widowhood
about 1210—12 (*Duchy of Lancaster Records*, Box B, No. 164). In
the *Register of Lanercost* he is witness to a charter (MS. vii. 17) while
he is Sheriff, and to another (MS. viii. 6) by Bishop Hugh (1219—23).

[4] This is the first Robert, in the early part of the 13th century, see
note on No. 46.

[5] All the witnesses point to the same date as Nos. 43 and 139,
i.e. the beginning of the 13th century, which is supported by the
probable identity of Robert de Mihers and Robert de Nuers as well
as by the date of Elyas (No. 149) father of the grantor.

153. CARTA WILLELMI FILII ELYÆ DE CROGLYN
FACTA MONACHIS DE WEDERHAL DE DUABUS BOVATIS
TERRÆ IN EADEM.

NOTUM sit omnibus legentibus vel audientibus literas
has quod Ego Willelmus filius Elyæ de Croglyn cum consensu et assensu Ysoudæ Uxoris meæ et hæredum et
amicorum meorum dedi et hac præsenti carta mea confirmavi pro salute Domini mei Rogeri de Bellocampo[1] et
mei et pro salute animarum Antecessorum meorum Deo et
Beatæ Mariæ et Ecclesiæ Sanctæ Trinitatis de Wederhal
et Monachis ibidem Deo servientibus in puram et perpetuam Elemosinam duas bovatas terræ in campo de
Croglyn scilicet totam decimam partem Villæ de Croglyn
tam in Dominicis meis quam in alijs locis et unum toftum
et croftum juxta vadum aquæ de Croglyn quod Gilbertus
avunculus meus aliquando tenuit libere et quiete ab omnibus terrenis servicijs et exactionibus cum omnibus libertatibus et aisiamentis decimæ parti Villæ de Croglyn
pertinentibus infra Villam et extra sine aliquo retenemento.

153. [1] Roger de Bellocampo, or Beauchamp, is here called the
"Lord" of the manor of Little Croglyn, and in the next charter
confirms these grants. In No. **172**, he is Lord of Stafhole. He
granted land in Cringeldic to the monks of Wederhal (No. **172**) on
account of which a lawsuit arose with his sisters Alice and Amabilla
(see No. **173**). He appears in the Pipe Rolls for Westmoreland as
Custos for Galfrid son of Peter, the Sheriff in 1200 (2 John); and in
1201 he and Grecia, widow of Thomas son of Gospatric (son of Orme)
are set down as owing 100 marcs for having the custody of the land
and heir of Thomas; and, in 1210, Grecia is given as the wife
of Roger. The Pipe Rolls for Cumberland in 1209 give his name as
having custody of the land of William son of Adam de Hotton
(probably not the same Adam as in No. **63**). He is witness to two
charters of Hugh de Morvill in the *Register of Lanercost* (MS. ii.
12, 13) with Thomas son of Gospatric, also to one of Adam Salsarius
(MS. v. 27) who attests his charter No. **154**. He gave his body to be
buried in the Church of Wederhal and land to provide vestments and
lights for the altar of the Virgin, see No. **172**, the date of the charter
being 1223—29.

Hanc vero Elemosinam Ego et hæredes mei prædictis
Monachis imperpetuum contra omnes gentes warantizabimus. Hijs Testibus, Roberto de Mihers tunc Vicecomite
Karlioli, Gilberto de Turribus, Alano de Caldebec, Roberto
Clerico, Alano de Cumreu, Willielmo de Aireminne, Radulpho Clerico, Willielmo Clerico, Umfrido de Wederhal et
multis alijs[2].

154. CONFIRMATIO ROGERI DE BELLOCAMPO FACTA
MONACHIS DE WEDERHAL DE TERRA QUAM HABENT IN
CROGLYN.

OMNIBUS Sanctæ Matris Ecclesiæ filijs Rogerus de
Bellocampo Salutem. Noverit universitas vestra me pro
salute animæ meæ et pro salute animarum Antecessorum
meorum concessisse et hac præsenti carta mea confirmasse
Deo et Beatæ Mariæ et Ecclesiæ Sanctæ Trinitatis de
Wederhal et Monachis ibidem Deo servientibus in puram
et perpetuam Elemosinam totam terram quam habent
præfati Monachi in Villa de Croglyn ex donatione Dominæ
Ybri et Simonis de Morvilla et ex dono Willelmi filij Elyæ
de Croglyn sicuti cartæ eorum testantur, scilicet totam
quintam partem[1] prædictæ Villæ integre et plenarie infra
Villam et extra Villam in omnibus locis et aisiamentis
prædictæ Villæ pertinentibus liberam et quietam ab omni
terreno servicio et exactione sicuti aliqua Elemosina liberius
dari vel confirmari potest. Insuper quinque acras terræ in
campo de Croglyn, quas Elyas de Croglyn præfatis Monachis in Elemosinam dedit. Hijs Testibus, Roberto de
Miers tunc Vicecomite, Roberto de Castelkairoc, Roberto
filio Willelmi de Korkeby, Adam Salsario[2], Alano de

---

[2] The date must be nearly the same as that of the preceding
charter, i.e. the beginning of the 13th century.

154. [1] The fifth, not the tenth part, as in the preceding charters;
perhaps all the grants named made up one fifth of the vill.

Adam Salsarius was a person of importance. He was proved,
by a trial at Carlisle held in 1210, to hold, by grant of King Richard I.

Cumreu, Willielmo de Aireminne, Laurentio de Agulunby
et multis aliis[8].

Ubrictebi (*hodie* Upperby) and the land of old Salhild (*hodie* Little
Salkeld) in the parish of Addingham (*Coram Rege Rolls*, 11 Joh.
No. 41, m. 9; Rec. Com. *Abbrev. Placit.* p. 66 *b*). In *Testa de Nevill*
(p. 380 *a*) Adam Salsarius is mentioned as holding lands under
the King (John) at an annual cornage rent of 27s. 11d., which was
pardoned to him ; also Adam, cook to the Queen, as holding Saulkill
under the King, by gift of King Richard, rendering annually 1 lb.
of pepper. These two Adams, it will be seen, are identical. In 1164
Olde Salchhild and Hobrihtebi, two carucates of land and a tanning
mill, appear among the escheats of the Crown in the *Pipe Rolls*
(*Carlisle*, 10 Hen. II.) ; and they appear again frequently in that
reign up to 1185. Tallage is also paid in that reign and the next for
Old Salekil and for Salekil (Salkeld Regis, *hodie* Great Salkeld,
see note 4 on No. 4). In the 5th year of King Richard (1194) on
April 20th, a grant was made by that King to Adam Cook to his
Queen Mother (Eleanor), of all the land of Old Salechild which had
returned annually to the Exchequer £4. 16s., and now to be held by
the payment of 1 lb. of pepper annually at Carlisle. The deed is
given in full in Machel's MSS. (iv. 131) taken from Sir William
Dugdale's MSS. Turning again to the *Pipe Rolls*, we find that
in 1193 and 1194 Adam Cook received by Royal writ 40s. in Uctredebi
(sometimes so spelled for Hubrichtebi) and Arphinebi (Farmanby in
the parish of Addingham) ; in 1195, 48s. in the lands given to him as
Cook to A. (Alienor) the Queen Mother ; in 1196, the sum is £4. 16s.,
as named in the deed above, and so in the years following to the end
of the reign of King John. Moreover in 1197, 1199 and other years,
he is pardoned the horn-geld, or cornage rent, of 27s. 11d., the sum
shewn above to be excused to Adam Salsarius. In 1201, the Sheriff
also accounted for £5 which Adam Salsarius had to pay for having
seisin of Old Salkil on production of the charter of King Richard. In
that and subsequent years, sometimes under the name of Adam le
Salseir, he pays small sums, *ne transfretet*, for cornage and for scutage.
Turning to the *Placita de quo Waranto* (Rec. Com. pp. 114 *b*, 117 *a*)
we find all these facts confirmed before the courts in November 1292,
that the vill of Old Salkeld was granted by charter of King Richard to
Adam le Sauser [or Adam le Ken (*sic*)] and confirmed by charter of
the 2nd year of King John, that it used to return £4. 16s. to the
exchequer, and, by these charters produced, was to be held on the
service of 1 lb. of pepper ; moreover, that the said Adam granted it to

155. Carta Willelmi de Croglin facta Monachis de Wederhal de duabus acris terræ in Croglyn.

UNIVERSIS Christi Fidelibus ad quorum notitiam præ-

Hugh, Bishop of Carlisle, he to pay to the King the 1 lb. of pepper ; that after the death of Bishop Hugh, it was claimed by Nicholas le Sauser and Henry son of Fulcher, the heirs of Adam, but it was decided at Westminster in 11 Henry III. that it belonged to Bishop Walter and the Church of S. Mary at Carlisle ; that Bishop Walter conceded to Henry and Nicholas and their heirs to hold it at a rent of £4. 16s. ; that in 14 Henry III. (see also *Close Rolls*, m. 11) the King quitclaimed the rent of 1 lb. of pepper ; that then Bishop Walter conceded all his right to the Canons and Church of Carlisle, which was confirmed by the charter of Henry III. in his 14th year. It also appears (*Placita de quo War.* Rec. Com. 116 *a*) that there was no church or advowson belonging to Old Salkeld, only a chapel which belonged to the mother church of the parish of Addingham. That Church "cum Capella sua de Salkeld" was granted to the Priory of Carlisle by Robert de Brus and Christiana, and confirmed by Bishop Radulf de Ireton in 1282 (*Register of Bp Halton*, p. 181), also confirmed by Edward I. July 8th, 1304. Adam Salsarius granted two charters of land in Kirkeosewald to the Priory of Lanercost, the former of which was attested by this Roger de Bellocampo. This land was quitclaimed by his widow Alicia, whose father's name was Alfrid (*Regist. Lanercost*, MS. v. 27 ; vi. 1, 2). Others of the name also appear there. In the reign of Edward I., about 1303, we find, among the *Exchequer Miscellanea*, Master John le Sausser of London, cook, giving us a hint as to the identity of Adam Salsarius, or Adam le Sauser, and Adam, cook, which is proved above. Thus we have our word "sauce," through the French, from the Latin *salsa*. Also in the same *Miscellanea* (see *Calend. Doc. Scot.* iv. 394) in the year 1305—6 we have mentioned Alan, the King's *salsarius*, to whom had been paid 9 quarters of wheat for certain things pertaining to his office. It is shewn by the *Fine Rolls* (5 Hen. III. m. 4, m. 3, 12 Hen. III. m. 9 ; ed. Roberts, i. 66, 70, 165) that Adam le Sauser was dead in 1221, and that his nephew Henry son of Fulcher and Nicholas le Sauser were his heirs, and were liable to a payment of 5 marcs to the King for the manor of Old Salkhill.

[3] Though a little later than the two preceding, the date of this charter must be about the same time, at the beginning of the 13th century.

sens scriptum pervenerit, Willelmus de Croglyn salutem æternam in Domino. Noverit universitas vestra me pro salute animarum Prædecessorum et Successorum meorum de assensu W. filij mei et hæredis dedisse et concessisse et præsenti carta mea confirmasse Deo et Abachiæ Sanctæ Mariæ Eboraci et Domui Sanctæ Trinitatis et Sancti Constantini de Wederhal et Monachis ibidem Deo servientibus duas acras terræ in alneto meo[1] juxta Domum meam in Villa de Croglyn illas videlicet quæ jacent propinquiores duccello quod dicitur Hellerbec versus Aquilonem. Habendas et tenendas in puram et perpetuam Elemosinam cum libero introitu et exitu, et licebit dictis Monachis dictas duas acras assarcare et boscum ibi crescentem habere et illas includere fossato vel alio modo sicut sibi viderint melius expedire ad omnimodum commodum suum faciendum sine aliqua contradictione mei vel hæredum meorum. Et Ego et hæredes mei illas duas acras sicut prædictum est dictis Monachis contra omnes homines imperpetuum warantizabimus et quietabimus et defendemus. In cujus rei Testimonium præsenti scripto sigillum meum apposui. Hijs Testibus, Domino R. Priore[2], W. Officiali Karlioli[3], W. de Daker[4], Domino R. de Castelcairoc, Petro de Tyllol, Heverardo Capellano, R. Clerico, Johanne de Hermine, Stephano de Westgart, Henrico de Hulvescuait, Willielmo Præposito de Cringildic[5] et multis alijs[6].

155. [1] *Alnetum*, a plantation of alder trees; the word occurs in *Domesday Book.*

[2] Radulph became Prior of Carlisle in 1231, see note 2 on No. 97.

[3] Walter de Ulvesby; see note 5 on No. 56.

[4] William de Daker, we observe, is not here Sheriff.

[5] Cringildic in the parish of Kirkoswald, between Staffield and Little Croglyn; about this time, it appears to have been in the hands of Roger de Bellocampo (see Nos. 172, 173) but the Priory had a mill there (see No. 171) and some other property.

[6] The date of this charter will be between 1231, when Radulph became Prior, and 1236 when William de Daker became Sheriff or Custos.

156. CARTA WILLELMI DE CROGLYN FACTA MONA-
CHIS DE WEDERHAL DE NATIVIS SUIS CUM SEQUELA
EORUM.

OMNIBUS Christi Fidelibus ad quorum notitiam presens
scriptum pervenerit Willelmus de Croglyn salutem æternam in Domino. Noverit universitas vestra [me] dedisse
concessisse et presenti carta confirmasse Deo et Monachis
Sanctæ Trinitatis et Sancti Constantini de Wederhal
Ranulphum filium Alani et Aliciam uxorem suam nativos
meos cum tota sequela eorum et cum omnibus catallis suis.
Habendos et Tenendos imperpetuum in liberam puram
et perpetuam Elemosinam quietos et solutos de me et
omnibus hæredibus meis. Ita quod nec Ego nec aliquis
hæredum meorum aliquam calumpniam versus dictum
Ranulphum et sororem[1] suam vel sequelam aut catalla
eorum movere poterimus imperpetuum. Quod si factum
aliquando fuerit auctoritate istius cartæ irritum sit et
inane. Et ut hoc scriptum perpetuæ firmitatis robur
optineat eidem scripto sigillum meum apposui. Hijs
Testibus, R. le Brun tunc Vicecomite Cumberlandiæ, R.
de Levington, Roberto de Hamton, Alano Buche, Ricardo
de Alneburg̃, Willelmo de Warthwic, Johanne de Stafhole
et alijs[2].

157. CARTA HENRICI DE ULVESWAIT FACTA RO-
BERTO DE GALVEDIA DE TOTA TERRA SUA IN PARVA
CROGLYN.

OMNIBUS hominibus ad quos presentes litteræ pervenerint Henricus de Ulveswait[1] salutem æternam in

156. [1] *Sororem* is an error for *uxorem*.

[2] The date of this charter is probably about the same as that
of the last ; Rich. le Brun was probably Sheriff, or Custos, before
Wm. de Daker in 1236 and after Robt. de Hampton in 1229.

157. [1] This is the Henry de Ulnesthwait, or Hulvesthuait,
mentioned in the charter of William de Croglyn, No. **151** ; he makes
another grant, No. **176**.

Domino. Noveritis me dedisse et concessisse et hac presenti carta mea confirmasse Roberto de Galwenhia et hæredibus suis vel suis assignatis totam terram illam quam Walterus Porter mihi dedit pro homagio meo et servicio in territorio de parva Croglyn per rectas divisas scilicet septem acras terræ quæ jacent propinquæ versus (*sic*) illius partis versus Villam de parva Croglyn cum omnibus pertinentijs et aisiamentis. Tenendam et Habendam de me et hæredibus meis ipse et hæredes sui vel eorum assignati libere quiete pacifice et integre cum omnibus libertatibus et aisiamentis ad Villam de Croglin adjacentibus. Reddendo inde annuatim mihi et hæredibus meis ipse et hæredes sui vel sui assignati tres solidos sterlingorum, scilicet medietatem ad Pentecosten et medietatem ad Festum Sancti Martini in yeme pro omnibus servicijs terrenis et accionibus et demandis. Et ego dictus Henricus et hæredes mei præfato Roberto et hæredibus suis vel suis assignatis præscriptas septem acras terræ contra omnes homines et fæminas warantizabimus et defendemus imperpetuum. In cujus rei Testimonium presenti scripto sigillum meum apposui. Hijs Testibus, Domino Thoma de Multon[2], Domino Willelmo de Vaus, Willelmo Salcoc tunc.tempore Vicecomite[3], Magistro Willelmo de Goldington[4], Thoma de

[2] This is the second Thomas de Multon of the name, mentioned in this *Register*; see note 4 on No. **47**; the first died in 1240.

[3] William Salcoc is not in the lists of sheriffs; he was, probably, pro-Sheriff or Custos. He is given as Sheriff of Carlisle, with William de Daker as Sheriff of York, in a confirmation of the Church of Crosthwaite to Fountains Abbey by William de Fortibus in the time of Bishop Silvester (1247—54) (*Archbp Gray's Register*, ed. Raine, p. 59 *n*.). He is witness as Sheriff of Cumberland to a grant to the Priory of Lanercost dated 1252 (*Regist. Lanercost*, MS. xii. 22) with Thomas de Multon and William de Vallibus. He must then have been Custos for John de Balliol.

[4] William de Goldington gives a "place" of land in Appleby to the Monastery in No. **222**. He is spoken of as one of "Robert de Veteripont's men of Westmerland" in 1256 (*Calcnd. Doc. Scot.* ed.

Beuchamp, Johanne de Stafol, Willelmo de Crogelin et multis alijs[5].

158. QUIETA CLAMATIO SYMONIS CAPELLANI DE WEDERHAL DE TERRA IN AINSTAPELIT CROGLYN ET RUCROFT.

OMNIBUS Christi Fidelibus ad quorum notitiam hoc præsens scriptum pervenerit Symon Capellanus de Wederhal salutem æternam in Domino.   Noverit universitas vestra me mea spontanea voluntate remisisse reddidisse et quietam clamasse de me et hæredibus meis imperpetuum Abbati et Conventui Sanctæ Mariæ Eborum et Monachis Sanctæ Trinitatis et Sancti Constantini de Wederhal totam terram sine aliquo retenemento quam tenui de eisdem Abbate et Conventu et Monachis in territorio Villarum de Ainstapelit[1] et de Croglyn et de Rucroft[2] cum toftis et croftis, Ita scilicet quod dicti Abbas Conventus et Monachi de Wederhal habeant et teneant totam prædictam terram imperpetuum cum omnibus pertinentijs suis liberam et

Bain, i. 403) ; as Mayor of Apelby, he attests a grant by Richard de Apelby, clerk, to Robert, son of John de Veteripont, who died in 1265 ; one of the name appears to have been alive in 1286 (see on No. 220) ; he is said to have founded the chantry of S. Mary in the Church of S. Laurence, Appleby (see *Machel MSS.* v. 522 sqq., where he appears in several documents). This cannot be the same William who was knight of the shire in 1307—8.

[5] The date seems to be fixed by William Salcoc as 1252, or very near that year, and with this the other witnesses agree.

158. [1] Ainstapelit, *hodie* Ainstable, is a parish and manor on the east of the river Eden ; the parish abutting towards the north on the Barony of Gilsland and divided from Kirkoswald on the south by the river Croglin. Ermynthwait (see No. **162**), *hod.* Armathwaite, is a manor in this parish. See on Adam son of Suan (note 4 on No. **14**) to whom Ainstable was granted by Henry I. The Church was appropriated to the nunnery at Ermynthwait (see No. **162**) and probably served by the chaplain there.

[2] Rucroft was in the southern part of the parish of Ainstable, bordering on the manor of Staffol in Kirkoswald.

solutam de me et omnibus hæredibus meis et assignatis. Et ne ego vel hæredes mei vel assignati de prædicta terra contra prædictos Monachos querelam movere vel aliquod vendicare possimus in posterum contra hoc scriptum meæ remissionis et quietæ clamationis eidem sigillum meum apposui. Hijs Testibus, Radulpho Priore[3], Magistro Gervasio Archidiacono[4], Magistro Waltero Officiali[5], Ricardo Brun tunc Vicecomite Karlioli, Ricardo de Levington, Alano Buch, Roberto de Castelkairoc, Petro de Tyllol, Johanne filio Willelmi, Johanne de Agulunby, Stephano de Nelmeslaie, Thoma janitore de Wederhal, Henrico Dispensatore[6] et multis alijs[7].

159. QUIETA CLAMATIO JOHANNIS FILIJ RADULPHI DE RUCROFT SUPER QUIBUSDAM TENEMENTIS IN EADEM.

OMNIBUS has Litteras visuris vel audituris Johannes filius Radulphi de Rucroft Salutem æternam in Domino· Noverit universitas vestra me remisisse et quietum clamasse de me et hæredibus meis imperpetuum Deo et Beatæ Mariæ Eboraci et Ecclesiæ Sanctæ Trinitatis de Wederhal et Monachis ibidem Deo servientibus totum jus et clamium quod habui vel habere potui in terra de Rucroft quam Simon Capellanus[1] eis dedit in Elemosinam et quam Ego aliquando de eadem Domo tenui. Et specialiter quietas clamavi omnes terras illas, scilicet Avantages et Fordales quæ continentur in quadam inquisitione pro voluntate Domini Prioris de Wederhal et mei factâ. Et ut omnia prædicta firmius observentur pro me et hæredibus meis

---

[3] Radulph became Prior of Carlisle in 1231, see note 2 on No. **97**.

[4] Gervase de Louther, see note 3 on No. **21**.

[5] Walter de Ulvesby, see note 5 on No. **56**.

[6] *Dispensator*, a steward generally, not only of the household, as *dapifer*.

[7] The witnesses are very similar to those in No. **97**, and the date of this charter is probably about the same, 1231—35.

159. [1] Symon Capellanus is the grantor of No. **158**.

tactis Sacrosanctis Evangelijs juravi. In cujus rei Testimonium presenti Scripto sigillum meum apposui. Hijs Testibus, Domino Radulpho Priore Karlioli, Domino W. Archidiacono Karlioli, Domino W. Capellano de Cumreu[2], Domino W. filio Rogeri Militis de Korkeby, Domino A. Milite de Cumreu[3], W. de Warthwic, R. de Cutun Clerico[4], Roberto de Hornebi, Johanne Stelfot, Galfrido fratre Johannis prædicti[5], W. de Langecost, Thoma Rouchclive et alijs[6].

160. SCRIPTUM DE PACE REFORMATA INTER PRIOREM DE WEDERHAL ET JOHANNEM FILIUM RADULPHI DE RUCROFT.

OMNIBUS Christi fidelibus hoc scriptum visuris vel audituris Johannes filius Radulphi de Rucroft salutem æternam in Domino. Noverit universitas vestra quod cum Dominus Prior de Wederhal me coram Judicibus a Domino propterea delegatis apud Eboracum inplacitasset tandem in hanc pacis formam devenimus; videlicet Quod coram multis probis viris et fide dignis tactis Sacrosanctis Evangelijs juravi quod nunquam in vita mea Domino Priori de Wederhal vel Domui de Wederhal per me vel per alium opere vel dicto forisfaciam, Et si instigante Diabolo contra hoc juramentum meum temere venire præsumpsero, dabo fabricæ Ecclesiæ Sanctæ Trinitatis de Wederhal viginti solidos sterlingorum nomine pœnæ subjiciens me et omnia bona mea jurisdictioni Archidiaconi vel Officialis Karlioli si Archidiaconus eo tempore non fuerit, ut ipsi

[2] Cumreu is a small parish in the Barony of Gilsland under the fells adjoining Croglin on the north, about 12 miles from Carlisle; see on W. de Kirketon No. **194.**

[3] A. Milite is Adam son of Alan de Cumreu; see on No. **131.**

[4] R. de Cutun should be Robert, clerk of Cutun, or Cucun, as in No. **143**, and in No. **171**, dated 1241.

[5] Galfrid is the brother of John de Rucroft, as in No. **160.**

[6] The date is rather later than No. **160**; the witnesses are similar to No. **115**, hence the date is probably very nearly 1240.

per quamcunque melius viderint expedire cohertionem possint compellere me ad solutionem prædictæ pœnæ. Ego autem in hac parte renuntiavi omni appellationi et exceptioni et privilegio fori civilis et privilegio crucesignatorum et brevi Regiæ prohibitionis de Catallis et de laico tenemento et omni re et facto quod possit objici contra scriptum hoc. In cujus rei Testimonium presenti scripto sigillum meum apposui. Hijs Testibus, Domino Radulpho Priore Karleoli, Domino W. Archidiacono Karlioli, W. Capellano de Cumreu, Domino W. filio Rogeri Milite, Domino A. de Cumreu Milite, W. de Warthwic, R. Clerico de Cutun, Roberto de Hornebi, Johanne Stelfot, Galfrido fratre prædicti Johannis de Ruccroft, Willielmo de Langecost, Thoma de Roucheclive, Willelmo filio Rogeri de Korkeby et alijs[1].

161. Carta Michaelis de Ainstapelit facta Monachis de Wederhal de IX acris terræ et dimidia cum morâ.

Omnibus Christi fidelibus ad quos presens scriptum pervenerit Michael de Ainstapelit[1] salutem in Domino. Noverit universitas vestra me Divinæ Caritatis intuitu et pro salute animæ meæ Antecessorum et Successorum meorum dedisse concessisse et hac presenti carta mea confirmasse Deo et Beatæ Mariæ de Eboraco et Beato Constantino de Wederhal et Monachis ibidem Deo servientibus novem acras et dimidiam cum Mora infra terram eandem jacente, Illas scilicet quæ jacent inter terram meam versus Austrum et terram Henrici de Terebi versus Aquilonem et inter Hallebanc et communem pasturam Villæ de Ainstapelit. Habendas et tenendas in liberam

---

160. [1] The witnesses here are identical with those of the preceding charter, and the date can only be very shortly before that of No. 159.

161. [1] Michael de Ainstapelit is the same as Michael son of David in the succeeding charters, and probably son of David de Valle in No. 170.

puram et perpetuam Elemosinam cum omnibus communis
libertatibus et aisiamentis ad eandem terram spectantibus
infra Villam et extra adeo libere honorifice et integre sicut
aliqua Elemosina possit dari vel possideri. Ego vero
Michael et hæredes mei dictam Elemosinam prædictis
Monachis sicut prædictum est contra omnes homines wa-
rantizabimus adquietabimus et defendemus imperpetuum.
Et ut hoc scriptum perpetuæ firmitatis robur optineat
præsens scriptum sigilli mei appositione roboravi. Testibus
Johanne de Levington[2], Adam de Cumreu, Thoma Heued,
Johanne de Hermiñe, Willelmo de Croglyn, Waltero porter,
Thoma filio Marville[3], Johanne filio Willelmi, Johanne de
Aglunby et alijs[4].

162. CARTA MICHAELIS FILIJ DAVID DE AIN-
STAPELYT DE TERRA PER PARTICULAS PROUT INFRA
PATET.

OMNIBUS Sanctæ Matris Ecclesiæ filijs ad quos præsens
scriptum pervenerit Michael filius David de Ainstaplid
salutem. Noverit universitas vestra me concessisse dedisse
et hac præsenti carta mea confirmasse Deo et Beatæ Mariæ
et Beato Constantino de Wederhal et Monachis ibidem
Deo servientibus unam dimidiam acram terræ cum tofto et
crofto in Villa de Ruccroft in feodo de Ainstapellid scilicet
inter terram Monachorum de Wederhal et terram Monialium de Ermynthwait[1] et dimidiam acram in Scichestoc-
landis, et dimidiam acram in Linwra et tres acras et

---

[2] This is not the John son of Robert of No. **44**, or the John, Dean
of Gillesland, a witness in the *Register of Lanercost* (MS. viii. 3, 4);
they are of earlier date.

[3] Marville should be Mabillæ, as in No. **164**.

[4] The date must be nearly the same as that of the succeeding
charters, shortly after 1236; several of the witnesses, as John de
Hermine and William de Croglyn, occur in 1241 (see No. **171**).

162. [1] Ermynthwait, or Ermitethait (No. **166**), later Armathwaite,
was the name of a convent of Benedictine nuns situated in the
southern angle of the parish of Ainstable, near the junction of the

dimidiam in Chareaire in territorio de Ainstapellid. Tenendas et Habendas prædictis Monachis de Wederhal in liberam puram et perpetuam Elemosinam cum omnibus libertatibus et aisiamentis in bosco in plano et in omnibus locis prædictæ Villæ de Ainstapellid et de Ruccroft pertinentibus, adeo libere et quiete sicut aliqua Elemosina alicui Domui Religionis liberius et quietius dari possit pro salute animæ meæ et Antecessorum meorum et Successorum. Et Ego Michael et hæredes mei prædictam terram cum omnibus pertinentijs suis sicut præscriptum est prædictæ Domui de Wederhal et Monachis ibidem Deo servientibus contra omnes homines et fæminas warantizabimus imperpetuum. Et ut hæc mea Donatio rata et stabilis permaneat presens scriptum sigilli mei impressione roboravi. Hijs Testibus, Waltero Officiali Karlioli, Domino W. de Daker Vicecomite, Domino R. de Castelkairoc, Domino W. de Warthwic, Galfrido de Ainstapellid, Johanne Stelfot, R. Clerico de Cutun, Roberto de Horneby, Willelmo de

river Croglin with the Eden. The nunnery is said to have been founded by William II. in the 2nd year of his reign, 1089; and this is stated in what purports to be the foundation charter given by Dugdale. But this charter "is spurious on the face of it," as Freeman has pointed out (*William Rufus*, ii. 506). William II. did not get possession of this district until 1092; he is made to call himself in the charter "Dux Normannorum," and the formula used is subsequent to the time of Edward III. Two royal charters, of Edward III. and Edward IV., are also given by Dugdale (*Monasticon*, iii. 270) and the names of three Prioresses, all in the 16th century. The names of two Prioresses occur in *Bishop Welton's Register* (MS. pp. 98, 99); Isabel, who died 1362, and in her place the nuns chose Katharine Lancaster, when the Bishop sent his mandate to instal her. At the Dissolution the convent consisted of a prioress and three nuns; among the items of the survey made 29 Henry VIII. is the annual rent of 12s. paid to the Priory of Wetherall. The site was afterwards called Nunnery, a name it retains to the present day. In 1317 the King, out of compassion for the poor nuns totally ruined by the Scots, granted them pasture for their cattle in Englewood forest (*Patent Rolls*, 4 Edw. II. p. 1, m. 25).

Langcost, Willelmo Pollard, Thoma de Roucheclive, Johanne Coquo et multis alijs[2].

163. CARTA MICHAELIS FILIJ DAVID DE AINSTA-PELIT DE TRIBUS ACRIS TERRÆ IN EADEM.

OMNIBUS Christi fidelibus ad quorum notitiam hoc præsens scriptum pervenerit Michael filius David de Ainstapellid salutem æternam in Domino. Noverit universitas vestra me pro salute animæ meæ et pro salute animarum prædecessorum et successorum meorum dedisse concessisse et præsenti carta confirmasse Deo et Abbachiæ Sanctæ Mariæ Eboraci et Monachis de Wederhal tres acras terræ in territorio de Ainstapellid quarum una dimidia acra jacet in Villa de Ruccroft inter terram dictorum Monachorum et terram Monialium de Hermithuait et una dimidia jacet in Linwra et una dimidia jacet in Skychestockelandis, et una acra et dimidia jacent in Yharere. Habendas et Tenendas in liberam puram et perpetuam Elemosinam cum omnibus libertatibus communis et aisiamentis ad Villas de Ainstapellid et Ruccroft spectantibus sine aliquo retenemento ad ædificandum et quodlibet aliud commodum faciendum sicut sibi melius viderint expedire sine aliqua contradictione mei vel hæredum meorum. Et Ego et hæredes mei totam prædictam terram sicut prescriptum est prædictis Monachis contra omnes homines imperpetuum warantizabimus acquietabimus et defendemus. In cujus rei Testimonium Sigillum meum apposui. Hijs Testibus, Domino [R.] Priore[1], [R.] Archidiacono[2],

---

[2] The date, from the Sheriff, must be in the years 1236—47, and from the other witnesses, as in the last charter and in No. **171**, about 1241.

163. [1] Transcript C supplies B(artholomew), but Radulph was Prior at this time ; compare No. **158**, an earlier charter ; and Radulph succeeded Bartholomew as Prior.

[2] Transcript C supplies R here, which is probably correct, for Robert de Otterington (see on No. **137**) who became Archdeacon in 1238. He occurs in No. **187**, with many of the same witnesses.

W. Officiali Karlioli[3], Willelmo de Dacre tunc Vicecomite, Ricardo de Levington, Petro de Tyllol, Roberto de Castelkairoc, Rolando de Vallibus, Willelmo filio Rogeri et Willelmo filio ejus, Everardo Capellano, Gilberto Parsona de Botil[4], Johanne filio Willelmi, Johanne de Agulunby, Henrico de Scalewra[5], Rogero Clerico et alijs[6].

164. CARTA JOHANNIS MUSEIE ET MATILDIS SPONSÆ SUÆ DE SEPTEM ACRIS TERRÆ IN AINSTAPELIT.

OMNIBUS Christi fidelibus ad quos præsens scriptum pervenerit Johannes Museie et Matildis Sponsa sua Salutem in Domino. Noverit universitas vestra nos Divinæ Caritatis intuitu et pro salute animarum nostrarum et Antecessorum et Successorum nostrorum, omnibus ingenij malivolenciæ retractionis et contradictionis articulis prætermissis mera et spontanea liberalitate nostra dedisse concessisse et hac præsenti carta nostra confirmasse Deo et Beatæ Mariæ de Eboraco et Beato Constantino de Wederhal et Monachis ibidem Deo servientibus septem acras terræ in territorio de Ainstapellid cum Mora infra eandem terram jacente, Scilicet quatuor acras quæ jacent inter terram quam Michael de Ainstapelid dedit in Elemosinam Domui de Wederhal et terram Henrici de Terribi super Hallebanc et unam acram et dimidiam quæ jacent inter terram Henrici de Terribi et terram Willelmi de Anand in Hallebanc, et unam acram in Ruccroft propinquiorem terræ paveie de Karliolo versus Aquilonem et dimidiam acram quæ jacet propinquior terræ Johannis hominis......versus Aquilonem in Ruccroft cum emendatione illius dimidiæ acræ scilicet dimidiam rodam quæ jacet ad caput crofti Johannis filij

---

[3] Walter de Ulvesby, see note 5 on No. **56.**

[4] Botil, or Bothill, or Bothel, was a township in the parish of Torpenhow; but there was no Church belonging to it. The name may refer to the parson of Botilton or Bolton, the parish adjoining.

[5] Henry de Scalewra is the same as Henry son of Warin, who grants the charters Nos. **187—189.**

[6] The date must be nearly the same as that of the preceding charter.

Leñy. Habendas et Tenendas in puram liberam et perpetuam Elemosinam cum omnibus communis libertatibus et aisiamentis ad eandem terram spectantibus infra Villam et extra adeo libere honorifice et integre sicut aliqua Elemosina liberius possit dari et possideri. Nos vero et hæredes nostri prædictam terram prænominatis Monachis sicut prædictum est contra omnes homines warantizabimus acquietabimus et defendemus imperpetuum. Et ut hæc nostra donatio et confirmatio perpetuæ robur firmitatis optineat præsens scriptum sigilli nostri munimine roboravimus. Testibus, Johanne de Levington, Adam de Cumreu, Thoma Heued, Johanne de Hermine, Willelmo de Crogelyn, Waltero porter, Thoma filio Mabillæ, Johanne filio Willelmi, Odardo Clerico et alijs[1].

165. QUIETA CLAMATIO JOHANNIS MUSEI FACTA MONACHIS DE WEDERHAL DE SEPTEM ACRIS TERRÆ IN AINSTAPELIT.

OMNIBUS Christi fidelibus ad quos præsens scriptum pervenerit Johannes Musei salutem in Domino. Noverit universitas vestra me remisisse et quietum clamasse Deo et Beatæ Mariæ Eborum et Domui Sanctæ Trinitatis et Sancti Constantini de Wederhal et Monachis ibidem Deo servientibus imperpetuum de me et hæredibus meis omne jus et clamium quod habui vel habere potui vel in posterum habere potero in septem acris terræ in territorio de Ainstapelit quarum quinque acræ jacent in Gefrariding et una acra et dimidia in Hallebanc et dimidia acra jacet juxta domum Willelmi viri Ysodæ[1] ex parte Aquilonis. Et insuper jus et clamium quod habui vel habere potui vel in posterum habere potero in quarta parte terræ domus

---

164. [1] The witnesses are practically the same as in No. 161, and again in No. 167 ; the date will be the same, after 1236, and probably about 1241.

165. [1] Willelmus vir Ysodæ is probably William de Croglyn, who was the husband of Ysouda, or Ysoda ; see No. 152.

Prioris de Wederhal juxta Migheldale continente in latitudine duodecim pedes et extendente se in longitudine prout
se extendit terra Michaelis filij David propinqua deč. terræ
versus occidentem. Et ad majorem securitatem affidavi et
tactis Sacrosanctis [Evangeliis] juravi pro me et hæredibus
meis omnia prædicta fideliter observare. Et in hujus rei
Testimonium præsenti scripto sigillum meum apposui.
Hijs Testibus, Domino Roberto de Castelkairoc Milite,
Magistro Johanne de Haiton, Willelmo filio Rogeri, Willelmo de Warthwic, et alijs[2].

166. CARTA HENRICI DE TERRIBI DE SEPTEM ACRIS
ET TRIBUS RODIS IN AINSTAPELIT.

OMNIBUS Christi fidelibus ad quorum notitiam hoc
presens scriptum pervenerit Henricus de Terribi salutem
in Domino. Noverit universitas vestra me caritatis intuitu
et pro salute animæ meæ et Prædecessorum et Successorum
meorum dedisse concessisse et hac presenti carta confirmasse Deo et Abbachiæ Sanctæ Mariæ Eboraci et
Monachis Sanctæ Trinitatis et Sancti Constantini de
Wederhal septem acras et tres rodas terræ in territorio
de Ainstapelit videlicet quatuor acras et unam rodam super
Hallebanc versus Orientem propinquiores terræ quam Johannes Musei dictæ Domui dedit in Elemosinam, et tres
acras terræ in Dalchangthe et illud essartum meum quod
jacet coram porta Monialium de Ermitethait pro dimidia
acra. Habendas et Tenendas imperpetuum in liberam
puram et perpetuam Elemosinam adeo libere et quiete in
omnibus ut aliqua Elemosina liberius et quietius dari possit
aut possideri. Et Ego et hæredes mei hanc Elemosinam
dictis Monachis imperpetuum contra omnes homines warantizabimus acquietabimus et defendemus cum omnibus
libertatibus pertinentijs communis et aisiamentis ad Villam
de Ainstapelit pertinentibus. Et ut hæc mea donatio

[2] The date must be about the same as that of the preceding
charters.

perpetuo tueatur munimine præsenti scripto cum sigilli mei appositione eam corroboravi. Hijs Testibus, Thoma filio Johannis tunc Vicecomite Cumberlandiæ, Petro de Tyllol, Roberto filio Willelmi, Roberto de Castelkairoc, Willelmo filio Rogeri, Roberto de Karlaton, Ynor de Hormesby, Michel del Dale[1], Waltero portario, Johanne Clerico et alijs[2].

167. CONFIRMATIO HENRICI DE TERRIBI DE VII ACRIS TERRÆ IN AINSTAPELIT.

OMNIBUS Christi fidelibus ad quos præsens scriptum pervenerit Henricus de Terriby salutem in Domino æternam. Noverit universitas vestra me Divinæ Caritatis intuitu pro salute animæ meæ Antecessorum et Successorum concessisse et hac præsenti carta mea confirmasse Deo et Beatæ Mariæ de Eboraco et Beato Constantino de Wederhal et Monachis ibidem Deo servientibus septem acras terræ in territorio de Ainstapelit quas Johannes Museye et Matildis sponsa sua Domui de Wederhal in Elemosinam dederunt, sicut carta[1] dictorum Johannis et Matildis inde confecta testatur. Habendas et Tenendas in puram liberam et perpetuam Elemosinam cum omnibus communis libertatibus et Aisiamentis ad præbdictam terram pertinentibus infra villam et extra adeo libere sicut aliqua Elemosina liberius possit dari et possideri. Et si forte prædicti Johannes et Matildis vel hæredes eorum prænominatam terram prædictæ Domui de Wederhal warantizare non possint, Ego Henricus et hæredes mei eandem terram dictæ Domui warantizabimus. Quod si forte facere non possimus dabimus eidem Domui septem acras in eadem villa de Ainstapelit ad valentiam illius terræ. Et ut hæc

---

166. [1] Michel del Dale held lands in Aynstapellyth (Ainstable), and we find his daughters Eda and Elena making grants of five acres to the Priory of Lanercost (*Regist. Lanercost*, MS. iv. 9, 10).

[2] From the Sheriff, the date of this charter must be 1230 or 1231.

167. [1] That is, No. **164.**

mea concessio et confirmatio rata permaneat et illibata
præsens scriptum sigilli mei appositione duxi muniendum.
Hijs Testibus, Johanne de Levington, Adam de Cumreu,
Thoma Heued, Johanne de Herminne, Willelmo de
Crogelyn, Waltero porter, Thoma filio Mabillæ, Johanne
filio Willelmi, Odardo Clerico, et alijs[2].

168. CARTA WILLELMI DE TERRIBI DE DUABUS
ACRIS TERRÆ IN AINSTAPELIT.

SCIANT omnes tam præsentes quam futuri quod Ego
Willelmus de Terribi dedi et concessi et hac præsenti carta
mea confirmavi Deo et Ecclesiæ Sanctæ Trinitatis et
Sancti Constantini de Wederhal et Monachis ibidem Deo
servientibus duas acras terræ in territorio de Ainstapelit
quarum una roda et quindecim particæ[1] jacent in Alder-
ruccrofte inter terram Michael filij David et terram Johannis
Muche et una roda in Linwra inter terram eorundem
Michael et Johannis, et dimidia roda et septem particæ in
Wyterays in Ssarrait inter terram dicti Michael et terram
Willielmi Chaumund et decem particæ ad finem dictæ
dimidiæ rodæ apud Boream, et dimidia roda inter
me ad horydh et terram dictorum Michael et Johannis et
dimidia roda et quatuor particæ juxta Langthorrave inter
terram dictorum Johannis et Michael, et dimidia roda in
Witelandes inter terram dictorum Michael et Johannis et
Willielmi Chaumund, et una roda tendens de Ssedestohelandes usque ad Birscohegarhe inter terram dictorum
Michaelis et Willielmi Chaumund et dimidia roda tendens
se de Ssedestohelandes usque ad ꞇne horydh inter terram
dictorum Michael et Willielmi Chaumund et una roda

---

[2] This charter is of later date than the preceding, and must be
nearly the same date as No. **164**, the witnesses being identical,
about 1241.

168. [1] *Pertica*, or *perca*, the land measure, "a perch"; it was
variously estimated at different times; in the time of Edward III.
5½ square yards; from the Latin *pertica*, a pole.

tendens se de Cheldehuspat usque ad Ssedestohelandes inter terram Wydonis de Boyvill[2] et dicti Michael et una roda juxta Marrays inter terram dictorum Wydonis et Michael. Tenendas et Habendas eisdem Monachis libere quiete pacifice et integre in liberam et perpetuam Elemosinam cum omnibus pertinentijs aisiamentis libertatibus ad dictam terram pertinentibus de me et hæredibus meis et assignatis meis. Et Ego præfatus Willelmus et hæredes mei warantizabimus prædictam terram dictis Monachis contra omnes gentes imperpetuum. In cujus rei Testimonium præsenti scripto sigillum meum apposui. Hijs Testibus, Domino Roberto de Castelkairoc, Ricardo filio suo, Johanne Parsona de Haiton[3], Alano de Cormaynoc, Johanne Muche de Ainstapelit, et alijs[4].

169. QUIETA CLAMATIO ALICIÆ FILIÆ DAVID DE TERRIBI DE DUABUS ACRIS TERRÆ IN CAMPO DE AINSTAPELIT.

OMNIBUS has litteras visuris vel audituris Alicia filia David de Terribi salutem æternam in Domino. Noverit universitas vestra me in libera viduitate mea et legitima potestate remisisse et quietum clamasse de me et hæredibus

[2] Wydo de Boyville is witness to a charter of Thomas de Multon in the *Register of Lanercost* (MS. ix. 1).

[3] Haiton, or Hayton, was a parish in the Barony of Gilsland about 7 miles east of Carlisle, adjoining the Parish of Wederhal. The name is formed with the common Anglo-Saxon suffix *ton* and *hay* or *haigh*, "a hedge," thence a place inclosed by a hedge, or an inclosure in the forest, for purposes of hunting, into which animals were driven to be killed. So we have the Anglo-Saxon *hecge*, "a hedge" and an "inclosure," and the French *haye*; compare the well known La Haye Sainte. In this sense the word *haia* occurs often in *Domesday Book*. The Church and a carucate of land were granted by Robert de Vallibus to the Priory of Carlisle, with whom it remained (see the charter of Henry III. in Dugdale, *Monasticon*, v. 144).

[4] The date of this charter is probably later than that of the preceding, but not much.

meis imperpetuum Deo et Beatæ Mariæ Eboraci et
Ecclesiæ Sanctæ Trinitatis de Wederhal et Monachis
ibidem Deo servientibus totum jus et clamium quod habui
vel habere potui in duabus acris terræ in campo de Ain-
stapelid quæ jacent in Scamelbrec juxta bercariam[1]
Monialium de Ermyngthait versus orientem. In cujus rei
Testimonium sigillum meum præsenti scripto apposui.
Hijs Testibus, Ricardo de Eboraco Capellano, Ricardo
Cervo, Galfrido de Crogelyn, Willelmo Tucemer[2], Johanne
Coquo, Thoma de Rowell[3] et alijs[4].

170. CARTA MAGISTRI ET FRATRUM HOSPITALIS SANCTI NICHOLAI DE KARLIOLO FACTA ALICIÆ FILIÆ RICARDI SAGITTARII &C.

OMNIBUS has Litteras visuris vel audituris Willelmus[1]
Capellanus Rector Hospitalis Sancti Nicholay[2] et fratres et
sorores ejusdem loci æternam in Domino Salutem. Noverit universitas vestra nos de communi assensu et consensu
Capituli nostri concessisse dedisse et hac nostra præsenti
carta confirmasse Aliciæ filiæ Ricardi Sagittarii de Ger-
sinton vel ejus assignatis vel cuicunque dare vel vendere
vel impignorare voluerit et quando, totam terram quam
Michael filius David de Valle[3] et totam terram quam

---

169. [1] *Bercaria*, or *bercheria*, a "sheepfold," from the Latin
berbex, or *vervex*, "a wether sheep"; compare the French *bergerie*.

[2] William Tucemer is no doubt identical with William Tussezemer,
or Tutzemer, in Nos. 53, 87.

[3] Thomas de Rowell is not improbably the same with Thomas
Rothwell in No. 87.

[4] A comparison of these witnesses with those of the charters
referred to above and No. 175, where Galfrid de Croglyn occurs, shews
that the date of this charter is the middle of the 13th century.

170. [1] This cannot be the William Chaplain of S. Nicholas who
attests No. 50, as that deed is about 1200.

[2] On the Hospital of S. Nicholas, Carlisle, see note 1 on No. 95.

[3] Michael son of David de Valle is apparently the same as Michael

Johannes Museie, et totam terram quam Willelmus filius Thomæ de Ainstapelit, et totam terram quam Cecilia filia David de Ainstapelit Nobis et Domui nostræ dederunt in puram et perpetuam Elemosinam infra feodum de Ainstapelid : Scilicet sex acras terræ et unam rodam et octo particas in Banco de Aykewelle, et duas acras cum pertinentijs de Dominico in cultura quæ vocatur Hallebanke, illas scilicet quas Alanus Capellanus quondam tenuit, et quatuor acras in assarto Radulphi super ripam Edene, et illam rodam quam Willelmus Clericus tenuit, et illam particulam terræ juxta terram Johannis Muse et quatuor acras sub Redehil, et unam acram in Hũnbirkis, et unam acram in Birkis, et unam dimidiam rodam ex opposito hostij Rogeri Carpentarij, et unam acram quæ vocatur Gateland, et dimidiam acram inter Hay et Gatelande et unam acram in Horiğ et unam dimidiam rodam in qua Aicus⁴ manebat, et unam acram ad caput crofti Rogeri Carpentarij et unam dimidiam rodam in qua nova domus Roberti de Lulington super est ædificata, et terram qua Willelmus Clericus quondam mansit, et terram Aliciæ Archer⁵, Habendas et Tenendas prædictæ Aliciæ vel cui assignare voluerit sicut præscriptum est de nobis et de Domo nostra in feodo et hæreditate adheo libere quiete et pacifice et integre cum omnibus libertatibus communis pertinentijs et aisiamentis prædictis terris pertinentibus ut cartæ prædictorum nobis melius et plenius testantur et confirmant, Reddendo inde annuatim nobis et Domui nostræ sex denarios, tres scilicet ad Festum Sancti Martini in Yeme, et tres ad Pentecosten pro omnibus demandis et consuetudinibus et secularijs servicijs. Et nos warantizabimus prædictas terras cum omnibus pertinentijs suis prænominatæ

son of David in the preceding charters (see on No. **161**), and perhaps the same as Michael de Vallibus in No. **150**.

⁴ Aicus is apparently here a proper name ; and compare the word in note I on No. **140**.

⁵ Alicia Archer is surnamed above Sagittarius.

Aliciæ vel assignatis suis quamdiu nobis ipsis warantizare poterimus. Testibus, Domino Radulpho Priore Karleoli, Waltero de Ulvesby tunc Archidiacono Karleoli, Willielmo Decano Karleoli[6], Roberto Decano Allerdal, Waltero Decano Cumberlandiæ, Henrico Berneval, Martino[7] Parsona de Kirkeoswald[8], Adam Parsona de Hedenhal[9] et alijs[10].

[6] This William Dean of Carlisle is not William de Kirkbride often mentioned before, but in the 12th century.

[7] Martin, Rector of Kirkeoswald, had a suit in 1246 against Radulph de Levington, and in 1258—59 against Helewisa wife of Richard de Vernun, concerning his rectorial rights (*Pedes Fin.* 30 Hen. III., *Coram Rege Rolls*, 43 Hen. III. No. 107, m. 3); he appears to have been rector in 1263, when a question was decided as to the right of patronage (*Bp. Nicolson MSS.* ii. 363).

[8] Kirkoswald was a parish and manor on the east of the river Eden, which divides it from Laysingby, or Lazonby, having Ainstable on the north and Addingham on the south. It is not very clear how it came to Hugh de Morvill; but he was in possession at the end of the 12th century, and after his death Kirkoswald and Lazonby were held by his widow, Helewisa de Stuteville; of this there is abundant evidence. In 1167, Kircoswald was in the hands of one of the Morvills, probably Simon father of Hugh, who then paid ½ marc (*Pipe Rolls*, 13 Hen. II.). In *Testa de Nevill* (p. 379 *b*) the daughters of Hugh, with their husbands, are recorded as being in possession of the lands of Hugh, which they held by cornage, £10. 2s. 10d., and which he had received from his ancestor Robert Trivers or d'Estrivers. The Church was also in the patronage of Hugh de Morvill and of several of his descendants.

[9] Hedenhal, or Edenhall, was a parish and manor on the immediate west of the river Eden, and north of the river Eamont; it was in the Forest of Inglewood, and joined the parishes of Penrith and Great Salkeld on the west and north. In 1159 it was in the possession of Henry, the younger brother of Adam son of Suan, or Suein (*Pipe Rolls*, 5 Hen. II.); but in a few years it passed again into the hands of the Crown. Henry II. gave it to Peter de Brus (*Testa de Nevill*, p. 379 *a*) and, from the *Pipe Rolls*, we learn that it was held by Robert de Brus and others of the family in the reigns of Richard and John, scutage of 1 marc being paid as late as the year 1214. The advowson of the Church of Edenhal was granted by Edward I. to the Priory of Carlisle, in whose hands it was in 1299

171. CONVENTIO FACTA INTER PRIOREM DE WE-
DERHAL ET ALANUM FABRUM DE GRINGELDIC.

ANNO Gratiæ Millesimo Ducentesimo Quadragesimo
primo ad Pentecosten facta est hæc conventio inter
Thomam Priorem de Wederhal[1] ex una parte, et Alanum
fabrum de Gringeldic ex altera videlicet Quod prædictus
Prior dimisit prædicto Alano totam terram suam in Ruccroft, videlicet novem acras quas Johannes de Ruccroft
aliquando tenuit de Priore de Wederhal usque ad terminum duodecim annorum plene completorum. Reddet
autem prædictus Alanus Domui de Wederhal singulis annis
sex solidos ad duos terminos medietatem ad Festum Sancti
Martini in yeme et aliam medietatem ad Pentecosten. Et
sciendum quod prædictus Alanus molet ad molendinum de
Gringeldic ad vicesimum vas totum bladum suum in prædicta terra crescentem similiter totum bladum quod alibi
adquirere poterit et solvet vicesimum porcum ad pannagium et sustinebit domos usque ad terminum prædictum.
Completis autem duodecim annis remanebit prædicta terra
cum omnibus ædificiis soluta et quieta a prædicto Alano et
omnibus suis. Et sciendum est quod si prædictus Prior
terram illam, quam Johannes de Ruccroft detenet injuste,
poterit adquirere, prædictus Alanus habebit illam cum prædictis novem acris pro prædicta firma. Et ut hæc Conventio rata sit et stabilis presenti scripto sigillum meum
apposui. Hijs Testibus, Johanne Capellano de Wederhal,
Gilberto Capellano de Warthwic, Roberto Clerico de Cutun,
Johanne de Hairminne, Willelmo de Crogelyn, Johanne
Stelfot, Roberto de Horneby, et multis alijs[2].

(*Register Bp Halton*, MS. p. 42), and it was appropriated to them
in 1303—4 (*Inquis. p. m.* 32 Edward I. No. 130).

[10] The date of the charter must be after 1239, when Walter de
Ulvesby became Archdeacon (see on No. 56), and, looking at the dates
of Martin of Kirkoswald, probably 1240—50.

171. [1] This is not Thomas de Wymondham, Prior in 1270 (see
note on No. 96), as other Priors came between (see Appendix E).

[2] The date of the charter is Pentecost, 1241.

172. Carta Rogeri de Bello-campo de tota
terra sua in Cringeldic.

Omnibus Sanctæ Matris Ecclesiæ filijs ad quorum
notitiam hoc præsens scriptum pervenerit Rogerus de Bellocampo[1] æternam in Domino Salutem. Noverit universitas
vestra me dedisse Deo et Ecclesiæ Sanctæ Mariæ Eborum
et Monachis Sanctæ Trinitatis et Sancti Constantini de
Wederhal corpus meum[2] in eorum Ecclesiâ sepeliendum et
cum corpore meo dedisse Deo et prædictæ Ecclesiæ et
Monachis ibidem Deo servientibus totam terram meam de
Cringeldic per rectas divisas suas cum toto servicio Johannis Golti. Habendam et Tenendam sibi in liberam
puram et perpetuam Elemosinam cum omnibus pertinentijs suis et cum omnibus libertatibus communis et aisiamentis ad Manerium de Stafhole[3] pertinentibus infra
Villam et extra absque ullo retenemento adeo libere et
quiete in omnibus sicut Elemosina liberius et quietius dari
possit aut possideri ad inveniendum Vestimentum[4] et
Luminare imperpetuum ad Altare Gloriosæ et perpetuæ
Virginis Mariæ per Priorem ejusdem Domus. Et ego et
hæredes mei prædictam terram cum pertinentijs prænominatis Deo et Abbachiæ Sanctæ Mariæ Eborum et Monachis
de Wederhal contra omnes homines warantizabimus acquietabimus et defendemus imperpetuum. Et ne quis hæredum meorum possit in posterum contra hanc donationem
meam venire eandem cum sigillo meo præsenti scripto

172.   [1] For Roger de Bello-campo, see note 1 on No. **153.**

[2] The grant is a singular one—his body to be buried in the Church
of the Priory of Wederhal, the land, carrying with it the services of
the serf John Golti—to provide vestments and lights for the altar
of the Virgin Mary.

[3] Stafhole, hodie Staffield, was a manor in the parish of Kirkoswald,
at the junction of the river Croglin with the Eden. In 1300, we find
that Sarra, widow of Richard de Levington, had lately held lands in
this vill (*Calend. Doc. Scot.* ed. Bain, iv. 361).

[4] *Vestimentum* in old inventories means, generally, the whole set
of altar or Eucharistic vestments.

apposito corroboravi. Hijs Testibus, Roberto filio Willelmi Vicecomite Cumberlandiæ, Magistro Gervasio Officiali Karlioli, Gilberto de Feritate, Symone de Aumdũc, Alano Coquo, Hugone Dispensatore, Johanne de Eyremiñe, Johanne filio Willelmi, Waltero janitore de Wederhal, Willelmo Præposito[5], et alijs[6]

173. FINIS FACTUS IN CURIA DOMINI REGIS INTER ALICIAM DE BELLO CAMPO ET ABBATEM EBORACI DE DUABUS CARUCATIS TERRÆ ET DIMIDIA IN CRINGELDIC.

HÆC est Finalis Concordia facta in Curia Domini Regis apud Karliolum a die Sancti Michaelis in tres Septimanas Anno Regni Regis Henrici filij Regis Johannis vicesimo quinto coram Roberto de Levington[1], Radulpho de Revclẽg, Willelmo de Culewrch et Sollano de Nevill[2] Justiciarijs Itinerantibus et alijs Domini Regis fidelibus tunc ibi presentibus inter Aliciam de Bello-campo et Amabillam sororem ejus petentes et Willelmum[3] Abbatem de Eboraco

---

[5] William was Præpositus of Cringeldic, see No. 155.

[6] From the Sheriff, the date of the charter must be 1223—29.

173. [1] Robert de Levington, or rather Lexinton, as in No. 226, was Justice Itinerant as early as 1230, when he was one of the judges in the great suit, Alan de Multon and his wife against Lambert de Multon and his wife, for the property of Richard de Lucy (*Pedes Finium*, 15 Hen. III. No. 12). The four justices mentioned here appear to have been at Carlisle also in 1242 (compare No. 226) when Alan de Multon and his wife were again before the court (*Pedes Finium*, 26 Hen. III. No. 31); but the names are evidently incorrectly copied here. Levington is Lexinton, Radulph de Revcleg' (in No. 226 Muthleg') should be Sutleg', William de Culewrch (in No. 226 Colewurth) is Culewurthe, and Sollan is Jollan de Nevill.

[2] Jollan de Nevill, in 1244, paid a fine of 20 marcs for permission to marry Sara widow of John Heriz; in October, 1246, he was dead and his son Jollan got seisin of his property (*Fine Rolls*, ed. Roberts, i. 426, 464). He has been supposed, and with fairly good reason, to have been the compiler of *Testa de Nevill;* see the Preface to the Record Com. edition, and an article in *The Genealogist*, v. p. 35.

[3] William Rundel, or de Roundell, was Abbot of S. Mary's at

tenentem per Willelmum de Leytun positum loco suo ad lucrandum vel perdendum de duabus carucatis terræ et dimidia cum pertinentijs in Cringeldic Unde assisa mortis Antecessorum[4] summonita fuit inter eos in eadem Curia Scilicet quod prædictæ Alicia et Amabilla recognoverunt totam prædictam terram cum pertinentijs esse jus ipsius Abbatis et Ecclesiæ suæ de Eboraco ut illam quam idem Abbas et Ecclesia sua habent de dono[5] Rogeri de Bello-campo fratris prædictarum Aliciæ et Amabillæ cujus hæredes ipsæ sunt et remiserunt et quiete clamaverunt de se et hæredibus suis prædicto Abbati et Successoribus suis et Ecclesiæ suæ prædictæ imperpetuum.   Et pro hac recognitione, remissione, quieta clamatione, fine[6] et Concordia, idem Abbas dedit predictis Aliciæ et Amabillæ tres Marcas Argenti[7].

174. FINIS FACTUS IN CURIA DOMINI REGIS DE DUABUS BOVATIS TERRÆ IN CRINGELDIC.

HÆC est Finalis Concordia facta in Curia Domini Regis apud Karliolum in crastino Nativitatis Beatæ Mariæ Anno Regni Regis Henrici filij Regis Johannis undecimo coram Rogero Bertram, Briano filio Alani[1], Simone de Hal,

York, from 1239 to 1244, and therefore at this time ; see note 5 on No. 46.

[4] *Assisa mortis antecessoris* is a certain form of legal writ ; see No. 92, note 5, and Jacob, *Law Dict. s. v.* "Assise."

[5] The grant is in No. 172.

[6] This document is from the *Pedes Finium*, or *Feet of Fines*, among the legal Records ; the *finis* or conclusion and agreement between the parties.

[7] The date is three weeks from S. Michael's day, 25 Hen. III., or October 20th, 1241.

174. [1] Brian son of Alan, or FitzAlan, was an important person in the reign of Henry III.   He was Sheriff for Northumberland from 1227 to 1235.   With Roger Bertram he formed part of the escort of Alexander II. King of Scotland, when he went to York in Lent 1228—29 to meet Henry III. (*Close Rolls*, 13 Hen. III. m. 17 d ; Rymer, *Fœdera*, new ed. i. 193), and was often employed in Scotch affairs.

Willelmo de Eboraco Justiciarijs Domini Regis Itinerantibus
et alijs Domini Regis Fidelibus tunc ibi præsentibus inter
Thomam de Maleton[2] et Adam uxorem ejus, Ricardum Gernun et Johannam uxorem ejus petentes, et
Robertum[3] Abbatem Sanctæ Mariæ de Eboraco tenentem
de duabus bovatis terræ cum pertinentijs in Cringeldick
Unde Assisa mortis Antecessorum summonita fuit inter
eos in eadem Curia : Scilicet quod prædicti Thomas et
Ada Ricardus et Johanna remiserunt et quietum clamaverunt de se et hæredibus ipsarum Adæ et Johannæ eidem
Abbati et successoribus suis et Ecclesiæ prædictæ totum
jus et clamium quod habuerunt in prædictis duabus bovatis
terræ cum pertinentijs imperpetuum. Et pro hac remissione et quieta clamatione fine et Concordia idem Abbas
recepit prædictos Thomam et Adam Ricardum et Johannam
et eorum hæredes in singulis Beneficijs et Orationibus quæ
de cetero fient in Ecclesia sua de Eboraco imperpetuum[4].

175. QUIETA CLAMATIO JOHANNIS DE HERMIÑE
FILIJ WILLELMI DE HERMIÑE DE DUABUS BOVATIS
TERRÆ IN KABERGH.

OMNIBUS Christi fidelibus ad quorum notitiam præsens
scriptum pervenerit Johannes de Hermiñe[1] filius Willelmi
de Hermiñe Salutem æternam in Domino. Noverit universitas vestra me pro salute animæ Patris mei et pro
animarum salute Antecessorum et Successorum meorum
reddidisse et quietas clamasse de me et hæredibus meis
imperpetuum Deo et Abbati Sanctæ Mariæ Eboraci et
ejusdem loci Conventui necnon et Monachis de Wederhal

---

² This is the first Thomas de Maleton, or Multon, for whom
and his relatives mentioned here, see on Nos. **47, 103, 104.**

³ Robert de Longo Campo, Abbot of S. Mary's at York, from
1197 to 1239 ; see note 3 on No. **10.**

⁴ The date is the morrow of the Nativity of the Blessed Mary,
11 Henry III., or September 9th, 1227.

175. ¹ On John de Hermiñe, see note 3, No. **64.**

duas bovatas terræ cum pertinentijs in territorio de Kaberch[2], Scilicet de illa terra quam teneo de dictis Monachis
de feudo de Raveneswic, videlicet totam terram a superiori
parte Mussæ[3] ad Neubussehill sicut le sikette descendit a
prædicta Mussa usque ad viam ad Surflatende, et sicut
dicta via tendit usque ad quoddam fossatum, et sicut
dictum fossatum tendit ex transverso linealiter usque ad
Regiam viam[4] quæ ducit ad Karleolum, et sicut dicta via
tendit usque ad divisam Dominici mei in Lechou et a dicta
divisa usque ad Hefdeland del Bochum et sicut divisa del
Hevefdland tendit sursum usque ad viam juxta Mussam,
et sicut semita ducit ad superiorem partem del Neubussehill, et in Bacstanegyle et in Bochum duas acras et dimidiam et quandam portiunculam terræ quæ vocatur le Gare
inter Regiam [viam] et magnam Mussam et ab angulo
fossati de Communa duas acras terræ in latitudine versus
Mussam et totam longitudinem sicut dicta terra se extendit
versus Neubussehille et totam medietatem Marisci Scalre-
manoch versus meridiem.   Hæc autem omnia præscripta
habebunt dicti Monachi pro duabus bovatis terræ libere
integre et quiete imperpetuum de me et hæredibus meis
cum omnibus communis libertatibus et aisiamentis suis
infra Villam et extra.   Et ego et hæredes mei prædictas
bovatas terræ cum pertinentijs dictis Monachis imperpetuum contra omnes homines warantizabimus et defendemus.   Et ne Ego vel hæredes mei contra hoc scriptum
meæ redditionis et quietæ clamationis imperpetuum venire
possimus, eidem sigillum meum apposui.   Hijs Testibus,
Symone Capellano, Johanne de Aglunby, Stephano de

[2] Kaberch, or Kaberge, *hodie* Cabers, adjoined Little Croglin on
the north (see Nos. 176, 177) and, as here stated, was in the fee
of Ravenswic, or Renwick.

[3] *Mussa*, "a moss" or marsh-ground, a swamp, Anglo-Saxon *meos*.

[4] See note 9 on No. 5 ; probably the same road as that from
Appleby to Carlisle, and here keeping the high ground on the other
side of the Eden ; see also note 3 on No. 179.

Helmesle, Radulpho et Willelmo de Cringeldic, Willelmo de Croglyn, Henrico de Hulvesthayt, Adam Scireloc[5], Galfrido de Croglyn, Alano de Herminne et alijs[6].

176. CARTA HENRICI DE ULVESTHUAIT DE TOTO PRATO SUO IN SMALWATHIS.

OMNIBUS Christi fidelibus ad quorum notitiam præsens scriptum pervenerit Henricus de Hulvesthuayt Salutem æternam in Domino. Noverit universitas vestra me Divinæ Pietatis intuitu et pro salute animæ meæ et pro salute animarum Prædecessorum et Successorum meorum dedisse concessisse et præsenti carta confirmasse Deo et Abbachiæ Sanctæ Mariæ Eboraci et Monachis de Wederhal in puram et perpetuam Elemosinam totum pratum meum de Smalewathis quod quidem pratum meum jacet inter divisam de Croglyn et de Kaberge. Habendum et Tenendum imperpetuum liberum solutum et quietum de me et hæredibus meis ad omnimodum commodum suum faciendum sicut sibi melius viderint expedire. Et Ego et hæredes mei dictum pratum prædictis Monachis imperpetuum warantizabimus acquietabimus et defendemus. In cujus rei Testimonium præsenti scripto sigillum meum apposui. Hijs Testibus, Johanne de Staffole, Thoma de Bellocampo, Willelmo de Croglyn, Johanne de Tabğe[1], Stephano de Westgard, Thoma de Raveneswic, Roberto de Ormesby, Alano de Caberge, Willielmo filio Willielmi, Gilberto de Laysinby, et alijs[2].

---

[5] Adam de Scireloc, or Schyrloc, is called of Ulvesby in No. **183.**

[6] In No. **161** John de Hermiñe appears with several of the witnesses here ; the date of this charter is probably about the same, shortly after 1236, or about 1240.

176. [1] John de Tabğe should be de Caberge, see No. **177,** where he appears with Alan "his brother," also see on No. **138.**

[2] Comparing this with the other charter of Henry de Hulvesthwayt about 1252 (No. **157**), we have evidently the same date here, and, from the witnesses, a date somewhat later than the charters preceding.

177. CARTA HENRICI DE ULVESTHUAYT FACTA
MONACHIS DE WEDERHAL DE QUODAM PRATO IN
SMALEUUAYES.

OMNIBUS Christi fidelibus ad quorum notitiam presens
scriptum pervenerit Henricus de Ulvesthuayt Salutem æternam in Domino. Noverit universitas vestra me Divinæ
pietatis intuitu pro salute animæ meæ et pro salute animarum Prædecessorum et Successorum meorum dedisse concessisse et presenti carta confirmasse Deo et Abbachiæ
Sanctæ Mariæ Eboraci et Monachis de Wederhal in puram
et perpetuam Elemosinam totum pratum meum de Smale-
uuays quod quidem pratum jacet juxta divisam de Crogelyn
et de Caberge. Habendum et Tenendum imperpetuum
liberum solutum et quietum de me et hæredibus meis ad
omnimodum commodum suum faciendum sicut sibi melius
viderint expedire. Et Ego et hæredes mei dictum pratum
prædictis Monachis imperpetuum warantizabimus acquietabimus et defendemus. In cujus rei Testimonium præsenti
scripto sigillum meum apposui. Hijs Testibus, Johanne
de Staffole, Thoma de Bellocampo, Willelmo de Croglyn,
Johanne de Caberge, Alano fratre ejus, Thoma de Raven-
wike, Stephano de Westgayt, Roberto de Horneby, Willelmo
filio Willelmi de Croghelyn, Gilberto de Laysingeby, Roberto Clerico et alijs.

178. QUIETA CLAMATIO JOHANNIS FILIJ WILLELMI
DE WEDERHAL DE DUABUS BOVATIS TERRÆ IN KABERGH.

OMNIBUS Christi fidelibus ad quorum notitiam præsens
scriptum pervenerit Johannes filius Willelmi de Wederhal
Salutem æternam in Domino. Noverit universitas vestra
me pro salute animæ meæ reddidisse et quietas clamasse de
me et hæredibus meis imperpetuum Deo et Abbati Sanctæ
Mariæ Eboraci et ejusdem loci Conventui necnon et Monachis de Wederhal duas bovatas terræ cum pertinentijs in
territorio de Kabergh quas ego aliquando tenui de dictis

Monachis de Wederhal ad inveniendum unum cereum[1] octo librarum imperpetuum per Priorem dictæ Domus de Wederhale ardentem singulis diebus coram Altari Gloriosæ et perpetuæ Virginis Mariæ quamdiu aliqua Missa celebrata in honore Gloriosæ Virginis ad dictum Altare duraverit. Ego autem et hæredes mei prædictam terram cum omnibus pertinentijs suis Deo et Abbachiæ Sanctæ Mariæ Eboraci et Monachis de Wederhal contra omnes homines warantiza-bimus acquietabimus et defendemus imperpetuum. Et ne quis hæredum meorum possit in posterum contra hanc Donationem meam venire, eandem cum sigillo meo præ-senti scripto apposito corroboravi. Hijs Testibus, Willelmo filio Rogeri de Korkeby, Willelmo filio ejus, Willelmo de Warthwic, Johanne de Caberch, Willelmo de Croghelyn, Radulpho Clerico et alijs[2].

179. CARTA RADULPHI DE HOF FACTA MONACHIS DE WEDERHAL DE QUADAM TERRA IN HUTESKOU IN PAROCHIA DE KIRCHOSWALD.

SCIANT omnes qui viderint vel audierint Litteras has quod Ego Radulphus de Hof cum consilio et assensu Uxoris meæ et hæredum meorum concessi et dedi et hac præsenti carta mea confirmavi Deo et Ecclesiæ Sancti Constantini de Wederhal et Monachis ibidem Deo servientibus quan-dam terram in Huttescou[1] in Parochia de Kirkeoswald,

---

178. [1] *Cereum*, "a wax candle"; the weight, 8 pounds, given here is worthy of note.

[2] A comparison of this charter with No. **142**, which John son of William de Wederhal attests, would seem to shew that it is not far from the same date, soon after 1239, or about 1240.

179. [1] Huttescou or Huddescoch (No. **180**), called later Huddles-keugh, was in the northern part of Kirkoswald, and adjoining Hareskeugh, which runs up into the eastern fells. Land in Hareskeugh was granted to the Priory of Lanercost by Ada Engayne, wife of Robert de Vallibus, when it is called "Little Haresco," and the grant was confirmed by Hugh de Morvill, when it is called "Little Harescou," and the bounds are set out (*Regist.*

scilicet quæ jacet juxta terram Hospitalis² et sicut Regia
via ducit in Raven³ et sicut Raven descendit in Becstervild
et de Becstervild contra Montem usque ad quandam quercum furcatam et de quercu furcata usque ad divisas Roberti
Huttescou et de divisis Roberti usque in Raven⁴, et sicut
Raven descendit usque ad divisas Willelmi Surrays et de
divisis Willelmi contra Montem usque ad quandam radicem
quercus in mora et de illa radice sicut sepes ducit usque ad
terram Hospitalis cum communi et aisiamentis de Kyrke-
oswald in puram et perpetuam Elemosinam liberam et
quietam imperpetuum a me et hæredibus meis pro anima
Domini mei Hugonis de Morevilla⁵ et pro salute animæ
meæ et Patris et Matris meæ et omnium Antecessorum
meorum.   Hanc vero Elemosinam Ego et hæredes mei
prædictis Monachis imperpetuum contra omnes gentes
warantizabimus.   Ne autem aliquis hæredum meorum in
præfata terra possit aliquid juris clamare vel inde calumpniam in posterum movere huic scripto sigillum meum
apposui in Testimonium.   Hijs Testibus, Symone Capellano de Croghelyn, Alano de Cumreu, Willelmo de Haire-
miñe, Willelmo filio Marchepetit de Melmorby, Johanne
fratre ejus, Yuone de Torvil, Alexandro Engain, Willelmo Clerico de Wederhal, Umfrido, Randulpho Clerico,

Lanercost, MS. ii. 11, 12 ; see also x. 12, 13).   These bounds are in
terms very similar to those used here of Huttescou.

² Probably S. Nicholas' Hospital, Carlisle, which had lands in
Ainstable (see No. 170).

³ The road from Appleby to Carlisle, as in No. 175.   In the grant
of Little Harescou by Hugh de Morvill referred to above, the bounds
are described—" sicut magna Via venit de Appelbi usque ad Raven et
inde sursum per Raven usque ad Caput ejusdem Aquæ."

⁴ The Raven is a small stream, which gives its name to Ravenswic, or Renwick, rising in the fells above Hareskeugh, and running
into the Eden near the town of Kirkoswald.

⁵ Hugo de Morvilla, who had died in 1202—3 (see note 8 on No.
101) was lord of Kirkoswald, and of Hareskeugh, as appears from the
grant in the *Register of Lanercost* (ii. 12) referred to above.

Waltero janitore, Johanne Coquo, Johanne filio Willelmi Clerici et alijs[6].

180. CARTA ABBATIS SANCTÆ MARIÆ FACTA ALICIÆ UXORI ROBERTI DE SALHILD DE QUADAM TERRA IN HUDDESCOCH.

SCIANT omnes tam presentes quam futuri quod Ego Robertus[1] Dei Gratia Abbas Sanctæ Mariæ Eboraci cum communi consilio et assensu Capituli nostri dedi et concessi et presenti carta mea confirmavi Aliciæ uxori Roberti de Salhild et uni de filijs suis cuicunque voluerit in feudo et hæreditate quandam terram in Huddescoch[2] quam Radulphus de Hof dedit nobis in Elemosinam tenere de nobis reddendo annuatim duodecim denarios pro omni servicio ad duos terminos, medietatem ad Festum Sancti Martini et aliam Medietatem ad Pentecosten. Testibus Hijs, Thoma de Wilton Dapifero, Willelmo...., Symone Capellano de Crogelyn, Roberto Vachel, Alano de Cumreu, Willelmo de Hermyñe, Willelmo Clerico de Wederhal, Ranulpho Clerico, Umfrido, Waltero janitore et multis alijs[3].

181. CARTA GERALDI DE MELMORBI FACTA MONACHIS DE WEDERHAL DE UNA BOVATA TERRÆ CUM TOFTO ET CROFTO IN MELMORBY.

UNIVERSIS Christi Fidelibus ad quorum notitiam præsens scriptum pervenerit Geraldus de Melmorby salutem æternam in Domino. Noverit universitas vestra me Divinæ

[6] The witnesses all point to the early years of the 13th century as the date of this charter, and this agrees with No. **153**, where several of the same witnesses occur.

180. [1] Robert de Longo Campo, Abbot from 1197 to 1239, see note 3 on No. **10**.

[2] The land in Huttescou, granted by the last charter, is now leased at an annual rent of 12*d*.

[3] This charter must be dated very shortly after the preceding, several of the witnesses being the same, i.e. the beginning of the 13th century.

Pietatis intuitu et pro salute animæ meæ et animarum
Prædecessorum et Successorum meorum dedisse concessisse et præsenti carta confirmasse Deo et Ecclesiæ Sanctæ
Mariæ Eboraci et Monachis de Wederhal ibidem Deo
servientibus unam bovatam terræ in territorio de Melmorby[1] cum tofto et crofto, Illam videlicet bovatam quæ
jacet propinquior terræ Adæ filij Henrici versus orientem,
Insuper autem unam acram et dimidiam terræ in Cumbre-
trute-wra.   Habendam et Tenendam in liberam puram et
perpetuam Elemosinam cum omnibus pertinentijs libertatibus et aisiamentis Villæ de Melmorby spectantibus ad
sustentamentum Luminaris Ecclesiæ de Wederhal.   Ego
vero et hæredes mei hanc Elemosinam dictis Monachis
contra omnes homines imperpetuum warantizabimus acquietabimus et defendemus.   Et ut hoc scriptum ratum
permaneat et inconcussum illud sigilli mei appositione
corroboravi.   Hijs Testibus, Symone Capellano, Ricardo
Diacono, Radulpho Clerico, Waltero janitore, Thoma Dispensatore, Johanne Coquo, Johanne de Aglunby, Johanne
filio Willelmi Clerici[2], Ranulpho filio Umfridi et multis
alijs[3].

181. [1] Melmorby, said to have been the *abode* of Melmor a Dane,
was a parish and manor on the east of the river Eden, lying under the
eastern fells between Ulvesby (or Ousby) and Gamelsby in the parish
of Addingham. At this time the manor was held by the second
Adam son of Odard, Baron of Wigton, or his father; and later in the
century we find it in possession of another Odard de Wygeton and his
son Walter; see on Odard note 5, No. 72. There is a curious petition
in the reign of Edward II., shewing that a fortress called the Tower
of Melmorby, capable of being guarded by 12 men-at-arms, had been
long held by John de Denum against the Scots, but his lands are
so wasted that he cannot provide a garrison, and he prays help of the
King. The petition is endorsed " Some marriage ward or farm to be
looked out, and the King will give him a reward " (*Calend. Doc. Scot.*
ed. Bain, iii. 163).

[2] John son of William, who was Clerk of Wederhal, as in No. 179.

[3] From the similarity of the witnesses, the date must be about the
same as that of No. 179, i.e. the early years of the 13th century.

182. Carta Willelmi filij Adæ de Mora de 2 bovatis terræ cum tofto et crofto in Melmorby.

Universis Christi Fidelibus ad quorum notitiam præsens Scriptum pervenerit Willelmus filius Adæ de Mora[1] Salutem æternam in Domino. Noverit Universitas vestra me Divinæ Pietatis intuitu et pro salute animæ meæ et animarum Prædecessorum et Successorum meorum dedisse concessisse et præsenti carta mea confirmasse Deo et Ecclesiæ Sanctæ Trinitatis de Wederhal et Monachis ibidem Deo servientibus illas duas bovatas terræ cum pertinentijs in Villa de Melmorby cum tofto et crofto quas Henricus Blanchard de me aliquando tenuit Illas scilicet quæ jacent inter terram Beatæ Mariæ Karleoli et Littilgilsic. Habendas et Tenendas dictæ Ecclesiæ et dictis Monachis de Wederhal in liberam puram et perpetuam Elemosinam cum omnibus pertinentijs libertatibus communis et aisiamentis Villæ de Melmorby spectantibus sine aliquo retenemento ad sustentamentum Luminaris prædictæ Ecclesiæ de Wederhal. Ego vero et hæredes mei totam prædictam terram prædictis Monachis contra omnes homines imperpetuum warantizabimus acquietabimus et defendemus. Et ut hoc scriptum ratum permaneat et inconcussum illud sigilli mei appositione corroboravi. Hijs Testibus, Domino Radulpho tunc Priore Karleoli, Domino Waltero Officiario Karleoli, Domino Roberto Decano de Croglyn, Michaele Capellano de Kirkeoswald, Henrico Capellano de Wederhale, Hugone Capellano de Warthwic et multis alijs[2].

182. [1] The family of de Mora, or de la More, was connected with Gilsland. This may be the same William de Mora who attests the charter of Matilda de Vallibus, No. 194, dated 1271 ; under the same date he, with his wife Agnes, quitclaimed property in Farlam and Little Camboc to the Priory of Lanercost (*Regist. Lanercost*, MS. xii. 13) ; he was also witness to several of their charters.

[2] The date of this charter will be after 1231, when Radulph became Prior, and before 1239, when Walter de Ulvesby probably became Archdeacon (see on Nos. 56, 97).

183. CARTA ROBERTI DE ROBERTBY FACTA MONACHIS DE WEDERHAL DE 3 ACRIS TERRÆ IN ULVESBY.

OMNIBUS Christi fidelibus has literas visuris vel audituris Robertus de Roberteby Salutem. Noverit universitas vestra me concessisse dedisse et hac presenti carta mea confirmasse Deo et Ecclesiæ Beatæ Mariæ Eboraci et Monachis de Wederhal Deo servientibus tres acras terræ et dimidiam in territorio de Ulvesby quarum una et dimidia jacent in crofto meo ubi horreum meum stat ex parte Australi et aliæ duæ super Borganessat ex parte Aquilonis quæ se extendunt de Sunnivegile usque ad fossatum de Castlel-slac ad sustentamentum Luminaris Altaris Sanctæ Mariæ Ecclesiæ de Wederhal. Tenendas et Habendas in puram et perpetuam Elemosinam cum omnibus pertinentijs et Aisiamentis et libertatibus pertinentibus ad Villam de Ulvesby salva multura vicesimi vasis molendino de Ulvesby debita. Ego vero Robertus et hæredes mei dictam terram dictis Monachis warantizabimus contra omnes homines et fœminas imperpetuum. Hijs Testibus, Willelmo de Daker tunc Vicecomite Karleoli, Waltero Parsona de Ulvesby tunc Officiali Karleolensi, Hamundo de Ulvesby, Adam Armstrang de eadem, Gervasio de Scrağ., Adam de Kempeley, Adam de Schyrloc de Ulvesby et multis alijs[1].

184. CARTA ADÆ FILIJ ALANI FACTA MONACHIS DE WEDERHAL DE DIMIDIA CARUCATA TERRÆ IN ORMESBY.

ADAM filius Alani omnibus legentibus vel audientibus litteras has tam præsentibus quam futuris Sanctæ Matris Ecclesiæ filijs Salutem. Sciatis me dedisse et præsenti carta confirmasse Deo et Beatæ Mariæ et Sancto Constantino de Wederhal et Monachis ibidem Deo servientibus

---

183. [1] From William de Daker, Sheriff 1236—47, and Walter, probably not Official after 1239, the date may be fixed as 1236—39.

dimidiam carucatam terræ in Ormesby[1] cum omnibus pertinentijs suis in puram et perpetuam Elemosinam ab omni exactione et servicio liberam et quietam. Similiter concessi eis communem pasturam præfatæ Villæ ad pecuniam Dominij sui pro anima Patris et Matris meæ et pro salute mea et uxoris meæ et omnium Parentum meorum tam vivorum quam defunctorum. Hijs Testibus, Willelmo fratre meo, Roberto de Hornesby[2], Huctredo Presbitero de Carlaton[3], Reinaldo Presbytero, Helya Sacerdote, Kettello Clerico, et multis alijs[4].

185. CARTA ADÆ FILIJ ROBERTI DE DIMIDIA CARU-CATA TERRÆ IN ORMESBY CUM PASTURA CCC. OVIUM.

SCIANT præsentes et futuri quod Ego Adam filius Roberti[1] cum consilio et assensu uxoris meæ Matildæ et hæredum meorum et amicorum dedi et concessi et præsenti carta mea confirmavi Deo et Abbachiæ Sanctæ Mariæ Eboraci et Monachis Sanctæ Trinitatis et Sancti Constantini de Wederhal pro salute animæ meæ et Antecessorum meorum dimidiam carucatam terræ in campis de Ormesby quæ dicitur Mirland cum omnibus pertinentijs et aisiamentis ad Villam de Ormesby ubique spectantibus infra Villam et extra sine aliquo retenemento in puram et perpetuam Elemosinam. Insuper autem præter communem pasturam

184. [1] Ormesby, or Hornsby, is in the southern part of the parish of Cumwhitton, see below on Cumquintyngton in No. 190.

[2] Robert de Hornesby may be the same as the Robert de Horneby, who attests No. 171, in 1241, and other charters in this Register.

[3] See on Karlaton in No. 189.

[4] There is nothing special to help to fix the date of this charter, unless the conjecture with regard to Robert de Hornesby be correct.

185. [1] Adam son of Robert, i.e. de Karliol, as shewn by his son, Eudo de Karliol, in the next charter. Robert was the grandson of Hildred de Carlel and son of Odard (see note 9 on No. 72). This Adam was therefore the brother of Odard de Hodema, who got seisin of some of his father's property in 1210 (see on No. 73). He gave a moiety of the tithes of Little Bampton to the Hospital of S. Nicholas, Carlisle (see on No. 95).

quæ ad prædictam dimidiam carucatam terræ pertinet dedi
et concessi et hac præsenti carta mea confirmavi predictis
Monachis in puram et perpetuam Elemosinam pasturam
ubique in predicta Villa de Ormesby proprijs animalibus
eorum et specialiter trecentis matricibus ovibus cum agnis
suis vel totidem multonibus.   Habendam et tenendam
imperpetuum sine aliqua contradictione vel impedimento
mei vel hæredum meorum.   Et Ego et hæredes mei hanc
prædictam Elemosinam præfatis Monachis contra omnes
homines warantizabimus et defendemus imperpetuum.   In
cujus rei Testimonium præsenti scripto sigillum meum
apposui. Hijs Testibus, Petro de Ditheric tunc Vicecomite
Karlioli, Duncano de Lascels², Roberto filio Willelmi³,

² Duncan de Lascels appears in the Pipe Rolls as early as 1200,
with Christiana his wife, as having "her land in Boultona which is
her heritage, since she cannot have a reasonable part of her heritage
in Scotland." This Christiana, there seems little doubt, was the
daughter of Walter de Wyndeshore ; see on this Walter in No. 134,
note 2, where it is shewn she had property in her own right in Scotland
and elsewhere. No doubt incorrectly, Waldef son of Gospatric is
spoken of as her "father" instead of her ancestor in a Final Concord
between Duncan de Lascelles and Christiana his wife and Hugh,
Abbot of Geddeworthe (Jedburgh) regarding the advowson of the
Church of Bastenethwait in 1208 (Pedes Finium, 10 Joh., ed. Hunter,
ii. 10). J. Denton (Cumberland, p. 52) speaks of Christiana as a
descendant of Gospatric, a bastard son of Waldeof and lord of
Boulton ; but I have been unable to find any authority for the
statement, or that this Gospatric had any son Waldef. Duncan
appears in the Pipe Rolls for Cumberland in 1205—6 as making
a payment in connection with the Church of Boulton ; and, with
Christiana, in the Pipe Rolls for Buckingham and Bedford, the next
year, as paying 240 marks for the whole land of Walter de Windlesores,
held of the King in capite ; and in the same Rolls for 1210—11 he
occurs as owing 60 marcs and a palfrey for getting seisin of his land
whereof he was disseised by the King's writ for not attending him
with horse and arms in the army of Scotland. The next year there is
a curious reference to this debt ; and in the autumn, among the
announcements of the justices, we find William Briwere in charge of
Christiana, the daughter of Duncan, and responsible for the debts
which Duncan and Ranulph de Hosdeng owed the Jews for Walter de

Alano de Cumreu, Willielmo Clerico, Umfrido, Waltero portario de Wederhal, Ricardo Caprun et alijs[4].

186. CARTA EUDONIS DE KARLEOLO FACTA MONA-CHIS DE WEDERHAL DE DIMIDIA CARUCATA TERRÆ IN ORMESBY.

SCIANT præsentes et futuri quod Ego Eudo de Karliolo[1] filius Adæ filij Roberti consensu et consilio hæredum meorum concessi et præsenti carta confirmavi Deo et Ecclesiæ Sanctæ Mariæ Eboraci et Domui Sanctæ Trinitatis et Sancti Constantini de Wederhal et Monachis ibidem Deo servientibus dimidiam carucatam terræ in campo de Ormesby quæ dicitur Mirland quam Pater meus eis dedit in Elemosinam. Adico autem ex dono meo prædictis Monachis totam illam terram quæ mihi pertinebat de qua tuli Breve de nova disseisina super Warinum de Mira qui prædictam terram tenuit. Habendam et Tenendam simul cum prædicta dimidia carucata terræ in puram et perpetuam Elemosinam cum omnibus pertinentijs libertatibus communis et aisiamentis infra Villam et extra prædictæ terræ pertinentibus. Ego vero et hæredes mei totam prædictam terram cum pertinentijs prædictis Monachis imperpetuum warantizabimus et defendemus. Et ut hæc mea donatio et confirmatio firma et stabilis perseveret præsenti scripto sigillum meum apposui. Hijs Testibus, Roberto de

Windlesores. Hence it is clear that Duncan de Lascels died in 1211. His daughter appears a little later as holding lands for 3 knights' fees, of the barony of Walter de Wyndesor in Buckinghamshire (*Calend. Doc. Scot.* ed. Bain, i. 96). Duncan de Lascels was witness to several charters of Robert son of Ranulph de Vallibus (the 2nd Robert) in the *Register of Lanercost* (MS. ii. 2, 3, 4, 5).

[3] Robert son of William, the son of Odard de Corkeby; he married Alicia de Lascels; see note 1 on No. 37.

[4] From Duncan de Lascels and other witnesses, the date will be before 1211, in the early years of the 13th century.

186. [1] For Eudo de Karliol, see on No. **75**; he was the son of the grantor of the preceding charter concerning the same land.

Hampton² tunc Vicecomite Karleoli, Ricardo de Leving-
ton, Elisio de Raveneswic, Roberto filio Willelmi³, Adam
Armstrang, Johanne filio Willelmi⁴, Alano de Langethwayt,
Willelmo janitore, Johanne de Aglunby, et alijs⁵.

187. Quieta Clamatio Henrici filij Warini de Scalewra de decem acris terræ in Ormesby.

UNIVERSIS Christi fidelibus ad quorum notitiam hoc
presens scriptum pervenerit Henricus filius Warini de
Scalewra salutem æternam in Domino.   Noverit Universitas me reddidisse et remisisse et quietas clamasse Deo
et Ecclesiæ Sanctæ Mariæ Eboraci et Monachis de Wederhal ibidem Deo servientibus decem acras terræ cum
pertinentijs in territorio de Ormesby, quæ quidem decem
acræ terræ sunt de illa dimidia carucata terræ quam
Adam filius Roberti dictæ Domui dedit¹ in Elemosinam.
Habendas et Tenendas imperpetuum cum omnibus libertatibus communis et aisiamentis ad Villam de Ormesby
spectantibus ad faciendum omnimodum commodum suum
sicut sibi melius viderint expedire.   Et Ego et hæredes
mei dictas decem acras terræ cum pertinentijs dictis Monachis contra omnes homines warantizabimus acquietabimus et defendemus imperpetuum.   Et ne Ego vel aliquis
hæredum meorum contra hoc scriptum in posterum venire
possimus eidem sigillum meum apposui.   Hijs Testibus,
R. Priore², R. Archidiacono³, W. Officiali⁴, Willelmo Vice-

---

² Robert son of William de Hampton, Sheriff, or Custos, 1223—29;
he attests No. 75, another charter of Eudo.

³ Robert son of William de Corkeby, as in No. 185.

⁴ John son of William is, probably, de Warthwic, brother of the
above, see on No. 39.

⁵ From the Sheriff, the date of the charter is 1223—29.

187. ¹ Given by Adam son of Robert de Karliol, in No. 185.

² Radulph, Prior of Carlisle, see note 3 on No. 97.

³ Robert de Otterington, Archdeacon of Carlisle, see note 3, No. 137.

⁴ Walter de Ulvesby, Official of Carlisle, see note 5 on No. 56.

comite Karlioli[5], Ricardo de Levington, Petro de Tyllol, Roberto de Castelcairoc, Radulpho de Feritate, Roberto de Hamton, Adam de Hotun, Willelmo filio Rogeri Militibus, Johanne filio Willelmi, Johanne de Aglunby, Henrico Præposito, N. serviente et multis alijs[6].

188. QUIETA CLAMATIO WILLELMI[1] FILIJ WARINI DE SCALEWRA FACTA MONACHIS DE WEDERHAL DE DECEM ACRIS TERRÆ IN ORMESBY.

UNIVERSIS Christi fidelibus ad quorum notitiam hoc presens scriptum pervenerit Henricus filius Warini de Scalewra salutem in Domino. Noverit universitas vestra me et reddidisse remisisse et quietas clamasse de me et hæredibus meis Deo et Ecclesiæ Sanctæ Mariæ Eboraci et Domui de Wederhal et Monachis ibidem Deo servientibus decem acras terræ cum pertinentijs in territorio de Ormesby quæ quidem decem acræ terræ jacent propinquiores alijs decem acris in eodem territorio quas eisdem Monachis reddidi et remisi et per cartam meam de me et hæredibus meis quietas clamavi. Tenendas et Habendas de me et hæredibus meis imperpetuum cum omnibus pertinentijs libertatibus communis et aisiamentis ad Villam de Ormsby spectantibus ad faciendum inde omnimodum commodum suum sicut viderint sibi melius expedire. Et Ego et hæredes mei istas decem acras terræ cum alijs decem acris quas idem Monachi per cartam meam habent de me cum omnibus pertinentijs contra omnes homines eisdem Monachis warantizabimus imperpetuum. Et ne Ego vel aliquis hæredum meorum in posterum contra hoc scriptum venire possimus huic scripto sigillum meum apposui. Hijs Testibus, Willelmo filio Rogeri, Willelmo de Warthwic, Gilberto de Schēpisheued, Elya Sacerdote de

[5] Probably William de Daker, Sheriff of Carlisle, 1236—47.

[6] From the Sheriff the date of the charter lies between 1236 and 1247, from the witnesses probably about 1240—47.

188. [1] This is an error for *Henrici.*

Wederhal, Ricardo et Radulpho Clericis de Wederhal, Adam de Hermesthwayt, Johanne Stelfot, Stephano de Wederhal, Ricardo Mansen[2], Johanne Coquo et alijs[3].

189. CARTA HENRICI FILIJ WARINI DE SCALEWRA FACTA RICARDO MAUNSEL DE TOTA TERRA SUA IN ORMESBY.

OMNIBUS Christi fidelibus ad quos præsens scriptum pervenerit Henricus filius Warini de Scalewra salutem in Domino. Noverit universitas vestra me dedisse et concessisse et præsenti carta mea confirmasse Ricardo Maunsel[1] et hæredibus suis vel suis assignatis totam terram meam quam habui in territorio de Ormesby cum omnibus ædificijs de marisco extra Villam de Karlaton[2] et cum omnibus

[2] Richard Mansen is, probably, the Richard Mansel, or Maunsel, of the next charter.

[3] From the witnesses, such as William son of Roger and John Stelfot, the date is, probably, only a little later than that of the preceding charter.

189. [1] Richard Maunsel is, probably, the same as the Richard Mansel, grantor of No. **77** and No. **190**.

[2] Karlaton, or Carlaton, must be distinguished from Karleton, or Carleton, about 3 miles south-east of Carlisle, and given by Henry I. to Walter his chaplain, afterwards a Canon, and perhaps Prior, of Carlisle (*Testa de Nevill*, p. 379 *b*, and see on Walter, Prior, No. **28**). Karlaton was a parish and manor in the Barony of Gilsland, adjoining on the north-east the parish of Cumwhitton in which this Ormesby was situated. This *mariscus*, or marsh, was probably on the south near the waste now existing. In the Pipe Rolls for 1158 Carlatun appears as being in the hands of Gospatric son of Mapbennoc, who pays one silver marc for it; in 1186 it appears among the escheats of the King, and is accounted for by the Sheriff; while later it is held from King John by Robert de Ros (*Testa de Nevill*, p. 379 *a*). It was one of the manors granted to Alexander King of Scotland by Henry III. (see on Scotby, note 9, No. **14** and on Robert de Ros, note 5, No. **44**). The Church of Karlaton was one of the Churches granted by Robert de Vallibus in the Foundation Charter of the Priory of Lanercost; but there must have been some difficulty, as it is given in *Testa de Nevill* (p. 379 *a*) among the Churches in the gift of the King; and later, after some controversy, it was granted by

alijs aisiamentis dictæ terræ pertinentibus sine aliquo retenemento, Illam scilicet terram quam teneo in puram et
perpetuam Elemosinam de Abbate et Conventu Eboraci
adeo libere et quiete sicut ego unquam tenui liberius et
quietius de dictis Abbate et Conventu. Reddendo inde
annuatim Domui de Wederhal duodecim denarios, scilicet
sex denarios ad Festum Sancti Martini in yeme et sex
denarios ad Pentecosten pro omnibus servicijs secularibus
consuetudinibus et demandis. Ita quod Ego præfatus
Henricus nec aliquis hæredum meorum contra hoc scriptum
meum venire poterimus et ad majorem securitatem præsenti
scripto sigillum meum apposui. Hijs Testibus, Domino
Thoma de Multon[3], Roberto de Castelkairoc, Willelmo de
Wallibus, Willelmo de Warthwic, Johanne Parsona de
Hayton, Ricardo de Salvage, Willelmo de Corkeby, Adam
Armstrang, Radulpho de Ormesby, Ricardo tunc Capellano
de Wederhal et alijs[4].

190. QUIETA CLAMATIO RICARDI MANSEL DE TOTA
TERRA SUA QUÆ VOCATUR MIRLAND IN ORMESBY.

UNIVERSIS Christi fidelibus ad quorum notitiam hoc
præsens scriptum pervenerit Ricardus de Hedon[1] dictus

Edward I. to the Priory of Lanercost when he was in Carlisle on
March 17th, 1307 (see *Bishop Halton's Register*, MS. pp. 56, 116, 140 ;
Register of Lanercost, MS. xii. 4 ; *Patent Rolls*, 35 Edw. I. m. 25 ;
Rymer, *Fœdera*, new ed. i. 1012). After the dissolution the parish
was merged in others, and the site of the Church alone remains.
Built into the farm house near is an interesting sepulchral slab with the
inscription : "Hic jacet Henricus de Newton qui fuit Vicarius de
Carlaton.   Orate pro anima ejus." He was made Vicar in August,
1320, presented by the Convent of Lanercost (*Register of Bp Halton*,
MS. p. 222). Huctred, presbyter of Carlaton, is a witness to No. **184.**

[3] This Thomas de Multon is the second of the name, called
"of Gilsland," he died in 1271 ; see note 4 on No. **47.**

[4] This charter is evidently later than the preceding, but must
be prior to 1271, when Thomas de Multon died.

190. [1] Richard de Hedon is the same as Richard Maunsel of the
preceding charters, and the grantor of No. **77.**

Maunsel salutem in Domino sempiternam. Noverit universitas vestra me reddidisse et relaxasse et omnino pro me et hæredibus meis quietam clamasse imperpetuum Deo et Ecclesiæ Sanctæ Mariæ Eboraci et Monachis ibidem Deo servientibus, et Domui Sanctæ Trinitatis et Sancti Constantini de Wederhal et Monachis Deo ibidem servientibus totam terram illam cum ædificijs suis et suis pertinentijs quæ vocatur Mirland in campo de Ormesby in Villa de Cumquintyngton² sine aliquo retenemento, Quam quidem terram cum ædificijs aliquando tenui de Abbate et Conventu Sanctæ Mariæ Eboraci et Domo Sanctæ Trinitatis et Sancti Constantini de Wederhal, Et quam quidem terram cum suis pertinentijs non tenui de eisdem nisi ad terminum vitæ meæ. Ita videlicet quod nec Ego Ricardus nec hæredes mei nec mei assignati nec aliquis nomine nostro in predicta terra cum suis pertinentijs de cætero aliquid juris vel clamij petere vel vendicare poterimus. In cujus rei Testimonium præsenti scripto sigillum meum apposui. Hijs Testibus, Domino Michaele de Hartecla³ tunc Vicecomite Cumberlandiæ, Thoma de Neuton et Johanne de Terribi tunc Coronatoribus ejusdem Comitatus Cumberlandiæ, Roberto de feritate, Waltero de Mulcastre, Willelmo de Boyvill Militibus, Roberto de Warthwic, Willelmo filio suo, Roberto de Crogelyn, Hugone de Talkan, Ricardo de Brakenthuayt, Johanne de Staffol, Roberto de Kirkeoswalde⁴ Clerico, et alijs⁵.

---

² Cumquintyngton, *hodie* Cumwhitton, lies on the east side of the river Eden, in the Barony of Gilsland, between the parish of Ainstable on the south and Corby, in the parish of Wetherhal, and the parish of Castlecarrock on the north. The place must be carefully distinguished from Cumquintin, *hodie* Cumwhinton, in the parish of Wetherhal, on the west side of the Eden ; see on No. 71 and following charters.

³ Michael de Hartecla, Sheriff of Cumberland 1285—98 ; see note on No. 78.

⁴ Robert de Kirkeoswald attests No. 199, dated 1291.

⁵ The witnesses are many of them the same as in No. 78; the date can only be fixed from the Sheriff, 1285—98.

191. Confirmatio Roberti de Wallibus facta Monachis de Wederhal de omnibus terris sibi datis in Gillesland.

Omnibus Christi fidelibus ad quorum notitiam præsens scriptum pervenerit Robertus de Wallibus[1] salutem. Sciatis me pro salute animarum Patris et Matris meæ et Antecessorum et Successorum meorum concessisse et presenti carta imperpetuum confirmasse Deo et Sancto Constantino de Wederhal et Monachis ibidem Deo servientibus omnia bona quæ Osbertus[2] et Willelmus filius Odardi Domini de Corkeby et cæteri liberi homines mei in Gillesland[3] dederunt eis in Elemosinam tam in terris quam

191. [1] This is Robert de Vallibus, the second Baron of Gillesland, who succeeded in 1164—65 ; see note 4 on No. **28.**

[2] Osbert, elder brother of William son of Odard, see note 1 on No. **35.**

[3] The Barony of Gillesland was the great district on the opposite side of the river Eden to Wetherhal, lying to the east and the far north-east. It included Corkeby. The boundaries of the Barony are set out in the local histories (see Nicolson and Burn, *History* ii. 479 ; *Cumb. Archæol. Trans.* iv. 452). According to Camden the first Lord of Gillesland was William Meschines, brother of Ranulph (see on No. **2**), but Gill son of Bueth held it by force of arms (*Britannia*, ed. Holland, p. 176). Of this he gives no evidence ; but there is no doubt that Gille son of Bueth had the land, and probably gave it the name (see on Robert son of Bueth in No. **107**). Henry II. on recovering the northern counties granted Gillesland to Hubert de Vallibus (*Testa de Nevill*, 379 *a*, and see on Robert de Vallibus in No. **28**. The charter is also given in full in the Illustrative Doc. XXII.). The names of the witnesses to the grant enable us to fix the date pretty closely. R. (Roger de Bishopbridge), Archbishop of York Oct. 1154—1181, R. (Robert de Chesney) Bishop of Lincoln 1147— Jan. 1167—68, H. (Hugh Pudsey), Bishop of Durham Dec. 1153— March 1195. These witnesses give limits from Oct. 1154 to Jan. 1167—68, and Hubert de Vallibus died in 1164. The grant must therefore have been made in 1155—64, and supports the suggestion (see on No. **28**) that Henry II. put Hubert in possession as soon as he got the land from King Malcolm in 1157. Hubert was succeeded by the first Robert, the grantor of this charter. The Barony passed into

in aquis et omnibus alijs locis sicut in eorum cartis plenius continetur. Volo itaque et firmiter præcipio qua-tenus prædicti Monachi de Wederhal fratres mei habeant communem pasturæ imperpetuum in Villa mea de Cro-gelyn[4] ubique cum meis animalibus dominicis et animalibus hominum meorum ad omnimoda animalia sua sine alicujus contradictione vel impedimento. Hijs Testibus, Waltero Priore Karleoli, Roberto Archidiacono[5], Hugone de Ner-burg[6], Johanne Camerario, Osberto de Bocland[7], et multis alijs[8].

192. CONFIRMATIO ROBERTI DE VALLIBUS DE TERRIS, REDDITIBUS, POSSESSIONIBUS ET PASTURIS UT PATET.

OMNIBUS Christi fidelibus ad quorum notitiam hoc præsens scriptum pervenerit Robertus de Vallibus filius Ranulphi[1] salutem in Domino. Noverit Universitas vestra me intuitu Dei et pro salute animæ meæ et Prædecessorum et Successorum meorum concessisse et præsenti carta mea confirmasse Deo et Ecclesiæ Sanctæ Mariæ Eboraci et Monachis Sanctæ Trinitatis et Sancti Constantini de Wederhal omnes terras redditus possessiones pasturas et libertates tam in terris quam in aquis quas dicti Monachi

the family of de Multon by the marriage of Matilda de Vallibus (see on No. **194**), and later to the Dacres and the Howards. There is a good account of the families by Chancellor Ferguson in the *Cumb. Archæol. Trans.* iv. 446 sq., but many of the details call for correction.

[4] Crogelyn, not Croglyn Parva, but the greater manor and parish, see note 7 on No. **14**.

[5] This is the first Robert, Archdeacon of Carlisle, see note 3 on No. **28**.

[6] This should be Neuburg, as in No. **44**.

[7] See on Osbert de Ocland in No. **44**, note 8.

[8] All these witnesses occur in No. **44**, whose probable date is 1165; as Hubert de Vallibus died in 1164, the date of this charter is probably 1165 or shortly after.

192. [1] This is the nephew of the first Robert de Vallibus who grants the preceding charter; see note 13 on No. **38**.

habent ubique in feudo de Gillesland de dono Prædecessorum meorum et de dono aliorum proborum hominum
in feudo prædicto qui eis res prædictas caritative contulerunt sicut in ipsorum cartis præfatis Monachis super
prædictis rebus factis et concessis plenius continetur. Insuper autem præter dimidiam carucatam terræ cum pertinentijs et pasturam trescentis ovibus et proprijs animalibus quam Adam filius Roberti dedit eis in Villa de
Ormesby in Elemosinam sicut in carta ejusdem Adæ[2]
plenius continetur, dedi et concessi prædictis Monachis
de dono meo proprio in puram et perpetuam Elemosinam
unum Mesuagium in Mira quod Garinus de Mora tenuit
et placeam ubi thoraillium[3] prædicti Garini situm est cum
libero introitu et exitu et totum mariscum qui jacet inter
Karu[4] et terram prædictorum Monachorum. Quare volo
et præcipio ut præfati Monachi hoc meum donum et insuper omnes terras redditus et possessiones pasturas et
libertates sicut scriptum est bene et pacifice et honorifice
habeant et teneant imperpetuum. Et Ego et hæredes mei
omnia præscripta contra omnes homines dictis Monachis
warantizabimus et defendemus imperpetuum. In cujus rei
Testimonium præsenti scripto sigillum meum apposui.
Hijs Testibus, Roberto filio Willelmi de Corkeby, Philippo
de Hastinges[5], Willelmo filio Rogeri, Huberto de Val-

----

[2] For the charter, see No. 185.

[3] *Thoraillium*, "species aggeris inter agros ducti," see Ducange
Gloss. s. v., from *torus*, "a heap."

[4] Karu, probably for Karn, *hodie* Cairn, a stream running through
Cumwhitton and part of Carlaton.

[5] According to John Denton, followed by Nicolson and Burn
(*History*, ii. 433), Croglyn was the freehold of Philip de Hastings
in the time of Henry II., and passed by marriage to the Whartons in
the reign of Edward I. This seems to agree with the claim of the
first Robert de Vallibus to be lord of Crogelyn in No. 191. Philip
is witness to charters of Robert de Vallibus, the present grantor,
and his father Ranulph in the *Register of Lanercost* (MS. i. 18, 19,
22, ii. 6); also to the confirmation of the church of Grenesdale by Hugo

libus[6], Alano filio Roaldi de Richemund[7], Roberto de
Leversdale, Petro de Corkeby, Willelmo de Rodes[9], Willelmo Clerico de Wederhal, Umfrido de Wederhal, Waltero
janitore, Odardo Clerico et alijs[9].

de Morvill (MS. ii. 17). He also attests, in the *Chartulary of Whitby*
(ed. Atkinson, i. 38) a charter of Thomas de Hastinges, probably his
brother, confirming the grant of the Church of Crosby Ravensworth ;
this Thomas in 1203 succeeded his father Hugh de Hastings, who had
married Helen daughter and heir of Alan de Alverstain (see note, No.
252). He also attests another charter of Thomas, granting land at
Crosby to the Hospital of S. Leonard at York, which is among the
Levens Hall MSS., see *10th Report, Hist. MSS. Com.* (4) p. 320.

[6] Hubert, the second of the name, was the son of the second
Robert de Vallibus, grantor of this charter, and was father of Matilda
de Vallibus, grantor of No. 194. His wife Matilda, or Maud, afterwards married William Everard (Dugdale, *Baronage*, i. 568).

[7] Alan de Richemund is witness to a charter of Robert de Veteriponte (who died 1228) in the time of Bishop Walter (1223—46) to the
Hospital of S. Peter at York (*Duchetiana* p. 125, from Dodsworth
MSS. vi. fol. 12). The family of Richmond appears to have been
connected with the family of Corkeby. We find Isabella, the daughter
of the witness here, Robert son of William de Corkeby, having
as her first husband Roald son of Alan (see note 5 on No. 47) ; and
according to a MS. of Lord William Howard (quoted by Hutchinson,
Hist. Cumb. i. 171) Thomas de Richmund was her son by Roald,
and another Thomas her grandson. From three deeds which were in
the Milbourne collection, and extracts from which are given at the end
of his copy of J. Denton's MS. on Cumberland (ed. Ferguson, p. 165),
it appears that Richard de Richemound released his right in the
manor of Corkeby to Sir Thomas de Richmund in 1312, and to
Andrew de Harcla, Earl of Carlisle in January, 1322, and that Roald
the son of Thomas released the manor to Andrew de Harcla in
September, 1321. Richard was probably the younger brother of this
Thomas. Compare also the pedigree p. 90.

[8] William de Rodes, or Rodis, quitclaims to this Robert de
Vallibus in the *Register of Lanercost* (MS. vii. 17) certain land in
Brampton, which Robert had granted him, in consideration of a sum
of money, which the said Robert had given him in his very great
need ; this, from the Sheriff, Alan de Caldebec, would be in 1214—15.
He is also witness there to several charters of this same Robert
(MS. ii. 2—5).

193. CONFIRMATIO ROBERTI DE VALLIBUS DE
TERRIS REDDITIBUS ET POSSESSIONIBUS UT PATET[1].

OMNIBUS Sanctæ Matris Ecclesiæ filijs ad quos præsens
scriptum pervenerit Robertus de Vallibus filius Ranulphi
de Vallibus salutem in Domino. Noverit universitas vestra
me intuitu Dei et pro salute animæ meæ et Antecessorum
et Successorum meorum concessisse et confirmasse Deo
et Beatæ Mariæ de Wederhal et Monachis ibidem Deo
servientibus omnes redditus terras et possessiones quas
habent in feodo meo in puram et perpetuam Elemosinam
et liberas a terreno servicio consuetudine et exactione
ad me vel ad hæredes meos pertinentibus, videlicet duas
bovatas terræ cum pertinentijs in Korkeby[2] et octo acras
cum pertinentijs in Denton[3], et unum Mesuagium cum
crofto in Neuby[4], et dimidiam carucatam terræ cum pertinentijs in Ormesby[5], et dimidiam carucatam terræ cum pertinentijs in Neuby[6], et duas bovatas terræ cum pertinentijs
in Talkan[7], et viginti acras terræ cum pertinentijs in
Bordosewald[8]. Præterea concessi et dedi et hac præsenti
carta mea confirmavi in puram et perpetuam Elemosinam
Deo et Beatæ Mariæ et prædictis Monachis de Wederhal
unum Mesuagium in Mira quod Garinus de Mora tenuit

---

[9] The date of this charter will be in the early years of the 13th
century, but after 1206 when this Robert de Vallibus came into
his lands, and from the witnesses probably about 1214.

193. [1] This charter specifies the places wherein lands were
granted by different persons to the Priory, and which owned Robert
de Vallibus as lord.

[2] In Corkeby, granted by Osbert son of Odard in No. **35.**

[3] In Denton, granted by John de Denton in No. **125.**

[4] In Neuby, granted by Anselm de Neuby in No. **141.**

[5] In Ormesby, granted by Adam son of Alan in No. **184.**

[6] In Neuby, granted by Walter de Neuby in No. **142.**

[7] In Talkan, granted by Alan son of William de Raveneswick
in No. **130.**

[8] In Bordosewald, granted by Walter Baynin in No. **127.**

et placeam ubi turaillium⁹ ejusdem Garini situm erat cum libero introitu et exitu et totum mariscum qui jacet inter Karu et terram ipsorum Monachorum. Quare volo et precipio ut ipsi Monachi omnes prædictas terras cum omnibus pertinentijs suis et aisiamentis bene pacifice et libere teneant sicut liberam Elemosinam meam. Et prohibeo ne aliquis Ballivus meus serviens vel minister eis injuriam gravamen vel molestiam super præfatis terris et Tenementis in aliquo inferre presumat. In cujus rei Testimonium præsenti scripto sigillum meum apposui. Hijs Testibus, Roberto filio Willelmi de Korkeby, Philippo de Hastinges, Willelmo filio Rogeri, Huberto de Vallibus, Rollando de Vallibus, Alano filio Roaldi de Richemund, Roberto de Leversdale, Waltero de Wyndesur, Roberto de Denton et Johanne fratre ejus, Petro de Korkeby, Willelmo de Rodes, Waltero de Wederhal, Umfrido de Wederhal, Odardo Clerico et alijs¹⁰.

194. CARTA MATILDIS DE VALLIBUS.

OMNIBUS Christi fidelibus hoc scriptum visuris vel audituris Matildis de Vallibus¹ Domina de Gillesland

---

⁹ *Turaillium*, for *thoraillium*, see note 3 on No. **192**.

¹⁰ The date must be very nearly the same as that of the preceding charter.

194. ¹ Matilda de Vallibus was, as she calls herself in two of her charters, "daughter of Hubert de Vallibus, Lady and heir of Gillesland, formerly wife of Thomas de Muleton" (*Regist. Lanercost*, MS. x. 5, 7). This Hubert was the second of the name, see note 6 on No. **192**. Matilda, his only child, married Thomas de Muleton, the second of the name, see note 4 on No. **47**. He died in 1271, the date of this charter ; but Matilda continued to rule and hold Gillesland independent of her son Thomas, who had seisin of the lands which his father had in his own right. She granted several charters in her widowhood to the Priory of Lanercost, calling herself sometimes de Multon, but generally de Vallibus ; some are dated, as in 1276, at Kircoswald (*Regist. Lanercost*, MS. x. 11) in 1285 (x. 18), in 1287 (xi. 8), in 1292 (xi. 6). In the writ of summons for military service issued April 16th,

salutem in Domino sempiternam. Noverit universitas vestra me in libera viduitate et potestate mea et pro salute animæ Domini mei Thomæ de Multon necnon et pro salute animarum Antecessorum et Successorum meorum concessisse et præsenti scripto meo confirmasse Deo et Ecclesiæ Mariæ Eboraci et Monachis Sanctæ Trinitatis de Wederhal omnes terras, redditus, et possessiones quas prædicti Monachi habuerunt die confectionis hujus scripti de dono et concessione Antecessorum meorum vel de dono hominum meorum de feodo meo de Gillesland. Tenendas et habendas predictis Ecclesiæ et Monachis ibidem Deo servientibus in liberam puram et perpetuam Elemosinam cum omnibus libertatibus et aisiamentis dictis terræ et Tenementis pertinentibus sicut in cartis et concessionibus Antecessorum meorum vel in cartis hominum meorum de feodo meo de Gillesland quas prædicti Monachi inde habent plenius et melius continetur. Et ut hæc mea concessio et confirmatio pro me et hæredibus meis perpetuum robur optineat firmitatis præsenti scripto sigillum meum apposui. Hijs Testibus, Domino Willelmo de Kirketon[2], Galfrido de Tyllol[3], Roberto de Tyllol tunc Senescallo de Gillesland, Roberto de Warthwic, Ricardo de Castelkairoc, Johanne de Denton, Willelmo de Leverisdal,

19 Edward I., 1291, both Thomas de Multon Senior and Junior are summoned, and Matilda de Multon Domina de Gillesland (F. Palgrave, *Parliamentary Writs*, i. 256). According to the *Chronicon de Lanercost* (ed. Stevenson, p. 159) she died on S. Dunstan's Day, May 19th, 1295; but according to the *Inquisitiones post mort.* (21 Edward I. No. 25) she was dead in 1293, "Thomas son of Thomas, above 30 years of age, being her heir."

[2] William de Kirketon, Dominus de Cumreu, granted a charter for the rent of 12*d.* from land in the vill of Talkan to the Priory of Lanercost (*Regist. Lanercost*, MS. x. 2) and witnessed two charters of Matilda de Vallibus (MS. ix. 16; x. 7). He also granted another charter, where Christiana his wife is mentioned (xiii. 7).

[3] Galfrid de Tyllol was the father of Robert de Tyllol, on whom see note 9, No. **47**, and the son of Peter de Tyllol. He died in 1295.

Ranulpho de Vallibus[4], Willelmo de Mora, Rogero de Levington[5], Thoma de Bellocampo, Roberto de Croglyn, Thoma de Blatern[6] et alijs. Hæc concessio et confirmatio factæ fuerunt die Apostolorum Petri et Pauli, Anno Gratiæ Millesimo Ducentesimo Septuagesimo primo[7].

195. CARTA ALEXANDRI DE CREUEQUER DE KIRK-ANDRES BOSCO TERRIS ET MOLENDINO IN CULGAIT.

NOTUM sit omnibus legentibus vel audientibus litteras has quod Ego Alexander de Creuequer[1] concessi et dedi Monachis de Wederhal ibidem Deo servientibus Kirkan-

---

[4] This is not Ranulph brother of the first Robert, and father of the second Robert de Vallibus; but, probably, the son of Alexander de Vallibus of Treverman; he was witness in 1273 to a charter of John de Denton with William de Mora and William de Leversdal (*Regist. Lanercost*, MS. ix. 15); and he granted several charters to the Priory of Lanercost shortly before this time (MS. ix. 18, 19, 20; x. 1) which are attested by several of these witnesses.

[5] It does not appear what relation this Roger de Levington is to others of the name in this *Register*. He was one of the jurors in an Inquisition held in 1246 on the lands of Peter de Tilliol, and again in 1272 on the lands of Helewysa widow of Eustace de Balliol (*Inquis. p. m.* 31 Hen. III. No. 46, and 56 Hen. III. No. 35). He is witness to a Convention in 1255 between the Priory of Lanercost and Thomas de Muleton and Matilda his wife, and grants a charter, where his name appears in the form Roger. fil. Rogeri de Levington (*Regist. Lanercost*, MS. ix. 12; iv. 24).

[6] Thomas de Blaterne attests three charters in the *Register of Lanercost*, with several of the witnesses here (MS. x. 15; xiii. 20, 21).

[7] The date is the day of the Apostles Peter and Paul, June 29th, 1271.

195. [1] Alexander de Crevequer married Amabil, or Mabilia, one of the two daughters of Adam son of Suan, the lord of the district in which Culgaith and Kirkandreas were, on the east of the river Eden (see on Adam in note 4 on No. 14). Little seems to be known of the family at this period; for some of the later members, see Dugdale, *Baronage*, i. 591. His wife Amabil afterwards married Galfrid de Nevill; and they confirmed the grants of Adam son of Suan to the Priory of Monk Bretton in Yorkshire, see the charter in Dugdale *Monasticon*, v. p. 138.

dreas² cum bosco usque ad locum qui dicitur Peyekyttoc
cum terris et cum omnibus libertatibus eidem loco pertinentibus in perpetuam Elemosinam. Insuper et molendinum meum de Culgait illis pariter dedi et concessi imperpetuum, Scilicet illam medietatem quæ ad me pertinet
in liberam Elemosinam sine omni terreno servicio cum
tota sequela pertinente. Et volo quod dicti Monachi habeant cum prædicto loco liberam communam ubique in
campo et bosco de Culgait³ sine aliquo retenemento, salvo
omnino eisdem prædicto bosco suo de Kirkandreas in

² From Nos. 14, 196, we see Kirkandreas included the Hermitage
and lands adjacent with a wood. This was conveyed to Michael de
Hartcla by Simon (de Warwicke) Abbot of S. Mary's at York for a
rent of 40s. to the monks of Wederhal (*Inquis. ad quod dam.* 17
Edw. III. No. 49, Record Com. p. 313). It was probably escheated to
the King on the arrest of his brother Andrew de Hartcla; for it was
reconfirmed to the Priory by Edward III. in 1369 (*Close Rolls*,
43 Edw. III. m. 33). The last lease of Kirkandreas on the part of the
Priory was made October 20th, 1538 to Christopher Crakenthorpe of
Nubigging, and bears the name of William (Thornton) Abbot of
S. Mary's, formerly Prior of Wetherhal (see MS. Registers of Dean
and Chapter of Carlisle, i. p. 20). In the survey at the time of the
Surrender, "the Herbage or Pannage of the wood of Kyrkander" was
valued at £1. 6s. 8d. In the Parliamentary Survey of the Manor
of Little Salkeld, made February 1649, the Mill and premises, called
Millridge Mille, were valued at £6. 13s. 4d. Bishop Nicolson (MSS.
vol. ii. p. 135) writes of S. Andrew's Hermitage: "This is now a small
piece of woody ground or copses at the bottom of Culgaith-Parks in
yᵉ Parish of Kirkland in lease under the Dean and Chapter of Carlisle
to Richard Crackenthorp of Newbiggin Esqʳᵉ."

³ Culgaith, or Culgarth, was a manor in the parish of Kirkland,
abutting on the county of Westmoreland, and part of the district
granted to Adam son of Suan. It was now, as we see in these
charters, held by his two daughters and their husbands. Culgaith in
early times was a distinct Chapelry (of All Saints) founded by the
predecessors of Christopher Moresby, as appears from a Bull of Pope
Calixtus III. dated May 5th, 1456, and copied by Bishop Nicolson
(MSS. vol. ii. p. 350, see also Nicolson and Burn, *History* ii. 446), who
says that in his time the original was in the hands of some of the
inhabitants.

usibus proprijs. Hanc autem Elemosinam feci prædictis
Monachis pro animabus Patris et Matris meæ et pro
liberis meis et pro animabus Antecessorum meorum.
Hijs Testibus, Adam de Mortebeg̃[4], Warino[5], Symone
de Creuequer, Jacobo Presbytero, Rogero de Plancha,
Warino de Scakargile, Roberto de Thoresby[6], Raynero
filio Ulfridi, Willelmo Walegrim, Gamello Houstino, Symone Boivylle[7], Herveio Nigro[8], Alexandro de Sancto
Andrea[9].

[4] This should be Montebeg̃, the abbreviated form of Montebegon.
Adam de Montebegon married Matilda, the other daughter of Adam
son of Suan. Adam de Munbegun appears in the Pipe Rolls in 1163
as paying 1 marc. He, together with his wife Matilda, confirmed the
grants of Adam son of Suan to the Priory of Monk Bretton in
Yorkshire (Dugdale, *Monast.* v. p. 138). A similar charter was
given by John Malherbe (not Manseil, as in No. **197**) and his wife
Matilda, the widow of Adam de Montbegon. Roger de Montbegon,
the son of Adam, also made a grant to that Priory (see on Adam son
of Suan, No. **14**). The name appears as Adam de Mundegame and
de Mondeg̃ in No. **233**, and other variations are found. He makes a
similar grant to the present in No. **233**, and probably at the same
time.

[5] After Warin, *presbytero*, as in No. **233**, is evidently omitted.
This can hardly be the same as Warin, Presbyter, in No. **103**; but is
probably identical with Warin de Kyrkeland who, with Adam son of
Suan, attests the charter of Bishop Athelwold (No. **15**). Kyrkeland
was the parish in which the property was situated. In the Pipe Rolls
for 1163 we find "Warin presbiter de Chirchelanda" making a
payment of 7 marcs.

[6] Robert de Thoresby attests No. **36**, between 1154—75, probably
1160—70.

[7] Simon de Boivylle, or Boivilla, was probably one of the family of
de Boyvill, who held the Barony of Levington, and some connection
with the preceding witness, Robert de Thoresby; see note 3 on No. **48**,
and under William de Bovilla in No. **78**.

[8] Herveus Niger attests a charter of Robert son of Colman before
1186, see note 6 on No. **252**.

[9] The date of the charter must be after the death of Adam son of
Suan, who was alive in 1159. We have Adam de Mortebeg̃ and
Robert de Thoresby between 1160—70, and this is about the date.

196. CARTA ADÆ FILIJ SUANI DE QUODAM HERMITORIO DICTO KIRKANDREAS.

ADAM filius Suani[1] omnibus hominibus suis et amicis Francis et Anglis et omnibus Christianis præsentibus et futuris salutem. Notum sit vobis me dedisse et concessisse Deo et Abbachiæ Sanctæ Mariæ Eboraci et Monachis Sanctæ Trinitatis et Sancti Constantini de Wederhal Heremitorium quod vocatur Kirkandreas cum terris eidem loco adjacentibus et cum bosco usque ad locum qui vocatur Pede[2] in liberam Elemosinam et quod Sanctus locus ille habeat liberam communam ubique in territorio de Culgait infra villam et extra. Do autem insuper eisdem Monachis molendinum meum de Culgait cum tota sequela in puram et perpetuam Elemosinam pro anima Patris mei et Matris meæ. Hanc autem Donationem et Elemosinam Ego A. et hæredes mei contra omnes gentes warantizabimus prædictis Monachis imperpetuum. Hijs Testibus, Roberto filio Troite, Suano Presbytero, Henrico fratre meo[3], Willelmo filio Godward, Uctredo filio Ravenchel, Normanno Obside, Augustino filio David, Reynero Clerico[4].

197. CARTA JOHANNIS MANSEIL FACTA MONACHIS DE WEDERHAL DE MEDIETATE MOLENDINI DE CULGAIT.

NOTUM sit omnibus audientibus vel legentibus litteras has quod Ego Johannes Manseil[1] cum consilio et assensu

196. [1] For Adam son of Suan, see note 4 on No. **14**.

[2] Pede is called Peyekyttoc in No. **195**, and Prestbancke in the Close Rolls ; see note 2 on No. **195**.

[3] Henry son of Suan was witness to the grant of Earl David to Holm Cultram in 1150 and granted a charter to the Abbey of Rievaulx (*Chart. Rievaulx*, p. 64, ed. Atkinson).

[4] The date of this charter will be before 1158 when Robert son of Troite was first sheriff, and before 1156 when Bp Athelwold died, who confirmed this grant (see No. **15**) and before 1147, prior to which David I. confirmed it (see No. **198**).

197. [1] There would seem to be some mistake here in the copying

Matildis uxoris meæ concessi et dedi totam medietatem
molendini de Culgait Deo et Abbachiæ Sanctæ Mariæ
Eboraci et Monachis ibidem Deo servientibus in puram
et perpetuam Elemosinam ut permaneat ad locum Sancti
Andreæ quem Adam filius Suani prius dederat præfatæ
Abbachiæ cum prædicto molendino et eandem donationem
quam ipse fecit tam de illo loco quam de molendino et
de terris præfato loco adjacentibus et de nemore quod
infra terrarum illarum terminos continetur Ego concedo
et hujus cartæ meæ munimine confirmo. Et ut locus ille
communem pasturam habeat sicut semper hactenus habuit
cum hominibus de Culgait. Testibus Normanno Clerico
de Mellinges², Johanne filio Essuf, Waltero Flandrensi,
Roberto le Swyni, Willelmo de Agnellis³, Roberto de
Uthexol, Henrico de Rokesby, Thoma de Bacon, Willelmo
Blanchard, Eustachio filio Johannis⁴, cum ceteris quam-
pluribus⁵.

198. CONFIRMATIO DAVID REGIS SCOTORUM SUPER DONATIONE A. FILIJ SUANI.

DAVID Rex Scotorum¹ Baronibus Vicecomitibus et

of the name. Manseil occurs frequently in this *Register*; but John
Malherbe was the second husband of Matilda, daughter of Adam son
of Suan (see note 4 on No. 195); as such he, with his wife, confirms
the grants of Adam to the Priory of Monk Bretton (Dugdale,
Monasticon, v. p. 138); they also confirmed the grant made by Henry
son of Suan to the Abbey of Rievaulx (*Chart. Rievaulx*, ed. Atkinson,
p. 62, see also p. 126).

² Malling in Lancashire, in the then Diocese of York.

³ William de Agnellis is witness to the charter in the *Chart.
of Rievaulx* mentioned above.

⁴ If this is the well-known Eustace son of John (see note 19 on
No. 5), he is believed to have died in 1157.

⁵ The date of the charter must be somewhat later than the
preceding, and after the death of the first husband, Adam de
Montbegon.

198. ¹ David I. was King of Scots from April 27th, 1124 to his
death on May 24th, 1153. As Earl David he granted the charter

omnibus probis hominibus suis totius Cumberlandiæ et Westmerlandiæ Francis et Anglis Salutem. Sciatis me concessisse et carta mea confirmasse terram et locum quam Adam filius Suani donavit in perpetuam Elemosinam Deo et Beatæ Mariæ de Eboraco et Monachis fratribus nostris ejusdem loci et de Wederhal. Et volo et firmiter præcipio quod Fratres et Ministri et omnia sua sint in mea firma pace et manutenentia qui in prædicto loco et terra habitaverint. Et prohibeo super meam plenariam defensionem quod nullus eis nec alicui eorum quicquam forisfaciat nec facere promittat. Testibus, Episcopo Johanne[2] et Jordano Cancellario, et Herberto Camerario apud Karliolum[3].

No. 106. By his accession, he united the northern and southern districts into one kingdom of Scotland (see Skene, *Celtic Scotland*, i. 459). In 1136 he invaded England, nominally on behalf of his niece the Empress Matilda, against Stephen, and received Carlisle and part of the district from that King. In 1138 the Scots again ravaged the northern counties. David was defeated in August at the Battle of the Standard, but Cumberland and other portions of the north were allowed to remain with him (see *Henry of Huntingdon*, Book viii.; John of Hexham, *Chron.* and Richard of Hexham, *Gesta Steph. in ann.* 1138, with the good notes of J. Raine, *Memorials of Hexham*, i. 77 seq. p. 113 seq., and *Chron. de Mailros in ann.* 1136 seq.). On September 26—29, 1138 David was at Carlisle, and a Provincial Council was held under Alberic, the Papal Legate, Bishop of Ostia, at which Bishop Athelwold was present (see the reff. given above). David founded several bishoprics and monasteries, among the latter Kelso, Melrose (refounded) and Jedburgh (see Skene, *Celtic Scotland*, ii. 376 seq.; Haddan and Stubbs, *Eccles. Doc.* vol. ii. Pt. i.). He died in 1153 at Carlisle (John of Hexham *in ann.* 1153).

[2] This was John, Bishop of Glasgow. He was consecrated by Pope Paschal II. about 1117, and was the strong opponent of the jurisdiction over Scotland of Archbishop Thurstin and the See of York. He appears to have held out, though enjoined to yield by successive Popes (see Haddan and Stubbs, *Eccles. Doc.* ii. 16 seq.). At the Council of 1138, referred to above, he was ordered to return to his See from the Abbey of Tiron, where he had retired in 1133. He died in 1147 (John of Hexham, *Chron. in ann.*; *Chron. de Mailros in*

199. CARTA HUGONIS DE TEMPILSOUREBY DE DUCTU AQUÆ IN CULTURA DE SANDWATH.

OMNIBUS Christi fidelibus presens scriptum visuris vel audituris Hugo de Tempilsoureby filius Adæ salutem in Deo sempiternam. Noveritis me dedisse concessisse et hac presenti carta mea confirmasse Abbati et Conventui Beatæ Mariæ Eboraci Cellæ de Wederhal Priori et Monachis ibidem Deo servientibus in puram et perpetuam Elemosinam pro me et hæredibus meis seu Assignatis meis quibuscunque aquæ ductum per medium culturæ meæ de Sandwath ad molendinum eorum de Culgayth dictæ Cellæ de Wederhal pertinens, Videlicet a capite cursus aquæ veteris vel ubi dimisso antiquo alveo aqua incepit fluere super terram meam de Sandwath prædictam cum omnibus aisiamentis profectibus et utilitatibus cursus aquæ prædictæ seu ductus per medium ut prædictum est culturæ meæ prænominatæ ad molendinum supradictum convenientibus et dictum stagnum tangentibus sine contradictione inquietatione vel perturbatione mei seu hæredum meorum aut assignatorum meorum ubicunque et quandocunque sibi et successoribus suis utilius et melius viderint expedire. Et Ego prædictus Hugo et hæredes mei seu mei assignati ductum Aquæ prædictum ut prædictum est dictis Abbati et Conventui Priori et Monachis Cellæ prædictæ de Wederhal contra omnes homines et fœminas warantizabimus acquietabimus et defendemus imperpetuum. In cujus rei Testimonium presenti scripto sigillum meum

ann., ed. Gale and Fulman, p. 167) having been the tutor of King David and his life-long friend.

³ The date of this charter must be before 1147, when Bishop John died. Bishop John was at Tiron from 1133 to 1138 (see the note above) and William Cumin was Chancellor, not Jordan, in 1124 and 1136 (Haddan and Stubbs, ii. 22, 28); from which we gather that, as the charter is dated at Carlisle, it must have been granted during one of the many times David held his court there after the first time in 1136. The date will therefore lie between 1138 and 1147.

apposui. Hijs Testibus, Dominis Michael de Hartcla tunc Vicecomite Cumberlandiæ, Thoma de Derwenwater[1], Willelmo de Strikeland[2], Roberto le Engleys[3] Militibus, Gilberto de Brunnolvesheued tunc Vicecomite Westmerlandiæ[4], Domino Waltero tunc Rectore de Neubiggin[5],

199. [1] Thomas de Derwentwater, knight, appears frequently as one of the jury in the Assize trials at Appleby in 1292 (see *Placita de quo War.*, Record Com., p. 123 *b et. al.*) and was himself called upon to shew *quo waranto* he held a market in his manor of Keswyk in Derwentfelles without license of the King. He attests the charter No. 203 dated 1292, and was member of Parliament for Westmoreland in 1297. He died in 1302—3 and was succeeded by his son John (*Inquis. post mort.* 31 Edw. I. No. 15).

[2] For William de Strikeland, or Stirkeland, see Nos. **201, 203.**

[3] Robert le Engleys (afterwards English), knight, was member of a family which long held lands in Little Askeby, or Asby, near Appleby. He was one of the inquisitors concerning the lands of Helewysa, widow of Eustace de Bayllol, in November 1272 (*Inquis. post mort.* 56 Hen. III. No. 35). He was one of the jurors, with some of these witnesses, at Appleby in 1292 (*Placita de quo War.*, Record Com., pp. 227, 790); and he was member of Parliament for the shire of Westmoreland in 1308 and 1310—12.

[4] Gilbert de Brunnolvesheued, or in more modern form Burneshead, belonged to Burneshead (*hodie* Burneside) in the parish of Kendal. He was custos, or deputy sheriff, for Westmoreland in 1290 and 1291. The sheriffdom of that county was hereditary in the family of de Veteriponte; after the death of Robert de Veteriponte, his daughters and heirs, Isabella and Idonea, had some dispute about the power of appointment of a deputy sheriff, and this Gilbert was in 1289 presented before the Barons of the Exchequer by Isabella de Clifford, see the extracts in Machel's MSS. vol. iv. p. 275 seq., also Nicolson and Burn, *History*, i. 273. Gilbert and his father Roger, with William de Stirkeland, attest a deed of Margaret de Ros in 1276 (see *Duchetiana*, by Sir G. Duckett, p. 274 from Dodsworth MSS. 90, fol. 146).

[5] Neubiggin, or Newbigging, one of several places of the same name in these counties, is a parish in Westmoreland, on the east of the river Eden, and divided on the north from the county of Cumberland and the parish of Kirkland by a small stream running down from Crossfell to the Eden. This Walter, Rector, or as he is there called, parson of Newebigginge Church, appears in the Coram Rege Rolls in 1258—59, on an

Hugone de Louther[6], Adam de Ulvesby, Adam de Derwenwater, Roberto de Neubiggin[7], Roberto de Kyrcos-
wald Clerico et alijs.   Datum Anno Domini MCCXCI⁰.

200. LITERA EPISCOPI KARLIOLENSIS DE SENTENTIA
EXCOMMUNICATIONIS FERENDA IN OMNES DIRUENTES
AQUAM, ETC.

VENERABILI Patri Domino Roberto Karliolensi Episcopo[1] vel suo Commissario sui in omnibus presbyteri parochiales de Kyrkeland, de Neubiggin et de Kyrkbithore
salutem in Domino cum Obedientia Reverentia et Honore.

action brought against him and Walrand de Soureby by Robert de
Veteripont, because they entered his park of Whynefel and there took
stags and bucks without his leave (*Calend. Doc. Scot.* ed. Bain, i. 420).

[6] Hugh de Louther was a person of importance in the reigns of
Edward I. and Edward II.; he was sheriff of Edinburgh about this
time, a justice itinerant in 1301 and 1307, and a knight of the shire of
Westmoreland in 1300 and 1305. The manor of Newton Regny was
granted to him by Robert Burnel, Bishop of Bath and Wells 1275—92,
and confirmed by Edward I.; the terms under which it was held under
the King are given in *Placita de quo War.*, Record Com., p. 115 *b*. From
him the present family of Lowther is descended, he having married a
daughter of Peter de Tylliol. He assisted in taking Andrew de Harcla
in 1323 and was rewarded by Edward II. (*Chronicon de Lanercost*, ed.
Stevenson, pp. 250, 251). There is more about him in Nicolson
and Burn (*History*, i. 429) taken from the Machel MSS.

[7] Robert de Neubiggin was one of the family who held the
manor of Newbiggin (see note 5 above); it was afterwards merged
in the family of Crakenthorp, the present holders (see on No. 207).
This Robert, according to Machel, married Agnes, a daughter of
Wackerfield. In a grant of his son Laurence to the Abbey of Holm
Cultram (Dugdale, *Monasticon*, v. 614) he is called "seneschal of
Neubigging."

200. [1] Bishop Robert Chause, 1258—78, see note 1 on No. **34**.
These letters of excommunication may have been procured in consequence of the failure of an action brought by the Abbot of S. Mary's
at York against Michael de Harcla and others (an "assize of novel
disseisin") touching a fosse destroyed in Culgethe in 1273 (see *Patent
Rolls*, 1 Edw. I. m. 11).

Noverit Paternitas vestra nos mandatum in hæc verba recepisse : Robertus miseratione Divina Karliolensis Ecclesiæ Minister humilis dilectis in Christo filijs de Kirkeland[2] de Neubyggin et de Kirkebithore[3] Ecclesiarum Presbyteris Parochialibus Salutem Gratiam et Benedictionem. Nonnulli iniquitatum filij sicut intelleximus accedentes ad molendinum de Culgayth et aquam per quam idem molendinum molere consuevit pura et perpetua Elemosina Domini Abbatis Sanctæ Mariæ Eboraci et Monachorum de Wederhal parietes ejusdem molendini et rotas et stagnum quoddam eorundem Monachorum factum ad conservationem dictæ aquæ temere diruerunt et quo voluerunt contra justitiam asportaverunt in animarum suarum periculum plorum et præjudicium dictorum Monachorum non modicum et gravamen ob quod delictum Excommunicationis sententiam latam per constitutionem[4] Domini Legati nuper

[2] Kirkeland is the most southern of the parishes of Cumberland on the east side of the Eden, in it Culgayth was situated, see on No. 195. The Church had long belonged to the Bishop of Carlisle, and was granted by Bishop Marmaduke Lumley to the Priory of Carlisle in the reign of Henry VI. between 1431—40 (*Inquis. ad quod dam.*, Record Com., p. 379), but as early as 1294 it paid to the Priory an annual pension of 20s. (*Bishop Halton's Register*, MS. p. 5).

[3] Kirkbythore is a large parish in Westmoreland, on the east of the river Eden and adjoining Newbiggin, mentioned above. The Church is about 5 miles from Appleby. Here was a well known Roman camp on the great Maiden Way, though the Roman name is uncertain. The present name is no doubt connected with Thor, the Norse deity, like such other places as Thursby. The Lord of the manor of Kyrkbithore towards the end of the 12th century (1179) was Waldiev, who made numerous grants to the Abbey of Holm Cultram (*Register*, MS. p. 126 seq. and Machel MSS. v. 471—479, where the witnesses are given) from which we learn that he was the son of Gamell the son of Whelp, and had a son Adam de Kyrkebythore (see note 8 on No. 117). This Adam sold the advowson of the rectory to Robert de Veteriponte; the purchase deed was at Appleby Castle, and is given in full in the Machel MSS. v. 509, with the witnesses and a copy of the seal attached.

[4] This would refer to the Constitutions of the Papal Legate,

in Anglia existentis in malefactores hujusmodi incurrerunt.
Hinc est quod vobis mandamus firmiter injungentes
quatinus ad Ecclesiam de Kirkeland per litteras accedentes ibidem tribus diebus festivis moveatis in genere
et efficaciter inducatis omnes dirutores et asportatores prædictos et alios quoscunque qui dampna aliqua præfatis
Monachis in dicto molendino vel aqua intulerint quominus
idem molendinum molere possit prout consuevit eorumque
auctores et fautores ut Domino Priori de Wederhal qui
quoad hoc pro prædicto Abbate est in partibus istis et
Monachis de Wederhal infra quindecim dies a dato præsentium de prædictis commissis satisfaciant competenter quod
si facere contempserint aut non fecerint ex tunc eosdem
dirutores asportatores dampna alia prædicta inferentes
auctores et fautores eorum in dictam sententiam Excommunicationis denuntietis singulis diebus Dominicis et festivis in genere sollempniter et pupplice incidisse. Ad hæc
quia dicti Prior et Monachi præfatum molendinum ni-
tuntur reficere et aquam purgare ac timeant sibi impedimentum in futurum per aliquos latenter in prædictis
quominus ea compleant ut deberent Vobis mandamus ut
prius quatenus in dicta Ecclesia vice et autoritate nostra
pupplice inhibeatis omnibus et singulis sub pœna Excommunicationis in eos ferendæ si impedimentum aliquod
præstiterint ne impedimentum aliquod præstent nec præstare
volentibus consentiant. Et si qui non obstante prohibitione
nostra impedimentum aliquod præstiterint in præmissis
quominus opus prædictum effectui debito mancipetur eosdem impedientes et eisdem consentientes auctoritate nostra
Excommunicationis vinculo generaliter innodetis. Inqui-
rentes nihilominus præfatorum dirutorum asportatorum et
alia dampna prædicta inferentium auctorum fautorum im-
pedientium et eis consentientium et cum ea inveneritis,
Citetis eos peremptorie quod compareant coram Nobis

Cardinal Othobon, which were promulgated at the Legatine Council
held in London in May, 1268.

vel Commissarijs nostris in Crastino Sancti Marci Evangelistæ in Karliolo Ecclesia Cathedrali Priori et Monachis
super præfatis commissis responsuri, et . . . .
suadebit. Et quid de præmissis feceritis Nobis vel Commissarijs nostris per litteras vestras patentes harum seriem
continentes ad dictos crastinum et locum fideliter intimetis.
Datum apud Rosam[5] XVI° Kal. Aprilis Anno Domini

---

[5] Rosa, or La Rose, later Rose Castle, about 7 miles south of
Carlisle, has been a residence of the Bishops of Carlisle since the 13th
century. Various derivations have been given of the name; the
simplest and most probable is the name of the flower, the rose being
an emblem of the Blessed Virgin Mary, to whom the Cathedral
Church of Carlisle was at first dedicated. It was usually stated in the
local notices of the Castle that the first mention of Rose was in connection with the writs issued in 1300 by Edward I., and dated "*Apud la
Rose, xxvi. die Septembris*" (see *Parliamentary Writs*, ed. Palgrave,
i. 90), and consequently that it was built by Bishop Halton (Hutchinson, *Cumberland*, ii. 433; *Cumberland Archæol. Trans.*, ii. 156, vi. 14);
but I pointed out some years ago that there are much earlier
references to the place. There is in the *Register of Lanercost*
(MS. ix. 14) a deed of concession of the Church of Laysingby to
which this Bishop Robert Chause is a party and which is dated *Apud
Rosam* 6to *Kal. Maii*, 1272; another deed, of the same Bishop in the
same *Register* (x. 8) is dated *Apud Rosam* 10° *Kal. Novem.* 1275; and
we have the present charter in April, 1274. But there is a still earlier
notice. A concession of Thomas Vipont, Bishop of Carlisle, to Alan
de Berwise to build a private chapel on his property in Berwise is
dated "Apud la Rose vii° Kalend. marcii Pontificatus nostri anno
primo," i.e. 1256. The deed is given in full in the Machel MSS.
v. 255 from the original in the possession of the family of Crakenthorp. We thus get within 10 years of Bishop Walter Malclerk, who
resigned in June, 1246 and to whom the manor was granted in 1230.
It seems pretty certain that the manor house, or one built by Bishop
Walter, was at once made an episcopal residence. On the Bishop's
residence at Lynstock see No. 239. In the 14th century, references to
Manerium nostrum de Rosa are frequent; and later we have the form
"The Rose" (1571). Rose was in the parish and manor of Dalston;
the advowson of the Church was granted with the manor of Dalston
by Henry III., in 1230, to Bishop Walter Malclerk (*Assize Rolls for
Cumberland*, 1278; *Placita de quo War.*, Record Com., p. 112 *a*; the

M.CC.LXXIV°. Quod quidem Mandatum vestrum in omnibus et per omnia secuti sumus Ita quod Willelmus de Lectoñ dicebat ipsum et Thomam de Starklay stagnum fregisse, qui Willelmus citatus fuit ad dictos crastinum et locum quod compareant coram vobis. Cum enim pro ammonitione nostra satisfacere non curant et post inhibitionem vestram dictum stagnum factum fuit per Procuratorem Prioris, venit quidam dirutor de Soureby[6] nomine Loure et quandam partem dicti Stagni fregit per consensum totius Villetæ de Soureby pro qua Villeta citatus est Walterus [Willelmus] prænominatus, Adam filius Roberti, Adam faber, Robertus de Clifburn qui sunt omnes de Soureby quod compareant coram vobis ut prius. In cujus rei Testimonium Litteras nostras vobis transmittimus patentes signis nostris signatas. Datum apud Kirke-

grant is given, but no reference, in Nicolson and Burn, *History*, ii. 541). There is no real authority for the statement that Rose was first built by Bishop Halton. Architects put the oldest remains in the 13th century, and it is more probable that one of the Bishops before 1292 did the work. Rose was crenellated under license to Bishop John de Kirkby in the 10th year of Edward III. (1336).

[6] The manor of Soureby, called Temple Soureby, even in 1291, was in the north-west of the parish of Kirkbythore, and adjacent to Neubiggin and to Culgayth in Kirkland here mentioned. The manor was held by the Knights Templars until their suppression by Papal Bull, May 2nd, 1312, and hence it claimed certain privileges to a late date. It was, like most of their possessions, transferred in 1320 to the Knights of S. John of Jerusalem, or Knights Hospitallers, with whom it remained until the Dissolution under Henry VIII. ; see the account of the Knights in Dugdale, *Monasticon*, vi. 786, 815 and the deed of transference p. 849. The amount of their possessions may be gathered from the list of 31 other places where they held property in Cumberland and Westmoreland, given in *Placita de quo War.*, Record Com., pp. 117 *b*, 792 *b*, see also pp. 786 *b*, 787 *b*. In the *Register of Bishop Kirkby* (MS. p. 382) under date 1338, there is a reference to a curious award made by Bishop Ralph de Irton, 1280—92, that the inhabitants of Temple Soureby were not to be called upon to aid in repairing the Church of Kirkbythore, unless the nave had to be enlarged, when they were to pay one-third of the expense.

land die Sancti Marci Evangelistæ Anno Domino Millesimo Ducentesimo Septuagesimo Quinto[7].

201. SCRIPTUM WALTERI DE STYRKELAND DE INDEMPNITATE MATRICIS ECCLESIÆ DE MORLUND PRO CANTARIA HABENDA IN CAPELLA SUA.

OMNIBUS Christi fidelibus ad quorum notitiam præsens
scriptum pervenerit Walterus de Styrkeland[1] Miles æternam
in Domino salutem. Noveritis me promisisse pro me et
hæredibus meis indempnitatem Matricis Ecclesiæ de More-
lund in omnibus pro Cantaria[2] habenda in Capella mea

---

[7] The date is S. Mark's Day, April 25th, 1275.

201. [1] The family of Strickland, or Styrkeland, took its name
from the vill of Stirkeland Magna (see No. 203) in the parish of
Morland in Westmoreland ; derived from Anglo-Saxon *styric*, " a stirk,"
a young heifer or bullock. Walter de Styrkeland appears in the Pipe
Rolls for Cumberland as paying an amercement of 1 marc in 1214. On
January 22, 1216, his " son or daughter and heir " is mentioned as
one of the hostages for Gilbert son of Roger son of Reinfrid to King
John for his fidelity (*Rot. de Oblat. et Finibus*, 17 Joh. Lancashire,
Record Com., p. 571 ; *Close Rolls*, Record Com. i. 248, 335). This
hostage was probably his son Adam, who attests the next charter, and
of whom nothing else seems to be known. Walter attests No. 210
about 1232—35. On April 24, 1212, Walter was witness to the
confirmation charter of Robert de Veteripont to the Abbey of Heppe,
or Shap, together with the above-named Gilbert, Randulph Deincurt,
Anselm de Furness and William de Thirneby (Dugdale, *Monasticon*,
vi. 869). He makes a grant to Wederhal of 4 acres in No. 202. There
does not seem to be any evidence that he married, as asserted, Cristina,
daughter of Roger son of Reinfrid. An elaborate pedigree of the family
is given by E. Bellasis, Lancaster Herald, in the *Cumb. and West.
Archæol. Trans.* x. 75, but no additional light is thrown on these
earlier members. Later the family was connected with Sizergh in the
parish of Kendal, but see more on William de Stirkeland in No. 203.
Walter and his son must have been dead when Robert, his grandson,
came into possession, see on No. 203.

[2] *Cantaria*, "a chantry," a benefice for the chanting of masses, often
a special altar where the Divine Offices were to be celebrated for the
souls of the donors or others. This chantry was to be in the private

quam habeo in curia mea de Styrkeland quam Cantariam tam R. Abbas[3] et Conventus Sanctæ Mariæ Eboraci Patroni ejusdem Ecclesiæ quam Michael[4] tunc temporis Vicarius ejusdem mihi concesserunt. Ita quod Capellanus meus quicunque pro tempore deserviet illi Capellæ jurabit fidelitatem et obedientiam Vicario Matricis Ecclesiæ de Morlund et Rectoribus ejusdem Ecclesiæ qui pro tempore fuerint et illis præsentabitur et per eos in Capella serviet. Ita tamen quod Ego et hæredes mei tam Capellæ quam Capellanis in omnibus competenter providebimus. Jurabit autem Capellanus meus in Capella mea ministraturus quod nullum Parœchianorum de Morlund nec aliquem extraneum recipiet ad confessionem vel ad alia divina officia vel Sacramenta in præjudicium Matricis Ecclesiæ de Morlund et Rectorum ejusdem qui pro tempore fuerint. Et quod omnes oblationes obventiones qualescunque fuerint et undecunque pervenerint fideliter et integre sine aliqua detentione Matrici Ecclesiæ persolvet et fidelis tam Matrici Ecclesiæ prædictæ quam Rectoribus ejusdem in omnibus existet. Præterea Ego Walterus juravi pro me et hæredibus meis quod sicut prædictum est nullum Parœchianorum vel aliorum permittam admitti ad Divina Officia vel oblationes vel obventiones a Capellano meo ibidem deteneri. Præterea juravi pro me et hæredibus meis quod fideliter persolvemus Matrici Ecclesiæ omnes decimas domus meæ tam majores

---

Chapel in the House at Styrkeland, the rights of the mother Church of Morland being carefully guarded. A similar permission was given by the Priory of Lanercost in 1293 to Robert de Denton to have a chantry in the Chapel in his manor of Lanerton ; he was to pay annually 1 lb. of wax, and all offerings were to go to the mother Church of Lanercost (*Regist. Lanercost*, MS. xii. 25). All the endowments of these chantrys were seized under 1 Edward VI. c. 14, and sold to private persons.

[3] Robert de Longo Campo, Abbot 1189—1239 ; see note 3 on No. 10.

[4] Michael is one of the witnesses to this deed. He is called Michael de Morlund, Dean of Westmoreland in 1240, see *Chart. Whitby*, ed. Atkinson, i. 274.

quam minores tam animalium quam servientium. Præterea juravi quod Ego et Uxor mea cum familia mea debitis et consuetis sollempnitatibus, scilicet die Natalis, Purificationis, Resurrectionis et Assumptionis cum debitis et consuetis oblationibus et obvencionibus Matricem Ecclesiam prædictam visitabimus. Præterea juravi pro me et hæredibus meis, quod si Ego vel hæredes mei vel Capellanus noster aliquando contra aliquem Articulum in hoc scripto insertum in aliquo excesserimus et post primam amonitionem competenter non satisfecerimus super prædicto excessu Licebit Rectoribus vel Vicarijs Matricis Ecclesiæ qui pro tempore fuerint me et Capellanum meum per sententiam Excommunicationis sive suspensionis in me et Capellanum meum et etiam in Capellam meam ferendam omni appellatione et cavillatione sive quolibet juris remedio remotis ad condignam compellere satisfactionem. Juravi et pro me et pro prædictis hæredibus meis quod nunquam aliquid impetrabimus contra Matricem Ecclesiam quominus hoc præsens scriptum ratum et stabile permaneat imperpetuum, Quod si aliquo casu impetratum fuerit auctoritate præsentis scripti irritum sit et inane. Insuper autem præter prædictam juratoriam cautionem per sigillum meum huic scripto appositum me et hæredes meos ad omnia præscripta fideliter observanda imperpetuum obligavi. Hiis Testibus, Radulpho Priore, Magistro G. Archidiacono[5], Domino W.[6] Officiali Karliolensi, Ricardo Brun, T. filio Johannis[7] tunc Vicecomitibus Cumberlandiæ et Westmerlandiæ, Michael[8] et Waltero[9] Vicarijs

[5] Gervase de Louther, see note 3 on No. 21.

[6] Walter de Ulvesby, see note 5 on No. 56.

[7] Thomas son of John, here deputy sheriff for Westmoreland, see note 8 on No. 56.

[8] It is Michael who is Vicar of Morland, and Walter of Appelby, see note 4 above and Nos. 203, 210.

[9] Walter, Vicar of Appelby, is the same as Walter, dean of Westmoreland, in No. 202, but not identical with the Vicar of S. Michael, Appelby, and Dean in No. 205.

de Appelby et de Morlund, Roberto de Castelkairoc, Thoma de Louther[10], Adam de Slegyle, Stephano et Roberto de Neuby, Thoma de Aslachby, Ricardo Overstrang et alijs multis[11].

202. Carta Walteri de Stirkeland facta Monachis de Wederhal de IV acris terræ in Stirkeland.

Omnibus Christi fidelibus ad quorum notitiam præsens scriptum pervenerit W. de Stirkeland Miles æternam in Domino salutem. Noverit universitas vestra me pro salute animæ meæ et animarum Prædecessorum et Successorum meorum dedisse et concessisse et præsenti carta mea confirmasse Deo et Ecclesiæ Sanctæ Mariæ Eboraci et Priori et Monachis de Wederhal quatuor acras terræ in territorio de Stirkeland scilicet duas acras et unam rodam et decem partatas in Alderderiding et quinque rodas a capud Villæ versus Occidentem et abuttatas super Leyrreberch et unam rodam et dimidiam super Ulsangeberch et dimidiam rodam subtus Skertoftis. Habendas et tenendas imperpetuum in liberam puram et perpetuam Elemosinam cum omnibus communis libertatibus et aisiamentis Villæ de Stirkeland pertinentibus, scilicet quantum pertinet ad tantam terram, Excepto bosco meo proprio tantum ; et quod licebit mihi et hæredibus meis frangere et extollere terram illam quæ partita est inter me et Rogerum filium Waldevi non ob-

---

[10] Of Thomas de Louther little is known, except that he cannot be identical with the witness of the same name to a grant by Liulf son of Liulf of Kirkbythore to the Abbey of Holm Cultram in the 12th century. He and his wife Beatrix paid a fine of a marc in 1259 to have a judicial writ (*Fine Rolls*, 43 Hen. III. m. 7, ed. Roberts ii. 300). He also attests No. **210**.

[11] The date of this charter must be after 1231, when Radulph became Prior, and when Thomas son of John was deputy sheriff for Cumberland, not Westmoreland, and agrees with 1234—36 when Richard le Brun was deputy sheriff (see note 5 on No. **97**).

stante ista carta. Prædicti autem Monachi et homines qui prædictam terram de eis tenebunt molent bladum quod crescet in prædictis quatuor acris et in alia dimidia acra terræ quam Sygherit vidua dedit eis in Elemosinam ad molendinum meum de Stirkeland liberum et quietum de multura. Ego autem Walterus et hæredes mei prædictam terram cum pertinentijs sicut prædictum est prædictis Monachis contra omnes homines warantizabimus acquietabimus et defendemus imperpetuum. Et ut hoc scriptum meæ donationis et concessionis perpetuæ firmitatis inconcussum robur optineat eidem sigillum meum apposui. Hijs Testibus, Radulpho Priore, Magistro G. Archidiacono, Domino W. Officiali Karliolensi, Ricardo Brun, Thoma filio Johannis, Vicecomitibus de Cumberlandia et de Westmerlandia, Roberto de Castelkairoc[1] fratre meo, Adam filio meo, Waltero Decano Westmerlandiæ[2], Michael Vicario de Morlund, Johanne filio Willelmi, Thoma de Louther, Thoma Francigena[3], Adam et Roberto filijs suis, Hugone Francigena[4], Adam de Slegyl, Stephano et Roberto de Neuby et alijs[5].

202. [1] Robert de Castelkairoc is the second of the name (see note 3 on No. 46), the words *fratre meo* probably imply that he was the brother-in-law of Walter de Stirkeland.

[2] Walter, dean, and Vicar of Appelby ; see on No. 201, this is evidently the same person.

[3] Thomas Francigena, or Franciscus, or le Franceys, or le Francaise, was one of a family settled in different places in the district, as Cliburn, Maulds Meaburn, Routhcliffe, and in Scotland. They are mentioned in early documents in connection with the family of Brus in Anandale, and probably, like them, came in from Normandy where the family was well known. This Thomas, whose two sons Adam and Robert are given here, probably belonged to the neighbouring parish of Cliburn ; of which we have a John le Francaise in No. 234. Referring to this John, it is said (see on No. 234) that he was the son of Robert le Franceys and Elizabeth de Talebois. That Robert may be the son, here mentioned, of Thomas Francigena.

[4] Hugh Francigena was probably the father of another John le

203. Confirmatio Willelmi de Stirkeland Facta Monachis de Wederhal de Terris et Tenementis in Magna Stirkeland.

OMNIBUS hoc scriptum visuris vel audituris Willelmus de Stirkeland[1] Miles Salutem æternam in Domino. Noveritis me pro salute animæ meæ et antecessorum et

Fraunceys, to whom the manor of Maulds Meaburn was given by Robert de Veteriponte in 1242, see Machel MSS. iv. 243 and below on No. 211.

[5] The date must be nearly that of the preceding charter, probably 1234—36.

203. [1] William de Stirkeland in this charter names Walter de Stirkeland as his great-grandfather ; and we saw (Nos. 201, 202) that Walter had a son Adam. The father of this William was Robert de Stirkeland, knight, who is a witness to No. 205. This Robert is called the son of Adam in a quitclaim to Alica de Levens (which I have not seen) among documents in the possession of the Stricklands of Sizergh ; and among the same documents is a settlement by Robert de Stirkeland of the manor of Great Stirkeland on this his son William and Elizabeth, daughter of Ralph Deincourt and Helen, daughter of Anselm de Furness, on their marriage, said to be dated June 23rd, 1239 (Bellasis). At the same time the manor of Sizergh was settled upon them by Ralph Deincourt, and became the residence of the family. [Can the above date be correct when we have his great-grandfather Walter alive and in possession 5 or 6 years before? see on No. 201 and note the dates following.] An Escheat given among the *Inquisitiones p. m.* (3 Edw. I. No. 74) shews that Elizabeth was the wife of William in 1275, and had brought him certain lands in Westmoreland from her father Ralph Ayncurt. Robert was an inquisitor concerning the lands of Walter de Lyndesay in 1272, and on the extent of the manor of Kyrkeby in Kendale in 1274 (*Calend. Doc. Scot.*, ed. Bain, i. 537, ii. 4) ; he died in 1278, when he was one of the coroners for the county. The son William, after his marriage referred to above, appears in numerous charters, many of which are referred to by Nicolson and Burn (*History*, i. 89), without giving their authority, but apparently taken by Machel from the Sizergh documents. Other deeds, about the date of this charter, are quoted by Sir G. Duckett (*Duchetiana*, p. 309). It appears that William released to his son Walter the manor of Sizergh and other lands which had come by his wife Elizabeth, who was dead in 1303 (see *Inquis. p. m.* 31 Edward I. No. 130).

hæredum meorum concessisse et confirmasse Deo et Beatæ Mariæ et Abbati Sanctæ Mariæ Eboraci et Monachis de Wederhal et Sanctæ Begæ de Coupland et Successoribus suis imperpetuum omnes terras et tenementa quas vel quæ habuerunt tempore confectionis præsentis scripti ex donis et concessionibus Domini Walteri de Stirkeland Proavi mei et omnium aliorum Antecessorum meorum in Villa et territorio de magna Stirkeland. Tenendas et Habendas sibi et successoribus suis de me et hæredibus meis in puram et perpetuam Elemosinam imperpetuum prout Cartæ quas inde habent de Prædecessoribus meis proportant et testantur. Ita quod nec Ego nec aliquis hæredum meorum aliquid juris vel clamij in prædictis terris nec tenementis nec in aliqua ejus parte de cætero exigere poterimus nec vendicare quoquo modo exceptis Orationibus et Beneficijs ad Deum. Et Ego Willelmus et hæredes mei warantizabimus Prædictis Abbati et Monachis de Wederhal et Sanctæ Begæ de Coupland et Successoribus suis omnes prædictas terras et tenementa acquietabimus et contra omnes homines imperpetuum defendemus. In cujus rei Testimonium præsenti scripto sigillum meum apposui. Datum apud Appilby in Westmerlandia die Jovis proxima post Festum Sancti Wilfridi[2] Archiepiscopi Anno Gratiæ M.CC.XCII°. et Anno Regni Regis Edwardi Vicesimo. Hijs Testibus, Michael de Hartcla, Thoma de Derwentwater, Hugone de Multon, Militibus, Roberto de Warthwic, Willelmo de Wyndesour[3], Willelmo filio ejus, Adam de Hairington[4] etc.[5]

---

[2] Wilfrid, Archbishop, or rather Bishop, of York, was consecrated in 665, but did not gain possession of the See till 669; he was driven out in 678 and died October 3rd or 12th, 709. His Feast was appointed to be held on February 12th. See J. Raine, *Fasti Eboracenses*, vol. i. p. 55.

[3] This is not the same as the William de Windeshore in No. **50**. He and his son William also attest No. **220**. He often appears in connection with William de Stirkeland, with whom he had a suit this

204. CARTA JOHANNIS DE VETERI-PONTE FACTA MONACHIS DE WEDERHAL DE XX KARREATIS BOSCI IN WINFEL.

OMNIBUS Christi Fidelibus ad quorum notitiam præsens scriptum pervenerit Johannes de Veteri-ponte[1] salutem

year, 1292.   But see the extracts, referred to above, in *Duchetiana*, p. 309 seq. where there is much about the family.

[4] Adam de Hairington, or Haverington, is not identical with the person of the same name in No. 135 ; but is, probably, the Adam who granted lands in Flemingby to the Abbey of Holm Cultram, and, with Robert his son, made a convention with Gervase Abbot of that Convent in 7 Edward I. (1279) (*Register Holm Cult.* Harleian MSS. 1881, p. 334).

[5] The date is the Thursday after February 12th, 1292.

204. [1] Robert de Veteriponte, Vieuxpont, or Vipont, the father of the grantor, was a strong supporter of King John, and received from that King, in the 4th year of his reign, a grant, dated at Rouen, March 31st, of the Barony of Westmoreland, with the Sheriffwick, and the castles of Apelby and Burgh, to be held during pleasure (*Patent Rolls*, 4 Joh. m. 2, Record Com. p. 27 *a*). The next year of his reign, by a deed dated October 28th, 1203, the King gave it to him in perpetuity (see Dugdale, *Baronage*, i. 347 ; Nicolson and Burn, *History* i. 267, who gives the deed in full from Dugdale MSS. in Machel, and many particulars about the Veteriponts ; see also for the deed Additional Charter No. 253). The deed bears upon the present charter, one of the saving clauses being : "et salvo quod dictus Robertus vel sui neque vastum neque exitium facere poterint in bruillis de Whinfell, vel in ipsis venari quamdiu vixerimus sine corpore ipsius Roberti." His father's name was William and his mother's Mahald, or Matilda, as is shewn in an *Inspeximus* of a charter of his to the Hospital of S. Peter (later S. Leonard) at York, granting land at Meburn (*Charter Rolls*, 22 Edw. I. m. 3 and 4). His mother, Matilda, was a sister of Hugh de Morville of Burgh (see note 8 on No. 101) and gave the name to Meaburn Matilda, or Mauds Meaburn, in the parish of Crosby Ravensworth (p. 13) ; she is also mentioned with Ivo his brother in his charter to the Abbey of Heppe, or Shap, dated Cliburn, Saturday, April 24th, 1212 (Dugdale, *Monast.* vi. 869). He was a justice itinerant in 1206, 1218 and 1226 (see the references in E. Foss, *Judges of England*, ii. 497). He married Idonea, daughter and heir of John de Builli, Lord of the Honor of Great Tickhill in Yorkshire, who

æternam in Domino. Noverit universitas vestra quod Ego pro salute animæ meæ et Sibillæ uxoris meæ necnon et pro salute animæ Roberti de Veteri-ponte Patris mei et pro salute animarum Prædecessorum et Successorum meorum dedi et concessi et præsenti carta² mea confirmavi Ecclesiæ Sanctæ Mariæ Eboraci et Priori et Monachis de Wederhal viginti karreatas de mortuo bosco jacenti capiendas annuatim in bosco meo de Winfel³ in West-

survived him and died in 1242 (Dugdale, *Baronage*, i. 347, 349 ; *Fine Rolls*, ed. Roberts, i. 168, 357). He was a witness to the Great Charter of Henry III. in 1225 (Stubbs, *Select Charters*, p. 354). He died in 1227, leaving his son and heir John still a minor, and a daughter Christiana. On February 1st, 1228, writs were issued to the Constables of Appelby, Malverstang and other castles, to deliver them up to Hubert de Burgo, who had the ward of the said John "till the heir's majority" (*Patent Rolls*, 12 Hen. m. 6 also *Fine Rolls*, ed. Roberts, i. 171). John de Veteriponte did not lead the stirring life of his father, or of his son Robert, but died comparatively young in 1241 (*Fine Rolls*, 25 Hen. III. m. 5, ed. Roberts, i. 349). He succeeded to the Barony of Appelby and the sheriffwick of Westmoreland, and married Sibilla, mentioned here, the daughter of William Ferrers, Earl of Derby. He left his son Robert, a minor, who was given by the King in ward to Walter, Bishop of Carlisle (see *Fine Rolls*, ed. Roberts, i. 385 and the references in Dugdale, *Baronage*, i. 349). John was one of the persons sent to escort the King, Alexander II., and Queen of Scotland to London in 1235 (Rymer, *Fœdera*, new ed. i. 221). We have him again in this *Register* as witness to No. 210, and affixing his seal to No. 223, both probably in 1232—35. For his grant of the Hospital of S. Nicholas, Appelby, to the Abbey of Shap, see note 5 on No. 27.

² This present charter of John de Veteriponte was confirmed by Edward II. (*Close Rolls*, 17 Edw. II. m. 38).

³ The importance of this chase, or forest, of Winfel is shewn by the care taken to protect it in the charter to Robert de Veteriponte, the elder, referred to above. It was in the parish of Brougham, in the northern border of the county, bounded by the rivers Eamont and Eden. The next reference, after the royal grant, is five years later, where in the Pipe Rolls (*Cumb.* 10 Joh.) in connection with a heavy debt, $\frac{3}{4}$ of which is pardoned, Robert de Veteriponte—"dimittit Regi Les Winefels." See other references in Nicolson and Burn, *History*,

merlandia, et habendas in liberam puram et perpetuam Elemosinam. Ita scilicet quod si mortuum boscum jacentem sufficienter invenire non possint licebit eis capere mortuum boscum stantem ad prædictas viginti karreatas plene perficiendas per visum Forestarij mei sine impedimento. Et ut hoc scriptum meæ donationis et Concessionis perpetuæ firmitatis robur optineat eidem sigillum meum apposui. Hijs Testibus, Domino Thoma de Alnon, Thoma filio Johannis, Johanne de Morevile⁴, Thoma de Musgrave⁵, Thoma de Caberga⁶, Adam Clerico, Willelmo de Oly, Ricardo de Denton, Waltero filio Johannis, Willelmo Clerico de Wederhal et alijs multis⁷.

i. 398. The care taken of this forest is illustrated by the case given in note 5 on No. **199,** where the second Robert prosecuted the Rector of Neubigging and another for poaching. An account of the bounds of the forest is given in Machel MSS. iv. p. **44,** and the partition between the sisters Isabella de Clifford and Idonea de Leyburn in 12 Edw. I. at p. 153.

⁴ John de Morevile, called knight in No. **205,** is witness with Thomas de Musgrave, Robert de Askeby and others mentioned in this *Register* to a quitclaim of the Church of Crosby Ravensworth to the Abbey of Whitby by Thomas de Hastynges (*Chart. Whiteby,* ed. Atkinson, i. 270). He was arraigned at an assize at Carlisle by Symon Buch. in 1237 and was an inquisitor with Thomas de Hastingges in 1271—72 concerning the lands of Walter de Lyndesay in Westmoreland (*Calend. Doc. Scot.* i. 240, 537, ed. Bain). This John must not be confounded with others of the name in earlier times, as in the Pipe Rolls for Westmoreland, 1176.

⁵ Thomas de Musgrave, one of the family from Musgrave in Westmoreland, appears as Sheriff, or deputy Sheriff, in No. **205,** an office which Nicolson and Burn (*Hist.* i. 591) say he held in 1252, one of the same name possessing a moiety of the manor of Orton in 1278. He arraigned certain parties at a special assize at Appelby in 1236, concerning a holding in Musgrave (*Calend. Doc. Scot.,* ed. Bain, i. 234). See also the preceding note. With John de Vescy, Abbot of Hepp, he was one of the executors of the second Robert de Veteriponte in 1264, July 5th (*Fine Rolls,* 48 Hen. III. m. 3, ed. Roberts, ii. 410).

⁶ For others of the family of Caberge see on No. **138.**

⁷ The date of the charter, limited by the grantor, must be between 1230 and 1241.

205. Carta Johannis filij Willelmi de Thrinneby facta Monachis de Wederhal de quadam parte tofti sui in Thrinneby.

Omnibus Christi fidelibus ad quos præsens scriptum pervenerit Johannes filius Willelmi de Thrinneby[1] salutem in Domino. Noveritis me pro salute animæ meæ Antecessorum et successorum meorum concessisse dedisse et hac præsenti carta mea confirmasse Deo et Ecclesiæ Sanctæ Mariæ Eboraci et Ecclesiæ Sanctæ Trinitatis et Sancti Constantini de Wederhal et Monachis ibidem Deo servientibus quandam partem tofti mei de Thrinneby[2], scilicet continentem in se quatuor particatas terræ et dimidiam in latitudine et in longitudine sex particatas cum quadam grangia super eandem sita. Tenendam et Habendam dictis Domibus et Monachis in puram et perpetuam Elemosinam adeo libere integre et quiete sicut aliqua terra liberius et quietius alicui Domui Religionis poterit dari vel concedi et quietam de multura. Et concessi eisdem liberum introitum et exitum ad prædictam grangiam per croftum meum sicut melius viderint expedire post blada asportata. Ego vero Johannes et hæredes mei prædictam terram cum dicta grangia et cum omnibus pertinentijs dictis Domibus et Monachis sicut dictum est contra omnes homines warantizabimus et defendemus imperpetuum. In cujus rei Testimonium præsenti scripto sigillum meum apposui. Hijs Testibus, Thoma de Musgrave tunc Vicecomite Westmerlandiæ, Domino Waltero[3]

---

205. [1] William de Thrinneby, or Tyrneby, came to an agreement with Robert, Prior of Watton, after a suit, on the Thursday after S. Michael's Day, 1202 (the *Finalis Concordia* is given in full, Illustrative Documents XXVI.), and was a witness in 1212, see on Walter de Stirkeland in No. 201. Alice, the widow of John his son, quitclaims a messuage in Thirneby to the Priory of Wederhal in No. 207.

[2] Thrinneby, or Thrimby, was a small vill in the parish of Morland.

[3] This is Walter, Vicar of S. Michael, Appleby ; not the same as

Vicario Sancti Michael de Appelby tunc Decano, Dominis Johanne de Morevill et Roberto de Stirkeland[4] Militibus, Ricardo de Aquila Vicario de Morlund, Domino Nicholao[5] Rectore Ecclesiæ de Cliburne, Hugone Capellano, Gilberto de Slegyle[6], Roberto Francisco[7] et Hugone de Tylia et alijs[8].

206. QUIETA CLAMATIO JOHANNIS FILIJ RICARDI DE COUPELAND FACTA MONACHIS DE WEDERHAL DE TERRA ET GRANGIA IN THIRNBY.

OMNIBUS Christi fidelibus ad quos præsens scriptum pervenerit Johannes filius Ricardi de Coupeland[1] salutem

Walter, Vicar of Appleby (i.e. S. Lawrence) in Nos. 201, 221. In No. 222 we find this Walter, Vicar of S. Michael, a co-witness with Jurdan, Vicar of S. Laurence, and in No. 201 Michael, not, as here, Richard de Aquila, is Vicar of Morland. This Walter is very probably identical with the Walter de Scaldwelle (or Fealdwell) who is Vicar of S. Michael in the deed of Bishop Vipont (see No. 27) dated 1256.

[4] For Robert de Stirkeland, see on William de Stirkeland in No. 203, note 1.

[5] This is the same as Nicholas Malveysyn, Rector of Clifburn, in No. 218, and as Nicholas Manneysyn in No. 206, where are several of the same witnesses.

[6] Gilbert de Slegyle had a brother William, but his relationship to Adam de Slegyle in No. 88 is not clear ; see on that charter, where a reference is given to Margaret, Gilbert's daughter, in 1292 ; his widow Maria confirms a grant by Gilbert to the Priory of a messuage, see No. 220.

[7] Robert Franciscus is evidently the same as Robert le Franceys in the next charter. He was the son of Thomas Francigena, see note 3 on No. 202.

[8] The witnesses, especially Thomas de Musgrave, Walter, Vicar of S. Michael's and Robert Franciscus, point to a date for this charter between 1250 and 1260.

206. [1] The family of Coupland, or Copeland, held Bootle, or Bothil, in Copeland. Coupland, or Allerdale above Derwent, was the Barony granted by Henry I. to William Meschin, afterwards part of the county of Cumberland (see note 5 on No. 2). The daughter of Richard de Coupland was one of the hostages of Gilbert son of Reinfrid in 1216 (see note 1 on No. 209).

æternam in Domino. Noverit universitas vestra me quietum clamasse de me et hæredibus meis totum jus et clamium quod habui vel aliquo modo habere potui in illa terra cum grangia quam Johannes filius Willelmi de Thirneby dedit et concessit Deo et Ecclesiæ Sanctæ Mariæ Eboraci et Ecclesiæ Sanctæ Trinitatis et Sancti Constantini de Wederhal et Monachis ibidem Deo servientibus in puram et perpetuam Elemosinam. Ita quod nec Ego nec aliquis hæres meus vel meorum in eadem terra aliquod jus vel calumpniam aliquo modo aliquo tempore exigere poterimus. In cujus rei Testimonium præsenti scripto sigillum meum apposui. Hijs Testibus, Domino Roberto de Askeby[2], Domino Willelmo filio Johannis, Domino Johanne de Moreville, Domino Ricardo de Aquila Vicario de Morlund, Nicholao Manneysyn[3], Roberto le Franceys, Henrico de Alneto, Hugone de Theyl et alijs[4].

207. QUIETA CLAMATIO ALICIÆ UXORIS JOHANNIS DE THIRNEBY FACTA MONACHIS DE WEDERHAL DE TENEMENTO IN THIRNEBY.

OMNIBUS Christi fidelibus hoc scriptum inspecturis vel audituris Alicia quæ fuit uxor quondam Johannis de Thyrneby salutem æternam in Domino. Noveritis me con-

---

[2] More than one of this name is mentioned as having belonged to Askeby (probably from *Aske*, a Norse proper name, with the termination *by*) *hodie* Asby, in Westmoreland; and one Robert witnessed a charter of John de Veteriponte to the men of Kirkbythore (Nicolson and Burn, i. p. 24 *n*.). See also on John de Morevile in No. **204**. This is probably the Robert who, as custos for the sheriff, is witness in 1246 to a grant by Thomas son of Henry de Redeman to the Abbey of Shap, see it given in full, Machel MSS. v. 261. He is identical with the Robert of No. **216**, but perhaps not of No. **210**; see there on the name.

[3] Nicholas Manneysyn is no doubt the Rector of Cliburne, see note 5 on No. **206**.

[4] The date of this charter, with so many of the same witnesses, must be very nearly the same as that of the preceding.

cessisse remisisse et quietum clamasse Abbati et Conventui
Beatæ Mariæ Eboraci et Priori et Monachis de Wederhal
ibidem Deo servientibus totum jus et clamium quod habui
habeo vel habere potero aliquo modo aliquo tempore in
illo Messuagio cum suis pertinentijs in Thirneby quod
quondam petij versus præfatum Abbatem per Breve in
Curia Domini apud Salopiam ratione dotis Quod quidem
Messuagium cum omnibus pertinentijs suis prædictus Johannes de Thirneby quondam vir meus prædictis Abbati
et Conventui et Priori et Monachis de Wederhal vendidit
et Ipsos inde feoffavit. Ita quod nec Ego Alicia nec
aliquis nomine meo aliquod jus vel clamium in prædicto
Messuagio vel ejus pertinentijs aliquo tempore aliquo modo
nobis exigere poterimus vel vendicare. In cujus rei
Testimonium hanc præsentem quietam Clamationem meam
sigilli mei impressione signavi. Hæc interlinearia de
Wederhal ponitur ante consignationem. Hijs Testibus,
Domino Willelmo de Cumbe tunc Vicecomite Westmerlandiæ, Domino Johanne de Rossegille[1] tunc Coronatore
Domini Regis in Westmerlandia, Roberto de Slegile[2],
Ricardo de Tyreth, Johanne Mauchael[3], Willelmo de

207. [1] John de Rossegille was a coroner for the county in 1278.
The family were lords of the manor of Rosgill in the parish of Shap.
He was one of the jurors in a plea against the Abbot of Bella Landa
(Byland) in 1292 (*Placita de quo War.*, Record Com. p. 789 *b*).

[2] Robert de Slegyle was a son of Adam de Slegyle (see note
on No. **88**); he is also a witness to No. **219**.

[3] John Mauchael is one of several of the name in the family of
Mauchael, or Machel, lords of the manor of Crackenthorp in the
parish of S. Michael, Appleby. An elaborate account of the family
is given by E. Bellasis, Lancaster Herald, in the *Trans. Cumb.*
Archæol. Society (vol. viii. p. 416 seq.). To it belonged Rev. Thomas
Machel, Rector of Kirkbythore, who compiled the Machel MSS. in
which are collected many facts connected with the family. This
John Mauchael cannot be the one who is witness to the sale of the
Church of Kirkbythore in the time of King John (see note 3 on
No. **200**); but in November, 1272, this John was an inquisitor

Crakenthorp[4], Adam de Haverington, Roberto de Neuby[5] et alijs[6].

208. COMPOSITIO FACTA INTER CONVENTUM DE WATTON ET RECTORES ECCLESI.E DE MORLUND SUPER QUIBUSDAM DECIMIS.

UNIVERSIS Sanctæ Matris Ecclesiæ filijs ad quos præsens scriptum pervenerit A. Abbas de Melsa[1] et H. Prior de Bridlynton[2] et Magister R. de Logyngton æternam

concerning the lands of Helewysa de Levington, widow of Eustace de Balliol (*Inquis. post mort.* 56 Hen. III. No. 35, and see *Calend. Doc. Scot.* i. 546). In 1292 he was defendant in a plea concerning a messuage and two bovates of land in Old Salkeld, which he claimed to hold as the inheritance of Beatrix his wife (*Placita de quo War.*, Record Com. p. 127 *b*). In 1292, in an Assize held with regard to the patronage of the two Churches of Appleby, claimed by the King against the Abbey of S. Mary at York, John Mauchael is one of the jurors with John de Rossegille, Wm de Crakenthorp, and others in this *Register* (see in the Illustrative Doc. XI.). His father's name was Alexander; John was living in 1298, but his son Thomas was in possession in 1309. He may be identical with the witness to No. **210**; but see the note there.

[4] William de Crakanthorp is with John Mauchael in 1272 in the inquisition referred to in the preceding note, and again in 1292; he also brought an action against the same John in 1266 concerning a promise to be allowed to grind his corn at the mill of John in Crakanthorp. The family were afterwards settled at Newbiggin, see note 7 on No. **199**.

[5] Robert de Neuby is of later date than the Robert in No. **202** and preceding charters.

[6] The date of the charter is not improbably 1278 (note 1) or a little later, as we see that several of the witnesses occur about 1291—92.

208. [1] This was Alexander the 4th Abbot of Melsa, from 1197 to 1210. Melsa, or Meaux, was a Cistercian Abbey in Holderness, in the East Riding of Yorkshire, a few miles from Watton. It was founded by William le Gros, Earl of Albemarle, in 1150. See Dugdale, *Monasticon*, v. 388; *Chron. de Melsa*, ed. E. A. Bond, i. 289 and Preface p. xxix.

[2] Hugh was Prior of Bridlington in 1189 and in 1192, and Helyas

in Domino Salutem. Noverit universitas vestra quod cum causa a Summo Pontifice nobis esset delegata inter Conventum de Watton[3] et Rectores Ecclesiæ de Morlund super retentione quarundam decimarum tam in terris conductis quam in proprijs in præjudicium privilegij a sede apostolica indulti ducentarum audienda et terminanda tandem amicabili compositione in præsentia nostra in hunc modum sopita est. Videlicet quod prædictus Conventus sine omni retentione et exactione tam in terris conductis quam conducendis vel quocunque titulo in Parœchia de Morlund possessis vel de cætero possidendis decimas bladi prædictæ Ecclesiæ de Morlund et ejusdem Rectoribus de cætero persolvent. Excepta una carucata terræ quam dictus Conventus in Thirneby in Dominio possidet, pro cujus decimarum solutione annuatim Ecclesiæ de Morlund et ejusdem Rectoribus unam markam argenti persolvet, Scilicet dimidiam ad Pentecosten, et dimidiam ad Festum Sancti Martini. Hanc autem amicabilem compositionem tam procuratores Domus de Watton ex consensu dicti Conventus quam memorati Rectores Ecclesiæ de Morlund de consensu Abbatis et Conventus Sanctæ Mariæ Eboraci firmiter imperpetuum observandam tactis Sacrosanctis Evangelijs juraverunt. Ne igitur questio semel sopita de cætero possit suscitari memoratam compositionem præsenti scripto et sigillorum nostrorum appositione, Cum sigilli Conventus de Watton appositione roboravimus[4].

was Prior in 1200. The latter is probably intended here. Bridlington was a Priory of Austin Canons in the East Riding of Yorkshire, founded by Walter de Gant in the reign of Henry I. See Dugdale, *Monasticon*, vi. 284 ; Burton, *Monast. Ebor.* p. 212.

[3] The Priory of Watton in the East Riding of Yorkshire was founded in 1150 by Eustace son of John (see note 19 on No. 5) for nuns and canons of the new English order of Gilbert de Sempringham (Dugdale, *Monasticon*, vi. 954, and for this singular order p. 945). The Priory held the Church and manor of Ravenstonedale in Westmoreland, besides this little property in Morland.

[4] From the names the date of the composition is clearly about 1200.

209. CONFIRMATIO GILBERTI FILIJ REINFREDI SUPER
ECCLESIJS UT PATET INFERIUS[1].

OMNIBUS Sanctæ Matris Ecclesiæ filijs ad quos præsens
scriptum pervenerit Gilbertus filius Reinfredi[2] et Elewisa

209. [1] A copy of this confirmation grant is given in Dugdale,
Monasticon, iii. 566 and is there said to be from the original in
the possession of Sir Walter Calverley of Calverley, Bart.

[2] Gilbert son of Reinfred, or more correctly, Gilbert son of Roger
son of Reinfrid, or Reinfrei, was a person of great importance in
Westmoreland in the reigns of Richard I. and John. Roger son
of Reinfrid, the father, was a justice itinerant in 1176, and was made a
justice by King Richard in 1189. He married Rohaise, niece of
Ranulf, Earl of Chester ; he and his two sons, Gilbert and Reinfrei,
were among those excommunicated by William Longchamp in 1191
(*Roger de Hoveden*, ed. Stubbs, ii. 87 ; iii. 16, 153). Gilbert was
married in August, 1189, to Helewisa, the daughter and heir of
William de Lancastre, second Baron of Kendal, and Helewisa de
Stuteville his wife (*Roger de Hoveden*, iii. 7 ; Benedict Abbas, *Gesta
Ricardi*, ed. Stubbs, ii. 73). He had a son William, who became the
third William de Lancastre, and Baron of Kendal in right of his
mother, and married Agnes de Brus (Dugdale, *Baronage*, i. 422, where
see the reff.). From the Pipe Rolls we find that Gilbert was Sheriff
of Durham in 1196—7, and of Westmoreland in 1199, of Lancashire
in 1207, and of York in 1210—12. For the privileges he had granted
to him in his great estates by Richard I. and John, see the references
given in Dugdale (*Baronage*, l.c.). He joined the Barons against
King John, and had to pay a fine of 12000 marcs *pro habenda benevo-
lencia Domini Regis*, and on January 22nd, 1216, he gave hostages for
the fine and for his fidelity (*Rot. de Oblatis et Finibus*, ed. Hardy,
p. 571) ; some of these hostages are elsewhere noted (see on Nos. 201,
206). Gilbert died in 1220, when his son William did homage for his
lands (*Excerpta de Rot. Finium*, ed. Roberts, i. 47, 48). Among the
numerous deeds connected with his name, one of great interest is the
agreement between Gilbert and his wife and Abbot Robert and the
monks of Furness in 1196, concerning the hills of Furness and the
hunting thereon, given in full in Dugdale, *Monasticon*, v. 249. He
was also a witness to the Confirmation Charter of Robert de Veteriponte to the Abbey of Shap in 1212 (see note 1 on No. **204**). The
charter of Richard I. granting him exemption from payment of
noutgeld is among the Levens Hall MSS. and is given by Nicolson
and Burn, *History*, i. 31.

uxor ejus salutem in Domino. Noverit universitas vestra
nos intuitu caritatis concessisse et hac præsenti carta nostra
confirmasse Deo et Ecclesiæ Sanctæ Mariæ Eboraci et
Monachis ibidem Deo servientibus Ecclesias[3] de Clapham
et de Kirkeby in Lonesdale, de Burton in Kendal, de
Beithum, de Everesheim, de Kirkeby in Kendale, de
Murland, de Brunefeld et Ecclesiam de Wirkynton.   Has
autem predictas Ecclesias confirmamus eis cum Capellis,
molendinis, terris, pasturis, possessionibus, libertatibus et
omnibus alijs pertinentijs suis sicut cartæ Antecessorum
nostrorum testantur.   Hijs Testibus Ricardo de Marisco[4],
Adam de Beithum, Rogero de Haversheim, Nicholao de
Kendale, Johanne de Lonesdale, Magistro Hugone Ruffo[5],

---

[3] Six of these churches, Clapham (in Yorkshire), Kirkeby in Lonsdale, Burton in Kendal, Beithum (*hod.* Beetham), Everesheim (*hod.*
Heversham) and Kirkeby in Kendale were given by Ivo de Taillebois
to the Abbey of S. Mary at York, as shewn by his charter (see
Illustrative Doc. XVI.), and the possessions of Ivo came to Gilbert son
of Reinfrid through his wife, though not in direct descent.   Ketell son
of Eltred gave to the same Abbey, Morlund and Wirchington (see
No. 235) ; and his lands seem afterwards to have been held by
William de Lancastre.   It is not so clear why the grant of Brunefeld
(*hod.* Bromfield in Cumberland) should have been confirmed by
Gilbert as it was granted to the Abbey by Waldiev son of Earl
Gospatrick (see No. 14 and Dugdale, iii. 550) ; but Orm the son
of Ketell married Gunilda sister of Waldiev which may be the
connection (see note 13 on No. 1).

[4] Richard de Marisco was the rapacious Chancellor of King John,
and, as Chancellor, he witnesses the grant by the King to the Abbey
of Holm Cultram, on March 1st, 1215, of the Hermitage of S. Hilda in
the Forest of Inglewood in the parish of Westward (*Register of Holm
Cultram*, MS. p. 163).   He was Archdeacon of Richmond in 1212,
and was styled Archdeacon of Richmond and Northumberland in
1213 (Hardy, *Fasti Eccles.* iii. 136, 305).   He was consecrated Bishop
of Durham on July 2, 1217.   He is witness, as Official, to two charters
of Bishop Bernard in the *Register of Lanercost* (MS. viii. 3, 4).   From
the *Chronicon de Lanercost* (p. 32) and *Annals of Waverley*, we learn
that he died in 1226, on May 1st.

[5] Hugo Ruffus was a collector of the "Fifteenth" in 1225—26

Gervas de Aincurt[6], Henrico de Redeman[7], Waltero de Bovinton[8], Johanne de Haverington, Petro Bleyn, Johanne Bleyn, Roberto Bachel, Magistro Gregorio de Eboraco, Roberto Supe, Johanne et Waltero cocis, Waltero de Pistr[ina], Osberto janitore, Turgis Granetario, Samsone Clerico et alijs multis[9].

(*Close Rolls*, 10 Hen. III. m. 29, Record Com. i. 85 *a*). He attests two deeds in the *Chartulary of Gyseburne* (ed. W. Brown, ii. 88, 91), and in one instance is called son of John Ruffus. The name was not uncommon in Yorkshire.

[6] Gervase de Aincurt, or Daincourt, or de Eincourt, appears often as a witness about this time. He attested the grant to the Abbey of Furness by Helewisa, daughter of William de Lancastre, in 1196 (see above note 2); also, together with Richard de Marisco, a grant of Levens in Westmoreland, by Gilbert son of Reinfrid, to Henry de Redman, cited from the Dodsworth MSS. by Sir G. Duckett (*Duchetiana*, p. 210). See also the note on Walter de Stirkeland in No. 201. To Gervase was granted, by William de Lancastre, in the reign of Richard I., the manor of Sizergh in Westmoreland, which passed into the family of Strickland when William de Stirkeland married Elizabeth, daughter of Ralph Deincourt (see the reff. on Nos. 201, 203). He was a juror in 1210 on an assize as to lands in Cumberland already often referred to, compare note 1 on No. 73.

[7] Henry de Redman got Levens, or part of it, or the confirmation of it, from Gilbert son of Reinfrid, see the preceding note; but Levens had been granted to Henry son of Norman de Redman in 1188 by Ketell son of Uchtred, see the quotation and reference by Sir G. Duckett (*Duchetiana*, p. 209) who has much information about the family. His son and heir Benedict was one of the hostages of Gilbert son of Reinfrid in 1216, see note 2 above. He also attested the charter of Robert de Veteriponte to the Abbey of Shap in 1212 (see note 1 on No. 204).

[8] Walter de Bovinton, or Boynton, is witness to a deed in the *Chartulary of Whitby* about 1220 (ed. Atkinson, pp. 202, 380); also to a grant of William son of Serlo of lands in Farnlay in Yorkshire, probably in 1196 (*Archbishop Gray's Register*, ed. Raine, p. 280 *n*.). We have J. de Bovingtun in 1220 in No. 19.

[9] The date of the charter must be after 1189, when Gilbert son of Reinfrid came into possession and probably before 1212 when Richard

210. COMPOSITIO FACTA INTER PRIOREM DE WE-DERHAL ET ALEXANDRUM DE WINDESOUR SUPER DI-VISIONE BOSCI DE MORLAND.

OMNIBUS Christi fidelibus ad quorum notitiam hoc presens scriptum pervenerit W. Prior de Wederhal[1] et Alexander de Windesour salutem æternam in Domino. Noverit Universitas vestra quod de communi et unanimi assensu mei et Domini Alexandri de Wyndesour[2] boscus de Morland, qui ad nos utrosque pertinebat in communi, partitus est in hunc modum, Videlicet quod totus boscus propior Villæ de Morland qui vocatur Linstouc remanebit Domino Alexandro et hæredibus suis imperpetuum usque ad quendam sikettum qui dividit Methilrig et Linstouc sicut cursus illius siketti se extendit in longum inter boscum de Methelrig et Linstouc. Totus autem boscus

de Marisco was Archdeacon. The other witnesses belong to the reign of John, so that the date lies probably in the early years of the 13th century.

210. [1] This is William Rundel, or de Roundell, who became Abbot of S. Mary's at York, in 1239 ; see note 5 on No. **46.**

[2] Alexander de Wyndesour is not identical with the Alexander who is witness to No. **38,** but is probably his grandson. The first Alexander was connected with Cumberland (see note 10 and refer-ences on No. **38**) ; and there seems little doubt that to him the first William de Lancastre, in the time of Henry II., gave his daughter Agnes in marriage, and with her whatever he possessed in Havershame, Grayrigge and Morlande. Part of Morland belonged to the Priory of Wederhal (see on No. **14**). The deed is given by Sir G. Duckett (*Duchetiana*, p. 15 *n.*) from the Rawlinson MSS. in the Bodleian (B. 437, fol. 71) and among the witnesses are R. the daughter of Hubert de Vallibus, and other persons of the period. The property in Morland thus descended to this second Alexander through his father William, who had married the niece of Gilbert son of Reinfrid ; and Alexander "son and heir" of William de Windlesore was one of the hostages of Gilbert in 1216 (see note 2 on No. **209**). Alexander appears in the Pipe Rolls for Westmoreland in 1246, as paying $\frac{1}{2}$ marc for default ; and he was succeeded by his son William.

qui dicitur Methelrig et totus boscus à Methelrig versus Orientem remanebit Priori et Successoribus suis imperpetuum usque ad Aquam de Lyvennc. Ita quod licebit Dicto Priori et Successoribus suis includere partem suam pro voluntate sua et redigere ad culturam sicut melius sibi viderint expedire sine impedimento aliquo prædicti Alexandri vel hæredum suorum. Similiter autem licebit prædicto Alexandro et hæredibus suis includere partem suam pro voluntate sua et redigere ad culturam sicut melius sibi viderint expedire sine impedimento aliquo dicti Prioris vel Successorum suorum. Ita tamen quod dictus Alexander et hæredes sui habebunt communam herbagij ad propria animalia tantum in bosco Prioris et Successorum quantum remanebit incultum sine nocumento bladorum dicti Prioris et Successorum suorum. Et dictus Prior et Successores sui habebunt communam herbagij tantum in bosco Alexandri et hæredum suorum quantum remanebit incultum sine nocumento bladorum dicti Alexandri et hæredum suorum. Dictus autem Prior et Successores sui respondebunt libere tenentibus suis de parte sua bosci. Et dictus Alexander et hæredes sui respondebunt libere tenentibus suis de parte sua bosci. Sciendum est autem quod quædam pars bosci de Morland in prædicta partitione non continetur Videlicet boscus à via de Appeltreholm sicut est in pendenti condorsi usque ad Amselbergile et iste boscus imperpetuum erit communis dicto Priori et Successoribus suis et dicto Alexandro et hæredibus suis ad Estomaveria sua capienda ibidem. Nec aliquis eorum sine altero aliquid inde dare poterit vel vendere. Et utræque Personæ tactis Sacrosanctis juraverunt quod nunquam venient per se vel per alias personas contra tenorem istius scripti. Et ut ista partitio ex utraque parte rata et stabilis sit imperpetuum, Prior pro se et Successoribus suis, et Dominus Alexander pro se et hæredibus suis sigilla sua hinc inde huic scripto apposuerunt. Hijs Testibus, Domino J. de Veteriponte, Domino R.

Priore³ et W. Officiali Karliolensi⁴, Thoma filio Willelmi, Thoma filio Johannis, Willelmo de Daker⁵, Waltero de Stirkeland, Johanne Maunchahel, Roberto de Askeby⁶, Thoma de Louther, Alano Pincerna, Roberto de Neuby, Michaele et Waltero Vicarijs de Morland et de Appelby, Waltero de Meburn⁷, Adam de Soureby, Johanne de Neubiching, Ricardo Overstrang, Hugone de Tayl, Thoma de Aselakebi et alijs⁸.

211. CARTA EPISCOPI KARLIOLENSIS FACTA NI-CHOLAO LEGAT DE DUABUS BOVATIS TERRÆ IN MOR-LAND.

OMNIBUS Sanctæ Matris Ecclesiæ filijs ad quos presens scriptum pervenerit W.¹ Dei Gratia Karliolensis Episcopus

³ Radulph, Prior of Carlisle from 1231 to 1247, see note 2 on No. **97.**

⁴ Walter de Ulvesby, Official of Carlisle, became Archdeacon about 1239, see note 5 on No. **56.**

⁵ William de Daker is not here Sheriff, which he was in 1236—47 ; see note 5 on No. **109.**

⁶ This may not be the same Robert de Askeby as in No. **206,** but is no doubt identical with Robert son of Gilbert de Askebi who is a party with the Hospital of S. Leonard at York to a deed among the Levens Hall MSS. (see 10*th Report of Hist. MSS. Commission,* p. 320) witnessed by Alexander de Windleshore, William de Daker and others in this *Register.*

⁷ Walter de Meburn, with his sons Walter and John, attests a deed concerning land in Crosseby Ravenswarthe about this time, to which Michael, Vicar of Morland, named above, is also a witness (*Chart. Whitby,* ed. Atkinson, p. 274), and where he is called Dean of Westmoreland. He is also a witness to another deed with Walter de Stirkland and several of the present witnesses—a grant of land in Crosby by Thomas de Hastings to the Hospital of S. Leonard at York ; see the Levens Hall MSS. referred to in the note above.

⁸ The date of the charter from the Prior of Wederhal and Walter Official, must be before 1239; from the Prior of Carlisle, after 1231 ; from William de Daker, before 1236; hence pretty certainly in 1232—35.

211. ¹ Walter Malclerk, a Canon of Southwell (*Papal Registers,*

salutem in Domino. Noverit universitas vestra Nos de consensu Capituli nostri concessisse dedisse et hac presenti carta nostra confirmasse Nicholao Legat[2] pro homagio et servicio suo duas bovatas terræ cum omnibus pertinentijs suis in Villa de Morland quas Gregorius de Neuby de nobis tenuit. Tenendas et Habendas sibi et hæredibus suis vel assignatis suis de nobis et successoribus nostris libere quiete et integre. Reddendo inde nobis et successoribus nostris dimidiam libram cumini in Nundinis Karlioli pro omni servicio et exactione seculari. Et ad majorem hujus rei securitatem presens scriptum sigilli nostri munimine corroboravimus. Testibus, G. de Louther, Archidiacono Karlioli, Magistro A. de Kirkeby juniore[3], Symone tunc Decano Karliolensi, Waltero tunc Decano Cumber-landiæ, Ricardo de Levington, Roberto de Hampton[4], Alexandro Bacun, Odardo de Wygeton[5], Johanne Franci-gena[6] Clerico et alijs[7]

ed. W. H. Bliss, i. 57 ; *Archbp. Gray's Reg.* ed. Raine, p. 134 *n.*), not Canon of Carlisle (as *Chron. de Lanercost*, p. 31), was consecrated Bishop of Carlisle by Archbishop Gray, soon after October 28th, 1223, when the temporalities were granted. He resigned and joined the Convent of Friars Preachers at Oxford, June 29th, 1246, where he died in 1248 (Matt. Paris, *Hist. Angl.*, ed. Luard, iv. 564, v. 16 ; *Annal. Waverley in ann.*).

[2] It appears from the Register of the Priory of Monk Bretton, in the West Riding of Yorkshire, founded by Adam son of Suan, that Nicolas Legat and his wife Dionisia gave lands in East Marham to that Priory ; also that Dionisia Lasceles, relict of Nicholas Legat, gave all her land at Becton in Derbyshire (Dugdale, *Monasticon*, v. 132, 134).

[3] A. de Kirkeby junior will probably be the son of Adam de Kirkeby, who was Official of Carlisle in 1220, see note 6 on No. 19.

[4] Robert de Hampton is the same who was Sheriff 1223—29 ; see note 4 on No. 54. The two preceding witnesses attest No. 54 with him when he was Sheriff, or Custos.

[5] Odard de Wygeton will be the third Odard (see note 5 on No. 72), the son of the second Adam, Baron of Wigton ; he died in 1238.

[6] John Francigena is called John Fraunceys in No. 213. This is probably not John a member of the family of Cliburn, who is of a

212. CARTA NICHOLAI LEGAT FACTA PETRO FRATRI SUO DE TOTA TERRA SUA IN TERRITORIO DE MORLUND.

OMNIBUS Christi fidelibus ad quos presens scriptum pervenerit Nicholaus Legat salutem in Domino. Noverit Universitas vestra me dedisse concessisse et hac presenti carta mea confirmasse Petro Clerico fratri meo et hæredibus suis vel assignatis suis totam terram meam cum pertinentijs quam habui in Villa de Morland Illam scilicet quam Venerabilis Pater in Christo Walterus Episcopus Karlio-

later date (see No. 234 and note 3 on No. 202), but probably the John Francigena, Parson of Caldbec, who (according to J. Denton, *Cumberland*, p. 55) was a kinsman of Gilbert Francigena, the Lord of Routhcliffe. This John, on payment of 20 marcs, got from the King, Henry III., in 1231, for the Church of the Blessed Kentigern of Caldebec, an inclosure in the border (*costera*) of Warnel in the Forest of Inglewood, formerly held by the Abbot of Holm Cultram. This led to difficulties which resulted in the King taking the property into his own hands, and then in John Francigena granting a defined portion of it to the Abbey of Holm Cultram. This grant was confirmed by Walter, Bishop of Carlisle, by the Prior and Convent of Carlisle, and by Henry III. on May 12th, 1232. See the references to this interesting case given in *Calend. Doc. Scot.*, ed. Bain, i. 210, 217, and for the charters *Register of Holm Cult.*, MS. pp. 166—168. For his portion, the parson of Caldbec still had to pay ½ marc to the Exchequer. This parson of Caldbec may be the same John Francigena who appears from 1244 to 1254 as one of the King's clerks and as Canon of Lichfield "of defective sight" (*Papal Registers*, ed. W. H. Bliss, i. pp. 262, 278). At a trial in 1268, it was shewn that John, who was then dead, was presented to the living of Caldbec by Walter, Bishop of Carlisle (*Coram Rege Rolls*, 52 Hen. III., m. 13 ; *Abbrev. Placit.*, Record Com. p. 169 *b*). But it is possible that this witness may be the John le Fraunceis, son of Hugo, to whom Robert de Veteriponte, the son of Ivo and nephew of Robert, Baron of Appelby, gave the manor of Meburn Matilda by charter in 1242—43 (see *Coram Rege Rolls*, 27 Henry III., m. 21 ; *Abbrev. Placit.* p. 120 *a*).

[7] The date of this charter can be fixed ; as, from No. 213, Bartholomew was Prior of Carlisle, who died in 1231, and as G. de Louther was not yet Archdeacon, and Richard de Hampton had ceased to be Sheriff, the date will be 1230—31.

lensis mihi contulit. Tenendam et Habendam libere quiete et pacifice prout illam terram liberius aliquo tempore tenui Reddendo inde annuatim Domino Episcopo Karliolensi dimidiam libram cumini ad Nundinas Karlioli pro omni servicio exactione et consuetudine. Quam terram dicto Petro contra omnes homines warantizabimus. In cujus rei Testimonium presenti scripto sigillum meum apposui. Testibus Domino Radulpho Priore Karliolensi, Domino Willelmo Rundel Priore de Wederhal[1], Domino Roberto Priore Sanctæ Mariæ Eboraci, Domino Guidone Priore de Sancta Bega, Domino W. de Ulvesby Officiali Karliolensi, Ricardo de Hardres senescallo Domini Episcopi Karliolensis, Domino Michael Vicario de Morland, Magistro Waltero de Stafford Parsona de Castelkairoc, Raginaldo Camerario[2], Elya de Ravenwic, Girardo Clerico et alijs[3].

213. Confirmatio Prioris et Conventus Karliolensis super collatione Episcopi de 2 bovatis Terræ in Morlund.

OMNIBUS Christi fidelibus ad quos presens scriptum pervenerit Bartholomeus Prior et conventus Karliolensis Salutem in Domino. Noverit universitas vestra nos unanimi totius Capituli nostri assensu ratam et gratam habere collationem[1] quam fecit Venerabilis Pater Episcopus Karliolensis Nicholao Legat super duabus bovatis terræ in Villa de Morlund secundum quod in carta dicti Domini Episcopi dicto Nicholao super hijs confecta continetur. In cujus rei Testimonium huic scripto sigillum Capituli nostri

212. [1] William Rundel, Prior, was afterwards Abbot of S. Mary's at York, 1239—44, see note 5 on No. 46.

[2] This is probably the same as Reginald, Camerarius of the Prior of Carlisle, in No. 63, about the same date.

[3] The date of the charter must be after 1231 when Radulph became Prior, probably shortly after, certainly before 1239.

213. [1] In the charter of Bishop Walter, No. 211.

apposuimus. Testibus, Domino Archidiacono Karliolensi[2], Magistro Thoma Buec, Magistro A. de Kirkeby[3], Domino T. Capellano, Johanne Fraunceys et alijs[4].

214. CONFIRMATIO PRIORIS ET CONVENTUS KAR-LIOLENSIS SUPER COLLATIONE QUAM NICHOLAUS FECIT PETRO FRATRI SUO.

OMNIBUS Christi fidelibus ad quos presens scriptum pervenerit R.[1] Prior Karliolensis et Conventus salutem in Domino. Noverit universitas vestra nos ratam et gratam habere Donationem[2] quam Nicholaus Legat fecit Petro Clerico fratri suo de duabus bovatis terræ in Villa de Morland quam Dominus Episcopus ei contulit pro servicio suo. In cujus rei Testimonium sigillum Capituli nostri apponi fecimus. Valete[3].

215. CARTA PETRI LEGAT FACTA HENRICO FRATRI SUO DE DUABUS BOVATIS TERRÆ IN MORLAND.

OMNIBUS Christi fidelibus ad quos presens scriptum pervenerit Petrus Legat[1] salutem in Domino. Noveritis me dedisse concessisse et hac presenti carta mea confirmasse Henrico Legat fratri meo et hæredibus suis de ipso procreatis illas duas bovatas terræ quas habui de dono Nicholai fratris mei in Villa de Morland. Tenendas et Habendas sibi et hæredibus suis libere et quiete ab

---

[2] Gervase de Louther.

[3] This is Adam de Kirkeby junior, as in No. **211**.

[4] The date of the charter will be practically the same as that of No. **211**.

214. [1] Radulph, Prior.

[2] By charter No. **212**.

[3] The date of the charter will be about the same as that of No. **212**.

215. [1] Peter Legat, or le Legat, was the brother of Nicholas and Henry (see No. **212**); he is probably the same who, in 1251, was called upon, with John de Boulton, to answer a plea concerning the manor of Lydel; see note 4 on No. **61** and *Calend. Doc. Scot.*, ed. Bain, i. 337.

omni servicio. Reddendo Domino Episcopo Karliolensi dimidiam libram cumini ad Nundinas Karlioli et mihi ad eundem terminum unum denarium in vita mea. In cujus rei Testimonium presenti scripto sigillum meum apposui. Testibus Adam de Musegrave[2], Roberto de Kirkeoswald[3], Willelmo de Branton, Rogero de Eston, Johanne de Crofton[4], Johanne de Brunthaithe, Roberto de Crofton[5].

216. CARTA HENRICI LEGAT FACTA MONACHIS DE WEDERHAL DE TOTA TERRA QUAM HABUIT EX DONO PETRI FRATRIS SUI IN MORLAND.

OMNIBUS Christi fidelibus ad quos præsens scriptum pervenerit Henricus dictus Legat Salutem æternam in Domino. Noverit universitas vestra quod Ego pro salute animæ meæ et pro anima Magistri Petri Legat fratris mei et pro salute animarum Prædecessorum et Successorum meorum dedi concessi et hac præsenti carta mea confirmavi

---

[2] Adam de Musgrave was no doubt of the same family as Thomas in No. **204**. He is mentioned in the Machel MSS. (iv. 14), as being witness to a grant of wood at Sandford by William son of Robert de Sandford to Robert de Veteriponte ; Machel ascribes it to the reign of King John, but it might be any time before 1228, when Robert died.

[3] This can scarcely be the same as the Robert who was witness to No. **199** in 1291.

[4] John de Crofton and Robert, who also attests this deed, were members of the family which held the manor of Crofton in the parish of Thursby in Cumberland, and which was afterwards merged in the family of Brisco. John, as we saw (note 5 on No. **95**), was witness to a charter of the Rector and Brethren of the Hospital of S. Nicholas, Carlisle, to which (according to J. Denton, *Cumberland*, p. 83 followed by Hugo Todd, MS. and Nicolson and Burn) his ancestor Gilbert de Dundraw, lord of Crofton, was a benefactor. John gave land "in Vico Francorum," Carlisle, to the Priory of Lanercost (*Register*, MS. vi. 12), and the deed is attested by G. (Gervase de Louther) Archdeacon of Carlisle, shewing that it is just about this period.

[5] The date of the charter must be later than that of No. **212**, i.e. after 1231, but before that of No. **216**, which is probably 1250—60.

Deo et Abbati et conventui Sanctæ Mariæ Eboraci et Priori et Monachis de Wederhal totam terram meam cum tofto et crofto cum omnibus pertinentijs suis in territorio et in Villa de Morland quam habui de dono Magistri Petri Legat fratris mei. Tenendam et Habendam dictis Abbati et Conventui Sanctæ Mariæ Eboraci et Priori et Monachis de Wederhal in liberam puram et perpetuam Elemosinam. Reddendo inde annuatim Domino Episcopo Karliolensi dimidiam libram cumini in Nundinis Karlioli pro omnibus servicijs exactionibus et secularibus demandis. Hoc dictis Abbati et Conventui Sanctæ Mariæ Eboraci et Priori et Monachis de Wederhal dedi et concessi et quietum clamavi de me et hæredibus meis et assignatis meis imperpetuum. In cujus rei Testimonium præsenti scripto sigillum meum apposui. Hijs Testibus, Domino Willelmo de Dakre, Domino Johanne de Morevill, Domino Roberto de Askeby, Domino Willelmo filio Johannis, Thoma de Musgrave tunc Vicecomite Westmerlandiæ, Ricardo Vicario de Morland[1], Nicholao Manneysyn[2], Willelmo de Wardcop[3], Roberto le Franceis, Gilberto de Sclegile, Roberto de Ormsheued[4], Johanne de Neuby et alijs multis[5].

216. [1] Richard de Aquila as in No. **88**, and, with many of these witnesses, in Nos. **205, 206**.

[2] Nicholas Manneysyn, Rector of Cliburn, see note 5 on No. **205**.

[3] William de Wardcop was one of the family which for long were lords of the manor of Warcop, a parish in Westmoreland. William is named by Nicolson and Burn (*History*, i. 602, 607), as being witness to a re-grant of property in Sandford (see note 2 on No. **215**), by Robert de Veteriponte to William de Sandford; this would be before 1228 when Robert died. He is spoken of in 1256 as one of the men of Robert de Veteriponte (grandson of the preceding), who held their land by cornage (*Fine Rolls*, 40 Hen. III. m. 2).

[4] Robert de Ormesheued, or Ormesheved, was lord of the manor of Ormesheved (*hodie* Ormside), in the parish of the same name, adjoining the parishes of Appleby and Warcop. He also is mentioned by Nicolson and Burn (*History*, i. 515) as Robert son of Guy, witness to a grant of Robert de Veteriponte (the younger) to Richard Clerke in 1251—52. He was one of the inquisitors, with John

217. CARTA PETRI LEGAT FACTA MONACHIS DE
WEDERHAL DE QUADAM TERRA SUA IN MORLAND
PROUT PRIUS.

UNIVERSIS Christi fidelibus ad quorum notitiam hoc
præsens scriptum pervenerit Petrus Legat Clericus salutem
æternam in Domino. Noverit universitas vestra me Divinæ
pietatis intuitu pro salute animæ meæ dedisse concessisse
et præsenti carta confirmasse Deo et Abbachiæ Sanctæ
Mariæ Eboraci et Domui Sanctæ Trinitatis de Wederhal
et Monachis ibidem Deo servientibus totam illam terram
in Villa de Morland quæ jacet inter culturam dictorum
Monachorum et terram Alexandri de Wyndeshour versus
Aquilonem et abuttat versus Ortum dictorum Monachorum.
Habendam et tenendam in liberam puram et perpetuam
Elemosinam cum omnibus pertinentijs suis et libertatibus
infra Villam [et] extra ad omnimodum commodum suum
faciendum. Et Ego P. et hæredes mei totam prædictam
terram dictis Monachis imperpetuum contra omnes homines
warantizabimus acquietabimus et defendemus. In cujus
rei Testimonium præsenti scripto sigillum meum apposui.
Hijs Testibus, Domino R. Priore[1], Magistro R. Archidiacono[2], Domino W. Officiali Karliolensi[3], Willelmo de
Daker tunc Vicecomite, Ricardo de Herdres tunc Sene-

de Moreville (see the ref. in note 4 on No. **204**), concerning the lands
of Walter de Lyndesay in 1271 ; also with John Mauchael (see the
ref. in No. **207**, note 3), concerning the lands of Helewysa de
Levington in 1272.

⁵ As William de Daker was Sheriff, 1236—47, the date of this
charter must clearly be after 1247, and from the earlier date when
some of the witnesses appear, as in Nos. **205, 206**, not very long
after, probably from 1250—60.

217. ¹ Radulph, Prior of Carlisle from 1231 to February 1247 ;
see note 2 on No. **97.**

² Robert de Otterington, Archdeacon of Carlisle in 1238 ; see note
3 on No. **137** ; Gervase de Louther, Archdeacon, was probably now
dead.

³ Walter de Ulvesby, Official of Carlisle.

scallo Domini Episcopi, Elya de Raveneswic, Willelmo de Crogelyn, Johanne filio Willelmi et M.[4] Vicario de Morland, M. Capellano, M. Serviente, Rogero Clerico et alijs[5].

218. OBLIGATIO RECTORIS ECCLESIÆ DE CLIFBURN DE PENCIONE DECEM SOLIDORUM PER ANNUM.

OMNIBUS Christi fidelibus ad quorum notitiam præsens scriptum pervenerit Nicholaus Malveysyn[1] Rector Ecclesiæ de Clifburn salutem æternam in Domino.   Noverit universitas vestra quod Ego teneor solvere annuatim Abbati et conventui Sanctæ Mariæ Eboraci et Monachis de Wederhal decem solidos nomine pensionis[2] prædictæ Ecclesiæ de Clifburn : Scilicet medietatem ad Pentecosten et medietatem ad Festum Sancti Martini in yeme.   Et ad hoc fideliter faciendum Sacramento meo me obligavi.   In cujus rei Testimonium præsenti scripto sigillum meum apposui. Hijs Testibus, Magistris Roberto de Saham, Rogero Pepin, Johanne de Popelton, Gilberto de Lincoln, Waltero de Gaugy, Johanne Malet, Johanne de Yuetot, Henrico Teutonico, Roberto Supe et T. de Karliolo Clerico et alijs[3].

[4] Michael, Vicar of Morland, see note 4 on No. 201.

[5] The date of the charter, from W. de Daker, Sheriff, must be between 1236 and 1247 ; from William de Crogelyn, who appears in 1241 and 1247, and from so many of the same witnesses being in No. 212 (before 1239) it is probably about 1240.

218. [1] Nicholas Malveysyn is no doubt the same as Nicholas Manneysyn in Nos. 206, 216, and as Nicolas, Rector of Cliburn, in No. 205.

[2] When this and other Churches were transferred to Walter, Bishop of Carlisle (Illustrative Doc. XVII.), and confirmed to Bishop Sylvester in 1248, these pensions to the Priory of Wederhal were specially reserved ; see on Cliburne, note 4 on No. 16.

[3] As we have Roger Pepin in 1246, 1247 (see note 4 on No. 26), and the three other charters in which the grantor occurs are between 1250—60, probably about the earlier date, 1250, is the date of this charter.

219. CARTA JOHANNIS FILIJ WALTERI DE RAVENS-
BY DE QUADAM PLACIA IN MEBURN REGIS.

OMNIBUS Christi fidelibus ad quorum notitiam præsens
scriptum pervenerit Johannes filius Walteri de Ravenesby[1]
salutem æternam in Domino. Noverit Universitas vestra
me Caritatis intuitu et pro salute animarum Antecessorum
et Successorum meorum dedisse concessisse et hac præsenti
carta mea confirmasse in puram et perpetuam Elemosinam
Deo et Abbati Sanctæ Mariæ Eboraci necnon et Monachis
Sanctæ Trinitatis et Sancti Constantini de Wederhale
ibidem Deo servientibus unam placeam in fine tofti mei
quod teneo de Episcopo Karliolensi in Villa de Meburn-
Regis[2] versus Aquilonem de longitudine quinquies viginti
et duodecim pedum ab Aquilone versus Austrum infra
fossatas cum fossatis ad utrumque capud. Et de latitudine
ad capud versus Aquilonem quinquaginta duorum pedum
et de latitudine versus Austrum septuaginta duorum pedum
infra fossatas cum fossatis ex utraque parte cum omnimodis pertinentijs eidem placiæ pertinentibus infra dictam
Villam de Meburn-Regis et extra. Tenendam et Habendam
dictam placeam cum omnibus libertatibus et aisiamentis
prædictæ placiæ quoquomodo pertinentibus dictis Abbati
et Monachis de Wederhal libere [et] quiete ab omni servicio

---

219. [1] Walter de Ravenesby was a juror in 1279 in an inquisition
on the property of Peter de Brus, quoted by Sir G. Duckett from the
Rawlinson MSS. B. 437, fol. 38. He was also witness to a deed of the
Abbey of Shap concerning land in Renegill, dated 1263 ; see 10*th*
Report Hist. MSS. Com. (iv) p. 324.

[2] Meburn Regis, so called to distinguish it from Meaburn Matildæ
(see note 3 on No. **4**), or Mauld's Meaburn, which was called also
Meaburn Gerardi (see No. **228**), was a manor in the parish of
Morland. It was granted by King John to Robert de Veteriponte
with the Barony of Westmoreland ; and in the division of the property
of the 2nd Robert between his two daughters, $\frac{3}{4}$ of the manor went to
Isabella de Clifford and $\frac{1}{4}$ to Idonea de Leyburne ; at that time the
whole manor was valued at £50. 6*s*. 3*d*. ; see some abstracts in
Machel's MSS. iv. pp. 43, 46 and 173.

seculari exactione et demanda in puram et perpetuam Elemosinam imperpetuum. Et Ego prænominatus Johannes et hæredes mei dictam placeam cum omnibus libertatibus et aisiamentis quæ ad eam pertinent vel pertinere poterint aliquo tempore pro eo quod dictus Abbas Beatæ Mariæ Eboraci et Monachi de Wederhal ceperunt nos et animas Antecessorum et Successorum nostrorum in orationibus suis warantizabimus acquietabimus et defendemus in puram et perpetuam Elemosinam sicut prædictum est contra omnes Gentes imperpetuum. In cujus rei Testimonium præsentem cartam meam pro me et hæredibus meis sigilli mei impressione signavi. Hijs Testibus, Dominis Roberto de Raveneswiche, Thoma de Derwentwater Militibus, Johanne de Helton, Roberto de Slegile, Alano le Buteler, Waltero de Boulton, Hugone de Colleby et alijs[3].

220. QUIETA CLAMATIO MARIÆ UXORIS GILBERTI DE SCLEGILE DE UNO MESSUAGIO IN EADEM.

OMNIBUS hoc scriptum visuris vel audituris Maria quæ fuit Uxor Gilberti de Slegile[1] salutem in Domino sempiternam. Noverit universitas vestra me in libera potestate et legia viduitate mea concessisse remisisse et omnino quietum clamasse imperpetuum Deo et Beatæ Mariæ et Abbati Beatæ Mariæ Eboraci et Monachis ibidem Deo servientibus totum jus et clamium quod habui habeo vel aliquo modo habere potero in uno Messuagio cum pertinentijs in Sclegile[2] quod quidem Messuagium idem Abbas et Monachi habuerunt et habent ex dono Gilberti de Slegyle. Ita videlicet quod nec ego Maria nec aliquis

---

[3] From Thomas de Derwentwater (see on No. 199) and some of the other witnesses, the date of the charter would seem to be about 1290.

220. [1] For Gilbert de Slegile, or Sclegile, see note 6 on No. **205.**

[2] Sclegile, or Slegile, was a manor in the parish of Morland, and was long held by the family of the name.

alius nomine meo aliquid juris vel clamij in prædicto Messuagio nec in aliqua ejus parte de cætero exigere poterimus nec vendicare quoquo modo. In hujus rei Testimonium præsenti scripto sigillum meum apposui. Hijs Testibus, Domino Michaele de Hartcle, Domino Thoma de Derwentwater, Domino Willelmo de Strikeland, Militibus, Roberto de Warthwic, Willelmo de Wyndesour, Willelmo filio ejus, Adam de Haverington, Stephano ad portam et alijs[3].

221. CARTA WALTERI FILIJ ROBERTI DE APPELBY DE QUADAM PARTE ORTI SUI.

UNIVERSIS Christi fidelibus ad quorum notitiam præsens scriptum pervenerit Walterus filius Roberti Burgensis de Appelby salutem æternam in Domino. Noverit universitas vestra me Divinæ Pietatis intuitu pro salute animæ meæ dedisse et concessisse et præsenti carta confirmasse Deo et Ecclesiæ Sanctæ Mariæ Eboraci et Monachis de Wederhal quandam partem Orti mei qui est propinquior Orto Vicarij de Appelby habentem viginti quatuor pedes in latitudine et in longitudine quantum prædictus ortus se extendit versus Occidentem usque ad viam quæ descendit de Appelby usque ad aquam de Edene. Habendam et Tenendam in puram et perpetuam Elemosinam imperpetuum ita libere et quiete sicut aliqua Elemosina liberius dari potest vel possideri, ad faciendum inde commodum suum prout sibi melius viderint expedire. Ego Walterus et hæredes mei hanc Elemosinam prædictis Monachis contra omnes homines imperpetuum warantizabimus et defendemus. Et in hujus rei Testimonium præsenti scripto sigillum meum apposui. Hijs Testibus,

---

[3] The date of the charter will probably be before 1285, when Michael de Hartcla became Sheriff (see note 2 on No. 78), and probably not long before, as some of the other witnesses occur about 1290.

Magistro Thoma tunc Officiali Karliolensi[1], Waltero Parsona de Ulvesby[2], Michaele Vicario de Morland, Waltero
Vicario de Appelby, Willelmo filio Symonis[3], Radulpho
filio Herberti, Willelmo Russel, Roberto et Radulpho
filijs Godefridi[4] et alijs[5].

222. CARTA MAGISTRI WILLELMI DE GOLDINGTON DE UNA PLACEA TERRÆ IN APPELBY.

OMNIBUS has litteras visuris vel audituris Magister
Willelmus de Goldyngton[1] de Appelby Salutem. Noverit
universitas vestra me de consensu totius Villæ de Appelby
dedisse concessisse et hac præsenti carta mea confirmasse
Deo et Ecclesiæ Sanctæ Mariæ Eboraci nec non Priori
et Monachis de Wederhal unam placeam terræ in Villa
de Appelby quam Robertus tixtor quondam tenuit in
liberam puram et perpetuam Elemosinam, illam scilicet
quæ jacet inter terram Hugonis Tinctoris et terram Petri
Aribridall in Schiterigate[2] in Villa de Appelby libere et

---

221. [1] This cannot be Thomas de Thorp, Official, at the end of the
12th century, as in Nos. 120, 123, and who appears as Thomas, Official
in Nos. 40 (see note 1 there), 49, 121. There is a judgment of Thomas,
Official of Carlisle, in September, 1269, on W. de Leversdale in the
Register of Lanercost (MS. xiv. 15), who may be the same.

[2] This is Walter de Ulvesby, afterwards Official, and about 1239
Archdeacon, see note 5 on No. 56. We find that he was Official as
early as 1230—31 in No. 129.

[3] William son of Symon appears in No. 225, as one of the
Burghers of Appleby, in the year 1225 ; so also do the three following
witnesses.

[4] For Robert son of Godefrid, see further on No. 223.

[5] The date of this charter will be before 1230—31 when Walter de
Ulvesby was Official, and, probably, from several witnesses who
occur in 1225, from 1225 to 1230.

222. [1] William de Goldington was Mayor of Appleby in the time
of the younger Robert de Veteriponte 1241—65 ; see note 4 on No.
157, where he is a witness about 1252.

[2] Schiterigate is mentioned in a deed referred to in Machel MSS.,
v. 522, wherein William Hoff grants a messuage in Skiterigate to the
Convent of Hepp, or Shap ; now called Scattergate.

quiete ab omni servicio exactione et demanda ad dictam
Villam de Appelby pertinente imperpetuum pro quadam
parte Crofti sui in dicta Villa de Appelby quæ se extendit a parte Orientali Ecclesiæ Sancti Laurentij a sinis-
tris versus aquam de Edene quam dicti Prior et Monachi
nobis ad augmentum cimeterij nostri dederunt. Ego vero
Willelmus et hæredes mei dictam placeam dictæ Ecclesiæ
Sanctæ Mariæ Eboraci et Priori et Monachis de Wederhal
sicut suprascriptum est contra omnes homines imperpetuum
warantizabimus et defendemus.   In cujus rei Testimonium
sigillum meum una cum sigillo Communitatis[3] de Appelby
huic scripto apposui.   Hijs Testibus, Magistro Rogero
Pepin, Ricardo Decano de Morland[4], Jurdano Vicario tunc
Sancti Laurentij de Appelby, Waltero Vicario Sancti
Michaelis de Appelby, Johanne et Roberto tunc Capel-
lanis, Ricardo Maunsell, Galfrido de Grangiis[5], Johanne
Clerico de Appelby et alijs[6].

223. CARTA ROBERTI FILIJ GODEFRIDI DE UNO MESSUAGIO ET DUODECIM ACRIS TERRÆ IN APPELBY.

OMNIBUS Christi fidelibus ad quorum notitiam hoc

---

[3] The word *Communitas* has a variety of meanings in our English
constitution. In the case of boroughs, "*Communitas* means sometimes
the whole body of burghers, sometimes the governing body or
corporation, sometimes the rest of the freemen, as in the form 'the
mayor, aldermen, and commonalty'" (Stubbs, *Constit. Hist.*, ii. 167).
We have the name used on the seal of the borough :

+ SIGILLUM : COMMUNITATIS : BURGII : DE APPILBI.

See an engraving of the seal in the *Trans. Cumb. Antiq. Society*,
vol. xiii., p. 6.

[4] Richard de Aquila, Vicar of Morland (see on No. 88), occurs
with some of these co-witnesses in Nos. 205, 206. If Dean is not an
error for Vicar, he was now Dean of Westmoreland ; but in No. 205
Walter, Vicar of S. Michael, Appleby, is Dean.

[5] Galfrid de Grangiis is one of the proctors in No. 27 in the year
1256.

[6] The date, from the witnesses, must be much the same as that of
Nos. 205, 206, that is, between 1250 and 1260.

præsens scriptum pervenerit Robertus filius Godefridi[1] Salutem. Noverit universitas vestra quod Ego teneo unum Messuagium et duodecim acras terræ in territorio de Appelby de Abbate et Conventu Sanctæ Mariæ Eboraci et Monachis de Wederhal, quod Messuagium et duodecim acræ terræ sunt pertinentes ad Ecclesiam Sancti Laurentij in eadem Villa. Ego vero pro prædicto Messuagio et pro prædicta terra teneor solvere Priori et Monachis de Wederhal annuatim quinque solidos, medietatem ad Festum Sancti Martini in yeme, et medietatem ad Pentecosten quamdiu placuerit dictis Priori et Monachis de Wederhale. Et ne aliquis meorum post decessum meum si in dicta terra me mori contigerit jus hæreditarium aliquo modo vendicare possit, hoc præsens tam in Comitatu[2] quam in Capitulo et in Burgamoto de Appelby[3] coram omnibus pupplice lectum feci et sigillo meo signatum. Insuper

223. [1] Robert son of Godefrid was a burgher of Appleby in 1225, see No. 225 ; he appears again in No. 226, in the year 1242, where an action is brought against him by the Abbot of S. Mary's at York.

[2] *Comitatus* is here the County Court or Shiremote.

[3] The Burgamote, or Burghers' Court, of the Community of Appelby, shews that they had now the *firma burgi*, and were free from the exactions of the Sheriff—Stubbs, *Constit. Hist.*, i. 424. The burghers of Appelbi appear in the Pipe Rolls for 1179 (Westmariland, 25 Hen. II.) as rendering "account of 40 marcs for having a charter of their liberties and customs the same as the citizens of York have in their city" ; and in the year 1200, as rendering account of 100 marcs "for having their liberties and for having the town of Appelbi to farm under the King." The two charters for which they thus paid are still in the possession of the borough of Appleby. A copy of them is given in Nicolson and Burn, *Hist.* i. 310 *n.* A copy of the latter, dated York, March 26th, 1200, and referring to the former, is in full in the Charter Rolls, 1 Joh. m. 19, ed. Hardy, p. 41 ; also in Machel, MSS., v. 519, and see also the *Inspeximus* in 14 Ed. I. at p. 533. Henry III. granted the borough a charter in 1232. The Burg of Appelbi paid 40 marcs for tallage in 1197 and various sums for tallage later. We have no mention of a Mayor before the William de Goldyngton of No. 222. The Town Hall still bears the name of the Moot, or Mote, Hall, from A.-S. *môtian*, "to summon," *môt*, "an assembly."

cum sigillis Domini Johannis de Veteri-Ponte et Thomæ
filij Johannis tunc Vicecomitis et Walteri de Ulvesby tunc
Officialis et communi sigillo Burgentium de Appelby.
[Testibus] Willelmo filio Symonis[4], Willelmo Russel,
Magistro Johanne, Waltero Badekoc, Waltero filio Roberti,
Alexandro de Berwis, Johanne filio suo, Radulpho filio
Godefridi, Willielmo Clerico de Wederhal et alijs multis[5].

224. CARTA NEPOTIS W. RUSSEL DE TRIBUS SOLIDIS
REDDENDIS PRO UNO BURGAGIO IN APPELBY.

OMNIBUS Christi fidelibus ad quorum notitiam presens
scriptum pervenerit Alanus nepos Willelmi Russel de
Appelby[1] Salutem. Noverit universitas vestra me tenere
in feudo et hæreditate de Abbate et Conventu Sanctæ
Mariæ Eboraci et Monachis de Wederhal unum Burgagium in Villa de Appelby, illud videlicet quod jacet inter
Burgagium Willelmi filij Bernardi versus Edene et Burgagium Willelmi Spirius. Reddendo inde annuatim Domui
de Wederhal tres solidos Sterlingorum medietatem ad
Pentecosten et medietatem ad Festum Sancti Martini in
yeme. Et Ego et hæredes mei et assignati dictos Abbatem
et Conventum et Monachos de Wederhal de omnibus
oneribus dictum Burgagium contingentibus acquietabimus
et defendemus imperpetuum. Illud autem sciendum est
quod Prior de Wederhal retenuit de dicto Burgagio quandam portionem quæ continet in latitudine viginti pedes
et in longitudine quantum dictum Burgagium se extendit
versus campum ad exitum suum faciendum. Et in hujus

---

[4] This witness and many that follow are stated to be burghers of
Appelby in No. **225**, in the year 1225.

[5] From John de Veteriponte the date of the charter must be
between 1228 and 1241 (No. **204**); from Walter de Ulvesby now
Official before 1239 (No. **56**); and from Thomas son of John, now
Deputy Sheriff, from 1234 to 1236 (see note 7 on No. **201**).

224. [1] William Russell is one of the burghers of Appelby in
No. **225**, dated 1225.

rei Testimonium presenti scripto sigillum meum apposui. Hijs Testibus, Waltero Vicario[2], Willelmo filio Symonis, Willelmo Russel, Johanne filio Roberti, Radulpho filio Herberti, Gilberto de Lãgedene[3], Willelmo Spirius, Elya filio Symonis, Thoma de Elemete, Adam filio Symonis, Radulpho et Roberto filijs Godefridi et alijs multis[4].

225. FORMA PACIS INTER ABBATEM EBORACI ET BURGENSES DE APPELBY DE PLACITO.

HÆC est Forma pacis provisæ inter Dominum Abbatem et Conventum Sanctæ Mariæ Eboraci ex una parte et Burgenses de Appelby ex alia istos videlicet Willelmum filium Symonis, S. Britone, W. Russel, Alexandrum de Berewys, W. de Eboraco[1], R. filium Herberti, S. de Morland, G. de Langedale, R. filium Godefridi, quos dictus Abbas et Conventus traxerunt in causam coram de Sancta Trinitate et de Sancto Andrea Prioribus[2] et Magistro G. Penetentiario[3] Eboraci auctoritate Litterarum Domini Papæ super destructione et asportatione domorum suarum de Appelby et retentione decimarum videlicet quod dicti Burgenses dabunt dicto Abbati et Conventui quadraginta

[2] Vicar of Appelby, see note 9 on No. 201.

[3] Gilbert de Lagedene, or Langedene, is probably identical with the Gilbert de Langedale of the next charter.

[4] Many of the witnesses are the same as those whose names occur in the preceding and succeeding charters, also in No. 221 ; and we may conclude that the date of the charter is between 1225 and 1235.

225.   [1] This may be the Canon of York, afterwards the justiciary ; see note 4 on No. 92.

[2] The Benedictine Priory of Holy Trinity at York, was refounded by Ralph Paganel in 1089, see Dugdale, *Monasticon*, iv. 680. The Priory of S. Andrew at York was founded by Hugh Murdac in 1200 for Canons of the Gilbertine order, see Dugdale, *Monast.* vi. 962.

[3] Godard, the Penancer, and also Canon of York, and probably the same as G. Canon in No. 119. Many instances of his name in the deeds of the period are given by J. Raine in his edition of *Archbishop Gray's Register* ; see pp. 139 *n.*, 252 *n.*, 277.

solidos sterlingorum ad reparandum domus prius dirutas scilicet unam marcam ad Purificationem Beatæ Mariæ proximo instantis, et unam marcam Dominicâ media Quadragesimæ proximo sequenti, et unam marcam Dominica Palmarum. Et ad pacandos istos denarios ad terminos prædictos manuceperunt W. filium Symonis, S. Britone, W. Russel fide interponita pro omnibus prædictis. Et de solutione decimarum de cætero plene facienda de omnibus Mercimonijs et rebus alijs manuceperunt omnes prædicti et de prædictis denarijs specialiter solvendis W. fil. Symonis, S. Britone, W. Russel non obstante morte mandatoris applicatione remota ad prædictos terminos pro omnibus alijs persolvere manuceperunt. Et ad hujus rei perpetuam firmitatem W. Prior de Wederhal procurator Abbatis et Conventus in Diœcesi Karliolensi, Willelmus filius Symonis, S. Britone et W. Russel signa sua cum signis Judicum unà apposuerunt huic scripto. Actum anno Gratiæ M.CC.XXV°. sexto Nonarum Octobris[4].

226. Finis facta in curia Regis inter Abbatem Eboraci et Robertum filium Godefridi de XIV acris terræ et uno Tofto in Appelby.

Hæc est Finalis Concordia facta in Curia Domini Regis apud Appelby in Octabis Omnium Sanctorum Anno Regni Regis Henrici filij Regis Johannis vicesimo sexto coram Roberto de Lexinton, Radulpho de Muthleg̃, Willelmo de Colewurth, et Sollano de Nevill, Justiciarijs itinerantibus[1] et alijs Domini Regis fidelibus tunc ibi præsentibus inter Willelmum Abbatem[2] Sanctæ Mariæ Eboraci Parsonam[3]

---

[4] Dated October 2nd, 1225.

226. [1] The justices are the same as in No. **173**, where see on the errors in the copying of these names.

[2] This is William de Rundel, formerly Prior of Wederhal, Abbot from 1239 to 1244 ; see note 5 on No. **46**.

[3] Here the Abbot of S. Mary's at York, as rector of the Church of

Ecclesiæ Sancti Laurentij de Appelby petentem per Willelmum de Leyrton positum loco suo ad lucrandum vel perdendum et Robertum filium Godefridi tenentem de quatuordecim acris terræ et uno tofto cum pertinentijs in Appelby unde assisa summonita fuit inter eosdem in eadem Curia ad recognoscendum utrum prædictæ 14. Acræ terræ et prædictum toftum cum pertinentijs essent libera Elemosina pertinens ad Ecclesiam ipsius Abbatis de Sancto Laurentio, an Laicum feodum ipsius Roberti, Scilicet quod prædictus Robertus recognovit totam prædictam terram et prædictum toftum cum pertinentijs esse jus ipsius Abbatis et Ecclesiæ suæ prædictæ.   Et pro hac recognitione fine et concordia idem Abbas concessit prædicto Roberto totam prædictam terram et prædictum toftum cum pertinentijs. Habendam et Tenendam eidem Roberto tota vita ipsius Roberti de prædicto Abbate et successoribus suis et Ecclesia sua prædicta, Reddendo inde annuatim quinque solidos et duos denarios ad duos terminos, scilicet medietatem ad Festum Sancti Martini et aliam medietatem ad Pentecosten pro omni servicio et exactione.   Et post decessum ipsius Roberti tota prædicta terra et prædictum toftum cum pertinentijs revertentur ad prædictum Abbatem et Successores suos et Ecclesiam suam prædictam quiete imperpetuum[4].

227. CARTA ABBATIS EBORACI FACTA ROBERTO CLERICO DE APPELBY DE UNA CARUCATA IN COLEBY.

NOTUM sit omnibus videntibus vel audientibus litteras has quod Ego Savaricus Abbas Ecclesiæ Sanctæ Mariæ Eboraci cum communi consensu et assensu totius Capituli nostri concessi Roberto Clerico de Appelby tenere de

S. Laurence, having the tithes appropriated to their Priory of Wederhal, is called *Parsona*.

[4] The date is the Octave of All Saints, 26 Henry III., or November 8th, 1241.

nobis in tota vita sua unam carucatam[1] terræ in Coleby[2]. Reddet autem nobis idem Robertus pro ipsa carucata terræ unoquoque anno quatuor solidos dimidium scilicet ad Pentecosten et dimidium ad Festum Sancti Martini. Hæc ei concedimus quamdiu se legaliter habuerit erga nos et bene reddiderit prædictos quatuor solidos[3].

228. CARTA ABBATIS EBORACI FACTA ALEXANDRO FILIO ROGERI CAPELLANI DE CROSSEBY DE 2[s] PARTIBUS DECIMÆ DE MEABRUN.

SCIANT omnes qui viderint vel audierint litteras has quod Ego Savaricus Abbas Ecclesiæ Sanctæ Mariæ Eborum cum communi consilio et assensu Capituli nostri concessi et dedi Alexandro Clerico filio Rogeri Presbyteri de Crosseby[1] tenere de nobis in Elemosinam in vita sua duas partes decimæ Dominij de Meabruna-Gerardi[2] Reddendo nobis pro eadem decima per annum duos solidos

---

227. [1] This is the carucate of land granted by Enisant son of Walter (see Additional Charters, No. **247**) and mentioned in the charter of Henry II. (No. **14**), and which was confirmed by William Britton in the time of Abbot Clement, 1161—84 (Additional Charters, No. **248**). This is a lease of the land.

[2] Coleby is a small manor on the west, in the parish of S. Laurence, Appleby.

[3] The date, from the Abbot, lies between 1132 and 1161.

228. [1] Crosseby Ravenswart (*hodie* Crosby Ravensworth) was a parish adjoining the parishes of S. Laurence, Appleby, and Morland. The Church was granted by Torfin de Alverstain, son of Uctred, son of Gospatric, to the Abbey of Whitby in Yorkshire and was confirmed to them by Bishop Adhelwald, and by Robert, Archdeacon, also by Alan the son of Torfin, the last on July 12th, 1174. Many interesting charters connected with this Church are given in the *Chartulary of Whitby* (ed. Atkinson, i. 35 *seq.*, 258 *seq.*).

[2] This is here called Meabruna Gerardi to distinguish it from Meaburn Regis in the parish of Morland (see note 2 on No. **219**). It was called later Meaburn Matildæ or Mauld's Meaburn. These two parts of the tithe had been granted to the Abbey of S. Mary at York by Ranulf Meschin (see note 3 on No. **4**).

integre ad Pentecosten. Hoc autem ei concedimus quamdiu se legaliter erga nos habuerit et præscriptum censum bene reddiderit[3].

229. Dimissio decimarum Ecclesiæ de Kirkbithore facta Alexandro de Milleburne per Abbatem et Conventum Eboraci.

Omnibus Christi Fidelibus ad quorum notitiam præsens scriptum pervenerit Magister A. de Milleburne Rector Ecclesiæ de Kirkbithore Salutem æternam in Domino. Noverit universitas vestra me tenere ad firmam de Abbate et Conventu Sanctæ Mariæ Eboraci medietatem decimarum de Dominico de Saureby[1]. Reddendo inde annuatim Monachis de Wederhale duos solidos per annum medietatem ad Festum Sancti Martini in yeme, et Medietatem ad Pentecosten. Ita quidem quod si ad aliquem istorum terminorum a solutione dictæ pecuniæ cessavero dabo fabricæ Ecclesiæ Sancti Petri Eboraci quinque solidos nomine pœnæ. Et ad hoc faciendum subjeci me jurisdictioni Prioris Sanctæ Trinitatis[2] et Præcentoris et Rectoris Scholarum Eboraci[3] qui pro tempore fuerint coram quibus dictus Abbas et Conventus autoritate Litterarum Domini Papæ traxerunt me in causam de prædictis decimis Ut ipsi perpetuata jurisdictione authoritate prædictarum Litterarum Domini Papæ possint compellere me per Censuram Ecclesiasticam prout melius viderint expedire tam ad

---

[3] The date, from Abbot Savaricus, is 1132—61 ; probably at the same time as the last charter.

229.   [1] Saureby, or Temple Sowerby, in the parish of Kirkbithore, see note 6 on No. 200. These tithes of the domain were given to the Abbey of S. Mary at York by Uctred son of Lyolf; see on No. 14 ; that this is the Saureby there referred to is shewn here by the mention of the rector of Kirkbithore.

[2] The Prior of the Priory of Holy Trinity at York ; see note 2 on No. 225.

[3] The Precentor and Rector Scholarum of the Cathedral Church of S. Peter at York.

solutionem dicti redditus quam ad solutionem pœnæ. Et
in hac parte renuntiavi omni appellationi et privilegio fori
et omni juris remedio tam Canonici quam Civilis. Et ut
hoc scriptum perpetuæ firmitatis inconcussum robur optineat præsenti scripto una cum sigillis judicum sigillum
meum apposui. Hijs Testibus, Symone Capellano de
Wederhal, Waltero janitore, J. filio Willelmi[4], Johanne
de Agullunby, Willelmo de Cringeldic, Ranulpho filio
Umfridi et multis alijs[5].

230. Conventio facta inter Dominam Idoneam de Layburn et Priorem de Wederhal de pastura juxta Appelby.

Anno ab Incarnatione Domini M.CC.XCII°. ad Festum
Sancti Martini in yeme facta est hæc conventio inter
Dominam Idoneam de Layburn[1] in sua viduitate et in

[4] This is, probably, from the other witnesses, John de Warthwic,
son of William son of Odard ; compare Nos. 58, 59.

[5] The first two witnesses occur often in the charters of Robert
brother of John, named above, as in No. 45, and the date is probably
about the same time, 1220—30.

230. [1] Idonea de Layburn, or de Leyburne, was the younger
of the two daughters and co-heirs of the second Robert de Veteriponte, son of John, and third Baron of Appleby, and his wife Isabella
Fitz-Peter.   Robert died, it is said, in 1265, of wounds received at the
battle of Evesham, leaving his two daughters, Isabella and Idonea,
mere children.   The King gave the guardianship of the two heirs and
their great estates to Roger de Clifford and Roger de Leyburne respectively, who in 1266—67 came to an agreement as to the partition of the
property.   Not long after, Roger de Clifford married Isabella to his
son Roger : and this Idonea became the wife of Roger, the son of Roger
de Leyburne. (On Roger, the father, see note 15 on No. 13.)   The
estates were divided between them much according to the agreement
before made (see the extracts in Machel MSS., iv. pp. 43, 46, and
especially p. 173 from the *Escheat Rolls*, 11 Edw. I. No. 36, Westd.).
Roger de Clifford died in 1283 (*Pipe Rolls* for Westd.) and Roger de
Leyburne in 1284.   The latter had no children, and his widow,
Idonea, afterwards married John de Crombwell, or Crumwelle (she
was his wife in 1299, see the *Pipe Rolls* for Westmoreland *in ann.*).

pura et legia sua potestate ex una parte et fratrem Willelmum de Tanefeld[2] Dominum Priorem de Wederhal ex
altera, Videlicet quod dicta Domina Idonea concessit et
ad firmam dimisit dicto Domino Priori quandam pasturam
quæ vocatur Milnesthoumor juxta Appelby prout jacet
juxta aquam quæ descendit de Bangelmibrigg versus
Colleby usque ad terram dicti Domini Prioris juxta
eandem aquam.   Et ex alia parte ascendendo versus
terram quondam Nicholai de Ormsheued, et sic in circuitu
contra cursum solis per capita diversarum terrarum abut-
tantium super eandem moram usque ad terram dicti
Domini Prioris in illa parte juxta viam quæ ducit de
Appelby versus Manerium suum ad grangias usque ad
terminum undecim annorum proximo sequentium plene
completorum pro quadam summa pecuniæ de qua dicta
Domina plenarie satisfacta est in principio hujus Conventionis.   Tenendam et Habendam dicto Domino Priori
et successoribus suis usque ad finem termini prædicti cum
omnibus libertatibus et aisiamentis suis libere quiete bene
et in pace.   Et prædicta Domina Idonea et hæredes sui
prædictam pasturam cum omnibus aisiamentis suis dicto
Domino Priori et Successoribus suis usque ad finem termini
supradicti contra omnes homines warantizabunt acquie-
tabunt et defendent.   In cujus rei Testimonium dicta

About this time, in 1292, Idonea had to answer at Appleby to a
plea *de quo waranto*, concerning her estates, Robert, the son and
heir of Roger and Isabella de Clifford, being then under age. Idonea
died without issue in 1309, when she ceases to appear in the Pipe
Rolls as joint-Sheriff for Westmoreland ; and her estates went to the
descendants of her sister, the family of the Cliffords. For many of
these particulars see Dugdale, *Baronage*, i. 349, Nicolson and Burn,
History, i. 272 *seq.*, most of whose information is taken from the
collection in Machel's MSS., made mainly of extracts from Sir Wm.
Dugdale's MSS.

   [2] William de Tanefeld, Prior of Wederhal, was made Prior of
Durham in 1309. There was another Prior of Wederhal of the same
name admitted in 1341. See the reff. in Appendix E.

Domina Idonea parti hujus scripti in modum Cirographi bipartiti penes dictum Dominum Priorem remanenti sigillum suum apposuit, et dictus Dominus Prior alteri parti penes dictam Dominam Idoneam residenti sigillum suum apposuit. Hijs Testibus, Domino Thoma de Hellebech tunc Vicecomite Westmerlandiæ[3], Domino Michael de Hartecla, Roberto de Engleys, Johanne de Holton[4], Henrico de Wardcop[5], Johanne filio Thomæ de Goldington[6] et alijs[7].

231. Carta Willelmi filij Gilberti de uno Tofto in Villa de Kirkebythore.

Sciant omnes qui viderint vel audierint litteras has quod Ego Willelmus filius Gilberti[1] dedi et concessi et

[3] Thomas de Hellebech, or Holebeck, was Deputy-Sheriff for Westmoreland in 1291—94. His wife's name was Avicia. He was one of the Coroners for the same County in 1278. The family held the manor of Helbeck in the parish of Brough under Stainmore ; a number of particulars are given in the Machel MSS., i. p. 407 a.

[4] John de Holton, or Helton (as in No. 219), was one of a family who held the manor of Burton, in the parish of Warcop. To him a grant was made in 1289 by John son of John de Sandford to which Henry de Warthecop and John Mauchael were witnesses, see Nicolson and Burn, *History*, i. 607.

[5] Henry de Wardcop is stated in the grant referred to in the preceding note to be the son of Richard. He was Deputy-Sheriff for Westmoreland in the years 1312 to 1318, and again in 1324.

[6] John son of Thomas de Goldington, together with William his brother, was sued by Isabella de Clifford and Idonea de Layburne in 1286, with other burghers of Appleby, for exceeding the privileges of the borough (Machel MSS., v. 530). This William, not the Mayor (see on No. 157), was probably the William de Goldington who was knight of the Shire in 1307. John de Goldington in 1286 occurs in a deed of Bishop Irton with regard to a chantry-priest in the Chantry of S. Mary in the Church of S. Laurence, Appleby, see Nicolson and Burn, *History*, i. 327.

[7] The date is S. Martin's Day, November 11th, 1292.

231. [1] William son of Gilbert may be son of Gilbert, the Lord of Kirkeby[thore], who is the first witness.

præsenti carta mea confirmavi Deo et Ecclesiæ Sanctæ Trinitatis et Sancti Constantini de Wederhal et Monachis ibidem Deo servientibus unum toftum in Villa de Kyrke-bythore, Illud videlicet quod Rogerus Abbot tenuit in eadem Villa subtus Boraiñs. Habendum et Tenendum in liberam puram et perpetuam Elemosinam cum communis libertatibus et aisiamentis ad Villam de Kirkebythore spectantibus infra Villam et extra adeo libere et quiete sicut aliqua Elemosina liberius dari possit aut possideri. Et Ego et hæredes mei hanc Elemosinam prædictis Mona-chis contra omnes homines warantizabimus et defendemus imperpetuum.   In cujus rei Testimonium præsenti scripto sigillum meum apposui.   Hijs Testibus, Gilberto Domino de Kirkeby[2], Waltero Vicario de Appelby, M. Vicario de Morland[3], J. de Neubygging, A. Forestario, Roberto de Broby, Warino de prato, Thoma filio Gerri, R. Overstrang[4].

232. DIVISIO TERRARUM PRIORATUS DE WEDER-HALE ET VICARIJ DE APPELBY[1].

Thursbĥt.   Prior versus solem, Vicarius versus umbram terræ et prati.

[2] Gilbert, Lord of the manor of Kirkebythore, was the son of Adam de Kirkbythore (see note 8 on No. **117**). He confirmed the grants of his father Adam, and grandfather Waldiev, to the Abbey of Holm Cultram, and granted additional lands there in 1247 (*Register*, MS. p. 139). His wife's name was Eva.

[3] Michael, Vicar of Morland ; see note 4 on No. **201**, where he occurs with Walter, Vicar of Appleby, and some of the present witnesses, as also in No. **210**.

[4] From a comparison of the witnesses, the date of this charter must be about the same as the dates of Nos. **201**, **210**, which lie between 1232 and 1236.

232. [1] Bishop Nicolson, in his MSS. vol. ii. p. 34, says : "These are divisions made (it would seem) by those Arbitrators directed to be indifferently chosen by the Bishop's Award in 1256." This was the award made by Bishop Thomas Veteriponte, or Vipont, and given in No. **27**, with regard to S. Michael's, Appelby, whereby the Vicar was to have a moiety of the arable and meadow land divided by trust-

Hormesheued sich. Prior versus solem, Vicarius versus umbram terræ et prati.

Brirestest. Prior versus umbram, Vicarius versus solem terræ.

Hulveber. Prior versus umbram, Vicarius versus solem terræ.

Hayberch. Prior versus solem, Vicarius versus umbram terræ.

Bethelomgh b̄gh. Prior versus solem, Vicarius versus umbram terræ.

Moreberch. Prior versus solem, Vicarius versus umbram terræ.

Calveshon. Prior versus umbram, Vicarius versus solem terræ et prati.

Brakenb̄. Prior versus umbram, Vicarius versus solem terræ.

Hutegarig̃h. Prior versus solem, Vicarius versus umbram terræ.

Galhebergh. Prior versus umbram, Vicarius versus solem terræ.

Grenegate. Prior versus solem, Vicarius versus umbram terræ.

Burchgarthes. Prior versus umbram, Vicarius versus solem terræ.

Langbelā. Prior versus solem, Vicarius versus umbram terræ.

worthy men chosen in equal numbers on each side. Bishop Nicolson also remarks concerning the MS. of this Register: "There is this title in a somewhat later hand than that wherein the book is generally written, ' *Divisio Terrarum nostrarum et Vicarii de......Appelby.*' After which follows in that elder hand (about the time of Edward the Third), wherein the grants are mostly registered." Then he gives the list of names. This blank serves to explain the omission of " S. Michaelis" before Appelby. Machel, MSS. iv. 465, makes a similar remark, and gives some of the names from another list later in the *Register* (fol. 197), e.g. Brakenbergh. Nicolson, an accurate copyist, has Bethalinghbergh, Hulverber, and Langbelam.

Kelderum. Prior versus solem, Vicarius versus umbram terræ.

Spitefeld. Prior versus umbram, Vicarius versus solem terræ[2].

N.B.   Quod cartæ sequentes recentiori scribuntur charactere.

233. CARTA DE KIRKANDRES.

NOTUM sit omnibus legentibus vel audientibus litteras has quod Ego Adam de Mundegame[1] consilio et assensu uxoris meæ[2] concessi et dedi Monachis de Wederhala ibidem Deo servientibus Kirkandreas cum omnibus libertatibus suis et pertinentijs quæ sunt in terris sive in silvis sive in aquis in liberam et perpetuam Elemosinam pro me et pro prædicta uxore mea et liberis meis et pro animabus Antecessorum nostrorum.   Insuper et molendinum de Culgaid illis pariter concessi, Scilicet, illam medietatem quæ ad me pertinet.   Si vero contigerit commutationem illis fieri pro eodem molendino, fiet illis ad opportunitatem, etiam quod æquè valeat et impensum suum quod expenderint in alleniatione prædicti molendini reddetur eis. Videlicet, quinque marcas et septem solidos et quatuor nummos.   Testibus Hijs, Adam de Mondeg̃, Roberto Vicecomite[3], Warino Presbytero, Symone de Cruaq̃r[4], Jacobo Presbytero, Adam de Brotun, Rogero de Planca, Warino de Scacargil, Roberto de Thorasby, Rainero filio Ulfridi, Willelmo Walegrim, Rainero Clerico, Gamello, Houstino,

---

[2] The date must be 1256, or very shortly after.

233.   [1] Adam de Mundegame, or Montebegon ; see note 4 on No. 195, which is the grant, corresponding to this, given by Alexander de Crevequer, who married the other daughter of Adam son of Suan.

[2] Matilda, daughter of Adam son of Suan.

[3] Robert Vicecomes is not among the witnesses in No. 195.   He is most probably Robert son of Troite, who was Sheriff of Cumberland in the years 1157—72 ; see note 8 on No. 36.

[4] This is Simon de Creuequer, as in No. 195.

Symone de Boivilla, Herveio Niger, Adam de Byrum, Alexandro de Sancto Andrea[5].

234. CARTA DE KIRKANDRES.

OMNIBUS Sanctæ Matris Ecclesiæ filijs ad quos præsens scriptum pervenerit Simon[1] permissione Divina Abbas Monasterii Beatæ Mariæ Eboraci, et ejusdem loci Conventus salutem in Domino. Noveritis Nos concessisse et hoc præsenti scripto nostro confirmasse Domino Michaeli de Hartcla Militi quendam locum nostrum qui vocatur Kirkandres cum bosco et terris eidem loco adjacentibus quas quidem terras et boscum Adam filius Suani et Alexander de Creuquer Abbachiæ Sanctæ Mariæ Eboraci et Monachis Sanctæ Trinitatis et Sancti Constantini de Wederale dederunt, et in liberam Elemosimam concesserunt unà cum quodam pendenti in territorio de Neubigging quod vocatur Prestbank, et una cultura terræ quam habuimus in eodem territorio. Habendum et Tenendum dicto Domino Michaeli, Joannæ uxori suæ et hæredibus ipsius Michaelis de nobis et successoribus nostris bene in perpetuum et in pace. Reddendo inde annuatim Priori Cellæ nostræ de Wederale qui pro tempore fuerit Quadraginta solidos argenti ad duos Terminos Anni, videlicet medietatem ad Pentecosten et aliam medietatem ad Festum Sancti Martini in hyeme pro omnibus exactionibus et demandis. Salvis Monachis supradictis Decimis majoribus et minoribus singulis annis de præfatis loco et terris provenientibus cum obventionibus debitis et consuetis. Et sciendum est quod non licebit dicto Michaeli Joannæ uxori suæ seu hæredibus ipsius Michaelis quo [ne] molendinum nostrum de Culgaid minus valeat annuatim in præfato loco aliquod molendinum construere vel levare.

---

[5] From the circumstances and from the witnesses, the date of this charter must be the same as that of No. 195, or 1160—72.

234. [1] Simon de Warewick was Abbot of S. Mary's, York, from 1258 to 1296; see note 2 on No. 91.

Scilicet prædicti Michael Joanna uxor ejus et hæredes dicti Michaelis, et homines dictorum Michaelis Joannæ et hæredum ipsius Michaelis molent bladum suum crescens in prædictis terris ad molendinum nostrum prædictum quietum tantummodo de multura. Hoc autem eis concedimus quamdiu erga nos legaliter se habuerint et prædictam firmam bene reddiderint. In cujus rei Testimonium uni parti istius scripti in modum Cirograffi confecti penes Dominum Michaelem remanenti Sigillum Capituli nostri apposuimus. Et predictus Michael alteri parti penes nos remanenti sigillum suum apposuit. Hijs Testibus, Dominis Thoma de Derwentwater, Roberto de Yevenewich, Johanne de Rossegile, Militibus, Roberto de Morevile[2], Roberto de Neubigging et Johanne le Francaise de Cliburn[3] et alijs[4].

235. CARTA DE MORLUND.

CHETELLUS filius Eltred[1] omnibus videntibus vel audientibus litteras has tam futuris quam præsentibus

---

[2] Robert de Morevill was presented before the Barons of the Exchequer as Deputy-Sheriff of Westmoreland on October 28th, 1287, by letters patent of Isabella de Clifford, *Vicecomitissa Westmerlandiæ*, for herself and sister Idonea, sharer of the hereditary right; see Machel's MSS. iv. 275. Robert was Deputy-Sheriff the following year, Edward the First's reign dating from November 20th. From the Pipe Rolls he appears to have been dead in 18 Edward I. (1290).

[3] John le Francaise of Cliburne was the son of Robert le Franceys of Cliburne (probably the Robert of No. 202) and Elizabeth de Talebois, to whose family the manor of Cliburne had belonged (see Machel's MSS. iv. 267); he was probably called " of Cliburne " to distinguish him from others of the name (see note 6 on No. 211); thus he appears as one of the jurors in 1292, to decide the claim made by the King to the two Churches of Appleby (see Illustrative Doc. XI.).

[4] Two of the witnesses appear with Mich. de Hartcla in No. 199, dated 1291, and the date must be very shortly before 1290 when Robert de Morevile is said to have been dead.

235. [1] For Chetell, or Hetell, son of Eltred, see note 13 on No. 1.

salutem. Notum sit vobis me dedisse et concessisse consilio amicorum meorum Deo et Ecclesiæ Sanctæ Mariæ Eborum et Monachis ibidem Deo servientibus Ecclesiam de Mor-lund cum omnibus suis pertinentijs et Ecclesiam de Wir-chington² et duas carucatas terræ in eadem Villa et unum molendinum et omnia quæ ad eam pertinent in liberam et perpetuam Elemosinam pro anima mea et hæredum meorum et pro animabus omnium Parentum meorum et omnium fidelium defunctorum. Quapropter censeo et pre-sentis Cartæ Testimonio confirmo ut hæc præfata Ele-mosina quieta et illibata ab omni terreno servicio absoluta usibus prædictorum Monachorum in perpetuum permaneat, Testibus Christiana uxore mea, Willelmo filio meo, Ar-chibaldo Senescallo et multis alijs³.

236. Hæ sunt Metæ et Bundæ circumscri-bentes territorium et Villam de Wederhal ac proprium solum ejusdem Dominij.

Prima Meta ejusdem Territorij incipit ad mediam partem aquæ de Edene subtus Pontem vulgariter vocatum Werwyke-bryge sicut eadem prædicta aqua de Edene abinde decurrit versus Occidentem, et ab inde ascendit usque ad

---

² These two Churches were confirmed to the Abbey of S. Mary by Gilbert son of Reinfrid in No. **209**. This seems to shew that the property of Ketell passed on to Gilbert through William de Lancastre. The parish of Wirchington lies on the west coast of Cumberland immediately to the south of the river Derwent. The manor and the Church have long been (since 1563) in the possession of the family of Culwen or Curwen, who claim descent from Ketell through his son Orme who married Gunilda sister of Waldiev son of Gospatric ; see the long account and pedigree by W. Jackson, *Papers and Pedigrees*, vol. i. p. 288.

³ There is little known about Chetell son of Eltred to fix the date of this charter. This may well have been about the time of other numerous grants to the Abbey of S. Mary at York, at the end of the 11th century, and agrees with the probable date of No. **1** to which he is witness.

unum torrentem vocatum Sawbeke[1] usque ad quandam crucem quæ vocatur Wederhal Gyrthcrosse[2] usque Occidentem et stantem super prædictum torrentem prius nominatum et ab hinc percurrit ad Holmemyr versus Carsike[3] sicut Gyrthcrosse de Wederhal extendit et ab hinc ascendit usque ad Scotbybeke[4] et ab eadem fossa usque ad Cumwhyntyngbeke[5] et ab inde ascendit usque ad Mauriscum qui vocatur Wragmyre et ab eodem percurrit usque ad Meresyke[6] et hoc ex parte Australi, et ab inde usque

236. [1] Sawbeke, probably Saurbek, or Sorbek, like Saurby (No. **14**, note 12), from Norse *sògrr*, "swampy," runs nearly north, and into the Eden, just below the present Warwick Bridge, draining the swamp or marsh under the hill.

[2] Wederhal Gyrth Crosse, or Grith Cross, was the Cross which fixed the boundary of the Sanctuary of Wederhal at this point. Here we see the boundary of the manor turns towards the west, and the Cross would be at the junction of the fields now numbered 216, 27, 16 on the Ordnance Survey map (xxiv. 2). On the Grith Cross and the Wederhal right of Sanctuary, see Appendix C ; this Cross is described as *juxta Sicketam de Waryewyke* (Illustrative Doc. XXX.).

[3] Carsyke is a name still known ; it is given as bounding the parish of Warwick (see Nicolson and Burn, *History*, ii. 326), and now runs as a hollow down to Scotby beck. Several of the adjoining fields preserve the name.

[4] Scotby Beke, which here runs through the parish of Wederhal, flows north from this point to the river Eden, and is called lower down, on the flats near the river, Pow Maughan Beck (from *pow*, "a swamp," Norse *pollr*, compare powdike, "a dike in the fens," and Maughan, or Maughon, an old proper name). It is the continuation of Cumwhinton Beck from the south.

[5] Cumwhyntyngbeke runs, as of old, out of Wragmire Moss, or Marsh, all along the boundary of the manor. In 1354 Bishop Welton granted 40 days' indulgence to any that would contribute to the repair of the high road through Wragmire, and to the support of John de Corbrig, a poor hermit, living somewhere on or near the said road, *Register of Bp Welton*, MS. p. 112.

[6] Meresyke is evidently the same as Moss Ditch (see Ordnance Survey Map, xxxi. 2), bounding Wragmire Moss, where it becomes the boundary of both the parish and the manor. This is as far south

ad Sandewath⁷ et ab eodem usque ad Takyngate⁸ et ab inde pertransit per Stratam Regiam⁹ quæ vocatur Hee-Strette quæ ducit de Carliĩ usque ad Appilby way et ab inde usque ad Drybeke, et a Drybeke descendit usque ad medium aquæ de Eden, et hoc ex parte Orientali ; et sic descendit per medium aquæ de Eden usque ad prædictum Pontem vocatum Werwykbrigg versus Borientalem.

237. TERRA SIVE CULTURÆ DE DOMINIO IN VILLA SEU TERRITORIO DE SALKELD REGIS DE QUIBUS PRIOR DE WEDERHALE HABET PERCIPERE DUAS PARTES Xᵐᵃᵉ. ET RECTOR UNAM¹.

IN the Croftes VI. acræ. Item in the Fittes XXXVI. acræ, videlicet in Holme. Item in Langrigg XVIII. acræ. Item in the Tathes VI. acræ. Item in Hapeshowe IX. acræ. Item in Halborwan vel in les Ranylandes XII. acræ. Item in Smekergilbanke XVIII. acræ. Item in le Wym XVIII. acræ. Item in the Northfeld inter vias VI. acræ. Item in le Kyngesflatt XII. acræ. Item in the Watelandes VI. acræ.

Summa acrarum CXLVII.

as the boundary goes, and it turns east at the junction of the fields numbered 683, 684.

⁷ There is now Stonywath, near the boundary ; see Ordnance Survey Map, xxxi. 6.

⁸ There is still Tackengate Stone on the edge of field No. 605 and near the field in which is Black Moss Pool (Map xxxi. 7).

⁹ The road is close by, which must have been the line of the old high road or King's highway, from Carlisle to Appleby (see note 9 on No. **5**) ; crossing the road the boundary of the manor runs eastwards down Drybec (see Maps, xxxi. 7, 8), the name which still obtains, into the river Eden, above what is now called Low House.

237. ¹ The two parts of the tithe of Salkeld Regis, or Great Salkeld, here mentioned, were granted by Ranulph Meschin in No. **4**, where (note 4) see more on this Church.

238. TERRÆ IN DIVERSIS LOCIS JACENTES IN WARTHWYK[1] PERTINENTES AD DOMUM DE WEDERHAL, VIDELICET.

UNA roda terræ jacens super le Strangfordrodes versus occidentem juxta aquam de Eden altera pars terræ [duæ acræ et tres rodæ] abuttans super le Bothomrode. Item III. acræ jacent super le...stanflatt buttantes super le Rodeflatte in longitudine ex parte Orientali et in latitudine de la Graystane usque le Schortbottes versus Austrum VI. acræ jacentes in le Stokflatte. Item II. acræ in le Potteflatte. Item I. acra quæ vocatur le Gotacre. Item I. acra jacens in les Halfacres in duobus locis. Item II. rodæ de les bottes. Item I. acra a les bottesbrume. Item ½ acra jacens super les Staynbrigrodes, IIII. rodæ ibidem. Item in le Schonpetreflatte I. acra et ½. Item III. acræ in Kenedyflatte. Item ½ acra super les Stanylandes et I. acra ibidem. Item III. acræ super le Skeubanke. Item una acra et ½ in le Fulwaylandes. Item I. acra de le Toftland. Item I. roda super Rouclefbank. Item III. rodæ super le Crokedbrome. Item tres rodæ de le Bromeland. Item una roda et ½ de le Stanetresrodes. Item I. a le Tondelache. Item in Henryholm una Roda.

Omnes terræ prædictæ erant pertinentes ad Tenementum in quo Robertus Schephird nuper inhabitavit.

Summa Acrarum XXXIII. acræ II. rodæ et ½.

239. METÆ ET BUNDÆ.

TERRÆ de Morehouse[1] jacentes in diversis locis infra Dominium de Warthewyk pertinentes Priori de Wedyr-

238. [1] For the parish of Warthwic, and the Chapel, see note 4 on No. 5.

239. [1] Morehouse was in the south-east of the parish of Warthwic, abutting on the boundary of the manor of Wederhal; but sundry of the lands appear to have been on the flats in the north of the parish towards the river.

hale de nuper bundatæ, videlicet xxvi⁰ die Januarii Anno
Domini MCCCCLV⁰. tempore fratris Thomæ Bothe² tunc
Prioris de Wedyrhale et Johannis de Warthewyk tunc
Domini de Warthewyk per Sacramentum Thomæ Lowson
de Warthewyk, Johannis Stabyll de eadem et Johannis
Ded de eadem tunc dictis die et tempore coram præfatis
Priore et Domino de Warthwyk pro bundatione dictæ
terræ juratorum, tunc ibidem præsentibus et astantibus
Thoma Vasy, Roberto Bowsted tunc Ballivo de Wedyr-
hale, Thoma Morpath tunc Ballivo dicti Domini de
Warthewyk et Johanne Wra tunc commorante in dicto
Tenemento de Morehouse.

Inprimis prædicti juratores præsentant et dicunt quod
sunt ibidem infra dictum Dominium I. acra vocata le
Toftlandakyr, cujus unus finis abuttat super Bromlands et
alius finis versus Lynstock.   Item ½ acra terræ cujus unus
finis abuttat super les Bromlands et alius finis versus
Lynstok.   Item III. rodæ de les Bromlands buttantes
super terram quæ vocatur le Bromylcroft.   Item I. roda
et ½ terræ buttantes super altam viam et super les Bromlands.   Item le Tendlatheakyr buttans super altam viam
et super communam de Warthewyk.   Item I. roda terræ
jacens super Roclyfbank et buttans super le Skewgh.
Item I. acra terræ jacens super Roclifbank et buttans super
le Skewgh.   Item III. acræ terræ jacentes super Roclifbank et super dictum Skewgh.   Item I. acra terræ parcell
de les Halfakyrs abuttans super Henry-holme et super les
Halfakyrs.   Item ½ acra terræ parcell de les Halfakyrs
abuttans super Henry-holme et super les Halfakyrs.   Item
I. acra terræ parcell de les Halfakyrs abuttans super
Warthewyk-wath et super les Halfakyrs.   Item le Showp-
treflat continens II. acras terræ parcell de les Halfakyrs

---

² Thomas Bothe, Prior of Wederhal, here on January 26th, 1455,
was elected Abbot of S. Mary's, at York, October 16th, 1464, where he
remained until 1485 (see Appendix E).

abuttantes super Roclifyate et super les Halfakyrs. Item
II. acræ parcell de les Halfakyrs abuttantes super altam
viam et super aquam de Eden. Item ½ acra terræ parcell
de les Halfakyrs abuttans super altam viam et super aquam
de Eden. Item ½ acra terræ parcell de les Halfakyrs
abuttans super altam viam et super Mydyleholmwath.
Item I. acra terræ vocata le Goteakyr jacens in longitudine per aquam de Eden. Item I. roda terræ vocata
Strawfordrode abuttans super aquam de Eden versus castellum de Lynstok et super les Bothomrodes. Item II.
acræ terræ vocatæ Grastanflatt jacentes super les Short-
butts, versus aquam de Eden. Item le Stockflatt continens
V. acras terræ abuttantes super le Soketflatt et super altam
viam. Item le Pittflatt continens II. acras terræ abuttantes super altam viam et super le Goteakyr. Item
dimidium acræ terræ abuttans super altam viam et super
le Syke vocatum Whetlandsyke. Item II. acræ jacentes
super le Butbrome et abuttantes super les Halfakyrs et
super altam viam. Item II. acræ terræ abuttantes super
terram de Aglunby et super terram vocatam ffulla-lands.
Item I. acra et ½ terræ vocatæ ffulla-lands abuttantes super
altam viam, et super les Halfakyrs et super Fulladub.
Item I. acra terræ vocata Stanbryglands.

ADDITIONAL CHARTERS

GIVEN IN TRANSCRIPT C, HARLEIAN MANUSCRIPTS, NUMBER 1881*.

240. CARTA ABBATIS EBORACI EPISCOPO KAR-
LIOLENSI FACTA DE ECCLESIJS DE ORMESHEVED MUS-
GRAVE BURGHE APULBY[1].

UNIVERSIS Christi fidelibus ad quos præsens Scriptum
pervenerit Thomas[2] Abbas et Conventus Sanctæ Mariæ
Eboraci Salutem in Domino. Noverit universitas vestra nos
unanimi assensu et consensu Capituli nostri dedisse et
concessisse venerabili Patri et Domino Silvestro Dei Gratia
Karliolensi Episcopo suisque successoribus jus Patronatus

---

240. [1] This assignment to the Bishops of Carlisle of the Churches
of Ormesheved (Ormside), Musgrave and Clibburne, and the Vicarage
of S. Michael, Appleby, is given in full by Bishop Nicolson (MSS.
vol. ii. pp. 17, 417), as being taken from the *Register of Wederhal*,
fol. 21 *a*. For the last Church see note 1 on No. **3**; and for
Ormesheved and Cliburn see No. **16**. This document, which has been
most carelessly copied in Transcript C, has been corrected from these
copies.

[2] Thomas de Wardhull, or Warterhille, was elected Abbot of
S. Mary's at York in 1244. He died in December 1257 (Dugdale,
Monasticon, iii. 538).

* These additions, probably from their later date or often doubtful
character, are not found in the two Transcripts in the Dean and Chapter
Library at Carlisle; but they seem to have been, at all events about 1702, in
the ancient manuscript of the Register, which was formerly in the possession
of the Dean and Chapter.

Ecclesiarum de Ormesheved de Musgrave et de Clibburne salvis nobis antiquis et consuetis pensionibus de eisdem et jus Patronatus Ecclesiæ de Burgo[3] absque aliqua pensione nobis solvenda et Vicariæ Ecclesiæ Sancti Michaelis de Appleby quæ quidem Vicaria taxabitur ad Valorem viginti Marcarum secundum Estimacionem bonorum virorum et legalium Salva tamen Nobis et Monasterio nostro antiqua et consueta pensione de dicta Ecclesia Sancti Michaelis de Appleby a Priore de Wedderhal qui pro tempore ibidem fuerit annuatim percipienda. Et nos et successores nostri dicto Episcopo et Successoribus suis advocationes dictarum Ecclesiarum et dictæ Vicariæ contra omnes homines imperpetuum warantizabimus. In cujus rei Testimonium præsenti scripto sigillum Capituli nostri duximus apponendum. Datum apud Eborum, octavo Idus Maij Anno Domini Millesimo ducentesimo quadragesimo octavo[4].

241. CONVENTIO DE DECIMIS DE MEABURN INTER ABBATEM DE WHITBY ET ABBATEM DE EBORACO[1].

OMNIBUS Christi fidelibus hoc scriptum visuris vel audituris P.[2] Abbas et Conventus de Whitby salutem in Domino sempiternam. Noverit universitas vestra nos tenere ad perpetuam firmam de Abbate et Conventu Beatæ Mariæ Eborum duas partes decimæ de Dominico de Mayburne[3]

---

[3] Burgh, or Brough, under Stanemore.

[4] Dated May 8th, 1248.

241. [1] The corresponding document will be found in the *Chartulary of Whitby* (ed. Atkinson, i. 216, No. cclxxii.), R. (Robert de Longo Campo, 1197—1239) Abbot of S. Mary's, York, being the other party; from this the above has been corrected.

[2] Peter, Abbot of Whitby, occurs 1190 to 1204, and is said to have died in 1211 (*Chart. Whitby*, i. p. lxxxvii.).

[3] Mayburne, or Meaburn, *hodie* Mauld's Meaburn in the parish of Crosby Ravensworth; this two-thirds of the tithe was granted by Ranulph Meschin (see note 3 on No. 4).

scilicet garbarum, et omnium aliarum decimacionum, Reddendo inde annuatim Monachis suis de Wederhala decem quartera frumenti boni et pacabilis apud domos suas de Appleby, die fori. Ita quidem quod dictum bladum persolvetur eis plene, vel eorum assignatis inter Festum Sancti Michaelis et Pascha proximo sequens. Si vero frumentum a Nobis oblatum bonum et pacabile non fuerit, dabimus eis precium boni frumenti et pacabilis secundum estimacionem fori de Appelbi. Si vero frumentum vel precium infra dictos terminos plene non solvimus dabimus fabricæ Beatæ Sanctæ Mariæ Karlioli nomine pœnæ dimidiam marcam argenti et nichilominus bladum non solutum vel precium. Si vero contigerit Abbaciam de Witeby esse in custodia Domini Regis, cum destituta fuerit Abbate, et custos Abbaciæ ex parte Regis deputatus, ut supra scriptum est, dictum bladum vel pretium non persolverit, Nos tempore substituti Abbatis sine aliqua difficultate et contradictione de blado non soluto vel pretio memoratis Monachis vel eorum Assignatis apud domos suas de Appelbi plenarie satisfaciemus. Si vero contigerit Nos aliquo casu per aliquem Ecclesia de Crosseby Ravenssuart esse destitutos, et occasione hujusmodi destitutionis a solutione dicti bladi vel pretij, prout scriptum est supra, cessavisse, licebit Abbati et Conventui Beatæ Mariæ Eborum et Monachis de Wederhala, non obstante Carta quam de eis habemus, liberum habere regressum ad perceptionem dictarum decimarum sine aliqua contradictione vel impedimento. Nos vero subjecimus nos et res nostras jurisdiccioni Officialis Karliolensis, qui pro tempore fuerit, ut ipse plenariam habeat potestatem compellandi Nos per censuram Ecclesiasticam omni appellatione remota, non obstante fori privilegio, ad omnia supradicta inviolabiliter observanda. Ut autem hoc præsens scriptum inconcussæ firmitatis robur optineat Commune Sigillum Domūs Nostræ eidem dignum duximus apponendum[4].

---

[4] The date of the Convention will lie between 1190 and 1211.

242. COMPOSITIO INTER CONVENTUM DE WATTON
ET RECTOREM DE MORLAND DE DECIMIS.

[The same as No. **208.**]

243. CARTA WILLELMI FILIJ ROGERI ET OSANNÆ
UXORIS DE CORKBY.

OMNIBUS etc., Willielmus filius Rogeri[1] et Osanna uxor
sua de Corkby salutem æternam in Domino. Noverit
universitas vestra nos Divinæ Pietatis intuitu, pro salute
animarum prædecessorum et successorum nostrorum, dedisse, concessisse, et præsenti charta nostra confirmasse Deo
et Abbaciæ Sanctæ Mariæ Eborum et Domui Sanctæ
Trinitatis et Sancti Constantini de Wedderal et Monachis
ibidem Deo servientibus in puram et perpetuam Elemosynam mortuum Boscum crescentem et siccum per totum
Boscum nostrum de Corkby, insuper et virides quercus
stantes quæ in croppo deficiant, et quaslibet alias quercus
stantes in dicto bosco, exceptis tantum illis querculis
quarum frondes virescunt per totum, tam in summo quam
in demisso, et sunt multum utiles ad glandem ferendam, et
sunt bonæ et faciles ad findendum ad longum maremium ad
Domos faciendum. Ita scilicet quod liceat dictis Monachis
in perpetuum capere predictum mortuum Boscum et quercus predictas per totum Boscum nostrum de Corkby ad
sustentationem Domus, sive ad comburendum ubi magis
fuerit ad commodum suum et Esgamentum, et kariare tam
per terram nostram quam per aquam sicut melius sibi
viderint expedire sine visu aliquo vel impedimento nostro
vel hæredum. Et licebit dictis Monachis habere liberum
ingressum et exitum tam in prædicto Bosco cum karris et
kareatis suis quandocunque voluerint, et congregare lignarium suum ubi voluerint in terra nostra, et facere et
securare sibi iter per totum prædictum Boscum ubi magis

---

243. [1] William son of Roger de Corkeby occurs in the year 1247
No. **144**), see also note 2 on No. **64.**

viderint expedire ad lignarium suum karriandum sine
aliquo impedimento, excepto nocumento bladorum semi-
natorum. Si autem karri et karreatæ dictorum Monachorum in Bosco vel in Campo de Corkby fracti fuerint,
quotiescunque hoc evenerit, licebit dictis Monachis capere
meremium quolibet viridi Bosco, quantum necesse fuerit
ad reparacionem eorum, sine alicujus visu vel impedimento
aliquo. Insuper autem dicti Monachi habebunt pasturam
ad boves et equos suos per totum Boscum et Campum de
Corkby sine aliquo retinemento vel impedimento, cum
boscum suum karriabunt. Insuper concessimus et confirmamus eisdem Monachis omnia Bona et omnes Ele-
mosynas quæ Antecessores nostri Domini de Corkby eis
dederunt, sicut in eorum chartis plenius continetur. Nos
vero et Hæredes nostri totam hanc prædictam donationem
nostram et confirmationem et concessionem prædictis Monachis warantizabimus in perpetuum. Et ad hoc faciendum sacramento corporaliter prestito Nos et Hæredes
nostros obligamus. Insuper autem ad majorem et ad
perpetuam securitatem præsenti scripto sigilla nostra apposuimus. Hijs Testibus, Radulpho Priore, Waltero Officiali, Richardo Vicecomite Karlioli, Ricardo de Levington,
Petro de Tyllol, Roberto de Castlecarrock, Willelmo de
Warthwick, Henrico Capellano, Gilberto Diacono, Johanne
filio Willelmi, Johanne de Aguluneby, Stephano de Holmes-
ley et alijs[2].

244. CONVENTIO INTER PRIOREM DE WEDDERHALE
ET RICARDUM SALKELD DE CORKBY, DE STAGNO.

Hæc Indentura facta inter Religiosos Viros Dominum
Wilhelmum de Tanfeld[1] Priorem Cellæ sive Prioratus de

---

[2] These witnesses are most of them the same as in No. **187**,
except Richard Sheriff (probably Richard le Brun, see note 5 on
No. **97**), and often occur with William son of Roger. From the
Sheriff and the Prior, the date is probably about 1235.
244. [1] William de Tanfeld was admitted Prior of Wederhal in

Wedderal et ejusdem loci Monachos ex una parte, et
Richardum de Salkeld[2] Dominum de Corkby ex altera
Testatur quod cum ante diem confectionis præsentium inter
dictas partes meta fuisset materia dissentionis controversiæ
et Brigæ super quodam Stagno[3] per dictos Religiosos in

November 1341. This was the second Prior of the name, see Appendix E.

    [2] Richard de Salkeld obtained the manor of Corkby by grant
from Edward III. October 15th, 1335, confirming the gift of his father.
The manor had been escheated to Edward II. on the attainder of
Andrew de Hartcla in March 1323 ; see the *Chronicon de Lanercost*
(ed. J. Stevenson, p. 251), whence it would appear that Richard
de Salkelde was one of those who seized the Earl, for which he was
rewarded with the vill of Magna Corkeby. He was succeeded, it
is said, by his son John ; but the account of his successors is not by
any means clear (see Nicolson and Burn, *History*, ii. 336, and the
inaccurate list of lords of Corby referred to before, given in a note by
Hutchinson, *Cumberland*, i. 170). There was another Richard de
Salkeld at Corby in the time of Edward IV. and Henry VII. He
married Jane Vaux, the daughter of Sir Roland Vaux of Tryermain.
In 1467 Edward IV. granted him the manors of Caldbek, Uldale and
Wigton and other property for his eminent services in rescuing the
city and castle of Carlisle from the rebels in the rebellion of James,
late Earl of Wilteshire (*Calend. Doc. Scot.*, ed. Bain, iv. 278). He died
in 1503, and was buried in the Church at Wetherhal on February 18th.
The effigy of himself and his wife in Wetherhal Church carries with it
this legend, as Bishop Nicolson copied it in 1703 (*Miscellany
Accounts*, p. 49, MS. p. 32), "over the Arch, betwixt the Quire and
ye North Isle, in old characters almost obliterated " ·

> "Here lyes Sir Richard Salkeld that Knight,
> Who in this Land was mickle of might.
> The Captain and Keeper of Carlisle was he,
> And also the Lord of Corkby.
> And now he lyes under this Stane,
> He and his Lady Dame Jane.
> The eighteenth day of Februere
> This Gentle Knight was bury'd here.
> I pray you all that this do see
> Pray for their Souls for Charitie,
> For as they are now so must we all be."

terra de Corkby noviter attachiato et constructo supra et extra locum, videlicet solitum ubi firmari seu figi antiquitus consueverit versus Corkby : Necnon petræ et ramorum perceptione, ac riparum concessione in ipsa terra de Corkby, prout in quadam Carta cujusdam olim Domini de Corkby inde confecta plenius continetur. Tandem communibus amicis pro utraque parte prædicta intervenientibus dicta dissensio conquievit in hunc modum : videlicet, quod præfatus Richardus, habito respectu ad dictorum Religiosorum cartas, munimenta et eorum jura concessit et confirmavit pro se et Hæredibus suis, quod ipsi Religiosi possint ipsum nominatum Stagnum sicut constructum et firmatum exaltare et reparare, illudque seu aliud vel alia eo majora et altiora in eodem loco et ab illo loco ubicunque quandocunque et quotiescunque voluerint, usque ad et in ripam cujusdam loci qui dicitur Munkwath versus le Brigend attachiare, firmare, facere, reparare, et exaltare, habere et tenere in perpetuum. Necnon diversa exclusagia coffinos seu piscarias in eisdem stagnis facere et construere : et de salmonibus et alijs piscibus quibuscunque in eis captis seu capiendis libere disponere modo quo viderint meliori. Concedit insuper et confirmat prædictus Richardus pro se et Hæredibus suis quod ipsi Religiosi possint quotiens voluerint ipsum Novum Stagnum sive aliud quodcunque infra metas prædictas facere reparare et exaltare; et petram et ramos capere sufficienter in territorio de Corkby, ubi capere solebant pro ipsis stagnis faciendis seu reparandis sine contradictione vel impedimento ipsius Richardi vel Hæredum suorum. Et quod dicti Monachi habeant et teneant totam aquam de Edene et totam piscariam a superiori parte dicti novi stagni versus Corkby usque prædictum locum vocatum Le Munkwath in usu suo separati, tanquam jus Ecclesiæ suæ in perpetuum : Itaque dictus Richardus nec Hæredes sui quicquid juris infra illas divisas ex nunc clamare possit

³ The *stagnum*, or pool, connected with the fishing weir is first mentioned in the grant of Ranulph Meschin, see note 2 on No. **2**.

quoquo modo. Nec licebit supradicto Richardo, Hæredibus suis, aut alicui suorum hominum præfatos Religiosos seu eorum famulos impedire quomodolibet quominus per bacillos, retia, et alia instrumenta piscandi et eadem trahendi, cum libero introitu et exitu, in ripis de Corkby, infra metas prædictas, videlicet a superiori parte novi stagni versus Corkby, usque Le Munkwath libere piscari poterint in futurum. Et præfatus Richardus et Hæredes sui supradictas concessiones et confirmationes prædictis Religiosis contra omnes gentes warantizabimus in perpetuum. In cujus rei Testimonium partes supradictæ partibus hujus indenturæ sigilla sua alternatim apposuerunt. Hijs Testibus, Dominis Hugone de Morriceby tunc Vicecomite Cumbriæ, Petro Tilliol militibus, Johanne de Stapleton, Johanne de Warthwick juniore, Alano de Kirkby et alijs. Datum apud Wedderhall die Lunæ in Festo Oswaldi Regis et Martyris[4] Anno Domini M. CCC. quadragesimo secundo, et Regni Regis Edvardi Tertij a Conquestu, sexto decimo[5].

245. DISTRIBUTIO CUMBERLANDIÆ AD CONQUESTUM ANGLIÆ[1].

REX Willielmus Dux Normanniæ, Conquestor Angliæ, dedit totam terram de Comitatu Cumbriæ Ranulpho de

---

[4] Oswald was the well known King of Northumbria, who defeated the heathen Ceadwalla a few miles north of Hexham in 634, and was killed in battle against the heathen Penda on the 5th of August, 642, that day being afterwards the day of his festival.

[5] The date of the charter is August 5th, 1342.

245. [1] This *Distributio Cumberlandiæ ad Conquestum Angliæ* is one of those common and inaccurate compilations found in so many of these old Registers and Chartularies. In the copy given by Dugdale (*Monasticon*, iii. p. 584), from the MS. *Reg. de Wetherhall penes D. Williel. Howard de Naworth an.* 1638, it has the title *Chronicon Cumbriæ.* Machel, who also gives a copy (MSS. vol. iv. p. 408), says "The title *Chronicon Cumbriæ* is writ in a late hand," and he refers to fol. clxi. All these copies have been very carelessly

Meschinis; et Galfrido fratri ejusdem Ranulphi totum Comitatum de Cestriæ; et Willielmo fratri eorundem totam terram de Coupland inter Duden et Derwynt.

Ranulphus de Meschinis feoffavit Hubertum de Vaux, de Baronia de Gillesland; et Ranulphum fratrem ejus de Soureby, Karlaton et Hubbradby[2]; et Robertum fratrem Eorundem de Baronia de Dalston. Et feoffavit Robertum de Estervers de Baronia de Burgo; et Richerum de Boyvill de Baronia de Levington; et Odardum de Logis de Baronia de Stainton. Et Feoffavit Waldevum filium Gospatrick Comitis de Dunbar de Scotia de tota Baronia de Allerdall in Wathpoll[3] et Derweynt.

Prædictus Willielmus de Meschinis, Dominus de Coupland feoffavit prædictum Waldevum filium Gospatricii de tota terra inter Kokyr et Derwynt simul cum quinque Villis; scilicet, Brigham, Eglesfield, Dene, Bramwhayt, Graysothen, et duo Clifton et Stainburn. Et feoffavit Odardum Le clefs[4] de quarta parte de Crossehayte pro custodia Austercorum suorum.

Galfridus de Meschinis Comes Cestriæ obijt sine Hærede de corpore suo; et Ranulphus de Meschinis fuit Comes Cestriæ; et reddidit Domino Regi totum Comitatum Cumbriæ, tali conditione, ut singuli feoffati sui tenuissent terras suas de Domino Rege in capite.

transcribed. It is here printed as in the Harleian MS. except a few manifest errors; some of the variations are noted below. It was evidently a late addition to the MS. *Register*, full of blunders; and far too much use has been made of it by some of the older local historians. There is a document curiously similar, and, if possible, more untrustworthy, in the *Tower Miscellaneous Rolls*, No. $\frac{459}{3}$, quoted by J. Bain (*Calend. Doc. Scot.* ii. 15); he places it about 1275, and has the not improbable conjecture that it was a statement by the monks of Holm Cultram, which its last clause and reference seems to support.

[2] Habbrughtly (Dugdale), Hubbrightby (Machel), *hod.* Upperby.

[3] Wathenpole (D., M.) *hod.* Wampool.

[4] le Clerke (D.), le Clarke (M.).

Prædictus Waldevus filius Comitis Gospatricij feoffavit Odardum de Logis de Baronia de Wygeton, Drundrey[5], Waverton, Blencoggen et Kirkbride : qui fundavit Ecclesiam de Wygeton. Et dedit Odardo filio Liolfe Talentir et Castlerig cum Foresta inter Greta et Calter : Et dedit Priori et Conventui de Giseburn, Appleton et Brydekirk cum advocatione ejusdem Ecclesiæ : Et dedit Adæ filio Liolfe, Ulnedale et Giterus[6] : Et dedit Gamello filio Brun nichil[7] : Et dedit Waldevo filio Gillemini cum Octreda[8] sorore sua Brochton, Ribeton et parvam Brochton. Et Gualī dedit[9] ad unam logam : Et dedit Ormo filio Ketelli, Seton, Camberton, Flemyngby, Graysothen cum Gimilda sorore sua : Et dedit Dolphino filio Ayleward cum Matella[10] sorore sua Aplewhayt et parvam Crosby Langrigg et Brigham, cum advocatione ejusdem Ecclesiæ. Dedit Melbethe Medico suo Villam de Brumfield, salva sibi advocatione ejusdem Ecclesiæ.

Alanus filius et Hæres ejusdem Waldevi dedit Ranulpho de Lindesey Blenrasset et Uckemanby cum Octreda[11] sorore sua. Et dedit Wilfrido[12] filio Fergusij Domino Galluyd[13] cum Gamilda sorore sua, Torpennou cum advocatione Ecclesiæ. Et dedit Ketello Le Despencer, Threpland. Et dedit Herberto Villam de Thornesby pro tertia parte unius Villæ[14] ; Et dedit Gamello Le Brun, Ysoll et

[5] Dondragt (D.), Dendraght (M.).   For Greta et Calter, Caltre et Greca (Dugdale, Machel).

[6] Gilcruce (D., M.).

[7] Bothill (D., M.).

[8] Ethreda (D., M.).

[9] Instead of " Et Gualī dedit," D. and M. have "et Dunwaldofe ac Bowaldofe."

[10] Matilda (D., M.).

[11] Etheldreda (D.), Etherela (M.).

[12] Ugthredo (D.), Uthredo (M.).

[13] Galwedia (D., M.).

[14] D. and M. here insert " Et dedit Cospatricio filio Ormi Altam Ireby pro tertia parte unius Villæ."

Ruthewhayt pro tertia parte unius Villæ. Et dedit Radulpho Engayne Yssoyl cum pertinentijs, Blencrayke cum servicio de Newton. Et idem Alanus habuit unum fratrem bastardum nomine Gospatricium, cui dedit Boulton, Bastenwayte et Estholm. Et dedit Odardo Newton cum pertinentijs. Et dedit tribus Venatoribus suis, scilicet Selip et socijs suis, Hayton, Et dedit Uctrido unam carucatam terræ in Aspatrick, ut esset summonitor in Allerdale : Et dedit Dolphino sex bovatas terræ in alta Crosby, ut esset Serviens Domini R[egis] in Allerdale. Et dedit Simoni de Sheftlings medietatem de Derham ; Et dedit Dolfino filio Gospatricij aliam medietatem. Et dedit Waldevo filio Dolfini Brackenthwayte. Et dedit Prioratui Sanctæ Begæ Stayneburn. Et dedit Prioratui Karlioli, cum corpore Waldevi filij sui, crucem sanctam, quam adhuc possident ; et Crosby cum advocatione Ecclesiæ ejusdem, et cum servicio Uchtredi, et advocatione Ecclesiæ de Aspatrick cum servicio Alani de Brenton[15], et advocatione Ecclesiæ de Ireby cum servicio Waldevi de Langthwayt.

Idem Alanus filius Waldevi dedit Domino H. Regi seniori landas Forestæ de Allerdall, una cum venatione Gospatricij[16] apud Holme coltram.

Cui Alano successit Willelmus filius Duncani Comes de Murres, nepos ipsius Alani et Hæres procreatus ex Octrida[17] sorore Waldevi.

Idem Willielmus filius Duncani qui desponsavit Aliciam filiam Roberti de Romeley Domini de Skypton in Cravene, Qui Robertus quondam desponsaverat filiam Willelmi de Meschinis, Domini de Coupland. Idem Willielmus procreavit ex predicta Domina[18] uxore sua Willielmum puerum de Egremond, qui infra ætatem obijt, et tres filias, quarum

---

[15] Brayton (D., M.).
[16] Instead of " Gospatricij," D. and M. have " quando hospitavit."
[17] Ethreda (D., M.).
[18] Alicia (D., M.).

prior nomine Sebilla [Cecilia][19] maritata fuit cum Honore
de Skypton Willelmo le Gross Comiti Albemarliæ, per
Dominum H. Regem Angliæ. Et secunda, nomine Amabilla maritata fuit Reginaldo de Lucy cum Honore de
Egermond per eundem Regem. Et tertia, nomine Alicia
de Romely maritata fuit Gilberto Pippard, cum Aspatrick,
et Baronia de Allerdall et Libertate de Kokerune[20], per
eundem Regem; et postea per Reginam Roberto de
Courtney, et obijt sine hærede.

Willielmus Grossus Comes Albemarliæ genuit ex Cecilia Halewissam; cui successit Willielmus de Fortibus
comes Albemarliæ; cui successit alter Willelmus de Fortibus; cui successit Avelina quæ desponsata fuit Domino
Edmundo fratri Domini Regis Edvardi, qui obijt sine
prole.

Reginaldus de Lucy genuit ex Amabilla Richardum de
Lucy, Amabilliam et Aliciam : et successit Amabilliæ Lam-
bertus de Multon; cui successit Thomas de Multon; et
successit Aliciæ, Thomas de Lucy.

246. RELAXATIO DE MESSUAGIO IN SLEGILL.

[An abstract of No. 220 badly transcribed.]

247. CARTA ENISANDI FILIJ WALTERI DE TERRIS IN COLBY[1].

SCIANT tam præsentes quam futuri, quod Ego Enisandus
filius Walteri, concessi et dedi et hac mea Carta confirmavi

---

[19] Cicilia (D., M.).

[20] Cokermouth (D., M.). There are considerable variations in the
last clauses in the several copies.

247. [1] This is the same charter as No. 251, and is the grant
referred to in No. 14, made by Constantine (Enisant) son of Walter;
see note 13 there, also note 1 on No. 227. His name is given as
Enisant Musart in No. 248 and is so copied by Machel (MSS., iv.
474), but with some doubt; it is clearly an error, and the mistake in
No. 252 (see note 3) shews that there was a difficulty in the MS.

Deo et Sanctæ Mariæ Eborum, et Monachis de Wedderhall, in puram et perpetuam Elemosynam unam carucatam terræ in Colby, cum prato adjacente et cæteris pertinentijs et aisiamentis, Tenendam libere et quiete ab omni terreno servicio. Hanc donationem feci prædictis Monachis pro salute animæ meæ et uxoris meæ et omnium parentum meorum. Testibus, Warrino Capellano de Bogtres, Turgestio de Rusdall[2], Willelmo de Harrais, Odardo Vice-Comite, Odone Walisca, Petro de Venice et Astius fratre ejus, Hugone de Ancavilla, Roberto de Lauda, Ricardo Sanard, et Willelmo fratre ejus, et multis alijs[3].

248. Carta Willelmi Brittan de terris in Colby.

[This is the same as No. 252, see page 392.]

249. Carta Gospatricij filij Ormi de terris in Flemingby[1].

Gospatricius filius Ormi[2] et Egelina uxor ejus, omnibus filijs Sanctæ Ecclesiæ salutem, Sciatis me dedisse et

---

[2] Turgest de Rusdall would seem to be the same as Turgis de Russedal, who, with Hugh de Morevil and Robert de Stutevill, is witness to the grant of Henry II. to Hubert de Vallibus in 1157 (see Illustrative Doc. XXII.). He can therefore scarcely be identical with Turgis Brundis (as Lysons, *Cumb.* p. 11), to whom, according to *Testa de Nevill* (p. 379 *b*), Ranulf Meschin gave the Barony of Lyddel before 1120. Robert de Stutevill founded the nunnery of Russedall, or Rosedale, in Yorkshire, and it will probably be learned that this Turgis de Russedal was connected with that place. He was certainly "Lord of the manor of Lydale" (*Inquis. ad quod dam.* 2 Edw. III. No. 3, Record Com. p. 288), and was not improbably the son of Turgis Brundis.

[3] For the probable date, see on Odard the sheriff in No. 72.

249. [1] This is a grant to the Priory of Carlisle which has been inserted here.

[2] Gospatric son of Orm was the grandson of Ketell, or Chetell, who granted Morland and Workington to the Abbey of S. Mary at York (see on No. 235). Waldiev, the son of Earl Gospatric and Baron

in perpetuam Elemosinam confirmasse Deo et Ecclesiæ
Sanctæ Mariæ Carlioli et Canonicis ibidem Deo servientibus totam terram illam quam Aculphus de nobis tenuit
juxta Flemingby inter duas Villas, cum bosco et pastura,
et omnibus alijs rebus prædictæ terræ juste pertinentibus,
pro salute animarum nostrarum et Parentum nostrorum,
liberam et quietam ab omni servicio et terrena exactione

of Allerdale below Derwent, had given to Orm with Gunilda in
marriage Seton, Camerton, Flemingby (Flimby), and Graysothen
(see No. 245, and on Waldiev in No. 1). Gospatric son of Orm attested
the Charter of Earl Henry, son of David, King of Scotland, with
Bishop Athelwold, to the Abbey of Holm Cultram in 1150 (Illustrative
Doc. XXIV.); and to that Abbey he gave Flemingby, "excepta
terra de Waytecroft, quam prius dederam Canonicis de Karliolo,"
which is probably the land mentioned in this Charter (see *Register of
Holm Cult.* MS. p. 34). His son and heir Thomas and another son
Alan are parties to the above grant. Another son Adam was parson
of Camerton (see note 3 on No. 28). His wife's name is here given as
Egelina. In the *Register of S. Bees* (Harleian MSS., No. 434, pp. 23,
24) there are charters of Gospatric, mentioning Egelina his wife,
Thomas his son and heir, Gilbert and Alan his sons, and Ebrea his
mother. His name appears in the earliest Pipe Roll of Henry II. (for
Cumberland) in 1158, and frequently afterwards. In the Pipe Rolls
for Westmoreland (which was then reckoned with Yorkshire) in 1176
and down to 1179, he appears as having to pay a fine of 500 marcs for
having surrendered the Royal Castle of Appelbi to William the Lion,
King of Scotland, in 1174. Others well known in the district were
fined with him. He is spoken of at that time by Jordan Fantosme in
his curious poem as "Cospatric le fiz Horm, un viel Engleis fluri"
(*Chronicle of the War in* 1173—74, ed. Surtees Soc., xi. 66). He
probably died in 1179. In the same Pipe Rolls for 1176, 1177, we
find William son of William paying 30 marcs "ut habeat duellum
versus Gospatricium fil. Orm," no doubt the same person. Thomas
son of Gospatric was the Founder of the Abbey of Shap, or Heppe,
and gave to that Abbey the Church of Shap. The grants are given in
Dugdale, *Monasticon*, vi. 868. Thomas must have died in 1201, or
very shortly before, as Roger de Bello Campo and Grecia the widow
of Thomas are then put in the Pipe Rolls as owing 100 marcs for having
custody of his lands and of his heir. Some of the local historians
wrongly place his death much earlier.

ad nos pertinentibus. Testibus, Michaele fratre Gospatricij, Ormo filio Dolfini, Waltero Probro de Wirchington,
Ricardo Probro, Alano Probro, Richardo Harsele, Mattheo
de Heppa, Edŏ serviente.

250. CONFIRMATIO WILLELMI REGIS SUPER CELLA
SANCTI CONSTANTINI, CUM MANERIO DE WEDDERALL
CUM PERTINENTIJS[1].

WILLELMUS Rex Angliæ Archiepiscopo T. Eborum,
Justiciarijs, Vice-comitibus et omnibus Baronibus fidelibus
suis Francis Eboracishire et de Carliolo salutem, Sciatis
me concessisse et confirmasse Deo et Ecclesiæ Sanctæ
Mariæ Eborum et Abbati Ricardo et Monachis ibidem
Deo servientibus, Cellam Sancti Constantini cum Manerio
de Wedderhall, et cum Capella de Warthwic, et cum
exclusagio et stagno et piscaria, et de Molendino de Wedderall quod fixum et firmatum in terra de Corkby: Quas
quidem terras habuerant ex dono Ranulphi Meschine
Comitis Cumbriæ[2] in puram et perpetuam Elemosinam.
Et confirmo eis ex Dono meo totam Pasturam inter Eden
et Regiam Viam quæ ducit de Karliolo ad Appleby apud
Wedderall usque ad Drybeck. Quapropter prohibeo ut
nulli alij perturbent aut rident [violent] hanc nostram confirmationem sive donationem prædictis Monachis factam.
Testibus hijs, Uxore mea Lucia, Henrico fratre meo,
Odardo, Hildredo Militibus, Enesaunt Muserd, cum alijs.

251. CARTA ONISANDI DE TERRIS IN COLLEBY.

[This is the same as No. **247.**]

250. [1] This document is an absurd combination of the charters of
Ranulf Meschin and the charter of Henry I. (No. **5**). In the first
edition of Dugdale's *Monasticon* (vol. i. p. 397) this is said to be
ex collectionibus August. Vincent e registro de Wederhale, and is
headed *Carta Willielmi Regis Conquestoris dicti*, though the name of
the Conqueror does not appear in the text of the charter.

[2] This title is never given to Ranulf Meschin in any genuine
charter.

252. CARTA WILLELMI DE BRETON DE TERRIS IN COLLEBY[1].

OMNIBUS Sanctæ Matris Ecclesiæ filijs tam præsentibus quam futuris, Willelmus Breton de Colleby[2] salutem: Sciatis me concessisse et hac mea præsenti carta confirmasse Deo et Sanctæ Mariæ de Eboraco et Abbati Clementi et successoribus ejus, et Monachis ibidem Deo et Sanctæ Mariæ servientibus in liberam et puram et perpetuam Elemosynam pro salute animæ meæ et Emmæ Sponsæ meæ et pro animabus Patris mei et Matris meæ et omnium Antecessorum et Successorum meorum totam illam carucatam terræ in Colleby quæ fuit Durandi cum omnibus pertinentijs suis et aisiamentis prædictæ Villæ adjacentibus, sicut carta quam habet de donatione ejusdem Durandi[3] testatur. Quare volo ut prædictus Clemens Abbas de Eboraco et Successores ejus, et Monachi ibidem Deo et Beatæ Mariæ servientes, habeant et teneant illam prædictam carucatam terræ de me, et de hæredibus meis tam liberam et quietam ab omni servicio et exactione

252.   [1] This is the same charter as No. **248** and refers to the carucate of land given by Enisand in No. **247** (or No. **251**).

[2] William Breton, or Brittan, de Coleby is, no doubt, identical with the William de Colebi who, in the Pipe Rolls for 1176, is fined 40s. for advising the surrender of Appleby Castle by Gospatric son of Orm (see on No. **249**). He is spoken of in a trial about this property as *consanguineus et hæres* of Enisand, or Emsand, son of Walter, who granted it to the Priory (see below). He made a grant of land at Colebi to the Regular Canons of Carlisle, and there is a curious entry of the particulars in the Pipe Rolls for 1198 (Westmoreland). See also the *Coram Rege Rolls*, 11 Joh. m. 9, *Abbrev. Placit.* Record Com. p. 67 a, where more details are given. Machel (MSS., iv. p. 475) gives an abstract of two pleas with regard to this property, one at Westminster in 1362, and one at Appleby in 1370, where the names of these parties are brought forward.

[3] *ejusdem Durandi* is apparently an error of the copyist for *Enisandi* simply, or for Enisant Musart, as in the copy No. **248**; but see note 1 on No. **247**.

sæculari, sicut aliqua datur liberius et quietius in tota Anglia. Hijs Testibus, Roberto Archidiacono Karlioli, Roberto Dristorell[4], Murdaco Decano de Appleby, Willelmo de Louther, Ada de Musgrave, Gospatricio filio Ormi, Thorstina de Battly[5], Thoma de Hellebeck, Roberto filio Petri, Roberto filio Coleman[6], Gamel de Sandford, Ada filio Uctredi de Botelton, Alano filio Torfin de Alvestain[7], Waldevo de Kirkebythore[8], Ulf de Apilby, Copsi Maurward[9].

[4] Robert Dristorell is called Aristotell in a copy of this charter made by Machel (MS. iv. 474), and quoted by Nicolson and Burn (*History*, i. 335), who omit this witness and several others. Robert Aristotil is witness with Robert Archdeacon and Gospatric son of Orm, to a confirmation by Hugh de Morville, Lord of Westmoreland and Knaresborough, of the grants of land in Crosby (Ravensworth) made by Thorphin de Alverstain and Alan his son (who is a witness here) to the Hospital of S. Peter at York. The originals are among the MSS. of Captain Bagot of Levens Hall, see 10*th Report Hist. MSS. Commission*, Appendix, Pt. iv. p. 319.

[5] Thorstin de Battly, Machel gives as Torfin de Wateby, no doubt correctly; Wadeby, or Wateby (*hodie* Waitby), is a manor in the parish of Kirkbystephen.

[6] Robert son of Colman was another of those who had to pay a fine (£10) for being concerned in the surrender of Appleby Castle in 1174 (*Pipe Rolls*, 1176, Westmoreland). He granted some land to the Hospital of S. Peter at York before 1186. The charter is among the MSS. at Levens Hall referred to above, and Murdac, dean of Appleby, William Brit. the present grantor, and Herveus Niger (see No. 195) are witnesses. He had sons Gilbert and Robert.

[7] Alan was the son of Thorfin de Alverstain of Yorkshire, who granted the Church of Crosby Ravensworth to the Abbey of Whitby. The charter and its confirmation by Alan, Bishop Adhelwald, and others form an interesting series in the *Chartulary of Whitby* (ed. Atkinson, p. 35 *sq.*). For the grants made by Thorfin and Alan to the Hospital of S. Peter at York, see note 4 above. Alan had a daughter Helen who was his heir and married Hugh de Hastings; their son Thomas about 1220—40 granted one of the above confirmations which Philip de Hastings (see note 5 on No. 192) witnessed.

[8] For Waldev de Kirkebythore, see on Adam de Kirkebithore, note 8, No. 117.

253. CARTA JOHANNIS REGIS FACTA ROBERTO DE
VETERI PONTE SUPER CUSTODIA HEREDITARIA BAL-
LIVÆ SIVE COMITATUS WESTMORIÆ[1].

JOHANNES Dei Gratia Rex Angliæ etc. Archiepiscopis, etc. salutem. Sciatis nos dedisse et præsenti carta
Nostra confirmasse dilecto et fideli nostro R. de Veteri
Ponte, Appilby et Burgh cum omnibus appendentijs suis,
et cum Balliva et Redditu Comitatus Westmorlandiæ, et
cum servicijs omnium inde tenentium de nobis qui non
tenent per servicium militare : Habendas et Tenendas
de Nobis et Hæredibus Nostris, sibi et hæredibus suis, qui
de ipso et Uxore sibi desponsata exierint per servicium
quatuor Militum pro omni servicio. Salvis, Nobis et
Hæredibus Nostris placitis omnibus quæ ad Coronam
Nostram pertinent, et salva dignitate Regali : et salvo quod
dictus Robertus vel sui neque vastum neque exitium
facere poterint in Brullijs de Winfell, vel in ipsis venari,
quamdiu vixerimus sine corpore ipsius Roberti. Quare
volumus et firmiter precipimus, quod ipse Robertus et
hæredes sui post ipsum habeant et teneant omnia prædicta
de Nobis et Hæredibus Nostris, ut dictum est in bosco,
in plano, in vijs et semitis, in pratis et pascuis, in moris
et mariscis, in stagnis et vivarijs, in aquis et molendinis
et in omnibus locis, libertatibus suis et liberis consuetudinibus, sicut prædictum est. Datum per manum Hugonis del Wall. apud Trant xxviii. die Octobris Anno
Regni Nostri quinto.

 ⁹ Maureward de Appelby, no doubt the same person, is witness to
a charter of Gerard de Lasceles with Robert the Archdeacon ; see
note I on No. **112.**

The date of the charter was after the death of Bishop Athelwold,
and no narrower limits can be fixed than Abbot Clement, 1161—84
(see note I on No. **44**).

253. [1] This is the grant to Robert de Veteriponte, made by King
John, of the Barony and Bailiwick of Westmoreland on October 28th,
1203, referred to in note I on No. **204.** It seems to have been added
here to the *Register* among other odds and ends in later times.

LIST OF ILLUSTRATIVE DOCUMENTS.

ILLUSTRATIVE DOCUMENTS.

I. GRANT OF ANANDALE BY DAVID, KING OF SCOTS (1124—53), TO ROBERT DE BRUS. [Facsimiles of National Manuscripts of Scotland, Part I. No. XIX.]

David Dei gratia Rex Scotorum Baronibus suis et hominibus et amicis Francis et Anglis, Salutem : Sciatis me dedisse et concessisse Roberto de Brus, Estrahanent et totam terram a divisa Dunegal de Stranit usque ad divisam Randulfi Meschin, Et volo et concedo ut illam terram et suum castellum bene et honorifice cum omnibus illis consuetudinibus quas Randulfus Meschin unquam habuit in Carduil et in terra sua de Cumberland illo die in quo unquam meliores et liberiores habuit. Testibus : Eustachio filio Johannis et Hugone de Morvilla et Alano de Perci et Willelmo de Sumervilla et Berengario Enganio et Randulpho de Sules et Willelmo de Morvilla et Herui filio Warini et Aedmundo Camerario. Apud Sconam.

II. MISSION OF RANULF MESCHIN AND OTHERS TO ESTABLISH THE LIBERTIES OF RIPON, 1106. [Ex Libello de Privilegiis ab Æthelstano Rege Ripensi Ecclesiæ concessis ; Memorials of Ripon, ed. J. T. Fowler, vol. i. p. 34 ; Dugdale, Monasticon, vol. ii. p. 133.]

Voluerat Osbertus vicecomes Eboracensis vim tulisse Libertati Ripensis ecclesiæ anno Domini MCVI, sed Gerardus Archepiscopus rem Regi detulit ; venerunt igitur a Rege missi, Robertus episcopus Lincoln., Radulphus Basset, Galfridus Ridel, Radulphus de Meschines, et Petrus de Valoniis qui causam ventilarent et tandem jura Wilfridi libera esse statuerunt.

III. EXTENT OF THE BISHOPRIC OF HEXHAM. [Prior Richard's History of the Church of Hexham, cap. v; Memorials of Hexham, ed. J. Raine, i. 20.]

Ut autem quidam ferunt, ab oriente mare, a meridie Tesa fluvius, ab occidente Wetherhala, a septentrione Alna fluvius, Hangustaldensis episcopatus termini fuerunt.

IV. THE RERE-CROSS OF STAYNMORE THE LIMIT OF CUMBERLAND. [Chronicles of the Picts and Scots, ed. W. F. Skene, 1867, p. 204 (from MS. Lib. C. C. C. Cantab. *circ.* 1280).]

Edmound, freir Athelstan, duna a cesti Donald, roy Descoce, tout Combirland, pur quoi lez Escoces ount fait clayme tanque al Reir croiz de Staynmore; mais cel doune ad este souent conquys puscedy et relesce en maint peise fesasent.

Translation. "Edmond (circ. A.D. 940), brother of Athelstan, gave to this Donald, King of Scotland, all Combirland, upon which the Scots laid claim as far as the Rere-Cross of Staynmore; but this donation was often conquered since then and released in making ofttimes peace[1]."

V. MEMORANDUM TOUCHING THE FOUNDATION OF THE PRIORY OF WEDERHAL. [Copied by Bishop Nicolson (MSS. vol. iii. p. 141) from the Register of Wetherhal, fol. 26 *a*.]

Carta Ranulphi Meschyni super fundatione de Wedderhal anno primo Regis Willi filii Willi Conquestoris.

Memorie merito commendandum quod Anno Dni M°LXXVI°[2] fundata fuit Abbatia Sancte Marie juxta Ebor. per Dominum

---

[1] The Rere Cross, or Rey Cross (King's Cross), of which the base and part of the shaft still exist, stands a little on the Yorkshire side of the boundary between that county and Westmoreland. It was, there seems little doubt, erected as a boundary mark between the two counties. As such it is not unfrequently referred to. Thus in 1258, John de Cheham, Bishop of Glasgow, asserted a claim "dicens usque ad Rer Cros in Staynmor ad diœcesem suam pertinere."—*Chron. de Lanercost*, ed. Stevenson, page 65. See also the "place called Rere Crosse upon Staynmore," referred to as the limit of the land at the time, in the document quoted from *Calend. Doc. Scot.* (ed. Bain ii. 15) in note 1 on No. **245.**

[2] Bishop Nicolson has here the note "it should be 1088," and correctly; "*in eodem anno*" for the Priory of Wetherhal is, of course, impossible.

Stephanum primum Abbatem ejusdem Anno Regni Willi filii Willi Conquestoris primo. Et in eodem anno Ranulphus Meschine fundavit et dedit in puram Eleemosynam sine omni terreno servicio quietum et liberum Manerium suum quod vocatur Wedderhala predicto Stephano Abbati et Abbacie Sancte [Marie] Ebor. in perpetuam possessionem. Hiis Testibus, Osberto Vicecom. et Waldeth filio Gospatricii Comitis et Ferna Ligulfi filio et aliis. Hec eadem Carta inter alias confirmata per Summos Pontifices, scilicet, Eugenium tertium, Celestinum secundum, Adrianum quartum, ac Bonifacium sub hac formidabili sententia. Si qua igitur in futurum Ecclesiastica Secularisve persona, hanc nostre Constitutionis paginam scienter contra ejus tenorem venire tempta-verit, secundo tertiove commonita, nisi presumptionem suam congrua satisfactione correxerit, potestatis honorisque sui dignitate careat, reamque se divino judicio existere de perpetrata iniquitate cognoscat, et a sacratissimo corpore et sanguine Dei et Dñi Redemptoris nostri Jhesu Xti aliena fiat, atque in extremo examine districte ultioni subjaceat. Cunctis autem eidem loco sua jura servantibus sit pax Dñi nostri Jhesu Xti quatenus et hic fructum bone actionis percipiant et apud districtum judicem premia eterne pacis inveniant. Amen.

VI. Plea against the Abbot of S. Mary's at York for raising the fish pool at Wederhale and contracting the fish pass, 1293. [Assize Roll, Northumberland, No. 651. 21 Edw. I., roll 36.]

Placita de Diuersis Comitatibus apud Nouum Castrum super Tynam coram H. de Cressingham et sociis suis, Justiciariis Itinerantibus in Crastino Sancti Hillarii anno xxj^{mo} (Jan. 14th, 1293).

Cumbria.—Idem dies datus est Abbati beate Marie Eboraci per attornatum suum, de audiendo Judicio suo apud Nouum Castrum super Tynam de quadam libertate quam clamat apud Wederhale, etc.

Idem Abbas summonitus fuit ad respondendum Domino Regi de placito quare exaltauit quoddam stagnum apud Wederhale vltra debitam assisam, de altitudine vnius pedis, per quod cursus aque de Edene nimis artatur extra solitum cursum, et ingenium quod vocatur Baye similiter artatur, vbi solebat esse tante largitatis quod vna sus cum quinque porcellis suis posset transire[1], etc., ad nocumentum, etc.

Et predictus Abbas per attornatum suum venit, et dicit quod inuenit ecclesiam suam seisitam de predicto stagno. Et dicit quod predictum stagnum est in consimili statu in quo illud fuit tempore predecessoris sui; et quod predictum stagnum per ipsum non exaltatur nec artatur, petit quod inquiratur per patriam, etc. Ideo preceptum est, etc.

Postea venerunt coram predictis W. [de Ormesby] et J. [Wogan] apud Karliolum, die Mercurii proxima post festum Sancti Jacobi Apostoli anno supradicto, tam predictus Abbas per attornatum suum quam predicti Jurati, etc. Et Jurati dicunt super sacramentum suum quod predictus Abbas non exaltauit stagnum predictum de Wetherhale, nec predictum ingenium artauit. Et quod predicta stagnum et ingenium sunt in eodem statu in quo fuerunt ante tempus predicti Abbatis, absque aliqua exaltacione predicti stagni vel artacione predicti ingenij, et est in eodem statu quo fuit ante tempus a quo non extat memoria, etc. Consideratum est quod predictus Abbas eat inde sine die, etc.

VII. Plea De Quo Waranto, the King against the Abbot of S. Mary's at York touching the right to have wreck and waif in Kirkeby, Whytothaven &c. and certain privileges in those towns and in Wederhale, Kringeldyk and Neuby. Carlisle, November 3rd, 1292. [This is too long to print. A full abstract is given in Placita de Quo Waranto, rot. 11 *d*, ed. Record Com. p. 122 *a*, to which reference can readily be made[2].]

[1] In the Assize Roll referred to in note 2 on No. 2 there is an order with regard to the fisheries in the County, and it is laid down that "in each pool where salmon may be taken, in mid-stream, by old custom, there shall be a pass wide enough for a sow with her five pigs." What was the exact size of this opening, I have been unable to determine.

[2] The Abbot and Convent lost their case to the King touching the wreck and waif, but retained all their rights and liberties in the several vills. An abstract of the further part of the hearing is given by Thomas Machel, MSS. iv. 432.

P. 26

VIII. Edward, Prince of Wales, at Wederhale in
1301 and 1306—7. [Calendar of Documents relating to Scotland
vol. ii. p. 319 from Chancery Miscellaneous Portfolios Nos. $\frac{41}{145}$,
$\frac{41}{149}$; vol. iv. p. 489, from British Museum, Addit. MSS. No.
22,923.]

1301. Edward Prince of Wales to Sir John de Langetone
the Chancellor. Asks a protection for Rotherik Despaigne his
chamberlain who is in constant attendance on him. Under his
privy seal. Wederhale, October 20th.

Edward Prince of Wales to Sir John de Langetone the
Chancellor. As Master Robert de Oydisterne his 'fisicien' is
going to London for certain matters required for his (the Prince's)
body and returns instantly, he asks a protection for him on
returning. Under his privy seal. Wederhale, October 20th.

Compotus Walteri Reginaldi Thesaurarii Domini Edwardi
Filii Regis, Principis Wallie, De Expensis [&c.] A° Regis E.
Patris Ejusdem Principis Tricesimoquinto Incipiente usque vij
Diem Julii quo die Idem Rex obiit [&c.].

1306—7. Dungallo Mak Dowil capitaneo exercitus Galewadie,
venienti ad curiam principis usque Wederhale et ducenti in comitiva sua dominos Thomam de Brus, Alexandrum fratrem ejus[1] et
Reginaldum de Crauford, proditores regis, per ipsum in prelio
captos, una cum capitibus quorundam aliorum proditorum de
partibus Hibernie et Kentire, per eundem Dungallum et exercitum suum amputatis, de dono et curialitate ipsius principis, in
recessu suo ab inde versus partes suas, per manus domini W. de
Boudon liberantis eidem denarios, simul cum uno cursore dato
eidem per eundem dominum apud Wederhal xix° die Februarii...
1 marcas.

---

[1] These were two brothers of Robert Brus, King of Scots, who were
hanged in the spring at Carlisle by the King's command (compare *Chronicon
de Lanercost*, ed. Stevenson, page 205). After the death of Edward I, in July,
Robert Brus led a foray in September, mainly to punish the MacDowals whose
chief had, as we see above, taken his brothers prisoner. In 1309 Sir Dungal
and his family had to take refuge in England.

IX. INJUNCTION TO EXCOMMUNICATE ROBERT DE GYSE-
BURGH AND PAPAL INTERDICT ON THE CONVENT OF WEDERHAL
IN 1313. [Register of Bishop Halton, MS. p. 168.]

Memorandum quod nos J. [John de Halton] Karl. Episcopus litteras reverendorum virorum Dominorum Agolanti de
Agolantibus Canonici Pistoriensis judicum...per Apostolicam
sedem deputatorum...die Mercurii in crastino Circumcisionis
Domini A.D. MCCCXIII. recepimus quarum auctoritate literarum
nobis extitit injunctum quod fratrem Robertum, Priorem de
Wederhal, excommunicatum publice denunciaremus totumque
Conventum suum suspensum et dictum Prioratum interdictum
&c. quousque Lotto Boethe, Matheo Matinghii &c. ac sociis suis
mercatoribus de Florencia de c marcis nomine sortis et aliis c
marcis nomine expensarum et interesse satisfecerit. Insuper fuit
nobis injunctum quod si dictus Robertus dicto Prioratui cederet
vel decederet dicta pecunia non soluta successor ipsius...terminum
competentem ad solucionem dicte pecunie...assignaremus et nisi
tunc persolveret ipsum in eandem sententiam involverimus. Cumque dictus Robertus...dictum Prioratum...resignasset non est
diu ac post modum Dño Gilberto de Botil ejus successori...
administrationem dicti Prioratus...commisimus, ac ipsum Priorem
instituimus XI Kal. Apl. A.D. supradicto eidem Fratri Gilberto
ad solvendum dictas ducentas marcas dictis mercatoribus festum
Sci Michaelis...assignavimus...sub pena excommunicationis et
penarum supradictarum.

X. TAXATION OF THE VICARAGE OF S. LAURENCE, APPLEBY,
AND AWARD BY BISHOP SILVESTER IN 1251. [Copied by Bishop
Nicolson, MSS. vol. ii. p. 21, from the Register of Wetherhal,
fol. 170 b.]

Omnibus S. Matris Ecclesie filiis Silvester Dei gratia Karl.
Episcopus Salutem in Domino. Noverit Universitas vestra quod
cum Hugo bone memorie predecessor noster quondam Karl.
Episcopus Vicariam Sti Laurencii de Appelby ad sex marcas
taxasset et nos ex officio nostro ad taxandam eam descenderemus,
et ipsam insufficientem, habito respectu ad facultates Ecclesie
predicte, inveniremus, de communi Assensu Dominorum Abbatis
et Conventus Sancte Marie Ebor. quibus per predecessores

nostros in usus proprios fuit assignata, dictam Vicariam sub forma subscripta taxavimus. Imprimis, assignavimus dicte Vicarie totum Altaragium illius Ecclesie cum omnibus decimis ferii et molendinorum, et cum mansione et domibus sitis juxta Ecclesiam predictam, ex parte occidentali, cum tota placia vasta prejacente eidem Mansioni et cum viginti acris quas Walterus Alũ. Capellanus ejusdem Ecclesie possidebat, et cum Communa totius Pasture et Bosci predictorum Abbatis et Conventus. Item, assignavimus dicte Vicarie omnes decimas de Hoff, scilicet, de farina decem eskeppas, de frumento quinque eskeppas et dimidiam et de braseo quinque eskeppas. Item de Crakanthorp, de farina quatuor eskeppas, de frumento unam eskeppam et de braseo tres eskeppas. Et quia hesitabatur utrum dicte eskeppe de Crakanthorp sint de parochia Sti Michaelis de Appelby vel de parochia Sti Laurencii, et pertinentes ad dictam Ecclesiam Sti Laurencii volumus quod si per Inquisitionem possit inveniri quod sint de parochia Sti Laurencii et ad eandem Ecclesiam dicti Laurencii pertinentes, stent per omnia quoad predicta nostra Taxatio. Si autem sint de parochia Sti Michaelis et ad eandem Ecclesiam pertinent, eidem Ecclesie, sicut de jure debetur, applicentur. Et quia ad eum spectare debet onus ad quem emolumentum et quedam terre, scilicet, quadraginta et octo acre cum pertinentiis que jacent in Campo de Appelby collate fuerunt Ecclesie predicte pro servitio faciendo singulis diebus per unum Capellanum in Capella Castelli de Appelby, et similiter triginta et septem acre cum pertinentiis que jacent in Campo de Hoff collate fuerunt Ecclesie predicte pro servitio faciendo in Capella de Hoff per tres dies in septimana, Volumus quod in optione dictorum Abbatis et Conventus sit, utrum velint terras predictas cum onere predicto per Priorem de Wedirhall retinere, an terras predictas cum onere Vicarie predicte assignare. Vicarii quoque qui pro tempore fuerint omnia onera Episcopalia et Archidiaconalia debita et consueta sustinebunt. Volumus autem quod Vicarii Sti Laurencii qui pro tempore fuerint sint penitus immunes a prestatione viginti solidorum qui debebantur Ecclesie Sti Michaelis tempore Willielmi Foliott Canonici Ecclesie Sti Petri Ebor. Rectoris dicte Ecclesie Sti Michaelis. Vicarii quoque in propriis personis decenter et honeste deservient Ecclesie supra-dicte, et fidelitatem dictis Abbati et Conventui qui pro tempore fuerint prestabunt corporalem. Hanc autem taxationem ita volumus perpetue firmitatis vices optinere, quod instrumentis predictorum Abbatis et Conventus a Venerabilibus predecessoribus nostris Ethelwaldo et Hugone Episcopis ac nobis et Capitulo Karliolensis Ecclesie optentis, quantum ad alios articulos in dictis instrumentis contentos, in nullo prejudicium generetur: Sed omnia instrumenta dictorum Abbatis et Conventus super omnibus concessionibus et confirmationibus aliis volumus et concedimus perpetuam habere firmitatem, instrumentis que de dictis Abbate et Conventu habemus in suo robore similiter duraturis. Item, volumus et concedimus quod predicti Abbas et Conventus habeant et possideant quiete et pacifice, quantum in nobis est, in usus proprios in perpetuum Ecclesiam Sti Michaelis de Appelby, cum omnibus pertinentiis suis, in Dioces' nostra sitam, secundum tenorem Cartarum Venerabilium Patrum Predecessorum nostrorum, Ethewaldi et Hugonis, quondam Karl. Episcoporum, excepta Vicaria viginti marcarum in eadem Ecclesia taxanda per nos, et a nobis et successoribus nostris in perpetuum conferenda. Insuper, quia dicti Abbas et Conventus offenderunt, eo quod, nobis contradicentibus, Ecclesiam Sti Michaelis de Appelby per Ricardum Priorem de Wedirhall et quosdam monachos fuerint ingressi, dicti Abbas et Conventus in hoc supposuerunt dictos Priorem et monachos gratie nostre, et in arbitrio nostro sit utrum velimus a dicto Prioratu ipsos penitus hac vice tantum amovere, vel gratiam eisdem ibidem remanendi facere. In cujus rei testimonium presenti scripto cirographato residenti penes nos et Successores nostros qui pro tempore fuerint signum nostrum, una cum signis tam Capituli nostri Karl. quam dictorum Abbatis et Conventus, ad eternam rei memoriam, apponi fecimus; et parti residenti penes dictos Abbatem et Conventum signum nostrum, una cum signo Capituli nostri Karl., similiter apponi fecimus. Hiis Testibus, Magistris Sewalo Decan. Ebor., Godefrido de Ludham precentori Ebor. Ecclesie, Symone de Hevisham Arch. de Estring., Steph. de Eglesfeld, Galfrido de Eylesbyrie, Johanne de Aseby et Dominis Waltero de Rudham et Elya Capellano Domini Karl. et aliis. Datum die Conversionis Sti Pauli Apostoli, Anno Domini Millesimo ducentesimo quinquagesimo primo.

XI. Plea De Quo Waranto, the King against the Abbot of S. Mary's at York touching the advowson of the two Churches of S. Laurence and S. Michael in Appleby. Apelby, Octave of S. Michael, 1292. [Placita De Quo Waranto, rot. 1 *d*, ed. Record Com. page 787 ; Bishop Nicolson, MSS. vol. ii. page 33, extract from Register of Wetherhal, fol. 121 *a*.]

Dom. Rex per Willielmum Inge petit versus Abbatem Eccle beate Marie Ebor. advocationem Eccle Sci Laurencii de Appelby et advocationem Eccle Sci Michaelis de Appelby in Bondegate ut Jus &c. Et unde dicit quod Dominus Henricus Rex proavus Domini Regis nunc tempore pacis presentavit quendam Adam Clericum suum ad predictam Ecclesiam Sci Laurencii, et quendam Willielmum Clericum suum ad predictam Ecclesiam Sci Michaelis de Appelby, qui ad presentationes suas fuerunt admissi et instituti in eisdem, capiendo inde explet̃. ut in decimis, oblationibus et aliis ad valent̃. &c. Et quod tale sit jus suum offert verificare pro ipso Domino Rege &c. Et Abbas per Attornatum suum venit et defendit jus ipsius Domini Regis qu. &c. et seisinam Antecessoris sui ut de feodo et jure et totum &c. Et ponit se in jurm. patrie loco magne Assise Domini Regis, et petit recognitionem fieri utrum ipse majus jus habeat in predictis advocationibus predictarum Ecclesiarum quam predictus Rex. Ideo fiat inde Jur̃. Et Thomas de Culwenne, Hugo de Multon de Hoffe, Willielmus de Stirkeland, Johannes de Rossegile, Robertus le Englays, Ricardus de Preston, Milites, Johannes Mauschael, Willielmus de Crakenthorp, Ricardus de Musgrave, Ricardus de Warthecop, Johannes Fraunceys de Clibburn, Ricardus Tyrel, Jur̃. dicunt super Sacramentum suum quod predictus Abbas majus jus habet in predictis Advocationibus quam predictus Dominus Rex. Ideo quoad hoc inde sine die &c.

XII. Inquisition held in Appleby in 1326 as to who ought to furnish the chantry in the Chapel of Bolton. [Copied by Thomas Machel, MSS. vol. iv. p. 497, from the Register of Wetherhal, fol. 105.]

Carta inquisitionis sive examinatio capta in Ecclesia Sancti Laurentii de Appelby, Quis debet invenire cantariam in Capella de

Bolton. Thomas Fibus de Bolton juratus et examinatus, de...
existens in Bolton...quem (*sic*) fuit donata predicte Ecclesie et ad
quid onerata. Dicit quod fuit donata per antecessores Dñi
Johannis de Derwentewatre, Domini de Bolton, ad inveniendum
Cantariam in Capella de Bolton sicut credit, et toto tempore suo
vidit quod quando deficiebant Cantarie Vestimenta vel alia
ornamenta, Dominus et Balivi sui Tenentes Prioris de Wederhal
in Bolton per catalla et animalia sua destringebant et tenebant
pro predictis. Et Tenentes Prioris conquerebant de hoc Priori,
et Prior destringebat Vicarium ad inveniendum Presbiterum, et
quicquid fuit inter Priorem et Vicarium, Dominus et Balivi sui
predicti semper tenebant destrictionem factam quousque habuerint
omnia predicta parata : Et sic audivit a patre suo et a senioribus
de villa. Sed an terra illa fuit specialiter onerata in donatione
prima ad inveniendum predicta nescit.

Requisitus, Quis invenit predicta, et quis debet invenire Prior
vel Vicarius? Dicit, quod nescit.

Requisitus et An Dominus habet jus sic distringuendi? Dicit
quod sic ; et hoc scit quod semper usus est per tempus cujus
contra' memoria non existit, et super hoc est fama communis in
villa de Bolton et locis vicariis.

Adam prepositus de Bolton, septuagenarius et ultra juratus et
examinatus et diligenter interrogatus super premissis omnibus et
singulis concordat cum Thoma conteste suo supradicto : Hoc
addito quod vidit totam carucam conjunctam constringi pro
predictis.

Rogerus de Bello Loco quinquagenarius ut dicit, juratus et
examinatus et diligenter interrogatus super premissis concordat
cum Thoma conteste suo supradicto : hoc addito quod dicit quod
Dominus Johannes de Gilling dudum Prior de Wederhal et post
Abbas de Ebor. demisit eidem XLVIII acras de predicta terra
Ecclesie de Bolton et predixit sibi in dimissione quod terra sua
deberet distringi si deficerent necessaria Cantarie predicte, Et
dixit sibi quod tunc deberet adire Vicarium de Morland, et ipse
deberet deliberare eum, et ponere averia sua pro averiis suis, et
palefridum suum proprium si necesse fuit.

Henricus Faber de Bolton quadrag. et ultra juratus examinatus et diligenter interrogatus super premissis concordat cum Adam conteste suo supradicto, Hoc addito quod requisitus an Dominus habeat jus sic destringere? Dicit quod sic ut credit et sic vidit fieri: Dicit etiam quod vidit Priorem per servos destringere animalia Vicarii ad liberandum destrictionem Tenentium suorum; et vidit Vicarium qui fuit an Vicarius qui nunc est invenire omnia necessaria et vestimenta predicta.

Adam Marshall de Kirkebythore, sexagenarius juratus exam. et diligenter inter. super premissis concordat cum Thoma primo conteste suo, quod ipse vidit talem districtionem semper in tempore suo sic fieri, et teneri quousque inventa fuerint omnia vestimenta et necessaria Cantarie; et Prior semper solebat deliberare districtionem ipsam; et dicit quod habet et habuit jur. sic destringere et hoc scit, et semper vidit et audivit; et pater uxoris sue ipsius juratoris qui fuit IX vigint. annorum sic sibi retulit, et multi alii; et super hec est communis fama in Patria.

Adam Clericus, sexagenarius jur. et exam. et diligenter inter. super premissis concordat cum omnibus et singulis contestibus suis supradictis. Et illa inquisitio capta fuit in Ecclesia Sancti Laurentii de Appilby die Jovis prox'. post Festum Translationis Sancti Thome Martyris Anno Domini millo. ccc^moxxvi° et coram Offic. videlicet Magistro Roberto de Southake. Et Anno Pontificatus nostri II°.

Joh. de Rosse.

XIII. The Chantry in the Castle of Appleby, also referred to in the assignment by Bishop Silvester in 1251 (No. **x**.). [From Abstracts made by Thomas Machel (MSS. vol. iv. p. 470) and Bishop Nicolson (MSS. vol. ii. p. 24) from an entry in the Register of Wetherhal, fol. 152 sq.]

1359. In this year sentence was given at York against Sir William Colyn, Vicar of S. Laurence in Appelby, who had endeavoured to throw the charges of serving the Chantry in the Castle of Appelby upon the Prior and Convent of Wedirhal. The Abbot and Convent of S. Mary at York pleaded by their proctor that they were free and discharged from any burden of finding and supporting the said Chantry and have been so beyond the memory of man ; and the Vicars of the said Church were wont to find the said Chantry and a Chaplain to celebrate every day in the Chapel of the Castle at their own proper cost: which being made appear sufficient to the Chancellor of York, definite sentence was passed against the said Sir W. Colyn, and the Abbot and Convent with the Prior and Monks of their Cell of Wedirhal were discharged on September 5th, 1359.

And on September 24th of the same year (1359) a decree, referring to the aforesaid sentence, sets forth the above privileges and immunity as having belonged to the Abbot and Convent time out of mind and the burden is wholly laid upon the Vicars, who though not ignorant by unjust ways and means endeavoured to secure it—Licet terre pro predicta Cantaria subvenienda predecessoribus et successoribus suis fuerint et sint assignate cum onere predicto. The Commissary at York considering the allegation of the Abbot sufficiently proved decreed it thus against the Vicar, that the Vicar of Appelby and his successors should support and find the said Chantry and a Chaplain to celebrate there every day &c.

In 1466 a difference arose between Sir Richard Appelby, Perpetual Vicar of the Parish Church of Appelby, and the Abbot and Convent of S. Mary at York about the provision of the necessary utensils for the said Chapel, Books, Chalices and Vestments, of which the then Chaplain was in need. But this was amicably settled by William Peteman, Doctor of Laws, and William Langton, Bachelor of Laws, arbitrators indifferently chosen, who ordered—Quod predictus Dominus Ricardus Vicarius quam alius comede poterit suis expensis unum vestimentum et unum calicem satis decentia pro usu Capellani predicti providebit: Et predicti Abbas et Conventus ad eundem usum Librum Missale etiam congruum competentem et decentem cum omni diligentia possibili suis sumptibus ordinabunt—which in case they fall into decay or happen to be lost by rapine or otherwise, the said Richard the Vicar was to replace and make them good during his stay in the said Vicarage. In quorum Testimon. &c. Datum Ebor. 7º die Mensis Junii Anno Dmi 1466.

XIV. The King's Forest. [Pipe Rolls for Cumberland 32 Hen. II. (1186) rot. 7, m. 1 d.]

De Placitis foreste de Cumberland per Aleẍ. fil. Nigeĩĩ. et Socios suos.

Idem Vicecomes (Hugo de Morewich[1]) reddit compt....

Et de dimidio marce de Priore de Wederhala pro Warda facta in foresta.

XV. Claim for puture in the Priory of Wederhale by a Forester of the King's Forest, 1337. [Assize Roll, Divers Counties, No. 1424 a, 11 Edw. III. roll 3.]

Assise capte apud Karliolum coram Ricardo de Aldeburghe, Thoma de Heppescotes, et Roberto Paruing, Justiciariis Domini Regis ad omnes assisas, juratas, et certificaciones in Comitatu Cumbrie arrainatas capiendas assignatis, die Mercurii proxima post festum Sancti Petri ad uincula anno regni Regis Edwardi tercij a conquestu vndecimo.

Roll 4 d.

Cumbria.—Assisa venit recognitura si Thomas Abbas[2] Beate Marie Eboraci et Frater Adam de Dalton[3], Commonachus eiusdem Abbatis, iniuste etc. disseisiuerunt Henricum de la Panetrie, Forester, de libero tenemento suo in Wederhale post primam etc. Et vnde queritur quod disseisiuerunt eum de putura[4] habenda in Prioratu de Wederhale, in Wederhale, videlicet, habendi pro seipso quolibet die Veneris in septimana per totum annum ministra- cionem de esculentis et poculentis ad mensam armigerorum predicti Abbatis in Prioratu de Wederhale, prout predicti armigeri habent ibidem, et pro garcione[5] suo esculenta et poculenta ad

---

[1] The forest was farmed at this time by the Sheriff at an annual rent of 10 marcs, but the fines went to the King.

[2] Thomas de Multon was Abbot from 1331 to 1359.

[3] Adam de Dalton became Prior of Wetherhal in 1318 and died or resigned in 1341, see Appendix E.

[4] *Putura*, puture, the custom of the keepers, or the bailiffs, of a forest to take meat for man and horse and dog from tenants or others within the perambulation of the forest.

[5] *Garcio*, French *garçon*, "a servant" or "attendant," generally those who followed the camp.

mensam garcionum predicti Abbatis in eodem Prioratu, sicut garciones Abbatis predicti habent ibidem, et habendi & asportandi quocumque sibi placuerit pro seipso quandam lagenam de meliori ceruisia de celario predicti Abbatis in Prioratu predicto, et duas candelas de sepo de Camera predicti Abbatis ibidem, et pro equo suo medietatem vnius busselli auenarum, et pro cane suo vnum panem nigrum, tanquam pertinentia ad balliuam suam Forestarie de Gaytsheles[1], in Foresta de Ingelwode, etc.

Et Abbas et Frater Adam, per Adam de Burton, attornatum ipsius Abbatis, veniunt. Et dic[unt] quod tenementa in visu posita sunt Celle & ecclesie sue Beati Constantini de Wederhale. Et pet[unt] quod predictus Henricus ostendat Curie hic si quid specialiter habeat per quod nititur ecclesiam et Cellam suas predictas de predicta putura onerare, etc. Et Henricus dicit quod quidam Rogerus de Wotton, quondam ballivus Forestarie predicte, et omnes alij qui balliuam predictam habuerunt, a tempore quo non extat memoria, seisiti fuerunt de putura illa, tanquam pertinenti ad balliuam suam predictam, qui quidem Rogerus forisfecit versus Dominum Edwardum nuper Regem, patrem etc., per cuius forisfactum idem Dominus Rex seisiuit in manum suam balliuam predictam, et per cartam suam eandem balliuam hactenus habuerunt ad totam vitam ipsius Henrici. Et profert hic predictam cartam que hoc testatur in hec verba :

Edwardus, Dei gratia, Rex Anglie, Dominus Hibernie, et Dux Aquitanie, Omnibus ad quos presentes litere peruenerint, salutem. Sciatis quod, ad requisicionem Isabelle Regine Anglie, consortis nostre karissime, concessimus dilecto nobis Henrico de la Panetrie, balliuam Forestarie de Gaytsheles, in Foresta nostra de Ingelwode : habendam eodem modo quo alij eandem balliuam hactenus habuerunt, ad totam vitam ipsius Henrici ; dum tamen idem Henricus bene et fideliter se habuerit in eadem. In cuius rei testimonium has literas nostras fieri fecimus patentes. Teste meipso, apud Thundrele, sexto die Junii anno regni nostri nono. Virtute cuius concessionis ipse Henricus seisitus est de balliua predicta, et de putura predicta fuit seisitus tanquam pertinent[i]

---

[1] Gaytsheles, *hodie* Gaitsgill in the parish of Dalston ; from A.-S. *gát*, "a goat," and probably Norse *skaale*, "a hut" or "shieling."

ad balliuam suam predictam, quousque predicti Abbas et Frater
Adam ipsum inde disseisiuerunt ; vnde petit assisam, etc.

Et Abbas et Frater Adam dicunt, quod ipsi sunt viri Religiosi,
et quod ipsi tenent ecclesiam et Cellam predictas in liberam,
puram, et perpetuam elemosinam ; et ex quo predictus Henricus
non ostendit Curie hic aliquod speciale factum predicti Abbatis,
nec aliquorum predecessorum suorum qui Cellam suam et ecclesiam predictas de predicta putura onerauerunt, nec aliquem titulum
sufficientem pro assisa habenda in hoc casu ostendit, petit iudicium
si assisam inde versus eos habere debeat, etc.......

Dies datus est eis de audiendo inde iudicio suo coram Justiciariis Domini Regis de Banco, a die Sancti Michaelis in xv dies, in
statu quo nunc, saluis partibus racionibus suis hinc inde dicendis,
etc. Et super hoc predictus Henricus ponit loco suo Thomam
Worship vel Thomam de Karliolo, etc.

XVI. Carta Ivonis Talliebois de diversis Ecclesiis
et Decimis. [Dugdale, Monasticon vol. iii. p. 553 ex Registro
Abb. S. Mariæ Ebor. fol. 124.]

Sciant omnes tam præsentes quam futuri quod ego Ivo
Talliebois pro salute animæ meæ necnon et uxoris meæ Luciæ
et pro anima patris mei et matris meæ omniumque fidelium
animabus concessisse et dedisse in puram et perpetuam elemosinam Deo et ecclesiæ S. Mariæ Ebor. et Stephano Abbati
omnibusque fratribus ibidem imperpetuum Deo servientibus dimidium dominii mei de Cherkaby-Stephan ac ecclesiæ ejusdem
villæ et decimam meam, in Wyntuna duas bovatas terræ et
decimam meam, et ecclesias de Cherkaby-Kendale et Eversham
et Cherkeby-Lonnesdala, et terras ac communias quæ ad easdem
ecclesias pertinent, et villam quæ vocatur Hutton, et ecclesiam
de Bethome, et terram quæ vocatur Halfrebek, et ecclesiam de
Burton et unam carucatam terræ cum communia, et ecclesiam de
Clepeam et unam carucatam terræ. Hiis testibus, Lucia uxore
mea, Ribaldo genero meo, Radulpho Taillebois, Roberto clerico,
Girardo de sancto Albano, et multis aliis.

XVII. Award made by the Prior of Carlisle and
others between Bishop Walter Malclerk (1223—46) and

THE ABBOT OF S. MARY'S AT YORK, TOUCHING THE CHURCH OF
KIRKBYSTEPHAN AND OTHER CHURCHES. [Register of Bishop
Halton, MS. page 67[1].]

Quomodo collaciones de Cliborne, Ormished et Musgrave
pervenerunt ad Episcopum Karliolensem.

Universis &c. Prior Karl. et Frater Thomas Elemosinarius
Beate Marie Ebor. et Magister Symon de Walton et Johannes de
Hamerton, Salutem. Noverit universitas vestra quod cum controversia mota esset inter Dm. W. Episcopum Karl. ex una parte
et Abbatem et Conventum Sancte Marie Ebor. ex altera super
Ecclesia de Kyrkebystephan cum suis pertinenciis tandem ut
litium contentiones sopiantur et ut panaium laboribus et expensis
consulatur: in nos tanquam in pacis provisores et arbitratores
sollempniter consenserunt ut super predictis contentionibus per
nos perpetua pax ordinetur conservando jus et possessionem
predictorum Abbatis et Conventus in ecclesiam de Kyrkebystephan cum suis pertinenciis et ipsius Episcopi et successorum
suorum et Ecclesie Karl. indempnitati prospiciendo. Nos igitur
habentes Deum pre oculis jure et possessione predictorum Abbatis
et Conventus in predicta Ecclesia diligenter inspectis tum super
collationibus et confirmationibus Romanorum Pontificum et super
possessione predicta inspectis et ponderatis lesionibus ipsius
Episcopi Karl. et successorum suorum necnon ipsius Ecclesie
Karl. sic ordinavimus. Ut Ecclesia de Kirkeby-Stephan cum
omnibus pertinentiis et Capellis suis (videl. cum Capella de Burg,
cum suis pertinentiis, et aliis, si que alie dici debent Capelle) salva
Vicaria infra scripta et taxata, et hac vice pro voluntate Episcopi
ipsius ad presentationem dictorum Abbatis et Conventus conferenda in usus ipsorum Abbatis et Conventus cedat in perpetuum.
Ordinavimus etiam super dictam Vicariam, que a predecessore
ipsius Episcopi ad centum solidos (see No. **19**) fuit taxata, ut
totum Altaragium cum omnibus pertinentiis ipsius Ecclesie et
suarum Capellarum, præter decimas Garbarum, Bladi et Legu-
minis extra Toftos et Ortos, penes Vicarium remaneat. Insuper
idem Vicarius habebit octo bovatas terre de Dominico ipsius
Ecclesie, et unum Mansum competentem, et solvet annuatim

---

[1] See the grant to Bishop Silvester in 1248, Additional Charters No. **240**.

dictis Abbati et Conventui, nomine Vicarii dimidium marce argenti, in Festo Sancti Martini. Verum cedente vel decedente Magistro J. de Ferentin qui Medietatem Altaragii in presenti habet ipsa Medietas ipso jure dicto Vicario accrescet, sine impedimento aliquo ipsius Abbatis et Conventus. Et ex tunc idem Vicarius et Successores sui prædictis Abbati et Conventui viginti solidos argenti annuatim persolvent in Festo S. Martini. Et idem Vicarius et Successores sui sustinebunt omnia onera et Archidiaconalia. Preterea, cedente vel decedente eodem Magistro Johanne, ipsa Medietas quam idem Johannes in presenti habet, excepta Vicaria, sine impedimento Episcopi Karliolensis, dictis Abbati et Conventui ipso jure accrescet. Similiter, cedente vel decedente Th. Boet, Capella de Burgh sue matrici Ecclesie de Kirkebystephan accrescat, sine aliquo impedimento Episcopi Karliolensis. Insuper ordinavimus ut idem Abbas in recompensationem lesionis ipsius Ecclesie Karliolensis ipsi Episcopo Karliolensi et Successoribus suis Jus Patronatus Ecclesie de Clibburn, Ecclesie de Ormesheued et Ecclesie de Musgrave, cum debita securitate conferet, Salvis debitis et consuetis pensionibus de predictis Ecclesiis Prioratui de Wederhal assignatis. Dictus vero Episcopus et Capitulum Karliolense prout a nobis ordinatum est confirmabunt. Et ut hec nostra Ordinatio perpetue firmitatis robur optineat eam Sigillorum nostrorum munimine roboravimus.

XVIII. THE CHAPEL OF S. MARY IN LE WYTH[1] IN THE PARISH OF MORLAND IN WESTMORELAND, 1405. [Copied by Thomas Machel (MSS. vol. iv. p. 495) from the Register of Wetherhal fol. 146*b*. He says "This I transcribed; the original in the Register is so worne out that it can hardly be discovered to after ages if they preserve it not."]

Collocatio Capelle Sancte Marie in Le Wyth in Parochia de Morlund, A.D. 1405.

Johannes de Stutton Prior Prioratus de Wederhale Karl. [Dioc.] dilecto nobis in Christo Rogero Peroy in annos senium elapso, Salutem in Domino, Attendentes et pensantes fervorem vivere

---

[1] Le Wyth is not now known; but there is a place still called "Chapel Garth" between Morland and King's Meaburn, close by the river Lyvennet.

solitarie et honeste ; hiis, experientia edocti, novimus te esse
deditum desiderio tuo commendabili et laudando Domino famu-
landi, Quantum possumus in hac parte duximus applaudend. ;
hinc est quod mores quibus te novimus insignitum nos excitant,
ut tuis votis gratulemur. Capellam igitur Beate Marie in Le
Wyth in Parochia nostra de Morland ad habitandum et orationibus insistendum in eadem pro nostro bene placito et tali honestatis
tempore......tibi conferimus, et ipsam Capellam in forma predicta
concedimus occupandam. Oblationibus et obventionibus in eadem
nobis et Prioratui nostro semper salvis. Datum sub sigillo nostro
apud Wedirhale quinto decimo die Aprilis anno Dom. milmo.
cccc^{mo} quinto.

XIX. AWARD MADE BY ABBOT WILLIAM BETWEEN THE
PRIOR OF WEDERHALE AND THE VICAR OF MORLAND CONCERNING
THE CHAPEL OF S. MARY IN LE WYTH, 1424. [Bishop Nicolson
(MSS. vol. ii. p. 407) from the Register of Wetherhal, fol. 164 a.]

Universis Sancte Matris Ecclesie filiis ad quos presentes Litere
indentate pervenerint Willielmus[1] permissione Divina Abbas Mon.
Beate Marie Ebor. Salutem in Domino. Noverit Universitas
vestra quod cum nuper inter dilectos nobis in Christo Priorem
Celle nostre de Wederhall Karl. Dioc. ad quam fructus et pro-
ventus Ecclesie parochialis de Morland dicte Dioc. provenientes
ab antiquo pertinent, salva portione Vicarii ejusdem pro tempore
existentis, ex una parte, et Dominum Johannem Richemont,
Vicarium perpetuum dicte Ecclesie, parte ex altera, de et super
perceptione et receptione oblationum in quadam Capella de
Wythe, in honorem beate Marie Virginis infra fines et limites dicte
Ecclesie de Morland erecta et constructa, ac super titulo, Jure et
possessione cujusdam dimidie acre jacentis super Litel Aynesbergh et buttantis super Commune Banc infra territorium dicte
Ville, diu et per longum tempus mota fuisset materia questionis.
Tandem dicti Prior et Vicarius, propter bonum pacis inter eos
firmandum, dictas materias nostro Arbitrio, Decreto et Laudo, in
alto et basso, submiserunt, et in nos meliore modo quo potuerint
compromiserunt ; Nosque volentes inter dictos Priorem et Vicarium in premissis Litium amfractus penitus extispare, et inter

---

[1] William Wellys, Abbot, 1423—36.

eos unitatis et pacis concordiam juxta vires plenarie confovere, ac eisdem juxta discretionem nobis a Deo datam justitiam ministrare, nonnullos testes fide dignos hinc inde productos, receptos, juratos et in forma juris diligenter examinatos, una cum aliis evidentiis in hac parte necessariis nobis exhibitis, admisimus; Ac dicta predictorum testium in Scriptis redigi fecimus; Deinde dicti Prior et Vicarius, nostro mediante et interveniente consensu et assensu, inter se super materiis prelibatis convenerunt, et amicabilem in hac parte compositionem inierunt, in hunc modum. Videlicet quod dictus Prior predictas Oblationes et dimidiam acram terre occuparet, reciperet et possideret pacifice et quiete sine impedimento perturbatione vel vexatione dicti Vicarii in futurum. Salvo semper et Proviso dicto Vicario quod si sepedictus Abbas aliquam Compositionem realem in premissis, quam, cum nobis tempus vacaverit ad hoc, bona fide scrutare et scrutari facere promittimus, in Archivis Monasterii nostri predicti invenire poterimus, per quam apparere valeat hujusmodi Oblationes in dicta Capella oblatas dicto Vicario pertinere et pertinere debere, quod veram ejusdem Compositionis copiam fideliter et absque fraude eidem liberari faciemus; et tunc licebit eidem Vicario easdem Oblationes in dicta Capella ut premittitur oblatas recipere, et secundum sue discretionis arbitrium in usus proprios convertere, presenti amicabili concordia in aliquo non obstante. Et ulterius dicti Prior et Vicarius consentierunt et fide sua media concordarunt, tunc et ibidem personaliter constituti, quod si aliqua inter eos emergere contingat controversia in futurum, sepedicti Prior et Vicarius duos viros in Jure egregie et profunde instructos, et arbitrandum amicabiliter in dicta controversia cum consilio nostro et assensu inter eos sine aliqua legis prosecutione assument. Et si ipsi duo Arbitri in hac parte concordiam facere non potuerint, tunc dicti Prior et Vicarius stabunt et parebunt nostro laudo et Arbitrio per nos fiendis, absque ulteriore legis prosecutione. Nos vero Willielmus Abbas supradictus dictas amicabilem compositionem, conventionem et concordiam, factas inter eos ut premittitur, quantum in nobis est, ratas habentes et gratas, eas sic compositas, conventas et concordatas, laudamus ratificamus et tenore presentium confirmamus. In quorum omnium et singulorum fidem et testimonium, presentes literas nostras indentatas, sive presens publicum instrumentum exinde fieri, et per Ricardum Marton, Clericum, Notarium publicum nostrum in hac parte scribam, subscribi nostrique sigilli appensione fecimus communiri. Data et acta sunt hec in Ecclesia parochiali de Moreland predicta, Anno ab Incarnatione Dñi secundum cursum et computationem Ecclesie Anglicane M°CCCC^mo vicesimo quarto, Indictione secunda Pontif. Sanctiss. in Christo Patris et Dñi nostri Dñi Martini Divina providentia P. P Quinti, anno septimo, Mensis Julii die xv^a, presentibus venerabilibus et religiosis viris Fratribus Johanne Salford sacre pagine Professore, et Roberto Spofford, Monachis Monasterii nostri predicti, Guidone Roucliff tunc seneschallo principali nostri Monasterii, Willielmo de Crakenthorp seneschallo Prioratus nostri de Wederhale, Roberto Cauce et Thoma Lovell Domicellis, et aliis pluribus testibus ad premissa vocatis specialiter et rogatis.

XX. RETURN OF THE PRIOR AND CHAPTER OF CARLISLE TO THE PRIOR AND CONVENT OF CONINGESHEUED IN 1343. [Duchy of Lancaster Records, Record Office, Box A. No. 416.]

Vniu̾sis X^i fidelibus p̾sentes lr̃as inspecturis Prior et Capłm ecc̃e Cathedralis Karłi słm̃ in Dño sēpit̾nam Ad vniu̾sitatis vr̃e Noticiam deducimꝰ ꝑ p̾sentes Qđ Nos Prior ⁊ Capitłm p̾dictꝫ quibusdam cronicis nr̃is siue libris antiquis ad ꝑpetuā rei memoriam ordinatis ad instanciā ⁊ rogatum specialē dilcorꝫ fr̃um nr̃orꝫ Prioris ⁊ Conuentꝰ de Conīgesheuid diligent̾ inspectis ⁊ scrutatis inuenimꝰ in eisdem euident̾ contineri Qđ Anno gr̃e M°.C^mo.xxxiij° Consecratus fuit Adelwaldus Prior ecc̃e Karłns in Ep̃m Karłi, Cui q^idem Adelwaldo postea inmediate successit Bernardus, ⁊ post Bernardum: Hugo, qui obijt Anno gr̃e M°.CC^mo.xxxiij°. [xxiii°]. Cuius temporibꝫ erat Dōpnꝰ Bartholomeus P^ior ecc̃e Karłn, qui cōsensu capłi sui cōfirmauit ecclesiam de Ouirtoñ ī Westmeria P^iori ⁊ Conuentui de Conīgesheuid Anno vero gr̃e M°.CC^mo.xxxiiij° ꝯsecratꝰ fuit Walterus in ep̃m Karłn Itē Anno gr̃e M°.CC^mo.xlvij° consecratus ē Siluester in ep̃m Karłn Itē Anno gr̃e M°.CC.^mo.lvj° consecratus fuit Thom^as ep̃s Karłn Itē Anno gr̃e M°.CC^mo.lviij° consecratus fuit Dñs Rob̃tus Ep̃s Karłn In cuiꝰ rei testimonium sigillū nr̃m cōmune p̾sentibꝫ ē appensum Datꝫ apđ Karłm in Capitło nr̃o xvij° die

Menš Septēbr̄ Anno Dñi Milesimo Trincentesimo Quadragesimo tercio.

[A portion of the seal is attached].

XXI. CONFIRMATION BY BERNARD, BISHOP OF CARLISLE, OF A GRANT BY ANSELM DE FURNESS, 1204-14. [Duchy of Lancaster Records, Record Office, Box A. No. 393.]

Vniu̇sis sc̄e mat⁹ˢ Ecc̄ie filiis has litt̃as uisuris ꝛ Auditᵘis. B. đi g͞ra Carleoȷ̇ns Ep̄c Salt̄m in Dño. Nouerit uniuersitas u͞ra nos diuini Amoris intuitu ᵒfirmasse đo ꝛ domui beate Marie quā Dñs Anselm⁹ de Furneš fundauit inꝉ Castelrig ꝛ aꝗᵃ q̃ appellatᵘ Lauther. ꝛ canonicis ibiđ đo seruientib₃. Castelrig. p diuisas in Carta ip̄ius nominatas. ꝛ om̄es ꝉras ꝛ possessiōes. ꝛ lib̄tates. ꝛ cōmunas. ꝛ pasturas. ꝛ ōia Aisiam̄ta eis a memorato A. collata. sicut in carta ip̄i⁹ ᵒtinetur. Et ut h̄ n͞ra ᵒfirmatio robur optineat firmitatis⸵ eam munimine sigilli n͞ri duxim⁹ roborandam.

L. S.

XXII. CHARTER OF HENRY II. TO HUBERT DE VALLIBUS. [Copied by Thomas Machel (MSS. vol. iv. p. 135) from Sir William Dugdale's Collections (vol. iii. p. 7) also given as an addition to the Transcript of the Register of Lanercost, MS. p. 270.]

Henricus Rex Angliæ Dux Normanniæ et Aquitaniæ Comes Andegaviæ, archiepiscopis, episcopis, abbatibus, comitibus, baronibus, justiciariis, vicecomitibus, ministris et omnibus fidelibus suis totius Angliæ Francis et Anglis, Salutem. Sciatis me concessisse dedisse et confirmasse Huberto de Vallibus in feodo et hereditate sibi et heredibus suis totam terram quam Gilbertus filius Boet tenuit die qua fuit vivus et mortuus de quocunque illam tenuisset, Et de incremento Korkeby cum piscaria et aliis pertinentiis quam Wescubrich filius Willielmi Steffan tenuit, et Kaderlenge cum

---

[1] The seal attached is in good condition, bearing the legend—
BERNARDUS : DEI GRACIA : CARLEOLENSIS : EPISC :

molendino quod Uchtredus filius Haldani tenuit: Et totam istam terram tenebit ipse et heredes sui de me et heredibus meis per servicium duorum militum. Quare volo et firmiter præcipio quod ipse et heredes sui supradictas terras de me et heredibus meis habeant et teneant bene et in pace libere quiete et integre et honorifice cum omnibus pertinentiis suis in bosco et plano in pratis et pascuis in viis et semitis in aquis et molendinis et piscariis et mariscis et stagnis infra Burgum et extra in omnibus rebus et locis cum thol et theam et socha et sacha et infangentheof et cum omnibus aliis libertatibus et liberis consuetudinibus quietas ab omni Neutegeldo. Testibus, R. Archiepiscopo Ebor. R. Epĩo Linc. H. Dunelm. Epĩo H. Comite Norff. Comite Alberico, Comite Galfrido, Richardo de Lucy, Manass. Biset, Dapifero, H. de Essex, Constabulario, Hugone de Morevil, Roberto de Dunstanvill, Willelmo filio Johannis, Simone filio Petri, Nigello de Broch, Willelmo Malet, Rogero filio Ricardi, Roberto de Stutevill, Turgi de Russedal. Apud Novum Castrum super Tynam[1].

XXIII. FOUNDATION CHARTER OF THE AUGUSTINIAN PRIORY OF LANERCOST. [Register of Lanercost, MS. Part i. i.]

Carta Roberti de Vallibus Senioris.

Universis Sanctæ Matris Ecclesiæ filiis Robertus de Vallibus filius Huberti de Vallibus, Salutem. Sciatis me concessisse dedisse et in liberam et perpetuam elemosinam assignasse et præsenti carta confirmasse Deo et Stæ Mariæ Magdalenæ de Lanercost et Canonicis Regularibus ibidem Deo servientibus eandem Landam de Lanercost per has Divisas, Scilicet inter Murum antiquum et Irthinam Et inter Burth et Poltros. Et præterea dedi eis villam de Walton infra has Divisas subscriptas Scilicet de Muro antiquo per longam sicam quæ est contigua Cospatricseye usque in Irthin et ita per Irthin usque ad locum ubi Camboc cadit in Irthin et sursum per Camboc usque ad sicam quæ descendit de nigra Quercu quæ est in via quæ ducit ad Cumquencath Et ex alia parte nigræ Quercus usque ad Sicam Polterheued quæ cadit in King Et per

---

[1] For the date, see note 4 on No. **28.**

King usque ad Murum et communem pasturam circumquaque Et Ecclesiam de ipsa Walton cum Capella de Treverman. Præterea dedi et concessi eis Ecclesiam de Irthinton et Ecclesiam de Brampton et Ecclesiam de Karlaton et Ecclesiam de Farlam cum omnibus quæ ad easdem Ecclesias pertinent. Et concessi eis Landam de Warthcoleman et Landam de Roswrageth et Landam de Apeltrethwayt per has Divisas, Scilt. sic Sechenent cadit in Herthinburn et deinde versus Tindale per has Divisas per quas Gille filius Bueth illam melius et plenius in vita sua tenuit Et per quas Domnus Henricus Rex secundus Huberto de Vallibus Patri meo et mihi dedit et Cartis suis comfirmavit Et Communem Pasturam totius moræ cum liberis Hominibus meis et unam Scalingam hyemalem in competenti loco ultra Herthingburn. Et concessi eis habere triginta Vaccas ubique in Foresta mea de Walton et viginti Sues cum Incremento duorum annorum et Pasturam Boum qui prædictas Landas arabunt Et liberum Pannagium de Porcis suis propriis tam de nutritis quam de emptis. Dedi etiam eis omnem Corticem de merremio meo proprio et de toto illo quod dedero cuicunque illud dedero in Boscis meis infra Baroniam meam de terra quæ fuit Gille filius Bueth. Et Lignum siccum et jacens ubique in Foresta mea ad sustinendam domum suam. Volo etiam et concedo ut prædicti Canonici et servientes illorum habeant Vias suas et Semitas sine aliquo impedimento Servientium meorum ad eundum ad Ecclesias et Domos suas Scilt. versus Brampton et versus Walton et versus Treverman et Wathcoleman et Roswrageth et de Landa ad Landam et versus Denton et versus Brenkibeth. Concessi autem eis et dedi quandam terram in Bosco meo de Brampton ad Horrea facienda et colligendas Decimas suas juxta sepem Laysing per easdem Divisas quibus ego ostendi eis et perambulavi coram pluribus Et de cætero si voluerint et necesse habuerint Molendinum vel Piscationes facere super Irthing vel King Hertingburn vel alibi in Terra sua propria. Concessi eis et dedi Licentiam firmare Stagnum suum super Dominium meum ubi Locum competentem et aptum viderint absque detrimento Molendinorum meorum. Quare volo ut prædicti Canonici habeant et teneant prædictas terras per præfatas Divisas et Ecclesias et Pasturas et Libertates in liberam et puram et perpetuam Elemosinam de me et Hæredibus meis liberas et quietas ab omni seculari Servitio pro Domino Henrico Rege Secundo et Hæredibus suis qui Donator et Warrantizator Patri meo et mihi terræ illius est De qua Elemosina ista supersit Exordinis Et pro animabus Antecessorum et Successorum illius Et pro anima Patris mei Huberti et Matris mei Greciæ et Antecessorum meorum et pro me et Successoribus meis. Hiis Testibus, Cristiano Candidæ Casæ Epo, Waltero Priore de Karlo, Roberto Archid. Ricardo Mala Terra, Robto Clerico de Leverton, Thoma Clco de Walton, Robto Capellano, Hudardo Dec. Petro de Teill. Alexandro de Wind. Will. fil. Hudard. Willo de la Kersuna. Radulpho de la Ferte, Bernardo le Flam. Gilberto Engain, Rad. Engain, Galter. de Wind. Hug. de Verburt, Roberto de Vall. minore, Willo Clico, Osberto Persona de Brampton, Israele Camerario, Johe Clico de Leverton, Joh. Camer. Thoma Pincerna, Jordano Camer. Eustachio de Wall. Galto. Flam. Robto fil. Asketil. Jordan. de Kerl. Petro de Leverton, Rogero de Vall. Stepho fil. Ric. Willo de Vall. fil. Robti de Vall. Gilberto Senzaner, Jocelino Aunger, Osberto de Pridevaus[1], Osberto de Bothl.[2] et multis aliis.

Note in Margin.—Anno ab Incarn. Dni 1169, 16 H. 2 dedicata fuit ista Ecclia a Dno Bernardo Epo Karl. Anno Pontificatus ejusdem xii°[3].

XXIV. FOUNDATION CHARTER OF THE CISTERCIAN ABBEY OF HOLM CULTRAM. [From a manuscript in the Library of Corpus Christi College, Cambridge, MS. cxi. 121; see also Harleian Manuscripts, No. 1881, but the witnesses are not there given.]

Carta Henrici Comitis Cumbriæ Davidis Regis Scotiæ filii.

H. Comes filius Davidis Regis Scotiæ, Episcopis, Abbatibus,

---

[1] The name is thus in the *Register of Lanercost*, MS. i. 6.

[2] The *Register* has in MS. i. 17 Osberto de Bocland.

[3] The date of the charter must be after Robert de Vallibus got possession in 1165 (see note 4 on No. **28**) and apparently from the witnesses, so many of whom occur in the *Register of Wetherhal*, before 1170, and probably earlier if anything, than the traditional date 1169. The note in the margin is manifestly incorrect; see Appendix D, on Bishop Bernard.

Comitibus, Justitiis, Baronibus, Vicecomitibus, Ministris et omnibus probis hominibus totius terræ suæ Clericis et Laicis, Francis et Anglis, Salutem. Sciatis me dedisse et concessisse in perpetuam Elemosynam duas partes Holme Coltriæ Abbati et Monachis ibidem Deo servientibus, quas ego et plures probi homines mecum perambulavimus, in primis inter eos et Alanum filium Waldeff quando ego tertiam partem prædictæ Holmcoltriæ prænominato Alano ad venationes suas concessi. Præterea vero concedo et hac mea carta confirmo donationem ejusdem Alani filii Waldeff, et Waldeff filii sui de illa tertia sua parte Holmcoltriæ quam illi ad venationes suas concesseram, quam ipse in præsentia Patris mei et mea et Baronum meorum apud Carleolum prædicti loci Abbati et Monachis in perpetuam Elemosynam dedit et concessit et Carta sua testante confirmavit. Volo itaque ut Abbas Holmcoltriæ et Monachi ibidem Deo servientes habeant plenarie Holmcoltriam per suas rectas divisas in nemore et plano, pratis et pascuis, piscationibus et aquis, et Rabi cum suis rectis divisis, sicut ego et Barones mecum ipsas perambulavimus inter prædictos Monachos et Aschetillum filium Udardi. Concedo etiam eis materiam in Foresta de Engleswoda ad ædificia sua et ad omnia domui suæ necessaria facienda et pasturam porcis eorum sine pasnagio. Cum hiis autem prædictis infra terminos Abbatiæ Holmcoltriæ et divisas suas tantam pacem et libertatem constituo, quantam Abbatia de Maylros et Abbatia de Neubotla concessione Patris mei tranquillius et sanctius et quietius possident et possessionibus suis infra perfruuntur. Hiis Testibus, Adulpho Carloli Episcopo, Waltero Priore, Waltero de Bydun Regis Cancellario, Engerram Comitis Cancell. Hugone de Moravilla, Willelmo de Somervilla, Willelmo de Heriz, Willelmo Engaine, Ranulpho de Soll. Ranulpho de Ludeseia, Waltero de Ridala, Cospatricio filio Ormi, Henrico filio Suani, Waltero filio Alani, Hugone Ridill, Alano de Laceles[1].

XXV. CHARTER OF BISHOP WALTER MALCLERK CONCERNING THE PENSION IN THE CHURCH OF NETHER DENTON, 1238. [Register of Lanercost, MS. x. 4.]

---

[1] The date of the foundation is given as 1150 in the *Chronic. de Mailros*, *in ann.* and see *Roger de Hoveden*, ed. Stubbs, i. 211.

Carta Domini Walteri Episcopi Karliol. de annua Pensione in Ecclesia de Denton.

Universis Sanctæ Matris Ecclesiæ filiis ad quorum Notitiam hoc præsens scriptum pervenerit W. Dei Gratia Karliolensis Episcopus Salutem in Domino. Noverit universitas vestra nos assensu Capituli nostri dedisse concessisse et præsenti carta confirmasse Priori et Conventui de Wederhal et Priori et Canonicis de Lanercost quinque marcas annuas de Ecclesia de Denton inperpetuum percipiendas per manum Vicarii qui pro tempore fuerit medietatem ad Pascham et medietatem ad Festum Sancti Michaelis quas dicti Monachi et Canonici æquali Portione divident inter se. Quislibet autem Vicarius successive instituendus statim post institutionem Juramento præstito dictis Monachis et Canonicis faciet securitatem de prædictis quinque marcis fideliter persolvendis ad duos terminos; ita tamen quod vacante Vicaria de prædicto redditu nihil eis depereat. - Et hoc ut Scriptum nostræ concessionis et confirmationis perpetuæ firmitatis robur optineat Sigillum nostrum eidem apposuimus. Datum apud Burgum sub Mora mense Octobris Pontificatus nostri Anno quinto decimo[1].

XXVI. Final agreement between the Prior of Watton and William de Tyrneby, in 1202, touching land and sheep in Tirneby (Thrimby). [Copied by Thomas Machel, MSS. vol. iv. p. 517, from the Register of Wetherhal, fol. 104 *b*.]

Hæc est finalis concordia facta in Curia Domini Regis apud Appelby die Jovis proximo post festum Sancti Michaelis anno Regni Regis Johannis quarto coram Domͫs L. Norwicensi Episcopo, Hugone Bardulf, Johanne de Gestelinges, Magistro Rogero Arundell, Willielmo filio Ricardi, Justiciariis et aliis fidelibus Domini Regis ibidem presentibus.

Inter Robertum Priorem de Watton conquerentem et Petrum Canonicum suum positum loco ipsius inde ad lucrandum vel perdendum. Et Willielmum de Tyrneby de warrantia cartæ j carucatæ terræ cum pertinentiis; et de pastura mille ovium in

---

[1] Brough under Stainmore, October, 1238.

Tirneby. Unde placitum fuit inter eos in predita curia sc. Quod predictus Willielmus recognovit prædictam carucatam terræ cum pertinentiis et Pasturam esse Jus et perpetuam elemosynam predicti Roberti Prioris, habendas et tenendas sibi et successoribus suis de predicto Willielmo et heredibus suis in perpetuum per servicium viginti solidorum reddendorum inde annuatim, sc. decem solidos ad Pentecosten et decem ad festum sancti Martini pro omni servicio. Preterea predictus Willielmus concessit predicto Roberto Priori et successoribus suis totam Culturam quæ fuit Gilberti de Lancastre et jacet proxima Bercariæ predicti Roberti Prioris versus Austrum. Et quinque acras in Cultura sua de Witerich propinquiores predictæ Bercariæ versus Occidentem jacere incultas ad communem pasturam averiorum suorum et totius villæ de Tirneby in perpetuum. Preterea idem Willielmus concessit predicto Roberto Priori et successoribus suis exitum predictæ Bercariæ qui est versus orientem super terram suam ad latitudinem quinque Perticarum secundum quod longitudo totius curiæ predictæ Bercariæ extendit versus Austrum. Preterea Willielmus concessit predicto Roberto Priori et successoribus suis pascere bona sua de rivulo qui currit extra et per medium Curiæ Grangiæ suæ pro voluntate et placito suis in quantumcunque ipse Willielmus vel heredes sui concedere possint. Et sciendum est quod predictus Willielmus vel heredes sui non possint a modo aliquid colere infra metas vastæ pasturæ predictæ de Tyrneby, nec ipse vel heredes sui possint attachiare alicujus hominis averia ad eandem pasturam nisi solummodo sua propria averia et hominum suorum de predicta villa de Tyrneby.

XXVII. CONFIRMATION OF THE PRIVILEGES AND CUSTOMS OF THE CHURCH OF YORK BY HENRY I., *cir.* 1110. [Registrum Magnum Album, apud Ebor. ii. 1. 62 *b*; Historians of the Church of York, ed. J. Raine, Rolls Series, iii. 34.]

Henricus Rex Angliæ archiepiscopis, episcopis, abbatibus, consulibus, proceribus, et universis fidelibus, Francis et Anglis, totius Angliæ salutem.

Possessiones et dignitates et libertatis consuetudines quas habuit Eboracensis ecclesia, concedo et regia auctoritate præsenti carta confirmo, sicut hic subscriptæ sunt.

Sub regibus antiquis et archiepiscopis, et, quod plerique meminisse possunt, Edwardo rege, et Aldredo archiepiscopo, fuit ecclesiæ Sancti Petri consuetudo egregiæ libertatis. Si quis enim quemlibet cujuscunque facinoris aut flagitii reum et convictum infra atrium ecclesiæ caperet et retineret, universali judicio vi. hundreth emendebat; si vero infra ecclesiam, xii. hundreth; infra chorum xviii. Pænitentia quoque de singulis, sicut de sacrilegiis, injuncta. In hundreth viii. lib. continentur. Quod si aliquis, vesano spiritu agitatus, diabolico ausu quemquam capere præsumerat in cathedra lapidea juxta altare, quam Angli vocant friðstol, id est cathedra quietudinis vel pacis, hujus tam flagitiosi sacrilegii emendatio sub nullo judicio erat, sub nullo pecuniæ numero claudebatur, sed apud Anglos boteles, hoc est sine emenda, vocabatur. Hæ emendæ nihil ad archiepiscopum sed ad canonicos pertinebant.

....
... .

Testibus, Thoma archiepiscopo, W. Giff. episcopo Wintoniensi, Roberto episcopo Lincolniensi, R. Flamb' episcopo Dunelmensi, W. Comite de Warr., R. Basset, G. Ridel, F. filio Sigulfi, apud Wintoniam.

XXVIII. AUTHORITY GRANTED BY EDWARD III. TO TAKE FOR MILITARY SERVICE IN SCOTLAND THE "GRITHMEN" OF WEDERHALE AND OTHER PLACES, 1342. [Rotuli Scotiæ, 16 Ed. III. m. 12, ed. Record Com. vol. i. p. 629b: Rymer, Fœdera, new ed. vol. ii. Pt. 2, p. 1203.]

Rex omnibus ad quos &c. Salutem. Sciatis quod assignavimus magnificum principem et dilectum consanguineum et fidelem nostrum, Edwardum de Balliolo, Regem Scotiæ, ad omnes homines vocatos Grithmen, apud Beverlacum, Ripon', Tynemuth et Wederhale, et alibi in libertate ecclesiastica, pro immunitate ibidem, ratione feloniarum, per ipsos factarum, optinenda, existentes, qui ad ipsum Regem venire et ad custus suos proprios, cum ipso ad partes Scotiæ, in obsequium nostrum proficisci voluerint, ibidem, quamdiu nostræ placuerit voluntati, moraturi, ad pacem nostram recipiendum, et ad eos arraiandum, et in comitiva sua ad easdem partes ducendum. Et ad sufficientem securitatem de eis super hoc capiendum, et ad cartas nostras de pardonatione quarumcunque feloniarum, per ipsos ante festum Sanctæ Trinitatis, proximo præteritum, perpetratarum, eis nostro nomine credendum. Quibus, ad certificationem ipsius Regis, nobis cum securitate prædicta factam, cartas nostras, de pardonatione feloniarum prædictarum, fieri faciemus absque mora. In cujus &c.

> Teste Rege apud Westm. xv die Julii.
>> Per ipsum Regem.

XXIX. LIBERTY OF SANCTUARY AT WETHERHAL, ASSIZE TRIALS, 1292. [Assize Roll, Cumberland, No. 135, 20 Edw. I.]

Placita Corone coram H. de Cressyngham et sociis [suis, Justiciariis itinerantibus,] apud Aldeyston, in comitatu Cumbrie, in Crastino Animarum anno regni Regis Edwardi vicesimo.

1. Roll 10.

Balliva de Cumberland' et Allerdale venit per xij Juratos.

Andreas filius Thome de Wardwyk' de die percussit Adam filium Andree Mangok' cum quodam baculo in capite, ita quod tercia die postea inde obiit. Et predictus Andreas statim post factum fugit usque Wetherhale, et ibidem [habuit] pacem in forma cuiusdam consuetudinis ibidem vsitate ab antiquo, ut dicitur; et malecreditur. Ideo exigatur et utlagetur. Catalla eius, v. s., vnde Vicecomes respondebit. Et quia nescitur quo waranto Prior de Wetherhale clamat habere huiusmodi libertatem, ideo preceptum est Vicecomiti, quod faciat venire predictum Priorem, et similiter Abbatem Sancte Marie Eboraci, ad ostendendum, etc. Et ipsi modo veniunt et dicunt, quod clamant ab antiquo habere talem libertatem apud Wetherhale infra banlucam[1], quod possint recipere quoscunque felones, et eos receptare infra libertatem predictam, prestito sacramento quod se bene gerent dum infra libertatem predictam moram fecerint, et illam non exierint, etc.

---

[1] *Banleuca,* or *banleuga,* "Modus agri, cujus finibus loci, seu oppidi, vel Monasterii alicujus immunitas, vel Jurisdictio terminatur"—Du Cange, *Glossarium*; the "precincts," compare Old French *banlieue.* From the Low Latin *bannum,* an "edict," a "district" or "jurisdiction," and *leuca* or *leuga,* a Gallic mile of 1500 Roman paces, a "league."

Et quod sic vsi sunt, et non aliter, a tempore quo non extat memoria petunt quod inquiratur, etc. Et Jurati dicunt super sacramentum suum, quod predicti Abbas et Prior et antecessores sui a tempore quo non extat memoria vsi sunt huiusmodi consuetudine in libertate predicta, in forma qua clamant. Ideo datus est dies de audiendo judicio suo apud Nouum Castrum super Tynam, in comitatu Northumbrie, in Octabis Sancti Hillarii, etc.

2. Roll 13, d.

Willelmus prepositus de Wederhale, Matheus de Wymundham, carettarius, Willelmus del Fyrhus, et Adam Stubber' noctanter occiderunt Robertum de Shawyl de Magna Corkeby in piscaria de Wederhale, infra libertatem Prioris de Wederhale. Et predictus Adam statim [post] factum fugit; et malecreditur. Ideo exigatur et utlagetur. Nulla habuit catalla. Et postea predicti Willelmus, Mattheus, et alii receptati fuerunt in predicta villa de Wederhale cum Thoma de Wymundham, Priore de Wederhale, qui obiit, per sex annos, ipso Priore sciente. Et post mortem ipsius Prioris predictus Willelmus prepositus per vnum mensem ante mortem suam cum Willelmo de Tannefeld', nunc Priore, receptatus fuit; et similiter Matheus carettarius per modicum tempus, et Willelmus del Fyrhus vsque adventum Justiciariorum nunc; ipso tamen Priore ignorante. Et tunc fugerunt. Et quia predicti Matheus et Willelmus del Fyrhus modo se subtraxerunt, et malecreduntur, ideo exigantur et utlagentur. Nulla habuerunt catalla. Et quidam Stephanus le Porter de Wederhale fecit inquisicionem de predicta morte, cum nullum ibidem habeant Coronatorem. Ideo preceptum est Vicecomiti, quod faciat eum venire, et Abbatem beate Marie Eboraci et predictum Priorem similiter, et Stephanum et totam vill[atam] de Wederhale. Post venit predicta villa, et finem fecit pro transgressione predicta per c s. Et Stephanus le Porter venit, et finem fecit pro transgressione per xx s., per plegium Willelmi de Wardwyk' et Simonis de Stuteuill'. Et predictus Abbas per attornatum suum dicit, quod nichil sciuit de predicta felonia, nec de receptamento predictorum felonum, nec de Inquisicione facta per predictum Stephanum de morte predicti Roberti; et dicit quod nullum clamat habere

Coronatorem in libertate predicta, nec clamat quod felones qui felonias fecerint in libertate illa aliquod habeant refugium, uel quod receptari poterunt in eadem.   Et Jurati hoc idem testantur. Dicit tamen quod ab antiquo omnes felones venientes ibidem causa refugij receptari solebant ibidem, pulsatis campanis in ecclesia, et sic accepta pace, pacifice infra banlucam eiusdem libertatis commorari, prestito tamen sacramento quod bene se gerent dum in eadem moram fecerint.   Et inde inuenit ecclesiam suam seysitam.   Et quod talis consuetudo in libertate illa fuit ab antiquo, petit quod inquiratur.   Et Jurati hoc idem testantur. Sed quia predicta consuetudo est contraria toti legi Anglie, et contra Coronam, etc., ideo datus est dies predicto Abbati apud Nouum Castrum super Tynam, in Comitatu Northumbrie, in Octabis Sancti Hillarii, de audiendo inde Judicio suo, etc.   Postea in Octabis Sancti Hillarii Abbas beate Marie Eboraci per attornatum suum optulit se, etc.   Et datus est ei dies de audiendo Judicio suo a die Pasche in v. septimanas apud Nouum Castrum super Tynam, etc.

3. Roll 17.

Villata de Karl[iolo] venit per xij Jur[atos].

Roll 17, d.

Ricardus Gener, Johannes Curur, [et] Clement Sutor venerunt prope domum Rogeri filii Martini carnificis, et predictus Ricardus percussit canem predicti Rogeri, et predictus Rogerus statim exiuit de domo sua et cum gladio percussit predictum Rogerum sub vmbiculo vsque ad cor, vnde statim inde obiit.   Prima inventrix venit, et non malecreditur.   Et predictus Clemens, qui presens fuit, non venit, et fuit attachiatus per Johannem et Adam filium Moryn, qui modo non habent ipsum.   Ideo ipsi in misericordia.   Et predictus Rogerus statim post factum fugit vsque ad libertatem Prioris de Wederhall', que est cella Abbacie Eboraci, et ibidem commorauit a die Purificacionis beate Marie anno vicesimo vsque festum Sancti Michaelis proximum sequens, quod propter adventum Domini Regis in partibus illis fugit in Scociam, et malecreditur.   Ideo exigatur et utlagetur.   Catalla eius, nulla. Et predictus Abbas venit per atturnatum suum, et super hoc allocutus, dicit quod predictus Rogerus post feloniam factam accessit ad libertatem suam predictam, et ad ecclesiam libertatis predicte pulsauit quamdam Campanam. Et coram Balliuis eiusdem libertatis jurauit quod inposterum bene et fideliter se haberet, et sic fuit admissus in libertate predicta pro voluntate sua commorand', ita quod non transiret terminos libertatis predicte. Et ea consuetudine vsus est ipse [Abbas] et predecessores sui in libertate predicta a tempore quo non extat memoria. Ideo inquiratur qualiter predictus Abbas et predecessores sui vsi sunt libertate predicta, et a quo tempore. Et xij Jurati de Lyth[dale] et Esk[dale], et similiter xij Jurati de Cumbria et Allerdale, et similiter Hugo de Multon' et Johannes de Hodeleston' et socij sui, dicunt super sacramentum suum, quod predictus Abbas et predecessores sui a tempore quo non extat memoria, sine aliqua temporis interrupcione, vsi sunt consuetudine predicta, quam idem Abbas modo clamat. Et datus est dies predicto Abbati apud Nouum Castrum super Tynam, in comitatu Northumbrie, in Octabis Sancti Hillarij, ad audiendum inde Judicium suum, etc.

XXX. LIBERTY OF SANCTUARY AT WETHERHAL: BOUNDS OF THE SANCTUARY AND OPINION OF COUNSEL. [Copied by Thomas Machel, MSS. vol. iv. pp. 425, 429 from the Register of Wetherhal fol. 124, 198.]

Libertas quam Abbas Eborum clamat de felonibus receptis apud Wederhal in Comit. Cumberlandiæ.

Abbas Beate Marie Ebor. clamat talem Libertatem et consuetudinem : Quod omnes felones ad Libertatem suam de Wederhal, pro felonia facta extra Libertatem suam predictam, et ad Ecclesiam predicte Libertatis accedentes, et quandam Campanam pulsantes et coram Balivis ejusdem Libertatis faciendo Sacramento quod in posterum bene et fideliter se habebunt, Et sic in Libertate illa infra divisas ejusdem Libertatis pro voluntate eorum commorand'. viz. Inter (⊞) Crucem quæ est in ripa de Eden versus Corkeby, et (⊬) Crucem quæ est juxta Capellam Sancti Oswaldi ex parte aquæ de Eden versus Corkeby. Et inter (†) Crucem quæ stat juxta le Loge super ripam predictæ aquæ: et (†) Crucem quæ stat juxta Sicketam de Waryewyke et (†) Crucem quæ stat inter villam de Scotteby et Grangiam Prioris de Wederhale ; Et sic per istum rivilum usque ad.........ad (⊞) Crucem quæ stat super ripam predicti rivili juxta Cumquintyn. Et sic de predicta Cruce usque ad Divisas Prioris de Wederhale et villæ de Cumquintyn super Lytilthwait, et sic de Lytilthwait usque ad Lencraike, quæ est super ripam aquæ de Eden, Et sic usque ad Wederhale et ad predictam Crucem in ripa de [Eden versus] Corkeby juxta Grangiam Prioris.

Avisamentum Consilii temporalis Domini Abbatis Stæ Mariæ Ebor. pro Libertatibus et franchasiis...de Wederhale conservandis in quibusdam casibus feloniæ, et aliorum si contingant &c.

Fyrst. The Temporal Counsaill learned saythe that the warrant or precept that comes from the Justice of Pees or any other that haithe authorite, with this clause—Quod non omittas propter aliquam libertatem—You must obey it without distorbance.

Also the said learned Counsail saith, That if there be ony man reseying and abideing within yᵉ Franches, and is no Chyrchman and he be a thefe and the Maynor with him ; ony man may take him and bring him to your Gauyll, and after that he may be brought befor the Justice of deliverance by writ, and so to be had out of the Franches.

Also they saye, that notwithstandying any Inditement, There shal no man be deliverd out of the Franches, without a non omittas, as is said afor.

Also they saie, That if siche a felony be don within franches, the Felone must be justifiede in your Court ; for he may nought clame Church there, as he has done felone : But if that he com to the Kyrke there he may clame preveleg of the Kyrke, by the common law of yᵉ Kyrke.

Also the said Counsail saith if ony Churchman that goos out and doth felone without, and cometh in agayn ; They thinke he should be punished within the Franches by emprisonment : for the Franches was never ordayned ne granted to be Spelunca Latronum. And in these poynts we counsail ye demean yowe after owre old precedent and not begyne newe thyngs ; for the said Counsail sayeth, That non of the Kynges offecers may enter your Franches in ony cas without warrant of Non omittas. But if you sew a felone That hath donne felone out of Franches, and freshely sewes hym into the Franches, than they may attache the felone and he aske no Church, and leve hym in your Prison to be sent for by writ.

XXXI. Heriots[1] not to be taken before the Mortuaries are paid, 1423–29. [Copied by Thomas Machel, MSS. vol. iv. p. 431, from the Register of Wetherhal p. 197*b*.]

Be it knowen to all manner of men that this present writynge shall see or here, That I Thomas Bampton of Threpland within the parish of T...[Torpenhow] 89 yeares and more of age saw and...knowledge That Robert Heghmore Lord of B...[Bowaldeth] presumptuously took in the name of a Heriot, a horse called a mare of the goods of John Oberhowse of Bowaldeth [a township of Torpenhow] affore the Kyrke took the mortuary. Wharfore he stoode accursed thowre the Diocese of Carlil and was cited to apper at Aspatry affore Mayster William Barowe Bishoppe of Carlil and Doctor of both Laws, whar he asked penance and absolucion, and there he made Restitucion of the sayde horse to Sir Robert Ellergill, Vicar of Torpenhowe. And in remembrance the sayde Robert Heghmore gaffe to the sayde Vicar vj Akes beste in his wodde whilke the sayde Thomas Bampton fellid and carred to Torpenhowe; and there the Bishopp oppynly gaffe a decre and a sentence to all thayme that aftyrward and from thens forthe tooke the Heriot affore the holy Kyrke war possessed, God's curse and his and all holy Kyrkks.

XXXII. Charter of Inspeximus and confirmation of charters to the Abbey of S. Mary, York, 1330. [Charter Rolls, 4 Edw. III. No. 14.]

Rex eisdem [Archiepiscopis &c.], salutem. Inspeximus cartam confirmacionis celebris memorie Domini E[dwardi], quondam Regis Anglie, patris nostri, in hec verba: Edwardus, Dei gracia

---

[1] Heriot, from Anglo-Saxon *here* "an army" and *geater*, "equipment," "apparel." The heriot was at first the military equipment escheated to the sovereign, or the lord of the manor, on the death of a vassal; in later times, a horse, or cow or other of his goods.

Rex Anglie, Dominus Hibernie, et Dux Aquitanie[1]......Inspeximus
eciam cartam Henrici Secundi, quondam Regis Anglie, progenitoris nostri, quam fecit predictis Abbati et Monachis in hec verba:
Henricus Dei gracia, Rex Anglie, et Dux Normannie et Aquitanie,
et Comes Andegavie[2]......Et ne alicuius heres vel successor
querat relevamen vel aliquod dominium preter orationes et preces
et elemosinam anime sue de beneficiis et elemosinis quas aliquis
dedit predicte Abbacie, que subscribuntur hic[3]:......Randulfus
Meschin [dedit] manerium de Wedarhala et ecclesiam eiusdem
ville, cum molendino et piscaria et bosco et ceteris pertinenciis;
capellam de Warthewic; terram que Camera Sancti Constantini
dicitur; in Corcabi ij. bouatas terre; aquam de Edene versus
Corcabi, necnon et ripam versus Corcabi in qua stagnum
firmatum est omnino; videlicet, liberas et quietas sine diminucione.   Randulfus Meschin [dedit] ecclesias de Apelbi, scilicet,
Sancti Michaelis et Sancti Laurencij, et terras earum, cum decimis
de dominiis eiusdem ville ex vtraque parte aque.   Adam filius
Suani Heremum Sancti Andree.   Vctredus filius Ligolf', iij. partem Crogeline, cum ecclesia et ceteris pertinentiis, et ij. bouatas
terre in Estuna, et molendinum de Scotebi.   In Cumquintina
dimidiam carucatam terre.   In Saurebi decimam de dominio.
Enisant filius Walteri, vnam carucatam terre que fuit Durandi in
Colebi.   Ketellus filius Eltreth ecclesiam de Morlund et iiij.
carucatas terre.   Walthef filius Gospatrici, ecclesiam de Brunne-
feeld, et corpus eiusdem Manerii.   In Salehild decimam de
dominio.   In Copelandia, Willelmus Meschin Chirkebibeccoch,
hoc est, vij. carucatas terre, cum omnibus pertinenciis suis, et
ecclesiam Sancte Bege, et quicquid ad eam pertinet, sicut carta
predicti Willelmi testatur.   Randulfus, filius eius, villam de Anan-
derdala, et dimidiam carucatam terre in Egremunt.   Reginaldus
faber aliam dimidiam carucatam terre in eadem villa.   Ketellus
filius Eltredi ecclesiam de Wyrchintuna, et ij. carucatas terre et i.
molendinum in eadem villa, et villam de Prestuna, cum bosco
et ceteris pertinenciis......Testibus hiis: T. Cantuariensi Archi-

---

[1] Edward II. begins by inspecting a charter of William II.

[2] See, for the first part of this charter of Henry II., No. 6.

[x] He first refers to the gifts of William I., William II. and Henry II.; what
follows here is similar to No. 14.

episcopo, Henrico Episcopo Wy[n]toniensi, Philippo Episcopo
Baiocensi, Herberto Episcopo Abri[n]censi, Thoma Cancellario,
Reinaldo Comite de Cornubia, Willelmo Comite de Albenia,
Henrico de Essex, Eust[achio] filio Johannis, Hugo de Gurn[ay],
Jurdano Tessun, Nichola de Hampt', apud Wudestocam......
Datum per manum nostram apud Langele, secundo die Junij,
anno regni nostri primo[1]. Nos autem donaciones, concessiones,
et confirmaciones predictas ratas habentes et gratas eas pro nobis
et heredibus nostris quantum in nobis est prefatis Abbati et
Monachis et eorum successoribus concedimus et confirmamus
sicut carte predicte racionabiliter testantur. Hiis Testibus ; venerabilibus patribus W. Archiepiscopo Eboracensi, Primate, Thesaurario nostro, J. Wyntoniensi, Cancellario nostro, W. Norwicensi,
Episcopis, Henrico Comite Lancastrie, consanguineo nostro,
Johanne de Warenna Comite Surrie, Henrico de Percy, consanguineo nostro, Radulpho de Nevill, Senescallo Hospicij nostri,
et aliis. Datum per manum nostram apud Westmonasterium,
xiiij. die Decembris[2].

Per peticionem de Consilio, et per
finem factum in alia carta.

XXXIII. CHARTER OF PRIVILEGES GRANTED BY KING
EDWARD III. TO THE ABBEY OF S. MARY AT YORK, MARCH 25th,
1331. [Charter Rolls, 5 Edward III. No. 66].

Rex Archiepis &c. Salutem. Inspeximus Cartam[3] quam
celebris Memorie Dnus Henricus quondam Rex Angl. pgenitor
nr fecit R...Abbati & Conventui Sce Marie de Ebor. in hec
verba : Henricus Rex Angl. T. Archiepo Ebor. & omnibus...
fidelibus & Ministris suis de Westmertland & de Cumbland
Saltm. Sciatis me concessisse, etc.

Inspeximus eciam quandam aliam Cartam quam Idem Pro-
genitor nr fecit Deo & Ecclie Sce Marie Eboraci et Abbati

---

[1] 1308. This is the date of Edward II.'s charter: that of Henry II. is not
dated, but the witnesses just given help to fix it, see note 10 on No. **6**.

[2] December 14th, 1330. The fine paid for this charter and the next
(No. **15**) was 40 marcs.

[3] Charter of Henry I. in the *Register*, No. **9**.

P.   28

Gaufrid et Monachis ibid. Deo servientibus in hec verba:
Henricus Rex Angl. Archiepo Ebor., etc.[1]...Nos autem Donaciones, Concessiones et Confirmaciones predcas ratas habentes et
gratas eas pro nobis et Heredibus nris quantum in nobis est
dilectis nobis in Xpo Abbati et Monachis Abbie predce et eorum
Successoribus concedimus et confirmamus sicut carte predicte
rationabiliter testantur.   Preterea cum in una cartarum predictarum contineatur quod predci Abbas et Monachi & Homines
sui habeant semper mortuum Boscum in Foresta predca ad
edificand. et comburend. Et in alia Carta ejusdem Progenitoris
nri similiter contineatur quod predci Abbas et Monachi habeant
Exclusagium et Stagnum de Piscaria et de Molendino de Wederhale et totam Pasturam inter Edene et regiam Viam que ducit de
Carleolo ad Appelby & a Wederhale usque ad Drybec, ijdemque
Abbas et Monachi quominus mortuum Boscum tam stantem quam
in eadem Foresta ad terram prostratum ad edificand. et comburend. pro se & Hominibus suis capere valeant, nec non
Exclusagium & Stagnum predca reparare et emendare, Ac eciam
Animalia et Pecora sua propria in pastura predca depasci et aliena
in eadem Pastura pro eorum Voluntate agistare et proficua inde
proveniencia ad Opus suum percipere possint et habere, per
Ministros nros Foreste predce jam de novo ut accepimus sint
impediti et multipliciter gravati, Et nobis supplicaverint ut nos pro
hujusmodi Impedimentis & Gravaminibus imposterum evitandis
velimus, Intencionem dicti Progenitoris nri in hac Parte declarare.
Nos ob Devocionem quam erga dcam beatam Virginem Mariam
in cujus Honore Abbia illa fundata existit gerimus et habemus, et
per Finem quem idem Abbas fecit nobis cum, volentes eisdem
Abbati & Monachis de Wederhale Graciam in hac Parte facere
specialem, Concessimus et hac carta nra confirmavimus pro nob.
& Heredibus nris quantum in nob. est eisdem Abbi et Monachis
qd ipsi et eorum successores mortuum Boscum tam stantem quam
in eadem Foresta ad terram prostratum ad edificand. et comburend. pro se et Hominibus suis capere valeant et habere nec
non Exclusagium et Stagnum predca reparare et emendare
quociens opus fuerit et prout eis videbitur expedire Ac eciam

---

[1] Charter of Henry I. in the *Register*, No. **5**.

omnimoda Animalia et Pecora sua propria in Pastura illa depasci et aliena in eadem pastura, pro voluntate eorundem Abbis & Monachorum agistare et proficua inde proveniencia ad Opus suum percipere possint & habere sine Occasione vel Impedimento nri vel Heredum nrorum aut Ministrorum nrorum predictorum tam Foreste quam aliorum quorumcumque. His Testibus Venerabilibus Patribus W. Archiepo Eborum Angl. Primate Thesaurario nro, J. Wynton Cancellario nro et W. Norwicen. Epis., Johe de Waren Comite Surr., Henr. de Percy, Willo de Monte Acuto, Willo de Clynton, Rado de Neyville Senescallo Hospicij nri et alijs, Dat. per Manum nram apud Westm. xxv. Die Marcii. (Cumbr.) Per Finem decem Marcarum.

XXXIV. Result of Inquisition ad quod Damnum 8 Edward III. (1334) No. 8.

Abbas Beatæ Mariæ Eboraci.

Rehabuit quatuor bovatas terræ et alias terras in Wederhale que captæ fuerunt in manu Regis occasione transgressionum &c.

XXXV. Petition of the Monks of Wederhale touching certain tenements in Wederhale seized by Sir John de Louthre, the King's Escheator, 8 Edward III. (1334). [Rolls and Pleas of Parliament, ed. Record Com., vol. ii. p. 77 *a*.]

A notre Seigneur le Roi et a son Conseil monstruont ses humbles Chapeleynes l'Abbe notre Dame d'Everwyck et ses Moignes de la Celle de Wederhale q̃. come par conge le Roi Edward prier notre Seigneur le Roi q̃. or est, et pour enquest retourne en la Chancellerie eyent purchace de William le fitz Johan de Benningham diverses teñz en la Ville de Wederhale, queux le dit William avoit purchace de diverses frank tenanntz de meisme la Ville; Sir Johan de Louthre, Escaetour le dit notre Seigneur le Roi, par colour d'un enquest de son office, pris par ascunes malvoilleauntz les avauntditz teñtz ad seisi en le maine le Roi, et encountre diverses maundementz q'il ad resceu a notre dit Seigneur le Roi les detent, et les issues par greivouses destresces fait lever a grant oppressioun de les Moines avauntditz. Dount ils priount q̃. convenable remedie les soit fait, issint q̃. le dit Eschetour en ost le main, et rent les issues q'il ad levez.

Responsio—

Sequatur Abbas ad communem legem.

XXXVI. Note of Inquisition ad quod Damnum, 29 Edward III. (1355) No. 27

Ada de Burton.

Dedit Abbati et Conventui Beatæ Mariæ Eboraci unum messuagium et quadraginta acras terræ &c. in Wederhale in partem satisfaccionis centum et quatuor viginti et quinque libratar' terræ &c.

XXXVII. Monition issued by Bishop Welton in a similar form to the Priories of Carlisle, Lanercost, and Wederhal for a special visitation under Mandate from the See of Rome[1], 1357. [Register of Bishop Welton, MS. page 44].

G. (Gilbert) &c. dilectis filiis Priori et Capitulo Ecclesie nostre Cathredalis beate Marie Karl. Salutem, gratiam et Bened. Quia de mandato Sedis Apostolice virtute literarum dicte Sedis nobis super directarum vobis exhibendarum et aliis quorum interest in eventum astricti sumus et artati sub penis et censuris in eisdem literis expressis, Clerum et populum nostre Diocesis visitare. Nos hujusmodi mandata Apostolica pretermittere non valentes, vos tenore presentium premunimus quod die Lune proxima post Dominicam qua cantatur Officium *Qui modo geniti* prox. futura in Domo Capitulari dicte Ecclesie nostre, auctoritate literarum hujusmodi, vos intendimus visitare. Quocirca vobis injungimus et mandamus, vosque tenore presentium peremptorie citamus, quod vos omnes et singuli dicto die tempestive coram nobis vel Commissariis nostris, in Domo Capitulari dicte Ecclesie nostre, compareatis ac vestram presentiam prebeatis, visitationem nostram nostraque salubria monita, correctiones et injungenda debita et devota reverentia recepturi. Concanonicos insuper vestros et Conversos, si qui fuerint, nunc absentes, qui in visitationibus hujusmodi debeant et consueverant interesse, faciatis

---

[1] The visitation of the Priory of Wederhal did not take place till 1358.

premuniri quod dictis die et loco coram nobis vel dictis Commissariis nostris, una vobiscum, compareant et intersint cum continuatione et prorogatione dierum subsequentium si necesse fuerint ad faciendum ea que superius exprimantur. Vobis etiam tenore presentium inhibemus ne quicquam quod in prejudicium dicte Visitationis nostre cedere poterit aliqualiter interim attemptetis, seu faciatis per vos vel per alium quomodolibet attemptari, Et nos de omni eo quod feceritis in premissis, una cum omnibus omnium et singulorum Concanonicorum vestrorum, tam presentium quam absentium, in scriptis fideliter redactis, citra dictam diem Lune distincte et aperte certificatis, per literas vestras patentes harum seriem continentes. Dat. apud Manerium nostrum de Rosa 13° die Martii, A.D. 1357 et nostre consecrationis quinto.

XXXVIII. EXTRACT FROM THE "COMPERTA" OR SUPPOSED FRAGMENTS OF THE LOST BLACK BOOK WHICH WAS SAID TO HAVE BEEN THE REPORT OF CRUMWEL'S VISITORS IN 1536. [Cottonian MSS. British Museum, *Cleopatra*, E. iv. page 147.]

Wetherall.

Sodom. {Nicholaus Barneston} per voluntar.
        {Robertus Goodon } pollut.

Fundator Dns. Rex.

Redditus annuus cxxx li.

Hic, ut putatur, partem habent Sancti (*sic*) Crucis, et lactis Beatæ Mariæ[1].

XXXIX. SURRENDER OF WETHERHALL PRIORY, OCTOBER 20th, 1538. [From the Record Office, No. 262.]

Omnibus Christi fidelibus ad quos presens Scriptum peruenerit Radolphus Hartley, Prior Prioratus de Wetherhall, in Comitatu Cumbrie, et eiusdem loci Conuentus, salutem. Sciatis nos, prefatos Priorem et Conuentum, vnanimibus nostris assensu et consensu, dedisse, concessisse, et hoc presenti Scripto nostro confirmasse excellentissimo ac invictissimo Principi et Domino nostro, Domino Henrico octauo, Dei gratia Anglie et Francie

---

[1] There are entries of the same character in regard to the other monasteries in the district. All have reference to the money value.

Regi, fidei defensori, Domino Hibernie, et in terra Supremo
Capiti Anglicane Ecclesie, totum Prioratum nostrum de Wetherhall predictum, ac totum Dominium nostrum de Wetherhall cum
suis membris et pertinentijs vniuersis, in Comitatu predicto,
aceciam Rectoriam nostram de Wetherhall, cum suis iuribus et
pertinentijs vniuersis, in eodem Comitatu, necnon totum Dominium nostrum de Morlande, cum suis membris et pertinentijs
vniuersis, in Comitatu Westmerland', ac Rectoriam nostram de
Morlande cum suis iuribus et pertinentijs vniuersis, in eodem
Comitatu Westmerland', necnon Rectorias Ecclesiarum parochialium Sancti Laurencij et Sancti Michaelis de Apleby, in dicto
Comitatu Westmerland', ac omnia maneria messuagia terras
tenementa prata pascuas pasturas boscos subboscos redditus
reuersiones seruicia rectorias vicarias ecclesias capellas aduoca-
ciones presentaciones donaciones et iura patronatuum ecclesiarum
capellarum et aliorum beneficiorum ecclesiasticorum quorumcumque penciones porciones decimas oblaciones feoda militum
escaetas releuia visus franciplegij Curias letas hundreda ac alia iura
possessiones et hereditamenta nostra quecumque tam spiritualia
quam temporalia, cuiuscumque sint generis nature vel speciei,
tam in dictis Comitatibus Cumbrie et Westmerland', quam in
aliquo alio Comitatu infra Regnum Anglie, seu alibi vbicumque;
ac omnia et singula ornamenta iocalia bona catalla et debita
nostra quecumque: HABENDUM tenendum et gaudendum omnia
et singula predicta Prioratum dominia maneria rectorias terras
tenementa et cetera omnia et singula premissa superius expressa
et specificata cum pertinentijs prefato Domino nostro Regi heredibus et successoribus suis imperpetuum. IN CUIUS rei testimonium
huic presenti Scripto nostro Sigillum nostrum commune apposuimus. DATUM in domo nostra Capitulari, vicesimo die Octobris
anno regni dicti Domini Regis nostri Henrici octaui tricesimo.

per me, Radulphum Hartley, Priorem monasterij siue Prioratus
de Wederhall.

per me, Johannem Clyston, monachum ibidem.

[Seal of Ralph Hartley.]

Recognitum coram me, Thoma Legh, xxviij die Januarij anno regni Regis Henrici octaui tricesimo.

per me, Thomam Legh.

XL. MEMORANDUM AND PETITION OF THE DEAN AND CHAPTER OF CARLISLE FOR THE RECTORY OF WETHERALL, MARCH 5th, 1546, AND PARTICULARS FOR GRANT. [From the Records of the late Augmentation Office, now in the Record Office.]

Particulars for grants, 37 Hen. VIII.

Memorandum, that we the Deane and Chapiter of the Cathedrall Churche of ye hollie Trynytie of Karlyll require to haue of the Kinges maiesties gyft and graunte the particler parcelles here unto annexed, being of the clere yerelie value of xiiij li. xiij s. iiij d., the tenth thereof not deducted, in recompence of the decaye and lacke of ye yerelie value of the holle possessions appoynted vs by the Kinges Majestie vpon the dotacion of the said Cathedrall Churche. In wytness where of to this present Byll we haue put our Chapter and Commen Seale, the vth daie of Mache (*sic*) in the xxxvijth yere of the raigne of our moost drad soueraigne lord King Henry theight by the grace of God Kynge of Englond, Fraunce, and Irelond, defendour of ye Faith, and of ye Churche of Englond and also of Irelond in earth the Supreme hedd.

Parcella possessionum
nuper Prioratus de } in Comitatu Cumbrie.
Wetherall................

Rectoria de Wetherall, cum pertinentijs, in Comitatu Cumbrie—

Valet in—

Firma Rectorie Ecclesie parochialis de Wetherall et Warwik, in dicto Comitatu Cumbrie, unacum decimis capellarum Sanctorum Anthonij et Severini eidem Rectorie annexarum, unacum omnibus domibus edificijs decimis oblacionibus proficuis commoditatibus et emolumentis quibuscumque eisdem Capellis et Rectorie pertinentibus siue spectantibus, sic concessa Radulpho Harteley, nuper Priori de Wetherall, pro termino vite sue, vel quousque idem Radulphus ad vnum vel plura beneficia ecclesiastica clari annui valoris xxx li. per Dominum Regem promotus fuerit; vltra xij li. per annum similiter concessas eidem Radulpho in recompen[sa]cionem pencionis sue per literas patentes Domini Regis magno Sigillo Curie Augmentacionum sigillatas, datas vltimo die Januarij anno regni Regis Henrici viijᵘⁱ xxxᵐᵒ, prout per easdem literas patentes plenius patet—xxvj li. xiij s. iiij d.

Reprise in—

Salario vnius presbiteri annuatim diuina celebrantis infra ecclesiam parochialem de Wetherall per annum.................vj li.

Salario vnius Capellani annuatim diuina celebrantis et curam obseruantis infra Capellam de Warwik per annum...............vj li.

[Summa,] xij li.

Et remanet vltra clare per annum—xiiij li. xiij s. iiij d., decima xxix s. iiij d., clare—xiij li. iiij s., whych the Kyng ys pleasyd to grawnt vnto the Deane and Chappyter of Carlyoll in recompense of their decayes vppon the dotacion.

Memorandum, the said parsonage of Wetherall was neuer surveyed by me sens I came in office.

Item, amongest the bokes remayning in my custody there bene ij, whereof one mencyoneth that the yerely valewe of the said parsonage is xl markes, making no mencion of reprises. In the other boke the said parsonage is charged but at xiij li. vj s. viij d. ouer and besides all deduccions and reprises going out of the same, soo that I am not certeyn neither of the yerely va[lue] ne of the yerely reprises going out of the said parsonage.

Item, the said parsonage is graunted to the late Prior of Wetherall for parte of his pencion as is abouesaid, but there is no somme mencyoned in the said patent of [the] yerely valewe of the said parsonage.

Exʳ per me, Ricardum Hochonsen, Auditorem.

vᵗᵒ Martij anno Regis Henrici viijᵘⁱ xxxvijᵐᵒ pro Decano et Capitulo Ecclesie Cathedralis Carliolensis.

The clere yerely value of the said parsonage is xiiij li. xiij s. iiij d., whereof deducted for the tenthe xxix s. iiij d. And so remayneth clere xiij li. iiij s., whiche the Kinges Majesty of his moste bountefull goodness is pleased and contente to gyve and graunte to the said Deane and Chapiter and to their successours for euer in recompence of suche decaies of yerelie value as they do wante of the somme appoynted vnto them vpon their dotacion. The said parsonage to come vnto thandes and possession of the said Deane and Chapiter after the death of the forsaid late Prior of Wetherall or soner, if the forsaid Deane and Chapiter can agree with hym for his intereste in the same.

Memorandum, that the forsaid decaye and lacke of value hath ben pervsed and examyned by Mr Hendeley, Mr Bacon, and Mr Hochonson.   Edward North.

Irrotulatum per Willelmum Burnell.

XLI. LETTERS PATENT OF HENRY VIII. GRANTING THE CHURCH OF WETHERALL AND THE CHAPEL OF WARWICK TO THE DEAN AND CHAPTER OF CARLISLE, DATED JANUARY 15th, 1547. [These are too long to print; a copy in full is given in the Minute Books of the Dean and Chapter of Carlisle, vol. x. p. 41, from the Record Office.]

XLII (a). ABSTRACT OF MINISTER'S ACCOUNTS, 30-31 HENRY VIII. (MARCH 4th, 1539) NO. 121, M. 20. [From the Public Record Office.]

WETHERELL NUPER MONASTERIUM, in Comitatu Cumberland.

COMPOTUS Thome Wentworth, militis, Collectoris Redditu[um] ibidem, per tempus predictum.

Arreragia.—Nulla, quia primus compotus dicti computantis.

Summa—nulla.

Scitus Monasterij, cum terris dominicalibus ac piscaria de Baye.—Sed respondet de xx li. viij d. de firma Scitus nuper Monasterij, cum terris dominicalibus gardinis pomarijs ac piscaria de le Baye, in manibus nuper Monasterij, nunc autem dimiss[i] Thome Wentworthe, militi, per Indenturam datam apud Westmonasterium, quarto die Marcij anno regni Regis Henrici octaui tricesimo, tenor cuius Indenture sequitur in hec verba, pro termino xxj annorum : *Hec Indentura* facta inter excellentissimum principem

et dominum Dominum Henricum octauum, Dei gracia Anglie et
Frauncie Regem, fidei defensorem, Dominum Hibernie, et in
terra Supremum Capud Anglicane Ecclesie, ex vna parte, et
Thomam Wentworth, militem, ex altera parte, testatur quod idem
Dominus Rex, per advisamentum et concensum Consilij Curie
Augmentacionum Revencionum Corone sue, tradidit concessit et
ad firmam dimissit prefato Thome Wentworth, militi, Domum et
Scitum nuper Monasterij de Wetherall, in Comitatu Cumbrie,
modo dissoluti, vnacum omnibus edifficijs oreis ortis pomerijs gar-
dinjs terris et solum (*sic*) infra Scitum septum ambitum circuitum
et precingtum dicti nuper Monasterij existencium (*sic*), ac tria parua
clausur' prati cum pertinentijs eidem Scitui adiacentia, continentia
per estimacionem tres acras, ac herbagium vnius bosci cum vna
parcella prati vocata Mirebanke[1] continente per estimacionem
octo acras, et vnam parcellam prati vocatam Syme Medow, cum
vno clauso terre vocato Conyngarth Hill, modo in tenura Nicholai
Ploughe, vnum clausum terre iacentis ante portas dicti nuper
Monasterij, continentis per estimacionem tres acras, ac vnum
terre vocatum Highefeld, alias dictum Priorfeld, continent' per
estimacionem [triginta] sex acras, vnum clausum terre vocatum
Turmyre et vnum alium terre vocatum...eidem adiacens, continent[ia] per estimacionem tres acras, modo in tenura Johannis
Broune, vnum clausur' terre vocatum Holmehouse Flatt cum
pertinentijs, continent' per estimacionem septem acras, vnum
clausur' terre vocatum Linghilles cum pertinentijs continent' per
estimacionem quatuor acras cum vno paruo clausur' terre eidem
adiacente, vnum clausur' vocatum Cotehouse cum pertinentijs,
cont[inens] per estimacionem tres acras terre, cum vno paruo
clausur' iacen[te] ante portam dicti nuper Monasterij, aceciam
vnam Capellam vocatam Saynt Anthonys Chapell, cum duabus
clausuris terre eidem Capelle adiacentibus, continentibus per
estimacionem iiij^or. acras, vnum clausur' pasture continens per
estimacionem vnam acram, vnam pasturam vocatam Calffe Close,
continentem per estimacionem ij acras, vnum clausur' pasture
vocatum Thornyfeld, continent' per estimacionem ij acras, unum
clausur' prati et pasture vocatum Swynestye Sykes, continens per

---

[1] These places may be compared with the description in **XLVI.**, the survey
on the surrender.

estimacionem vnam acram et dimidiam, vnum pratum vocatum Trodmyrebanke, continens per estimacionem duas acras, ac herbagium vnius bosci et subbosci vocati Parke, vnam parcellam prati iacentem iuxta le Myrebanke modo in tenura Thome Thomson, continentem per estimacionem dimidiam acram, ac vnam pasturam Shepehethe vocatam Frodell Croke et Thoppell Syke, vnum mollendinum aquaticum adiacens iuxta dictum nuper Monasterium, ac totam piscariam apud le Bay: que omnia et singula premissa scituantur, iacent, et existunt in Wetherall, in Comitatu predicto, et dicto nuper Monasterio spect[ab]ant et pertinebant, ac in manibus cultura et occupacione propria nuper Prioris dicti nuper Monasterij, tempore dissolucionis illius nuper Monasterij et antea, reseruata et occupata fuerunt: *Exceptis* tamen et dicto Domino Regi heredibus et successoribus suis omnino reseruatis omnibus grossis arboribus et boscis de et super premissis crescentibus et existentibus, ac omnibus turribus et edificijs huiusmodi que dictus Dominus Rex ibidem imposterum prosterni et afferri mandauerit: Habendum et tenendum &c.... Reddendo inde annuatim dicto Domino Regi heredibus et successoribus suis xx li. viij d. legalis monete Anglie, videlicet, &c.[1]...

Summa—xx li. viij d.

Wetherall villa.—*Et de*—iiij s. de firma vnius tenementi in tenura Richerdi Twentiman, cum ij acris terre ac pertinentijs ibidem, ad voluntatem Domini Regis per annum, ac dat annuatim domino vnum gallum ij gallinas ac iij precarias[2] in authumpno, soluendis ad terminos Sancti Martini et Penthecostes per equales porciones. *Et de* &c.... [The other tenants are here given.]

Summa—xiij li. xix s. ij d.

Morland town, Colbye-Lathes,...township, St. Michael's and St. Lawrence's, Appulbye. [The particulars as to these are given.]

---

[1] The annual values here given are the same as in **XLVI**. making up £20. 0s. 8d.

[2] *Precaria*, the day's work which the tenants on some manors were bound, under their tenure, to render as service to the lord. The old English term is *biden-day*. Compare the word "precarious," doubtful, obtained by prayer, as a favour. In addition to the annual money-rent, all these customary tenants rendered 1 cock, 2 hens and 3 days' work in autumn as in 1490 (see **XLIV**.).

Rectoria de Wetherall.—De xxvj li. xiij s. iiij d. de exitibus sive proficuis Rectorie Ecclesie paroch[i]alis de Wetherall hic non respondet, eo quod dicta Rectoria concessa est Radulpho Harteley, nuper Priori Prioratus predicti, ut in parte pencionis sue, per litteras patentes Domini Regis datas apud Westmonasterium vltimo die Januarij anno regni Regis predicti tricesimo, pro termino vite eiusdem Radulphi.

Summa—nulla.

Penciones.—Sed respondet de—iiij li. de annuali pencione exeunte de Rectoria de Crossebye Ravenswaith, nuper pertinente Monasterio de Whitbye, soluendis ad terminos Sancti Martini in Ieme et Penthecostes per equales porciones. *Et de*—xv s. de annuali pencione exeunte de decimis granorum de Salkeld pertinentibus Archidiacono Carliolin', soluendis ad terminos predictos equaliter.

Summa—iiij li. xv s.

Perquisita Cur[iarum].—*Et de*—xix s. provenientibus de placitis et perquisitis Cur[iarum] hoc anno tent[arum], prout patet per extractus Cur[iarum] examinatos super hunc compotum cum Rotulis Cur[iarum] predict[arum], et Rem[anent].

Summa—xix s.

Summa totalis Recepte.— Cxxxiiij li. x s. iij d. ob. [There follows a list of payments.]

XLII (b). ABSTRACT OF MINISTERS' ACCOUNTS, 30-31 HEN. VIII., NO. 218, M. 2 d.

WETHERALL NUPER PRIORATUS.

COMPOTUS Thome Whartone, militis, et Jacobi Rokebie, Commissionariorum Domini Regis super surrend' nuper Prioratus ibidem, vltimo die Decembris Anno regni Regis predicti xxx^{mo}., tam de omnibus vendicionibus ibidem factis, quam omnimodis denariorum summis prouenientibus de dissolucione predicta diuersis personis solutis et distributis, prout inferius patet.

Arreragia.—Nulla, quia primus compotus dict[orum] Computant[ium].

Summa—nulla.

Vendicio vtensilium domorum.—*Sed* recept' compotum de liij s. iiij d. de precio diuersorum vtensilium Ecclesie, videlicet, iij tabule alabastri x s., ij candlestickes erea ij s., divers' imag' lignia iij s. iiij d., divers' stall' in choro vj s. viij d., j vestimentum viridi dornex[1] iij s. iiij d., j vestimentum veteris damas cum j avbe v s., ij vetera vestimenta cum albis vj s. viij d., iij panna alteria ij s., j perclose[2] frat' vj s. viij d., ij parr' cencr' ij s., j cloke veter' ibidem vij s., et vnum letteron'[3] viij d., sic vendit[orum] Thome Wentfurthe militi. *Et de* ij s. viij d. de precio ij veterum matressarum ij veterum couerlett' et j parr' veterum sheittes ibidem invent[orum] in Cameria vocata Inner Chaumer, sic vendit[orum] Thome Wentfurthe predicto. *Et de* viij s. iiij d. de precio veterum stufferarum, videlicet, ij veterum mattressarum ij s., ij bolsters xvj d., j parr' blankettes xx d., ij veterum couerlettes ij s., et ij pillowes xvj d., ibidem inventorum in Camera vocata Vtter Chambre, sic venditorum Thome Wentfurthe, militi. *Et de* xiij s. iiij d. de precio veterum stufferarum [et?] vtensilium inventorum in magna noua Camera, videlicet, j veteris fetherbedd x s., j bolster viij d., ij couerlettes xvj d., et j parr' blankettes xvj d., sic venditorum Thome Wentfurthe, militi. *Et de* viij s. iiij d. de precio stufferarum inventarum in the Buttere, videlicet, iij veterum table clothez lineij iij s., iiij d., iiij veterum candel' v s., sic venditorum Thome Wentfurth, militi, predicto. *Et de* xxvj s. viij d. de precio diuersarum stufferarum inventarum in lez Kitchine, videlicet, iij olla erea x s., iiij lez pannez v s., j lez brandrethe vj s. viij d., iij lez speittes iij s. iiij d., et j parr' rakkes xx d. in toto, sic venditarum predicto Thome Wentfurthe, militi. *Et de* xij s. viij d. de precio diuersarum stufferarum inventarum in lez Wete Larder, videlicet, ij leade sistrons x s., ij veter' tubbis xij d., et ij le bordes xx d., sic venditarum predicto Thome Wentfurthe, militi. *Et de* xxvj s. viij d. de precio diuersarum stufferarum inventarum in lez Breuhouse, videlicet, j bruyng leade x s., j culing leade x s., et diuers' veter' tubbz vj s. viij d., in toto sic venditarum sepedicto Thome Wentfurthe militi *Et de* xiiij s. viij d. de precio veterum stufferarum

---

[1] *Dornex,* coarse damask made at Doornik (Tournai) in the Netherlands.

[2] *Perclose,* or *parclose,* the division or railing separating the portion of the monks from the rest of the Church.

[3] *Letteron',* a lectern.

inventarum in lez Hall, videlicet, iij tabul' fract' vj s. viij d., diuers' lez formez iij s. iiij d., j veter' cupborde iij s. iiij d., et j skrene xvj d., sic venditarum Thome Wentfurthe, militi. *Et de* xxiij s. iiij d. de precio diuersarum stufferarum husbandrie, videlicet, ij plaustr' xvj s. viij d., iiij lez temez vj s. viij d., sic venditarum Thome Wentfurthe, militi. *Et de* xxvj s. viij d. de precio diuersarum stuffurarum inventarum in lez Kylne, videlicet, j lez stepe leade xx s., et j lez Kylne haire vj s. viij d., sic venditarum Thome Wentfurthe, militi.

Summa—x li. xvj s. viij d.

Vendicio granorum et cattallorum.—Et de xj li. vj s. de precio diuersorum generum granorum, videlicet, xij bz silinginis xij s., ij loodes feni iiij s., xij skepe ordei iiij li. iiij s., avene intritur[ate] xv s., ij skepe di' brasij xvij s. vj d., di' skepe ordeii iij s. vj d., iiij^{or} quart' tritici xxvj s. viij d., v acrez tritico seminat' xxxiij s. iiij d., iiij acrez di' silingine seminat' xxx s., sic venditorum Thome Wentfurthe, militi, vt supra. *Et de* xx li. vij s. de precio diuersorum cattallorum, videlicet, boues viij li. xj s., ix vacce lx s., viij vituli xiij s. iiij d., ij pull' x s., iiij^{xx} oves matrices iiij li. xij s. iiij d., agnelli xliiij s. iiij d. et xiij porcelli xiij s., sic venditorum Thome Wentfurthe, militi.

Summa—xxxj li. xiij s.

Denarie nuper Prioratui predicto debit'.—xxiiij li. xvij s. iiij d.

Vendicio Jocalium.—De precio vnius calecis, iiij bocliar[iorum], et vnius salsamen' de argento albo, ponderancium......vncias, non respondet, eo quod nulla huiusmodi jocalia ibidem vendita fuerint (*sic*) super dissolucionem predictam, sed liberantur Willelmo Grene, Receptori Domini Regis ibidem, et responsurus est inde per pondus, prout patet per compotum Receptoris in Comitatibus Northumbrie Cumbrie et Westmerl' de anno regni Regis Henrici viij^{ui} xxxj^{mo}.

Summa—nulla.

Summa totalis Recepte—lxvij li. vij s.

De quibus—

Regard[a] Confratrum et seruiencium, cum eorum expensis in Hospicio ibidem a die Sequestracionis usque diem Dissolucionis.— *Idem computat in* regardijs datis nuper confratribus super dissolucionem dicti nuper Monasterij, videlicet, Johanni Clistone, presbitero, xl s., Thome Hartleye, presbitero, xxvj s. viij d., Johanni Gaille, presbitero, xxvj s. viij d., et dicto nuper Priori, scilicet [Radulpho] Hartleye iiij li.—viij li. xiij s. iiij d. *Et in* regardijs datis diuersis seruicienc' &c...

Soluciones debitorum.

Summa—xxvj li. iiij s. vij d.
Summa—xlj li. viij d.

Liberacio denariorum.

Summa—ij s. j d.

Summa allocacionum et liberacionum — lxvij li. vij s. Que summa coequalis est cum summa Recepte.

Et eque.

XLII (c). ABSTRACT OF MINISTERS' ACCOUNTS, 32–33 HEN. VIII., L. R. 1010, M. 15.

WETHERELL NUPER PRIORATUS.

COMPOTUS Thome Wentworthe, militis, Collectoris Reddit[us] et Firmarius ibidem, &c....scilicet, pro vno anno integro, prout inferius patet.

Arreragia.—*Nulla*—quia in pede vltimi compoti sui anni proximi precedentis plene liquet.

Summa—nulla.

Redditus et Firme.—*De* Cxxxiij li. xj s. iij d. ob. de firma Scitus &c.[1]...hic non respondet, eo quod omnia et singula premissa inter alia conceduntur Decano et Capitulo Ecclesie Cathedralis Carliolij et successoribus suis imperpetuum per litteras Domini Regis nunc Henrici viij[ui] Dei gratia Anglie Francie et Hibernie Regis fidei defensoris ac in terra Supremi Ca[pitis Anglicane et] Hibernice Ecclesie patentes sub magno sigillo Anglie, datas apud Westmonasterium...die...... (MS. torn.)

Wetherell Rectoria.—*Nec respondet de*—xxvj li. [xiij s. iiij d.]...is Rectorie Ecclesie Parochialis de Wetherell hic non respondet, eo quod &c.[2]...

Summa—nulla.

Summa oneris....... (MS. torn.)

---

[1] The details and amounts are the same as in the Survey **XLVI.**
[2] The remainder is as in **XLII (a).**

XLIII. Taxatio Ecclesiastica P. Nicholai IV. 1292; also Nova Taxatio 1817–18. [From ed. Record Commission, pp. 319, 320.]

Taxacoes sive estimacoes...facte in Dioc. Karl. per Ric. de Wyteby Archid. Karl. et Adam de Levington Rectorem Ecclie de Skelton ejusdem Dioc.

Decanatus Karl.	*Karliolens. Sp.*		
	£.	s.	d.
Ecclia de Wedirhale	32	0	0
Decanatus Westm'land.			
Ecclia Sci. Laur. de Appleby	15	0	0
Ecclia Sci. Michis de Appleby . . .	30	0	0
Ecclia de Morlund	80	0	0
Pens. Abbis de Ebor. in Vicar. Sci. Laur. de Appleby.	1	6	8
Pens. ejusdem in Vicar. de Morlund . .	2	13	4
Pens. Prioris de Wederhale in Ecclia de Crossebiravesuart pro x qtiis fri . . .	2	0	0

Taxatio bonor. tempalm dni Karl. Epi et Religiosor. vim ejusdem Karl. dioc. facta anno Dni Millimo cc^{mo} nonagesimo sedo per magros Petrum de Insula Archid. Exon. et Adam de Aston Reorem ecclie de Bekingham...

Prior de Wedirhal. het	52	17	6

Nova Taxatio, 1318[1].

	Karliol. Sp.		
Ecclia de Wedirhale	1	0	0
Ecclia Sci Laurencij de Appleby . . .	4	0	0
Vicar. ejusdem non sufficit pro omibs ordinar. supportand.			
Ecclia Sci Michis de Appleby . . .	5	0	0
Vicar. ejusdem	1	0	0

---

[1] This "Nova Taxatio" only affected some of the Border districts wherein the Clergy were unable to pay the former tax on account of the invasions of the Scots and other troubles. The Mandate (Oct 26, 11 Ed. II.) was addressed by the King to Bishop Halton.

	Karliol. Sp.		
Ecclia de Morlund	13	6	8
Vicar. ejusdem	4	0	0
Pens. Abbis de Ebor. in Vicar. Sci Laur. de			
Appleby.	1	6	8
Pens. ejusdem in Vicar. de Moreland . .	2	13	4
Pens. Prioris de Wederhale in Ecclia de			
Crossebiravesuart	2	0	0
Tempalia Prioris de Wedirhale . .	4	0	0

XLIV. RENTAL OF THE CELL OF WEDYRHALE, OCTOBER, 1490. [From the original Parchment in the "Chest" of the Dean and Chapter of Carlisle.]

Rentale omnium firmarum decimarum pensionum et porcionum pertinencium Celle de Wedyrhale factum per fratrem Ricardum Esyngwalde priorem ejusdem mensis Octobris Anno Domi Millmo quadrigesimo nonagesimo.

Firme de Wedyrhale⎱ Thomas Veller tenet ad volunt. Dni ad voluntat. Dni ⎰ duo Cotagia cum duab. acr. ter. nuper in tenura Johan. Ormesby et reddit per annu ... ... 4s.

Idm Thomas dat pro eisdem tres precarias[1] unum gallum et duas gallinas.

[*With each tenant comes a similar clause.*]

Ricardus West tenet ut supra du. Cotagia et tre. acr. ter. nuper in tenura Matth. Whitebrowe et red. per annu ... 4s.

Johes Grayson un. tentn. et octo acr. ter....Roger Haton   8s.

Thomas Milner un. tent. et octo acr. ter....Willi Milner   8s.

Willms Barne du. Messuagia et sexdec. acr. ter....Willi Waynhope   ...   .   16s.

Johes Macleney du. Cotagia cum quinque acr. ter. et dim.... Archebalde Noble   ...   .   5s.

Johes Barne unu. tent. et octo acr. ter....Johes Ormesby   8s.

Johes Linewray unu. tent. et octo acr. ter....Ricardi Archer   8s.

Willmus Lowicke un. tent. et octo acr. ter... Willi Sclater   8s.

Thomas Ormesby unu. tent. et octo acr. ter. cum uno Cotagio... Willi Sharparowe   ...   .   10s.

---

[1] On these *precariæ*, see **XLII (a)**, p. 443, note 2.

Robtus Sharparow un. tent. et octo acr. ter....Th. Sharparow 10s.

Robtus Pavy un. tent. et octo acr. ter. cum du. Byggs...Th. Blythe ...   .   8s. 6d.

Thomas Blythe unu. tent. et octo acr. ter....Thom. Waynopp 8s.

Thomas Hardkneys unu. tent. cum un. Cotagio adjacent.... Th. Whelpedale   ...   .   8s.

Idm Tho. tenet quadm parcell. ter. de divsis terr. vocat. Fostane flatt prope Myrebanke 4s

Idm Tho. tenet ibm un. Croftum vocat. Smithy Croft 18s. 8d.

Idm Tho. tenet du. Cotlands ibm   ...   ...   3s. 8d.

Ricardus Vauxe du. tent. et sexdecim. acr. ter....Joh. Smithe 16s.

Idm Ric. tenet un. Cotland   ...   .   3s.

Robtus Grayson un. Cotland in un. Gryslande...Johis Walker 5s.

Johes Mershell un. tent. et octo acr. ter....Willi Portar   8s.

Robtus Collynson un. tent. et octo acr. ter ...Johi Walker 8s.

Johes Richmond unu. tent. et octo acr. ter....Tho. Newlands 8s.

Idm Johes tenet di. tent. cum trib. acr. ter. et dim. et redd. per annu. pret. ali. trib. acr. et di. terr. in tenura Willi More   4s.

Robtus Ormesby du. Cotagia et un. acr. et dim. ter....Johi Anderson   ...   .   5s.

Willmus West un. Cotag. et di. acr. ter....Edwardi Crabe   3s.

Idm Willmus tenet ali. di. acr. ter. quod pertinet Cotag. jam vastat. ...   .   6d.

Johes Donwethy un. tent. un. Cotag. cum di. acr. ter.... Adde Donwethy   ...   .   3s.

Johes Browne un. tent. et octo acr. ter....Johis Browne   8s.

Relict. Willi Archer unu. Cotag. cum di. acr. ter....Willi Archer ...   .   3s.

Eadm Relict. tenet sept. perticatas ter. vocat. sept. Rodelands super Le Sandys   ...   .   1s. 6d.

Willmus Watson unu. Cotag. cum di. acr. ter....Thome Peert 3s.

Johes Valles un. Cotag. cum di. acr. ter....Rob. Ormesby   3s.

Crofer Waynhopp du. tent. et sexdec. acr. ter....Johis Taylro 16s.

Johes Archer un. tent. et octo acr. ter....Tho. Sclater ...   8s.

Robtus Thompson du. tent. et sexdec. acr. ter....Rich. Penrith   ...   .   16s.

Johes Andrason un. tent. et octo acr. ter....Thom. Locke-smith ...   .   8s.

Willmus Moore di. tent. cum tribus acr. et di. ter. præter alia tr. acr. et di....Johan. Richmond ... ... 4*s.*

Isabella Ormesby un. Cotag. cum quinque rod. ter.. .Johis Ormesby ... ... 3*s.*

Willmus Atkinson de Scoteby tenet molendinum de Gylmyln¹ ... ... 26*s.* 8*d.*

Robtus Endrew un. tent. ex novo fact. cum dec. acr. ter.... Willi Dobinson ... ... 8*s.*

SUM. TOTAL. HUJUS VILLE £14 15*s.* 6*d.*

Morehouse. Willms Sclater un. tent. vocat. Morehouse cum trigint. quat. acr. et di. ter. ... ... 20*s.*

Holmehouse. Thomas Lowson un. tent. vocat. Holmehouse cum trigint. quatuor acr. et di. ter. et pratis ... ... 20*s.*

Corkby. Robtus Lowson un. tent. cum du. acr. et di. ter. 8*s.*

Newby. Relict. Rob. Stavyll de Newby un. tent. cum sexdec. acr. ter. ... ... 8*s.*

Cowhintyng. Willmus Smith de Comwhintinge un. Cotag. cum un. acr. et di. ter....Joh. Browne ... ... 3*s.*

Carliell. Willms Shythyngton de Carliell nuper tenuit un. Cotag. in Carliel et solebat redd. per ann. 2*s.* modo nl quia vast. et non ædificat.

Bochardby. Robtus Holme de Bochardby un. Clausur. vocat. Well Close in Bochardby...Willi Sewell et continet du. acr. ter. 2*s.*

Frodelcrocke. Robtus Ricardby de frodelcroke un. tent. cum crtis ters...Willi Browne ... ... 4*s.*

Willms Ricardby de eadem tenet un. tent. ... ... 4*s.*

Penrith Cotes. Thomas Agloneby de Carlile tenet pro liba firma de Penrith Cotes ... ... 8*s.*

Agloneby. Itm idm Tho. Agloneby tenet pro liba firma in Agloneby per ann. ... ... 1*s.*

Brigend. Katrina Smith de brigend quat. acr. ter....Johis Smithe ... ... 4*s.*

GYLLYSLANDE.

Bordeswald. Radulphus et Walterus Baymn dederunt dmi de Wederhale vigint. acr. ter. in Bordeswald que occupat. per Rowlande Vauxe et nihil dat.

¹ The clause mentioned above is now omitted.

29—2

Cringildike. Ricardus Mershall tenet ut supra certas tras et un. perc. silve ... ... 13*s.* 4*d.*

Anastable. Vicarius de Anastable quond. tenuit un. garden qd solebat red. per ann. 6*d.* modo nihil quia vast.

Armathwaite. Priorissa de Armathwaite tenet ut supra certas tras .. .. 1*s.*

Newby. Robtus Warthwicke de Newby tenet libe certas acr. terre ... ... 3*s.*

Farlame. Thomas Gyle de eadem quatuordec. acr. ter. 2*s.*

Rucroft. Willus Ullesby tenet ad voluntat. dni octo acr. ter. ... ... 4*s.*

Caberge. Rolandus Browne de eadem tenet libe pro du. bovat. ter. in Caberge ... ... 3*s.* 4*d.*

Gyllowfield. Itm Idm Rolandus tenet libe in Gyllowfield
1*s.* 8*d.*

Scaldyrmalaghe. Relict. Tho. Waldar tenet ad volunt. pro certis tris in Scaldyrmalaghe ... ... 2*s.*

Talkan. Thomas de Lamore tenet du. bov. ter. in Thalkane vocat. Surland et solebat red. per ann. 3*s.* modo nihil quia credit devast.

Kirkbythore. Nicholaus Radcliffe tenet un. toft. ibm...et prope predictam villam juxta molend. q. solebat dare per ann. 1*s.* modo nihil quia vast.

Johes Crakenthorpe tenet medietatem alterius tofti ibm et sol. red. per ann. 6*d.* modo ... ...

Johes Wharton tenet aliam medietatem dict. toft. et solebat red. per ann. 6*d.* modo nl quia vast.

Summa £05 12*s.* 4*d.*

Morlande. Robtus Coke et Willms Bakehouse de Morland ten. dominicas tras ejusdem ville continent. nonagint. quatuor acr. tre jacent. in diversis flats scilicet quatuor acr. in Clothmanflat, quinque acr. in Overcroft, decem acr. in Espland, viginti acr. in Byrks, octo acr. in Scalyflatte et fullhyle, octo acr. in Scalow, quinque acr. in Sulbarr, quatuor acr. in Bugflatt, octo acr. in Jackflatt, tr. acr. in Holeyeng, et quinque acr. in Jacdyke, itm le Kempleyflatt jacet in coi tenentib. utrisque dm et continet trigint. acr. pasture et redd. pro eisdem singulis annis ad terminos Marten. et Pent. equis portionibus ... ... 53*s.* 4*d.*

Johes Colston tenet tredec. acr. tre ... ... 8s.

Willmus Addison octo acr. et tr. rod. ... ... 6s. 8d.

Henricus Wilkinson tenet novedec. acr. ... 13s. 4d.

Rolandus Wilkinson tenet sexdec. acr. et tr. rodd. ... 9s.

Johes Winter Junior tenet septem acr. ... ... 4s.

Itm Idm Johes tenet le Smethy ... ... 1s.

Thomas Colson Junior tenet unu. acr. ... ... 2s.

Relict. Johis Coke alit. Ric. Jackson tenet vigint. sex
acr. .. .. 18s.

Jake Coke tenet quatuor acr. ... ... 3s. 4d.

Willmus Richardson tenet quatuordec. acr. ... 10s. 8d.

Willmus Bakehouse tenet sexdec. acr. ... ... 11s. 8d.

Johes Winter Senior tenet sex et vigint. acr. ... 13s. 4d.

Willmus Coke Senior tenet duo et vigint. acr. ... 13s. 4d.

Willmus Coke Junior tenet septem acr. et tr. rod. 6s. 8d.

Robtus Coke tenet du. acr. ... ... 2s. 6d.

Robtus Addison tenet du. acr. . . .. 3s. od.

Ricardus Winter tenet dec. acr. ... ... 9s. od.

Johes Nicolson tenet dec. acr. ... ... 9s. 8d.

Thomas Addison tenet du. et vigint. acr. ... 12d. : ob : qª.

Thomas Colyton tenet octo acr. ... ... 7s. od.

Willmus Bethome ten. molendinum ibm ... 13s. 4d.

Sum. Total. hujus Ville £11 10s. 10d. : ob : qª.

Bolton. Willms Thompson de eadem tenet du. bov. scilicet
vigint. acr. terr. ... ... 11s. 8d.

Robtus Bryswood tenet du. bov. sc. vigint. acr. 11s. 8d.

Johes Threlkeld ,, ,, ,, 11s. 8d.

Adde Cady ,, ,, ,, 11s. 8d.

Itm diversi tenentes ibm ten. decim. ejusdem ville 5s. od.

Sum. £2 10s. 8d.

Kirkandres. Johes Crakenthorpe de Newbigynge ten. et dat
pro firma de Kirkandres per ann. ... ... £1 6s. 8d.

Idm Johes tenet et dat pro decima eadm Kirkandres per
ann. ... ... 16d.

Sum. £1 8s. od.

Culgaith Milne. Henricus Smithe de eadem tenet molendinum de le Culgaithe ... ... 10*s.*

Sum. 10*s.*

Appylby. Dns Ricardus Benson vicarius Sci. Laurencii in Appleby tenet le Kirkcroft ... ... 3*s.*

Idm Vicarius ten. un. pert. ortum ibm nuper in tenura Johis Day de eadm ... ... 3*d.*

Johes Smyth de eadem tenet un. ortum ibm qui solebat redd. per ann. 1*s.* 8*d.* modo ... ... 10*d.*

Relict. Tho. Warcoppe de Colby pro le Mylne green ... 1*s.*

Johes Machell de Crakenthorpe pro le Mylne dame ibm 1*s.*

C. fribs. Carmel.[1] in Appleby pro quadam tra ibm ... 1*s.*

Sum. 7*s.* 1*d.*

Sum. total. firmar. tam libe qu. ad voluntatem

£36 15*s.* 5*d.* : ob : q^a.

Decimæ, Pensiones et Porciones infra Comitat. Westmorland et alibi pertin. Dicte Celle de Wedyrhall.

Ecclesie de Wedyrhall et de Warwicke stant in man. Prioris.

Robtus Coke de Morland et socii sui ten. decim. ville de Morland que solebat redd. per ann. £4 modo £6

Rolandus Robinson tenet decim. Newby de Stanes et red. per ann. £4

Dns Xristoferus Moresby Miles tenet decim. de Parva Strickland £2

Magister Ric. Cliford tenet decim. de Magna Strickland que solebat redd. £3 6*s.* 8*d.* modo £4

Thomas ffallowfield tenet decim. dominii sui ibm 13*s.* 4*d.*

Decima de Kings Meaburne in manu Prioris ad proficu. Celle que solebat red. per ann. £5 10*s.*

Dns Ric. Salkeld miles tenet decim. de Thirneby £2 13*s.* 4*d.*

Thomas Radcliffe tenet decim. de Bolton £7 6*s.* 3*d.*

Thomas Colsone tenet decim. de Slegill £3 6*s.* 8*d.*

Ricardus Musgrave tenet decim. de Drybeke £1 16*s.* 8*d.*

M. Robtus Machell tenet decim. de Colby £2 6*s.* 8*d.*

[1] There was a Convent of Carmelite Friars at Appleby.

M. Hugo Gryndon tenet decim. de Skittergate £3 6s. 8d.
Idm M. Hugo tenet decim. de Bongett et Langton
£6 13s. 4d.
Rogerus Hilton et Nicolaus Harrison ten. decim. de Hilton et
Morton ... ... £2 13s. 4d.
Johes Machel tenet decim. de Crakenthorpe £2 13s. 4d.
Thomas Prest cosyn ten. decim. de Rutto. ... 3s. 4d.
Dns Ricardus Salkeld miles tenet di. decim. de Mikyll
Corkby £1
et altr. dimidia decim. est in manu Prioris ex prof. Celle.
Idm Dnus Salkeld tenet decim. de Brigend £1 6s. 8d.
et habet hanc decim. annuati. pro feodo ten. ... ...
Dns Willms Benson Capellanus tenet decim. de Berwis 10s.
Thomas Hylle de Colby Lathes tenet decim. de Bewly 13s. 4d.

Sum. deciman. £53 3s. 4d.

PENSIONES ET PORCIONES.

Pensio ecclie de Ville Morland q. solebat rede per ann. Celle
de Wedyrhall £2 13s. 4d. modo nihil q. jam solvitur ad manus
Dni Prioris Mon. Ebor.
Dnus Thomas Bakehouse Capellanus ecclie de Ryppon pro
pensione Eccle de Cliburne per ann. ... ... 10s.
Dnus Edwardus Crakenthorpe Rector Ecclie de Musgrave pro
pensione ejusdem per annum ... ... 5s.
Abbas et Conventus de Whitby Rector ecclie de Crosby
Ravenswathe pro pensione ejusdem ecclie sol. per manus Dne
Margarete Clyford firmar. eorund. Abbtis et Conventus per
annum ... ... £3 6s. 8d.
M. Hugo Dacre Archidiaconus et Rector de Magna Salkeld
pro porcione terrar. Dmcalm ejusdem ecclie per ann. ... 15s.

Sum. £4 16s. 8d.

Sum. total. decimar. pensionum et porcionum ... £58

Sum. omi. Recepcionum tam firmar. decimar. pensionum et
porcionum predictar. £94 15s. 6d. : ob : qª.

XLV. VALOR ECCLESIASTICUS MADE UNDER THE AUTHORITY OF 26 HEN. VIII. C. 3 (1534) WHICH GAVE THE FIRST FRUITS AND TENTHS TO THE KING. [From ed. Record Commission, vol. v. p. 10.]

COM. CUMBR.

CELLA S'C'E TRINITATIS DE WEDERHALE IN COM. CUMBRIE.

RICUS WEDERHALL, INCUMBENS.

Temporalia valent in
Scit. Celle pdict valet in terr.   £   s.   d.   £   s.   d.
dnic. cu. claus. ibm per annu.   vj xiij iiij

Reddit. et firm. in Wederhall cu. molendin ibm et aliis ptin. per ann. xiiij^{li} xij^s Brigend iiij^s Piscaria de Wederhall viij^{li} Botcherby iiij^s Murns xx^s Holmus xx^s Rukecrofte per annum iiij^s Cryngledyke cu. ptin. per annum xiij^s iiij^d Scattmallege per annu iiij^s Cabage cu. ptin. iij^s iiij^d Farlam et Penrith Cot^s cu. ptin. per annum viij^s Frudell Crook cu. ptin. xxvj^s viij^d Corby viij^s et Quityn cu. ptin. iij^s iiij^d.   xxviij vij vij   xxxv — xj

CUMBR.

Spiritualia valent in

Exit. et profic. decim. garbar. et feni ac aliar.   £   s.   d.
decimabil. et oblac. ecclie de Wedhall cu. capella de Warwyk coibus ann.   x

Reddit. et firm. in Morland cu. ptin. p. ann xi^{li} x^s x^d ob. q. Bolton cu. ptin. p. ann lj^s viij^d Kirkanders cu. ptin. p. ann xxvj^s viij^d Appleby cu. ptin. xiij^s iiij^d Culgarth Myln cu. ptin. xiij^s iiij^d et Colby-lathes cu. ptin. p. ann lxvj^s viij^d.   xx ij vj ob. q.

Westm'l'.

Vendic. Bosc. valet in

Vendic. Bosc. ibm communibus annis—xxvj^s viij^d.

Spiritualia valent in

	£	s.	d.	£	s.	d.
Exit et profic. Decim. Eccliar. de Morland xxxix^{li} xiij^s iiij^d Sci Michis in Appleby vi^{li} et Sci Laurencij in Appleby pdict. x^{li} vj^s viij^d.	lvj					
Penc. annuatim recept. de ecclijs de Crosby Ravenswath iiij^{li} et Salkeld xv^s.	iiij	xv		lx	xv	—

Cumbr.

Pquis. cur. Celle pdict. communibus annis.	—	xx	—	—	xx	—
Sma valoris hujus Celle				cxxviij	v	ij ob. q.

Repris.

Resoluc. videlt.

Prior de Carliel. pro terr. in Scotby Parke p. ann	—	x	—			
Dno Comiti Cumbr. pro terr. in Colby Lathes p. ann	—	iij	iiij	—	xiij	iiij

Foed. videlt.

Willmo Dno Dacres sen^{lo} terr. Celle pdict. p. ann.	—	xl	—			
Georgio Mires sen^{lo} cur. ibm	—	xxvj	viij			
Edwardo Walles ballivo de Wederhall et rec. pecuniar. ibm et in Westm.	—	liij	iiij			
Roberto Watson ballivo de Morland	—	xxvj	viij	vij	vj	viij

Elemosia videlt. in

Elemosina distribut paupibus ex fundacoe	£	s.	d.
Willi Meschyn fundatoris imppm per ann		˙ liij	iiij
Sma repris.	x	xiij	iiij
Et valet clare	cvij	x	x ob. q.
Xma ps inde	xj	xv	ij q.

XLVI. SURVEY OF THE PRIORY OF WETHERHAL, MADE DECEMBER, 1538. [From the Paper Surveys late in the Augmentation Office, now in the Record Office.]

Com. Cumbriæ. Wetherall.

In the Surrendre ther mad the last day of Decembre anno regni regis Henrici viij xxx^mo inter alia continetur.

The Demanez.

The scite of the howse with edificez and iij littell closez of medoo adionyng the sayme scite contenynge iij acrez and is worth by yere   ...   .   viij^s.

Itm ther is a woodd with a parcell of medoo callyd Mirebank cont. viij acrez and the herbage thereof is worth by yere xvj^s. iiij^d.

Itm a parcell of medoo called Syme medoo with a close callyd Conygarthe Hill in the holding of Nichol. Pleughe and rent by yere ...   .   viij^d.

Itm a close lienge before the Yats (of the monastery, page 442) cont. iij acrez and is worth by yere   ...   .   vj^s.

Itm a close callyd the Highfeld or Priorfeld cont. xxxvj acrez and is worth by yere   ...   .   ij^li. j^s. iiij^d.

Itm j close callyd Turmyre and j close adionyng contenyng in all iij acrez lettyn unto John Bonus and rents by yere at Martm. and Pent.   ...   .   x^s.

Itm j close callyd Holmehouseflatt cont. vij acrez land arrable and is worth by yere   ...   .   vij^s. viij^d.

Itm j. close callyd Lynghills contenyng iiij acrez with a littell close adionyng and is worth by yere   ...   ...   iiij^s. vj^d.

Itm j close callyd Cotehowsse cont. iij acrez with a littell close affore the Yate (of the monastery, page 442)   iij^s. iiij^d.

Itm a chappell callyd Sanct Anthony's chappell with ij close adionyng cont. iiij acrez   ...   .   v^s.

Itm a cloose of leez cont. j acre ... ... xvj^d.

Itm a pasture callyd Calf close contenyng ij acrez and is worth by yere ... ... iiij^s.

Itm j cloose callyd Thornyfeld contenyng ij acrez pasture and is worth by yere ... ... ij^s. vj^d

Itm j close callyd Bromeclose cont. xij acrez pasture xvj^s.

Itm j. close of medoo and pasture called Swynestye Syks cont. j acre di. and is worth by yere ... ... ij^s. iiij^d.

Itm j medoo callyd Trodmyre bank cont. ij acrez ... iiij^s.

Itm a woodd called the Park set with oke and underwodd the herbage of which is worth by yere ... ... n^l.

Itm a parcell of medoo lyeng beyond the Mirebank in the tenure of Thomas Thomson cont. di. acre ... ... xij^d.

Itm there is a shepe heth called Frodell Crok and Toppell Syke and is worth by yere ... ... n^l.

Summa vj^{li}. xiiij^s.

The Water Mill.

Itm there is a water corne mill nere adionyng the same howse late in the holding of the prior and convent and is worth by yere ... ... lxvj^s. viij^d.

The Fishing.

Itm there is a fishyng at the bay ther late in the hands of the late monastery and is worth by yere ... ... x^{li}.

Summa totalis xx^{li}. viij^d

Per me JACOBUM ROKEBY, Audit^r.

Com. Cumbriæ.

Wetherell nuper Prioratus sive Cella in Com. Cumbriæ nuper Monasterio Beatæ Virginis Ebor. pertinens.

Temporalia.

Scitus dicti nuper prioratus cum terris dominicalibus, &c. ... ... £29 0s. 8d.

Redd. et Firm. Ten. et Tentorum in villa de Wetherell

£13 19s. 2d.

Redd. et Firm. Ten. et Tentorum in villa de Morland

£12 9s. 5d.

Redd. unius Tenti sive Grangiæ in Colby Leathez

£10 0s. 0d.

Redd. et Firm. in		Morehouse	...	...	£1	0s.	0d.
,,	,,	Holmehouse	...	...	£1	0s.	0d.
,,	,,	Corkeby	...	...	£0	8s.	0d.
,,	,,	Newby	...	...	£0	8s.	0d.
,,	,,	Cumwhynten	...	...	£0	3s.	0d.
,,	,,	Civit. Carliell	...	...	£0	2s.	4d.
,,	,,	Bocherby	...	...	£0	3s.	0d.
,,	,,	Frodelcroke	...	...	£1	13s.	4d.
,,	,,	Pereth Cott	...	...	£0	8s.	0d.
,,	,,	Brigend	...	...	£0	4s.	0d.
,,	,,	Cryngledyke	...	...	£0	13s.	4d.
,,	,,	Armatwhaitt	...	...	£0	1s.	0d.
,,	,,	Newby	...	...	£0	3s.	0d.
,,	,,	Farlam	...	...	£0	2s.	0d.
,,	,,	Caybry'g	...	...	£0	3s.	4d.
,,	,,	Gallowfeld	...	...	£0	1s.	8d.
,,	,,	Rukecrofte	...	...	£0	4s.	0d.
,,	,,	Skalmallok	...	...	£0	2s.	0d.
,,	,,	Bolton	...	...	£2	13s.	4d.

Herbag' sive Pannag' Silvæ de Kyrkander £1 6s. 8d.

Culgarth pro Molend' ... ... £0 13s. 4d.

Appulby in vico voc' Bondgate ... ... £0 16s. 8d.

Spiritualia.

Decim' Rector' de Morland ... ... £10 5s. 4d.

Decim' Rector' S. Michis de Appulby ... £14 0s. 0d.

Decim' Rector' S. Laurenc' de Appulby £5 10s. 8d.

Exit' sive Profic' Rector' de Wetherell ... £26 13s. 4d.

Pensio Rector' de Crosseby et (sic) Ravenswath £4 0s. 0d.

Pensio decim' gran' in Salkeld ... ... £0 15s. 0d.

XLVII. ENDOWMENT CHARTER OF THE CATHEDRAL CHURCH OF CARLISLE, DATED MAY 6TH, 1541. [This Charter is too long to print. The original with the broad seal attached is now in the "Chest" in the Dean and Chapter Registry. It sets out all the lands, properties &c. including those transferred from the dissolved Priory of Wetherhal. There is a copy in the same MS. volume as Transcript A. of the *Register*, and another among the loose papers in the Registry.]

XLVIII. ABSTRACT OF LEASE BY THE DEAN AND CHAPTER OF CARLISLE TO JOHN BLAKLOCKE OF THE HOUSE AND LANDS OF THE LATE MONASTERY OF WETHERALL, DECEMBER 14TH, 1541.

The Indenture was made at Carlisle on the xiiith day of December in "the thretty and thre yeare" of the reign of Henry VIII., "under God Supreme Head of the Church of England," betwixt Lancelot Salkeld, Dean of the Cathedral Church of the Holy and Indivisible Trinity in Carlisle and the Chapter of the same and John Blaklocke of Henryby (Harraby) in the County of Cumberland, yeoman.

The Lease is granted for a term of 37 years unto the foresaid John of the "House and site of the lait Monastery of Watherall" with all houses edifices barns orchards and land within the same site and compass circuity and "pertiguite" of the said lait monasterie, Also the three little closes &c. [The same as in **XLVI.**] The rents are £6. 14s. 0d. for the lands, £3. 6s. 8d. for the mill and £10 for the fishing, payable in equal portions at Lady Day and Michaelmas. [The same value as in **XLVI.**] The said John is to do the repairs, having timber allowed, also hedgeboote[1], fyreboote, ploughboote and cartboote[2].

---

[1] Boote from A.-S. *bót*, "profit," "amends," here wood to repair hedges, &c.

[2] Dean and Chapter of Carlisle, *Registers* vol. ii. p. 77 *b* (numbered at the bottom). This is the earliest document in their *Registers* after the foundation of the Dean and Chapter on May 8th, 1541. The dissolved Priory of Wetherhal was transferred to them by the Endowment charter dated May 6th, 1541. The late Mr Henry Bradshaw, Librarian of the Cambridge University Library, conjectured that, as in some other instances, there had been an error in copying

XLIX. Parliamentary Survey of the Rectories of
Weatherall and Warwick within the County of Cumberland made April, 1650.

A Survey of the Mannour of Weatherall[1] with the Rights
Members and appurtenances thereof lying and being within the
County of Cumberland late parcell of the possessions or late
belonging to the late Deane and Chapter of the Cathedrall
Church of St Maries of Carlisle made and taken by vs whose
names are hereunto subscribed in the Moneth of Aprill one
thousand six hundred ffifty By vertue of a Comission to vs
graunted vpon Act of the Commons of England assembled in
Parliament, for the abolishing of Deanes Deanes and Chapters
Cannons Prebends and other officers and titles of or belonging to
any Cathedrall or Collegiate Church or Chappell within England
and Walles vnder the handes and seales of fiue or more of y^e
Trustees in ye said Act named & appointed.

The Rectorie of Weatherall and Warwick within the County of
Cumberland. All that the Rectory of Weatherall and Warwicke
with thappurtenances to the same Rectory and Church of
Weatherall annexed belonging or appertaining wth all manner
of tythes oblacons obvencons pencons porcons fruites Emoluments and profitts whatsoever to the said Rectory and parish
Churches of Weatherall or Warwick or either of them by any
meanes or wayes belonging or appertaining All which said
Rectory with all and singular the tythes belonging to the
aforesaid Churches were late in the possession of Sr Ffrancis
Howard of Corby Castle within the County of Cumberland Kn^t.
but now sequestred, and in the possession of Thomas Sewelland

---

and that the date should be 35 Henry VIII. (1543) and not 33 Henry VIII.
(1541). But really the interval of the seven months between May and December,
when the lease was granted, was a very natural time to have elapsed after the
acquisition of the property.   There is one lease existing, before the Priory of
Carlisle was dissolved, of the tithes of S. Nicholas Church, Newcastle on Tyne,
dated August 1st 1537, Lancelot Salkeld being then Prior of the Cathedral
church of the Blessed Mary of Carlisle.

[1] The Survey of the Manor has not been found.

and others for the vse of the Comonwealth and is worth p. Annum one hundred eighty six pounds.

Memorandum that the aforesaid Sr Ffrancis Howard Son and assignee of William Lord Howard late of Nauorth within the County of Cumberland deceased, By Indenture of Lease dated the Twenty eight day of August in the fourteenth yeare of the late King Charles graunted by Thomas Cumber, Deane and the Chapter of Carlisle vnto the aforesaid Lord William Howard his Executors and assignes holds all that last menconed premisses from the date for the tearme of one and twenty yeares yeilding and paying therefore vnto the said Deane and Chapter and their Successors the annuall rent of fourteene poundes thirteene shillinges foure pence at the feasts of St Michael and the annunciacon or within fforty dayes But are worth vpon improuem^t ouer and aboue the old Rent comunibus annis one hundred seauenty one pounds six shillinges eight pence.

With Couenant to pay six poundes p. Anum to the Curate of Weatherall and six poundes to the Curate of Warwicke yearely, Provided, that if the aforesaid yearely Rent be behind and vnpaid at ye ffeasts and dayes at which it ought to be paid then the Lease to be void.

There were to come of the aforesaid lease the Twenty eighth day of August last ten yeares.

A true copy Exami...
Nouember 3^a 1659.

L. Certain entries in the Household Books of Lord William Howard of Naworth Castle relating to Wetherhal and Warwick. [Surtees Society, vol. 68.]

1618. April 18. Rec. of Mr George Skelton for the Easter booke of Wetherall and Warwick, x^l. xviij^s. j^d. ob. For small dues thear xxvj^s. ij^d For tith hay of Aglionby, vj^s. viij^d. Tith hay of Scotby, xlvi^s. viij^d. For tith hay of Warwick, xx^s. [p. 68, see also p. 152].

Aug. 23. Wetherall, Aglionby and Warwick. To Blaylock for vj. dayes d. gathering tithes iij^s. iiij^d. To Jo. Storrow for iij dayes, ij^s. To Coleman and Iveston for other 2 dayes, ij^s. [p. 90, where are several similar entries].

Octob. 4. To Mr Bellwood, Curate of Wetherall, for one quarter due at Michaelmas last past, 1618, xxx^s. To Mr Alleson, Curate of Warthwick for one quarter due 18 of this Octob^r. xxx^s. [p. 98, similar entries p. 99].

Nov. 23. To the Prebends (of Carlyle) for one hallf yeare's rent for the tithes of Wetherall and Warwick due at Michaelmas 1618, vij^{li}. vj^s. viij^d. [p. 99].

1618—9. Bread and wyne at Wetherall at Easter, xviij^s. Their diners thear at the same tyme x^s. [p. 99].

25 of March, 1620. Rec. of Rob. Stapleton, xxx^s. and v^{li}. which was paid to Mr Peele, as curate and preacher at Wetherall, at our Ladye day last, 1621, reckoned in my former booke pag. 65, A^o. 1620, *in toto*, vj^{li}. x^s. [p. 151].

March 25, 1622. To Mr Peele for one quarter as curate of Wetherall due at our Ladye Day 1622, xxx^s.; and for one hallf year as preacher thear, due the same tyme, v^{li}. *in toto* vj^{li}. x^s. April 22, 1622. Wine: for xxx quarts of Wine for communicants at Wetherall at Easter xx^s. iiij^d. Bread for them, ij^s. vi^d. The dinner there, x^s. 27. To Mr Allyson, curatt of Warwick for serving the cure thear for one quarter ended xviij. of April, 1622, xxx^s. [p. 181, see also p. 219].

1625. July 6. Bread and wyne for the communicants at Wetherall church, xix^s. iij^d. The curat's and clark's dinner upon Easter Day, x^d. [p. 228].

1629. Aug. 26. To the Deane and Prebends of Carlile for a new Lease of the Tythes Wetherall, Warwick &c. c^{li}. [p. 260].

April 3. To the Prebends of Carlile for the halfe yeare's rent of the tythes of Wetherall, Warwick, Cotehill &c. and the rent of my Lord's house in Fishergate at Carlile due at the Annunciation of B. Ladie, 1630, vij^{li}. xiij^s. iij^d. [p. 269, see also pp. 338, 340].

December 9. To Sr John Sewell, Vikar of Wetherall for one quarter's wages due at Christenmas, 1629, xxx^s.

Januari 18. To James Pawston, Vicar of Warwicke, for one quarter serving the cure at Warwicke, due the 18th of Januari, 1629, xxx^s.

Septem. 6. To Sr Robert Raylton for one halfe yeare's pention for preaching at Wetherall, due at Michelmas, 1630, v^{li}. More to him for one quarter's wages for servinge the cure ther, xxx^s. [p. 270, see also p. 339].

June 6. Rec. of Water Rosewarren, for the Easter booke and other Church dues at Wetherall, due at Easter, 1634, xiij^{li}. viij^s. Rec. more of him for mortuaries, xvj^s. viij^d. [p. 282].

LI. ABSTRACTS FROM THE PATENT ROLLS AND CLOSE ROLLS RELATING TO WETHERHAL REFERRED TO BY TANNER, NOTITIA MONASTICA p. 75. [From the Public Record office.]

Patent Rolls.

(*a*) 11 Edw. 2, pt. 2, m. 25. Licence to William son of John de Berningham to give 7 mess. 6 bov. and 6^a of land and 12^d. rent in Wederhale and to other persons to give land and rent elsewhere to the Abbot and Convent of S^t. Mary's York. 18 March.

(*b*) 29 Edw. 3, pt. 2, m. 18. Licence to Adam de Burton and Laurence de Sutton to give one mess. 3 cottages 46^a of land and 4^a. meadow in Wederhale to Abbot and Conv. of S^t. Mary's, York. 28 June. (Compare the Inquisition **XXXVI.**)

(*c*) 31 Edw. 3, pt 3, m. 8. Licence to W^m. de Wyluyby and Agnes his wife to give 4 mess. 50^a. of land and 2^a. meadow in Wederhale to the Abbot and Conv. of S^t. Mary's.

(*d*) 40 Edw. 3, pt. 2, m. 34 (33 d.) see **LII.**

(*e*) 16 Ric. 2, pt. 2, m. 30. Licence to the Vicars (named) of Kirkeby in Lonsdale and Appilby and others to give lands and tenements in York, Knapton and other places and in Kirkeby in Lonsdale, Kirkeby, Becoke, Gosford, Bolton and Distington to the same Abbot and Convent. 27 Sept. (nothing as to Wetherhall).

Close Rolls.

(*f*) 17 Edw. 2, m. 38. Touching the charter of John de
Veteri Ponte, granting to the Priory of Wederhale, 20 cartloads of
dead wood in his wood of Wynnesell, yearly. [The charter is
given in No. 204.]

(*g*) 43 Edw. 3, m. 33. Priory of Wetherhall, a Cell of S^t.
Mary's, York ; and a tenement called Kirkandros next Blenkarne
apppertaining thereto.

LII. INQUIRY FOR THE KING, EDWARD III., CONCERNING
THE FOUNDATION OF THE PRIORY OF WEDERHALE AND ITS
RIGHTS, SEPT. 5TH, 1366. [Patent Rolls, 40 Edw. III. part,
m. 33.]

De inquirendo pro Rege.

Rex dilectis et fidelibus suis, Thome de Whiterig', Johanni de
Warthewyk', Clementi de Skelton', Ade de Blenkhowe, et Ade
de Anglounby, salutem. Quia datum est nobis intelligi, quod
Prior de Wederhale agistamenta animalium in foresta nostra de
Ingelwod', que ad nos pertinent, et de quibus nos et progenitores
nostri a tempore quo non extat memoria seisiti eramus, sibi et
Prioratui suo predicto vsurpauit, et proficua agistamentorum
eorundem ad opus suum proprium leuari facit ; et quod idem
Prior quoddam rete in aqua de Eden' ex transuerso eiusdem aque
iam de nouo exaltari fecit, sic quod pisces propter impedimentum
retis predicti in aqua illa versus mare, vt solebant, transire non
possunt ; dictusque Prior animalia que dicuntur waif' in foresta
predicta, et eciam blodewites, que ad nos pertinent, ad se
pertinere vendicat, et easdem wainas vendit, et pro predictis
blodwites distringit ; et quoddam stagnum vocatum la Baye de
Wederhale multo alcius quam esse solebat et debet exaltari fecit,
et illud tempore debito et solito aperire et claudere non facit ; et
tenentes nostros quominus viam suam per villam de Wederhale,
sicut totis temporibus retroactis habuerunt, ad buscam in foresta
predicta querendam, et ad domos suos ducendam, habere possint,
impedit minus iuste, tam in nostri preiudicium et contemptum,
quam nostri et tocius populi nostri parcium illarum dampnum

non modicum et iacturam ; et quod cum in dicto Prioratu, qui de fundacione progenitorum nostrorum, quondam Regum Anglie, existit, duodecim Monachi iuxta fundacionem eiusdem esse solebant, iam in Prioratu illo nisi quatuor Monachi existunt ; et in ecclesijs de Wederhale et Warthewyk', in quibus Prior loci predicti, qui pro tempore fuerit, duos Capellanos parochiales, videlicet, in qualibet ecclesia vnum Capellanum, iuxta formam fundacionis predicte, inuenire tenetur, iam nullus Capellanus ibidem inuenitur, set dictus Prior omnes exitus et prouentus ecclesiarum illarum, absque aliquo onere eisdem ecclesijs incumbente inueniendo, percipit, contra formam fundacionis predicte ; et eciam cum tota multura de molendino de Eden' proueniens pauperibus in elemosinam pro animabus progenitorum nostrorum predictorum distribui debeat et solebat, et similiter cum in dicto Prioratu due distribuciones duobus diebus in qualibet septimana pro animabus dictorum progenitorum nostrorum in elemosinam pauperum fieri debebant (*sic*) et solebant, eedem elemosine et distribuciones adiu subtracte extiterunt, et adhuc existunt, in animarum dictorum progenitorum nostrorum periculum, et nostri dedecus, et dampnum manifestum : Nos, volentes super premissis plenius informari, assignauimus vos, quatuor, tres, et duos vestrum, ad inquirendum per sacramentum proborum et legalium hominum de Comitatu Cumbrie, per quos rei veritas melius sciri poterit, super premissis omnibus et singulis et alijs circumstancijs ea tangentibus plenius veritatem. Et ideo vobis mandamus, quod ad certos etc. quos etc. ad hoc prouideritis, inquisiciones super predictis faciatis, et eas distincte et aperte factas nobis in Cancellaria nostra, sub sigillis vestris quatuor, trium, vel duorum vestrum, et sigillis eorum per quos facte fuerint, sine dilacione mittatis, et hoc breue. Mandauimus enim Vicecomiti nostro Comitatus predicti, quod ad certos etc. quos etc. ei scire facietis, venire faciat coram vobis, quatuor, tribus, vel duobus vestrum, tot etc. de balliua sua per quos etc. et inquiri. In cuius etc. Teste Rege, apud Claryndon', quinto die Septembris.

per breue de priuato sigillo.

APPENDIX A.

Ranulf Meschin, or Ranulf "Junior," was probably so named
to distinguish him from his father Ranulf. This and not "le
Meschin" is the form used in all documents to which he is a
party[1]. He is called Ranulf of Bayeux, or Ranulf de Briscasard,
by Ordericus Vitalis (Lib. xi. c. 20; Lib. xii. c. 14 *et al.*) and
Ranulf de Micenis, or de Meschines, by Matthew of Westminster
(*in ann.* 1072) and Matthew Paris (*Chron. Maj.* ed. Luard, ii. 8
marg.). He was Viscount of the Bessin, or territory of Bayeux
in Normandy. His father, Ranulf, was, there is little doubt,
identical with that Ranulf of Bayeux who joined the Norman
Viscounts in their rebellion against William of Normandy, and
was defeated at the battle of Val-ès-Dunes in 1047 (*Orderic.
Vital.* Lib. vii. c. 15; *William of Malmesbury*, Lib. iii. § 230;
Freeman, *Norman Conquest*, ii. 250). His mother's name was
Matilda or Maud (Mahald, in the *Liber Vitæ* of Durham, ed.
Surtees Society, p. 78), the sister of Hugh, Viscount of Avranches
and Earl of Chester (*Orderic. Vital.* Lib. xii. c. 28). His brother
Richard is mentioned in the first charter of this *Register* and in
the *Liber Vitæ* of Durham; and his brother William is a witness
to the two following charters. He married Lucia, the widow of
Roger de Romara and daughter of Ivo Taillebois (see below), and

---

[1] Among the witnesses to the Great Charter of David, King of Scots, to
Melrose (1124—53) is Robert Brus Meschin (*Facsimiles of National MSS. of
Scotland*, No. xvii).

her name appears in three of these early charters. His sister Agnes married Robert de Grantmesnil (*Orderic. Vital.* Lib. viii. c. 16). By his wife, Lucia, he had a son, William Ranulf, who must have been born before 1108, as he was of age before 1129 when he succeeded his father. Other children are ascribed to Ranulf, but on no very good evidence.

The historical details about Ranulf Meschin are only scanty. It is not known how or when he came over from Normandy. But in 1093, we find him with his uncle, Hugh, Earl of Chester, the strong supporter of William Rufus. He then, as "Ranulph, nephew of the Earl," witnessed the charter granted by Earl Hugh to the monastery of St Werburgh, at Chester, when the Earl expelled the secular Canons, and placed there monks of the Benedictine Rule (see the charter in Dugdale, *Monasticon*, ii. 386, No. iv.).

Ranulf appears in these early charters of our *Register* as Lord of the district or power (*potestas*) or Honor of Carlisle and in possession of the castle of Appelby. He must have been placed in command here by William Rufus after the conquest of the country in 1092 (see below), or by Henry I. between 1100 and 1112, the limit of the date of our first charter. The former is by far the more probable; and if the reference to King William in the first charter be correct, it is beyond doubt. To protect his province against the Scots, he founded three Baronies—Lyddale, he gave to Turgis Brundis, Burgh by Sands, to Robert de Trivers (*Testa de Nevill*, p. 379 *b*), and Gillesland, to his brother William Meschin (Camden, *Britannia*, ed. Holland, p. 176). The last named does not seem ever to have got the land entirely out of the power of its original possessor, Gill son of Bueth, or Boet (see on William Meschin in No. 2, note 5). In the year 1106 Ranulf was in Normandy with King Henry I., and he commanded one of the three divisions of the army at the battle of Tinchebrai on September 28th, when Duke Robert was so signally defeated. He is then spoken of as a great Baron, and not one of the four Earls who were present (*Orderic. Vital.* Lib. xi. c. 20). In the same year, Osbert de Archis, Sheriff of York, made some attack on the liberties of the monastery of Ripon. Archbishop Gerard complained to the King, and Radulph le Meschines, as he is called in the Chronicle, was sent down with Robert Bloet, Bishop of Lincoln, Radulph Basset and others to investigate the matter (Illustrative Documents, II.). Between the years 1108 and 1111 Ranulf was a party to a Convention[1] made at Doura, on May 17th, between Henry I. and Robert, count of Flanders. The deed is given in Rymer (*Fœdera*, new edn. i. 6), a portion of it in facsimile, and his name is there spelt Rañ. Meschin.

In the year 1119, King Henry was in Normandy quelling a revolt, and among the nobles who were loyal to him Ordericus (Lib. xii. c. 14) specially mentions "Richard, Earl of Chester, and Ranulf de Bricasard, his cousin and successor"; and speaks of their fortresses of Avranches and Bayeux. In the same year, as Ranulf Meschin, together with his brother William Meschin, he attested the charter granted by Earl Richard to the Abbey of St Werburgh at Chester (Dugdale, *Monasticon*, ii. 387, No. v.).

In the year following, 1120, the fatal wreck of the "White Ship" made a great change in the fortunes of Ranulf. With the King's son, William the Ætheling, perished Richard, Earl of Chester, and his wife Matilda. Ranulf obtained the Earldom of Chester with all the patrimony of Earl Richard, being next heir in right of his mother, Matilda, sister of Earl Hugh (*Orderic. Vital.* Lib. xii. c. 28). But he had to give up the lordship of Carlisle to the King, and, perhaps, the Barony of Kendal held in right of his wife Lucia (see below). Ten years later the District or Honor of Carlisle appears in the earliest extant Pipe Roll, that of 31 Henry I., divided into the two Shires of Carlisle and Westmarieland. He was, moreover, charged with the payment of a heavy fine; of this fine a thousand pounds "due for the land of Earl Hugh" remained still to be paid by his son after his death (*Pipe Roll for Lincoln*, 31 Hen. I. ed. J. Hunter, p. 110).

We find Ranulf once more with King Henry in Normandy, in the winter of 1123—24; and he was one of the leaders against the rebels at the battle of Bourgtheroulde (*Orderic. Vital.* Lib. xii. c. 38, 39). "Ranulf, Earl of Chester" granted a charter to the

---

[1] On the date of this treaty, see Lappenberg, *Anglo-Norman Kings*, ed. Thorpe, page 301.

Abbey of St Werburgh, at Chester, whither he had caused the body of Earl Hugh to be transferred, and he directed his own body to be buried there (Dugdale, *Monasticon*, ii. 387, No vi.). He died in 1129 (Dugdale, *Baronage*, i. 37) and was interred in the Abbey in acordance with his wish. He was succeeded by his son, the Earl Ranulf who played such an important part in the reign of Stephen (*Orderic. Vital.* Lib. xii. c. 28; Durham *Liber Vitae*). From these scattered notices, we get the outlines of a distinguished soldier and of a man of great influence with the reigning monarchs of England.

It does not appear that Ranulf Meschin ever had the title of "Earl" before he became Earl of Chester, or that the land of Carlisle was termed the "Earldom of Carlisle" in his time. We have seen above that he was distinguished by Ordericus from the four Earls who were present in Normandy. In this *Register of Wetherhal* he is spoken of as holding the "power" (*potestas*) or the "honor" of Carlisle (No. 1 and No. 8), not the earldom. In *Testa de Nevill* he is called "Lord (*Dominus*) of Cumberland," and elsewhere his district is called "his land of Cumberland" (see below p. 476). Freeman and others seem to have taken the title from Matthew of Westminster, who says of Ranulf (*in ann.* 1072) "regebat comitatum Carlioli comes Ranulphus de Micenis"; but the whole passage is so full of errors as to be quite devoid of authority. Dugdale (*Baronage* i. 37) quotes from the spurious charter of William II. (Additional Charter No. 250), and others from the equally valueless *Distributio Cumberlandiae* (No. 245). The title occurs in no genuine charter.

The arms of Ranulf Meschin are given by Lysons (*Cumberland*, page lv.) as "Or, a lion rampant, gules."

We now turn to the wife of Ranulf, Lucia, or Lucy. She was the daughter of Ivo Taillebois, or Taleboys, who came from Anjou, and of Lucia, his wife. The identity of names has given rise to many difficulties. The elder Lucia was descended from one Torold, Sheriff of Lincolnshire, and from him she inherited large property in that county. This property Ivo enjoyed in right of his wife, as would appear from a grant by Ivo, in 1085, to the Priory of Spalding of the Church of St Nicholas of Angers and other privileges (Dugdale, *Monast.* vol. iii. pp. 216, 217). It was also in the hands of Ivo, together with lands in Norfolk, at the time of the Domesday survey, when he is called, Ivo Taillgebosc. (*Domesday Book*, ed. Record Com. vol. i. p. 350 sq., ii. p. 244.) Ivo Taillebois had but one child, his daughter Lucia, who inherited these and other estates at his death (in 1114, according to Peter Blessensis, but probably earlier). This younger Lucia married first, Roger son of Gerold, or Roger de Romara, by whom she had a son, William de Romara (*Orderic. Vital.* Lib. xii. c. 28, 34). Ranulf Meschin was her second husband, and by him she had a son, William Ranulf, called also Ranulf Gernons, who succeeded his father as Earl of Chester. There is much doubt as to the existence of any other children of Lucia[1]. She appears in the earliest extant Pipe Roll for Lincolnshire (31 Hen. I. ed. J. Hunter, p. 110) as Lucia Comitissa Cestr., liable for a fine of £246. 13s. 4d. for livery of the lands in Lincolnshire of her father. She is called "Lucia, Countess of Bolingbroc" in *Testa de Nevill* (p. 313 a), but the title "Countess Lucia" is generally applied to her in right of her husband after he had become Earl of Chester. A charter of the Countess Lucia, granting the manor of Spalding to the monastery there, mentions Ivo de Taleboys, Roger son of Gerald and Earl Ranulf, and is evidently after the death of her second husband, the Earl (Dugdale, *Monasticon*, iii. 217).

When Ivo Taillebois died, Ranulf Meschin, in right of his wife, succeeded to Ivo's possessions. Among them, besides the property in Lincolnshire, was what was known later as the Barony of Kendal, as appears from the grant of Ivo to the Abbey of

---

[1] The following table will explain the relationships :

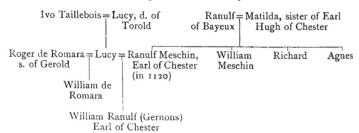

St Mary at York (Illustrative Documents, XVI.). This came to Ivo after the Domesday survey (1085—86) when the Barony was in the hands of the Crown, and was, there is little doubt, given to him by William Rufus about the time William put his son-in-law Ranulf Meschin in command of the frontier district. But this Barony, together with the land of Carlisle, passed into the hands of the Crown when Ranulf succeeded to the Earldom of Chester. With considerable difficulty and during the lifetime of Lucia, her son, William de Romara, obtained a portion of her domains which the Crown had taken, probably those in Lincolnshire (*Orderic. Vital.* Lib. xii. c. 34). In 1130 Lucia paid to the King 500 marks that she should not be compelled to marry again within five years (*Pipe Rolls*, Lincoln, 31 Hen. I. ed. J. Hunter, p. 110). It is said that she was buried in the monastery of Spalding in the year 1141 (Dugdale, *Baronage*, i. 37 *a*). On the confusion of names and the opinions concerning her descent, see Freeman, *Norman Conquest*, ii. 682, iii. 778 and *Pipe Rolls for Cumberland &c.*, ed. Hodgson Hinde, p. xvi. sq. Everthing that can be said as to the identity of the two Lucias is ably said by R. E. G. Kirk is an exhaustive set of papers in *The Genealogist* (New Series v. 60, 131, 153); but his evidence does not carry conviction against the great improbability of the case and the evidence on the other side.

The "lordship," or "power" (*potestas*, No. 1), or "honor" (No. 8) of Carlisle, over which Ranulf Meschin ruled, was not, we have seen, an earldom[1]. It had formed the southern part of ancient Cumbria, or Strathclyde. The name Cumbria does not appear to be used before writers of the 11th century, or the term Cumbri to be applied to the Britons of Strathclyde[2]. The latter designation first appears about the middle of the 9th century[3]. Cumbria, or its Saxon equivalent Cumbraland, was granted in 945 to Malcolm I., King of Scots, by Eadmund, King of the West Saxons, after the defeat of Donald, or Dunmail, King of Cumbria. Malcolm held it as a fief of the English Crown, for

---

[1] See also note 4 on No. **8**.

[2] They are called *Strœcled Wealas* in the *Anglo-Saxon Chronicle, in ann.* 875.

[3] See, on both names, W. F. Skene, *Celtic Scotland*, i. 325.

which he did homage, though it was not yet a part of England[1]. The heir apparent, or one of the royal house of Scotland, seems often to have governed the land. In the year 1070, Malcolm III., Malcolm Ceanmor, held Scotland proper together with Cumbria; passing through the latter province, he invaded and laid waste Northumbria. William the Conqueror, who had ravaged Yorkshire in the winter of 1069, again came north in 1072, and advanced beyond the Forth, when Malcolm did homage to him as his vassal. It should be noted that William did not return through Cumbria, but by the eastern coast. At this time Gospatric, Earl of Northumberland, who had harried Cumbria in 1070, was deprived of his earldom by King William, and betook himself to Malcolm, who gave him Dunbar and other possessions[2]. It would appear to be his son Dolfin who is found a few years later ruling the district of Carlisle under Malcolm.

We come now near the date of our first charter. In the year 1092, William Rufus went north with a large force and drove out Dolfin. He seized the southern part of Cumbria, to which the name of Cumbraland was soon applied, and made it for the first time part of England[3]. The northern part remained under the Scottish King, Malcolm, as the vassal of the King of England. He acknowledged the English supremacy both as regards northern Cumbria and as regards Lothian, which was then essentially a part, not of Scotland proper, but of England. At the date of the first charter of the *Register*, that is between 1092 and 1112, probably before 1100, we find Ranulf Meschin in possession of the land, and guarding at his castle of Appelby the road by which the Scots had so often invaded Teesdale and Yorkshire. No other lord of the land is mentioned. His grants of property in this district to the Abbey of St Mary at York are very natural in the son-in-law of Ivo Taillebois, who about this time was himself a benefactor to the Abbey, and a strong supporter of William

---

[1] *Anglo-Saxon Chronicle, in ann.* 945; Skene, *Celtic Scotland,* i. 362; Lappenberg, *Anglo-Saxon Kings,* ed. Thorpe, ii. 122; Freeman, *Norman Conquest,* i. 123, 125.

[2] Skene, *Celtic Scotland,* i. 424 sq. Freeman, *Norman Conquest,* iv. 516 sq. E. W. Robertson, *Scotland under her Early Kings,* i. 136 sq.

[3] *Anglo-Saxon Chronicle, in ann.* 1092; compare *Florence of Worcester, in ann.* 1092, and see below p. 482.

Rufus. Moreover the King himself took much interest in the Abbey of St Mary, and laid the foundation stone of the new buildings in 1089. We have seen that Ranulf was often engaged with King Henry I. in Normandy early in the century, the beginning of Henry's reign; he could hardly have left this important command had he been lately appointed to it. We may, therefore, conclude that Ranulf was placed in charge when the land was conquered by William Rufus; and under that King the monastery of Wetherhal was probably founded.

The limits of this district have been pretty clearly defined. The boundaries of ancient Cumbria in the year 1069 are given on excellent authority. In the return made to the King's writ by the Prior and Convent of the Cathedral Church of Carlisle in the reign of Edward I. (1291) there is this statement, under that year, sent by the hand of Alan de Frysington, "Cocanonicus et Precentor Ecclesiæ nostrae," from their chronicles and writings—"A.D. 1069. Cumbria dicebatur, quantum modo est Episcopatus Karliolensis et Episcopatus Glasguensis et Episcopatus Candide case et insuper ab Episcopatu Karliol usque ad flumen Dunde (Duddon)......ibi in passu illo[1]." Hence it can be shown that ancient Cumbria at that date stretched from the Firth of Clyde on the north to the river Duddon on the south. David, afterwards King of Scotland, who from 1107 to 1124 ruled as Earl over Scotland south of the Clyde and the Forth, made an Inquisition in 1120, or 1121, into the lands belonging to the Church of Glasgow. This Inquisition is given in full in the *Registrum Episcopatus Glasguensis*[2]. The inquiry was made "in each of the provinces of Cumbria which were under his dominion and power, for he did not rule over the whole of the Cumbrian region" (*non enim toti Cumbrensi regioni dominabatur*). It clearly shews by the places mentioned that the Bishopric of Glasgow stretched on the south as far as the Solway Frith and the Cheviots, the boundaries of England. The limit of Earl David's dominion towards the south at this time is further

---

[1] Palgrave, Sir F., *Documents and Records illustrating the History of Scotland*, 1837, vol. i. p. 70.
[2] Page 3, ed. Cosmo Innes, and Haddan and Stubbs, *Eccles. Doc.* ii. p. 17.

proved by another act of his, a grant of land in Anandale (Estrahanent) to Robert de Brus, the first of the line in Scotland. This grant speaks of the land "from the bounds of Dunegal of Strathnith (Stranit) to the bounds of Randulf Meschin......with all those customs which Randulf Meschin had at any time in Carlisle (Carduil) and in his land of Cumberland" (Illustrative Documents, I.). This clearly points to the boundary of the Solway; and the date of the grant must have been shortly after David became King of all Scotland in 1124.

The southern boundary of ancient Cumbria towards the west in 1069 was, we see, the river Duddon; but shortly after, probably in the reign of William I., the boundary of England proper was advanced northward to the Derwent. Part of the intervening country, that lying between the Duddon and the Esk, is even found in *Domesday Book* in 1085—86 (ed. Record Com. vol. i. p. 301 *b*). The Derwent was the boundary in that direction of the Diocese of Carlisle when the See was founded, and was almost certainly the limit also of this district or "honor of Carlisle." On the south-east the hills, through which ran the passes into the valley of the Tees and into Yorkshire, marked the natural boundary of the "honor"; and these passes were well guarded by the castle of Appleby, and probably by the castles of Brough and Mallerstang (Pendragon). The *Chronicles of the Picts* speak of "Cumbirland," or Strathclyde, "as far as the Rerecross (*Reir croiz*) of Staynmore[1]." There was again a natural boundary on the east, the hills of the Pennine range; this soon after became the boundary of the Diocese and of the Shires, excepting the peculiar parish of Alston in Northumbria. Even the Bishopric of Hexham, which ceased to be a See in 821, only claimed to reach westward as far as Wetherhala (Illustrative Documents, III.).

The limits of this district, or "honor" of Carlisle, were practically identical with those of the Diocese founded in 1133. When to this district were added the Barony of Kendal, the land between the Derwent and the Duddon, and the parish of Alston, the whole made up the two Shires of Carlisle and Westmoreland.

---

[1] See, and for other reff., Illustrative Documents, IV.

These shires must have been formed after 1120, when Ranulf succeeded to the Earldom of Chester and the whole district came into the hands of the Crown. The two shires, or counties, as well as "the mines of Carlisle" in the parish of Alston, appear in the Pipe Roll of 31 Henry I.; but Cumberland as the name of the shire, or county of Carlisle, I have not found before January 25th 1176, when it occurs in the appointment of justices recorded by Benedict Abbas (ed. Stubbs, i. 108); it is also given in the Pipe Roll of 23 Henry II. (1177). Benedict there names Coupelanda as independent of Cumberlanda.

APPENDIX B.

It is generally asserted in the local histories that the Priory
of Carlisle was founded in the year 1102 by Henry I. None of
the early English Chroniclers appear to refer to the foundation.
There is the following passage in the Scottish Chronicle of John
de Fordun—" Henricus persuasione et consilio ipsius Reginæ,
anno MCII, constituit Canonicos Regulares in Kaerliel"—
Scotichronicon v. 39. Even this is not a part of John de Fordun's
Chronicle, but is an interpolation by his Continuator, William
Bower, Abbot of Inchcolm, in the 15th century[1].

The Anglo-Saxon Chronicle, Florence of Worcester, Simeon
of Durham, Richard of Hexham and John of Hexham, William
of Malmesbury, Ordericus Vitalis and Henry of Huntingdon do
not mention the subject, although the first three speak of the
restoration of the City of Carlisle and the building of a castle by
William Rufus in 1092[2].

These Regular Canons were supposed to have adopted the
Rule and name of S. Augustine, though the great Augustine of
Hippo can have had little to do with the Rule. It is generally
allowed that they had their origin about the middle of the 11th
century, and were not introduced into England before the 12th
century, in the reign of Henry I.[3] The first Priory of Augustinian
Canons in England was founded at Colchester, certainly not

[1] See W. F. Skene's edition of Fordun's *Chronica Gentis Scotorum.*
[2] See below, note 1, p. 482.
[3] See Dugdale, *Monasticon*, vi. 37.

before 1105. Priority has been claimed for Nostell, but on no good ground. Probably in the North of England, the first Augustinian monastery was Hexham, due to Archbishop Thurstin, and therefore not before December 1114, for in that month he was enthroned, though not yet consecrated. There is no trustworthy evidence that the House at Carlisle was founded before that date.

There is a special interest for us about the Augustinian Priory of S. Oswald at Nostell, near Pontefract, in the West Riding of Yorkshire. It was the mother House from which came, undoubtedly, the first Bishop of Carlisle, in the person of Athelwold, the Prior of that monastery. It is alleged that he was also the first Prior of Carlisle. These points call for closer examination.

Athelwold, as he is called in this *Register*, or Æthelwulf, or Aldulf, for his name appears in many forms, was consecrated 1st Bishop of Carlisle at York, by Thurstin, Archbishop of York, on August 6th, 1133. He was at the time Prior of S. Oswald's at Nostell, or Nostla, in Yorkshire, and as such was a Canon of York, holding the prebend of Bramham (Hardy, *Fasti Eccles*. iii. 177), and he was confessor to King Henry I. Thus John of Hexham writes—"Anno MCXXXIII, mense Augusto, ante Assumptionem Sanctæ Mariæ apud Eboracum a Turstino archiepiscopo consecrati sunt episcopi Galfridus, cancellarius Regis Henrici, ad episcopatum Dunelmensem, Aldulfus, Prior de Nostla, ad urbem Karleol, quam Rex Henricus initiavit ad sedem episcopalem, datis sibi ecclesiis de Cumberland et Westmariland quæ adjacuerunt archidiaconatui Eboracensi" (i.e. of Richmond).— *Memorials of Hexham*, ed. J. Raine, i. 109. Also in the *Annals of Waverley* (*in ann.* 1133)—"Fecit Rex Henricus novum Episcopatum apud Karduil, in finibus Angliæ et Scotiæ, et posuit ibi Episcopum Adulfum, Priorem Canonicorum Regularium Sancti Oswaldi, cui solitus erat confiteri peccata sua. Hic autem Canonicos Regulares posuit in Ecclesia sedis suæ."—*Annales Monastici*, ed. Luard, ii. 223 [1]. The date, August 6th, is the day

---

[1] Other authorities are—Henry of Huntingdon (*in ann.* 1133); Robert de Monte, who gives the same account as the *Annals of Waverley*; *Chron. de Mailros, in ann.* 1133—"Gaufridus Regis Cancellarius Ecclesiæ Dunelmensis et

on which Galfrid Rufus is known to have been consecrated, and, as we see, John of Hexham says before the Assumption, August 15th.

The Priory of Nostell was founded by Robert de Lacy in the reign of Henry I., and partly endowed by him; his charter is extant. It is not clear whether there was an earlier foundation or not; but the confirmation charters of Henry I. and Henry II. distinctly state that Regular Canons were placed there by Archbishop Thurstin. The date of foundation was probably in or shortly after the year 1121[1]. It is asserted that Athelwold was the *second* Prior of Nostell. However that may have been, it is certain that he came from Nostell to Carlisle; and therefore, whether as Prior of Carlisle or Bishop, it must have been long after 1102. In fact it would be scarcely credible that, as he died in 1156, he should have held the important posts of Prior, and then Bishop, of Carlisle for the long space of 54 years.

But was Athelwold ever Prior of Carlisle? If so, at what date? He was certainly Prior of S. Oswald (Nostell) early in 1123, when he was sent by Archbishop Thurstin on a mission to William de Corbeil, Archbishop Elect of Canterbury[2]. As Prior of Nostell he often appears in the history of that period in connection with, and as a friend of, Archbishop Thurstin[3]. It is remarkable that he is invariably spoken of in the older accounts

Adulfus Ecclesiæ Carleolensis a Turstino Archiepiscopo Eboracensi consecrati sunt Episcopi." Matthew Paris, *Historia Anglorum* (ed. Madden, i. 245)— " Anno Domini Mᵒcᵒxxxᵒiiᵒ (*sic*) rex Henricus novum fecit episcopatum apud Karleolum, in limbo scilicet Angliæ et Galwalliæ. Et posuit ibi primum episcopum, nomine Athelulphum, sancti Oswaldi priorem, cui peccata solitus fuerat confiteri. Hic autem creatus antistes, in ecclesia sedis suæ canonicos posuit regulares, et eam multis honoribus ampliavit." Similarly *Chron. Major.* ed. Luard, ii. 158. Thos. Stubbs (ed. Twysden, col. 1717) and John Bromton (ed. Twysden, col. 1019) also refer to the event *in ann.* 1133.

[1] The date of the Nostell charter of Henry I. must be between June, 1121, and August, 1127, as it is witnessed by Ebrard, Bishop of Norwich, and by Richard de Capella, Bishop of Hereford; see the charter in Dugdale, *Monasticon*, vi. 92. For Archbp Thurstin's life, see Hugh the Cantor in *Historians of the Church of York*, ii. 129, Rolls Series, also *Fasti Eboracenses*, ed. J. Raine, p. 170.

[2] Thos. Stubbs, ed. Twysden, col. 1717.

[3] See also *Fasti Eboracenses*, ed. J. Raine, pp. 192, 201.

as Prior of Nostell or Prior of S. Oswald, and not as Prior of Carlisle. One important document, among the Duchy of Lancaster Records[1], is an exception, and speaks of Adelwald as being Prior of the Church of Carlisle at the time of his consecration. It is a return made Sept. 17th, 1343, by the Prior and Chapter of the Cathedral Church of Carlisle in reply to an inquiry of the Prior and Convent of Coningesheved in Lancashire, after a careful inspection of their chronicles and other evidences. This testimony should perhaps be received with some little suspicion. Even if Athelwold were Prior of Carlisle for a time before the foundation of the See, he could scarcely have occupied the position for 31 years and then be spoken of habitually as Prior of Nostell. Burton quotes a statement which, if correct, would explain the fact of Athelwold always being spoken of as Prior of Nostell[2]. He says that Athelwold founded the Cathedral in Carlisle for Canons of his own order, which Pope Calixtus II.[3] granted him the privilege of holding along with his Priory of Nostell for his life, but that it should cease at his death. Thus, although Prior of Carlisle, the better known title would be used, especially by the Yorkshire historians. It is worthy of note that the charter of Bishop Athelwold (*Chart. Whitby*, i. 38) confirming the Church of Crosby Ravensworth to the Abbey of Whitby is addressed to Elyas Archdeacon and the Chapter of S. Mary, but does not mention any Prior of Carlisle, yet we find that Walter was Prior in 1150 and attested the Foundation Charter of Holm Cultram with Bishop Adulph (Illustrative Doc. xxiv.). Hence it is quite possible that Athelwold, while holding the Priory of Nostell, may have gone to found or to confirm the Priory of Carlisle ; and, when the See of Carlisle was founded in 1133, he may have joined, at all events for a time, the offices of Prior and Bishop of Carlisle with that of Prior of Nostell. This is supported by the fact that Savardus, the next Prior of Nostell, was appointed about the time of the death of Athelwold in 1156.

Let us now turn to the reputed founder of the Priory of Carlisle, Henry I. In the first year of his reign, on November

---

[1] Box A. No. 416 : see Illustrative Docum. xx.

[2] *Monasticon Eboracense*, p. 310, quoting J. Bronolt, script. 257.

[3] Pope from Feb. 2, 1119 to Dec. 15, 1124.

11th, 1100, he married the Princess Eadgyth, or Matilda, the daughter of Malcolm Ceanmor, King of Scots, and the "good Queen Margaret." The nominal Scottish Chronicler, perhaps naturally, spends a good deal of time in recounting the pious deeds of Queen Margaret and of her daughter. But he is in error when he gives Queen Matilda credit for persuading King Henry to place Regular Canons in Carlisle in 1102. Indeed, as Bishop Tanner says referring to another event, "this is not the only mistake he has made with regard to our English affairs." No doubt there was much communication between the English and Scottish Courts in the early years of Henry's reign. He was, however, at that time far too much occupied in the southern part of his kingdom to trouble himself about the ecclesiastical affairs of a northern border town, which ten years before had been for two centuries an uninhabited heap of ruins[1]. Matilda had been, till the time of her marriage, in the Benedictine Abbey of Ramsey, in Hampshire. Her sympathies would not be with the new foreign order of Augustinian Canons, even if at that time she had ever heard of them.

---

[1] The following are some of the authorities.—*Anglo-Saxon Chronicle, in ann.* 1092 (ed. B. Thorpe, i. 359, trans.): "In this year King William, with a large force, went north to Cardeol, and restored the town and raised the castle, and drove out Dolfin, who previously had ruled the land there, and garrisoned the castle with his own men, and then returned south hither. And very many country folk, with wives and with cattle, he sent thither, there to dwell and to till the land." Simeon of Durham, *Hist. Regum*, ed. T. Arnold, ii. 220: "His actis Rex in Northimbriam profectus civitatem quæ Britannice Cairleil, Latine Lugubalia vocatur restauravit, et in ea castellum ædificavit. Hæc enim civitas, ut illis in partibus aliæ nonnullæ, a Danis paganis ante cc. annos diruta, et usque ad id tempus mansit deserta." Florence of Worcester (ed. B. Thorpe, ii. 30) uses the same words, probably the original statement; and Roger de Hoveden (ed. Stubbs, i. 145) and Ralph de Diceto (ed. Stubbs, i. 217) copy from Simeon. The *Annals of Waverley, in ann.* 1092, here copy from the *A.-S. Chronicle*, the variations are to be noted: "Rex Willelmus ivit in Nord apud Cardeol, et burgum ædificavit, et castellum incepit, et Dolfinum fugavit, cujus terra illa fuit; et misit homines suos in castello, et postea reversus est Sud, et misit illuc multos villanos cum uxoribus et animalibus suis, ut in illa terra manerent."—*Annal. Monastici*, ed. Luard, ii. 202. Henry of Huntingdon writes (ed. T. Arnold, p. 216): "Succedente anno (1092) Rex reædificavit civitatem Carleol, et ex australibus Angliæ partibus illuc habitatores transmisit."

With the advent of the famous Thurstin, Archbishop of York, began a great increase of religious activity in the North of England. Though elected and enthroned at York, in 1114, he was not consecrated until October 19th, 1119. Thurstin, after many differences with the King, at length arrived at York, early in 1121, with his strong friendship and approval. The next year, in October, 1122, the King himself went down into the north. He turned aside from York, as Simeon of Durham tells us[1], towards the western sea, and having inspected the ancient city of Carleol, ordered it to be fortified with a castle and towers, giving money for that purpose. He then returned to York. We can scarcely doubt, when all things are considered, it was after this visit that Henry I., at the instigation of Thurstin, founded the Priory of Regular Canons at Carlisle. He made a grant by charter to S. Mary of Carlisle and the Canons there of the Churches of Newcastle-on-Tyne and Newburn, and the Churches then held by Richard de Aurea Valle on his death. Richard was his Chaplain; and the Churches were Warkworth, Corbridge, Whittingham, and Rothbury, all in Northumberland. From the charters[2], we gather that the grant to the Chaplain was made before January 10th, 1123, when one of the witnesses, Robert Bloet, Bishop of Lincoln, died; and the grant to the monastery certainly between 1116 and 1128, two of the witnesses being William de Giffard, Bishop of Winchester, and Bernard, Bishop of S. David's. It is worthy of note that the latter charter is dated from Rouen, where according to Ordericus Vitalis (Bk xii. c. 34) the King went in 1123 to quell the revolt which had broken out in Normandy[3]. Henry I., as appears from a charter of Henry II., also granted to the monastery, probably at a later

---

[1] "Hoc anno (1122) Rex Henricus post festum Sancti Michaelis Northymbranas intrans regiones ab Eboraco divertit versus mare occidentale, consideraturus civitatem antiquam quæ lingua Brittonum Cairleil dicitur, quæ nunc Carleol Anglice, Latine vero Lugubalia appellatur, quam data pecunia castello et turribus præcepit muniri."—*Hist. Regum* (ed. T. Arnold, ii. 267). Also "Henricus Rex ad Carleil venit."—*Chronica de Mailros, in ann.* 1122.

[2] Given in Dugdale, *Monasticon*, vi. 144.

[3] See also the *Anglo-Saxon Chronicle* where, *in ann.* 1123, the bishops above named are mentioned.

date, a mill on the bridge over the river Eden and a fishery therein[1].

The interest felt by Archbishop Thurstin in the new Order is proved by the fact that during his tenure of the See of York at least eight other houses of Augustinian Canons were founded in the north, some of them avowedly at his instigation; and none were founded before his time. These were Hexham, Nostell, Drax, Embsay (afterwards Bolton), Giseburn, Kirkham, Wartre, and Bridlington, probably all before the foundation of the See of Carlisle in 1133. We can well understand Thurstin pressing upon Henry I. in 1122 the claims of Carlisle, which the King had lately visited, and those of his friend Athelwold, the Prior of Nostell, who was also the Confessor of the King. The anxiety of Thurstin to establish his jurisdiction over the Diocese of Glasgow, and the violent opposition at this very time of John, Bishop of Glasgow, may have also been a reason for fixing an ecclesiastical outpost of strong adherents, like these Regular Canons, upon the border. It was certainly one reason for the foundation of the Bishopric of Carlisle a few years later[2].

There is clear proof that, a little later, works were going on in connection with the Church of Carlisle, including, no doubt, the monastic buildings. In the earliest Pipe Roll extant, ascribed to 31 Henry I. (1130–31), there is the payment by Royal writ to the Canons of S. Mary of Carlisle of £10, *ad operat. Ecclesie sue,*

---

[1] There is a letter from Henry III. to Pope Honorius III. in the Close Rolls (3 Hen. III. *m.* 11) dated Feb. 17th, 1219, which says that these six Churches "ex concessione bonæ memoriæ Regis Henrici primi *in prima fundatione Ecclesiæ Carleolensis* eidem collatas fuisse, et in Episcopatu Carleolensi ecclesiam de Penret cum quibusdam aliis, et confirmatum fuit dictæ Carl. Eccles. per cartas Regum Angliæ scilicet predicti Regis Henrici primi et secundi, &c.," and that these had been alienated through the neglect of the Canons when the See was vacant, Bishop Hugh having been lately appointed (see also the Patent Rolls 3 Hen. III. m. 5). There is also a confirmation in the Papal Registers (*Calend.* ed. Bliss, i. 91) by Pope Honorius III. to Hugh Bishop of Carlisle of the bishopric and parish of Carlisle, dated May 2nd, 1223. The possessions of the See are set out and reference is made to the divisions settled between the Bishop and the Prior and Convent of Carlisle and certain arbitrators, several of whom are well known.

[2] See Haddan and Stubbs, *Eccles. Docum.* ii. pp. 15, 19.

also the remittance to them twice of 37s. 4d. of the noutgeld, of which more will be said below. The same Pipe Roll contains items of gifts by the King towards the works on the wall and the tower of the city. Coupling this with the statement of Simeon of Durham given above, we see the strong interest felt by the King after his visit to Carlisle in 1122, not only in the fortifications of the city, but in the works of the Canons upon their monastery buildings.

There is another statement which can be traced back as far as John Leland, the antiquary, who about 1540 wandered over England picking up strange traditions. The story was taken up by Bishop F. Godwin with variations, and is followed by Hutchinson, Lysons, and other local historians[1]. It is said that Walter, a rich Norman ecclesiastic, who had come to England with the Conqueror, was set over the city by William Rufus, and that he began to build a religious House in honour of the Blessed Virgin Mary; but, Walter dying before his design was completed, Athelwold, Prior of Nostell, spent the wealth left by Walter in finishing the structure, and placed there Regular Canons.

It is possible that a monastery of some kind was commenced here in the rebuilt city before Athelwold had anything to do with Carlisle; but it would be years after the time of William Rufus. There would seem, however, to be some connection between the above tradition and the following fact. We have it on the good authority of the *Testa de Nevill*[2], that Henry I. gave to one Walter, his Chaplain, Linstoc and Carleton (near Carlisle) at a yearly cornage rent of 37s. 4d., that Walter, by permission of the King, took the religious habit in the Priory of Carlisle, and with his consent gave all the aforesaid land to the religious House;

---

[1] Leland, *Collectanea*, i. 120; F. Godwin, *De Presulibus Angliæ* (p. 144, Pt ii. ed. 1616).

[2] Ed. Record Com. p. 379 b. "H. Rex avus H. patris Dñi Regis dedit quondam Waltero capellano suo Linstoc et Karleton reddendo annuatim de cornagio xxxvijs. iiijd.; predictus Walterus voluntate et concessione Dñi Regis suscepit habitum religionis in prioratu Sancte Marie de Carleol et voluntate et assensu predicti Dñi H. Regis dedit totam predictam terram predicte domui religionis in puram perpetuam elemosinam per predictum servicium. Predictum servicium pardonatum est viris religiosis predicte domus per cartas predecessoris Dñi Regis."

and the aforesaid service was pardoned to the religious of that House by Royal charters. But this service of 37s. 4d. cornage is the exact amount of the noutgeld, or *geldum animalium*, which we saw, in the Pipe Roll quoted above, was remitted by Royal writ to the Canons of S. Mary of Carlisle. The item appears again long after, in the time of Henry II., in the Pipe Rolls for 1158 and following years. The reference is clearly to the same property[1]. Here then we have another instance of the active interest taken by Henry I. about this time in the monastery at Carlisle.

We have seen that there could not have been a foundation of Regular Canons at Carlisle in 1102. It is well to note that the position of affairs in the district points altogether to a later date. Ten years before, in 1092, the Normans under William Rufus had taken possession of the land. The castle, which he had ordered to be built at this important military point, may have been completed. The city, long uninhabited, was being re-peopled, partly by settlers whom the King had sent from the south[2]. Ranulf Meschin, the experienced Norman soldier, was set over the newly acquired district. The sympathies of Ranulf and of his family were with the Benedictine Monks, not the Augustinian Canons. They had been large benefactors to the Abbey of S. Mary at York. He had at once placed a Benedictine Priory, at Wetherhala, 5 miles from Carlisle, close to the great road which led from that city to Appleby[3]. At his "castle of Appelby," he ruled the district. In 1120 Ranulf succeeded as Earl of Chester. The lordship of the "honor of Carlisle" which he held passed into the hands of the King. And shortly, as we have seen, Henry I. came down from York to look over this part of his kingdom. The time would seem to have been opportune, and the place well fitted, for founding a House of the new order of Regular Canons.

We come therefore to the following conclusions. We have evidence that a House of Regular Canons was founded at

---

[1] This Walter has been said to be the Walter who succeeded Athelwold as Prior of Carlisle, but this is very improbable, see note 1 on No. **28**.

[2] See the quotations p. 482, note 1, above.

[3] See Appendix A, p. 469.

Carlisle by Henry I., not in 1102 but in or about the year 1123; that he acted to a certain extent under the advice of Thurstin, Archbishop of York; also that Athelwold, the friend of Thurstin, and Prior of Nostell, may have been made Prior of Carlisle not many years before his consecration to that new See; that he probably held for a time the two offices together, and may have continued to be also Prior of Nostell until his death in 1156.

The Priory of Carlisle was dedicated to S. Mary—a dedication which the Cathedral Church retained until the refoundation in 1541, and which has led to some confusion. There is not the slightest evidence of the existence at this period, 1123, or for some time after, of the two Carlisle parishes of S. Mary and S. Cuthbert. The circuit of 15 miles granted to S. Cuthbert by King Ecgfrid in 685 (p. 95 note) may have formed roughly an ecclesiastical district with a radius of from 2 to 3 miles; and it may have been worked from the monastery at Caerluel instituted by S. Cuthbert; for the existence of parishes, as now understood, before the 10th century is very doubtful[1]. But we know that war and disorder prevailed generally until 875, when Eadred the Abbot fled away[2] and when the city was destroyed by the Danes and became deserted until 1092. No parishes could therefore be formed until near the date of the foundation of the Priory, when the inhabitants would at first be served from that centre. We cannot gather how long this ministration lasted; but in the 14th century we do find mention of ministers of those parishes. Then they appear as Chaplains, not Vicars, who were appointed by the Priory. We should have expected to hear of such long before. The charter of Henry II. does not mention the parishes or their Churches. However, out of the immediate district two parishes were constituted, probably in the 12th century, and were under the ecclesiastical superintendence of the Priory. A Church was built for the parish of S. Cuthbert. The nave of the Cathedral, a not unfrequent instance, was allowed for a Church of

---

[1] See Lord Selborne, *Ancient Facts and Fictions*, p. 292; Bp. Stubbs, *Dict. Christian Biog.* iii. 930.

[2] "Ascito ergo probandæ sanctitatis viro Eadredo, qui ab eo quod in Luel, in monasterio dudum ab ipso Cuthberto instituto, educatus officium abbatis gesserit, Lulisc cognominabatur."—Simeon of Durham, ed. Arnold, i. 56.

the parish of S. Mary, but their cemetery was the "cemetery of the Canons of S. Mary" and was regulated by the Priory and later by the Dean and Chapter. For the statement that the parish of S. Mary was constituted before the Cathedral, or that the nave, which was used as the parish Church, was independent of the Cathedral, there is no historical foundation, and all the reliable evidence is against it[1].

We may now consider the later history of Bishop Athelwold. In 1120 we find that Bishop Athelulf was witness, with Bishop Nigell of Ely and others, to the famous Charter of Liberties granted by King Stephen (Stubbs, *Select Charters*, p. 120; Richard of Hexham, ed. J. Raine, i. 74). Bishop Adthelwlfus accompanied Alberic, the Papal Legate, and Robert, Bishop of Hereford, in September, 1138, to Carlisle, where David, King of Scots, was then holding his court (Richard of Hexham, ed. J. Raine, i. 99, and see note 1 on No. 198). Adelulph, Bishop of Carlisle, attended an important council at Winchester in 1143 (W. Thorn, ed. Twysden, col. 1803). He was also one of the minority who voted for Henry Murdac, Abbot of Fountains, to be Archbishop of York, in opposition to the will of the King; and Murdac was consecrated by the Pope in December, 1147 (*Chron. Mailros, in ann.*; John of Hexham, ed. Raine, i. 155, 158). He was present at the coronation of Henry II. in December, 1154; and he died in 1156, on the morrow of Ascension Day, the second year of Henry II. (*Annals of Waverley*, vid. *Annal. Monastici*, ed. Luard, ii. 237; Benedict Abbas, ed. Stubbs, i. 349, who gives the date incorrectly MCLVII). The next year, 1157, the land of Carlisle, which had been held as a fief of the English Crown since 1136, was ceded to Henry II. by Malcolm IV., King of Scots. Bishop Athelwold would thus occupy a difficult position for almost the whole of his episcopate, a suffragan of York and yet his diocese under the rule of a Scottish King. His appointment was at first strongly objected to by John, Bishop of Glasgow; but John of Hexham, in his account

---

[1] As to the legend told by J. Denton (*Cumberland*, p. 97) of the heap of coins buried under the steeple of S. Cuthbert's Church at its first foundation before the advent of the Danes and of their being found in later times, it may be taken, like many of Mr Denton's statements, for what it is worth.

of the Council held at Carlisle in 1138, under King David I., says of Alberic, the Papal Legate : "Aldulfum Episcopum in gratiam ejusdem Regis et in sedem suam de Karlel recipi impetravit" (ed. J. Raine, i. 121). A letter is given in Raine's *Memorials of Hexham* (vol. i. Appendix, p. xii) from Pope Innocent II. to King Stephen, urging him to complete the work of Henry I., and to arrange the affairs of the Diocese of Carlisle. Athelwold, besides being recognized as an English Bishop, is constantly in evidence as discharging the duties of his Diocese. Thus, in addition to the two Confirmations in this *Register*, we find Adhelwald confirming the Church of Crosseby Ravenswart in Westmoreland to the Monastery of Whitby (*Chart. Whitby*, ed. Atkinson, i. 38) and as witness to a charter of the liberties of the same Monastery, granted by Henry I. between 1133 and 1135 (i. 214). He also attests the charter granted by Earl Henry to the Abbey of Holm Cultram in 1150 (Illustrative Documents, xxiv.).

APPENDIX C.

The bounds of the Sanctuary of Wetherhal were marked by six crosses. One of these, which also stood upon the boundary of the manor, is called, Wederhal Gyrth Crosse or Gryth Crosse, "juxta sicketam de Waryewyke" (No. 236, Illus. Docum. xxx). *Gryth*, or *grith*, is the Anglo-Saxon word for "peace," but differs from *frith*, a general peace—"*Grith* is immunity from molestation, special *frith* or localised peace" (Bp Stubbs); it is peace or protection such as was given by the King to official men, also the privilege of sanctuary within a certain space. Hence we have also *grithstole*, a seat of peace, a sanctuary, *grithbreke*, a breach of the peace, and *grithmen*, or *girthmen*, men who had taken sanctuary and had obtained "grith" or "peace."

The privilege of sanctuary was granted to Wetherhal under the charter of Henry I., and confirmed by later Kings, the same as was enjoyed by the Church of S. Peter in York and S. John in Beverley—"et omnes easdem libertates habeant quas habent istæ duæ Ecclesiæ." These two Churches had liberty of sanctuary granted to them (it is supposed) by King Æthelstan (924—940) though the Revised Charters called Æthelstan's have no authority, but belong to the 13th century (see Dugdale, *Monasticon*, ii. 129). There is a charter of Henry I. to York about 1110, confirming a deed by Edward the Confessor and granting this liberty (see Illustrative Documents, xxvii.).

Three cases of considerable interest concerning the Sanctuary at Wetherhal came before the justices in 1292. Andrew son of Thomas de Wardwyk' struck one Adam on the head with a stick so that he died on the third day. Andrew at once fled to Wetherhale, and there had peace. The Prior of Wetherhale was called upon to shew *quo waranto* he claimed this liberty. The Prior and the Abbot of S. Mary's at York appeared and claimed that of old time they had at Wetherhale this liberty *infra banlucam* to receive any felons who had taken an oath that they would conduct themselves well within the Liberty, and would not go out of it. The jury found that they and their predecessors had had such a custom time out of mind. In the second case, four men, one of them William the prepositus of Wederhale, had killed in the night Robert de Shawyl of Great Corkeby in the fishery at Wederhale within the Liberty. They had been received for six years, but, before the coming of the justices, the survivors had lately fled. The matter was complicated by an informal coroner's inquest which had been held upon the body. In this case it was affirmed that no claim was made to have a coroner within the Liberty, or to receive felons who committed a felony within the Liberty. The jury assented to this, but said that by old custom all felons coming there had been received and, having rung the bell in the Church, and so accepted "peace," dwelt peacefully *infra banlucam* of the said Liberty, having sworn to conduct themselves well while they remained. In the third case, three men, Richard Gener, John Curur and Clement Sutor, came near the house of Roger son of Martin, and Richard struck Roger's dog, upon which Roger rushed out of his house and stabbed Richard to the heart with his sword. Roger at once fled to the Liberty of the Priory of Wederhalle, and dwelt there for some months. The Abbot of S. Mary appeared by his attorney and allowed that the said Roger after the felony came within the Liberty and rang a certain bell in the Church, and swore before the Bailiff of the liberty that he would in future conduct himself well and faithfully; so he was admitted and permitted to remain so long as he did not go outside the bounds of the Liberty. The Abbot claimed that he and his predecessors had used this custom time without mind and without interruption. The jury found to this effect (Illustrative Documents, xxix.).

The bounds of the Sanctuary are set out in the Illustrative Documents (xxx.); also a curious opinion of counsel with regard to the liberties of Wetherhal, but at what date it was given does not appear.

We find that Edward III., on the 15th of July, 1342, empowered Edward Balliol, King of Scots, to take the "grith-men" at Beverley, Ripon, Tynemuth, Hextildesham (Hexham) and Wederhale; and if they would fight in Scotland, they should receive the Royal pardon (see Illustrative Documents, XXVIII.).

An account of these sanctuary men at Beverley and Durham, and their offences, will be found in *Sanctuarium Dunelmense et Sanctuarium Beverlacense* (ed. Surtees Society, vol. 5). There is also an interesting account of a breach of sanctuary with an appeal to the Legate Otho and to the King, with the punishment of the violators in the *Annals of Waverley, in ann.* 1240 (*Annales Monast.* ed. Luard, ii. 325).

This liberty of sanctuary does not appear to have been common, if it was not unique, in the district. It has been claimed for the Nunnery of Ermynthwait, or Armathwaite, on the strength of an old stone having been found there with a cross and the word *Sanctuarium* cut on it (see Hutchinson, *Hist. Cumberland*, i. 192). The extant charters do not confirm it; and as I have pointed out the charter of William II. to Armathwaite is clearly spurious (see on No. 162). It is singular that in that charter is quoted the latter of two lines from Æthelstan's Revised Charter referred to above:

> "And in all thyngges be als free
>   as herte may thynk or eghe may see,"

which run, as given in the longer Revised Charter:

> "Swa mickel freedom give I ye
>   Swa hert may think or eghe see."

This helps to confirm the idea of its fabrication. A sort of claim has also been put forward for a sanctuary at Ravenstonedale in Westmoreland (see Nicolson and Burn, *History*, i. 520) on the ground of the manor belonging to the Gilbertine Priory of Watton, but there is no real evidence of its existence. At Hexham in Northumberland there was of course a very ancient and famous sanctuary, defined in Prior Richard's *History of the Church of Hexham*, Bk. ii. c. 14; see *Memorials of Hexham*, ed. Raine, i. 61.

APPENDIX D.

It is generally affirmed, especially in the local histories, that Bishop Bernard immediately succeeded Athelwold, the first Bishop of Carlisle, who occupied the See from 1133 to 1156. Nothing is stated as to his consecration, but his death is frequently placed in 1186. The very existence of a Bernard, Bishop of Carlisle, has been doubted or denied by modern writers of eminence (see Hardy in *Fasti Ecclesiæ*, vol. iii. p. 230; Haddan and Stubbs, *Eccles. Doc.* vol. ii. pp. 34, 48). The error as to his existence arose, it is alleged, from the fact of the temporalities of the See having been given by King John to a Bernard, Archbishop of Slavonia, or Ragusa, early in the 13th century. There is, however, ample evidence of a Bernard, Bishop of Carlisle, who performed many episcopal acts in connection with the Diocese. The questions to be decided are—Did a Bernard, Bishop of Carlisle, ever exist? Was there a second Bernard, living in the 12th century, distinct from the Archbishop of Ragusa? During what period did Bishop Bernard exercise his episcopate? These questions are of no small importance to the history of the Diocese in those early times.

Bishop Athelwold died on the morrow of Ascension Day, 1156 (see page 488). For 20 years the District of Carlisle had been again an appanage of the Scottish crown with an English Bishop exercising jurisdiction in it. The land was reclaimed in 1157 by Henry II., and retained by him. No successor to Athelwold was appointed. We have proof that the Bishopric was vacant for a long period, and that no Bishop

Bernard occupied the See.   In the *Register of Wetheral* there
is a document (No. **44**) concerning a chapel at Corkeby,
wherein Robert, Archdeacon of Carlisle, is addressed by Clement,
Abbot of S. Mary, York (1161—84), as being the person in
authority.   Walter, Prior of Carlisle, is one of the witnesses, and
the date of the document is almost certainly between 1161 and
1165.   In the *Chartulary of Whitby* (ed. Atkinson, No. xxxvi)
there is a confirmation charter of Bernardus Karleolensis Episcopus in regard to the Church of Crosseby Ravenswart (in
Westmoreland) to which I shall have again to refer.   The point
here is that Bishop Bernard speaks in the charter of " Adelwold
our predecessor " and Roger, Archbishop of York, as being both
dead, also of Robert, Archdeacon of Carlisle, having instituted to
the living, under the mandate of Archbishop Roger, " when the
See of Carlisle was vacant."   Roger de Pont l'Evêque was
Archbishop from 1154 to 1181.   In the same *Chartulary* (No.
xxxiii) is a confirmation charter of Robert, Archdeacon, which
speaks of Bishop Adelwold as dead, and of Robert having given
seisin of the Church of Crosseby to the Abbot and monks of
Wyteby by direction of Archbishop Roger.   The first witness is
Walter, Prior of Carlisle.   In the *Register of Holm Cultram* (MS.
p. 239) there is a charter of confirmation by Pope Clement III.
(1187—91) of grants made to that Abbey.   He therein speaks of
the grant of the chapel of Flemingby by Gospatric son of Orm,
and of an agreement between the Convent and Adam, son of
Gospatric, ratified by Robert, Archdeacon, acting as Diocesan,
the Bishopric being vacant (Agreement, MS. p. 36).   The date of
this agreement would be between 1170 and 1180.   The same
Archdeacon and Prior are witnesses to the Foundation Charter of
Lanercost, about 1169, as the names of the other witnesses seem
to shew (Illustrative Documents, xxiii.).   This is an important
point.   It is generally stated that the Priory of Lanercost was
dedicated in 1169 by Bishop Bernard in the 12th year of his
Episcopate.   The reference given is to the 1st edition of
Dugdale's *Monasticon*.   This would seem to prove that Bishop
Bernard filled the Bishopric at that time.   By this many have
been led astray.   Dugdale gives as his authority the *Register of
Lanercost* in the possession of Lord William Howard at Naworth.

Of this *Register* an old Transcript is now in the possession of the Dean and Chapter of Carlisle. The statement there is as follows, in the same hand as the Transcript—"Anno ab incarnatione Domini 1169, 16 H. 2, dedicata fuit ista Ecclesia a Domino Bernardo Episcopo Carl. anno Pontificatus ejusdem xii°." But this is only a marginal note, due to the invention of the writer, who took the death of Athelwold as his starting point. The first witness to the charter is Cristian, Bishop of Candida Casa, a natural position if he were engaged in episcopal matters connected with the district of Carlisle, though he had no episcopal jurisdiction there. This appears to have been the case (see note 9 on No. 38). It would be difficult to understand the part he played in the Diocese, if Bernard or any other person were Bishop of Carlisle. The matter is quite simple, if he were acting for the Archbishop of York and the See were vacant at the time.

We learn from the Chronicles of Benedict Abbas and of Roger de Hoveden, that when Henry II. was at Carlisle in 1186, he granted the petition of the Canons Regular of the Church of S. Mary to be allowed to elect a Bishop. They chose Paulinus de Ledes, Master of the Hospital of S. Leonard at York. Paulinus refused the bishopric, although the King offered to add 300 marcs annually to the endowment from certain rents which he named from the Church of Bamburg, the Church of Scartheburg (Scarborough), the chapel of Tikehil and two manors of the King near Carlisle (Rog. de Hoveden, ii. 309). From this statement Bishop F. Godwin (*De Præsul. Angl.* p. 145) concluded that Bishop Bernard must have died about this date, 1186, and he has been followed by too many writers. Benedict, indeed, goes on to say that the election was received with great satisfaction, for the See of Carlisle had been vacant nearly 29 years (elsewhere "nearly 30 years") from the death of Adelwold the first Bishop (see Benedict Abbas, ed. Stubbs, i. 344, 349, 360).

The Pipe Rolls prove that the See was vacant and the revenues were in the hands of the King in the years 1187 and 1188 (Cumberland, 33 and 34 Hen. II.). The Sheriff renders a most interesting account of receipts from the Bishopric and of payments made by him, partly for oil for the Sacrament at Easter, and partly for works on the Cathedral and the Priory buildings. His receipts were from the Churches of Dalston, Carleton and Meleburn (Derbyshire) and the School of Carlisle. There is no similar account beyond these two years; and if the revenues were collected for the King, they were not accounted for by the Sheriff.

The attempt to fill the Bishopric failed, and the death of Henry II. in July 1189 probably led to the abandonment of all efforts in this direction. There were ecclesiastical difficulties in the reign of King Richard, especially those connected with the Archbishopric of York, which would no doubt stand in the way, besides the poverty of the See.

We pass on, and we still find that there is no Bishop of Carlisle. Two charters in the *Register of Wetheral* (Nos. 120, 123) are granted by Peter de Ros, Archdeacon of Carlisle, as "Custos Episcopatus," during the vacancy of the See. From the names in these charters it is clear that their date must be between 1180 and 1192. In 1196 Aumeric de Taillebois was Archdeacon, and certainly confirmed Churches and vicarages; and he held this Archdeaconry until 1203. From a confirmation charter by him in the *Register of Lanercost* (MS. viii. 2) of Churches belonging to that Priory, it is evident that there was no Bishop of Carlisle at the time.

Again, it admits of no doubt that the See was vacant in the year 1200, and the temporalities in the King's hand. In the Charter Rolls for that year there is the record—"Dominus Rex concessit Archiepis. Sclavoniæ Episcopatum Carleoli ad se sustentandum donec Dominus Rex ei in ampliori beneficio providerit" (*Rot. Cart.* 2 Joh. m. 35 *d*, ed. Hardy, p. 96 *b*). This grant was not carried out, for we find in the Patent Rolls for 1202 that the King commands the Bishop of Coventry to admit and institute Henry de Duly, chaplain to Hugh Bardulf, to the Church of Meleburn (in Derbyshire) "vacant and in our gift from the Bishopric of Carlisle being in our hands" (*Rot. Pat.* 3 Joh. m. 4, Rec. Com. i. 7 *a*, dated March 18). The next year, June 8th, 1203, he granted "Episcopatum de Carleol." (apparently only the temporalities) to Alexander de Lucy, and the Archdeaconry of Carlisle on the 18th of November following (*Rot. Pat.* 5 Joh. m. 9, m. 5, Rec. Com. i. 30 *b*, 35 *b*). But in answer to a pressing letter from Pope Innocent III., dated May 15th, 1203, on behalf of the Archbishop of Ragusa, the King gave him the Bishopric of Carlisle on January 10th, 1204. The Archbishop of Ragusa, or Sclavonia, was consecrated at Rome, November 19th, 1189 (Bp Stubbs, quoting Farlati, *Illyricum Sacrum*, vi. 83)[1]. We learn from the Patent Roll, where the above letter is cited (*Rot. Pat.* 5 Joh. m. 4, Rec. Com. i. 37 *b*) that he had been absolved by the Pope from the care of the Church at Ragusa, as he could only live there at the risk of his life. The Pope begged King John to give him for the relief of his poverty the Bishopric of Carlisle, to which the Archbishop of York might collate him, and the Church of Meleburne (in Derbyshire). The Patent is addressed by the King to Geoffrey, Archbishop of York, commanding him to attend to this matter, as he had granted the Bishopric of Carlisle to the Archbishop of Ragusa (not by the Pope's authority) *de munificentia et liberalitate Regia*. Here then we have the distinct appointment of Bishop Bernard to Carlisle. This is further confirmed. In the Close Rolls (7 Joh. m. 13, Rec. Com. i. 52 *b*) under date March 23rd, 1205, there is an order from the King to W. Treasurer, to pay B. Bishop of Carlisle 20 marcs annually, the Church of Meleburne to remain to the said Bishop. Also we find in the Patent Rolls (9 Joh. m. 5, Rec. Com. i. 76)—"To the Barons of the Exchequer. We have given to our Venerable Father, Bernard, Bishop of Carlisle, 20 marcs yearly from our Exchequer as long as he lives." On July 8th, 1214, the custody of the Bishopric of Carlisle was given to Aymeric (de Taillebois) Archdeacon of Durham (and Carlisle) who is mentioned above (*Rot. Pat.* 16 Joh. m. 15, Rec. Com. i. 118). At this time, therefore, Bishop Bernard must have been dead or have resigned the See. On May 26th, 1215 (it should be noted that May 26 occurs twice in the 16th year of King John), the custody was given to the Prior of Carlisle during pleasure (*Rot. Pat.* 16 Joh. m. 1, Rec. Com. i. 138 *b*); and on May 27th and May 31st letters

---

[1] It is stated in the *Annals of Bermondsey*, perhaps not very good authority, that Bernard, formerly Archbishop of Ragusa, came into England with King Richard (*Annales Monastici*, ed. Luard, iii. 450).

were sent to Gerard de Rodes, also to all holding benefices in the Diocese, announcing that the Bishopric was vacant and the custody granted to the Prior of Carlisle (*Rot. Pat.* 16 Joh. m. 24, Rec. Com. i. 142 *a*; 17 Joh. i. 142 *b*). The vacancy continued until August 1st, 1218, when Henry III. gave his assent to the election of Hugh, Abbot of Beaulieu (de Bello Loco) in Hampshire (not in Burgundy as *Chron. de Lanercost*, p. 27, see Dugdale, *Monasticon*, v. 560). Bishop Hugh was consecrated at York on February 24th, 1218—19; and orders were sent to the Sheriff of Cumberland to give seisin to the Elect of Carlisle of lands and tenements belonging to the Bishopric, such as Bernard, Archbishop of Sclavonia, formerly Custos of the said Bishopric had (*Close Rolls*, 2 Hen. III. m. 2, Rec. Com. i. 369 *b*). We have therefore, from January 10th, 1204, to July 8th, 1214, a period of about 10 years during which Bernard, Archbishop of Sclavonia, may have been, and during part of which he certainly was, Bishop of Carlisle. He not only held the temporalities of the See, but we have abundant evidence that he exercised episcopal functions in the Diocese. Of the numerous charters and documents in which his name occurs, all fall within this period. The following may be quoted :—

(1) In the *Register of Wetherhal* (No. **17**) " B[ernardus] Dei gratia Karliolensis Episcopus " confirms to the Abbey of S. Mary, York, all the Churches and ecclesiastical benefices in the Diocese of Carlisle belonging to them.

(2) The next charter (No. **18**) is a confirmation by Pope Honorius III., dated April 8th, 1226, of the concessions made to the Abbey of S. Mary, York, by Athelwold and Bernard, Bishops of Carlisle, of whom he speaks as being dead.

(3) No. **25** is a Bull of Pope Gregory IX., dated March 14th, 1239, concerning the Churches of S. Michael and S. Lawrence, Appleby, in which he speaks of B[ernard] and H[ugh], Bishops of Carlisle to whom the right of institution belonged, both now dead.

(4) There is an interesting series of charters in the same *Register* about the Church of Nether Denton, in Cumberland. A controversy having arisen concerning this Church between the Monks of Wederhal and the Canons of Lanercost, they entered

into an important Composition (No. 119). Among the names which appear in the document are those of men well known in the history of this period (see the notes there). From these names, the date of the Composition must be from 1198 to 1214. But there is a confirmation (No. 117) of this Composition by Bernard, Bishop of Carlisle, with the assent of his Chapter; among the witnesses are those who can be proved to have lived in the first few years of the century.

(5) The next charter (No. 118) is a confirmation by Bishop Hugh (1218—23) of this concession to the Houses of Wederhale and Lanercost made by his predecessor B[ernard], formerly Bishop of Carlisle.

(6) We then have (No. 122) the assent of Chapter, referred to above, or confirmation of John, Prior and the Convent of S. Mary, Carlisle, of the concession made by " B. Episcopus noster " to the Convent of S. Mary, York, and the Houses of Wederhal and Lanercost concerning the Church of Denton "as is more fully contained in the instrument of the same which our Bishop executed in this matter."

(7) In the *Register of Lanercost* (MS. viii. 3) there is a confirmation charter of " B[ernardus] Karleolensis Episcopus." Among the witnesses are John, Prior of Carlisle, and Alexander de Daker, whose names appear in the charter of Bishop Bernard in the *Register of Wetherhal*.

(8) The next charter (MS. viii. 4) is the confirmation by the Prior and Convent of Carlisle of the above concession of "Venerabilis Pater noster B[ernardus], Karleolensis Episcopus," the witnesses being nearly the same, including John, the Prior of Carlisle.

(9) There is in the same *Register* (MS. xiv. 21) the confirmation by Odard, son of Adam (de Wigton, died 1208—9), of a grant of land in Ulveton to the Canons of Lanercost. The first witness is " Dominus Bernardus, Karliolen. Episcopus "; another witness, among several of the period, is Walter Beinin, who often appears about this time and in the Pipe Rolls as late as 1214.

(10) In the *Chartulary of Whitby* (ed. Atkinson, No. xxxv) " Bernardus, Karleolensis Episcopus " confirms to the Monks of

S. Peter and S. Hylda of Wyteby the Church of Crosseby Ravenswart (in Westmoreland). The first witnesses are Symon, Dean
of York, and Hamund (or Hamo), Treasurer of York, witnesses
to the Composition (No. 119) referred to above. Another
witness is Laurence, Prior of Gyseburne, who occurs in 1211.

(11) and (12)   The two next charters (Nos. xxxvi, xxxvii) are
similar confirmations by Bishop Bernard about the same time and
with nearly the same witnesses.

(13)   Then follows (No. xxxviii) a charter which speaks of
"Venerabilis Pater noster Bernardus Karliol. Episcopus" as
being then dead. It is a confirmation by H. the Prior and the
Convent of Carlisle of Bishop Bernard's concession of the Church
of Crosseby Ravenswart referred to above. H. the Prior is
probably Henry de Mariscis, who became Prior in 1214
(*Chronicon de Lanercost,* p. 14).

(14)   Another charter in the same *Chartulary* (No. cclxx) is the
confirmation of the Church of Engleby in Cleveland to the same
monastery by Gaufrid, Archbishop of York (1191—1207). The
first witness is B[ernard], Bishop of Carlisle.

(15)   There is also an *Inspeximus* (No. cccxiii) by Radulf
Irton, Bishop of Carlisle, dated 1281, recapitulating the several
grants and confirmations referring to the Church of Crosseby,
among which, in full, is that of "Bernard our predecessor"
quoted above.

(16)   In the *Register of Holm Cultram* (Dean and Chapter
MS. p. 14) there is a confirmation by B[ernard], Bishop of
Carlisle, of the grant by Hugh de Morevilla of the Church of
Burgo. The only witness given is Thomas, Prior of Wederhall.
Hugh de Morevilla died in 1202—3, and his grant (MS. p. 13) is
attested by Thomas, son of Gospatric, who died in 1201 (p. 390 *n.*),
and Thomas de Brumefeld who is witness to the first charter
of Bishop Bernard mentioned above (No. 17).

(17)   Another confirmation of the same grant (Harleian MS.
p. 304) by B[ernard], Bishop, is also given, in somewhat different
terms and with no witnesses.

(18)   In the *Register of Archbishop Walter Gray* there is the
confirmation (No. ccxlviii. ed. J. Raine, p. 58) in the year 1233 of
the grants made by B., H. and W., Bishops of Carlisle, to the

Abbey of Fountains, of the Church of Crosthwayt (in Cumber-land). These are evidently Bernard, Hugh and Walter, successive Bishops of Carlisle, Bishop Walter being then alive. Although these confirmation grants of the Bishops have not been found, we have the copy of the original grant of this Church to the Abbey (MSS. Cotton, Tiberius C. xii. p. 97) by "Alicia de Rumely, daughter of William, son of Dunecann." This grant she makes "in mea viduitate et ligia potestate." This was her first widow-hood in the years 1193 to 1196, as is shown by the grant being confirmed with others in a charter of Richard I. (Dugdale, *Monasticon*, No. lxxvi. vol. v. p. 310), who died in April, 1199.

(19) There is a deed of the institution, by Gaufrid, Arch-bishop of York (1191—1207) of Robert de Langar, Clerk, to the Church of Langar, Notts. This is given in Raine's edition of *Archbishop Gray's Register* (p. 73 *n.*). The first witness is B[ernard], Bishop of Carlisle, others of the witnesses also belong to this period.

(20) Among the Duchy of Lancaster Records (Box A. No. 393) there is the original deed of Confirmation by B[ernard], Bishop of Carlisle, of a grant by Anselm de Furness to the House of the Blessed Mary which he founded between Castlerig and the water which is called Lauther. Anselm de Furness appears in the Pipe Rolls for Westmoreland in 1198; he also attests a confirmation by Robert de Veteriponte, dated April 24th, 1211, of the grants of Thomas, son of Gospatric and his son Thomas to the Abbey of Heppe (Shap). His daughter Helena married Ralph D'Aincourt. There is no date, and there are no witnesses to the confirmation of Bishop Bernard; but his seal is appended, bearing the legend—BERNARDUS: DEI: GRACIA: CARLEOLENSIS: EPISC: (Illustrative Documents, XXI.).

(21) Among the same *Records* (Box A. No. 416) there is a document dated September 17th, 1343—a return of the Prior and Chapter of Carlisle (Illustrative Documents, xx.). They state among other things: "Cui quidem Adelwaldo postea im-mediate successit Bernardus, et post Bernardum, Hugo."

(22) Bishop Nicolson says in his Manuscript Collections (vol. iii. p. 127; vol. ii. pp. 379, 402, 487) that it appears from original grants in his possession Bishop Bernard confirmed the

grant of the Rectory of Shap, or Heppe, and certain lands, to the Abbey of Heppe, made by Thomas, son of Gospatric, the Founder. This Thomas died in 1201. He names some of the witnesses to the confirmation, among them John de Hardcla, parson of Moreton (Long Marton in Westmoreland), who is also witness to the charter of Robert de Veteriponte in 1211 referred to above on No. (20). These original documents of Bp Nicolson's are not forthcoming.

(23) and (24) Two similar charters of Alicia de Rumely, daughter of William, son of Duncan, are given by Dugdale (*Monasticon*, vi. 271), in which she grants in her widowhood the Churches of Bridekirke and Derehame in Alredale (Cumberland) to the Church of S. Mary of Gyseburne and the Canons there. The former is given more fully from the Dodsworth MSS. in the *Chartulary of Gyseburne* (ed. W. Brown, ii. 319). The first witness is B[ernard] then Bishop of Carlisle. This was in her second widowhood; for her two husbands Gilbert Pipard and Robert de Curtenay are mentioned. The former died in 1193, the latter in 1209—10: and she appears as a widow in the Pipe Rolls for Cumberland in 1210. The date of the charters therefore lies between 1210 and July 1214, when we know that the See was vacant. Other witnesses are J. (John de Ebor), Abbot of Fountains 1203 to 1211, Alexander de Dacre, Adam de Aspatric, Dean of Alredale and others of the period.

(25) and (26). Among the *Regesta* of Pope Honorius III. are two confirmations to the Prior and Canons of Giseburn, under date April 27th, 1218, of the grants to them of the Churches of Bridekirke and Deram in the Diocese of Carlisle made by B[ernard] sometime Bishop of Ragusa, when Bishop of Carlisle, with the assent of his Chapter and the consent of A[licia] the patron (*Calendar of Papal Registers*, ed. W. H. Bliss, i. 54). These Papal Letters are important as proving the identity of the Archbishop of Ragusa with Bernard, Bishop of Carlisle, who confirmed grants made in that Diocese. They also shew that he issued deeds of confirmation of the two charters, No. (23) and No. (24) mentioned above, to which he was also witness.

(27) In an Inquisition held at Carlisle in January, 1328—29 (*Inquis. ad quod damnum*, 2 Edw. III. No. 3), it was shewn that

the Church of Arturethe (Arthuret) was granted to the convent of Geddeworthe (Jedburgh) in Scotland by Turgis de Russedale, Lord of the manor of Lydale, and appropriated with the consent of Lord Bernard, second Bishop of Carlisle, and his Chapter.

We see from this long series of documents that Bishop Bernard, formerly Archbishop of Ragusa, discharged episcopal functions in his own right in the Diocese of Carlisle. He was recognised as Bishop of Carlisle by the Prior and Chapter, by Popes, and by his successors in the See, and as being of equal authority with his predecessor Bishop Athelwold and his successor Bishop Hugh. He was also recognised as Bishop of Carlisle in the Diocese of York. It is clear from some of those deeds in which his name appears that he must have been collated in 1204, soon after the Letters Patent were issued; and from others that he retained the Bishopric for some years, probably until very nearly the time of the vacancy which is noted in July, 1214. No evidence is yet forthcoming as to whether he vacated the office by death, or resignation, or deprivation.

It seems therefore to admit of no doubt that Bernard was not Bishop of Carlisle in the 12th century, but that he filled the See in the reign of King John, probably from 1204 to 1214.

APPENDIX E.

The Priors of Wetherhal.

1. Richard de Reme is said by Leland to have been the first Prior of Wetherhal ("primus inter Priores ibi numeratus," *Collectanea* i. p. 25). Todd also says, "Primus qui Prioratui præfuit erat Richardus temp. Willi. II." (*Notitia*, MS.). Leland gives no authority and is not reliable. Todd puts *Reg. Wed.* in the margin, but as there is no such statement in the *Register of Wetherhal*, no reliance is to be placed upon him.

2. Radulph, Prior of Wederhale, occurs in a Concession in the *Register of Wetherhal* (No. 72) of some land and wood by Hildred de Carlel, from the names of the many witnesses about 1130.

3. Thomas, Prior of Wederhall, is witness to a charter, in the *Register of Holm Cultram* (MS. p. 14) of Bernard, Bishop of Carlisle, between 1204 and 1214, confirming the grant by Hugo de Morvilla of the Church of Burgo (Burgh) to the Abbey of Holm Cultram.

4. Suffred, Prior of Wederhala, is witness to a Charter in the *Chartulary of Whitby* (ed. Atkinson, No. xxxix) of Hugh, Bishop of Carlisle, between 1218 and 1223, confirming the Church of Crosseby Ravenswart to the Abbot and Monks of Wyteby. This Charter is also quoted in an *Inspeximus* of the Official of the court of York (No. cccxiii) dated 1281. In the *Register of Lanercost* (MS. viii. 8), S. Prior of Wedderhall is a witness to the Assent of the Prior and Convent of Carlisle to the Confirmation by Bishop Hugh of certain Churches to the Prior and Convent of Lanercost. The said Confirmation (MS. viii. 7) is witnessed by G. Prior of

Wederhal, an evident error of the copyist for S., the other witnesses being identical in the two documents.

5. William Rundel, Prior of Wederhal, is witness to a Charter of Nicholas Legat in the *Register of Wetherhal* (No. 212) concerning certain land in Morland. The Charter refers to Walter, Bishop of Carlisle; and its date must be between 1223 and 1239 when this William Rundel, or Runndele, was made Abbot of S. Mary's, York. As Abbot of S. Mary's, he appears in a Final Concord in the same *Register* (No. 226) dated November 8th, 1241. He died November 29th, 1244 (Dugdale, *Monasticon* iii. 538). W. Prior of Wederhal appears as Proctor in a Form of Peace (No. 225) entered into between the Convent of S. Mary's, York, and the Burgesses of Appelby, dated October 2nd, 1225; also in two Agreements (Nos. 46, 210) the same W. is found, and William in a third (No. 116); all clearly about the same period. In the *Register of Lanercost* (MS. ii. 21) William, Prior of Wederhall, is witness to a Charter of Rolland de Vallibus together with Bishop Walter and several of the witnesses to the first Charter (No. 212) referred to above.

6. Thomas, Prior of Wederhal, is party to a Convention with Alan faber of Gringeldic in the *Register of Wetherhal* (No. 171) dated Pentecost, 1241. This cannot be the same with Thomas de Wymondham (see below) as two Priors clearly came between.

7. Richard de Rotomago (Rouen), Prior of Wederhal, is witness to a charter of Beatrix, widow of Robert de Neuby, in the *Register of Wetherhal* (No. 87) concerning her land at Wederhal. From the names, the date is evidently about 1250 or a few years later. Richard, Prior of Wederhal, occurs in an Assignment by Bishop Silvester (de Everdon) of a taxation of the Church of S. Laurence, Appleby, for the Vicar of the same, dated January 25th, 1251 (see Illustrative Documents, x.).

8. Henry de Tutesbiri (Tutbury, Staffordshire), Prior of Wederhal, is party to a Convention with John Spendlime in the *Register of Wetherhal* (No. 66) concerning some land at Wederhal, dated November 11th, 1257. Henry, Prior of Wederhal, also occurs in a Charter of Adam son of Roger de Karliol in the same *Register* (No. 76) and about the same date.

9. Thomas de Wymundham, Prior of Wederhal, is party to a Convention with Symon, Master of the Hospital of S. Nicholas, near Carlisle, in the *Register of Wetherhal* (No. 96) dated Monday before Ash Wednesday 1270. The Assize Rolls for Cumberland (see Illustrative Documents, XXIX. 2) shew that in November, 1292, Thomas de Wymundham had been not long dead, that he had been Prior of Wederhale for the six previous years, and had been succeeded by William de Tannefeld.

10. William de Tanefeld, Prior of Wederhal, is a party to a Convention with Lady Idonea de Layburn, in the *Register of Wetherhal* (No. 230) concerning a pasture near Appleby, dated November 11th, 1292. From the note on the preceding Prior, we see that he had not been long appointed. At an ordination held at Hautwysell (*hodie* Haltwhistle) on December 18th, 1293, W. Prior of Wederhale, presented William de Morlund, the Bishop of Carlisle ordaining *vice* the Bishop of Durham (*Register of Bp Halton*, MS. p. 12). In the same Bishop's *Register* (p. 7 *b*) there is the following: "Memorandum, quod XV Kal. Aprilis A.D. MCCC tercio (March 18th, 1303) admissus fuit Dominus Will. de Tanefeld ad Prioratum de Wederhal et commissa fuit (eidem) cura ecclesiarum parochialium pertinentium ad Prioratum antedictum." There seems to be an error here as to the date or more probably the name, as at this time John de Gilling was Prior (see below). It would appear that W. de Tanefeld had resigned the office, but there is no record of the date of his resignation or when John de Gilling succeeded. As Abbot of S. Mary's, York, the latter nominated William de Tanefeld as his proctor to attend the Parliament held in Carlisle on the Octave of St Hilary, 35 Edward I. (January 20th, 1307) and calls him "Fratrem Will. de Tanefeld monachum meum" not "Priorem" (*The Parliamentary Writs*, ed. Sir F. Palgrave, vol. i. p. 186 : *Rolls of Parliament*, Record Com. vol. i. p. 188). William de Tainfelde, formerly monk of S. Mary's, York, and Prior of Wederhall, was appointed Prior of Durham by Papal provision, dated February 22nd, 1308 (*Papal Registers*, ed. W. H. Bliss, ii. 40) and installed September 14th, on the Feast of S. Cuthbert. Durham was also a Benedictine convent. A contemporary writer, Robert de Graystanes, who was also

Sub-Prior, asserts that the collation was purchased for 3000 marcs to the Pope and 1000 marcs to the Cardinals. He thus describes William de Tanefelde—"Erat statura procerus, vultu decorus, moribus placidus, sumptibus largus, sed in providendo minus sciens. Lætabatur in magnitudine familiæ, in multitudine et frequentia conviventium; et unde talia sustineret non satis provide cogitabat." Two of the Durham monks formally waited on him at Wetherhal begging him to accept the provision. He is spoken of as if he were then the Prior of Wetherhal, though John de Thorp had been nominated to the office after the promotion of John de Gilling to be Abbot of S. Mary's. The large sums mentioned above had to be found by the Priory. These with other debts seriously impoverished them, and they had to have recourse to the money-lenders. The whole account gives a good idea of the rapacity of the Papal Court. The new Prior was not one to consider the poverty of the House "sed sumptibus excessivis debita domus auxit potius quam diminuit" (*Hist. Dunelm. Scriptores Tres*, Surtees Soc. vol. 9, pp. 85—89).

William de Tanefeld resigned the Priory of Durham in 1313; and is said to have died in February, 1342 (Dugdale, *Monasticon*, i. 230), but so late a date seems improbable. In the *Registrum Palatinum Dunelmense* (ed. Hardy, i. 355, 361 seq.) there is given the petition of the Sub-Prior and Convent of Durham to elect a Prior in place of William de Tanefeld, their late Prior, who had resigned; it is dated June 14th, 1313; also the form of resignation and the provision made (the cell of Jarrow and other property) for him on account of his age and infirmities. In the *Depositions of the Court of Durham* (Surtees Society, vol. 21, p. 9), also in the *Registrum Palatinum* (i. 476), there is a Licence to William de Tanefeld, late Prior of Durham, "declinans in senectam et senium," to be excused fasting at Advent, dated December 2nd, 1314.

11. John de Gilling, or Gylling, Prior of Wederhal, was made Abbot of S. Mary's, York, and received the temporalities, August 19th, 1303; he died May 24th, 1313 (Dugdale, *Monasticon*, iii. 538). In an Inquisition made in 1326, we find it stated—"Rogerus de Bello Loco dicit quod Dominus Johannes de Gilling dudum Prior de Wederhal et post Abbas de Ebor. &c." (see Illustrative Doc. XII.).

12. John de Thorp was nominated to be Prior of Wederhal on November 10th, 1303, by J. (John de Gilling) Abbot of S. Mary's, York, in the following form :—

"Venerabili in Christo Patri ac Dño suo semper reverendo, Dño J. Ep̄o Karliol. suus devotissimus J. permissione Divina Abbas Monasterii beate Marie Ebor. Salutem cum omni reverentia et honore tam debitis quam devotis. Quia Prioratus Celle nostre de Wederhal cujus nuper Prior existimus (*sic*) vestre Diocesis per creationem vestram in Abbatem dicti Monasterii jam vacat ne Cella predicta in spiritualibus et temporalibus per defectum regiminis ulterius detrimentum patiatur, dilectum nobis in Christo fratrem J. de Thorp nostri monasterii commonachum quem ad regimen dicti prioratus idoneum reputamus, vobis in Priorem dicti loci tenore presentium presentamus; devote supplicantes quatinus ipsum in Priorem dicti loci sine difficultate velitis admittere, secundum formam compositionis ultimo initæ inter vestros et nostros predecessores, ac ulterius exercere circa eum, cum gratia et favore, quod vestrum fuerit in hac parte. Vos ad regimen Ecclesiæ sue conservet Deus in prosperitate jocunda per tempora diuturna. Dat. Ebor. iiij Id. Novembris A.D. mccciii" (*Register of Bp Halton*, MS. p. 73).

The Composition here spoken of is that entered into with Bishop Chause in 1266 and given in the *Register*, No. 34.

13. Robert de Gyseburgh was appointed to the Priory of Wetherhal by Papal provision in 1309, but John de Thorp, as we see above, being nominated by the Abbot of S. Mary's, York, was already in possession and opposed him. Writs from the King to the Bishop followed, prohibiting John de Thorp from obeying any Papal mandate until the matter should have been heard in the King's Court. John de Thorp appears to have resigned, for in 1313 we find Robert, Prior of Wederhal, was in possession. Prior Robert would seem to have been early familiar with debt. In April, 1309, he obtained a licence from the Pope to contract a loan of 2000 gold florins to meet his expenses at the Apostolic See. A mandate was issued in March, 1312, by the Pope to warn Robert de Giseburn, Prior, and the Convent of Wederhale "who have been allowed to contract a loan up to the amount of 2000 florins and have borrowed from a firm of Florentine

merchants a sum of 100 marcs, to repay the same" (*Papal Registers*, ed. W. H. Bliss, ii. 53, 94.) In 1313 Prior Robert was excommunicated, and the Convent was put under a Papal interdict for not paying the 100 marcs to certain merchants of Florence; Robert then resigned (see Illustrative Documents, IX. and *Register of Bp Halton*, MS. pp. 125, 131, 168).

14. Gilbert de Bothil was instituted Prior of Wederhal on March 22nd, 1313, on the resignation of Robert de Gyseburgh. Upon him was also laid the above debt of 100 marcs with interest and expenses amounting to another 100 marcs. He was called to the office of Prior of S. Mary's, York, in 1318 (*Register of Bp Halton*, MS. pp. 168, 214).

15. Adam de Dalton, monk of S. Mary's, York, was presented by the Abbot to the Priory of Wederhal in 1318 (*Register of Bp Halton*, MS. p. 214). Dugdale (*Monasticon*, iii. 581) gives a reference to Harleian MSS. 6971, fol. 165 (*Ex Registro penes Dec. Capit. Ebor. R.*). There he is said to be Prior de Wederhale in 1340. In 1341 he seems to have been engaged in a great controversy with the Chapter of York (see *Register of Bp Kirkby*, MS. pp. 421, 422), and in the same year to have died or resigned.

16. On November 19th, 1341, William de Tanfeld, a second evidently of the name, was admitted into the Priory of Wederhal (*Regist. of Bishop Kirkby*, MS. p. 428). This cannot be the same as William de Tanefeld who became Prior of Durham. We saw the latter was an old man broken with infirmity 28 years before. He had received a valuable pension from Durham, and would not in any case have been allowed to return to the Priory of Wetherhal. In the *Register of Bishop Welton* (MS. p. 6) there is a record of the institution of this second William on June 21st, 1354; but it does not appear what was the cause of this delay or second institution. He is a party to a Convention with Richard de Salkeld, Lord of Corkby, concerning a fishery, dated Monday, August 5th, 1342 (*Register of Wetherhal*, No. 244). Dr Todd (MS. *Notitia*) calls him incorrectly William de Santfield, giving the authority of the Bishop's Register. A copy of a seal of this Prior, said to have been appended to a deed of 1342, is given in Hutchinson, *History, Cumberland*, i. 348.

17. William de Brudford, or Brydford, "sacræ paginæ professor" and Monk of S. Mary's, York, was admitted into the Priory of Wederhal in August 1373 (*Register of Bp Appleby*, MS. p. 258). He was made Abbot of S. Mary's, York, in 1382, and he died in August, 1389 (Dugdale, *Monasticon*, iii. 539).

18. Richard de Appilton, Monk of S. Mary's, York, was instituted to the Priory of Wederhale in 1382, there being at the time some dispute about the Churches of Wetherhal and Warwick (*Register of Bp Appleby*, MS. p. 342).

19. Thomas Pygott, or Pigot, was admitted to the Priory of Wederhale on October 12th, 1386 (*Register of Bp Appleby*, MS. p. 362). He appeared in court at York in 1392, being Prior of Wederhale, as Proctor for the Abbot and Convent of S. Mary at York, in a trial concerning the repairs of the chancel of the Church at Brumfeld (*Register of Bp Appleby*, pp. 365—367). He was confirmed Abbot of S. Mary's, York, on May 24th, 1399 (Dugdale, *Monasticon*, iii. 539, quoting Pat. 21 Ric. II. p. 1, and Harleian MS. 6961, fol. 253).

20. John de Stutton, Prior of the Priory of Wederhale, is party to an arrangement concerning the Chapel of S. Mary in Le Wyth in the Parish of Morland dated April 15, 1405 (see Illustrative Documents, XVIII.).

21. Thomas Stanley, Abbot (*sic*) of Wederhill, was returned by the Commissioners in a List of Gentry of the County of Cumberland in 12 Henry VI. 1434 (S. Jefferson, *Leath Ward* p. 495).

22. Robert Hertford, Prior of Wederhal, is a party to an agreement with John de Warthwick, September 21st, 1444 (Extract from Carlisle Dean and Chapter *Registers*).

23. Thomas Bothe, Prior of Wedyrhale, appears in an Account of the lands of Morehouse, in the lordship of Warthewyk, belonging to the Priory, dated January 26th, 1455, and given in the *Register of Wetherhal* (No. 239). He was elected Abbot of S. Mary's, York, Oct. 16th, 1464, and his name occurs as late as 1481 (Dugdale, *Monasticon*, iii. 539, quoting Pat. 4 Ed. IV. p. 1);

his successor, William Sever, afterwards Bishop of Carlisle, was appointed in 1485.

24. Robert Esyngwalde, Prior of Wedyrhall, occurs in an original Parchment Rental dated October, 1490 (see Illustrative Documents, XLIV.).

25. In the Carlisle Dean and Chapter *Minute Books* (vol. ii. p. 11, also in vol. i. p. 16ᵃ) there is a lease of the tithes of Morland, dated January 25th, 155⁸⁄₉, which refers to the grant of a lease by W. (William Thornton), Abbot of S. Mary's, York, on October 17th, 1535, at the expiration of a lease for 41 years granted by Robert Allonbye, Prior (of Wederhal). This would bring the date of the Prior to about 1494.

26. William Thornton, Prior of Wederhale, was made Abbot of S. Mary's, York, in March, 1530 (Dugdale, *Monasticon*, iii. 539, quoting Orig. 22 Hen. VIII. MS. Lands. p. 62). Over the south window of the chancel of Wetherhal Church is the inscription

"Orate p a'i'a Willi'mi Thornton Abbatis."

27. Richard Wederhall, Prior of Wederhall, appears in the *Valor Ecclesiasticus*, 26 Hen. VIII. 1534—35 (Illustrative Documents, XLV.). Over the chancel door of Wetherhal Church is the inscription

"Orate p anima Richardi Wedderhall."

28. Radulphus, or Ralph, Hartley was Prior of Wetherhall at the surrender of the Priory on October 20th, 1538. The Surrender, signed by him, has a seal with the initials R. H. (Illustrative Documents, XXXIX.). He was party to a lease dated June 20th, 1538, and referred to in a lease dated January 25th, 155⁸⁄₉ (Carlisle Dean and Chapter *Minute Books*, vol. i. p. 16). He received a pension of £12 per annum, but beyond this he had a life interest in the Rectory of the Churches of Wetherhal and Warwick together with the tithes of the Chapels of S. Anthony and S. Severin. These were secured to him by Royal Letters Patent under the seal of the Court of Augmentations and were valued at £26. 13s. 4d. (Illustrative Documents, XL.). He was alive in 1555 for in the Roll of Payments to the Religious in 2 & 3 Philip and Mary his name appears—"Wetherail, *nuper*

Mon. Annuit. Edwardi Waller, per annum xl s. Penc. Radulphi Hartley, per annum xij li."

List of Priors.	Known Dates and Limits.
1. Richard de Reme (?)	circ. 1100
2. Radulph	circ. 1130
3. Thomas	temp. Bp Bernard 1204—14
4. Suffred	temp. Bp Hugh 1218—23
5. William Rundel	1225 ; 1223—39 ; elected Abbot of S. Mary's, York 1239
6. Thomas	1241
7. Richard de Rotomago	1251
8. Henry de Tutesbiri	1257
9. Thomas de Wymundham	1270 ; ob. 1292
10. William de Tanefeld (1)	1292 ; 1293 ; elected Prior of Durham 1309
11. John de Gilling	In 1303 elected Abbot of S. Mary's, York
12. John de Thorp	1303
13. Robert de Gyseburgh	1313
14. Gilbert de Bothil	1313 ; 1318
15. Adam de Dalton	1318 ; 1340 ; 1341
16. William de Tanfeld (2)	1341 ; 1342 ; 1354
17. William de Brudford	1373 ; elected Abbot of S. Mary's 1382
18. Richard de Appilton	1382
19. Thomas Pygott	1386 ; 1392 ; confirmed Abbot of S. Mary's 1399
20. John de Stutton	1405
21. Thomas Stanley	1434
22. Robert Hertford	1444
23. Thomas Bothe	1455 ; elected Abbot of S. Mary's 1464
24. Robert Esyngwalde	1490
25. Robert Allonbye	circ. 1494
26. William Thornton	Elected Abbot of S. Mary's 1530
27. Richard Wederhall	1534—35
28. Radulph Hartley	1538 ; alive 1555

GENERAL INDEX.

THE principal note on any place or subject will be found, as a rule, under the first mention of the same in the *Register*.

P.

33

INDEX OF PERSONAL NAMES.

The letter *c* after a numeral denotes that the person is a party to the charter.

The principal note on any person will, as a rule, be found under the first mention of the person in the *Register*.

P. Abbot of Whitby, 378
P. Prior, 48; *see* John Prior
P. sub-prior of Durham, 213
Pagan, knt., 145
— s. of John, 19, 26
Paganel, Jordan, 27
Palmer, William, 176
Paris, Robert de, 135, 163
Pateshull, Simon de, justiciary, 94
Penda, 384 *n*
Penereth, Normann de, 149
Peninton, Alan de, 131 *n*, mayor of
    Carlisle, 181 *n*
Penrith, Eliphe de, 5
Pepin, Roger, 60, 350, 355
Perci, Galfrid de, 38
— Robert de, justiciary, 94
Peroy, Roger, chaplain of le Wyth
    (Morland), 43 *n*, 414
Peter, Abbot of Whitby, 378
— chaplain, 57
— s. of William, 83
— vicar of Burgo, 194
Petricurta, J. de, 61
Peverel, Pagan, 19, 26
— William, 19 *n*, 23
Pippard, Gilbert, 388, 502
Pistrina, Walter de, 339
Plancha, Roger de, 310, 368
Pointū, Alexander de, justiciary, 95
Pollard, William, 244, 269
Ponte, Werri de, 133 *c*
Pontefract, William de, 53
Pope of Rome, Alexander III., 72 ;
    Gregory IX., 58 *c*; Honorius III.,
    49 *c*, 484 *n*
Popelton, John de, 350
Porta, Adam de, justiciary, 94
— Stephen de, 169, 170
Porter, Jordan, 179
— Walter, 262
Prato, Warin de, 366
Preston, Radulph de, 236
Pygott, Thomas, prior of Wetherhal,
    510

R. Abbot, *see* Robert
R. Archdeacon, *see* Robert
R. Bishop, *see* Robert
R. clerk, 260
R. Dean, *see* Roger
R. Prior, *see* Radulph
R. s. of William, 174
Racī, Simon de, 159
Radulph, 277
— chaplain, 12, 13, 89, 127
— clerk, 129, 135, 163, 175, 183,
    205, 206, 207, 231, 255, 257,
    287, 288, 290
— clerk of Burgo, 188
— clerk of Wetherhal, 298
— or R. (Barri), Prior of Carlisle,
    182, 200, 205, 206, 207, 208,
    230, 238, 260, 264, 265, 269,
    278, 291, 296, 323, 325, 342,
    345, 346, 349, 381
— Prior of Wetherhal, 144, 145,
    504
— s. of Galfrid, 146
— s. of Godefrid, 354, 357, 358
— s. of Herbert, 354, 358
— s. of Landric, 26
— s. of Theobald, 241 *c*
— s. of Umfrid, 185
— s. of Wido, 146
Raginald, camerarius, 345
Raimbald s. of William, 145
Rainald, monk, 144
Raneswic, *see* Raveneswic
Ranulph, 147
— Bishop of Durham, 23
— clerk, 114, 122, 289
— præpositus, 250
— s. of Alan (nativus), 261; Alicia
    w. of, 261
— s. of Henry, justiciary, 171
— s. of Umfrid, 129, 290, 363
Raveneswic, or Raveneswiche, Adam
    de, 197, 199; Alan s. of, 198,
    217, 219; Thomas s. of, 198, 217,
    219

Tymparun, William, 179, 181

Tyrer, Simon de, vicar of Camboc, 198 *n*

Tyreth, Richard de, 334

Tysun, Gilbert, 12, 14

Uctrid, summonitor, 387

— s. of Fergus, *see* Huctred

— s. of Lyolf, 39, 143 *n*

— s. of Ravenchel, 311

Udard, *see* Odard

Ulnesby, or Ulvesby (Ousby), Bernard, parson of, 220; Walter, parson, 354

— Adam de, 201, 316

— Hamund de, 292

— Richard de, 252

— Robert s. of William de, 253

— Walter de, Archdeacon of Carlisle, 278; Walter de, Official, 124, 292, 345, 357; *see* Walter

— William de, 178 *n*

Ulvesthwaite, or Hulveswait, Henry de, 254, 261 *c*, 286 *c*

Umfraius, 255

Umfrid, 212, 288, 289, 295

Uthexol, Robert de, 312

Vachel, Robert, 289

Valle, Michael s. of David del, 276

Vallibus, or Vaus, Eustace de, 103 *n*

— Hubert de, (1) 65 *n*, 196 *n*, 301 *n*, 385, 389 *n*; grant to, 418; (2) [s. of Robert (2)], 88 *n*, 303, 306; Matilda w. of, 304 *n*

— John de, 131 *n*

— Ranulph de, (1) 87 *n*, 224, 225; (2) [s. of Alexander], 308

— Robert de, (1) sheriff, 64, 83, 85, 101, 150 *n*, 186 *n*, 210 *n*, 301 *c*; grant to Lanercost, 419; Ada w. of, 66 *n*; (2) [s. of Ranulph (1)], 66 *n*, 87 *n*, 224, 225, 233 *n*, 302 *c*, 304 *n*, 305 *c*; (3) 107; (4) juvenis, 86

Vallibus, Matilda de [d. of Hubert (2)], 106 *n*, 302 *n*, 306; *see* Multon

— Roland de, (1) 88 *n*, 120, 232, 237, 270, 306; (2) 382 *n*; Alexander s. of, 120 *n*

— William de, 131, 136, 138, 152, 160, 239, 262, 299

Vasy, Thomas, 375

Venise, or Venice, Peter de, 389; Astius, b. of, 389

Verdun, John de, 38

Vernun, Richard de, *see* Gernun

Verrar, or Werrer, Gamell, 158, 159, 161

Vescy, John de, Abbot of Shap, 330 *n*

Veteriponte, or Vipont, Ivo de, 233 *n*, 328 *n*, 344 *n*

— John de, 62 *n*, 328, 333 *n*, 341, 357; Sibilla w. of, 329

— Robert de, (1) 62 *n*, 328 *n*, 329, 347 *n*, 348 *n*, 351 *n*, 394 *c*; Idonea (de Builli) w. of, 328 *n*; Christiana d. of, 238 *n*, 329 *n*

— Robert de, (2) [s. of John], 38 *n*, 315 *n*, 316 *n*, 321 *n*, 326 *n*, 330 *n*, 348 *n*, 351 *n*, 363 *n*; Isabella d. of, 315 *n*, 330 *n*, 351 *n*, 363 *n*, 370 *n*; Idonea d. of, *see* de Leyburne

— Thomas, Bishop of Carlisle, 61 *c*, 319 *n*

— William de, 13 *n*, 328 *n*; Matilda w. of, 13 *n*, 328 *n*

Vitalis, priest, 145

Vivat, 147

Vivian, Papal legate, 85 *n*

W. Archdeacon of Notingham, 211, 214 *c*; *see* Testard

W. Archdeacon of Carlisle, *see* Walter

W. Bishop, *see* Walter, Bishop; 210, 212, *see* Bernard, Bishop

W. chaplain, 55, 213

— — of Cumreu, 265, 266

THE REGISTER OF
THE PRIORY OF WETHERHAL,

BY THE

VENERABLE ARCHDEACON PRESCOTT, D.D.,

CARLISLE.

LIST OF SUBSCRIBERS

Banks, E. H., Highmoor House, Wigton.
Barnes, Henry, M.D., 6, Portland Square, Carlisle.
Barrow-in-Furness, The Right Rev. the Bishop of
Bethell, W., Rise Park, Hull.
5 Birkbeck, R., F.S.A., 20, Berkeley Square, London.
Blakesley, G. H., 12, Old Square, Lincoln's Inn.
Bower, Rev. R., St. Cuthbert's Vicarage, Carlisle.
Bowman, A. N., Portland Square, Carlisle.
Brown, W., Trenholme, Northallerton.
10 Brown, Rev. William, Old Elvet, Durham.
Burnyeat, William, Millgrove, Moresby.
Burrow, Rev. James J., Ireby Vicarage, Mealsgate,
    Carlisle.

Calverley, Rev. W. S., F.S.A., The Vicarage, Aspatria.
15 Carlisle, The Right Rev. the Lord Bishop of, Rose
    Castle, Carlisle. (2 copies)
Carlisle, The Very Rev. the Dean of, The Abbey, Carlisle.
Carlisle Public Library, Tullie House.
Carlisle, The Earl of, Naworth Castle.
Carruthers, Richard, Eden Grove, Carlisle.
20 Collingwood, W. G., M.A., Lane Head, Coniston.
Constable, W., Holme Head, Carlisle.
Cowie, The Very Rev. Dean, The Deanery, Exeter.
Cowper, H. S., F.S.A., Yewfield, Outgate, Ambleside.
Creighton, Miss, 13, Warwick Square, Carlisle.
25 Crowder, W. J. R., Jun., 4, Portland Square, Carlisle.

Diggle, Ven. Archdeacon, The Abbey, Carlisle.
Dudgeon, W. L. G., 65, Evelyn Gardens, South Kensington, S.W.

Ecroyd, Edward, Armathwaite, Cumberland.
Eyre and Spottiswoode, 5, Middle New Street, E.C.

30 Farrer, William, Marton House, Skipton-on-Craven.
Ferguson, The Worshipful Chancellor, F.S.A., LL.M., Carlisle. (2 copies)
Ferguson, R., F.S.A., Morton, Carlisle.
Ferguson, G. H. H. Oliphant, Broadfield House, Carlisle.

35 Gilbanks, Rev. G. E., Abbey Town, Carlisle.
Grainger, Francis, Southerfield, Abbey Town, Carlisle.
Guildhall Library, London, E.C.

Hair, Martin, 13, Abbey Street, Carlisle.
Harrison, James, Newby Bridge, Ulverston.
40 Harrison, J., Dunthwaite, Cockermouth.
Harvey, Rev. Canon, Lincoln.
Haswell, Francis, M.B., C.M., Penrith.
Haverfield, F., M.A., F.S.A., Christ Church, Oxford.
Hawkesbury, Lord, F.S.A., Kirkham Abbey, York.
45 Helder, Augustus, M.P., Corkickle, Whitehaven.
Heysham, A. Mounsey, Carlisle.
Hibbert, Percy, Plumtree Hall, Milnthorpe.
Hills, His Honour Judge, Corby Castle, Carlisle.
Hinds, James P., 20, Fisher Street, Carlisle.
50 Hoare, Rev. J. N., St. John's Parsonage, Keswick.
Hudleston, F., 57, Inverness Terrace, Hyde Park, London.
Hudleston, Gilbert John, St. Benedict's Abbey, Fort Augustus, Inverness.
Hudson, Rev. J., Crosby-on-Eden, Carlisle.

Irwin, Col., (High Sheriff of Cumberland), Lynehow.

55 Jackson, Mrs., 10, Duke Street, Southport.
Johnson, James H., J.P., Hall Garth, Over Kellet.

Lediard, H. A., M..D, Lowther Street, Carlisle.
Lindsay, W. A., Windsor Herald, Coll. of Arms.
Ling, C., Wandales, Wetheral.
60 Little, William, Chapel Ridding, Windermere.
Loftie, Rev. A. G., Great Salkeld, Penrith.
Lonsdale, Earl of, Lowther Castle, Penrith.
Lonsdale, Earl of, Whitehaven Castle.
Lonsdale, H. B., 25, Lowther Street, Carlisle.

65 Maclaren, Roderick, M.D., Portland Square, Carlisle.
Mac Innes, Miles, Rickerby, Carlisle.
Magrath, Rev. J. R., D.D., Provost of Queen's Coll.,
Vice-Chancellor, Oxford.
Markham, Captain, Morland, Penrith.
Martindale, James Henry, Moor Yeat, Wetheral.
70 Metcalfe, Rev. R. W., The Vicarage, Ravenstonedale.
Moore, Stewart, F.S.A., 6, King's Bench Walk, The
Temple, London.
Muncaster, Lord, F.S.A., Muncaster Castle, Ravenglass.
Mylne, Rev. R. S., M.A., B.C.L., F.S.A., Great Amwell,
Herts.

Neilson, George, F.S.A., Scot., 34, Granby Terrace,
Glasgow.

75 Pearson, A. G. B., Lune Cottage, Kirkby Lonsdale.
Peile, John, Litt. D., Master of Christ's Coll., Cambridge.
Postlethwaite, Geo. B., Hollybrake, Chislehurst.

Richmond, Rev. Canon, The Abbey, Carlisle.
Richardson, Rev. G., The College, Winchester.
80 Robinson, Robert, C.E., Beechwood, Darlington.
Robinson, John, M.Inst.C.E., Vicarage Terrace, Kendal.
Rymer, Thomas, Calder Abbey, via Carnforth.

Saul, S. G., Brunstock Park, Carlisle.
Scott, Wm. Hudson, Red Gables, Carlisle.
85 Scott, Benjamin, Linden House, Stanwix.
Scott, Daniel, 26, Graham Street, Penrith,
Senhouse, H. P., Netherhall, Maryport.
Sewell, Col. F. R., Brandling Gill, Cockermouth.
Sherwen, Rev. Canon, Dean Rectory, Cockermouth.

90 Simpson, J., Cockermouth.
   Steel, James, Wetheral, Carlisle.
   Steele, Major General, 28, West Cromwell Road, London, S.E.
   Stephenson, Rev. William, The Rectory, Kendal.
   Sykes, Rev. W. S., M.A., Millom.

95 Thompson, Andrew, 22, Lowther Street, Carlisle.
   Thurnam, Charles and Son, Carlisle.
   Tyson, E. T., Wood Hall, Cockermouth.

   Waugh, E. L., The Burroughs, Cockermouth.
   Wheatley, James A., 65, English Street, Carlisle.
100 White, George, 8, Botchergate, Carlisle.
   Whitwell, Robert, Banbury Road, Oxford.
   Wilde, R. W., Bowden.
   Wilson, Rev. James, M.A., Dalston Vicarage, Carlisle.
   Wilson, T. Aynam Lodge, Kendal.
105 Wrigley, Robert, Brampton.

Printed in Great Britain
by Amazon